Schott's Almanac

2007

LIBER PRAETERITORUM ET POSTERITATIS CARMEN

Everyone spoke of information overload,
but what there was, in fact, was a non-information overload.
— RICHARD SAUL WURMAN, *What-If, Could-Be*, 1976

COPYRIGHT © BEN SCHOTT 2006 · All rights reserved

Published by Bloomsbury USA, New York
175 Fifth Avenue, New York, NY 10010, USA
Distributed to the trade by Holtzbrinck Publishers

www.schottsalmanac.com · www.benschott.com

First US Edition 2006

1 2 3 4 5 6 7 8 9 10 · [see p.160]

Hardback – ISBN-10 1-59691-171-9 · ISBN-13 978-1-59691-171-0 [see p.162]
Book Club Edition – ISBN-10 1-59691-359-2 · ISBN-13 978-1-59691-359-2

Library of Congress Cataloging-in-Publication Data have been applied for.

All papers used by Bloomsbury USA are natural, recyclable products made from
wood grown in well-managed forests. The manufacturing processes conform to
the environmental regulations of the country of origin.

Designed and typeset by BEN SCHOTT
Printed in the USA by R.R. DONNELLEY & SONS, HARRISONBURG, VIRGINIA

* * * *

Also by BEN SCHOTT
Schott's Original Miscellany
Schott's Food & Drink Miscellany
Schott's Sporting, Gaming, & Idling Miscellany
Schott's Miscellany Diary (with Smythson of Bond St, London)

British and German Editions of *Schott's Almanac 2007* are also available

Schott's
Almanac

2007

· *The book of things past and the song of the future* ·

Conceived, edited, and designed by

BEN SCHOTT

US Assistant Editor · Bess Lovejoy

Series Assistant Editor · Claire Cock-Starkey

BLOOMSBURY

Preface

Schott's Almanac offers a biography of the year – its aim is to select, record, and analyze the significant events of the past. In the modern information age, however, the role of the almanac has changed. Just as C20th almanacs were less concerned with astronomical and ecclesiastical data than their C18th and C19th predecessors, so the C21st almanac must adapt to its time. *Schott's Almanac* reflects the age in which it has been written: an age when information is plentiful, but selection and analysis are more elusive. So, while *Schott's Almanac* hopes to include all of the essential data one would expect to find in such a volume, it has not attempted to be comprehensive. Perhaps in contrast to some of its venerable forerunners [see p.6], rather than simply presenting encyclopedic listings, *Schott's Almanac* aspires to provide an informative, selective, and entertaining analysis of the year.

— *Schott's* is an almanac written to be read.

THE ALMANAC'S YEAR

In order to be as inclusive as possible, the *Schott's Almanac* year runs until late August.

Data cited in *Schott's Almanac* are taken from the latest sources available at the time of writing.

CHERISH TRUTH, PARDON ERROR

Every effort has been taken to ensure that the information contained within *Schott's Almanac* is both accurate and up-to-date, and grateful acknowledgment is made to the various sources used. However, as Goethe once said: 'Error is to truth as sleep is to waking'. Consequently, the author would be pleased to be informed of any errors, inaccuracies, or omissions that might help improve future editions.

Please send all comments or suggestions to the author, care of:

Bloomsbury USA, 175 Fifth Avenue, New York, NY 10010, USA

or email *useditor@schottsalmanac.com*

In keeping with most newspapers and journals, *Schott's Almanac* will publish any significant corrections and clarifications each year in its Errata section [see p.368].

Contents

―――――――――― EARLY ALMANACS OF NOTE ――――――――――

Solomon Jarchi.................. *c.*1150	Zainer (at Ulm) 1478
Peter de Dacia................... *c.*1300	Francis Moore's Almanack. 1698–1713
John Somers (Oxford) 1380	Poor Richard's Almanack 1732
Nicholas de Lynna 1386	Almanach de Gotha............... 1764
Purbach..................... 1150–1461	The Old Farmer's Almanac 1792
After the invention of printing	Whitaker's Almanack 1868
Gutenberg (at Mainz)............. 1457	The World Almanac 1868
Regiomontanus (at Nuremberg) . 1474	Information Please Almanac...... 1947

―――――――――― ALMANAC vs ALMANACK ――――――――――

The spelling and etymology of 'almanac' are the subject of some dispute. The *Oxford English Dictionary* notes the very early use of 'almanac' by Roger Bacon in 1267, though Chaucer used 'almenak' in *c.*1391; and Shakespeare, 'almanack' in 1590. Variations include almanach(e), amminick, almanacke, almanack, &c. A number of etymologies for *almanac* have been suggested: that it comes from the Arabic *al* [the] *mana(h)* [reckoning or diary]; that it comes from the Anglo-Saxon *al-moan-heed* ['to wit, the regard or observations of all the moons'], or from the Anglo-Saxon *al-monath* [all the months]; or that it is linked to the Latin for 'sundial', *manachus*. In 1838, *Murphy's Almanac* made the bold prediction that January 20 of that year would be 'Fair, prob. lowest deg. of winter temp'. When, on the day, this actually turned out to be true, *Murphy's Almanac* became a best seller.

―――――――――― SYMBOLS & ABBREVIATIONS ――――――――――

> ....greater than	≈ ....approximately equal to
≥ ....greater than or equal to	km.............................. kilometer
< .... less than	m .... meter
≤ ....less than or equal to	mi.................................mile
♂ ....male/men	'/" ....feet (ft)/inches (in)
♀ .... female/women	C.................. century (e.g. C20th)
c...... *circa*, meaning around or roughly	m/bn ....million/billion

Throughout the *Almanac*, some figures may not add to totals because of rounding.

―――――――――― 'AVERAGES' ――――――――――

With the following list of values: 10, 10, 20, 30, 30, 30, 40, 50, 70, 100 = 390

MEAN or AVERAGE.....	the sum divided by the number of values...............	39
MODE..................	the most popular value	30
MEDIAN................	the 'middle' value of a range, here: (30+30)/2..........	30
RANGE	the difference between the highest & lowest values	90

Chronicle

To every thing there is a season, and a time to every purpose under the heaven:
A time to be born, and a time to die.
— ECCLESIASTES 3:1–8

―――――――――― SOME AWARDS OF NOTE ――――――――――

TIME magazine Persons of the Year [2005]
BONO and BILL & MELINDA GATES
'For being shrewd about doing good, for rewiring politics
and re-engineering justice, for making mercy smarter and hope
strategic and then daring the rest of us to follow ...'

Miss Universe ....Zuleyka Rivera Mendoza, Puerto Rico
International Best Dressed [*Vanity Fair*]....................................Kate Moss
NAACP Hall of Fame Award.. Carlos Santana
NFL's Sexiest Man .... Brett Favre, Green Bay Packers
Best Hospital [*US News & World Report*] ....Johns Hopkins Hospital, Baltimore
National Teacher of the Year............................Kimberly Oliver, Maryland
Intel Science Talent Search ....Shannon Babb (18 years old, Utah)
Principal of the Year .... Ellen Minette (Heidelberg Middle School, Germany)
Airline of the Year [Skytrax]...British Airways
Airport of the Year [Skytrax] .... Singapore Changi Airport
Most Beautiful Bulldog..................................... Hannah (Des Moines, Iowa)
Tabbie Award [for trade publications] ....*Legal Business* magazine
Ernest Hemingway Look-alike Award ....Chris Storm (Texas)
Odor-Eaters Rotten Sneaker Award.......................McKenna Dinkel (Alaska)
Best of Show, Dog Show USA.........................Tillie, dachshund-cocker mix
Dog Writers Assoc. of America Poetry Award ...... *Corgi Haiku* · Andy Bergstrom
Car of the Year [caroftheyear.org].......................................Renault Clio III
Wine of the Year [2005] .... Joseph Phelps, Insignia Napa Valley 2002
American Cheese Society Best of Show...............Cabot Clothbound Cheddar
Australian of the Year Award ....Professor Ian Frazer (clinical immunologist)
US National Air Guitar Champion ....Craig 'Hot Lixx Hulahan' Billmeier
High Sierra Beard and Moustache Champion..........................Jack Passion

―――――――――― DOUBLESPEAK AWARD ――――――――――

The National Council of Teachers of English Doublespeak Award for 2005 went
to Philip A. Cooney, former Chief of Staff for the White House Council on
Environmental Quality. Cooney was honored for his 'commitment to doublespeak',
and for using 'well-placed modifiers and hedges' in his editing of scientific reports.

——— MISC. LISTS OF 2006 ———

MADAME TUSSAUDS
*New wax figures for
2006 at Madame
Tussauds, New York*

———

Hillary Rodham Clinton
Bono
Johnny Cash
Lindsay Lohan
Britney Spears
Shiloh Nouvel Jolie-Pitt†
Johnny Depp
Brandon Routh
(as Superman)

† Shiloh was Tussauds' first
wax baby, and appeared in an
'African' nursery.
[See p.118]

GREATEST SIDEKICKS
Entertainment Weekly

———

1 .... Ed McMahon
2 .... Robin
3 ...... George Costanza
4 .... Chewbacca
5 .... Ethel Mertz
6 .... Dr Watson
7 ...... Samwise Gamgee
8 .... Ed Norton
9 .... Tattoo
10 ...... Dwight Schrute

HAPPIEST COUNTRIES
New Economics Fndn.

———

Vanuatu · Colombia
Costa Rica · Dominica
Panama · Cuba
Honduras · Guatemala
El Salvador · St Lucia
Vietnam · Bhutan
W. Samoa · Sri Lanka
Antigua & Barbuda
Philippines · Nicaragua

BEST PLACES TO LIVE
Money *magazine's most
livable places in the US*

———

1 ...... Fort Collins, CO
2 .... Naperville, IL
3 .... Sugar Land, TX
4 .... Columbia/
Ellicott City, MD
5 .... Cary, NC
6 .... Overland Park, KS
7 .... Scottsdale, AZ
8 .... Boise, ID
9 .... Fairfield, CT
10 .... Eden Prairie, MN

BEST GOLF COURSES
chosen by Golf Digest

———

*Pine Valley Golf Course
Augusta · Shinnecockhills
Cypress Point Club
Oakmont Country Club*

IMPORTANT TOOLS
Forbes.com's *list of tools
that have 'most impacted
human civilization'*

———

the knife · the abacus
the compass · the pencil
the harness · the scythe
the rifle · the sword
eyeglasses · the saw
the watch · the lathe
the needle · the candle
the scale · the pot
the telescope · the level
the fish hook · the chisel

SWEATIEST CITY
*The Old Spice 2006
'sweatiest city in America'
was* Phoenix, AZ, *where
on average residents sweat
26 ounces per hour.*

—2007 WORDS—

The following words
celebrate anniversaries
in 2007, based upon the
earliest cited use traced
by the venerable Oxford
English Dictionary:

{1507} *banishment*
(expelling from a state)
{1607} *archaeology*
(the study of ancient
history) · *glossographer*
(a writer of commentaries)
· *morological* (relating to
foolish words) ·
nightcapped (wearing said
bed-wear) · *thimbleful* (as
much as a thimble will hold)
{1707} *bourgeoisie*
(the freemen of a French
town) · *dustman* (one
who disposes of refuse) ·
vivisection (cutting part of
a living organism) · {1807}
mispunctuation (faulty
punctuation) · *whimsy-
whamsy* (fanciful nonsense)
· {1907} *anorexic*
(characterized by a lack of
appetite) · *chemotherapy*
(treatment of disease with
chemicals) · *unk* (colloquial
abbreviation of uncle) ·
{1957} *bleep* (to make a
high-pitched bleeping sound)
· *Sputnik* (unmanned
[Russian] artificial earth
satellite) · *transsexual*
(pertaining to transsexualism)
{1997} *blamestorming*
(investigating or
apportioning blame) ·
Muggle (in J.K. Rowling's
work, one with no magical
powers, and by extension,
anyone lacking in skill)

SOME SURVEY RESULTS OF 2006

%	*of adult Americans (unless otherwise noted)*	*source & month*
93	think some, about half, or most, members of Congress accept bribes	[CBS/*NYT*; Jan]
90	of New Yorkers hold open doors for other people [see p.79]	[*Reader's Digest*; Jul]
80	of Americans believe Abu Ghraib-type abuse is still going on	[World Pub. Opinion; Jul]
78	think the national anthem should be sung only in English [see p.260]	[Fox News; May]
73	think Martin Luther King Jr's birthday should be a national holiday	[AP/Ipsos; Jan]
70	favor televising sessions of the Supreme Court [see p.306]	[Fox News; Apr]
67	consider left-wing leaders in Latin America a threat to the US	[Pew; Feb]
67	think immigration is good for the US [see p.28]	[Gallup; Jun]
65	of women shoppers regularly consult food labels	[AP/Ipsos; Jul]
64	use the 'F' word (8% several times per day)	[AP/Ipsos; Mar]
64	approve of doctor-assisted suicide for terminally ill patients	[Gallup; May]
61	of the French forgave Zidane for his World Cup headbutt [see p.230]	[*Le Parisien*; Jul]
60	favor allowing gays and lesbians to serve openly in the military [see p.101]	[Pew; Mar]
59	think global warming requires some or immediate action	[NBC News/*WSJ*; Jun]
58	of workers have purloined office supplies for personal use	[Harris Interactive; May]
57	have never played golf	[CNN/*USA Today*/Gallup; Jan]
56	think America is ready to elect a female President	[Diageo/Hotline; Feb]
53	would not vote for a Muslim presidential candidate [see p.335]	[*LA Times*; Jun]
51	think the death penalty is not imposed often enough [see p.116]	[Gallup; May]
48	specifically celebrate American independence on July 4	[Zogby; Jun]
48	approve of drilling for oil in Alaska's Arctic wildlife refuge	[CBS News/*NYT*; May]
46	think America is safer than it was before 9/11	[Zogby; Jan]
45	would like affirmative action programs ended or phased out	[CBS News; Jan]
44	consider the federal income tax they pay to be about right [see p.313]	[Gallup; Apr]
44	consider paying for prescription drugs to be a major problem [see p.105]	[Pew; Mar]
44	of Japanese consider sexual relationships to be tiresome	[Japan Family Plan. Assoc.; Jun]
43	think the US penny should be withdrawn [see p.321]	[*USA Today*/Gallup; Jun]
42	rate the overall state of moral values in the US as poor [see p.26]	[Gallup; May]
40	of women would choose not to menstruate	[Assoc. of Reproductive Health Pros; May]
34	think the US health care system requires complete rebuilding	[CBS News/*NYT*; Jun]
33	consider the 9/11 film *United 93* to be 'inappropriate'	[Fox News; Apr]
31	consider Iran to be America's greatest enemy [see p.34]	[Gallup; Feb]
25	think the US spends too little on the military [see p.270]	[Gallup; Feb]
21	believe the 1st Amendment enshrines the right to own pets [see p.307]	[Synovate; Jan]
21	believe it likely their phone calls have been wiretapped	[CNN/*USA Today*/Gallup; Feb]
14	have no confidence in the US govt to respond to natural disasters	[CBS News; Feb]
14	would not vote for a Jewish presidential candidate	[*LA Times*; Jun]
11	rate the quality of the US environment as poor	[Gallup; Mar]
11	consider it acceptable to lie on a résumé [see p.26]	[AP/Ipsos; Jun]
10	ate less chicken and turkey because of bird flu [see p.19]	[Fox News; Mar]
8	have no confidence at all in the news media [see p.131]	[CBS News/*NYT*; Jan]
6	have no understanding at all about the 'greenhouse effect'	[Gallup; Mar]
5	consider polygamy to be morally acceptable [see p.96]	[Gallup; May]
5	want the US space program to be ended	[*USA Today*/Gallup; Jun]
1	consider France to be America's greatest enemy	[Gallup; Feb]

—————————— SIGNIFICA · 2006 ——————————

Some (in)significa(nt) footnotes to the year ❦ If all the Lego in the world were evenly divided, we would each receive 30 pieces [*Prospect*] ❦ William Shatner sold a kidney stone to raise $25,000 for a housing charity [BBC] ❦ Bangladeshi authorities ordered cellphone providers to stop free calls after midnight, after parents complained that children were using the service to form premarital romantic attachments [BBC] ❦ In New Delhi, microchips were inserted into the stomachs of cows so that, if

lost, they could be traced and returned to their owners [*Wall St Journal*] ❦ 'Sonic fiber', a textile woven from cassette tape, was invented by artist Alyce Santoro; when tape heads are run over the material, the clothes will play [*Guardian*] ❦ Benedict XVI had his library of 20,000 books photographed shelf-by-shelf, so they could be re-assembled in the Vatican precisely as they were in his apartment [*NYT*] ❦ The President of Turkmenistan (His Excellency Saparmurat Niyazov 'Turkmenbashi') declared that those who read his book of moral and spiritual guidance (the *Rukhnama*) three times ('at home, at sunset, and at dawn')

President Niyazov

will go to heaven [*Guardian*] ❦ The world's smallest vertebrate was discovered in Sumatra; *Paedocypris progenetica,* a member of the carp family, grows to a maximum length of 1cm [*New Scientist*] ❦ Former Italian PM Silvio Berlusconi took a vow of sexual abstinence for the 10 weeks leading up to the general election [BBC] ❦ Uzbekistan banned fur-lined underwear, deeming it likely to cause 'unbridled fantasies' [*Telegraph*] ❦ 40 Austrian songbirds thought to have died of avian flu were actually drunk; having gorged on fermented berries, they flew into windows [*NYT*] ❦ Taiwanese drunkdrivers were given the option of playing Mah Jong with the elderly instead of paying a fine [*Guardian*] ❦ Mattel unveiled a makeover for Barbie's companion, Ken; in addition to facial resculpting, Ken was given torn jeans and board shorts to reflect the time he spent 'exploring the world and himself' [BBC] ❦ Willie Nelson released a song about gay cowboys, to coincide with *Brokeback Mountain* – 'Cowboys Are Secretly, Frequently (Fond of Each Other)' [BBC] ❦ Supreme Court Justices upheld the use of the hallucinogenic *hoasca* tea in a four-hour, twice-monthly church service in New Mexico [MSNBC] ❦ The US military funded a computer game to teach troops how to decipher Iraqi body language; other games in development include Tactical Pashto (Afghanistan) and Tactical Levantine (Lebanon) [BBC] ❦ In Baghdad's Al Hakimiya prison, a 'price list' of bribes was reported, including: $30,000 to be released; $200 to make a cellphone call; and $13 for an hour of sunlight. Victims of torture rich enough could buy painkillers from their guards [*Newsweek*] ❦ 42,578 MySpace.com users declared themselves a 'friend' of Madonna [*Guardian*] ❦ Romanian soccer team *Regal Hornia* bought defender Marius Cioara for 15 kilos of pork sausages [*Seattle Times*] ❦ The Chinese government announced it would introduce a 5% chopstick tax to preserve its forests [BBC] ❦ Conservative peer Lord Inglewood suggested that British children be encouraged to eat gray squirrels in school dinners to preserve the red variety [BBC] ❦ Emergency services in Las Vegas invested in a fleet of 'bariatric ambulances' (equipped with a winch) to deal with increasing numbers of obese patients; in just 6 months, medics had collected 75 patients over 497lb [*USA Today*] ❦ It was alleged that Dick Cheney requires TVs in his hotel rooms to be pre-tuned

SIGNIFICA · 2006 cont.

to Fox News [*thesmokinggun.com*] ❦ After complaints of rude behavior, it was announced that Russian police would be taught table manners and an appreciation of poetry, literature, art, music, and dance [ananova.com] ❦ The venture capital arm of the CIA is named 'In-Q-Tel' in honor of 'Q', the inventor and tinkerer in the James Bond films [*Washington Post*] ❦ A California good Samaritan returned a bag containing a Cartier watch, diamond and ruby rings, pearl earrings, diamond necklaces, and hundreds of dollars in cash, worth >$1m, to a woman whose husband had lost the bag while they were sightseeing [ABC] ❦ Pope Benedict XVI blessed a fleet of 45 Ferraris in St Peter's Square [Catholic News Agency] ❦ A judge in Manila was removed from the bench after it emerged he was consulting three imaginary mystical dwarves – Armand, Luis, and Angel [Reuters] ❦ Rains in Penglai City, China, created a rare mirage in which a whole section of the city, including buildings and crowds of people, appeared to float above the shore [chinadaily.com] ❦ The 888-foot retired aircraft carrier USS *Oriskany* was sunk to the bottom of the Gulf of Mexico to create the world's largest artificial reef [CNN] ❦ Because of a visit by Pope Benedict XVI, the Polish town of Wadowice restricted the sale of alcohol and ice cream, and halted TV ads for contraceptives and tampons [BBC] ❦ FIFA forced Dutch football fans at the World Cup to remove their bright orange trousers (leeuwenhose) before entering a Stuttgart stadium, since they bore the name of a Bavarian brewery, a rival of tournament sponsor Budweiser [*Guardian*] ❦ A British insurance agency withdrew a £1m policy that covered three Scottish nuns in the event that they immaculately conceived the Second Coming [*Times*] ❦ In the week before Valentine's Day, people were more likely to search online for the key words 'love poems' than for 'flowers' or 'lingerie' [*New York Times*] ❦ The perm, invented in 1906 by German emigré Karl Nessler, celebrated its 100th anniversary [*Guardian*] ❦ David Beckham revealed that he had spent months battling obsessive-compulsive disorder; he disclosed that he has to have his belongings arranged in straight lines, and buys exactly 20 packets of 'super noodles' every time he visits the supermarket [*Independent*] ❦ After a survey predicted the last fluent Sissenton-Wahpeton speaker would die in 2025, the Dakota Sioux set up an interschool Scrabble tournament to prolong the use of its language [MSNBC] ❦ While playing James Bond, Sean Connery wrote a ballet called *Black Lake*, according to his ex-wife's autobiography [*Guardian*] ❦ A host of celebrities (including writer Stephen King) urged J.K. Rowling not to 'kill off' Harry Potter in the last (planned) book of the series [BBC] ❦ Concerned about the promotion of 'feudalism and feudal beliefs', Chinese authorities banned the sale of voodoo dolls from Beijing shops [*Newsweek*] ❦ Zimbabwe introduced a $100,000 bill, worth US$1 at official exchange rates [BBC] ❦ Residents of Hell (pop. 72), MI, celebrated 6·6·06

J.K. Rowling

with '666' branded T-shirts and mugs, and sold deeds to 1 sq. inch of Hell for $6·66 [MSNBC] ❦ The average consumer spends $88·80 on Father's Day and $122·16 on Mother's Day [NRF Survey] ❦ The Turkmenbashi [see p.10] had a melon named in his honor during Turkmenistan's national and annual Melon Day [AFP] ❦ In August, Iranian President Mahmoud Ahmadinejad [see p.34] launched his own blog – ahmadinejad.ir – which is translated into Persian, Arabic, English, and French.

———————————— WORDS OF THE YEAR ————————————

BROWNSPLOITATION · nickname for the profusion of products cashing in on the success of Dan Brown's books.

IED · Improvised Explosive Devices, like roadside bombs, that have proved so devastating to Allied forces in Iraq. To check for IEDs, US soldiers perform '5s AND 25s' when leaving their vehicles: walking 5 meters, and visually scanning a 25-meter perimeter. *Also* VBED · Vehicle-Born (Improvised) Explosive Device.

SLOWRINO · comment on the leisurely pace of the Torino Winter Olympics.

CASSEURS · French for 'smashers', used to describe the rioters who infiltrated the Paris labor law demonstrations.

YO, BLAIR · Bush's friendly/belittling (depending on your viewpoint) private greeting for Blair, caught by the press when a microphone at the Moscow G8 conference was left on. (Discussing the Israel-Lebanon crisis, Bush was overheard telling Blair, 'What they need to do is to get Syria to get Hezbollah to stop doing this SHIT and it's over'.)

CIVIL WAR · controversial description of the state of post-invasion Iraq.

HANNIBAL DIRECTIVE · *Nohal Hannibal* · rumored to be the unofficial Israeli order for soldiers to open fire on those kidnapping a comrade, even at the cost of his/her life, on the basis that a dead soldier is better than one whose life can be bartered for political gain.

BELOW THE CNN LINE · Rumsfeld's definition of pre-invasion air strikes on Iraq that would inflict damage, but not so much as to feature on the US news.

TRASH · Annie Proulx's mischievous reference to *Crash* – the film that beat (her story) *Brokeback Mountain* to the Best Picture Oscar [see p.152].

BIG BLU · a 30,000lb, bunker-busting bomb (ready for use in 2007), that some claim will be the weapon of choice for a US attack on Iranian nuclear facilities.

DRAWING DOWN · military term for reducing troop levels (e.g. in Iraq).

COLLECTIVE PUNISHMENT · controversial description of Israel's attack on Gaza and Lebanon [see p.32]. Collective punishments are banned by Article 33 of the 4th Geneva Convention, 1949.

NAHR · Arabic word for the slaughter of sheep, used by 'Islamic' extremists as a euphemism for beheading victims.

JAMES BLAND · disparaging nickname for Daniel Craig's James Bond.

WARLORDISTAN · nickname for post-2001 Afghanistan. *Also* HAMASTAN · nickname for Hamas-run Palestine. *Also* TEHRANGELES · nickname for LA based on its large Iranian population.

BINNERS · British Ministry of Defence nickname for Osama bin Laden. *Also* KSM · nickname for alleged Al Qaeda chief Khalid Sheikh Mohammed. In Spain, €500 notes are known as 'bin Ladens', because they are the highest value euro notes, thought to be used in crime, and no one ever sees them.

ANOMALY · Tony Blair's description of Guantánamo Bay.

ANTI-ANTI-AMERICANS · the people against the people against America.

—————————— WORDS OF THE YEAR cont. ——————————

PAYOLA SIX · nickname for the scandal surrounding the *New York Post*'s 'Page Six' gossip column and Jared Paul Stern (aka JPS or THE NIGHTCRAWLER).

PHARM ANIMAL · GM animals bred to make transgenic drugs for humans.

MUFFIN TOP · a roll of abdominal fat that spills from the top of tight jeans.

UNPLUGGING · to rescind a public endorsement or plug – notably, Oprah Winfrey 'unplugged' James Frey's *A Million Little Pieces* [see p.27].

AROUND-SOURCING · where work (in developing nations) is outsourced from cities to nearby villages.

LETHAL AMBIGUITY · where military 'rules of engagement' are deliberately left unclear to provide soldiers a degree of protection from prosecution.

HOTSPUR · codename for the US-UK mock 'war game' invasion of Iran, held at Fort Belvoir, VA, in July 2004.

THE POODLE PROBLEM · Whitehall slang for the perception that Tony Blair is merely George Bush's lapdog.

SIDESTABBER · one who warns a potential victim that a backstabber is about to strike but, by swearing the victim to secrecy, protects both themself and the backstabber. *Also* FRENEMY · one who pretends to be your friend, but is really your enemy.

GRAY MAIL · legal tactic of deliberately seeking classified evidence (that will not be released) in order to claim that an adequate defense cannot be mounted · *Also* suspected spam email [see p.197].

THE LONG WAR · Pentagon's replacement for the abstract 'War on Terror'.

FRATIRE · male equivalent of *chick lit*, emphasising sex, drinking, sport, &c; part of the MENAISSANCE rejection of metrosexuality and gender ambiguity.

KATYUSHA ('little Katherine') ROCKETS · Soviet-era-design, unguided rockets deployed in July and August against targets in N. Israel by Hezbollah, and alleged to be supplied by Iran [see p.32].

GURGITATOR · one who participates in eating competitions [see p.251].

LEONARDOS · marketing term for 30-somethings who like arts *and* sciences.

HOUSE FLUFFING · titivating a house to entice prospective buyers.

FRANKENBITING · a technique used by 'reality' TV, wherein clips are doctored to make for better viewing.

HAJJI · honorific title for one who has made the Hajj [see p.337], used by US soldiers as a generic term of abuse for Iraqis (as they called the Viet Cong 'gooks'). *Also* HAJJINET · small-scale informal internet services set up by US soldiers in Iraq to provide internet access for their comrades. *Also* MUJ · nickname for the Mujahideen.

COCKTAIL NO. 4 · the combination of urine, feces, semen, and spit that, it has been claimed, some Guantánamo Bay inmates throw at their guards.

ISLAMOFASCISM · comparison of certain 'Islamic' extremists (like Al Qaeda) with the Nazis, both for their violent methods and their anti-Semitism.

———————— WORDS OF THE YEAR cont. ————————

QUAILGATE · nickname for Dick Cheney's accidental shooting of Harry Whittington while quail hunting, and the subsequent fallout [see p.29].

PIMPFANTS · children dressed up like pimps [see p.137]. *Also* GRUPS · adult kids, & CHILEBRITIES · kids of celebs.

LOCATIONSHIP · a relationship based on geographical proximity rather than true attraction (e.g. dating roommates).

ECOGLITTERATI · green celebrities.

BILLANTHROPHY · spectacular form of philanthropy practiced by Bill Gates, Warren Buffett, and the like.

VOLUNTARY FASTING · US military term for a hunger strike (defined by them as missing ≥9 consecutive meals).

SMUM · Smart Middle-class Uninvolved Mother – a new breed of moms who show little interest in their children.

PUSH PRESENTS · gifts given to (and increasingly expected by) women who have just given birth.

SOCK-HER MOMS *or* KILLER MOMS · mothers who take a fiercely competitive approach to raising their children. *Also* HELICOPTER PARENTS · those ever hovering over their offspring.

SMIRTING · flirting between those who have been banished outside to smoke.

PREGAME · to drink at home before going out to drink in public.

CHOICE FEMINISM · the notion that traditional roles (e.g. child care) can be 'feminist' if freely chosen by women.

BOOMERITIS · sports-related injuries suffered by the baby-boom generation.

ABORTION TOURISM · moving from one country (or state) to another to seek a legal abortion. *Also* HEALTH, FERTILITY, & TRANSPLANT tourism.

ELBOW BUMP · the pandemic-friendly greeting to replace the handshake.

GHETTO TAX · the additional financial burden of living in poor areas, caused by the higher costs of insurance, check cashing, loans, &c.

FREEMIUM · a business model where users sign up for a free service, and are then tempted or persuaded to pay for advanced or premium features.

HEZBOLLYWOOD · allegation that the media is taken in by Hezbollah's spin.

FRACTIONALS · new real-estate jargon for highend timeshares.

AEROTROPOLI · areas surrounding airports (like Schiphol, Amsterdam) that are increasingly becoming mini-cities in themselves.

VICE MAIL · the scam of leaving chatty and supposedly 'accidental' voicemails praising a stock, in the hope that investors will think they have stumbled on 'inside' information and buy.

FRENCH FRIES · back on the menu in Congress cafeterias, replacing the Franco-phobic 'freedom fries' that had been introduced just before the Iraq war.

MASS-CASUALTY ATTACKS · intelligence term for attacks like 9/11 & 7/7 designed for maximum loss of life.

—————— OBJECT OF THE YEAR · THE VIBRATOR ——————

On March 15, 2006, Senator Ralph Davenport [SC-R] proposed a bill to the South Carolina General Assembly to ban the sale of 'sexual devices'. If passed, SC will join a number of states (including AL, TX, MS, & GA) with laws restricting sex toys – defined in the SC bill as objects 'designed or marketed as useful primarily for the stimulation of human genital organs and solely for the sale of prurient interest in sex'. ❦ This political move is part of a realignment of public attitudes to sexuality in general and sex toys specifically. According to Durex's 2005 Global Sex Survey, 45% of American adults have used a vibrator – the global average is 22% – and only 11% of Americans would not buy one. Similar results were obtained by the magazines *Glamour* and *More*, and in June 2006, Oprah's magazine, *O,* ran an article titled '*Everything You Wanted to Know About Sex Toys*'. At the vanguard of this trend is the internet, which allows browsing and purchasing outside the realm of (male, seedy) 'adult stores'. 59% of sex toys in the US were purchased online, according to Durex. In May 2006, the best-selling toy in *Amazon.com*'s 'Sex and Sensuality' section was the Vibratex *Rabbit Habit,* made famous by *Sex and the City*. And, sex toys [like Durex's *Little Gem*, shown here] are often now designed with women shoppers in mind. ❦ As the internet has opened the closet, so 'adult stores' have evolved. Female-friendly shops-cum-boudoirs such as *Babeland, Myla,* and *Kiki de Montparnasse* are flourishing in New York and elsewhere, representing a confident step out of the shadows. *Fred Segal, Catriona MacKechnie, Selfridges, Harvey Nichols,* and a host of high-end stores stock sex toys – like Jimmy Jane's $350 *Little Gold* vibrator which Kate Moss was spotted buying in April. At the other end of the market, CVS and Walgreens sell Trojan's *Vibrating Ring* – 'designed to enhance the pleasure of both partners through intimate vibrations'. A number of devices are sold to transform iPods into vibrators that pulse to the beat, and the latest trend takes the sex toy/internet relationship to its logical conclusion. 'Teledildonics' is the online control of sex toys, allowing remote and even anonymous sexual s(t)imulation. Steve Rhodes, president of cybersex firm Sinulate Entertainment, told ABC News that teledildonics 'is not something that just the lunatic fringe does', and added 'the Iraq war ... was kind of a boom for our company'. The current state of US sexuality [see p.100] indicates a wider range of activity than some might suppose. Research by Jean Twenge, at San Diego State U., shows that between 1943–99, the age of first sexual intercourse fell from 19 to 15 [♀]; and 18 to 15 [♂]. The percentage of sexually active young women rose from 13% to 47%, and 'feelings of sexual guilt plummeted, especially among young women'. ❦ There is nothing new about sex toys – their first incarnation in the 1880s was as 'pelvic massagers' to treat hysterical women. Yet, the current debate not only illuminates trends in female sexuality; it also highlights a duality in American society: *laissez-faire* sex shops in some states, sumptuary laws on morality in others. In contrast to South Carolina, the Australian Taxation Office decreed in 2006 that prostitutes may claim sex toys (as well as 'consumable items like condoms, lubricants, gels, oils and tissues') as valid work-related expenses.

———— 2005 PAKISTAN–KASHMIR EARTHQUAKE ————

DATE: Saturday, October 8, 2005 · TIME: 08:50:40 at epicenter
QUAKE MAGNITUDE: 7·6 Richter scale [see p.77] · DEPTH: 26km (16·2miles)
LOCATION: Pakistan, 34·493°N, 73·629°E · [Source: US Geological Survey]
105km NNE of Islamabad, Pakistan · 115km ESE of Mingaora, Pakistan
125km WNW of Srinagar, Kashmir · 165km SSW of Gilgit, Kashmir

The earthquake that struck Pakistan-adminstered Kashmir killed >86,000, wiped out entire villages, and devastated the local infrastructure. The immediate problem facing the Pakistani government was galvanizing a coordinated response to the tragedy. The quake struck a remote mountainous region and destroyed many of the access roads, making rescue and recovery difficult and hazardous. As temperatures dropped and the delivery of aid stalled, increasing numbers of desperate refugees fled their homes to gather in camps in the Kashmiri valleys. A harsh winter loomed and, with *c*.3 million feared to be homeless, provision of shelter and food became urgent. ❦ The delicate relationship between India and Pakistan, who both lay claim to the entire Kashmir region, was further tested by the disaster. Pakistan's President Musharraf suggested that the earthquake might be an opportunity to resolve the long-running dispute; and in a gesture that further raised hopes of a reconciliation, India pledged $25m of aid to Pakistan. ❦ Aid agencies feared that the international response to earlier disasters (southeast Asia's tsunami, Darfur, &c.) had depleted national annual aid budgets. And, a month after the quake, it emerged that just 30% of the UN's aid target had been pledged, a response derided by UN Secretary-General Kofi Annan as 'weak' [see p.65]. Stung into action, the international community promised $5·4bn to Pakistan (exceeding the $5·2bn requested), with Muslim nations accounting for the majority of the donations. The US pledged a total of $510m, which comprised $300m from USAID, $110m in military support, and up to $100m from private contributions. In addition, >1,200 US personnel were sent to assist in the relief operation, and further humanitarian support was promised. ❦ It is feared that the widespread desertion of the mountainous communities in Kashmir could severely affect the reconstruction of the area, leaving a region of ghost towns with many thousands permanently displaced. Current estimates from Pakistan suggest that recovery might take as long as a decade.

MUHAMMAD CARTOON CRISIS

On September 30, 2005, the Danish national newspaper *Jyllands-Posten* printed twelve cartoons on the subject of Muhammad – many of which contravened strict Islamic tradition by actually portraying images of the Prophet. The cartoons were commissioned to explore why a Danish author had struggled to find artists willing to illustrate his children's book about the Prophet. Under the headline 'The Face of Muhammad', the paper's culture editor wrote: '*The modern, secular society is rejected by some Muslims. They demand a special position, insisting on special consideration of their own religious feelings. It is incompatible with contemporary democracy and freedom of speech, where you must be ready to put up with insults, mockery, and ridicule*'.

The cartoons represented Muhammad in a variety of ways, including one of the Prophet refusing suicide bombers entry to heaven, saying: 'Stop, stop, we have run out of virgins!' Yet, the most iconic and controversial image was that by artist Kurt Westergaard, who depicted Muhammad as a terrorist, wearing not a turban but a bomb with a lit fuse, inscribed in Arabic with the Muslim declaration of faith. ❦ A fortnight after publication, a peaceful protest was held in Copenhagen, but quickly the controversy proved another example of political 'chaos theory', where local incidents can rapidly have global repercussions. By early 2006, demonstrations of increasing violence had erupted in Europe and across the Islamic world, from Afghanistan, Libya, and Iran to Somalia, Nigeria, and Pakistan. In a professed show of solidarity for press freedom, newspapers in dozens of countries reprinted the cartoons. Each new publication sparked further protest, and several editors were sacked. Danish embassies were attacked, Danes were advised to leave Indonesia and warned against traveling to the Middle East, and a Muslim-wide boycott of Danish goods was attempted. Danish PM Anders Fogh Rasmussen declared the incident to be Denmark's worst international crisis since World War II.

❦ At the heart of the crisis was the clash of two 'self-evident' and 'inalienable' rights: the right to free expression and the right to religious respect. Though much of the hurt expressed by Muslims was genuine, some suggested the crisis had been deliberately fomented. It was claimed that certain Islamic states found it useful to attach themselves to a popular cause (an Iranian newspaper solicited cartoons satirizing the Holocaust), while radical Islamists used the crisis as an aid to recruitment (Osama bin Laden called for the cartoonists to be tried by Al Qaeda and executed). However, the February 2006 jailing of David Irving for Holocaust denial [see p.63] led many to question whether liberal Europe had a double standard: Islam could be 'defamed' with impunity whereas Judaism had legal protection. ❦ Although the direct attribution of casualties to the cartoons is complex, it is thought that *c.*823 were injured and *c.*139 killed by the time the protests had faded in April–May. Speaking at the World Editor's Forum in Moscow in June 2006, *Jyllands-Posten* editor-in-chief Joern Mikkelsen reflected on his decision to print the cartoons: 'Would we do it again? I have been asked time and time again. It is very hard to tell, I have said that we wouldn't do it if we had known the consequences'.

——————— ENRON, SKILLING, & LAY ———————

Another chapter of the Enron scandal closed in May 2006, when founder Kenneth Lay and former CEO Jeffrey Skilling were convicted on multiple charges of fraud and conspiracy. Six weeks later, Lay died suddenly from heart disease. ❦ Prior to bankruptcy in 2001, Enron was America's 7th-largest company, employing *c.*21,000 in >40 countries, and declaring revenues of $100bn (2000). For six consecutive years *Fortune* declared Enron to be *America's Most Innovative Company*; at its peak, Enron stock traded at *c.*$90. Although it began as a gas pipeline company, Enron took advantage of market de-regulations to trade in myriad fields, from natural resources and energy to broadband internet capacity and fluctuations in the weather. Yet, as Enron grew, exactly what it did and how it made such massive profits were unclear. A *Fortune* article in March 2001 is credited with exposing chinks in the company's armor. Under the prescient headline '*Is Enron Overpriced?*', journalist Bethany McLean called the firm's operations 'mind-numbingly complex', and quoted one financial analyst who described Enron as 'a big black box'. ❦

With Enron's collapse came a rapid unraveling of the convoluted and arcane techniques to maximize the appearance of profits, while shifting debts and losses 'off balance-sheet'. ❦ Six years later, the consequences of Enron are still being assessed. The demise of Arthur Andersen, WorldCom, and others stemmed from Enron, as did the 2002 Sarbanes-Oxley Act, which tightened the US law on corporate governance. Enron may also have led to a harsher treatment of white-collar criminals, now denied the privilege of a discreet arrest and paraded in handcuffs on the 'perp walk'. ❦ At the time of writing, Skilling had not been sentenced and planned to appeal, and the consequences of Lay's death were still being assessed. Yet the Enron trial (and those that followed) served notice on corporate America that prosecutors were willing to take on the wealthy and well-connected in highly complex cases, and focus their charges in a way that juries could understand. It was in this way that Enron's arrogant and criminally corrupt culture was distilled to the personal liability of those who led what the London *Financial Times* called 'a virtual company with virtual profits'.

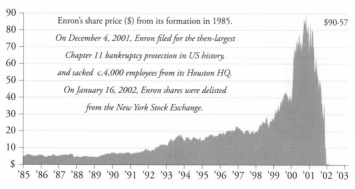

Enron's share price ($) from its formation in 1985. $90·57

On December 4, 2001, Enron filed for the then-largest

Chapter 11 bankruptcy protection in US history,

and sacked c.4,000 employees from its Houston HQ.

On January 16, 2002, Enron shares were delisted

from the New York Stock Exchange.

90 · 80 · 70 · 60 · 50 · 40 · 30 · 20 · 10 · $

'85 '86 '87 '88 '89 '90 '91 '92 '93 '94 '95 '96 '97 '98 '99 '00 '01 '02 '03

AVIAN FLU

As of August 9, 2006, the World Health Organization (WHO) had confirmed 236 human cases of avian influenza A(H5N1) – 138 of which had been fatal (a mortality rate of *c.*59%) [see chart]. Although some of the most dire predictions of a human pandemic have failed yet to materialize, governments around the world continue to stockpile drug treatments [see p.181]. And though most human cases have been caused by direct contact with diseased animals, international organizations continue to monitor the emergence of disease 'clusters' that might give an early warning of human-to-human transmission. ✻ Avian influenza (or bird flu) is a naturally occurring bird disease caused by flu viruses that closely resemble those affecting humans. It is spread by secretions in saliva and feces, and can quickly be passed between poultry flocks. The most pathogenic strains of avian flu have a 90–100% mortality rate within 48 hours, though, crucially, some infected animals can remain healthy while passing on the virus to others. ✻ The H5N1 strain was initially identified in birds in 1961 – and the first human infections were in Hong Kong in 1997; of the 18 people infected, 6 died, and only the swift destruction of Hong Kong's entire poultry population (*c.*1½m birds) averted a possible pandemic. The latest H5N1 outbreak is thought to have begun with a number of undetected and unreported cases in

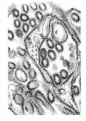

The H5N1 *virus*

Asia in mid-2003. By January 2004, Korea, Vietnam, Japan, Thailand, Cambodia, and Laos had all reported H5N1 in poultry, and the first human cases had been confirmed. Throughout Asia, tens of millions of birds died from the disease, and in mass culls to prevent its spread. However, avian migration (and possibly the international poultry trade) has spread H5N1 around the globe. August 2006 data from the World Organisation for Animal Health (OIE) show H5N1 in >50 countries. As the virus spreads and more animals are infected, the risk that H5N1 will mutate to cause human-to-human infections grows. ✻ According to the WHO, seasonal flu epidemics hit 5–15% of the world population every year, killing between ¼–½ million, mostly the sick and elderly. However, flu *pandemics* typically occur every 10–50 years, with much more devastating results. The C20th saw 3 flu pandemics: the 1918 Spanish Flu (*c.*40m deaths); the 1957 Asian Flu (>2m deaths); and the 1968 Hong Kong Flu (*c.*1m deaths). For obvious reasons, many organizations are reluctant to estimate potential death tolls for a hypothetical H5N1 pandemic. Yet the WHO states that modeling of the current population suggests that 'at a minimum' 2–7·4m might die in the next pandemic, a statistic that does not take into account nonfatal morbidity, nor the potentially catastrophic socioeconomic toll of a pandemic.

Human Cases of H5N1

at 8/9/06	cases	deaths
Azerbaijan	8	5
Cambodia	6	6
China	20	13
Djibouti	1	0
Egypt	14	6
Indonesia	56	44
Iraq	2	2
Thailand	24	16
Turkey	12	4
Vietnam	93	42
Total	236	138

World Health Organization

US OVERVIEW 2001–2006

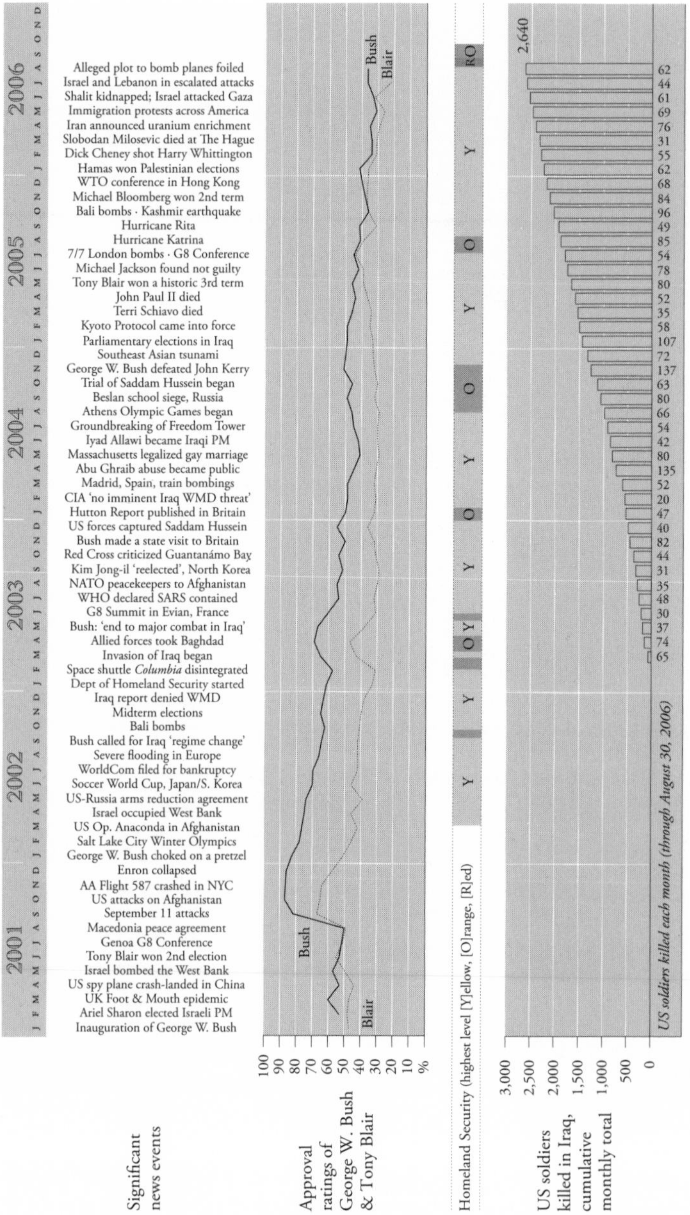
2001 2002 2003 2004 2005 2006
Alleged plot to bomb planes foiled
Israel and Lebanon in escalated attacks
Shalit kidnapped; Israel attacked Gaza
Immigration protests across America
Iran announced uranium enrichment
Slobodan Milosevic died at The Hague
Dick Cheney shot Harry Whittington
Hamas won Palestinian elections
WTO conference in Hong Kong
Michael Bloomberg won 2nd term
Bali bombs · Kashmir earthquake
Hurricane Rita
Hurricane Katrina
7/7 London bombs · G8 Conference
Michael Jackson found not guilty
Tony Blair won a historic 3rd term
John Paul II died
Terri Schiavo died
Kyoto Protocol came into force
Parliamentary elections in Iraq
Southeast Asian tsunami
George W. Bush defeated John Kerry
Trial of Saddam Hussein began
Beslan school siege, Russia
Athens Olympic Games began
Groundbreaking of Freedom Tower
Iyad Allawi became Iraqi PM
Massachusetts legalized gay marriage
Abu Ghraib abuse became public
Madrid, Spain, train bombings
CIA 'no imminent Iraq WMD threat'
Hutton Report published in Britain
US forces captured Saddam Hussein
Bush made a state visit to Britain
Red Cross criticized Guantanámo Bay
Kim Jong-il 'reelected', North Korea
NATO peacekeepers to Afghanistan
WHO declared SARS contained
G8 Summit in Evian, France
Bush: 'end to major combat in Iraq'
Allied forces took Baghdad
Invasion of Iraq began
Space shuttle *Columbia* disintegrated
Dept of Homeland Security started
Iraq report denied WMD
Midterm elections
Bali bombs
Bush called for Iraq 'regime change'
Severe flooding in Europe
WorldCom filed for bankruptcy
Soccer World Cup, Japan/S. Korea
US-Russia arms reduction agreement
Israel occupied West Bank
US Op. Anaconda in Afghanistan
Salt Lake City Winter Olympics
George W. Bush choked on a pretzel
Enron collapsed
AA Flight 587 crashed in NYC
US attacks on Afghanistan
September 11 attacks
Macedonia peace agreement
Genoa G8 Conference
Tony Blair won 2nd election
Israel bombed the West Bank
US spy plane crash-landed in China
UK Foot & Mouth epidemic
Ariel Sharon elected Israeli PM
Inauguration of George W. Bush
Significant news events
Approval ratings of George W. Bush & Tony Blair
Bush
Blair
100 90 80 70 60 50 40 30 20 10 %
Homeland Security (highest level [Y]ellow, [O]range, [R]ed)
Y Y O Y Y O Y O Y O Y O Y RO
US soldiers killed in Iraq, cumulative monthly total
3,000 2,500 2,000 1,500 1,000 500 0
2,640
62 44 61 69 76 31 55 62 68 84 96 49 85 54 78 80 52 35 58 107 72 137 63 80 66 54 42 80 135 52 20 47 40 82 44 31 35 48 30 37 74 65
US soldiers killed each month (through August 30, 2006)

US OVERVIEW 2001–2006 cont.

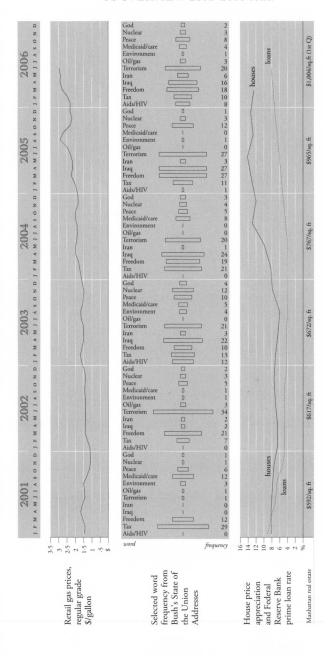

Retail gas prices, regular grade $/gallon

3·5 · 3 · 2·5 · 2 · 1·5 · 1 · ·5 · $

Selected word frequency from Bush's State of the Union Addresses

word   *frequency*

word	2006	2005	2004	2003	2002	2001
God	2	1	3	4	2	1
Nuclear	3	3	4	12	3	1
Peace	8	12	2	10	5	6
Medicaid/care	4	0	8	5	1	12
Environment	1	1	0	4	2	3
Oil/gas	3	0	0	0	3	1
Terrorism	20	27	20	21	34	1
Iran	6	3	1	3	2	0
Iraq	16	27	24	22	2	0
Freedom	18	27	19	10	21	12
Tax	10	11	21	13	7	29
Aids/HIV	8	1	0	12	0	

House price appreciation and Federal Reserve Bank prime loan rate

16 · 14 · 12 · 10 · 8 · 6 · 4 · 2 · %

houses / loans

	2001	2002	2003	2004	2005	2006
Manhattan real estate	$592/sq. ft	$617/sq. ft	$672/sq. ft	$767/sq. ft	$965/sq. ft	$1,004/sq.ft (1st Q)

Debate & dispute surround some entries. Approval rating for Bush, source: *New York Times*/CBS News Poll; rating for Blair, source: Mori. US troops killed in Iraq, source: Dept of Defense; the Brookings Institution. Retail US gas prices are for regular, all formulations, including all taxes, source: US Dept of Energy. Word frequency is analyzed from White House transcripts of Bush's State of the Union Addresses and, in 2001, his 'Budget Message' before a joint session of Congress. Word count is calculated using all relevant iterations of a word, for example: 'tax' includes 'taxes', 'taxpayer(s)', 'tax-cut(s)', 'taxation', &c. House price appreciation data from same quarter one year earlier, source: Office of Federal Housing Enterprise Oversight. Manhattan real estate prices from average $ per square foot for co-ops and condos, source: Prudential Douglas Elliman.

—IRAQ CONFLICT · CASUALTIES & TROOP NUMBERS—

There are no official figures for civilian deaths in Iraq. Neither the Americans nor the British count civilian deaths (or, if they do, they decline to publish the data). The British Foreign Office states there is no Geneva Convention obligation to log civilian casualties; General Tommy Franks is quoted to have said, 'We don't do body counts'. Filling this vacuum of official data are independent organizations, like the Iraq Body Count (IBC), which piece together figures from military, press, hospital, and mortuary reports. However, as the IBC notes, 'Any parties to this conflict will have an interest in manipulating casualty figures for political ends. There is no such thing (and will probably never be such a thing) as a "wholly accurate" figure, which could be accepted as historical truth by all parties'. Below are the IBC's maximum and minimum figures of civilian deaths in Iraq – alongside US military fatalities:

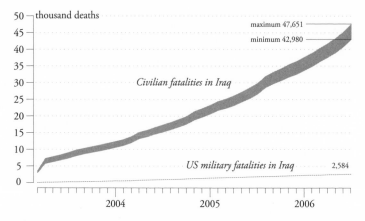

Data on troop deployment, although easier to obtain, are no less controversial, since the ongoing complexity of the conflict in Iraq (and Afghanistan) has so far limited the options for 'drawdown' [see p.12]. Below is charted the strength of US forces in Iraq since May 2003, from the Department of State's *Iraq Weekly Status Report*:

As of August 2006, the US had 133,000 troops in Iraq. 27 other countries had contributed a further *c.*19,000, including: UK 7,200; South Korea 3,277; Italy 1,600; Poland 900; Australia 900; Georgia 900; Romania 860; & Denmark 530.

—— BAROMETER OF WORLD OPINION OF THE US ——

OPINION OF AMERICA & AMERICANS

The shift between 2000–06 in those with a favorable opinion of the US

% favorable	2000	2006
China	—	.47
Egypt	—	.30
France	.62	.39
Germany	.78	.37
GB	.83	.56
India	—	.56
Indonesia	.75	.30
Japan	.77	.63
Jordan	—	.15
Nigeria	.46	.62
Pakistan	.23	.27
Russia	.37	.43
Spain	.50	.23
Turkey	.52	.12

The difference in 2006 between those with a favorable opinion of America vs Americans

% favorable	America	Americans
China	.47	.49
Egypt	.30	.36
France	.39	.65
GB	.56	.69
Germany	.37	.66
India	.56	.67
Indonesia	.30	.36
Japan	.63	.82
Jordan	.15	.38
Nigeria	.62	.56
Pakistan	.27	.27
Russia	.43	.57
Spain	.23	.37
Turkey	.12	.17

[Pew Global Attitudes Project 15-nation study · June 2006]

THE 'SPECIAL RELATIONSHIP'

63% of the British said Blair had tied GB too closely to the White House; 30% called the relationship 'just right'.

[*Guardian*/ICM · July 2006]

GUANTÁNAMO, RENDITION, & HUMAN RIGHTS

The % that said the US policies of detention at Guantánamo Bay are not legal

Germany	85
United Kingdom	65
Poland	50
India	34

The % that said the US should not be allowed to use their airspace for rendition [see p.25]

United Kingdom	66
Germany	55
Poland	48
India	42

The % that said the US does a bad job of advancing human rights abroad

Germany	78
Russia	66
United Kingdom	56
Poland	33
India	19

[WorldPublicOpinion.org/ Knowledge Networks · July 2006]

VIEW OF THE US's WORLD INFLUENCE

The % that said the US has a mainly negative influence on the world and world events

France	65
Germany	65
Finland	65
Iran	65
Argentina	62
Canada	60
Brazil	60
Australia	60
Great Britain	57
Iraq	56
Mexico	55
Spain	53
South Korea	53
Russia	52
Turkey	49
Indonesia	47
Italy	46
Saudi Arabia	38
Congo	28
Zimbabwe	28
Senegal	25
Ghana	20
Sri Lanka	20
China	20
South Africa	18
Nigeria	17
India	17
Tanzania	16
Poland	15
Afghanistan	14
Kenya	12
Philippines	10

This 33-nation poll found that only Iran was viewed less favorably internationally.

[BBC World Service/Globescan/ PIPA · January 2006]

— THE LANGUAGE OF DETENTION & INTERROGATION —

Since the 2003 invasion of Iraq, controversy has surrounded the US techniques of detention and interrogation – catalyzed by reports and images of abuse in Abu Ghraib, Guantánamo Bay (Gitmo), and elsewhere. The early classification of terror suspects as 'Illegal Enemy Combatants' has allowed the US to justify abrogations from conventions (including Geneva, 1949) that proscribe cruel and degrading treatment. America's use of 'enhanced interrogation techniques' has been defended by President Bush, who argued that a 'new paradigm' was required to crack 'the worst of the worst'. (According to a US official, Guantánamo Bay was designed to be the 'legal equivalent of outer space'.) ❦ It is beyond the remit of *Schott's Almanac* to detail the ongoing allegations, investigations, and prosecutions of mistreatment – some of which go well beyond so-called 'torture lite' into severe physical, sexual, and psychological abuse. Yet, one of the novel features of this reappraisal of detention and interrogation is the vocabulary of its practitioners. For example, when three Gitmo inmates committed suicide in June 2006, the camp commander called it an 'act of *asymmetrical warfare* waged against us'. Another spokesman described the deaths as '*a good PR move*'. Below are some other terms that have recently emerged:

HOODING · covering prisoners' heads to render them docile and deprive them of sensory input. The wearing of gloves, goggles, and headphones can produce hallucinations within 48 hours.

FUTILITY MUSIC · violent, aggressive, repetitive, and 'culturally insensitive' music played at high volume for hours on end, often combined with strobe lights. Various reports have listed bands that were inflicted on suspects, including: Eminem, Bruce Springsteen, Metallica, Limp Bizkit, Christina Aguilera, Britney Spears, and, bizarrely, Barney the Dinosaur. Other noises used include 'Halloween sounds', cats meowing, and babies crying inconsolably.

THE BLACK ROOM · 'a windowless jet-black garage-size room' (formerly a Saddam torture chamber) in Camp Nama, Baghdad, where US troops 'beat prisoners with rifle butts, yelled and spit in their faces and, in a nearby area, used detainees for target practice in a game of JAILER PAINTBALL', where, according to a printed sign, the rule was 'NO BLOOD, NO FOUL' [*NY Times*].

SLEEP ADJUSTMENT · manipulating and repeatedly interrupting the sleep of prisoners, while theoretically allowing them adequate overall hours of sleep. In Gitmo, the technique of moving detainees from cell to cell every few hours to disrupt their sleep was known as the FREQUENT FLYER PROGRAM.

INTERNAL NUTRITION · US military euphemism for force-feeding.

WATER-BOARDING · where prisoners are strapped to an inclined board and made to feel they will drown – either by submerging them in water or by wrapping their faces with plastic and pouring water over them. Senator John McCain said, 'I believe that [water-boarding] is torture, very exquisite torture', and, according to ABC News, CIA operatives who underwent this technique lasted just 14 seconds. *Also* THE WATER CURE · where prisoners are strapped down with a rag in their mouths onto which water is poured. *Also* WATER PIT · a void filled with water in which prisoners have to stand on tiptoe to avoid drowning.

—————— LANGUAGE OF DETENTION &c. cont. ——————

TICKING TIME BOMB · a justification for torture, premised on the scenario of a prisoner who has vital information on an *imminent* explosion that can be extracted only by the use of torture.

ATTENTION GRAB · where an interrogator forcefully grabs the clothes of a prisoner and shakes him. *Also* ATTENTION SLAP · an open-handed slap to cause pain and trigger fear. *Also* BELLY SLAP · a hard, open-handed slap to the stomach, to cause pain, but not internal injury. *Also* SISSY SLAP · where prisoners are touched with an inflated latex glove labeled 'sissy slap glove'.

MOCK BURIAL · where prisoners are made to think they will be buried alive. *Also* FAKE EXECUTION · convincing prisoners they are about to be killed.

DIETARY MANIPULATION · where a prisoner's rations are changed (e.g. cold instead of hot food), not as deprivation but to upset routine. *Also* ENVIRONMENTAL MANIPULATION · where the prisoners' cells are made uncomfortable (e.g. with noxious smells, excrement, temperature changes, sounds, &c.).

EXTRAORDINARY RENDITION (aka RUMSFELD PROCESSING) · moving suspects from countries where torture is banned to those where it is not. It is alleged that the US OUTSOURCES TORTURE to countries like Syria, and operates an archipelago of secret prisons (BLACK SITES) in eastern Europe, Thailand, Afghanistan, &c. It has been claimed that the CIA owns a number of private jets to fly GHOST PRISONERS around the world. *Also* REVERSE RENDITION · when foreign powers arrest suspects in noncombat areas and hand them over to the US.

FORCED GROOMING · shaving off body hair – especially effective against Muslims, for whom hair is sacred.

PRIDE AND EGO DOWN · employing humiliation to crush a prisoner's sense of pride and self (e.g. abusing copies of the Koran or wrapping prisoners in the Stars and Stripes). Recent allegations against US forces include the 'invasion of space by a female' – e.g. enforced nudity in front of female soldiers, lap-dancing, making prisoners wear female underwear, and daubing prisoners with perfume and fake menstrual blood.

STRESS POSITIONS · forcing prisoners into discomfort for hours on end, or keeping them in confined spaces where they can neither sit nor stand. *Also* SHORT SHACKLE · where prisoners' wrists and ankles are fixed to eyebolts in the floor, forcing them to crouch. *Also* LONG-TIME STANDING · making prisoners stand and denying them sleep. *Also* COLD CELL · keeping prisoners naked in 50ºF cells and dousing them in water. *Also* FORCED EXERCISE · gratuitous physical training. *Also* CLAUSTROPHOBIC TECHNIQUES · like tying prisoners into sleeping bags or cramming them into metal lockers.

REMOVAL OF COMFORT ITEMS · denial of items that, though not essential, give prisoners a sense of self or comfort (e.g. cigarettes); recently, the removal of prayer rugs and Korans from Muslims.

EXPLOIT PHOBIAS · using factors that play on a prisoner's fears (e.g. directing dogs to growl, bark, and show teeth).

[Sources: *New York Times*; *Guardian*;
Amnesty Int.; ACLU; MSNBC; *New Yorker*;
BBC; HRW; ABC; US Dept of Defense; &c.]

—————— BAROMETER OF US MORALITY ——————

The charts below give a snapshot of the, often contradictory, state of US morality:

42% rate the overall state of moral values in the US as 'poor'
†

81% think the state of US morality is getting worse
†

71% think the death penalty is morally acceptable
†

62% think buying and wearing fur clothes are morally acceptable
†

60% think gambling is morally acceptable
†

5% think polygamy is morally acceptable
†

61% think medical research on human stem cells is morally acceptable
†

51% think having a baby outside marriage is morally acceptable
†

15% think suicide is morally acceptable
†

8% think cloning humans is morally acceptable
†

3% think having an adulterous affair is morally acceptable
‡

22% think sex outside of marriage is morally acceptable
‡

35% think smoking marijuana is not a moral issue
‡

79% think underreporting income on taxes is morally wrong
‡

32% think overeating is morally wrong
‡

61% think drinking alcohol to excess is morally wrong
‡

52% think lying can never be justified
§

44% think it 'okay' to exaggerate to make a story interesting
§

65% think it 'okay' to lie to avoid hurting someone's feelings
§

37% think it 'okay' to lie about one's age
§

11% think it 'okay' to lie on a résumé
§

9% think it 'okay' to lie to a spouse or partner about an affair
§

33% think it 'okay' to lie about being sick to take a day off work
§

39% say they never feel they have to lie or cheat
§

17% judge morality to be the most important issue when deciding whom to vote for
◊

92% think Americans are becoming too materialistic
∞

76% agree that Americans have 'gotten too far away from God and family'
∞

22% think 'kids not raised with the right values' is the most serious moral crisis
∞

4% think 'abortion & homosexuality' are the most serious moral crises
∞

12% think being a moral person involves 'honoring religious tradition and faith'
∞

[Key to sources: † = Gallup Poll, May 2006 · ‡ = Pew Research Center, March 2006 · § = Ipsos/AP, June 2006
◊ = National Public Radio Poll, July 2006 · ∞ = Center for American Progress, June 2006]

──────PUBLISHING & TRUTHINESS──────

2006 witnessed a series of publishing scandals that dented authorial identity and credibility, and provided further examples of 'truthiness' – Stephen Colbert's elegant description of the triumph of gut feeling over fact. ❦ After a number of publishers rejected his novel addressing drug abuse, alcoholism, pain, and suicide, James Frey found a publisher (Doubleday) for *A Million Little Pieces*, presenting the book as his memoir. Such literary sleight of hand (used by Hemingway, &c.) might have gone unexposed had not Frey's book been catapulted to No. 1 in 2005 by Oprah Winfrey's Book Club. Resulting sales of >3m prompted the blogosphere to investigate suspicions voiced in early reviews (in 2003, Germaine Greer called Frey's book 'the greatest load of old crap'). In January 2006, *thesmokinggun.com* reported that Frey had spent hours, rather than months, in jail and had made up or exaggerated other aspects of his life and 'criminal' past. Oprah's vigorous defense of Frey (including on *Larry King Live*) was swiftly reversed in a riveting live *Oprah* special, where she accused Frey and his publisher to their faces of deceiving millions. Admitting he had erred, Frey attempted various justifications, including a note inserted into later editions: 'My mistake … is writing about the person I created in my mind to help me cope, and not the person who went through the experience'. (Inevitably, legal action was threatened against Frey, including a suit seeking compensation for time lost both in reading his book and in filing the suit.) ❦ Publishing's dalliance with truthiness continued with the exposure of J.T. LeRoy, the author of a series of successful and celebrity-

James Frey

endorsed books, including *The Heart Is Deceitful Above All Things*. In October 2005, *New York* magazine suggested that LeRoy was not in fact an HIV-positive, previously homeless, child prostitute, drug-abusing, gender-confused 25-year-old man, but actually a 40-year-old woman, Laura Albert. In 2006, the *New York Times* ran an interview with Albert's partner of 16 years, Geoffrey Knoop, who admitted, 'The jig is up … I do want to apologize to people. … It got to a level I didn't expect'. (It seems that LeRoy's public persona, a man in a blond wig with dark glasses, was played by Knoop's half-sister Savannah.) Albert has neither confirmed nor denied her involvement in the LeRoy hoax. ❦ Harvard student Kaavya Viswanathan (*b.*1987) became mired in controversy when it emerged that her debut Indian American coming-of-age novel, *How Opal Mehta Got Kissed, Got Wild & Got a Life*, contained numerous plagiarized passages. Viswanathan called her appropriations 'unintentional and unconscious'; her publishers declined to print a revised edition and canceled her second book. ❦ Other publishing skirmishes in 2006 included: the admission of Raytheon CEO Bill Swanson that 17 of his 33 *Unwritten Rules of Management* were lifted from a 1944 text; Dan Brown's *Da Vinci* victory [see p.164]; the suggestion that the memoirs of Native American Nasdijj were the work of a white Michigander writer of gay erotica; and allegations that Vladimir Putin's 1997 PhD stole from a 1978 US management study. ❦ In the light of such incidents, it seems that Stephen Colbert may have been a little generous when he said: 'I don't trust books. They're all fact, no heart'.

──────────────── IMMIGRATION ────────────────

The Pew Hispanic Center estimated that ½–1m illegal immigrants entered the US in 2005 (mostly via the porous 2,000-mile Mexican border), adding to the *c.*11·5m illegal immigrants already in the country (*c.*3·6% of the population). This represented a rise of 185% from 1992, when there were *c.*3·9m illegal immigrants. The heated political debate over immigration in 2006 focused on the issues of border security, programs for temporary workers, criminal penalties for existing illegals, measures requiring employers to verify the status of employees, and, most controversially, a path for illegal immigrants to become legal US citizens. The House and Senate were deadlocked over most of these issues – even the length of border fencing. In May 2006, President Bush attempted to find a solution with a range of initiatives, including sending 6,000 National Guardsmen to the Mexican border. However, it seemed that in the run-up to the midterms, the political impasse would not easily be broken, especially with polls illustrating the strength of public feeling:

57% .... considered illegal immigration to be a very serious problem [1]
46% ....thought immigrants have a bad influence in the US [2]
19% ....said immigrants were more likely to be involved in crime [2]
51% .... said immigrants worked harder than those born here [2]
45% .... thought immigration hurt the US more than it helped [3]
56% ....disapproved of the way George W. Bush was handling immigration [4]
63% ....favored using the National Guard to patrol the Mexican border [1]
79% ....favored allowing illegal workers a way into legal citizenship [5]
77% .... thought the US was not doing enough to halt illegal immigration [6]

Of course, tension between American citizens and those aspiring to citizenship is nothing new. Below is a schematic of legal immigration into the US (1900–2004) – with a few of the landmark events that have influenced the flow of immigrants.

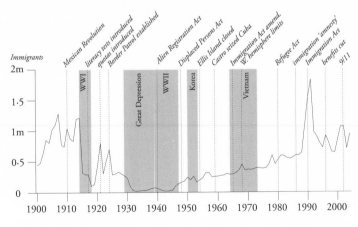

[Polls: 1. Fox News, May 2006; 2. AP, May 2006; 3. NBC News, June 2006; 4. CBS, June 2006; 5. CNN, May 2006; 6. ABC News/*Washington Post*, May 2006. Graph data: US Census]

OTHER MAJOR STORIES IN BRIEF

Abramoff & Lobbying

Jack Abramoff was one of K Street's most powerful lobbyists until allegations surfaced in 2004 that he had tried to bribe lawmakers with gifts, meals, excursions, and vast campaign contributions. On January 3, 2006, he pleaded guilty to tax evasion, defrauding his clients (notably, some tribal casinos), and conspiracy to bribe public officials. In a plea bargain, Abramoff promised to testify against former associates, broadening further one of the most far-reaching corruption investigations. (Additionally, in March, Abramoff and business partner Adam Kidan were sentenced to 70 months in prison for the fraudulent purchase of SunCruz Casinos in Miami.) ❦ House majority leader Tom DeLay and Rep. Bob Ney announced their retirements in the wake of the scandal, which also led to the arrest of federal procurement administrator David Safavian. ❦ Although Congress has since legislated to clean up lobbying, it is unclear what effect these events will have on the 2006 midterms or on public perception of political integrity. At the time of writing, about 20 officials were thought to be under investigation.

Wiretapping & the Executive

The National Security Agency has been required since 1978 to obtain judicial warrants before tapping phone calls, when at least one party is in the US. Yet, in December 2005, the *New York Times* reported that in 2002 President George W. Bush had authorized 'warrantless wiretaps'. Critics regarded this secret program as a major threat to civil liberties, and a potentially unlawful overstep of power. Administration officials argued that judicial checks were no longer practical in the 'war on ter-

ror', and that their actions were authorized by the broad antiterror resolution passed by Congress days after 9/11. On August 17, a federal judge ruled the program violated the 4th Amendment and the 1978 law, but the program was set to continue pending a September appeal. ❦ In May, *USA Today* reported that the NSA had collected millions of phone records with the help of 3 phone companies (2 later denied participation). And, in June, the *New York Times* reported on a CIA program involving access to millions of US financial records. These revelations of controversial surveillance look set to test the limits of Executive power, and challenge the balance between national security and the privacy of the individual.

'Quailgate' · Whittington & Cheney

On February 11, 2006, Vice President Dick Cheney accidentally shot his 78-year-old lawyer friend Harry Whittington in the face, neck, and chest with an Italian 28-gauge Perazzi shotgun, while hunting quail in Texas. Whittington was rushed to the hospital in Corpus Christi, where, a few days later, he suffered a mild heart attack caused by a pellet lodged in his heart. The controversy surrounding the incident was exacerbated by allegations of Cheney's obfuscatory delay in informing the police, the President, and the media. As he left the hospital a week after the shooting, Whittington noted 'accidents do and will happen', and he apologized 'for all that Vice President Cheney and his family have had to go through'.

ETA Cease-fire

At midnight on March 24, 2006, the Basque separatists ETA (Euskadi Ta Askatasuna, 'Basque Homeland & Freedom') began a 'permanent cease-fire'. The

──────────OTHER MAJOR STORIES IN BRIEF cont.──────────

group promised to 'promote a demo-cratic process in the Basque country', a pledge greeted with caution – since earlier ETA cease-fires had ended within months. Spain, the US, and the EU classify ETA as a terrorist organization, and the group is held responsible for >800 deaths since it was founded in 1959. Although ETA's campaign had been in decline, it seems likely that their rejection of terror was catalyzed by the arrest of a swath of members, and by a shift in Spanish public opinion after the 2004 Madrid train bombings.

Dubai Ports Deal

In February 2006, the British-owned Peninsular & Oriental Steam Navigation Co. (P&O) approved a takeover bid by the United Arab Emirates-controlled Dubai Ports World. The deal was controversial because P&O managed operations at 6 US cargo terminals. Notwithstanding accusations of racism, critics of the takeover claimed it jeopardized national security, noting the UAE had been home to two 9/11 hijackers, and that money for the attacks had flowed through the country. Although the takeover had passed government review, several key Congressmen promised legislation to block the deal. On February 21, Bush vowed to veto any such move, but on March 8, the House Appropriations Cmte voted 62–2 against the takeover. Dubai Ports World averted a political showdown by agreeing, on March 9, to transfer operations of US ports to a US company – and later deciding to sell all of its US port assets to an 'unrelated' US buyer.

French Labor Law Demonstrations

In March 2006, French PM Dominique de Villepin pushed through a controversial new labor law in an attempt to revivify the country's stagnant economy and reduce high rates of youth unemployment (>22% of French 18–25 are unemployed). The law created a 2-year trial contract for those under 26 (*Contrat Première Embauche,* CPE) that employers could terminate without explanation and with minimum notice. This attempt to create a more flexible youth workforce was immediately rejected by unions and students, who feared the CPE would be exploited by large employers. During March and April, mass protests and strikes swept across France – and violent rioting saw shops damaged and cars burned. Despite a tough initial stance, de Villepin and President Chirac were shocked by the vehemence of the public's rejection of the contracts and, on April 10, the CPEs were withdrawn. It is thought that this embarrassing *volte-face* may have seriously damaged de Villepin's chance of succeeding Chirac in the 2007 French presidential elections.

Haditha &c.

Allegations that US Marines killed *c.*24 Iraqi civilians in Haditha, Iraq, on 11·19·2005 came to light in March 2006. The claims shocked Americans and drew comparisons with Vietnam's My Lai massacre. ❧ The initial report of the incident stated that a roadside bomb that killed 20-year-old US Marine Miguel Terrazax and wounded 2 others, also killed 15 civilians and sparked a gun battle in which 8 insurgents died. However, eyewitnesses later alleged that the Marines went on a rampage after the bomb exploded, deliberately shooting *c.*24 civilians at close range. Film shot by a local journalist the day after the attack led to several military inquiries and extensive press investigation. On April 7, three

──────OTHER MAJOR STORIES IN BRIEF cont.──────

officers in overall charge at the time of the deaths were relieved of their command. On June 1, the senior US general in Iraq ordered ethical training for his troops. Members of Iraq's Cabinet have said they will launch their own investigation. At the time of writing, press reports suggested evidence existed of wrongdoing by US soldiers, but no charges had been brought. ❦ During 2006, a series of further allegations of serious misconduct by US troops came to light. One of the most shocking involved claims as-yet-unproven that on 3·12·2005 US soldiers gang-raped and killed a 14-year-old girl in Mahmudiya, before killing her family and burning their house to destroy any evidence. ❦ At the time of writing, a number of military investigations were ongoing.

Java Earthquakes

On May 26, 2006, at 22:53:58 UTC, a 6·3 Richter earthquake occurred under the Indian Ocean, 10 miles SSE of Yogyakarta, on the S. side of Java. The worst-affected area, Bantul, was densely populated, and the latest estimate was of *c.*5,782 deaths, *c.*36,299 injuries, and *c.*600,000 homeless. The international aid response was hindered by poor local coordination. ❦ On July 17, at 08:19:28 UTC, a 7·7 Richter earthquake caused a 6½-ft tsunami to hit a 125-mile stretch of Java's S. shore near Pangandaran. >500 are thought to have died in the tsunami – a death toll made worse by the Indonesian government's unwillingness and inability to pass on the early warning it had received.

Embryonic Stem Cell Veto

On July 19, 2006, George W. Bush exercised his first Presidential veto to halt the Stem Cell Research Enhancement Act. The Act would have reversed

Bush's 2001 ban on federal funding for new embryonic stem cell research, and allowed federal researchers to harvest surplus embryonic stem cells left over from IVF treatments. ❦ Many scientists viewed Bush's veto as perverse, since privately funded research remains legal, and surplus IVF stem cells would be destroyed anyway. Some campaigners saw it as a lost opportunity for US science to be at the vanguard of new treatments for Alzheimer's, Parkinson's, &c. Bush, however, remained resolute, saying the Bill 'crosses a moral boundary that our decent society needs to respect, so I vetoed it'. The House voted 235–193 to override the President, but failed to get the ⅔ majority required.

Alleged Transatlantic Terror Plot

On August 10, 2006, British police announced that an alleged plot to blow up *c.*9 aircraft in mid-air between Britain and America had been foiled. *c.*21 were arrested in raids across Britain and 7 were detained in Pakistan. ❦ It emerged that the plan involved the use of liquid explosives. In response, Britain raised its security state to *Critical* [see p.268], and airports adopted unprecedented security measures – refusing all carry-on luggage save for a few small items, and prohibiting any liquids or gels onboard. The US Homeland Security threat was raised to *Severe* (red) for UK flights bound for the US, and *High* (orange) for flights in or destined for the US. ❦ The disclosure that all of those arrested were followers of, or recent converts to, Islam added to British concerns about the radicalization of sections of the Muslim community. ❦ At the time of writing, 11 suspects had been charged in Britain (others remained in custody), and airport security had been relaxed only slightly.

———————————— ISRAEL, GAZA, & LEBANON ————————————

In summer 2006, a long history of skirmishes along Israel's borders with Gaza and Lebanon escalated into a major conflict after 3 Israeli soldiers were kidnapped in two separate raids that left 10 Israeli soldiers dead. ❦ On June 25, Corporal Gilad Shalit was seized by Palestinian militants who tunneled into Israel under the S. Gaza border. Rejecting as 'extortion' the kidnappers' demands for a prisoner swap, Israeli PM Ehud Olmert ordered attacks on Gaza and the arrest of dozens of Hamas politicians. On July 12, Hezbollah fighters in S. Lebanon launched a cross-border raid and kidnapped Israeli soldiers Ehud Goldwasser and Eldad Regev. Olmert declared this an 'act of war', and said that the Lebanese government (of which Hezbollah is a part) was 'responsible for the consequences'. His cabinet ordered 'severe and harsh' retaliation that would, in the words of one Israeli colonel, 'turn Lebanon's clock back 20 years'. In response, Hezbollah's leader, Hassan Nasrallah, promised 'open war' on Israel. ❦ Israel enforced an air and sea blockade of Lebanon, and for 34 days Israeli forces conducted thousands of air and ground attacks, hitting any targets they suspected of harboring or helping Hezbollah. In retaliation, Hezbollah conducted guerilla attacks, and indiscriminately fired thousands of rockets into densely populated northern Israeli cities. ❦ While the West denounced Hezbollah's provocation and defended Israel's right to self-defense, the scale of the Israeli response quickly drew condemnation – especially after bridges, roads, TV and phone antennas, water treatment centers, and powerplants were destroyed. Israel justified its attacks claiming that Hezbollah was 'mixing in' with the general population and firing rockets from civilian locations. Israel insisted that, unlike Hezbollah, it did not deliberately target civilians, and even dropped leaflets warning of raids. But Israel's standing was not helped by attacks like that on the S. Lebanese village of Qana on July 30, when *c*.28 Lebanese civilians, including *c*.16 children, were killed; or by the negligent killing of 4 unarmed UN observers on July 25. Some described the magnitude of Israel's attacks (where *c*.10 Lebanese died for every Israeli) as 'disproportionate', and even as a 'collective punishment' – significantly, the Geneva Convention defines the latter as a war crime. ❦ As the fighting intensified, the international community moved slowly into action. A UN-led summit in Rome on July 26 failed to demand an immediate cease-fire, a decision that Israel claimed authorized their offensive. An 'immediate' cease-fire was supported by the UN, France, Germany, Italy, Spain, Greece, Jordan, Russia, Saudi Arabia, Canada, Egypt, and Cyprus; it was rejected by the US and Britain, who instead called for a 'sustainable' cease-fire. This crucial semantic difference effectively granted Israel 3 further weeks of attacks. In Britain, Blair again faced accusations of slavishly following US foreign policy; opponents of Bush condemned what they saw as his uncritical support of Israel. Some suggested that America viewed the conflict as a proxy war against Tehran and Damascus; Bush himself said 'responsibility for the suffering of the Lebanese people also lies with Hezbollah's state sponsors, Iran and Syria'. Writing in the *New Yorker*, Seymour Hersh claimed that the US 'was closely involved in the planning of Israel's retaliatory attacks'. ❦ On August 11, after intense negotiation, the UN Security Council approved Resolution 1701, which called for the 'full cessation of hostilities' and a 15,000-strong UN force to replace Israeli troops south of the River Litani. The resolution received a guarded welcome from Israel, Lebanon, and Hezbollah, and the cease-fire came into effect at 0500 GMT

———————— ISRAEL, GAZA, & LEBANON cont. ————————

on August 14. ❦ As c.600,000 refugees poured back into Lebanon, and tensions eased in Israel's northern towns, all sides claimed victory. Hezbollah, Syria, and Iran argued that Israel had been fought to a standstill, and Nasrallah mocked its 'failure and impotency'. Conversely, Bush boldly declared, 'Hezbollah started the crisis, and Hezbollah suffered a defeat in this crisis'. Olmert's reaction was muted by continuing insecurity in Gaza, a sharp swing in Israeli public opinion against his handling of the war, and surprise and anger at the shortcomings of Israel's army and intelligence. Olmert claimed that the 'strategic balance' in the region had shifted against Hezbollah, but he could not dodge his failure to achieve his stated war aims: to return the Israeli hostages, to disarm Hezbollah, and to secure S. Lebanon. ❦ At the time of writing, the fragile cease-fire was holding, despite skirmishes on both sides. However, the formation of the UN's peacekeeping mission was beset by delays and disputes as to the composition of the force and its precise mandate.

As of 8·24·06, Israel claimed that 43 Israeli civilians had died and c.1,340 had been wounded; 119 Israeli soldiers had died and c.400 had been wounded. Hezbollah reported that 74 of its soldiers had been killed, however Israel claimed >500. The Lebanese government claimed that c.1,130 civilians had been killed, and c.3,800 injured. According to the BBC, at the time of the cease-fire on August 14, Israel had hit c.7,000 targets in air strikes, and c.3,700 Hezbollah rockets had landed in Israel.

Hezbollah kidnappings

Approximate range of most Hezbollah rockets

≈ deepest Hezbollah rocket attack in Israel

Shalit kidnapped

————— PROFILE: MAHMOUD AHMADINEJAD —————

Since becoming President of Iran in August 2005, Mahmoud Ahmadinejad has adopted a provocative stance. He has questioned the Holocaust, demanded the elimination of Israel and the re-settlement of Israelis, insinuated a US conspiracy in 9/11, fomented the crisis between Israel and Hezbollah, insisted that Iran has the right to a peaceful program for nuclear power, and threatened that this program may not remain peaceful if Iran is attacked. Yet, his speeches and interviews (and his personal letter to George W. Bush) are embellished with exhortations to harmony, peace, justice, spirituality, equality, compassion, and tranquility. In 2006, this (calculatedly) mercurial mix of firebrand and philosopher fortified his position on the world stage. ❦ Ahmadinejad was born in 1956, in a small village near Garmsar, the fourth son of a blacksmith and one of seven children. He moved with his family to Tehran, where he attended school. In 1979 he was admitted to study civil engineering at Tehran's Science and Technology University (where he obtained a PhD in traffic and transportation in 1997). Uncertainty surrounds Ahmadinejad's activities during the 1979 Revolution and the 1980–88 Iran-Iraq War. His official biography states he engaged in 'political activities' and 'was actively present as a member of the [Revolutionary Guard] in different parts and divisions of the battlefronts'. Other accounts allege involvement in covert operations in Iraq, assassinations of dissidents, and executions in Tehran's bloody Evin prison. (The US claims he led the seizing of the American embassy in Tehran in 1979.) After serving regional governorships in the 1980s, Ahmadinejad was appointed Mayor of Tehran in 2003, where he reversed many earlier reforms, closing fast-food restaurants, requiring women to use separate elevators, ordering male city employees to wear beards, &c. (In 2005, Ahmadinejad was a finalist in the World Mayor contest, alongside NYC's Michael Bloomberg.) ❦ Ahmadinejad's deliberately modest 2005 Presidential bid focused on Islam, social justice, poverty, and corruption. But he also used the campaign to attack the US and challenge the UN, which he said was 'stacked against the Islamic world'. To the surprise of many, he beat ex-President Rafsanjani, 62% to 36%. At his inauguration, Ahmadinejad demonstrated his loyalty (and subjugation?) to Iran's Supreme Leader by kissing Ayatollah Khamenei's hand – an unusual public gesture of respect. ❦ Ahmadinejad's domestic policy has combined reaction (banning Western music) with reform (allowing women to watch sports), and he continues to struggle with Iran's economic inequalities and poverty. But it is internationally that Ahmadinejad has made his mark, strengthening relations with Islamic neighbors, fixing deals with China and Russia, and challenging the West by pursuing a nuclear fuel cycle. Time will tell whether Ahmadinejad's defiance of the IAEA is designed to extract concessions and credibility from the West, or give Iran time to weaponize its research. If the latter, the US commitment to neutralize the threat may be circumscribed by military overstretch in Afghanistan and Iraq, and by the ability of a weakened President to persuade the world that *this* time WMD exist. Israel, however, is likely to feel no such constraints.

—SCHEMATIC · SOME WORLD EVENTS OF NOTE · 2006—

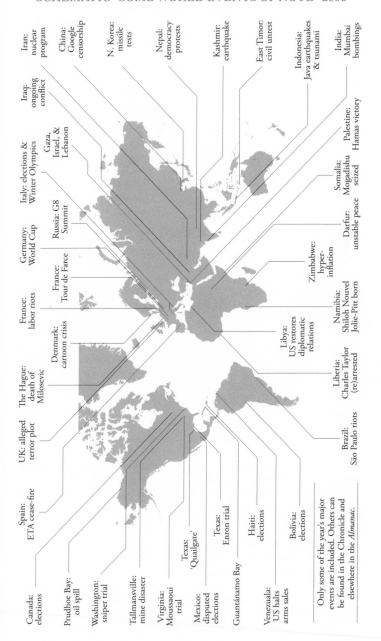

Iran: nuclear program

China: Google censorship

N. Korea: missile tests

Nepal: democracy protests

Kashmir: earthquake

East Timor: civil unrest

Indonesia: Java earthquakes & tsunami

India: Mumbai bombings

Iraq: ongoing conflict

Gaza, Israel, & Lebanon

Palestine: Hamas victory

Italy: elections & Winter Olympics

Somalia: Mogadishu seized

Russia: G8 Summit

Darfur: unstable peace

Germany: World Cup

France: Tour de Farce

Zimbabwe: hyper-inflation

France: labor riots

Namibia: Shiloh Nouvel Jolie-Pitt born

Denmark: cartoon crisis

Libya: US restores diplomatic relations

The Hague: death of Milosevic

Liberia: Charles Taylor (re)arrested

UK: alleged terror plot

Brazil: São Paulo riots

Spain: ETA cease-fire

Canada: elections

Prudhoe Bay: oil spill

Washington: sniper trial

Tallmansville: mine disaster

Virginia: Moussaoui trial

Texas: 'Quailgate'

Mexico: disputed elections

Texas: Enron trial

Guantánamo Bay

Haiti: elections

Venezuala: US halts arms sales

Bolivia: elections

Only some of the year's major events are included. Others can be found in the Chronicle and elsewhere in the *Almanac*.

——————IN BRIEF · JANUARY 2006——————

JANUARY · {2} An explosion at a Tallmansville, WV, coal mine trapped 13 miners 260ft underground; dangerous gases delayed a rescue attempt. {3} Iran announced plans to resume its 'peaceful nuclear energy program', suspended in 2004.
❦ Republican lobbyist Jack Abramoff pleaded guilty to conspiracy, mail fraud, and tax evasion. {4} Bombs in central Iraq killed >50; 30 Shiites died in a Miqdadiyah attack.
❦ Despite initial reports that 12 of the 13 trapped miners in WV had been found alive, it was announced that only 1 had survived. ❦ Abramoff pleaded guilty to 2 felony charges of conspiracy and fraud at a second federal court. ❦ Israeli PM Ariel Sharon suffered a massive stroke. {5} Ehud Olmert was named acting PM of Israel. ❦ >100 Iraqis died in Ramadi and Karbala, Iraq. {6} The Congressional Research Service reported that Bush's eavesdropping program 'does not seem to be as well-grounded' as government lawyers had suggested. ❦ Sharon underwent a 5-hour brain operation. {7} 12 were killed after a US Black Hawk helicopter crashed in N. Iraq. ❦ *Christian Science Monitor* reporter Jill Carroll was kidnapped in Baghdad and her translator was killed; Carroll was threatened with death unless the US released

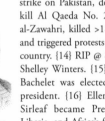

Jack Abramoff

Maybe [Ariel Sharon] will be able to understand and to speak.
– neurosurgeon JOSE COHEN

female Iraqi prisoners. ❦ Rep. Tom DeLay [TX-R] said he was giving up plans to resume his post as House majority leader. {9} Supreme Court nominee Samuel A. Alito Jr began his confirmation hearing before the Senate Judiciary Cmte. {10} Iran opened the seals on 3 nuclear facilities; the US condemned the action. {11} Israel announced it would no longer do business with Pat Robertson after he called Sharon's stroke 'divine retribution' for pulling out of Gaza; Robertson later apologized. {12} 345 pilgrims were trampled to death in the annual pilgrimage to Mecca [see p.337]. {13} A US missile strike on Pakistan, designed to kill Al Qaeda No. 2, Ayman al-Zawahri, killed >18 civilians and triggered protests across the country. {14} RIP @ 85, actress Shelley Winters. {15} Michelle Bachelet was elected Chilean president. {16} Ellen Johnson Sirleaf became President of Liberia, and Africa's first female head of state. {17} 2 civil rights groups filed lawsuits seeking a ban on the National Security Agency's eavesdropping program. ❦ The Supreme Court upheld an OR law allowing assisted suicide. {18} The Justice Dept demanded *Google* release 1m website addresses and all search queries from a 1-week period, to test the effectiveness of 1998 anti-child-pornography legislation; *Google* refused. ❦ Tokyo's stock exchange closed early for the first time ever, after a fraud investigation catalyzed panic selling. ❦ The bodies of 36 Iraqis were found in mass graves N. of Baghdad. {19} Aljazeera aired an audiotape of Osama bin Laden threatening further attacks on the US but hinting a 'truce' was possible. ❦ RIP @ 64, soul legend Wilson Pickett [see p.56]. ❦ NASA launched the first mission to Pluto. {20} Official results confirmed that the Shiite-led United Iraqi Alliance had won 181 of 275 seats in December's Iraqi parliamentary elections; Sunnis won 58 seats. ❦ RIP @ 61, President of Kosovo Ibrahim Rugova. ❦ Neil Entwistle's wife and daughter were found murdered in Hopkinton, MA. {21} Evo Morales was

──── IN BRIEF · JANUARY – FEBRUARY 2006 ────

sworn in as President of Bolivia, the first indigenous Bolivian to hold the post. {23} Conservative Stephen Harper was elected Canadian PM, ending 13 years of Liberal rule. ❦ A new judge, Raouf Rasheed Abdel Rahman, was appointed in Saddam Hussein's trial [which began 10/18/2005]. {24} The Senate Judiciary Cmte voted 10–8 to endorse Alito's nomination. ❦ An audit by the Special Inspector General for Iraq Reconstruction found evidence that millions of dollars meant for Iraqi reconstruction were misused. ❦ Bush refused to turn over internal correspondence concerning Hurricane Katrina, citing confidentiality. ❦ RIP @ 40 [?43], actor Chris Penn. ❦ RIP @ 91, tap-dancing pioneer Fayard Nicholas. {25} Pope Benedict XVI issued his first major papal teaching, on love and charity. ❦ Hamas won a landslide victory in the Palestinian parliamentary elections; Fatah PM Ahmed Qurei resigned. {29} ABC news anchor Bob Woodruff and his cameraman were seriously injured by a bomb in N. Iraq. ❦ Hussein's trial descended into chaos when he walked out with his defense team. ❦ Sheikh Sabah al-Ahmad al-Sabah was elected Kuwait's 3rd new ruler in a fortnight. ❦ Acting Israeli PM Olmert said Israel would no longer negotiate with the Palestinian government unless Hamas recognized Israel and renounced violence. {30} Aljazeera aired a videotape of Al Qaeda's Ayman al-Zawahri taunting Bush and warning of new attacks. ❦ RIP @ 78, Coretta Scott King [see p.56]. ❦ RIP @ 55, playwright Wendy Wasserstein. {31} Enron founder Kenneth Lay and former CEO Jeffrey Skilling began their criminal trial in Houston for fraud and

Samuel Alito

The judge's only obligation, and it's a solemn obligation, is to the rule of law.
– SAMUEL ALITO

conspiracy. ❦ The Senate voted 58–42 to confirm Alito; he was then sworn in as 110th Justice of the Supreme Court [see p.306]. ❦ A former postal worker killed 7 and then herself in a Santa Barbara postal center [see p.314]. ❦ A Danish paper apologized after its publication of cartoons depicting Muhammad led to diplomatic sanctions and death threats [see p.17]. ❦ The Senate confirmed Ben Bernanke as the new Federal Reserve chief. ❦ Bush delivered his State of the Union address [see pp.294–5].

FEBRUARY · {1} The House passed a $39bn deficit-reduction bill, including cuts to Medicaid and student loans. {2} Rep. John A. Boehner [OH-R] was elected House Majority Leader, replacing Rep. Tom DeLay [TX-R]. ❦ Gunmen occupied the offices of the EU in Gaza to protest the Muhammad cartoons. {3} Arsonists burned 5 Baptist churches in central AL. ❦ An Egyptian passenger ferry sunk in the Red Sea; c.1,000 drowned. {4} The IAEA voted to report Iran to the UN Security Council over its nuclear program. ❦ Protesters burned the Danish Mission in Lebanon to protest the Muhammad cartoons; 1 died. ❦ RIP @ 85, feminist Betty Friedan [see p.56]. {6} 'Detective to the stars' Anthony Pellicano was charged with 110 counts of racketeering and conspiracy for eavesdropping on celebrities, journalists, and executives. ❦ 5 died and c.12 were injured in Afghanistan in Muhammad cartoon protests. ❦ Congressional hearings began on the NSA's domestic eavesdropping program; Attorney General Alberto Gonzales said Bush acted legally when authorizing the program. ❦ Bush

—————— IN BRIEF · FEBRUARY 2006 ——————

released his budget proposals, calling for increased defense spending and cuts in domestic programs. {7} Arsonists burned 4 more Baptist churches in AL. {8} Africa's first case of bird flu was confirmed in Nigeria. {9} Bush revealed details of a foiled 2002 Al Qaeda plot to fly a plane into an LA skyscraper. ❦ Kuwaiti TV aired a video of Carroll pleading for her captors' demands. {10} The XX Winter Olympic Games began in Turin [see pp.228–99]. {11} VP Dick Cheney accidentally shot his friend Harry Whittington in the face while hunting quail in TX (the press later questioned why the news was delayed) [see p.29]. ❦ A 10th Baptist church was burned in AL. ❦ The EU announced its first bird flu cases [see p.19]. ❦ The press reported on a plan to cede operations of 6 US ports to Dubai Ports World; the deal later drew criticism from several senators [see p.30]. {12} RIP @ 65, *Jaws* author Peter Benchley. {13} Preliminary Haitian election results showing René Préval's defeat caused widespread protests and violence. {14} Whittington suffered a mild heart attack as a result of birdshot lodged in his heart. {15} Australian TV broadcast previously unseen images of Iraqi prisoner abuse at Abu Ghraib in 2003.

Harry Whittington

❦ Cheney spoke for the first time about his hunting accident, taking full responsibility and defending the delay in disclosure. ❦ A House report on failures during Katrina blamed all levels of government; a Senate Cmte. chastised Homeland Security Sec. Michael Chertoff in particular. {16} A UN Human Rights Cmsn report calling for the closure of Guantánamo Bay was dismissed by the White House. ❦ Bush said Cheney had handled the disclo-

I turned and shot at the bird and at that second saw Harry standing there.
– DICK CHENEY

sure of his hunting accident 'just fine'; the Kenedy County, TX, Sheriff's Dept said the incident's investigation was closed with no charges filed. ❦ Preval was declared winner of Haiti's Presidential elections after an agreement between the interim government and the electoral council. {17} *c.*1,400 were missing after a mudslide destroyed the Philippines village of Guinsaugon. ❦ Whittington was released from hospital. {19} Israeli leaders voted to withhold $50m per month in customs and tax revenues from the Palestinians. ❦ 65 coal miners were trapped by a blast near San Juan de Sabinas, Mexico. {20} Bombs in Iraq killed *c.*26. ❦ An Austrian court sentenced British revisionist historian David Irving to 3 years in prison for Holocaust denial [see p.63]. ❦ Bin Laden's Jan 19 remarks were posted in full online; he claimed he would never be captured alive and that the US military was as barbaric as Hussein's. ❦ RIP @ 86, sportscaster Curt 'Voice of the Red Sox' Gowdy. {21} Hamas chief Ismail Haniya was appointed PM. ❦ Harvard Pres. Lawrence H. Summers announced his resignation. ❦ RIP @ 68, writer of the *Sesame Street* theme song Bruce Hart. ❦ Bush defended the Dubai Ports World deal, and vowed to veto any Congressional attempt to block it. {22} A bomb attack heavily damaged the al-Askari shrine in Samarra, one of Iraq's most famous Shiite sites, dramatically heightening sectarian tensions. ❦ 8 workers at a Nebraska ham-processing plant shared $365m, the largest lottery jackpot in US history. {23} The White House official report into Hurricane Katrina blamed lack of experience, planning, discipline, and leadership

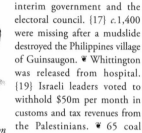

─── IN BRIEF · FEBRUARY – MARCH 2006 ───

for the federal response failures. ❧ Several days of violence after the al-Askari bombing in Iraq led to *c.*138 deaths. ❧ 2 days of rioting in Nigeria over the Muhammad cartoons killed >80 [see p.17]. {24} RIP @ 81, actor Don Knotts. ❧ RIP @ 58, sci-fi author Octavia Butler. {25} Mine owners declared there was no hope for 65 miners trapped in N. Mexico on 2/19. ❧ RIP @ 69, Ethiopian Poet Laureate Tsegaye Gabre-Medhin. {27} ❧ RIP @ 78, *LA Times* publisher Otis Chandler. ❧ Bosnian genocide hearings began at The Hague. ❧ The US agreed to pay $300,000 to Ehab Elmaghraby, an Egyptian living in NY who was jailed and deported after 9/11, despite having no links to terrorism. ❧ The EU offered $144m of emergency aid to the Palestinian Authority. ❧ Police in Riyadh killed Fahd Faraaj al-Juwair, the leader of Al Qaeda in Saudia Arabia. ❧ *The Da Vinci Code* author Dan Brown's plagiarism trial opened in London [see p.164]. {28} *c.*75 Iraqis were killed in sectarian violence, including 5 bombings in Baghdad. ❧ RIP @ 85, Nobel Prize physicist Owen Chamberlain.

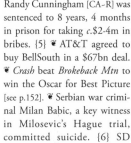

Barry Bonds

The Senate voted 89–10 to renew the Patriot Act. ❧ The largest oil spill to hit Alaska's North Slope was discovered. {3} The Pentagon was forced to reveal the names and nationalities of some Guantánamo inmates. ❧ Former Rep. Randy Cunningham [CA-R] was sentenced to 8 years, 4 months in prison for taking *c.*$2·4m in bribes. {5} ❧ AT&T agreed to buy BellSouth in a $67bn deal. ❧ *Crash* beat *Brokeback Mtn* to win the Oscar for Best Picture [see p.152]. ❧ Serbian war criminal Milan Babic, a key witness in Milosevic's Hague trial, committed suicide. {6} SD banned all abortions except when necessary to save the mother's life [see p.101]. ❧ The trial of alleged 9/11 conspirator Zacarias Moussaoui opened in VA. ❧ The Supreme Court ruled that federal financing to universities can be cut if they do not allow military recruiters access to students equal to other employers. ❧ US health officials authorized the development of a 2nd bird flu vaccine. ❧ RIP @ 44, advocate for the disabled and widow of Christopher, Dana Reeve. ❧ RIP @ 45, legendary baseball outfielder, Kirby Puckett. ❧ After legal delays, demolition began on homes hit by Katrina. {7} *Sports Illustrated* published excerpts from the book *Game of Shadows*, that alleged extensive steroid use by Barry Bonds and others [see p.234]. ❧ 3 college students were arrested in connection with the AL church arsons. ❧ RIP @ 93, *Shaft* director, Gordon Parks [see p.56]. ❧ Bombs in the Hindu holy city of Varanasi, India, killed *c.*14 and wounded >100. ❧ The House voted 280–138 to renew the Patriot Act. {8} Dublin's Roman Catholic Archdiocese admitted that 102 of its

M ARCH {1} · Authorities took control of the main high-security prison in Afghanistan after a 4-day, riot in which 6 died and >40 were injured. ❧ On the first visit to Afghanistan by a US President in 50 years, Bush vowed to capture bin Laden. ❧ The government announced plans to buy antiviral drugs to treat 14m people for bird flu [see pp.19 & 181]. {2} Bush and Indian President Manmohan Singh announced a deal to share US nuclear knowledge and fuel with India. ❧

We had a tiny picture, and we opened at the wrong time.
— PAUL HAGGIS on *Crash*

—— IN BRIEF · MARCH 2006 ——

priests were suspected of abusing >350 children since 1940. ❦ Gunmen kidnapped 50 employees of a security firm in Baghdad. ❦ The House Appropriations Cmte voted 62–2 to bar Dubai Ports World from holding leases or contracts at US ports. ❦ N. Korea reportedly test-fired 2 short-range missiles toward China. ❦ The IAEA reported Iran's nuclear activity to the UN Security Council; Iran said the US could face 'harm and pain' for its opposition [see p.34]. {9} The US announced plans to close Abu Ghraib within 3 months. ❦ Iraq hanged 13 insurgents, the first executions since the invasion. ❦ Homeland Security Sec. Chertoff warned that bird flu could hit the US within months. ❦ SoS Condoleezza Rice called Iran a greater challenge than any other nation to the US, and the 'central bank for terrorism'. ❦ Bush signed the renewed Patriot Act; he also issued a 'signing statement' with his own interpretation of the law. ❦ Dubai Ports World withdrew from the ports deal, promising to transfer its leases to a US company. ❦ A federal jury found Iraq contractor Custer Battles LLC guilty of defrauding the US of $3m. ❦ American aid worker Tom Fox, kidnapped in Iraq [on 11/26/05], was found dead in Baghdad. ❦ Claude A. Allen, Bush's former domestic policy adviser, was charged with theft. ❦ Top Baghdad commanders launched a criminal investigation into alleged Marine killings of *c.*24 civilians in Haditha, Iraq, on 11·19·05. {10} Interior Secretary Gale Norton announced her resignation. {11} Slobodan Milosevic was found dead (aged 64) in his Hague cell. {12} Car bombs killed *c.*46 and injured

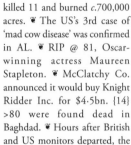

Slobodan Milosevic

>90 in Sadr City, Baghdad. {13} Tornadoes in the Midwest killed >10 and displaced >150. ❦ Moussaoui's trial judge abruptly adjourned the hearing after learning that a government lawyer had 'coached' witnesses. ❦ Wildfires in Texas killed 11 and burned *c.*700,000 acres. ❦ The US's 3rd case of 'mad cow disease' was confirmed in AL. ❦ RIP @ 81, Oscar-winning actress Maureen Stapleton. ❦ McClatchy Co. announced it would buy Knight Ridder Inc. for $4·5bn. {14} >80 were found dead in Baghdad. ❦ Hours after British and US monitors departed, the Israeli army raided a Palestinian prison and seized 6 inmates, including Ahmed Saadat; Palestinians kidnapped 9 foreigners in response. ❦ Thousands of students marched in France, protesting new labor laws. ❦ Milosevic's trial was formally closed; speculation lingered regarding his cause of death. ❦ S. Korean PM Lee Hae-chan announced his resignation after he was caught golfing on the first day of a railway strike. {15} Moussaoui's trial judge restarted the hearing, after rejecting evidence 'contaminated' by witness coaching. ❦ The UN General Assembly voted to create the Human Rights Council to replace the controversial Human Rights Commission (the US voted against the proposal). ❦ Hussein testified at his trial for the first time, urging Iraqis to focus their attacks on the US instead of each other. {16} The US launched its biggest air attack in Iraq since 2003, near Samarra. ❦ The Iraqi parliament convened its inaugural session, which lasted *c.*30 minutes and was adjourned indefinitely. ❦ *March Madness* began [see p.239]. ❦ Protests over youth

[Iran] is a country determined to develop a nuclear weapon.
– CONDOLEEZZA RICE

—————IN BRIEF · MARCH 2006—————

labor laws in France turned violent, leading to the arrest of *c.*150. ❦ Congress approved $92bn in new money for Iraq and Afghanistan, lifted the ceiling on the national debt to $9 trillion, and approved a $2·8 trillion budget blueprint for the upcoming year. ❦ The UN War Crimes Tribunal announced that Milosevic's body had no traces of poison. ❦ A Govt Accountability Office's review of post-Katrina relief contracts found millions of dollars of waste. ❦ Iran offered to meet with the US to discuss ways of stabilizing Iraq, the first offer of negotiation with the US since 1979. {17} A federal judge ordered *Google* to release 50,000 web addresses, but denied a Justice Dept request for specific search wording. ❦ RIP @ 92, fashion designer Oleg Cassini. {18} Milosevic was buried in his hometown of Pozarevac; thousands attended a Belgrade ceremony. ❦ RIP @ 75, veteran ABC anchorman Bill Beutel. {19} Alexander Lukashenko won Belarus's Presidential election in a vote international monitors called fraudulent; >10,000 protested the result. {20} On the 3rd anniversary of the Iraq invasion, Bush asked Americans to look beyond bloodshed for signs of progress. ❦ Former Congolese warlord Thomas Lubanga became the first person to stand trial at the Int. Criminal Court in The Hague. {21} The US military announced it was investigating allegations that US forces had killed a number of civilians in Ishaqi, Iraq, on March 15. ❦ Bush denied that Iraq had descended into 'civil war', but predicted US troops would remain in Iraq after his Presidency. ❦ A court martial convicted Sgt Michael Smith of using his dog to

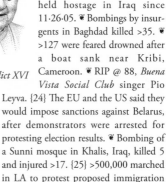

Pope Benedict XVI

The expectation of privacy by some Google users may not be reasonable.
— Federal Judge JAMES WARE

terrify inmates at Abu Ghraib. ❦ Gunmen stormed an Iraqi prison near the Iranian border, freeing 33; *c.*30 were killed. {22} Basque separatists ETA announced a permanent cease-fire [see p.29]. ❦ The Supreme Court ruled that police without a warrant cannot search a house if one resident agrees but another does not. {23} British and US troops freed 3 peace activists held hostage in Iraq since 11·26·05. ❦ Bombings by insurgents in Baghdad killed >35. ❦ >127 were feared drowned after a boat sank near Kribi, Cameroon. ❦ RIP @ 88, *Buena Vista Social Club* singer Pio Leyva. {24} The EU and the US said they would impose sanctions against Belarus, after demonstrators were arrested for protesting election results. ❦ Bombing of a Sunni mosque in Khalis, Iraq, killed 5 and injured >17. {25} >500,000 marched in LA to protest proposed immigration reforms. ❦ A shooting at a party in Seattle left 7 dead and 2 wounded. ❦ RIP @ 76, *Hee Haw* star Buck Owens. ❦ Pope Benedict XVI appealed to Afghan President Hamid Karzai for clemency in the case of Abdul Rahman, facing execution for converting to Christianity. ❦ RIP @ 89, director Richard Fleischer. {26} 17 Iraqis died and 18 were captured in a raid on a Baghdad mosque. ❦ 30 Iraqis were found dead on a village road N. of Baghdad. ❦ RIP @ 30, Indy Racing League driver Paul Dana. {27} A suicide bomber killed *c.*40 inside a military base near Mosul, Iraq. ❦ Abdul Rahman was freed after he was deemed mentally unfit to stand trial. ❦ Iraqi Shiite leaders suspended talks on the formation of a new government. ❦ Charles Taylor disappeared. ❦ RIP @ 84, sci-fi author

─────────IN BRIEF · MARCH – APRIL 2006─────────

Stanislaw Lem. ❦ Moussaoui testified that he was supposed to fly a 5th plane into the White House on 9/11. ❦ Pro-Russian forces won Ukraine's parliamentary elections but failed to get a majority. ❦ The Senate Judiciary Cmte approved a bill to create a guest-worker program and allow illegal aliens to stay in the US. {28} *c.*1·5m demonstrated against France's new youth labor law. ❦ White House Chief of Staff Andrew Card resigned; he was replaced by former Budget Director Joshua Bolten. ❦ RIP @ 88, former Sec. of Defense Caspar Weinberger [see p.56]. ❦ 3 groups of gunmen kidnapped 24 Iraqis from Baghdad businesses. ❦ Taylor was captured and returned to Liberia. ❦ The Senate began debating the Senate Judiciary Cmte's immigration reform bill. ❦ Israelis voted in a general election; Kadima won, but failed to secure a majority. {29} Millions in Brazil, Africa, and Asia saw the first total solar eclipse in 2 years. ❦ Abdul Rahman was granted asylum in Italy. ❦ A Florida judge sentenced Abramoff to 5 years, 10 months in prison. ❦ American Ahmed Omar Abu Ali was sentenced to 30 years in prison by a US jury for joining Al Qaeda and plotting to assassinate Bush. ❦ The UN Security Council urged Iran to suspend uranium enrichment, but did not threaten sanctions. ❦ The Senate banned lobbyists from giving meals and gifts to lawmakers, among other restrictions. ❦ The coach of Duke University men's lacrosse team resigned, following days of protests after the alleged rape of a dancer on March 13. ❦ Rep. Cynthia McKinney [GA-D] allegedly struck a Capitol police officer who tried to prevent her from entering a

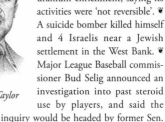

Charles Taylor

House office building. {30} Hostage Jill Carroll was freed. ❦ MA's Supreme Judicial Court ruled that same-sex couples from other states cannot legally marry in the state. ❦ Gunmen killed 8 workers in Iraq's main oil refinery in the northern city of Baiji. ❦ Iran rejected UN Security Council calls to halt uranium enrichment, saying its activities were 'not reversible'. ❦ A suicide bomber killed himself and 4 Israelis near a Jewish settlement in the West Bank. ❦ Major League Baseball commissioner Bud Selig announced an investigation into past steroid use by players, and said the inquiry would be headed by former Sen. George Mitchell [see p.234]. {31} *c.*70 people were killed and 980 injured by earthquakes in W. Iran. ❦ New York City released harrowing recordings of *c.*130 911 calls made during the 9/11 attacks.

A PRIL · {2} Thunderstorms and tornadoes in the Midwest killed *c.*28. ❦ Iran tested a high-speed underwater missile, one of several during days of war games. ❦ French President Jacques Chirac signed a controversial youth labor law [see p.30]. {3} A federal jury found Moussaoui directly linked to the 9/11 attacks, and thus liable to the death penalty. ❦ The Florida Gators beat UCLA 73–57 to take the NCAA championship [see p.239]. ❦ Taylor pleaded not guilty to a Sierra Leone war crimes court. {4} Tom DeLay announced his resignation from Congress. ❦ Thai PM Thaksin Shinawatra announced his resignation. ❦ *c.*1m protested the youth labor law in France. ❦ Hussein was charged with genocide for a 1998 military campaign that killed >50,000

I am much chastened and profoundly remorseful.
– JACK ABRAMOFF

—————— IN BRIEF · APRIL 2006 ——————

Kurds. {5} Katie Couric announced she was leaving NBC's *Today* to anchor the CBS *Evening News*. ❧ RIP @ 65, singer-songwriter Gene Pitney [see p.56]. ❧ Apple unveiled software that allows Macs to run Windows. ❧ The Senate created a compromise immigration bill, including a path to citizenship for those in the country ≥5 years. {6} Britain's first case of bird flu was confirmed. ❧ *New York Post* gossip writer Jared Paul Stern was suspended from his job, after allegedly trying to extort billionaire Ron Burkle. ❧ A group of scientists claimed to have found a 375-million-year-old fossil that may be the 'missing link' between fish and land animals. {7} Dan Brown's trial ended [see p.164]. ❧ A triple-suicide bomb attack on a Shia mosque in Baghdad killed *c.*70 and injured >150. ❧ The compromise immigration bill collapsed when Senators failed to agree on amendments. ❧ 3 officers in charge of troops in Haditha, Iraq, were stripped of command and reassigned. {9} A stampede in Karachi, Pakistan, killed 30 and injured >70. {10} Chirac announced he would repeal the country's controversial youth labor law. ❧ Pro-immigration demonstrations were held across the US. {11} A bomb at a prayer service in Karachi, Pakistan, killed *c.*56. ❧ Iran declared it had successfully enriched uranium. ❧ Romano Prodi's coalition was declared winner of the Italian elections, but Silvio Berlusconi refused to concede defeat. {12} The Israeli Cabinet ended Sharon's premiership, declaring him permanently incapacitated by his January stroke. ❧ MA Gov. Mitt Romney signed the first state legislation providing universal health coverage. {13} ❧

Jared Paul Stern

I'm the decider, and I decide what is best. – GEORGE W. BUSH
defending Donald Rumsfeld

IAEA director Mohamed ElBaradei met with senior Iranian officials, but failed to convince them to abandon nuclear activities. ❧ *c.*350 died in a Sudanese rebel assault on N'Djamena, Chad. {14} Bush defended Defense Sec. Rumsfeld after a sixth retired military commander called for his resignation. ❧ RIP @ 88, novelist Muriel Spark [see p.56]. {16} Iran promised the Palestinian government $50m after the US and EU froze financing. {17} A suicide bomber killed 9 and wounded *c.*49 at a falafel restaurant in Tel Aviv; Hamas called the act 'legitimate'; Palestinian President Mahmoud Abbas condemned it. ❧ The Supreme Court rejected an appeal from 2 Chinese Muslims held in Guantánamo since 2001. {18} Bush nominated Trade Representative Rob Portman for White House Budget Director, and Susan Schwab for Trade Representative. ❧ 2 Duke University lacrosse players were arrested on charges of raping and kidnapping a dancer hired for a March 13 party. ❧ Katie Holmes and Tom Cruise had a daughter, Suri, in LA [see p.118]. ❧ Former IL Governor George Ryan was convicted of corruption in a federal trial. {19} White House Press Sec. Scott McClellan announced his resignation; Deputy Chief of Staff Karl Rove gave up policy oversight to focus on the midterm elections; Joel Kaplan replaced Rove. ❧ The Italian Supreme Court confirmed Prodi's victory. {20} Chinese President Hu Jintao met with Bush at the White House; a protester disrupted the welcoming ceremony. ❧ Iraqi PM Ibrahim al-Jaafari dropped his bid to remain in power. ❧ RIP @ 84, Scott Crossfield, the first pilot to fly at twice the speed of

―――――――― IN BRIEF · APRIL – MAY 2006 ――――――――

sound. {21} >10,000 protesters demonstrated in Katmandu; Nepalese King Gyanendra offered to transfer executive power to a prime minister. {22} Iraq's Parliament chose 7 new political leaders, including Jawad al-Maliki as PM; Maliki was given 30 days to form a new cabinet. ❦ New Orleans voted in mayoral election; Ray Nagin failed to win a majority, necessitating a May 20 runoff. ❦ Nepalese opposition groups rejected King Gyanendra's offer. {23} In an audiotape message, bin Laden accused the West of waging a 'Zionist-crusader war'.

Z. Moussaoui

{24} 7 car bombs in Baghdad killed *c*.10; 30 Iraqis died in other incidents. ❦ 3 explosions in Dahab, Egypt, killed *c*.30 and wounded >115. ❦ RIP @ 91, Grand Rabbi of the Satmar Hasidim Moses Teitelbaum. ❦ King Gyanendra agreed to reinstate Nepal's parliament; 13 total had died in 19 days of protests. {25} RIP @ 89, urban theorist Jane Jacobs. ❦ A CA federal jury convicted US citizen Hamid Hayat of supporting terrorists and lying to the FBI. ❦ A suicide bomber in Sri Lanka killed 9; the government launched an air strike against Tamil Tiger areas. ❦ Head of Al Qaeda in Iraq, Abu Musab al-Zarqawi, appeared in an internet video mocking US troops and vowing their defeat. {26} Bush named Fox News commentator Tony Snow his new Press Secretary. ❦ Iranian Supreme Leader Ayatollah Ali Khamenei threatened a 'twofold' response to any American attacks. ❦ Rove testified for the 5th time during the grand jury investigation into the Valerie Plame affair. ❦ EU investigators accused the CIA of flying >1,000 flights over EU states since 2001, allegedly transporting terror suspects [see

Iran will respond twofold to any attack.
– AYATOLLAH ALI KHAMENEI

pp.24–25]. {27} ❦ Mayson Ahmed Bakir, sister of the Iraqi Vice President, was killed by gunmen in SW Baghdad. {28} Bin Laden's deputy, Ayman Zawahiri, appeared in an internet video claiming that the Iraqi insurgency had 'broken America's back.' ❦ The IAEA reported that Iran had enriched uranium and had not cooperated with inspectors. {29} RIP @ 97, economist John Kenneth Galbraith [see p.57]. {30} Afghan President Karzai pardoned all prisoners with <1 year still to serve, including one American.

MAY · {1} >1m demonstrated in favor of immigration reform in cities across the US. ❦ Bolivian president Evo Morales nationalized the country's oil and gas fields. ❦ DC sniper John A. Muhammad's MD trial began; Muhammad had previously been sentenced to death by a VA court in 2004. {2} Berlusconi resigned as Italian PM. {3} Moussaoui was sentenced to life in prison; he shouted, 'America, you lost!' and 'I won!' as he left the courtroom. ❦ The House passed lobbying reform legislation requiring increased disclosure and ethics training for lawmakers. {4} Olmert was sworn-in as Israeli PM, and his governing coalition was approved by Parliament. {5} CIA Director Porter Goss resigned unexpectedly. ❦ The Sudanese government signed a peace agreement with the rebel Sudan Liberation Army; 2 other rebel groups refused to sign. ❦ Moussaoui said he lied about his 9/11 involvement and asked to withdraw his guilty plea; the judge refused. {7} Car bombs in Baghdad and Karbala, Iraq, killed *c*.14 and wounded >40. {8} Bush nominated

—————————— IN BRIEF · MAY 2006 ——————————

former NSA chief Gen. Michael Hayden as CIA Director. ❦ Iranian President Ahmadinejad sent an 18-page letter to President Bush; it was dismissed by the White House [see p.34]. {9} 17 died in a suicide bombing in Tal Afar, Iraq. ❦ The US endorsed a European plan to aid Palestinian civilians. {10} Giorgio Napolitano was elected President of Italy. ❦ The House passed a *c.*$70bn tax cut bill. {11} The Senate approved a version of the tax cut bill. ❦ *USA Today* reported that Verizon, AT&T, and BellSouth had given tens of millions of phone records to the NSA; Verizon and BellSouth later denied providing any data. ❦ RIP @ 71, boxer Floyd Patterson [see p.57]. {12} A gasoline pipeline in Nigeria exploded after villagers tried to steal fuel; *c.*200 died. {14} 14 were killed in 2 suicide bombings near Baghdad airport. ❦ Preval was sworn in for a 2nd term as President of Haiti. ❦ New England suffered its worst flooding in 70 years. ❦ Israeli troops killed 6 Palestinians in raids on the West Bank. ❦ RIP @ 100, former Poet Laureate Stanley Kunitz. {15} The US announced it would restore normal diplomatic relations with Libya, citing the country's renunciation of terrorism and nuclear weapons. ❦ Hussein was formally charged with crimes against humanity in his trial for the 1982 execution of 150 Shiites; he refused to enter a plea. ❦ The Pentagon released the first list of all prisoners held at Guantánamo Bay. ❦ A 3rd Duke lacrosse player was indicted in the college's rape allegations. ❦ Bush gave a major address on immigration, proposing to send 6,000 National Guardsmen to the Mexican border; he also proposed a path to citizenship for illegal immi-

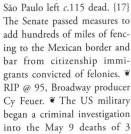

Barbaro

This is the best lead I've seen come across in the Hoffa investigation.
— Special Agent DANIEL ROBERTS

grants who met certain requirements [see p.28]. ❦ The US said it would no longer sell military equipment to Venezuela, because the country was not co-operating with counterterrorism efforts. {16} 5 days of gang attacks and police reprisals in São Paulo left *c.*115 dead. {17} The Senate passed measures to add hundreds of miles of fencing to the Mexican border and bar from citizenship immigrants convicted of felonies. ❦ RIP @ 95, Broadway producer Cy Feuer. ❦ The US military began a criminal investigation into the May 9 deaths of 3 Iraqi detainees. ❦ Bush signed the *c.*$70bn tax cut package. {18} *c.*100 died, including 1 American, in a major escalation of violence in Afghanistan. ❦ The FBI began searching a MI farm for the body of former Teamster boss Jimmy Hoffa. ❦ 1m were evacuated and *c.*50 killed when typhoon Chanchu hit S. China. ❦ 6 Guantánamo Bay detainees were hurt in fighting. ❦ The House voted to end royalty incentives for oil and gas companies drilling in public waters. {19} The Senate approved 2 amendments to the immigration bill to make English the US national language [see p.260]. ❦ The UN Cmte Against Torture denounced CIA handling of terror suspects, and recommended closing Guantánamo. {20} Ray Nagin was re-elected Mayor of New Orleans. ❦ Barbaro broke his ankle at the Preakness Stakes [see p.250] ❦ Barry Bonds hit his 714th home run at a game in Oakland, CA, tying Babe Ruth's career total [see p.234]. ❦ Iraqi Parliament approved PM Maliki's cabinet; 3 key posts remained vacant. ❦ The FBI conducted a controversial overnight raid of the office of Rep. William Jefferson

───────────── IN BRIEF · MAY 2006 ─────────────

[LA-D] as part of a bribery investigation. {21} 20 died in Baghdad bombings and shootings. ❦ Montenegro voted to separate from Serbia. ❦ RIP @ 96, pioneering choreographer and activist Katherine Dunham. {22} The Senate authorized sending National Guardsmen to police the Mexican border. ❦ US planes bombed a S. Afghanistan village, killing *c*.16 civilians and wounding >15; 20–80 Taliban also died. ❦ RIP @ 61, World Health Organization leader Dr Lee Jong Wook. ❦ Veteran Affairs announced a laptop containing 26·5m Social Security numbers and other personal data had been stolen. {23} In an internet video, bin Laden declared that neither Moussaoui nor any Guantánamo prisoners were involved in 9/11. ❦ RIP @ 85, former TX Sen. and Treasury Sec. Lloyd Bentsen. {24} An Israeli raid on the West Bank killed 4 Palestinians and wounded *c*.50. ❦ Shahawar Matin Siraj was convicted by a Brooklyn federal jury of plotting to blow up a NYC subway station in 2004. {25} Under pressure from members of Congress, Bush sealed the documents from the FBI raid of Rep. Jefferson's office for 45 days. ❦ Enron's Lay and Skilling were convicted of fraud and conspiracy [see p.18].

❦ A Russian court sentenced Nur-Pashi Kulayev to life for his role in the 2004 Beslan school siege. ❦ Bush and British PM Tony Blair held a joint news conference, in which they acknowledged mistakes in the war in Iraq. ❦ The Senate passed an immigration bill including a path to citizenship for *c*.11m illegal immigrants, the creation of a guest worker program, and enhanced border security with Mexico. {26} The Senate voted to confirm Gen. Hayden as

Michael Hayden

CIA chief. ❦ Attorney General Gonzales and FBI Director Robert Mueller held a meeting with internet company execs to propose record-keeping to fight child pornography and terrorism. ❦ R. David Paulison approved as FEMA director, and Idaho Gov. Dirk Kempthorne confirmed as Sec. of the Interior. {27} An earthquake at Yogyakarta, Indonesia, killed >5,000, wounded >15,000, and displaced *c*.100,000. ❦ Angelina Jolie gave birth to Shiloh Nouvel Jolie-Pitt in Namibia [see p.118]. {28} 75 Guantánamo Bay inmates went on a hunger strike. ❦ Álvaro Uribe was reelected President of Colombia. {29} A Baghdad car bomb killed 2 British members of a CBS News crew and seriously wounded US journalist Kimberly Dozier. ❦ A traffic accident caused by a US military vehicle killed *c*.5 in Afghanistan and sparked anti-American riots that killed *c*.15. {30} An Israeli helicopter fired a missile at Palestinian militants in Gaza, killing 3 and wounding 4. ❦ Treasury Sec. John Snow resigned; Bush nominated Henry M. Paulson Jr as his replacement. ❦ The FBI ended the search of a MI farm after finding no trace of Hoffa. ❦ John A. Muhammad was found guilty on 6 counts of first-degree murder in MD. ❦ The Supreme Court ruled that public employee 'whistle-blowers' do

Shiloh will receive a Namibian passport, so we shall return.
– BRAD PITT

not have free speech protection for statements they make in the course of performing their duties. ❦ Car bombs in Baghdad killed 54 and wounded >120. ❦ East Timor PM Mari Alkatiri seized control of the country's army and announced emergency rule, after 10 days of unrest in the capital killed *c*.30. {31} PM Maliki declared a state of emergency in Basra. ❦

———————— IN BRIEF · MAY – JUNE 2006 ————————

Coalition forces shot and killed 2 women N. of Baghdad after their car failed to stop at a security checkpoint. ❧ The Dept of Homeland Security announced new antiterrorism funding, including a 40% cut in funding for NYC and Washington, DC; the move was criticized by officials in those cities. ❧ The US agreed to join European talks with Iran, if the country first halted uranium enrichment.

J UNE · {1} A MD court sentenced John A. Muhammad to 6 consecutive life terms in prison with no possibility of parole. ❧ The US and 5 other nations agreed on incentives to encourage Iran to halt uranium enrichment; Iran welcomed talks with the US but rejected their preconditions. ❧ The number of Guantánamo inmates on a hunger strike rose to 89. ❧ Dog handler Sgt Santos A. Cardona was convicted of using his animal to torment Abu Ghraib prisoners. ❧ N. Korea invited Asst SoS Christopher R. Hill to participate in bilateral discussions; the US refused, insisting N. Korea return to 6-nation talks. ❧ Bush pledged a full investigation into the events in Haditha, and the military ordered 'ethical' training for all US and coalition forces stationed in Iraq. ❧ The Pentagon cleared US troops of misconduct allegations regarding a March 15 raid that killed 15 civilians; the Iraqi government rejected the findings. {3} In June 2–3 raids near Toronto, Canadian police arrested 17 men and boys allegedly planning 'Al Qaeda-inspired' bomb attacks on the city. {4} Gunmen stopped 2 minivans carrying students near Baghdad and killed 21 Shiites. ❧ The US military announced

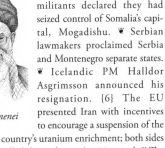

Ali Khamenei

that the number of Guantánamo inmates on a hunger strike had fallen to 18. ❧ Khamenei warned that oil shipments from Iran would be 'jeopardized' if the country was punished for its nuclear program. ❧ Alan García was elected President of Peru. {5} Islamic militants declared they had seized control of Somalia's capital, Mogadishu. ❧ Serbian lawmakers proclaimed Serbia and Montenegro separate states. ❧ Icelandic PM Halldor Asgrimsson announced his resignation. {6} The EU presented Iran with incentives to encourage a suspension of the country's uranium enrichment; both sides called the package a 'positive step'. ❧ The CIA released documents showing that the Agency knew Nazi war criminal Adolf Eichmann's location and pseudonym in 1958, but made no attempt to arrest him. ❧ RIP @ 88, photographer Arnold Newman. ❧ Federal investigators searched the home of Arizona Diamondback Jason Grimsley; he later admitted to using performance-enhancing drugs and was suspended for 50 games [see p.234]. ❧ PM Maliki said the Iraqi government would release 2,500 prisoners not involved in the insurgency, in an attempt to ease sectarian tensions. {7} The Senate voted down a constitutional amendment to ban gay marriage [see p.88]. ❧ Diplomats involved in Iranian nuclear talks asked that uranium enrichment be suspended, rather than halted – a key compromise in the negotiation. ❧ PM Maliki released *c.*590 Iraqi prisoners. ❧ A Council of Europe report claimed 14 European nations colluded with the CIA to transport terror suspects to secret detention facilities. ❧ A US attack killed

[Canada is] not sheltered from the terrorist threat.
– Canadian PM STEPHEN HARPER

—————— IN BRIEF · JUNE 2006 ——————

al-Zarqawi, leader of Al Qaeda in Iraq. {8} The US released 33 prisoners from Afghanistan's Bagram air base. ❧ The FDA approved a vaccine to prevent cervical cancer. ❧ The Iraqi parliament approved ministers for defense, the interior, and national security. ❧ The Senate voted to keep the estate tax. {9} The 2006 soccer World Cup began in Germany [see p.230]. ❧ Alleged Israeli shelling killed 6 Palestinians on a N. Gaza beach; Israel apologized but later denied responsibility. {10} 3 detainees hanged themselves at Guantánamo Bay [see p.24]. {11} 200 prisoners were

A.M. al-Zarqawi

released from Abu Ghraib. ❧ Palestinians bombed S. Israel in retaliation for the Gaza beach blast, injuring >1 and ending a 16-month cease-fire; an Israeli air strike killed 2 Hamas militants. ❧ 32 Iraqi insurgents were killed and 178 captured in raids by US troops over several days. {12} 9 were killed and >3 wounded in a raid NE of Baghdad. ❧ The US military announced that autopsy results had confirmed al-Zarqawi's death from internal injuries. ❧ Karl Rove was told he would not be charged in the Valerie Plame investigation. ❧ The Supreme Court ruled that death row inmates could challenge lethal injection as a 'cruel and unusual punishment' [see p.116]. ❧ Al Qaeda named the previously unknown Abu Hamza al-Muhajir its Iraq leader. ❧ RIP @ 83, composer György Ligeti [see p.57]. {13} Bush paid a surprise visit to Baghdad, where he urged Iraqis to 'seize the moment' and end sectarian conflict. ❧ >24 Iraqis died in 6 bombings in Kirkuk. ❧ Israel missiles in Gaza killed *c.*10. {14} Palestinians stormed their parliament, demanding to have their

If I see First Amendment violations, I will speak up.
— DONALD HALL

wages paid. ❧ The Library of Congress named Donald Hall the 14th Poet Laureate. {15} The US military announced that Abu Hamza al-Muhajir was the *nom de guerre* [see p.161] of Egyptian militant Abu Ayyub al-Masri. ❧ The US military death toll in Iraq reached 2,500 [see p.22]. ❧ A land mine explosion in N. Sri Lanka killed 64 and wounded 86; the Sri Lankan military bombed rebel outposts in response. ❧ The Supreme Court ruled that evidence gathered by officers who search homes following 'knock and announce' procedures was admissible in court. ❧ Bush signed a major overhaul of mine safety laws. ❧ Bush granted national monument status to a large section of the NW Hawaiian islands [see p.215]. ❧ Bill Gates announced he would step down from day-to-day Microsoft operations in 2 years. {16} A shoe bomber killed 11 and wounded >25 at a Shiite mosque in Baghdad. ❧ The Pentagon released a study that found that Special Operations troops had used unauthorized interrogation on Iraqi detainees in 2004. ❧ An insurgent attack in Yusufiya, Iraq, killed 1 soldier and led to the disappearance of 2, who were feared kidnapped. ❧ The House approved a resolution rejecting a timetable for Iraqi withdrawal and vowing 'completion of the mission'. {18} Katharine Jefferts Schori was elected the first female bishop of the Episcopal Church. ❧ Militants killed the former district chief of Afghanistan's Helmand province; *c.*40 relatives traveling to his funeral were also later killed. ❧ Gustav Klimt's 1907 *Adele Bloch-Bauer I* was sold for the highest sum ever paid for a painting [see p.170]. {19} The chief prosecutor

—————————— IN BRIEF · JUNE 2006 ——————————

at Hussein's trial delivered his closing arguments, calling for the death penalty for Hussein and his co-defendants. The trial was adjourned until July 10. ❦ The US military said 3 soldiers had been charged with premeditated murder and obstruction of justice in the May 9 deaths of 3 Iraqi detainees. ❦ 500 prisoners were freed from Abu Ghraib. ❦ Italian prosecutors requested the indictment of a US soldier for the 2005 shooting of Italian agent Nicola Calipari in Baghdad. ❦ 30 civilians and *c*.11 militants died in Afghanistan. {20} The military said the bodies of the 2 soldiers missing since June 16 had been found near Yusufiya, Iraq; officials said they had been tortured and killed 'in a barbaric way'. ❦ Federal procurement officer David Safavian was convicted of lying to investigators about his ties to Abramoff. ❦ Japan announced it would withdraw its troops from Iraq. ❦ Israeli missiles killed 3 children in Gaza. ❦ 300 National Guard troops and 60 state police were dispatched to New Orleans after 6 shootings in the city. ❦ Dan Rather left CBS after 44 years. {21} Israeli missiles killed 1 woman and wounded 13 in Gaza. ❦ A senior member of Hussein's defense team, Khamis al-Obeidi, was abducted and killed, allegedly by Shiite militants. ❦ 7 US Marines and a sailor were charged with premeditated murder, kidnapping, and conspiracy in the April 26 death of an Iraqi civilian. ❦ A fourth soldier was charged in the May 9 deaths of 3 Iraqi detainees. {22} The Senate rejected 2 Democratic proposals to begin troop withdrawal from Iraq. ❦ The Red Cross approved the Red Crystal symbol and the entry of the Israeli Magen

Warren Buffett

I am not an enthusiast of dynastic wealth.
– WARREN BUFFETT

David Adom and Palestinian Red Crescent societies [see p.70]. ❦ The House voted to abolish the estate tax for all but the wealthiest families. {23} 7 were arrested in Miami for allegedly plotting to blow up the Sears Tower and other US buildings. ❦ The *New York Times* reported on a US counterterrorism program involving access to the SWIFT international financial database; several politicians, including Bush, condemned the decision to run the story. ❦ RIP @ 83, TV producer Aaron Spelling [see p.57]. {24} The US released 14 Saudi Arabian prisoners from Guantánamo Bay. {25} Palestinian militants tunneled out of Gaza, killed 2 Israeli soldiers, and captured Israeli Corporal Gilad Shalit. ❦ An Iraqi militant group posted an internet video apparently showing the killing of 2 Russian embassy workers kidnapped June 3. ❦ PM Maliki presented his 'national reconciliation plan'. ❦ Warren Buffett announced he would give away $37bn (85% of his wealth), with the largest share going to the Gates Foundation; it was reportedly the largest single charitable donation in US history. {26} Bombings in Hillah and Baqouba, Iraq, killed *c*.40. ❦ Palestinian militant groups called for the release of female and child prisoners in exchange for information on Shalit; Olmert rejected the demand. ❦ East Timor PM Alkatiri resigned after months of political crisis and violence. {27} Palestinian groups Fatah and Hamas agreed on a common political strategy; there was controversy over whether the accord implicitly recognized Israel. ❦ Israeli troops entered S. Gaza, attacking 3 bridges and a power station; SoS Rice urged Israel to give

IN BRIEF · JUNE – JULY 2006

diplomacy a chance. {28} Flooding across the NE states forced >200,000 to evacuate; *c*.12 died. ❦ Israel claimed that the Fatah-Hamas plan rejected the 2-state solution and did not recognize Israel. ❦ The Senate narrowly defeated a constitutional amendment to prohibit flag desecration [see p.259]. {29} Israeli forces arrested Hamas officials in the West Bank, including the Deputy PM; Israeli air strikes on Gaza destroyed the office of the Palestinian Interior Minister; 1 militant leader was killed. ❦ The Supreme Court ruled that terror suspects could not be tried in military tribunals without Congressional authorization, and that so doing would violate international and federal law. ❦ Veteran Affairs announced that the laptop with *c*.26·5m Social Security numbers and other personal data been recovered and that none of the information had been copied. {30} Bin Laden paid tribute to Abu al-Zarqawi in an audio message posted on the internet.

Gilad Shalit

exchange for Shalit's life. ❦ Intelligence officials confirmed that 'Alec Station', the CIA unit charged with tracking bin Laden, had been disbanded. {4} Space shuttle *Discovery* launched safely from the Kennedy Space Center. ❦ Palestinian militants fired a rocket into an empty high school in Ashkelon, Israel. {5} North Korea fired *c*.6 missiles over the Sea of Japan, including one long-range missile, which failed after launching. ❦ RIP @ 64, disgraced Enron founder Kenneth Lay [see p.18]. {6} Official tallies showed Felipe Calderón had narrowly won Mexico's presidential election; rival López Obrador vowed a legal challenge. ❦ Israeli troops killed *c*.19 Palestinians in Gaza. ❦ The top US military commander in Iraq and the country's US Ambassador issued a joint apology for the March 12 rape and murders in Mahmudiya. ❦ New York's Court of Appeals ruled against same-sex marriage. {7} US authorities announced that a plot to bomb NY train tunnels and flood lower Manhattan had been thwarted, and a suspect arrested. ❦ RIP @ 60, *Pink Floyd* cofounder Syd Barrett [see p.57]. {8} Nobel Laureate José Ramos-Horta was named PM of East Timor, following months of violence between police and former soldiers. ❦ The Palestinian government called for a cease-fire, but refused to release Shalit; Israel rejected the offer. ❦ 4 Palestinian civilians were killed in a blast near Gaza City; Israel denied responsibility. {9} Gunmen killed >14 in a Sunni area of Baghdad; 2 car bombs near a Shiite mosque killed >19 and wounded >59. ❦ Italy defeated France to win the World Cup [see p.230]. ❦ 4 further US

JULY · {1} In another audio message posted online, bin Laden endorsed the new leader of Al Qaeda in Iraq. ❦ A suicide car bomber in Baghdad killed >62; a Sunni member of parliament was kidnapped. {2} Israeli soldiers killed 3 Palestinian gunmen near Gaza's airport. ❦ Mexicans voted in Presidential elections. {3} A former US soldier was charged with murder and rape for a March 12 attack on an Iraqi family in Mahmudiya. ❦ A subway train derailed in Valencia, Spain, killing 41. ❦ Israel rejected an ultimatum from Palestinian militants demanding the release of 1,500 Palestinian prisoners in

The CIA's efforts to locate bin Laden ... [have] not been downgraded.
– *White House spokesman* TONY SNOW

IN BRIEF · JULY 2006

soldiers were charged with rape, murder, and arson in the March 12 Mahmudiya killings; a 5th was charged with dereliction of duty. ❧ Israeli missiles killed 1 Palestinian civilian. ❧ India test-fired its longest-range missile, which failed. ❧ A plane crash in Siberia killed *c*.122. {10} 6 of Milosevic's top aides began a war crimes trial at The Hague. ❧ Chechen rebel leader Shamil Basayev, organizer of the 2002 Moscow theater and 2004 Beslan school seizures, was killed in the Republic of Ingushetia, Russia. ❧ A federal judge ruled that the FBI raid on Rep. William Jefferson's office

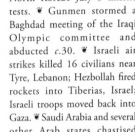

Ehud Olmert

was legal. {11} 8 bombs on commuter trains in Mumbai, India, killed *c*.200 and wounded >400. ❧ The White House announced that terrorism suspects in US military custody are legally protected by the Geneva Conventions. {12} The Israeli military killed *c*.22 in Gaza and injured the leader of Hamas's military wing. ❧ Hezbollah captured 2 Israeli soldiers and killed 3 in a surprise raid, and Israel attacked S. Lebanon in retaliation; 8 Israeli soldiers died. ❧ Russia and China said they would join the US and Europe in seeking a Security Council resolution ordering Iran to end nuclear activities or face sanctions. {13} Israel announced an air and sea blockade; Hezbollah rockets hit Haifa; *c*.35 Lebanese and 2 Israelis died. ❧ Gang violence in São Paulo killed 100 in *c*.71 attacks over 3 days. ❧ The White House agreed to let the Foreign Intelligence Surveillance Court conduct a constitutional review of the NSA eavesdropping program. ❧ RIP @ 87, character actor Red Buttons. {14} Tropical storm Bilis hit China; *c*.92 were killed. ❧ Israel attacked Hezbollah head-

quarters in Beirut, leading Hezbollah leader Hassan Nasrallah to threaten 'open war'; Israeli toops left central Gaza; the UN Security Council called an emergency meeting. {15} The UN Security Council passed a resolution condemning North Korea's July 5 missile tests. ❧ Gunmen stormed a Baghdad meeting of the Iraqi Olympic committee and abducted *c*.30. ❧ Israeli air strikes killed 16 civilians near Tyre, Lebanon; Hezbollah fired rockets into Tiberias, Israel; Israeli troops moved back into Gaza. ❧ Saudi Arabia and several other Arab states chastised Hezbollah for 'inappropriate and irresponsible acts' at an Arab League summit. {16} The 32nd G8 summit began in St Petersburg, Russia. ❧ N. Korea rejected the UN Security Council resolution and vowed to continue building its military arsenal. ❧ Hezbollah missiles killed 8 in Haifa; Israeli bombardment in S. Lebanon killed *c*.45, including 8 Canadians; mass evacuations began; G8 leaders outlined cease-fire requirements. ❧ 27 were killed by a suicide bomber at a N. Iraq café. ❧ Gunmen kidnapped a top oil official in Baghdad. {17} A tsunami in Java killed >80. ❧ Gunmen killed *c*.48 at a market in Mahmudiya, Iraq. ❧ Space shuttle *Discovery* returned safely to Cape Canaveral [see p.191]. ❧ *c*.43 Lebanese were killed in Israeli attacks; *c*.30 Hezbollah rockets attacked Israel, wounding *c*.6; mass evacuations continued. ❧ Bush was caught on an open microphone sharing frank words with Tony Blair at the G8 summit [see p.12]. ❧ RIP @ 88, author Mickey Spillane [see p.57]. {18} The death toll from the July 11 Mumbai train bombings rose to 207. ❧ A New Orleans

Our children will not be the only ones to die.
— HASSAN NASRALLAH

Schott's Almanac 2007

doctor and 2 nurses were charged with killing 4 patients at a flooded hospital after Hurricane Katrina. ❦ Israeli warplanes in Lebanon killed 30; Hezbollah rockets in Israel killed 1; Israel withdrew from N. Gaza. ❦ A suicide bomber near a Shiite shrine in Kufa, Iraq, killed *c*.53. ❦ Iraqi officials announced that Abu al-Afghani, killer of the 2 US soldiers captured in Yusufiya, had been killed by security forces. ❦ The Senate passed a bill to expand the number of stem cell lines available for federal financing. {19} The death toll from the Java tsunami rose to *c*.550; 275 remained missing. ❦ Israeli raids killed >60 Lebanese civilians; Israeli ground combat began in Lebanon, with 2 Israeli soldiers killed; Hezbollah rockets killed 2 in Nazareth; Israeli tanks entered central Gaza; *c*.1,000 Americans were evacuated to Cyprus. ❦ *c*.49 were found dead or killed in Iraq; 20 government employees were kidnapped in Baghdad. ❦ Bush vetoed the stem cell research bill; the first veto of his Presidency [see p.31]. {20} Bush addressed the NAACP for the first time in his Presidency. ❦ The Senate voted to extend the Voting Rights Act for 25 years. ❦ Israeli forces pulled out of a Gaza refugee camp after killing *c*.14; US Marines arrived in Lebanon for the first time in 20 years; >1,000 further Americans were evacuated to Cyprus; UN Secretary General Kofi Annan condemned Israel's 'excessive use of force'. {21} Hezbollah rockets injured >20 in N. Israel; Israel continued its bombardment of Lebanon and called up reservist troops. {22} Israeli troops moved into the S. Lebanon village of Maround al-Ras; Hezbollah rockets in N. Israel

George W. Bush

Israel has a right to defend itself [but] the excessive use of force is to be condemned. – KOFI ANNAN

wounded *c*.10. {23} Bombings killed *c*.57 in Baghdad and Kirkuk, Iraq. ❦ Hussein was hospitalized and fed on the 17th day of his hunger strike. ❦ Israeli warplanes struck fleeing civilians in S. Lebanon, killing 3; *c*.8 other Lebanese were killed in the region, including a Lebanese photographer; Hezbollah rockets in N. Israel killed 2. ❦ Saudi officials met with Bush and SoS Rice at the White House to discuss the Israel-Lebanon conflict. {24} The death toll from tropical storm Bilis in China rose to 612, with 208 missing. ❦ Fighting between Israeli troops and Hezbollah militants in S. Lebanon killed 2 Israeli soldiers and an unspecified number of militants; air strikes on Tyre killed 7; Hezbollah rockets wounded *c*.20 in N. Israel; Israeli shelling killed 8 Palestinian civilians. ❦ SoS Rice visited Lebanon and met with Lebanese PM Fouad Siniora to discuss the Israel-Lebanon crisis. ❦ EU science ministers agreed that member states could continue stem cell research; Germany had earlier proposed a ban. {25} An Israeli air strike on Khiam killed 4 UN observers; Israelis killed *c*.30 Hezbollah in Bint Jbail and Marun al Ras and 7 people in Nabatiye; Hezbollah rockets killed 1 in Mughar; Israel announced plans to occupy a 1·2-mile strip of S. Lebanon as a 'security zone'. ❦ PM Maliki made his first visit to the White House; Maliki and Bush announced a plan to bolster Baghdad security by adding 4,000 US soldiers to city. ❦ An Indiana teenager confessed to the 4 highway sniper attacks that killed 1 on 7/23. {26} The UN said top officials had repeatedly telephoned Israel during the 7/25 attacks on its

— IN BRIEF · JULY – AUGUST 2006 —

observation post. ❦ A Houston jury found Andrea Yates not guilty by reason of insanity for her children's 2001 drowning. ❦ Washington's Supreme Court upheld the state's gay marriage ban. ❦ Chad and Sudan signed a peace agreement, forbidding 'the presence of rebel elements' and calling for a joint military commission to monitor the border. ❦ Hezbollah forces killed >9 Israeli soldiers; Hezbollah rockets wounded *c.*10 Israeli civilians; dozens of Hezbollah were reported killed; Israeli raids killed *c.*23 in Gaza; talks between the EU, US, and Arab countries in Rome failed to result in a plan to end the fighting. ❦ PM Maliki addressed Congress, calling Iraq a frontline in the war on terror. {27} Hussein's trial adjourned, with a verdict expected in October 2006. ❦ Bush signed a 25-year extension of the 1965 Voting Rights Act. ❦ Zawahri released a videotaped speech decrying the 'Zionist crusader war' and calling for renewed attacks on 'Jewish and American interests'. ❦ Israeli warplanes bombed Lebanon, killing *c.*1; Hezbollah rockets attacked Israel; 3 Palestinians were killed in Gaza City fighting. ❦ Tour de France winner Floyd Landis was suspended by his team after test results showed unnaturally high levels of testosterone [see p.245]. ❦ A rocket attack and car bomb in Baghdad killed 32. ❦ Bush signed the Adam Walsh Child Protection and Safety Act of 2006, which authorized a nationwide online database of sex offenders' homes and workplaces. {28} Israeli strikes killed *c.*12 in S. Lebanon; Bush called for an international force to be sent to the area. ❦ Mel Gibson was arrested in Malibu on suspicion of

Saddam Hussein

drunk driving, and reportedly made anti-semitic remarks to a police officer. {29} Israeli air raids in S. Lebanon killed *c.*7; an Israeli strike wounded 2 UN monitors in their observation post. {30} An Israeli air strike killed >28 civilians in Qana, Lebanon; the UN Security Council expressed 'extreme shock and distress'; *c.*5,000 in Beirut protested the attack; the Israeli military killed 5 in Yaroun, Lebanon; France, China, Jordan, Egypt, the EU, Saudi Arabia, and Kuwait called for an immediate cease-fire in the Israel-Lebanon conflict [see p.32–33]. ❦ Congo held its first multiparty election in 46 years. {31} Israel announced a 48-hour halt on air strikes in S. Lebanon; limited strikes continued, however, killing *c.*1; PM Olmert apologized for the Qana attack but said there would not be a cease-fire in the 'coming days'; Lebanon asked the UN Security Council for an inquiry into the Qana bombing. ❦ The US military transferred command of S. Afghanistan to NATO forces. ❦ Fidel Castro temporarily transferred power to his brother Raúl Castro after undergoing surgery. ❦ The UN Security Council passed a resolution demanding that Iran suspend uranium enrichment by August 31 or face sanctions. ❦ German police found 2 suitcases containing unexploded bombs on trains in Dortmund and Koblenz.

> *What has happened in Qana shows this is a situation that simply cannot continue.* – TONY BLAIR

AUGUST · {1} >70 died in bombings and shootings in Iraq. ❦ Israel sent *c.*7,000 soldiers into Lebanon; 3 Israeli soldiers and an unspecified number of Hezbollah were killed in Lebanon. ❦ EU foreign ministers meeting in Brussels called

—————————— IN BRIEF · AUGUST 2006 ——————————

for an 'immediate cessation of hostilities' and 'sustainable cease-fire' in the Israel-Lebanon conflict. {2} Russian oil company Yukos was declared bankrupt by a Moscow judge. ❦ Hezbollah fired >230 rockets into Israel; Israel claimed to have captured 5 Hezbollah in Baalbek, where *c*.15 civilians were killed; PM Olmert said fighting would continue until international peacekeepers were deployed in S. Lebanon. ❦ Ukrainian President Viktor Yushchenko nominated former rival Viktor Yanukovych as PM. {3} Hezbollah launched >100 rockets on N. Israel in <1 hour, killing *c*.8 civilians; 4 Israeli soldiers died in Lebanon. ❦ Israel killed *c*.8 Palestinians in Gaza. ❦ Hillary Rodham Clinton called for Donald Rumsfeld's resignation at a hearing of the Senate Armed Services Cmte. ❦ A suicide bomber in S. Afghanistan killed 21 civilians and injured *c*.14 others. ❦ RIP @ 90, soprano Elisabeth Schwarzkopf [see p.57]. ❦ *c*.17 civilians were killed in Sri Lanka, part of several days of clashes between rebels and Sri Lankan security forces. {4} Phoenix authorities arrested 2 in connection with the city's 'serial shooter' case. ❦ The Israeli military killed 26 in the Lebanese village of Qaa, 5 N. of Beirut, and 7 in S. Lebanon; Hezbollah rockets killed 3 in N. Israel. {5} Landis was

Fidel Castro

I think the President should choose to accept Secretary Rumsfeld's resignation.
— HILLARY RODHAM CLINTON

fired by his team after a second steroid test showed excessive levels of testosterone [see p.234]. ❦ An Israeli raid in Tyre, Lebanon killed 8 Israeli soldiers, several Hezbollah, *c*.1 Lebanese soldier, and *c*.4 civilians; Hezbollah rockets killed 3 in Arab al-Aramshe and wounded 5 in Haifa, Israel. ❦ The UN Security Council met to discuss a draft peace resolution for the Israel-Lebanon conflict. {6} Hezbollah rockets killed 12 in Kfar Giladi and 3 in Haifa; Israeli bombing killed *c*.14 in Lebanon. ❦ Iran's security chief said the country refused to halt uranium enrichment by the UN Security Council's end of August deadline. ❦ A preliminary military hearing into the Mahmudiya rape and murders began in Baghdad. {7} BP Exploration Alaska began closing the Prudhoe Bay oil field for repairs after discovering severe pipe corrosion. ❦ *c*.49 Lebanese died in Israeli raids; 5 Israeli soldiers and 5 Hezbollah were killed in Bint Jbeil, Lebanon; *c*.100 Hezbollah rockets hit N. Israel. ❦ Lebanese PM Siniora rejected the draft UN cease-fire proposal, demanding that Israel withdraw from Lebanon before a peacekeeping team arrived, and offered to send 15,000 soldiers to patrol the south. {8} Speculation increased that Castro's medical condition was serious. ❦ Sen. Joe Lieberman lost to Ned Lamont in the Connecticut Democratic primary, but declared he would run as an Independent; Rep. Cynthia McKinney lost a runoff election for Georgia's Fourth Congressional District to Democrat Hank Johnson. ❦ Bombings and shootings killed *c*.33 in Iraq. ❦ The Lebanese death toll for 8/7 rose to 77; *c*.13 Lebanese were killed in the village of Ghaziyeh; *c*.4 Israeli soldiers died fighting with Hezbollah; Israel announced that vehicles moving S. of the Litani River would be destroyed; aid convoys were disrupted. ❦ Roger Goodell was elected NFL commissioner, replacing Paul Tagliabue. {9} The US military said 4 Iraqis had been arrested in connection with Jill Carroll's kidnapping. ❦ 15 Israeli soldiers and

──IN BRIEF · AUGUST 2006──

*c.*40 Hezbollah died; Israel approved a major expansion of the ground war in Lebanon but delayed its implementation. ❦ RIP @ 83, ballerina Melissa Hayden. {10} UK officials announced that 24 had been arrested in connection with a foiled plot to blow up *c.*10 airplanes [see pp. 31, 210]. ❦ Israeli air strikes killed 2 Lebanese civilians; Hezbollah rockets killed 2 civilians in N. Israel. ❦ A suicide bomber killed *c.*35 in the Shiite holy city of Najaf, Iraq. ❦ Typhoon Saomai killed >100 in China. {11} The UN Security Council approved resolution 1701 [see p.32]; 11 civilians and 1 Israeli soldier were killed in Lebanon. ❦ A German newspaper revealed that Günter Grass admitted serving in the Nazi 'Waffen SS'. {12} Nasrallah said Hezbollah accepted the UN cease-fire, but would fight while Israel remained in Lebanon; 24 Israeli soldiers died. {13} The Israeli cabinet endorsed the cease-fire, but said its forces would remain in Lebanon until peacekeepers were deployed; *c.*22 Lebanese and 1 Israeli were killed. ❦ Car bombs in Baghdad killed >50. {14} The UN cease-fire took effect; displaced Lebanese began returning home. ❦ The threat level on UK–US flights was downgraded to 'high'. ❦ 2 Fox news journalists were kidnapped in Gaza City. ❦ Dell recalled 4·1 million laptop batteries. {15} Israeli troops began to withdraw from Lebanon as the cease-fire solidified, despite limited skirmishes. ❦ {16} John Mark Karr was arrested in Thailand in connection with the 1996 death of JonBenet Ramsey. {17} The Lebanese army began deploying past the Litani River. ❦ A federal judge ruled that the NSA wiretapping program violated

Tony Blair

This feeling of shame burdened me … It had to come out finally.
— GÜNTER GRASS

the constitution and ordered a halt; the Justice Dept filed an appeal. ❦ A federal judge ruled that several leading tobacco companies had conspired to deceive the public about the dangers of smoking for 50 years. ❦ Bush signed a major overhaul of pension and savings rules. ❦ Mel Gibson pled no contest to his drunk driving charge; he was sentenced to 3 years probation and ordered to attend AA meetings. {19} Iran began test-firing missiles and conducting war-games. {20} Lebanon's Defence Minister said anyone firing rockets into Israel would be considered a traitor; Olmert said he would not accept peacekeepers from countries with whom Israel did not have diplomatic relations. ❦ 71 militants died in fighting with Afghan and NATO forces in Afghanistan. {21} Hussein began a second Baghdad trial, on genocide charges for his 1988 anti-Kurdish campaign. ❦ British authorities charged 11 in connection with the alleged airline terror plot. ❦ Bush announced a $230m aid package to rebuild Lebanon. {22} Iran formally responded to the incentives package and offered 'serious talks' on its nuclear program, but did not address whether it would halt uranium enrichment by the 8/31 UN deadline. ❦ 170 died in a plane crash in Donetsk, Ukraine. ❦ The US Marine Corps said it had been authorized to recall thousands of reservists to active duty in Iraq and Afghanistan. ❦ Amnesty International accused Israel of war crimes in its attacks on Lebanon [see pp.32–33]. ❦

───────────

The daily chronicle will continue in the 2008 edition of Schott's Almanac

————————————SOME GREAT LIVES IN BRIEF————————————

WILSON 'WICKED' PICKETT
3·18·1941–1·19·2006 (64)

A gospel singer lured by rhythm and blues, Pickett achieved fame with a string of soul classics, including *Land of 1,000 Dances*, *In the Midnight Hour*, *Mustang Sally*, *634-5789*, and *Everybody Needs Somebody to Love*. Although his career dwindled, and he had a number of altercations with the law, Pickett will be remembered, in the words of Aretha Franklin, as 'one of the greatest soul singers of all time'.

CORETTA SCOTT KING
4·27·1927–1·30·2006 (78)

King was a tireless civil rights advocate, who became an icon of the movement after the 1968 assassination of her husband, Martin Luther King Jr. Raised in poverty in Alabama, she met Dr King when studying music in Boston. Her love of the subject led her to stage more than 30 fund-raising 'Freedom Concerts'. After her husband's death, King founded the Atlanta Center for Non-violent Social Change in his honor, and led the campaign to make Dr King's birthday a national holiday.

BETTY FRIEDAN
2·4·1921–2·4·2006 (85)

Credited with founding feminism's 'second wave', Friedan opened her influential book *The Feminine Mystique* with a survey of her former Smith classmates. She found a dissatisfaction with suburban female roles that she termed 'the problem that has no name'. Adopting an increasingly activist stance, Friedan made an indelible mark on US sexual politics. As she told *Life*, 'Some people think I'm saying, "Women of the world unite, you have nothing to lose but your men". It's not true. You have nothing to lose but your vacuum cleaners'.

GORDON PARKS
11·30·1912–3·7·2006 (93)

Often billed as Hollywood's first black director, Parks is famed for creating the Blaxploitation genre with his 1971 classic, *Shaft*. A poor, orphan childhood gave Parks a strong sense of social justice that he championed in his early career as a *Life* photojournalist. By his death, Parks had mastered a host of skills, and was a respected writer, poet, composer, and musician. As Richard Rowntree, who portrayed John Shaft, said, 'There's no one cooler than Gordon Parks'.

CASPAR WEINBERGER
8·18·1917–3·28·2006 (88)

An implacable Cold War warrior, 'Cap' served three Republican Presidents and, as Reagan's Defense Secretary, presided over unprecedented peacetime military spending. He was indicted in the Iran-Contra affair and charged with lying to Congress, but received a pardon from Bush Sr before the trial.

GENE PITNEY
2·17·1941–4·5·2006 (65)

A tenor crooner whose quavering voice captured the pathos of teenage love, Pitney wrote and performed an array of songs and had 16 Top 20 hits, 1961–8. Among his most famous songs were *That Girl Belongs to Yesterday*, *Town Without Pity*, *(The Man Who Shot) Liberty Valance*, and *24 Hours from Tulsa*.

DAME MURIEL SPARK
2·1·1918–4·13·2006 (88)

Best known for her semi-autobiographical novel *The Prime of Miss Jean Brodie*, Spark was a waspish, witty, and prolific Scottish writer. Her prose style (at once crisp, elegant, sinister, and macabre) was heavily influenced by Roman Catholicism, to which she converted at 36.

——————SOME GREAT LIVES IN BRIEF cont.——————

JOHN KENNETH GALBRAITH
10·15·1908–4·29·2006 (97)

A 'renegade economist', Harvard professor, and advisor to Democratic presidents, Galbraith was both a pillar of the American liberal establishment and its frequent critic. He rose to prominence with his 1958 bestseller, *The Affluent Society*. Admired for his fluent, witty, sharp-tongued style, Galbraith championed the 'countervailing power' of institutions, and critiqued America as a 'democracy of the fortunate'.

FLOYD PATTERSON
1·4·1935–5·11·2006 (71)

Despite a diminutive stature (6ft; 71" reach; 190lb), Patterson won Olympic middleweight gold in 1952, took the world heavyweight title in 1956, and, in 1960, became the first man to regain the title, after losing it in 1959.

GYÖRGY LIGETI
5·28·1923–6·12·2006 (83)

Ligeti rose to fame as a composer with complex, idiosyncratic, and anarchic works that defined one strand of post-War classical music. Some of his compositions attracted derision, including one that called for the smashing of a tea service, and a work for 100 metronomes. His popular fame derives from the pieces Stanley Kubrick used in his films, notably *2001: A Space Odyssey*.

AARON SPELLING
4·22·1923–6·23·2006 (83)

Spelling found early work acting in *Gunsmoke* and *Dragnet*. But he found fame and fortune behind the lens, producing glitzy dramas like *Dynasty*, *Charlie's Angels*, and *Beverly Hills, 90210* – an oeuvre of excess he called 'mind candy', but which gave him the world record for hours of TV produced.

HARRIET
c.1830–6·23·2006 (*c*.175)

One of the world's oldest known living creatures, Harriet (a giant Galápagos tortoise) died of heart failure in an Australian zoo, at age *c*.175. At the time of her death, she weighed 322lb and was 'roughly the size of a dinner table'. It has been suggested that Harriet might have been one of a number of tortoises studied by Charles Darwin and taken by him to Britain on the *Beagle*.

ROGER 'SYD' BARRETT
1·6·1946–7·7·2006 (60)

Barrett was the creative force of early *Pink Floyd* (writing their first two hits); he was also responsible for the band's name (a fusion of the bluesmen Pink Anderson and Floyd Council). Yet, Barrett found himself unable to handle the band's success or his drug addiction, and in 1968 he quit. After a short-lived solo career, Barrett entered a reclusive retirement that lasted thirty years.

MICKEY SPILLANE
3·9·1918–7·17·2006 (88)

A failed attempt to be a lawyer, a stint as a circus trampolinist, summer jobs as a lifeguard, time spent as a fighter pilot, and undercover work for the FBI all gave Spillane the perfect crime-writer's training. Blasted by critics but loved by readers, Spillane's hard-boiled pulp fiction sold by the million to become, in his words, 'the chewing gum of American literature'.

DAME ELISABETH SCHWARZKOPF
12·9·1915–8·2·2006 (90)

One of the C20th's greatest singers, Schwarzkopf's lyrical soprano graced opera and concert halls around the world, and was matched only by her fiery and uncompromising personality.

The World

*The world is not merely the world. It is our world. It is not merely
an industrial world. It is, above all things, a human world.*
— AGNES E. MEYER

THE PLANETS

symbol	name	diameter	no. of moons	surface gravity	rings?	distance from Sun	mean temp.	day length
		miles		ft/s²		miles (m)	°F	hours
☿	Mercury	3,032	0	12·1	N	36	332.33	4,222·6
♀	Venus	7,521	0	29·1	N	67	854.33	2,802·0
⊕	Earth	7,926	1	32	N	93	57	24·0
♂	Mars	4,222	2	12·1	N	142	–81	24·6
♃	Jupiter	88,846	63	68·5	Y	484	–234	9·9
♄	Saturn	74,898	47	23·6	Y	888	–288	10·7
♅	Uranus	31,763	27	27·7	Y	1,784	–353	17·2
♆	Neptune	30,778	13	35·1	Y	2,799	–322·87	16·1
(♇	Pluto†	1,413	1	2·7	N	3,674	–355·63	153·3)

† On August 24, 2006, a Prague meeting of the International Astronomical Union voted to strip
Pluto of its status as a planet, by defining planets as any 'celestial body that is in orbit around the
sun, has sufficient mass for its self-gravity to overcome rigid body forces so that it assumes a ... nearly
round shape, and has cleared the neighborhood around its orbit'. The reclassification of Pluto as a
'dwarf planet' required a host of text-books and mnemonics (such as the one below) to be rewritten.

Mercury Venus Earth Mars Jupiter Saturn Uranus Neptune Pluto
My Very Eager Monkey Just Sets Up Nine Planets

THE EARTH

Equatorial radius..........3,963·19mi
Polar radius................3,949·90mi
Temperature at core........*c.*12,000 °F
Core constituents ....nickel & iron
Core radius..................*c.*2,100mi
Axial tilt........................ 23·5°
Atmosphere.............78% Nitrogen
         21% Oxygen · 1% trace gases
Planetary satellites 1
Mass...............5·9736 x 10²¹ tons

Diameter ....7,926·2mi
Distance to moon.......... 238,855mi
Density......................5.52g/cm³
Earth orbits sun............66,600mph
Age (approximately) .....4,500m years
Surface area total............ 197m mi²
— *land* ....58m mi²
— *water*.................... 139m mi²
Water/land ....70·8%/29·2%
Coastline 372,000mi

THE CONTINENTS

Continent	square miles	est. population	population density
Asia	17,212,000	3,776m	83·4
Africa	11,608,000	832m	27·4
North America	9,449,000	501m	20·3
South America	6,879,000	357m	20·0
Antarctica	5,100,000	(some scientists)	—
Europe	3,837,000	727m	73·3
Australia†	3,132,000	20m	2·6

† Australia is usually considered a continent because it is a continuous landmass, though this leaves Polynesia, New Zealand, and many other areas unclassified. Consequently, some prefer the usage of 'Oceania' – a continental grouping that includes all the Pacific islands surrounding Australia. ❧ Geographically, there are six continents, but the Americas are generally split into two. ❧ *c.*225m years ago the only continent was Pangaea – a supercontinent surrounded by the Panthalassa Ocean. *c.*180m years ago Pangaea split into two, Laurasia and Gondwanaland, before shifting plate tectonics created the still-evolving landmasses we have today.

THE OCEANS

Oceans are the largest bodies of water, making up more than 70% of the globe's surface. The structure of the continents demarcates the Pacific, Indian, and Atlantic oceans, to which maritime organizations added the Arctic. In 2000, the International Hydrographic Organization, the body responsible for charting the oceans, defined the Southern (or Antarctic) Ocean, due to its unique ecosystem.

Ocean	square miles	greatest known depth at	depth (ft)
Pacific	60,045,000	Mariana Trench	36,220
Atlantic	29,630,000	Puerto Rico Trench	28,232
Indian	26,463,000	Java Trench	23,812
Southern	7,846,000	South Sandwich Trench	23,737
Arctic	5,426,000	Fram Basin	15,305

DESERTS

Deserts cover roughly 33% of Earth's landmass, and this is increasing. Deserts can be hot or cold; about one sixth of deserts are permanently covered in snow and ice. The characteristics common to all types of desert are: irregular rainfall of <10" per year; low humidity; and very high evaporation rates. Some major deserts are:

Desert	location	area mi²
Sahara	N. Africa	3,500,000
Gobi	Mongolia/China	500,000
Patagonian	Argentina	260,000
Rub al-Khali	Saudi Arabia	250,000
Kalahari	SW Africa	225,000
Chihuahuan	Mexico/USA	140,000
Taklimakan	N. China	140,000

——————————— A WORLD OF SUPERLATIVES ———————————

Highest city	La Paz, Bolivia	1,099ft
Highest mountain	Everest, Nepal/Tibet	29,035'
Highest volcano	Ojos del Salado, Chile	22,572'
Highest dam	Rogan, Tajikistan	1,105'
Highest waterfall	Angel Falls, Venezuela	3,212'
Biggest waterfall (volume)	Inga, Dem. Rep. of Congo	1,500,000 ft³/s
Lowest point	Dead Sea, Israel/Jordan	–1,312'
Deepest point	Challenger Deep, Mariana Trench	36,220'
Deepest ocean	Pacific	average depth 14,100'
Deepest freshwater lake	Baikal, Russia	5,314'
Largest lake	Caspian Sea	149,200mi²
Largest desert	Sahara	3,500,000mi²
Largest island	Greenland	840,000mi²
Largest country	Russia	6,592,800mi²
Largest population	China	1·3bn people
Largest monolith	Uluru, Australia	1,099' high; 6·25mi base
Largest landmass	Eurasia	21,137,356mi²
Largest river (volume)	Amazon	28bn gal/min
Largest peninsula	Arabian	1,249,523mi²
Largest rainforest	Amazon, South America	1·2bn acres
Largest forest	Northern Russia	1·87bn acres
Largest atoll	Kwajalein, Marshall Islands	6·5mi²
Largest glacier	Vatnajökull, Iceland	3,150mi²
Largest concrete banana	The Big Banana, Australia	42·7' x 16·4'
Largest archipelago	Indonesia	17,508 islands
Largest lake in a lake	Manitou, on an island in Lake Huron	60mi²
Largest city by area	Mount Isa, Australia	15,821mi²
Smallest country	Vatican City	0·20mi²
Smallest population	Vatican City	770 people
Smallest republic	Republic of Nauru	8·1mi²
Longest coastline	Canada	151,485mi
Longest mountain range	Andes	5,500mi
Longest suspension bridge	Akashi-Kaikyo, Japan	6,532'
Longest rail tunnel	Seikan, Japan	34mi
Longest road tunnel	Laerdal, Norway	15·2mi
Longest river	The Nile	4,150mi
Tallest inhabited building	Taipei 101, Taiwan	1,667'
Tallest structure	KVLY-TV Mast, USA	2,064'
Most land borders	China & Russia	14 countries
Most populated urban area	Tokyo, Japan	26·5m
Most remote settlement	Tristan da Cunha	1,450mi from neighbors
Least populous capital city	Tórshavn, Faroe Islands	pop. 16,300
Warmest sea	Red Sea	average temp. *c.*77°F
Longest bay	Bay of Bengal	1,300mi
Largest banknote	Brobdingnagian bills, Philippines	14" x 8½"

Unsurprisingly, a degree of uncertainty and debate surrounds some of these entries and their specifications.

—————— WORLD BIRTH & DEATH RATES ——————

Births	time unit	deaths	change
130,860,569	*per* YEAR	56,579,396	+74,281,173
10,905,047	*per* MONTH	4,714,950	+6,190,098
358,522	*per* DAY	155,012	+203,510
14,938	*per* HOUR	6,459	+8,480
249	*per* MINUTE	108	+141
4·1	*per* SECOND	1·8	+2·4

[Source: US Census Bureau, 2006 · Figures may not add to totals because of rounding]

————————— WORLD POPULATION MILESTONES —————————

According to the US Census Bureau, it took 118 years for the world's population to grow from 1 to 2 billion (1804–1922). Since then, total population has increased dramatically, and is still increasing despite the prevalence of AIDS, a decrease in the global rate of growth, and the fall of fertility levels in many countries. Below are some estimated milestones, with the number of years elapsed between each billion rise:

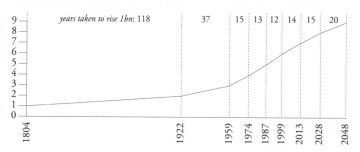

—————— THE TOP TEN MOST POPULOUS COUNTRIES——————

Rank	1950	2002	2050 (est.)	rank
1	China	China	India	1
2	India	India	China	2
3	United States	United States	United States	3
4	Russia	Indonesia	Indonesia	4
5	Japan	Brazil	Nigeria	5
6	Indonesia	Pakistan	Bangladesh	6
7	Germany	Russia	Pakistan	7
8	Brazil	Bangladesh	Brazil	8
9	United Kingdom	Nigeria	Congo	9
10	Italy	Japan	Mexico	10

[Source: US Census, Global Population Profile, 2002]

—————————— NOBEL PEACE PRIZE ——————————

The 2005 Nobel Peace Prize was awarded to the INTERNATIONAL ATOMIC
ENERGY AGENCY and its Director General, MOHAMED ELBARADEI (1942–), for

*their efforts to prevent nuclear energy from being used for military purposes and
to ensure that nuclear energy for peaceful purposes is used in the safest possible way*

Born in Egypt in 1942, Mohamed
ElBaradei studied law in Cairo before
joining the Egyptian Ministry of
Foreign Affairs in 1964. He ascended
the diplomatic ladder, and received a
doctorate in International Law
from New York University.
ElBaradei joined the International Atomic Energy Agency
(IAEA) in 1984 and succeeded
Hans Blix as Director General
in 1997. ❦ The IAEA was established in 1957 in Vienna to
promote the development of
peaceful nuclear research and
oversee controls governing the
misuse of nuclear power for military
ends. The IAEA employs *c.*2,200 from
>90 countries, and has 139 member
states. ❦ Since becoming Director
General, ElBaradei has argued passion-
ately for a stronger global stance on
nuclear nonproliferation. At present,
efforts toward worldwide nuclear disarmament have reached an impasse, but
ElBaradei has been unafraid to attack
the hypocrisy of those states who hold
nuclear weapons while criticizing other
countries for pursuing their own
nuclear ambitions. During his leadership, ElBaradei has had to guide the
agency through difficult times, most
notably the unsuccessful efforts to
establish the presence of nuclear weap-

ElBaradei

ons in Iraq. Recently, the IAEA has been
working to prevent Iran and North
Korea from developing or procuring
nuclear weapons [see p.67]. In 2005,
ElBaradei was reappointed Director
General for a third four-year
term – despite reported efforts
by the United States to have
him replaced. Washington's
impatience with ElBaradei
stems from his unwillingness
to denounce Iran's alleged
nuclear arms program until he
has absolute proof of its existence. ❦ Over the years, the
Nobel Committee has often
rewarded those who have campaigned
for the abolition of nuclear weapons
and other weapons of mass destruction
[see below]. Currently many thousands
of nuclear warheads wait armed and
ready – approximately as many as there
were when the first Non-Proliferation
Treaty was signed in 1970. Many saw
the Nobel Committee's 2005 decision
as particularly appropriate and timely,
since that year marked the 60th anniversary of the atom bomb attacks on
Hiroshima and Nagasaki. ❦ On accepting his Laureate, Mohamed ElBaradei
declared, 'The award gives me lots of
pride and also lots of responsibility. It
sends a very strong message: keep doing
what you are doing'.

*Some Nobel Peace Laureates who
received the Prize for their work
toward nuclear disarmament:*
1962......................Linus Pauling
1975.........Andrei Sakharov [see p.63]

1982......Alva Myrdal; Garcia Robles
1985....*International Physicians for the
Prevention of Nuclear War*
1995.........Joseph Rotblat; *Pugwash
Conferences on Science & World Affairs*

HOLOCAUST DENIAL

Holocaust deniers question the Nazis' genocide of 6 million Jews and often assert that a Jewish conspiracy has perpetuated the myth of the Holocaust for political and financial gain. Germany introduced a Holocaust denial law in 1985, making it a crime to deny the organized extermination of Jews. These laws were tightened in 1994 so that anyone who publicly endorses, denies, or denigrates the Holocaust can be jailed for up to five years. The law in Austria, introduced in 1946 to prevent the possible resurgence of a fascist regime, is the most stringent of all Holocaust denial laws. This so called 'forbidding law' prevents anyone from questioning the Holocaust or glorifying the Nazis by, for example, displaying the swastika. In 2004, the Austrian authorities charged 724 people under this law – those convicted face ten years in prison†. The following countries have laws banning Holocaust denial:

Austria · Belgium · Czech Republic · France · Germany · Israel
Lithuania · Poland · Romania · Slovakia · Switzerland

† British academic David Irving was jailed by an Austrian court in February 2006 for a speech he made in 1989 questioning the existence of gas chambers in Auschwitz. Irving pleaded guilty, and was sentenced to three years in prison – a punishment that was hailed by some as a victory against Holocaust denial, and derided by others as a denial of the rights to freedom of thought and speech.

TOP TEN RECIPIENTS OF US AID

The top 10 US aid† beneficiaries, according to latest (2004) figures from the OECD:

Iraq $2,286m	Jordan $666m	Israel $525m
Congo DR $804m	Afghanistan $632m	Ethiopia $500m
Egypt $767m	Pakistan $590m	
Russia $737m	Colombia $536m	† Total development aid

SAKHAROV PRIZE

Awarded by the European Union since 1988, the Sakharov Prize for Freedom of Thought aims to reward individuals and organizations who challenge oppression and campaign for human rights. It is named in honor of the Soviet physicist Andrei Sakharov (1921–89) who helped to develop the hydrogen bomb, but later won the Nobel Peace Prize for his work campaigning against nuclear weapons. In 2005, the European Parliament's €50,000 prize was shared by the following three: Nigerian lawyer HAUWA IBRAHIM, for defending women who face execution by stoning for committing adultery · REPORTERS WITHOUT BORDERS, a group that works to protect from persecution and censorship those working in the media [see p.133] · and the LADIES IN WHITE, the wives and families of 75 Cuban dissidents who were imprisoned in 2003. The Ladies in White hold weekly vigils and peaceful demonstrations to try to gain the freedom of their relatives. Ironically, the Cuban State barred the Ladies in White from traveling to Europe to accept their award.

———————————— UN PEACE AMBASSADORS ————————————

United Nations Secretary General Kofi Annan personally recruits 'Messengers of Peace' – individuals with widely recognized talents in art, literature, music, or sports who have agreed to help focus attention on the United Nations' projects. In 2006, renowned cellist Yo Yo Ma joined their ranks. The other UN Messengers of Peace are:

Muhammad Ali · Vijay Amritraj · Anna Cataldi · Michael Douglas
Jane Goodall · Enrico Macias · Wynton Marsalis · Luciano Pavarotti · Elie Wiesel

Individual UN agencies appoint their own envoys – who are known as Goodwill Ambassadors.

———————————— AGING POPULATION ————————————

In 2005, 65 countries had fertility rates that were below the global replacement level of 2·1 children per woman (i.e. the rate a country needs to sustain in order to replace its population). The following United Nations figures show the countries with the oldest and the youngest populations by median age over time:

1950	1975	2005
OLDEST POPULATION	OLDEST POPULATION	OLDEST POPULATION
rank *median age*	*rank* *median age*	*rank* *median age*
1 .. Austria .... 35·8	1 .. Germany .... 35·4	1 .. Japan .... 42·9
2 .. Channel Is...... 35·7	2 .. Sweden .... 35·3	2 .. Italy .... 42·3
3 .. Belgium .... 35·6	3 .. Latvia .... 34·8	3 .. Germany .... 42·1
YOUNGEST POPULATION	YOUNGEST POPULATION	YOUNGEST POPULATION
rank *median age*	*rank* *median age*	*rank* *median age*
1 .. St Vincent...... 15·4	1 .. Yemen .... 15·0	1 .. Uganda......... 14·8
2 .. Tonga .... 15·5	2 .. Kenya .... 15·1	2 .. Niger .... 15·5
3 .. Djibouti........ 16·5	3 .. Botswana....... 15·5	3 .. Mali .... 15·8

———————————— WORLD ECONOMIC FORUM · 2006 ————————————

For the past 30 years, political and economic leaders have gathered annually in Davos, Switzerland, at the World Economic Forum to discuss 'improving the state of the world.' 2006 participants included former president Bill Clinton, Bill Gates of Microsoft, Michael S. Dell of Dell Computers, Larry Page of Google, and actress Angelina Jolie. Iran's nuclear plans, Middle East peace, and the rise of gas prices were key points for discussion. Some of the other debates from Davos:

Beyond Short-termism: Not on My Watch · Economics Misbehaving
Multilateral Development Banks (Get Their) Act Together
Exuberant Consumers of Last Resort · Risks and the Liquidization of Everything
Jobs! Where Will They Come from Next? · Digital Inclusion: To 'e' or Not to 'e'?

TSUNAMI AID

In response to the 2004 Asian tsunami, governments worldwide pledged vast sums of money in aid. However, figures released in March 2006 by the Organisation for Economic Cooperation and Development (OECD) revealed that many countries had paid out only a small proportion of the money they had initially promised:

Country	$m pledge	paid	%
Australia	193	117	60·6
Canada	176	131	74·4
France	243	109	44·9
Germany	313	82	26·2
Greece	33	33	100·0
Ireland	26	23	88·5
Italy	94	42	44·7
Japan	601	539	89·7
Netherlands	156	82	52·6
New Zealand	37	37	100·0
Norway	139	132	95·0
Portugal	13	7	53·8
Spain	114	17	14·9
UK	149	130	87·2
USA	792	277	35·0

GLOBAL FREEDOM

The US pressure group Freedom House annually compiles a *Freedom in the World Survey*, classifying countries by the political rights and civil liberties their citizens enjoy. Countries are judged to be: FREE, PARTLY FREE, or NOT FREE. The survey showed 27 countries became more free and only 9 regressed in 2006. The following countries have been classified by *www.freedomhouse.org* as still being NOT FREE:

Algeria · Angola · Azerbaijan · Belarus · Bhutan · Brunei · Burma · Cambodia Cameroon · Chad · China · Congo (Kinshasa) · Côte d'Ivoire · Cuba · Egypt Equatorial Guinea · Eritrea · Guinea · Haiti · Iran · Iraq · Kazakhstan · Laos Libya · Maldives · Nepal · North Korea · Oman · Pakistan · Qatar · Russia Rwanda · Saudi Arabia · Somalia · Sudan · Swaziland · Syria · Tajikistan · Togo Tunisia · Turkmenistan · UAE · Uzbekistan · Vietnam · Zimbabwe

INTERNATIONAL DEVELOPMENT & AID

Figures released by the Organisation for Economic Cooperation and Development showed that development aid had risen from $69bn in 2003 to $79·5bn in 2004, the highest-ever level. However, only 5 of 22 major donors have hit the UN's target of giving 0·7% of their Gross National Income to Overseas Development Aid:

Country	ODA $m	% GNI
Australia	1,460	0·25
Canada	2,599	0·27
Denmark	2,037	0·85
France	8,473	0·41
Germany	7,534	0·28
Ireland	607	0·39
Japan	8,906	0·19
Luxembourg	236	0·83
Netherlands	4,204	0·73
Norway	2,199	0·87
Spain	2,437	0·24
Sweden	2,722	0·78
UK	7,883	0·36
US	19,705	0·17

[Latest released figures: 2004]

——COMMONWEALTH OF INDEPENDENT STATES (CIS)——

The CIS was formed in 1991 to aid cooperation between the former Soviet states:

Armenia · Azerbaijan · Belarus · Georgia · Kazakhstan · Kyrgyzstan
Moldova · Russia · Tajikistan · Turkmenistan · Ukraine · Uzbekistan

——————————MYANMAR/BURMESE CAPITAL——————————

The Myanmar/Burmese government declared a sudden, surprise switch of capital city on November 6, 2005, giving startled officials no choice but to pile into buses and relocate from bustling Rangoon (pop. *c.*4m) to sleepy Pyinmana (pop. *c.*50,000) – a remote, half-built city surrounded by mountains and jungle. Pyinmana was swiftly renamed Naypyidaw Myodaw ('The Royal Capital') – a curious decision since the country has no king. The first official event to be held in Naypyidaw Myodaw took place in March 2006, when General Than Shwe addressed 12,000 of his troops in celebration of Armed Forces Day. It is thought that the abrupt change of capital was prompted by the junta's fear of invasion, a general desire for secrecy, and the prognostications of fortune-tellers, who wield great influence within government.

——————————LANDLOCKED COUNTRIES &c——————————

Afghanistan · Andorra · Armenia · Austria · Azerbaijan · Belarus
Bhutan · Bolivia · Botswana · Burkina Faso · Burundi · Central African Rep.
Chad · Czech Republic · Ethiopia · Holy See (Vatican City) · Hungary
Kazakhstan · Kyrgyzstan · Laos · Lesotho · Liechtenstein[†] · Luxembourg
Malawi · Mali · Moldova · Mongolia · Nepal · Niger · Paraguay · Rwanda
San Marino · Slovakia · Swaziland · Switzerland · Tajikistan
The Former Yugoslav Republic of Macedonia · Turkmenistan
Uganda · Uzbekistan[†] · West Bank · Zambia · Zimbabwe
[† *'double landlocked' countries, being those surrounded by landlocked countries*]

——————————SYMBOL OF CYPRUS——————————

The Republic of Cyprus announced in February 2006 that the cyclamen (*Cyclamen cyprium*) had been chosen as the national plant, and the golden oak (*Quercus alnifolia*) the national tree. The choice was hampered by stipulations that the symbols be native to the island and not be used by another country. Whereas the golden oak was an easy choice (the only other indigenous tree is the cedar, which is the symbol of Lebanon), Cypriot officials took 15 years to choose the cyclamen from a list of 140 native plants. Both will now be used to promote tourism and the environment.

In 2006 Venezuela's legislators acquiesced to President Chávez's proposals to change the national symbols. The galloping 'Imperialist' horse on the coat of arms will now face left rather than right. Commentators have suggested that the change illustrates the new political direction of the country.

─────── NUCLEAR PROLIFERATION ───────

The nuclear proliferation stakes were raised in 2006, as Iran continued its game of cat and mouse with the international community [see p.34] and tensions increased with North Korea. Below is a snapshot of the *estimated* stockpiles of nuclear warheads held by the nine declared, suspected, or professed nuclear states:

· CHINA ·	· ISRAEL ·	·· RUSSIA ·
declared nuclear state	*suspected nuclear state*	*declared nuclear state*
first test in 1964	alleged test in 1979	first test in 1949
≈200 warheads	≈?200 warheads	≈16,000 warheads
[≈130 deliverable]	[≈?200 deliverable]	[≈6,000 deliverable]
· FRANCE ·	· NORTH KOREA ·	· UNITED KINGDOM ·
declared nuclear state	*professed nuclear state*	*declared nuclear state*
first test in 1960	no confirmed test	first test in 1952
≈350 warheads	≈?10–15 warheads	≈<200 warheads
[≈350 deliverable]	[≈?10 deliverable]	[≈<200 deliverable]
· INDIA ·	· PAKISTAN ·	· UNITED STATES ·
declared nuclear state	*declared nuclear state*	*declared nuclear state*
first test in 1974	first test in 1998	first test in 1945
50–150 warheads	≈50–100 warheads	≈10,000 warheads
[≈100 deliverable]	[≈80 deliverable]	[≈5,700 deliverable]

The respected *Bulletin of the Atomic Scientists* regularly charts the 'global level of nuclear danger and the state of international security' via its aptly named 'doomsday clock'. In 1947 the clock was inaugurated at 7 minutes to midnight (–7), and has shifted with risk every few years since then. The clock hit –3 in 1949, when the Soviets exploded their first atomic bomb, and –2 in 1953 when US and Soviet tests occurred within nine months of each other. Over the decades, the clock has ticked closer to and further from doomsday – slipping back to –17 in 1991 with the US–Soviet Strategic Arms Reduction Treaty. The clock currently stands at –7. [Sources: Center for Nonproliferation Studies; US Congressional Research Service; globalsecurity.org; *Bulletin of the Atomic Scientists*]

―――――――――――――― GENOCIDE ――――――――――――――

According to Article 6 of the Rome Statute of the International Criminal Court:

... 'genocide' means any of the following acts committed with intent to destroy, in whole or in part, a national, ethnical, racial, or religious group, as such:
(a) Killing members of the group;
(b) Causing serious bodily or mental harm to members of the group;

(c) Deliberately inflicting on the group conditions of life calculated to bring about its physical destruction in whole or in part;
(d) Imposing measures intended to prevent births within the group;
(e) Forcibly transferring children of the group to another group.

―――――― THE STATE OF THE WORLD'S MOTHERS REPORT ――――――

The disparity between the health of mothers and their babies in the developing and the Western worlds is highlighted by Save the Children's annual Mothers' Index – which reveals that *c.*4m newborn babies die each year. The latest report, released in May 2006, ranked the status of mothers and babies in 125 countries, based on 10 indicators relating to health and education. The best and worst countries were:

Best countries		*Worst countries*	
1 . . . . Sweden	4= . . . . Norway	125 . . . . Niger	120 . . . . Sierra Leone
2= . . . . Denmark	7= . . . . Australia	124 . . . Burkina Faso	119 . . . . Ethiopia
2= . . . . Finland	7= . . . . Netherlands	123 . . . . Mali	118 . . . . Yemen
4= . . . . Austria	9 . . . . Canada	122 . . . . Chad	117 . . C African Rep
4= . . . . Germany	10= . . . . USA	121 . . Guinea-Bissau	115= . D Rep Congo
	10= . . . . UK		115= . . . . Liberia

Compared to a mother in the top 10 countries, a mother in the bottom 10 countries is 28 times more likely to lose her child in the first year of its life; and >750 times more likely to die during pregnancy or childbirth. Simple solutions (providing midwives, &c.) could reduce deaths by 70%.

―――――――――――― ERADICATION OF POLIO ――――――――――――

In February 2006, the World Health Organization (WHO) announced that the number of countries with indigenous polio had dropped to an all-time low, and that the indigenous polio virus had not circulated in Egypt or Niger for over 12 months. Therefore, only 4 countries are currently affected by polio: AFGHANISTAN, INDIA, NIGERIA, and PAKISTAN. ☙ The Global Polio Eradication Program was launched in 1988 (with 166 member states) to rid the world of the virus by 2000. Despite missing this target, the program has reduced cases of polio by 99% and, by implementing mass immunization with 'next-generation' vaccines, it soon hopes to achieve total eradication. ☙ Poliomyelitis is an acute infectious disease (mainly affecting children) caused by a virus that can attack the central nervous system. Symptoms include sore throat, headache, vomiting, and stiffness of neck and back. Polio can cause muscle atrophy, paralysis, and deformity, and can prove to be fatal.

─────────── INTERNATIONAL SHARK ATTACKS ───────────

The International Shark Attack File (ISAF) is a record of all known worldwide shark attacks against humans; it is collated by the American Elasmobranch† Society and the Florida Museum of Natural History. The file contains 4,000 investigations into shark attacks from the 1500s to the present day. The ISAF reported that in 2004 there were 109 shark-related incidents worldwide – 61 of which were confirmed cases of unprovoked attacks. The majority of these incidents (27 attacks) took place in North American waters. Other locations that suffered multiple attacks were Australia (12), Brazil (5), South Africa (5), and Reunion Island (3). The following table shows the total number of shark attacks worldwide between 1990–2004:

Year	attacks	deaths
2004	61	7
2003	57	4
2002	63	3
2001	68	4
2000	78	11
1999	56	4
1998	51	6
1997	49	9
1996	43	3
1995	67	10
1994	57	7
1993	41	11
1992	48	6
1991	33	3
1990	35	2

† Elasomobranch are cartilaginous fish; members of this class include sharks, rays, and skates.

Three Florida women died in alligator attacks between May 9–14, 2006. Such attacks were previously rare: the Florida Fish & Wildlife Conservation Commission reports only 17 alligator-related deaths since 1948. The 2006 deaths were linked to warm weather – which tends to make alligators hungry.

─────────────── THE RED LIST · 2006 ───────────────

The World Conservation Union (IUCN) publishes an annual 'Red List' of species that are under threat worldwide – classifying them from those considered to be at a minor risk of extinction ('Least Concern'), to those actually rendered extinct:

*Least Concern → Near Threatened → Vulnerable → Endangered →
Critically Endangered → Extinct in the Wild → Extinct*

In 2006, the number of known threatened species reached 16,119 – and 784 species were declared extinct. The status of 871 species on the Red List was reassessed: 172 declined in status; 139 improved. Below are some recent successes and failures:

Species	previous status	2006 status
Common hippopotamus	Least Concern (1996)	Vulnerable
White-tailed eagle	Near Threatened (2004)	Least Concern
Common skate	Endangered (2000)	Critically Endangered
Dama gazelle	Endangered (1996)	Critically Endangered
Thick-billed ground dove	Critically Endangered (2004)	Extinct
Abbott's booby	Critically Endangered (2004)	Endangered
Angel shark	Vulnerable (2000)	Critically Endangered
Polar bear	Low Risk (1996)	Vulnerable
Kirtland's warbler	Vulnerable (2004)	Near Threatened

────── RED CROSS, CRESCENT, & CRYSTAL ──────

On June 22, 2006, the 29th International Conference of the Red Cross and Red Crescent (ICRC) amended its statutes to incorporate the 'Red Crystal' and afford it the same status as the Red Cross and Red Crescent. The significance of this decision went well beyond graphic design, since it allowed Israel to join the Red Cross movement (despite objections from some Muslim countries). Israel's equivalent to the Red Cross, the Magen David Adom, had previously had only 'observer status', since its logo, a red Star of David, was not accepted under the Geneva Conventions.

The Red Cross, a reversal of the Swiss Flag, was designed in 1864, and given official international status of battlefield neutrality by the Geneva Conventions.

The Red Crescent was adopted c.1877 as a rejection of the Red Cross which had associations with the Christian Crusades. It is currently used by 32 countries.

The religiously neutral Red Crystal was adopted in 2006, and can be used alone, or in combination with the Cross, Crescent, or other symbols such as the Star of David.

At the same conference, Palestinian humanitarian societies were included (they had previously been excluded for not representing an internationally recognized state).

────── WORLD'S TEN WORST DICTATORS ──────

The weekly magazine *Parade* annually publishes a list of the world's worst dictators, based on their record of human rights abuse. The top ten from 2006 follows:

No.	dictator	age	country	years reign	facial hair?
1	Omar al-Bashir	62	Sudan	17	goatee
2	Kim Jong-il	63	North Korea	12	none
3	Than Shwe	72	Burma/Myanmar	14	none
4	Robert Mugabe	81	Zimbabwe	26	Hitler-esque
5	Islam Karimov	67	Uzbekistan	16	none
6	Hu Jintao	63	China	4	none
7	King Abdullah	82	Saudi Arabia	11	cavalier beard
8	Saparmurat Niyazov†	65	Turkmenistan	16	none
9	Seyed Ali Khamenei	66	Iran	17	bushy beard
10	Teodoro Obiang Nguema	63	Equatorial Guinea	27	none

† Niyazov's regime is as repressive as it is curious. For example, since declaring himself President for Life in 1999, he has banned opera, ballet, theater, car radios, gold fillings, and long hair or beards. He has renamed the days of the week and the months of the year – April is named after his mother.

—— UNIVERSAL DECLARATION OF HUMAN RIGHTS ——

[1] Right to equality and dignity. [2] Freedom from discrimination. [3] Right to life, liberty, personal security. [4] Freedom from slavery. [5] Freedom from torture and degradation. [6] Right to recognition before the law. [7] Equality before the law. [8] Right of appeal by competent tribunal. [9] Freedom from arbitrary arrest or exile. [10] Right to fair public hearing. [11] Presumption of innocence; freedom from retrospective law. [12] Freedom from interference with privacy, family, and correspondence. [13] Right of free movement. [14] Right to asylum from persecution. [15] Right to a nationality and freedom to change it. [16] Right to free marriage and family. [17] Right to own property. [18] Freedom of thought, belief, conscience, and worship. [19] Freedom of opinion and expression. [20] Right of peaceful assembly and association. [21] Right to participate in government; free elections under universal suffrage. [22] Right to social security. [23] Right to choose employment; join trades union; equal pay. [24] Right to rest and holidays. [25] Right to adequate living standards; protection of children. [26] Right to free elementary education. [27] Right to participate in cultural and scientific life. [28] Right to a social order that assures these rights. [29] Rights may only be limited by law to secure protection for others or the community. [30] Freedom from state or other interference in the above rights.

Condensed from the
1948 UN Universal Declaration

—— THREE WORLDS THEORY ——

Developed during the Cold War, the 'three worlds' theory asserted that the world might usefully be divided into blocs based upon economic status: the FIRST WORLD of developed capitalist economies (e.g. USA and western Europe); the SECOND WORLD of developed communist countries (e.g. the Soviet Union); and the THIRD WORLD of underdeveloped countries (e.g. Latin America and Africa). It was assumed in terms of the Cold War that much of the third world could safely be considered neutral (for reasons of poverty perhaps more than ideology). The FOURTH WORLD was a term used to describe the world's 25 poorest nations. The International Monetary Fund (IMF) employs its own tripartite world classification:

Advanced Economies . . . . *e.g. Australia, Norway, Sweden, UK, US*
Countries in Transition . . . . *e.g. Albania, Croatia, Poland, Russia*
Developing Countries . . . . *e.g. Afghanistan, Ethiopia, Swaziland*

A range of other groupings are employed by nation states and international organizations to categorize the (often rapid) shifts in global economic prosperity:

Developed Countries (DCs) . . . .*e.g. France, Canada, UK*
Former USSR & eastern Europe (FORMER USSR/EE) . . . . . . *e.g. Armenia, Uzbekistan*
Less Developed Countries (LDCs) . . . . *e.g. Egypt, Sierra Leone, Yemen*
Newly Industrializing Economies (NIEs) . . . . *e.g. Singapore, Taiwan, Brazil*
Heavily Indebted Poor Countries (HIPCs) . . . .*e.g. Burkina Faso, Zambia*

———————————— THE FBI'S MOST WANTED ————————————

Fugitive [as of 8·29·2006]	*allegation*	*reward*
Osama bin Laden	terrorism	$25,000,000†
Diego Leon Montoya Sanchez	drug running	$5,000,000
James J. Bulger	murder; racketeering	$1,000,000
Victor Manuel Gerena	armed robbery	$1,000,000
Warren Steed Jeffs	child abuse	$100,000
Robert William Fisher	murder; arson	$100,000
Glen Stewart Godwin	murder; prison escape	$100,000
Richard Steve Goldberg	child abuse	$100,000
Jorge Alberto Lopez-Orozco	murder	$100,000
Donald Eugene Webb	murder	$100,000

† An extra $2m is offered by the Airline Pilots Association and Air Transport Association.
(Contact your local FBI office or the US Consulate with any information on the above.)

———————————— FOREIGNERS WITHIN POPULATIONS ————————————

2005 OECD figures indicating the percentage of foreigners in these countries:

Australia........% 23·0	Germany...........12·5	Spain .... 5·3
Canada ....19·3	Japan ....*c.*1·5	Switzerland.........22·4
Finland .... 2·5	Luxembourg........32·6	UK................... 8·3
France ....10·0	New Zealand.......19·5	USA ....12·3

———————————— THE CIA'S WORLDVIEW ————————————

The US Central Intelligence Agency annually publishes its *World Factbook*, which tabulates statistical, political, geographical, and sociological data on the countries of the world. One of the entries details the 'comparative area' of each country, providing a comparison based on the entire US, or one of its individual states:

Afghanistan	slightly smaller than Texas
China	slightly smaller than the US
France	less than twice the size of Colorado
Iran	slightly larger than Alaska
Iraq	slightly more than twice the size of Idaho
Israel	slightly smaller than New Jersey
Japan	slightly smaller than California
Korea, North	slightly smaller than Mississippi
Mexico	slightly less than three times the size of Texas
Pakistan	less than twice the size of California
Russia	approximately 1·8 times the size of the US
United Kingdom	slightly smaller than Oregon
Vietnam	slightly larger than New Mexico

———— DEPLOYMENT OF UN PEACEKEEPERS ————

There have been 60 United Nations peacekeeping missions since 1948, although the majority of these were established after 1991. The UN's peacekeeping troops are loaned voluntarily by member states, who pay troops at their own national scales but are reimbursed by the UN at a flat monthly rate *c*.$1,000 per soldier. The map below indicates ongoing UN peacekeeping missions, as of June 2006.

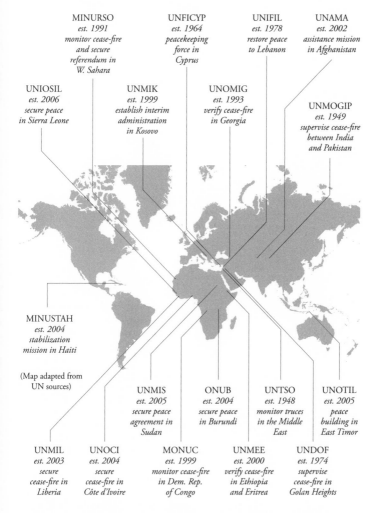

MINURSO
est. 1991
monitor cease-fire
and secure
referendum in
W. Sahara

UNFICYP
est. 1964
peacekeeping
force in
Cyprus

UNIFIL
est. 1978
restore peace
to Lebanon

UNAMA
est. 2002
assistance mission
in Afghanistan

UNIOSIL
est. 2006
secure peace
in Sierra Leone

UNMIK
est. 1999
establish interim
administration
in Kosovo

UNOMIG
est. 1993
verify cease-fire
in Georgia

UNMOGIP
est. 1949
supervise cease-fire
between India
and Pakistan

MINUSTAH
est. 2004
stabilization
mission in Haiti

(Map adapted from
UN sources)

UNMIS
est. 2005
secure peace
agreement in
Sudan

ONUB
est. 2004
secure peace
in Burundi

UNTSO
est. 1948
monitor truces
in the Middle
East

UNOTIL
est. 2005
peace
building in
East Timor

UNMIL
est. 2003
secure
cease-fire in
Liberia

UNOCI
est. 2004
secure
cease-fire in
Côte d'Ivoire

MONUC
est. 1999
monitor cease-fire
in Dem. Rep.
of Congo

UNMEE
est. 2000
verify cease-fire
in Ethiopia
and Eritrea

UNDOF
est. 1974
supervise
cease-fire in
Golan Heights

72,724 uniformed personnel (from 109 countries) are deployed in 18 peacekeeping and peace-building operations. Since 1948, 2,272 UN personnel have been killed.

———————————— VANISHING DELTAS ————————————

Research led by Jason Ericson at the Virginia Department of Conservation and Recreation, published in 2006 by the journal *Global & Planetary Change*, revealed the adverse effect that rising sea levels may have on river deltas. Deltas are formed when river sediment settles in a large fanlike shape at the mouth of a river (they are so named because the Nile delta resembles the Greek letter). Ericson sampled 40 deltas worldwide and, by extrapolating rising sea level data, suggested that by 2050, 10,810 mi² of land and 8·7m people could be at risk from rising seas, land sinkage, or storms. According to Ericson's data the most vulnerable deltas worldwide are:

Delta	*people at risk by 2050*
Bengal delta, Bangladesh	.........3·4m
Mekong delta, Vietnam	..........1·9m
Nile delta, Egypt	.................1·3m

Yangtze delta, China	.... 0·48m
Mississippi delta, USA	.... 0·48m
Godavari delta, India	.... 0·45m

[Source: *New Scientist*]

———————————— DISAPPEARING FORESTS ————————————

A 2006 report by E. Katsigris et al. in the *International Forestry Review* suggests that current logging rates (in many cases driven by China's growing demand for imported wood) may deplete 'economically accessible mature natural forests' in the very near future. Of special concern are Cambodia (with *c.*4–9 years of logging left); Myanmar (with *c.*10–15 years); and Papua New Guinea (*c.*13–16 years).

———————————— ECOLOGICAL FOOTPRINT ————————————

Ecological footprints are a measure of the amount of land required sustainably to support the population. A country's footprint can be measured by comparing the total area required to grow the food it consumes, absorb the waste created from its energy consumption, and house its infrastructure. According to the World Wildlife Federation (WWF), the *global* ecological footprint in 2001 was 2·2 hectares per person. However, the world's footprint exceeds its biocapacity by 21%, so that humans are using more of the world's resources than are being regenerated. The following shows a selection of countries' footprints and their deficits (those with a negative deficit have a surplus of resources, and thus are living within their means):

Footprint (global ha/person)	*deficit*
7·7 .... Australia	.........−11·5
2·2 .... Brazil	.... −8·0
6·4 .... Canada	.... −8·0
1·5 .... China	.... 0·8
7·0 .... Finland	.... −5·4
5·8 .... France	.... 2·8
1·7 .... Gabon	...........−18·4
4·8 .... Germany	.... 2·9

0·8 .... India	..............0·4
4·3 .... Japan	..............3·6
4·4 .... Russia	.... −2·6
2·8 .... South Africa	..........0·8
9·9 .... UAE	.... 8·9
5·4 .... UK	................3·9
9·5 .... USA	................4·7

(Therefore, the USA uses 4·7 hectares per person more than it can support.)

INTERNATIONAL RECYCLING SYMBOLS

PETE	HDPE	V	LDPE	PP	PS	
polyethylene terephthalate	*high-density polyethylene*	*PVC*	*low-density polyethylene*	*polypropylene*	*polystyrene*	*other/hybrid materials*

THREATENED BY CLIMATE CHANGE

Environmental groups have alerted UNESCO, the body that oversees World Heritage [see p.214], that four sites are under threat from climate change. (Rising temperatures and the acidification of oceans are considered to be the cause.) The sites at risk are:

Sagarmatha National Park in Nepal (the location of Mount Everest)
Belize Barrier Reef · Huascarán National Park, Peru
Waterton-Glacier International Peace Park, on the USA-Canada border

UN MILLENNIUM DEVELOPMENT GOALS

By the year 2015, all 191 member states of the United Nations have pledged to meet the following 8 Millennium Development Goals to help the world's poor:

Eradicate extreme poverty and hunger · Achieve universal primary education
Promote gender equality and empower women · Reduce child mortality
Improve maternal health · Combat HIV/AIDS, malaria, and other diseases
Ensure environmental sustainability · Develop a global partnership for development

ENVIRONMENTAL PERFORMANCE

A team of environmental experts from Yale and Columbia universities has ranked countries around the world on their environmental performance. The system known as the Environmental Performance Index (EPI) works by scoring 133 countries on 16 indicators across 6 policy categories: environmental health; air quality; water resources; biodiversity; productive natural resources; and sustainable energy. The research was presented to the World Economic Forum in January 2006 in an effort to encourage policy making on environmental issues. The following table shows the countries with the best and worst environmental performance scores:

The best		*The worst*	
1 ....New Zealand	6 ....Austria	133 .... Niger	128 ....Angola
2 ....Sweden	7 ....Denmark	132 .... Chad	127 ...... Pakistan
3 ....Finland	8 ....Canada	131 ... Mauritania	126 . Burkina Faso
4 ......Czech Rep.	9 ....Malaysia	130 .... Mali	125 ... Bangladesh
5 ....UK	10..........Ireland	129 ...... Ethiopia	124 ....Sudan

──SAFFIR-SIMPSON HURRICANE INTENSITY SCALE──

Category	wind (mph)	storm surge (ft)	description	example
1	74–95	3–5	Minimal	Gaston (2004)
2	96–110	6–8	Moderate	Frances (2004)
3	111–130	9–12	Extensive	Ivan (2004)
4	131–155	13–18	Extreme	Charley (2004)
5	>156	>18	Catastrophic	Katrina (2005)

With 27 named storms and 15 hurricanes, the 2005 Atlantic basin hurricane season (Jun 1–Nov 30) was the worst on record. Hurricanes are usually named from a pool of 21 names, which are recycled every 6 years. However, the freak conditions of 2005 forced the World Meteorological Organization (WMO) to call into service the letters of the Greek alphabet (e.g. Tropical Storm Alpha). ❦ Each year the names of particularly violent storms are permanently 'retired' – in 2006 the WMO declared that the names Dennis, Katrina, Rita, Stan, and Wilma would be replaced on the 2011 roster by with Don, Katia, Rina, Sean, and Whitney. Since naming began in 1953, 67 names have been retired; 2005 had the most retired in a single season.

Atlantic basin	Dean	Jerry	Pablo
hurricane names	Erin	Karen	Rebekah
for 2007:	Felix	Lorenzo	Sebastien
Andrea	Gabrielle	Melissa	Tanya
Barry	Humberto	Noel	Van
Chantal	Ingrid	Olga	Wendy

──────────VOLCANIC EXPLOSIVITY INDEX──────────

Below is the Volcanic Explosivity Index (VEI) used to classify volcanic eruptions:

VEI	category	plume	frequency	classification
0	Nonexplosive	<100m	daily	Hawaiian
1	Gentle	100m–1km	daily	Hawaiian/Strombolian
2	Explosive	1–5km	weekly	Strombolian/Vulcanian
3	Severe	3–15km	yearly	Vulcanian
4	Cataclysmic	10–25km	10s years	Vulcanian/Plinian
5	Paroxysmal	>25km	100s years	Plinian
6	Colossal	>25km	100s years	Plinian/Ultra-Plinian
7	Super-colossal	>25km	1,000s years	Ultra-Plinian
8	Mega-colossal	>25km	10,000s years	Ultra-Plinian

No VEI 8 volcano has exploded in recorded human history. The last VEI 8 event took place *c.*74,000 years ago, when Toba erupted in Indonesia; it is speculated that this explosion may have pushed mankind to the very brink of extinction. Scientists continue to debate the risks posed by the supervolcano in Yellowstone National Park, USA, which has the potential to reach VEI 8. Explosions of that size take place every *c.*600,000 years, and one has not occurred at Yellowstone for 620,000 years. Were a VEI 8 event to hit Yellowstone, the global consequences would be dire.

BEAUFORT WIND SCALE

Beaufort Scale	sea height feet	wind knots	wind (mph)	description
0	—	<1	<1	calm
1	¼	1–3	1–3	light air
2	½	4–6	4–7	light breeze
3	2	7–10	8–12	gentle breeze
4	3½	11–16	13–18	moderate breeze
5	6	17–21	19–24	fresh breeze
6	9½	22–27	25–31	strong breeze
7	13½	28–33	32–38	near gale
8	18	34–40	39–46	gale
9	23	41–47	47–54	strong gale
10	29	48–55	55–63	storm
11	37	56–63	64–72	violent storm
12	—	64	73	hurricane

EARTHQUAKE SCALES

RICHTER	MERCALLI SCALE & DESCRIPTION	SEVERITY
<4·3	i ..... *barely noticeable; doors may swing* ii .... *detected by some; slight* iii................... *traffic-like vibration*	Mild
4·3–4·8	iv .... *cars rock; pictures move* v .... *buildings tremble; trees shake*	Moderate
4·8–6·2	vi .... *plaster cracks; hard to stand* vii ....*alarm; moderate building damage* viii.......... *fright; considerable damage*	Intermediate
6·2–7·3	ix .... *panic; landslides, earth shifts* x ....*ground cracks; buildings collapse*	Severe
>7·3	xi .... *destruction; few buildings stand* xii .. *devastation; ground moves in waves*	Catastrophic

[The relationship between Richter and Mercalli scales is approximate]

SIEBERG–AMBRASEYS SEAWAVE INTENSITY SCALE

1	Very Light	*perceptible only on tide-gauge records*
2	Light	*noticed by those living along the shore*
3	Rather Strong	*generally noticed; flooding of sloping coasts; boats carried away*
4	Strong	*shore flooding; light scouring; solid structures on the coast injured*
5	Very Strong	*shore flooding to some depth; solid structures damaged; light structures destroyed; severe scouring; people drowned; strong roar*
6	Disastrous	*partial or complete destruction of structures far from shore; coast flooding to great depths; big ships severely damaged; many casualties*

WORLD WONDERS & OTHER 7s

7 MODERN WONDERS
(American Society of Civil Engineers)
The Empire State Building
The Itaipu Dam · The CN Tower
The Panama Canal · Channel Tunnel
The North Sea Protection Works
The Golden Gate Bridge

7 CAUSES OF GREATNESS IN CITIES
The palace of a Prince
A navigable river
The residence of the nobility
The seat of justice
Public schools of good learning
Immunities from taxes
Opinion of sanctity

7 THINGS NOT
TO BE TRUSTED
A strong dog · A hired horse
A prattling woman · A proud servant
The deepest place of a river
The flattery of an enemy
The report of a far traveler

7 PREMODERN WONDERS
Stonehenge · The Colosseum
The Catacombs of Kom el Shoqafa
The Great Wall of China
The Porcelain Tower of Nanjing
The Hagia Sophia
The Leaning Tower of Pisa

7 WONDERS OF THE
ANCIENT WORLD
The Pyramids of Egypt
The Colossus of Rhodes
The Hanging Gardens of Babylon
The Mausoleum of Halicarnassus
The Statue of Zeus at Olympia
The Temple of Artemis at Ephesus
The Pharos of Alexandria

7 NATURAL WONDERS
(according to CNN)
The Grand Canyon
The Harbor of Rio de Janeiro
The Northern Lights
The Great Barrier Reef
Victoria Falls · Mount Everest
Paricutin Volcano

7 SORTS OF PEOPLE GREAT
IN TITLE BUT POOR IN PURSE
The Dons of Spain
The Monsieurs of France
The Bishops of Italy
The Nobility of Hungary
The Lairds of Scotland
The Earls of Germany
The Knights of Naples

'No one can remember more than seven of anything.' — St Robert Bellarmine, on why his catechism omitted the eight beatitudes.

The New 7 Wonders Foundation is a privately funded organization that is attempting to create a new list of world wonders. Since 2001, more than 19 million people worldwide have voted for their favorite landmarks. In January 2006 a short-list of 21 potential wonders was announced, to be voted on during the year. The new wonders will be revealed January 1, 2007. The shortlist comprises:

Acropolis, Greece	Eiffel Tower, France	Petra, Jordan
Alhambra, Spain	Great Wall, China	Pyramids of Giza, Egypt
Angkor, Cambodia	Hagia Sophia, Turkey	Statue of Liberty, USA
Chichén Itzá, Mexico	Kyomizu Temple, Japan	Stonehenge, UK
Christ Redeemer, Brazil	Kremlin, Russia	Opera House, Australia
Colosseum, Italy	Machu Picchu, Peru	Taj Mahal, India
Easter Island Statues	Neuschwanstein, Ger.	Timbuktu, Mali

——EXPENSIVE CITIES—— | ——POLITE CITIES——

The Economist Intelligence Unit annually charts the cost of living in cities around the world. The survey revealed that in 2005 Oslo usurped Tokyo after 14 years as the world's most expensive city. Eight of the most expensive cities are in Europe, with the first US city, New York, coming in at 27. The top ten most expensive cities were (2004 position in brackets):

In 2006 *Reader's Digest* sent reporters onto the streets to test which cities around the globe were the most polite. Researchers dropped papers in the street to see if anyone helped, and counted how often doors were held open for them and whether shop assistants said thank you. The investigation concluded that Mumbai was the rudest city, and the most polite cities were:

1 (3)..........Oslo	6 (5). Copenhagen	1 ...... New York	4=........ Zagreb
2 (1)........Tokyo	7 (7)......London	2 .... Zurich	7=..... Auckland
3 (8).... Reykjavik	8 (6)....... Zurich	3 ....Toronto	7=....... Warsaw
4= (2) ...... Osaka	9 (8).......Geneva	4=......... Berlin	9 .... Mexico City
4= (4) ....Paris	10 (10) ...Helsinki	4=..... São Paulo	10..... Stockholm

——————— NOTES TO THE GAZETTEER ———————

Few countries, if any, are more thoroughly gazetteered than France.
— THE CHAMBERS ENCYCLOPEDIA, 1890

The gazetteer on the following pages is designed to allow comparisons to be made between countries around the world. As might be expected, some of the data are tentative and open to debate. A range of sources has been consulted, including the CIA's *World Factbook*, Amnesty International, the US Treasury, &c.

Size km²	*sum of all land and water areas delimited by international boundaries and coastlines*
Population	*mainly July 2006 estimate; some vary*
Life expectancy at birth	*in years; mainly 2006 estimate*
Infant mortality	*deaths of infants <1, per 1,000 live births, per year; mainly 2006 estimate*
Median age	*mainly 2006 estimate*
Birth & death rates	*average per 1,000 persons in the population at midyear; mainly 2006 estimate*
Fertility rate	*average theoretical number of children per woman; mainly 2006 estimate*
HIV rate	*percentage of adults (15–49) living with* HIV/AIDS*; mainly 2003 estimate*
Literacy rate	*definition (especially of target age) varies; mainly 2003 estimate*
Exchange rate	*spot rate at 6·30·06*
GDP per capita	*($) GDP on purchasing power parity basis/population; mainly 2005*
Inflation	*annual % change in consumer prices; years vary, generally from 2005*
Unemployment	*% of labor force without jobs; years vary, generally from 2005*
Voting age	*voting age; (U)niversal; (C)ompulsory for at least one election; *=entitlement varies*
Military service	*age, length of service, sex and/or religion required to serve vary*
Death penalty	*(N) no death penalty; (N*) death penalty not used in practice;*
	(Y) death penalty for common crimes; (Y) death penalty for exceptional crimes only*
National Day	*some countries have more than one; not all are universally recognized*

—— GAZETTEER · ALGERIA – SOUTH KOREA · [1/4] ——

Country	Size (km²)	Population (m)	Capital city	± GMT	Inhabitants
United States	9,631,418	298·4	Washington, DC	−5	Americans
Algeria	2,381,740	32·9	Algiers	+1	Algerians
Argentina	2,766,890	39·9	Buenos Aires	−3	Argentines
Australia	7,686,850	20·3	Canberra	+9½	Australians
Austria	83,870	8·2	Vienna	+1	Austrians
Belarus	207,600	10·3	Minsk	+2	Belarusians
Belgium	30,528	10·4	Brussels	+1	Belgians
Bolivia	1,098,580	9·0	La Paz	−4	Bolivians
Brazil	8,511,965	188·1	Brasilia	−3	Brazilians
Bulgaria	110,910	7·4	Sofia	+2	Bulgarians
Burma/Myanmar	678,500	47·4	[see p.66]	+6½	Burmese
Cambodia	181,040	13·9	Phnom Penh	+7	Cambodians
Canada	9,984,670	33·1	Ottawa	−5	Canadians
Chile	756,950	16·1	Santiago	−4	Chileans
China	9,596,960	1·3bn	Beijing	+8	Chinese
Colombia	1,138,910	43·6	Bogotá	−5	Colombians
Cuba	110,860	11·4	Havana	−5	Cubans
Czech Republic	78,866	10·2	Prague	+1	Czechs
Denmark	43,094	5·5	Copenhagen	+1	Danes
Egypt	1,001,450	78·9	Cairo	+2	Egyptians
Estonia	45,226	1·3	Tallinn	+2	Estonians
Finland	338,145	5·2	Helsinki	+2	Finns
France	547,030	60·9	Paris	+1	French
Germany	357,021	82·4	Berlin	+1	Germans
Greece	131,940	10·7	Athens	+2	Greeks
Haiti	27,750	8·3	Port-au-Prince	−5	Haitians
Hong Kong	1,092	6·9	—	+8	Hong Kongers
Hungary	93,030	10·0	Budapest	+1	Hungarians
India	3,287,590	1·1bn	New Delhi	+5½	Indians
Indonesia	1,919,440	245·5	Jakarta	+8	Indonesians
Iran	1,648,000	68·7	Tehran	+3½	Iranians
Iraq	437,072	26·8	Baghdad	+3	Iraqis
Ireland	70,280	4·1	Dublin	0	Irish
Israel	20,770	6·4	Jerusalem/Tel Aviv	+2	Israelis
Italy	301,230	58·1	Rome	+1	Italians
Japan	377,835	127·5	Tokyo	+9	Japanese
Jordan	92,300	5·9	Amman	+2	Jordanians
Kazakhstan	2,717,300	15·2	Astana	+4	Kazakhstani
Kenya	582,650	34·7	Nairobi	+3	Kenyans
Korea, North	120,540	23·1	Pyongyang	+9	Koreans
Korea, South	98,480	48·8	Seoul	+9	Koreans

———— GAZETTEER · KUWAIT – ZIMBABWE · [1/4] ————

Country	Size (km²)	Population (m)	Capital city	± GMT	Inhabitants
United States	9,631,418	298·4	Washington, DC	−5	Americans
Kuwait	17,820	2·4	Kuwait City	+3	Kuwaitis
Latvia	64,589	2·3	Riga	+2	Latvians
Lebanon	10,400	3·9	Beirut	+2	Lebanese
Liberia	111,370	3·0	Monrovia	0	Liberians
Lithuania	65,200	3·6	Vilnius	+2	Lithuanians
Malaysia	329,750	24·4	Kuala Lumpur	+8	Malaysians
Mexico	1,972,550	107·4	Mexico City	−7	Mexicans
Monaco	195	32·6k	Monaco	+1	Monegasques
Morocco	446,300	33·2	Rabat	0	Moroccans
Netherlands	41,526	16·5	Amsterdam	+1	Dutch
New Zealand	268,680	4·1	Wellington	+12	New Zealanders
Nigeria	923,768	131·9	Abuja	+1	Nigerians
Norway	324,220	4·6	Oslo	+1	Norwegians
Pakistan	803,940	165·8	Islamabad	+5	Pakistanis
Peru	1,285,220	28·3	Lima	−5	Peruvians
Philippines	300,000	89·5	Manila	+8	Filipinos
Poland	312,685	38·5	Warsaw	+1	Poles
Portugal	92,391	10·6	Lisbon	0	Portuguese
Romania	237,500	22·3	Bucharest	+2	Romanians
Russia	17,075,200	142·9	Moscow	+3	Russians
Rwanda	26,338	8·6	Kigali	+2	Rwandans
Saudi Arabia	1,960,582	27·0	Riyadh	+3	Saudis
Singapore	692·7	4·5	Singapore	+8	Singaporeans
Slovakia	48,845	5·4	Bratislava	+1	Slovaks
Slovenia	20,273	2·0	Ljubljana	+1	Slovenes
Somalia	637,657	8·9	Mogadishu	+3	Somalis
South Africa	1,219,912	44·2	Pretoria/Tshwane	+2	South Africans
Spain	504,782	40·4	Madrid	+1	Spaniards
Sudan	2,505,810	41·2	Khartoum	+3	Sudanese
Sweden	449,964	9·0	Stockholm	+1	Swedes
Switzerland	41,290	7·5	Bern	+1	Swiss
Syria	185,180	18·9	Damascus	+2	Syrians
Taiwan	35,980	23·0	Taipei	+8	Taiwanese
Thailand	514,000	64·6	Bangkok	+7	Thai
Turkey	780,580	70·4	Ankara	+2	Turks
Ukraine	603,700	46·7	Kiev	+2	Ukranians
United Kingdom	244,820	60·6	London	n/a	British
Venezuela	912,050	25·7	Caracas	−4	Venezuelans
Vietnam	329,560	84·4	Hanoi	+7	Vietnamese
Zimbabwe	390,580	12·2	Harare	+2	Zimbabweans

——— GAZETTEER · ALGERIA – SOUTH KOREA · [2/4] ———

Country	Male life expectancy	Female life expectancy	difference	Infant mortality	Median age	Birth rate	Death rate	Fertility rate	Adult HIV rate	Literacy
United States	75·0	80·8	−5·8	6·4	36·5	14·1	8·3	2·1	0·6	99
Algeria	71·7	74·9	−3·2	29·9	24·9	17·1	4·6	1·9	0·1	70
Argentina	72·4	80·1	−7·7	14·7	29·7	16·7	7·6	2·2	0·7	97
Australia	77·6	83·5	−5·9	4·6	36·9	12·1	7·5	1·8	0·1	99
Austria	76·2	82·1	−5·9	4·6	40·9	8·7	9·8	1·4	0·3	98
Belarus	63·5	75·0	−11·5	13·0	37·2	11·2	14·0	1·4	0·3	100
Belgium	75·6	82·1	−6·5	4·6	40·9	10·4	10·3	1·6	0·2	99
Bolivia	63·2	68·6	−5·4	51·8	21·8	23·3	7·5	2·9	0·1	87
Brazil	68·0	76·1	−8·1	28·6	28·2	16·6	6·2	1·9	0·7	86
Bulgaria	68·7	76·1	−7·4	19·9	40·8	9·7	14·3	1·4	0·1	99
Burma/Myanmar	58·1	64·0	−5·9	61·9	27·0	17·9	9·8	2·0	1·2	85
Cambodia	57·4	61·3	−3·9	68·8	20·6	26·9	9·1	3·4	2·6	74
Canada	76·9	83·7	−6·8	4·7	38·9	10·8	7·8	1·6	0·3	99
Chile	73·5	80·2	−6·7	8·6	30·4	15·2	5·8	2·0	0·3	96
China	70·9	74·5	−3·6	23·1	32·7	13·3	7·0	1·7	0·1	91
Colombia	68·2	76·0	−7·8	20·4	26·3	20·5	5·6	2·5	0·7	93
Cuba	75·1	79·9	−4·8	6·2	35·9	11·9	7·2	1·7	0·1	97
Czech Republic	72·9	79·7	−6·8	3·9	39·3	9·0	10·6	1·2	0·1	99
Denmark	75·5	80·2	−4·7	4·5	39·8	11·1	10·4	1·7	0·2	99
Egypt	68·8	73·9	−5·1	31·3	24·0	22·9	5·2	2·8	0·1	58
Estonia	66·6	77·8	−11·2	7·7	39·3	10·0	13·3	1·4	1·1	100
Finland	75·0	82·2	−7·2	3·6	41·3	10·5	9·9	1·7	0·1	100
France	76·1	83·5	−7·4	4·2	39·1	12·0	9·1	1·8	0·4	99
Germany	75·8	82·0	−6·2	4·1	42·6	8·3	10·6	1·4	0·1	99
Greece	76·7	81·9	−5·2	5·4	40·8	9·7	10·2	1·3	0·2	98
Haiti	51·9	54·6	−2·7	71·7	18·2	36·4	12·2	4·9	5·6	53
Hong Kong	78·9	84·5	−5·6	3·0	40·7	7·3	6·3	1·0	0·1	94
Hungary	68·5	77·1	−8·6	8·4	38·7	9·7	13·1	1·3	0·1	99
India	63·9	65·6	−1·7	54·6	24·9	22·0	8·2	2·7	0·9	60
Indonesia	67·4	72·5	−5·1	34·4	26·8	20·3	6·3	2·4	0·1	88
Iran	68·9	71·7	−2·8	40·3	24·8	17·0	5·6	1·8	0·1	79
Iraq	67·8	70·3	−2·5	48·6	19·7	32·0	5·4	4·2	0·1	40
Ireland	75·1	80·5	−5·4	5·3	34·0	14·5	7·8	1·9	0·1	99
Israel	77·3	81·7	−4·4	6·9	29·6	18·0	6·2	2·4	0·1	95
Italy	76·9	82·9	−6·0	5·8	42·2	8·7	10·4	1·3	0·5	99
Japan	78·0	84·7	−6·7	3·2	42·9	9·4	9·2	1·4	0·1	99
Jordan	76·0	81·1	−5·1	16·8	23·0	21·3	2·7	2·6	0·1	91
Kazakhstan	61·6	72·5	−10·9	28·3	28·8	16·0	9·4	1·9	0·2	98
Kenya	49·8	48·1	1·7	59·3	18·2	39·7	14·0	4·9	6·7	85
Korea, North	68·9	74·5	−5·6	23·3	32·0	15·5	7·1	2·1	—	99
Korea, South	73·6	80·8	−7·2	6·2	35·2	10·0	5·9	1·3	0·1	98

———— GAZETTEER · KUWAIT – ZIMBABWE · [2/4] ————

Country	Male life expectancy	Female life expectancy	difference	Infant mortality	Median age	Birth rate	Death rate	Fertility rate	Adult HIV rate	Literacy
United States	75·0	80·8	–5·8	6·4	36·5	14·1	8·3	2·1	0·6	99
Kuwait	76·1	78·3	–2·2	9·7	25·9	21·9	2·4	2·9	0·1	84
Latvia	66·1	76·9	–10·8	9·4	39·4	9·2	13·7	1·3	0·6	100
Lebanon	70·4	75·5	–5·1	23·7	27·8	18·5	6·2	1·9	0·1	87
Liberia	38·0	41·4	–3·4	155·8	18·1	44·8	23·1	6·0	5·9	58
Lithuania	69·2	79·5	–10·3	6·8	38·2	8·8	11·0	1·2	0·1	100
Malaysia	69·8	75·4	–5·6	17·2	24·1	22·9	5·1	3·0	0·4	89
Mexico	72·6	78·3	–5·7	20·3	25·3	20·7	4·7	2·4	0·3	92
Monaco	75·9	83·7	–7·8	5·4	45·4	9·2	12·9	1·8	—	99
Morocco	68·6	73·4	–4·8	40·2	23·9	22·0	5·6	2·7	0·1	52
Netherlands	76·4	81·7	–5·3	5·0	39·4	10·9	8·7	1·7	0·2	99
New Zealand	75·8	81·9	–6·1	5·8	33·9	13·8	7·5	1·8	0·1	99
Nigeria	46·5	47·7	–1·2	97·1	18·7	40·4	16·9	5·5	5·4	68
Norway	76·9	82·3	–5·4	3·7	38·4	11·5	9·4	1·8	0·1	100
Pakistan	62·4	64·4	–2·0	70·5	19·8	29·7	8·2	4·0	0·1	49
Peru	68·1	71·7	–3·6	30·9	25·3	20·5	6·2	2·5	0·5	88
Philippines	67·3	73·2	–5·9	22·8	22·5	24·9	5·4	3·1	0·1	93
Poland	71·0	79·2	–8·2	7·2	37·0	9·9	10·0	1·3	0·1	100
Portugal	74·4	81·2	–6·8	5·0	38·5	10·7	9·9	1·5	0·4	93
Romania	68·1	75·3	–7·2	25·5	36·6	10·7	11·8	1·4	0·1	98
Russia	60·5	74·1	–13·6	15·1	38·4	10·0	14·7	1·3	1·1	100
Rwanda	46·3	48·4	–2·1	89·6	18·6	40·4	16·1	5·4	5·1	70
Saudi Arabia	73·7	77·8	–4·1	12·8	21·4	29·3	2·6	4·0	·01	79
Singapore	79·1	84·5	–5·4	2·3	37·3	9·3	4·3	1·1	0·2	93
Slovakia	70·8	78·9	–8·1	7·3	35·8	10·7	9·5	1·3	0·1	100
Slovenia	72·6	80·3	–7·7	4·4	40·6	9·0	10·3	1·3	0·1	100
Somalia	46·7	50·3	–3·6	114·9	17·6	45·1	16·6	6·8	1·0	38
South Africa	43·3	42·2	1·1	60·7	24·1	18·2	22·0	2·2	21·5	86
Spain	76·3	83·2	–6·9	4·4	39·9	10·1	9·7	1·3	0·7	98
Sudan	57·7	60·2	–2·5	61·1	18·3	34·5	9·0	4·7	2·3	61
Sweden	78·3	82·9	–4·6	2·8	40·9	10·3	10·3	1·7	0·1	99
Switzerland	77·7	83·5	–5·8	4·3	40·1	9·7	8·5	1·4	0·4	99
Syria	69·0	71·7	–2·7	28·6	20·7	27·8	4·8	3·4	0·1	77
Taiwan	74·7	80·5	–5·8	6·3	34·6	12·6	6·5	1·6	—	96
Thailand	70·0	74·7	–4·7	19·5	31·9	13·9	7·0	1·6	1·5	93
Turkey	70·2	75·2	–5·0	39·7	28·1	16·6	6·0	1·9	0·1	87
Ukraine	64·7	75·6	–10·9	9·9	39·2	8·8	14·4	1·2	1·4	100
United Kingdom	76·1	81·1	–5·0	5·1	39·3	10·7	10·1	1·7	0·2	99
Venezuela	71·5	77·8	–6·3	21·5	26·0	18·7	4·9	2·2	0·7	93
Vietnam	68·1	73·9	5·8	25·1	25·9	16·9	6·2	1·9	0·4	90
Zimbabwe	40·4	38·2	2·2	51·7	19·9	28·0	21·8	3·1	24·6	91

——— GAZETTEER · ALGERIA – SOUTH KOREA · [3/4] ———

Country	Currency	Currency code	$1 =	GDP per capita $	Inflation %	Unemployment %	Fiscal year end
United States	Dollar=100 Cents	USD	—	40,100	2·5	5·5	Sep 30
Algeria	Dinar=100 Centimes	DZD	72·4	6,600	3·1	25·4	Dec 31
Argentina	Peso=10,000 Australes	ARS	3·1	12,400	6·1	14·8	Dec 31
Australia	Dollar=100 Cents	AUD	1·3	30,700	2·3	5·1	Jun 30
Austria	euro=100 cent	EUR	0·8	31,300	1·8	4·4	Dec 31
Belarus	Ruble=100 Kopecks	BYB	2143·0	6,800	17·4	2	Dec 31
Belgium	euro=100 cent	EUR	0·8	30,600	1·9	12	Dec 31
Bolivia	Boliviano=100 Centavos	BOB	8·0	2,900	5·4	8	Dec 31
Brazil	Real=100 Centavos	BRL	2·3	8,100	7·6	11·5	Dec 31
Bulgaria	Lev=100 Stotinki	BGN	1·5	8,200	6·1	12·7	Dec 31
Burma/Myanmar	Kyat=100 Pyas	MMK	450·0	1,700	17·2	5·2	Dec 31
Cambodia	Riel=100 Sen	KHR	4,079·0	2,000	3·1	2·5	Dec 31
Canada	Dollar=100 Cents	CAD	1·1	31,500	1·9	7	Mar 31
Chile	Peso=100 Centavos	CLP	532·0	10,700	2·4	8·5	Dec 31
China	Renminbi Yuan=100 Fen	CNY	8·0	5,600	4·1	9·8	Dec 31
Colombia	Peso=100 Centavos	COP	2,477·0	6,600	5·9	13·6	Dec 31
Cuba	Peso=100 Centavos	CUP/C	0·9	3,000	3·1	2·5	Dec 31
Czech Republic	Koruna=100 Haléru	CZK	21·5	16,800	3·2	10·6	Dec 31
Denmark	Krone=100 Øre	DKK	5·8	32,200	1·4	6·2	Dec 31
Egypt	Pound=100 Piastres	EGP	5·8	4,200	9·5	10·9	Jun 30
Estonia	Kroon=100 sents	EEK	12·2	14,300	3	9·6	Dec 31
Finland	euro=100 cent	EUR	0·8	29,000	0·7	8·9	Dec 31
France	euro=100 cent	EUR	0·8	28,700	2·3	10·1	Dec 31
Germany	euro=100 cent	EUR	0·8	28,700	1·6	10·6	Dec 31
Greece	euro=100 cent	EUR	0·8	21,300	2·9	10	Dec 31
Haiti	Gourde=100 Centimes	HTG	37·9	1,500	22	c.65	Sep 30
Hong Kong	HK Dollar=100 Cents	HKD	7·8	34,200	−0·3	6·7	Mar 31
Hungary	Forint=100 Fillér	HUF	204·2	14,900	7	5·9	Dec 31
India	Rupee=100 Paisa	INR	46·1	3,100	4·2	9·2	Mar 31
Indonesia	Rupiah=100 Sen	IDR	9,200·0	3,500	6·1	9·2	Dec 31
Iran	Rial	IRR	8,229·0	7,700	15·5	11·2	Mar 20
Iraq	New Iraqi Dinar	NID	1,476·2	3,500	25·4	30	Dec 31
Ireland	euro=100 cent	EUR	0·8	31,900	2·2	4·3	Dec 31
Israel	Shekel=100 Agora	ILS	4·5	20,800	0	10·7	Dec 31
Italy	euro=100 cent	EUR	0·8	27,700	2·3	8·6	Dec 31
Japan	Yen=100 Sen	JPY	112·3	29,400	−0·1	4·7	Mar 31
Jordan	Dinar=1,000 Fils	JOD	0·7	4,500	3·2	15	Dec 31
Kazakhstan	Tenge=100 Tiyn	KZT	123·0	7,800	6·9	8	Dec 31
Kenya	Shilling=100 Cents	KES	72·1	1,100	9	40	Jun 30
Korea, North	NK Won=100 Chon	KPW	—	1,400	—	—	Dec 31
Korea, South	SK Won=100 Chon	KRW	945·3	19,200	3·6	3·6	Dec 31

—————— GAZETTEER · KUWAIT – ZIMBABWE · [3/4] ——————

Country	Currency	Currency code	$1 =	GDP per capita $	Inflation %	Unemployment %	Fiscal year end
United States	Dollar=100 Cents	USD	—	40,100	2·5	5·5	Sep 30
Kuwait	Dinar=1,000 Fils	KWD	0·3	21,300	2·3	2·2	Mar 31
Latvia	Lats=100 Santims	LVL	0·5	11,500	6	8·8	Dec 31
Lebanon	Pound=100 Piastres	LBP	1,501·0	5,000	2	18	Dec 31
Liberia	Dollar=100 Cents	LRD	49·0	900	15	85	Dec 31
Lithuania	Litas=100 Centas	LTL	2·7	12,500	1·1	8	Dec 31
Malaysia	Ringgit=100 Sen	MYR	3·6	9,700	1·3	3	Dec 31
Mexico	Peso=100 Centavos	MXN	11·3	9,600	5·4	3·2	Dec 31
Monaco	euro=100 cent	EUR	0·8	27,000	1·9	22	Dec 31
Morocco	Dirham=100 centimes	MAD	8·6	4,200	2·1	12·1	Dec 31
Netherlands	euro=100 cent	EUR	0·8	29,500	1·4	6	Dec 31
New Zealand	Dollar=100 Cents	NZD	1·6	23,200	2·4	4·2	Jun 30
Nigeria	Naira=100 Kobo	NGN	128·0	1,000	16·5	—	Dec 31
Norway	Krone=100 Øre	NOK	6·0	40,000	1	4·3	Dec 31
Pakistan	Rupee=100 Paisa	PKR	60·1	2,200	4·8	8·3	Jun 30
Peru	New Sol=100 Cénts	PEN	52·8	5,600	3·8	9·6	Dec 31
Philippines	Peso=100 Centavos	PHP	3·3	5,000	5·5	11·7	Dec 31
Poland	Zloty=100 Groszy	PLN	3·1	12,000	3·4	19·5	Dec 31
Portugal	euro=100 cent	EUR	0·8	17,900	2·1	6·5	Dec 31
Romania	New Leu=100 New Bani	ROL	2·8	7,700	9·6	6·3	Dec 31
Russia	Rouble=100 Kopecks	RUR	27·0	9,800	11·5	8·3	Dec 31
Rwanda	Franc=100 Centimes	RWF	551·5	1,300	7	—	Dec 31
Saudi Arabia	Riyal=100 Halala	SAR	3·7	12,000	0·8	25	Dec 31
Singapore	Dollar=100 Cents	SGD	1·6	27,800	1·7	3·4	Mar 31
Slovakia	Koruna=100 Halierov	SKK	29·4	14,500	7·5	13·1	Dec 31
Slovenia	Tolar=100 Stotin	SIT	186·5	19,600	3·3	6·4	Dec 31
Somalia	Shilling=100 Cents	SOS	—	600			
South Africa	Rand=100 Cents	ZAR	6·7	11,100	4·5	26·2	Mar 31
Spain	euro=100 cent	EUR	0·8	23,300	3·2	10·4	Dec 31
Sudan	Dinar= 100 Piastres	SDD	220·0	1,900	9	18·7	Dec 31
Sweden	Krona=100 Øre	SEK	7·2	28,400	0·7	5·6	Dec 31
Switzerland	Franc=100 Centimes	CHF	1·2	33,800	0·9	3·4	Dec 31
Syria	Pound=100 Piastres	SYP	50·7	3,400	2·1	20	Dec 31
Taiwan	Dollar=100 Cents	TWD	32·0	25,300	1·7	4·5	Dec 31
Thailand	Baht=100 Satang	THB	38·2	8,100	2·8	1·5	Sep 30
Turkey	New Lira=100 New Kurus	TRL	1·6	7,400	9·3	9·3	Dec 31
Ukraine	Hryvena=100 Kopiykas	UAH	5·0	6,300	12	3·5	Dec 31
United Kingdom	Pound=100 Pence	GBP	0·5	29,600	1·4	4·8	Apr 5
Venezuela	Bolivar=100 Centimos	VEB	2,150·0	5,800	22·4	17·1	Dec 31
Vietnam	Dong=100 Xu	VND	15,955·0	2,700	9·5	1·9	Dec 31
Zimbabwe	Dollar=100 Cents	ZWD	119,500·0	1,900	133	70	Dec 31

—— GAZETTEER · ALGERIA – SOUTH KOREA · [4/4] ——

Country	Voting age	Driving side	UN vehicle code	Internet country code	Military service	Death penalty	National Day
United States	18 U	R	USA	.us	N	Y	Jul 4
Algeria	18 U	R	DZ	.dz	Y	N*	Nov 1
Argentina	18 UC	R	RA	.ar	N	Y*	May 25
Australia	18 UC	L	AUS	.au	N	N	Jan 26
Austria	18 UC*	R	A	.at	Y	N	Oct 26
Belarus	18 U	R	BY	.by	Y	Y	Jul 3
Belgium	18 UC	R	B	.be	N	N	Jul 21
Bolivia	18 UC*	R	BOL	.bo	N/Y	N	Aug 6
Brazil	16 U*	R	BR	.br	Y	Y*	Sep 7
Bulgaria	18 U	R	BG	.bg	Y	N	Mar 3
Burma/Myanmar	18 U	R	BUR	.mm	N	N*	Jan 4
Cambodia	18 U	R	K	.kh	Y	N	Nov 9
Canada	18 U	R	CDN	.ca	N	N	Jul 1
Chile	18 UC	R	RCH	.cl	Y	Y*	Sep 18
China	18 U	R	RC	.cn	Y	Y	Oct 1
Colombia	18 U	R	CO	.co	Y	N	Jul 20
Cuba	16 U	R	CU	.cu	N	Y	Dec 10
Czech Republic	18 U	R	CZ	.cz	N	N	Oct 28
Denmark	18 U	R	DK	.dk	Y	N	Jun 5
Egypt	18 UC	R	ET	.eg	Y	Y	Jul 23
Estonia	18 U	R	EST	.ee	Y	N	Feb 24
Finland	18 U	R	FIN	.fi	Y	N	Dec 6
France	18 U	R	F	.fr	N	N	Jul 14
Germany	18 U	R	D	.de	Y	N	Oct 3
Greece	18 UC	R	GR	.gr	Y	N	Mar 25
Haiti	18 U	R	RH	.ht	N	N	Jan 1
Hong Kong	18 U*	L	CN/HK	.hk	N	N	Oct 1
Hungary	18 U	R	H	.hu	N	N	Aug 20
India	18 U	L	IND	.in	N	Y	Jan 26
Indonesia	17 U*	L	RI	.id	Y	Y	Aug 17
Iran	15 U	R	IR	.ir	Y	Y	Apr 1
Iraq	18 U	R	IRQ	.iq	N	Y	Jul 17
Ireland	18 U	L	IRL	.ie	N	N	Mar 17
Israel	18 U	R	IL	.il	Y	Y*	May 14
Italy	18 U*	R	I	.it	N	N	Jun 2
Japan	20 U	L	J	.jp	N	Y	Dec 23
Jordan	18 U	R	HKJ	.jo	N	Y	May 25
Kazakhstan	18 U	R	KZ	.kz	Y	Y	Dec 16
Kenya	18 U	L	EAK	.ke	N	N*	Dec 12
Korea, North	17 U	R	DVRK	.kp	N	Y	Sep 9
Korea, South	20 U	R	ROK	.kr	Y	Y	Aug 15

———— GAZETTEER · KUWAIT – ZIMBABWE · [4/4] ————

Country	Voting age	Driving side	UN vehicle code	Internet country code	Military service	Death penalty	National Day
United States	18 U	R	USA	.us	N	Y	Jul 4
Kuwait	21 C	R	KWT	.kw	Y	Y	Feb 25
Latvia	18 U	R	LV	.lv	Y	Y*	Nov 18
Lebanon	21 C*	R	RL	.lb	Y	Y	Nov 22
Liberia	18 U	R	LB	.lr	N	N	Jul 26
Lithuania	18 U	R	LT	.lt	Y	N	Feb 16
Malaysia	21 U	L	MAL	.my	N	Y	Aug 31
Mexico	18 UC	R	MEX	.mx	Y	N	Sep 16
Monaco	21 U	R	MC	.mc	N	N	Nov 19
Morocco	18 U	R	MA	.ma	Y	N	Mar 3
Netherlands	18 U	R	NL	.nl	N	N	Apr 30
New Zealand	18 U	L	NZ	.nz	N	N	Feb 6
Nigeria	18 U	R	WAN	.ng	N	Y	Oct 1
Norway	18 U	R	N	.no	Y	N	May 17
Pakistan	18 U	L	PK	.pk	N	Y	Mar 23
Peru	18 UC*	R	PE	.pe	Y	Y*	Jul 28
Philippines	18 U	R	RP	.ph	Y	N	Jun 12
Poland	18 U	R	PL	.pl	Y	N	May 3
Portugal	18 U	R	P	.pt	N	N	Jun 10
Romania	18 U	R	RO	.ro	Y	N	Dec 1
Russia	18 U	R	RU	.ru	Y	N*	Jun 12
Rwanda	18 U	R	RWA	.rw	N	Y	Jul 1
Saudi Arabia	21 C	R	SA	.sa	N	Y	Sep 23
Singapore	21 UC	L	SGP	.sg	Y	Y	Aug 9
Slovakia	18 U	R	SK	.sk	Y	N	Sep 1
Slovenia	18 U*	R	SLO	.si	N	N	Jun 25
Somalia	18 U	L	SO	.so	N	Y	Jul 1
South Africa	18 U	L	ZA	.za	N	N	Apr 27
Spain	18 U	R	E	.es	N	N	Oct 12
Sudan	17 U	R	SUD	.sd	Y	Y	Jan 1
Sweden	18 U	R	S	.se	Y	N	Jun 6
Switzerland	18 U	R	CH	.ch	Y	N	Aug 1
Syria	18 U	R	SYR	.sy	Y	Y	Apr 17
Taiwan	20 U	R	RC	.tw	Y	Y	Oct 10
Thailand	18 UC	L	T	.th	Y	Y	Dec 5
Turkey	18 U	R	TR	.tr	Y	N	Oct 29
Ukraine	18 U	R	UA	.ua	Y	N	Aug 24
United Kingdom	18 U	L	GB	.uk	N	N	—
Venezuela	18 U	R	YV	.ve	Y	N	Jul 5
Vietnam	18 U	R	VN	.vn	Y	Y	Sep 2
Zimbabwe	18 U	L	ZW	.zw	N	Y	Apr 18

Society & Health

No man is an Island, entire of itself;
every man is a piece of the Continent, a part of the main.
— JOHN DONNE, *Devotions on Emergent Occasions,* 1624

─────────────────── GAY MARRIAGE ───────────────────

In his weekly radio address on June 3, 2006, President Bush sought to galvanize support for a Senate attempt to amend the Constitution to define marriage as a 'union between a man and woman' – thereby banning same-sex marriages. *'Marriage is the most enduring and important human institution, honored and encouraged in all cultures and by every religious faith. ... today, 45 of the 50 states have either a state constitutional amendment or statute defining marriage as the union of a man and a woman. ... Unfortunately, activist judges and some local officials have made an aggressive attempt to redefine marriage in recent years. ... These court decisions could have an impact on our whole Nation. The Defense of Marriage Act declares that no state is required to accept another state's definition of marriage. If that act is overturned by activist courts, then marriages recognized in one city or state might have to be recognized as marriages everywhere else. That would* mean that every state would have to recognize marriages redefined by judges in Massachusetts or local officials in San Francisco, no matter what their own laws or state constitutions say. This national question requires a national solution'.* ❦ Some commentators accused Bush of political opportunism and cynicism in the run-up to the midterm elections – using issues like gay marriage (and flag burning [see p.259]) as a rallying call for Republicans and a tactic to divert attention away from more troublesome topics like gas prices and Iraq. The *New York Times* pithily dismissed the endeavor as 'wasting the nation's time'. ❦ A Constitutional amendment requires the approval of ⅔ of both houses of Congress and ¾ of all the States. On June 7, 2006, the Senate effectively rejected the amendment by 49 votes to 48 – well short of the votes required. ❦ Below are some recent measures of American public opinion on the issue of gay marriages:

48% think the issue of gay marriage should be decided at the state level; 38% at the federal level; and 13% were unsure [Fox News, June 2006] ❦ 39% would be less likely to vote for a candidate who favored a Constitutional ban on gay marriage; 37% more likely; 22% no difference; and 2% unsure [NBC News/*Wall St Journal*, June 2006] ❦ 45% of Democrats favor gay marriage, compared to 38% of Independents and 16% of Republicans [Fox News, April 2006] ❦ 58% think that gay marriages should not be recognized by the law as legally valid [Gallup, May 2006] ❦ 45% think that homosexuals should be allowed to form civil unions [ABC News, June 2006]

──────── US RESIDENTIAL POPULATION ────────

April 2006 estimate...... 298,615,562	1996... 265,228,572	1946... 141,388,566
– 1 birth every .... 8 secs	1986... 240,132,887	1936... 128,053,180
– 1 death every .... 13 secs	1976... 218,035,164	1926... 117,397,000
– 1 net foreign migrant every .... 31 secs	1966... 196,560,338	1916... 101,961,000
– net gain of 1 person every ...... 11 secs	1956... 168,903,031	1906.... 85,450,000

──────── US POPULATION BY SEX & AGE ────────

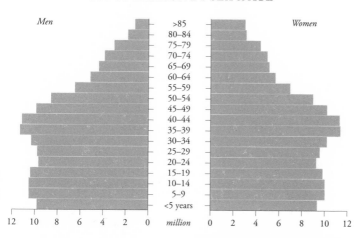

Men · 138,053,563 · 49·1%	Women · 143,368,343 · 50·9%

──── US LIFE EXPECTANCY AT BIRTH BY SEX & RACE ────

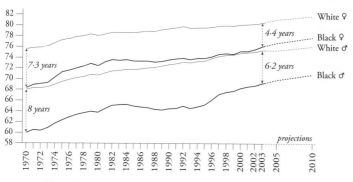

[Source: US Census Bureau, Statistical Abstract of the United States, 2006]

———————————— ANCESTRY OF US CITIZENS ————————————

Ancestry	millions	%	Ancestry	millions	%
German	42·9	15·2	Arab	1·2	0·4
Irish	30·6	10·9	Portuguese	1·2	0·4
English	24·5	8·7	Greek	1·2	0·4
US or American	20·6	7·3	Swiss	0·9	0·3
Italian	15·7	5·6	Ukrainian	0·9	0·3
Polish	9·0	3·2	Slovak	0·8	0·3
French	8·3	3·0	Lithuanian	0·7	0·2
Scottish	4·9	1·7	Other ancestries	91·6	32·6
Dutch	4·5	1·6			
Norwegian	4·5	1·6	*Total population*	281·4	100·0
Scotch-Irish	4·3	1·5	*Total reported*	287·3	102·1
Swedish	4·0	1·4			
Russian	2·7	0·9			
French Canadian	2·4	0·9			
West Indian	1·9	0·7			
Sub-Saharan African	1·8	0·6			
Welsh	1·8	0·6			
Czech	1·7	0·6			
Danish	1·4	0·5			
Hungarian	1·4	0·5			

Includes both single and multiple ancestries. French includes Alsatian but excludes Basques. French Canadian includes Acadian/Cajun. West Indian excludes Hispanic groups. Irish includes Celtic. Czech includes Czechoslovakian.

[Source: US Census, 2000]

———— TOP LANGUAGES ————
SPOKEN AT HOME

Speak only English	80·6%
Speak another language	19·4
of which	
Spanish or Spanish Creole	62·0
Chinese	4·4
French (incl. Patois, Cajun)	2·7
Tagalog	2·6
German	2·2
Vietnamese	2·2
Korean	2·0
Italian	1·9
Russian	1·6
Polish	1·2
Arabic	1·3
Portuguese or Portuguese Creole	1·3
French Creole	1·1

[Source: American Community Survey, 2005, based on a sample of households. For population age >5]

—— NATIVE vs FOREIGN- ——
BORN POPULATION

Native population
249,376,000 (88·1%)

Foreign-born pop.
33,534,000 (11·9%)

Below are the states with the highest and lowest % foreign-born population:

California	% 26·5
New York	20·8
Florida	17·6
Nevada	17·2
Hawaii	17·0
Wyoming	2·2
Montana	1·8
South Dakota	1·7
Mississippi	1·6

[Source: American Community Survey, 2003]

———————US POPULATION BY RACE & ETHNICITY———————

The racial and ethnic breakdown of the US, according to the latest (2000) Census:

	%	
TOTAL POPULATION		281,421,906
ONE RACE	97·6	274,595,678
· White	75·1	211,460,626
· Black or African American	12.3	34,658,190
· Am. Indian and Alaska Native	0·9	2,475,956
· Asian	3·6	10,242,998
Asian Indian	0·6	1,678,765
Chinese	0·9	2,432,585
Filipino	0·7	1,850,314
Japanese	0·3	796,700
Korean	0·4	1,076,872
Vietnamese	0·4	1,122,528
Other Asian	0·5	1,285,234
· Native Hawaiian & other	0·1	398,835
Native Hawaiian	<0·1	140,652
Guamanian/Chamorro	<0·1	58,240
Samoan	<0·1	91,029
Other Pacific Islander	<0·1	108,914
· Some other race	5·5	15,359,073
TWO OR MORE RACES	2·4	6,826,228

Race alone or with >1 other race

	%	
Total population		281,421,906
White	77·1	216,930,975
Black or African American	12·9	36,419,434
American Indian and Alaska Native	1·5	4,119,301
Asian	4·2	11,898,828
Native Hawaiian & other	0·3	874,414
Some other race	6·6	18,521,486

Hispanic or Latino & Race

	%	
Total population		281,421,906
Hispanic or Latino (of any race)	12·5	35,305,818
Mexican	7·3	20,640,711
Puerto Rican	1·2	3,406,178
Cuban	0·4	1,241,685
Other Hispanic or Latino	3·6	10,017,244
Not Hispanic or Latino	87·5	246,116,088
White alone	69·1	194,552,774

According to the US Census 2006 Special Report into American Indians and Alaska Natives, 4,315,865 people (1·53% of the entire US population) reported that they were American Indian or Alaska Native, of whom 2,447,989 (0·87% of the population) reported only American Indian or Alaska Native as their race.

─────────── IMMUNIZATION SCHEDULE ───────────

The following schedule provides an elementary guide to childhood immunizations:

Vaccine	*standard doses*	*age of child*
Hepatitis B	3	birth · 1–4 months · 6–18 months
Hib	4	2 months · 4 months · (6 months) · >12–15 months
Polio	4	2 months · 4 months · 6–18 months · 4–6 years
DTaP	5	2 months · 4 months · 6 months · 15–18 months · 4–6 years
Pneumo	4	2 months · 4 months · 6 months · 12–15 months
MMR	2	12–15 months · 4–6 years
Varicella	1	12–18 months
Hepatitis A	2	2 doses >6 months apart, between 1–18 years

This chart is based upon the recommended immunization schedule published by the Department of Health & Human Services, 2006. For up-to-date information and for advice relevant to high-risk groups, parents are strongly advised to contact the Centers for Disease Control or their pediatrician.

─────────── NEW FIRST NAMES OF THE YEAR ───────────

The Social Security Administration annually lists the most popular names given to babies, based on applications for Social Security cards. The top 2005 names were:

Jacob	*from Hebrew Yaakov*	1	*from the Latin Aemilia*	Emily
Michael	*who is like God*	2	*from Germanic ermen, 'universal'*	Emma
Joshua	*Jehovah saves*	3	*son of Maud*	Madison
Matthew	*God's gift*	4	*my father is joy*	Abigail
Ethan	*Hebrew for solid, enduring*	5	*feminine form of Oliver*	Olivia
Andrew	*from Greek for 'warrior' or 'man'*	6	*Spanish form of Elizabeth*	Isabella
Daniel	*God is my judge*	7	*from Hebrew for 'grace'*	Hannah
Anthony	*from the Latin Antonius*	8	*combination of Sam and Anthea*	Samantha
Christopher	*bearer of Christ*	9	*possible variant of Eve*	Ava
Joseph	*he will add*	10	*Old English for 'Ash tree clearing'*	Ashley

Top names of 1880	*Top names of 1920*	*Top names of 1970*
John & Mary	John & Mary	Michael & Jennifer
William & Anna	William & Dorothy	James & Lisa
James & Emma	Robert & Helen	David & Kimberly
Charles & Elizabeth	James & Margaret	John & Michelle
George & Minnie	Charles & Ruth	Robert & Amy

In 2005, 'Nevaeh' became the 70th most popular girl's name, with 4,457 registrations. In 1991 only 8 babies were called Nevaeh. The name's current vogue has been ascribed to an MTV interview (in 2000) with 'Sonny' Sandoval, singer with the Christian metal band P(ayable) O(n) D(eath). Sandoval disclosed that he named his first daughter Nevaeh because it was 'Heaven' spelled backward. Since then, Nevaeh has made the fastest climb since records were first kept in 1880. ❦ Oddly, in 2005 the 73rd most popular name for a boy was Jesus, and for a girl, Mary.

─────────── AMERICA'S CHILDREN · A SNAPSHOT ───────────

According to the 2006 report of the Forum on Child and Family Statistics, in 2004 there were 73·3m children (aged 0–17) in the US – *c.*25% of the population:

Children (0–17) by race & ethnicity   %
White....................................76·5
White, non-Hispanic..............58·9
Black................................15·5

Asian ....3·9
All other races......................4·1
Hispanic (of any race) ....19·2

Key National Indicator of Well-Being	*previous value*	*most recent value*	*significant change*
Number of children (0–17) in the US population	73·1m ['03]	73·3m ['04]	↑
Children (0–17) as % of the US population	25% ['03]	25% ['04]	–
Children (5–17) in non-English-speaking households	19% ['03]	19% ['04]	–
Children (5–17) with difficulty speaking English	5% ['03]	5% ['04]	–
Children (3–5) read to every day by a family member	58% ['01]	60% ['05]	–
Children (0–17) living with 2 married parents	68% ['04]	67% ['05]	–
Children born to women aged 15–17 [per 1,000]	22·4 ['02]	22·1 ['03]	↓
All births to unmarried women [see p.101]	35% ['03]	36% ['04]	↑
Children (4–11) exposed to 2nd-hand smoke	88% ['88–'94]	59% ['01–'04]	↓
Children (0–6) in households with a regular smoker	19% ['99]	11% ['03]	↓
Children (0–17) living in poverty	17% ['03]	17% ['04]	–
Children (0–17) covered by health insurance [see p.105]	89% ['03]	89% ['04]	–
Children (0–17) with no usual source of health care	5% ['03]	5% ['04]	–
Children (0–17) in very good or excellent health	83% ['03]	82% ['04]	–
Children (4–17) with emotional/behavioral problems	5% ['03]	5% ['04]	–
Children (6–17) who are overweight [see p.108]	17% ['01–'02]	18% ['03–'04]	–
Children (19–35 months) properly vaccinated [see p.92]	81% ['03]	83% ['04]	–
Infants born underweight [<5lb 7oz at birth]	7·9% ['03]	8·1% ['04]	↑
Children who die before 1st birthday [per 1,000]	7·0 ['02]	6·8 ['03]	↓
Children who die aged 1–4 [per 100,000]	31 ['02]	32 ['03]	–
Children who die aged 5–14 [per 100,000]	17 ['02]	17 ['03]	–
Adolescents who die aged 15–19 [per 100,000]	68 ['02]	66 ['03]	–
Children who smoke daily – 8th grade [see p.109]	4% ['04]	4% ['05]	–
– 10th grade	8% ['04]	8% ['05]	–
– 12th grade	16% ['04]	14% ['05]	↓
Youths (18–24) who have completed high school	87% ['03]	87% ['04]	–
Youths (16–19) neither in school nor working	8% ['04]	8% ['05]	–
Youths (12–17) the victim of violent crime [per 1,000]	18 ['03]	11 ['04]	↓

─────────────── SPANKING CHILDREN ───────────────

The General Social Survey asks if respondents think it is 'sometimes necessary to discipline a child with a good, hard spanking.' The latest (2004) results show that 22·9% *strongly agree* and 48·4% *agree*, 21·5% *disagree* and 7·2% *strongly disagree*.

—————————————SCHOOLS · PUBLIC & PRIVATE———————————

The National Center for Education Statistics (NCES) estimates 48,375,400 students were enrolled in public elementary and secondary schools in the fall of 2005 (44,840,481 in 1995). Below are some recent statistics relating to public schools:

Race/ethnicity: K–12 (2004)	%
White	57·4
Black	16·0
Hispanic	19·3
Other	7·3

Teachers' average full-time experience	%
<3 years	13
3–9 years	29
10–20 years	29
>20 years	30

Average pupil/teacher ratio (2003)	
Public schools	16:1
Private schools [see below]	12:1

Highest qualification of teacher (2000)	%
Bachelor's	52
Master's	42
Education specialist	5
Doctorate	1

High school security (2002)	%
Had security guards	30
Had metal detectors	4
Had security cameras	18
Had fencing around school	18

Average annual salary (2004–5)	$
Elementary teachers	47,487
Secondary teachers	48,100

In 2003, 1·1m children (2·2%) were homeschooled: 77% were white, and 81% lived in two-parent households. Of parents who homeschooled, 85% cited concerns about the school environment for removing their children; 72% cited a desire to provide their own religious or moral guidance.

The average US 10th-grader's perceptions of their school's environment were [NCES]:

Statement (2002)	% agree
When I work hard on schoolwork, my teachers praise my effort	63·2
In class I often feel 'put down' by other students	16·7
In class I often feel 'put down' by my teachers	13·5
Misbehaving students often get away with it	53·5
Disruptions by other students get in the way of my learning	46·7
Students make friends with students of other racial/ethnic groups	89·6
Fights often occur between different racial/ethnic groups	28·0
I don't feel safe at this school	12·6

The latest NCES report shows that 5,122,772 students were enrolled in private schools in the fall of 2003 – c.10% of all students. In 2003, there were 28,384 private elementary and secondary schools – c.23% of all US schools. 95% of private schools were coeducational; 2% were all-girl and 3% all-boy. The average length of the private school day was 6·7 hours; the average year was 180 days. 28% of private schools were Catholic, 48% had other religious affiliations, and 24% were nonsectarian. 76% of pupils at private schools were white. Below are the latest (2000) NCES data for annual private school tuition fees:

Average $4,689 · *Catholic* $3,236 · *Other religious* · $4,063 · *Nonsectarian* $10,992

———————————— COLLEGE ENROLLMENT ————————————

Below are the recent rates of college enrollment amongst those who graduated from high school in the preceding 12 months (1985–2003), analyzed by race and sex:

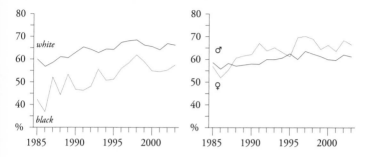

[Source: US Census Bureau, Statistical Abstract of the United States, 2006]

———————————— TOP US & WORLD COLLEGES ————————————

Rank	United States	Rank	Worldwide
1	Harvard University · MA	1	Harvard University · US
1	Princeton University · NJ	2	Massachusetts Inst. of Tech. · US
3	Yale University · CT	3	Cambridge University · UK
4	University of Pennsylvania	4	Oxford University · UK
5	Duke University · NC	5	Stanford University · US
5	Stanford University · CA	6	U. of California, Berkeley · US
7	California Institute of Technology	7	Yale University · US
7	Massachusetts Inst. of Technology	8	California Inst. of Tech. · US
9	Columbia University · NY	9	Princeton University · US
9	Dartmouth College · NH	10	Ecole Polytechnique · France

[Source: *US News & World Report*, 2006]   [Source: *Times Educational Supplement*, 2005]

———————— EDUCATIONAL ATTAINMENT OF AMERICANS ————————

Highest qualification (2004)	all %	♂	♀	white	black
Not a high school graduate	14·8	15·2	14·6	14·2	19·4
High school graduate	32·0	31·1	32·8	32·2	36·0
Some college, but no degree	17·0	16·8	17·3	17·0	19·2
Associate's degree	8·4	7·5	9·3	8·5	7·8
Bachelor's degree	18·1	18·6	17·6	18·4	12·3
Advanced degree	9·6	10·8	8·5	9·8	5·3

[For population ≥25 · Source: US Census Bureau, Statistical Abstract of the United States, 2006]

MARITAL STATUS OF THE US POPULATION

2004 status	population	%	male	%	female	%
Married		58·5		60·3		57·1
Widowed		6·4		2·5		10·0
Divorced		10·2		8·6		11·5
Never married		24·8		28·5		21·3

Marriages by race 2004   *marriages*
All married couples 59,064,000
All interracial couples 2,157,000
White & Black 413,000
   (*White ♂ & Black ♀* ... 287,000)
   (*Black ♂ & White ♀* ... 126,000)
White & other† 1,622,000
Black & other† 122,000

By Hispanic origin 2004   *marriages*
Hispanic & Hispanic 5,611,000
Hispanic & non-Hispanic .. 2,076,000
All other couples 51,378,000
All married couples 59,064,000

[† Any race other than White or Black, for example: American Indian, Chinese, &c. Source: US Census, Statistical Abstract, 2006]

MARRIAGE TERMINOLOGY OF NOTE

Adelphogamy .... *marriage between brothers and sisters*
Bigamy .... *having more than one husband or wife at once (a crime in many cultures)*
Coenogamy ...... *group marriage between two or more men and two or more women*
Deuterogamy...................... *a second marriage after the termination of the first*
Digamy................................... *a second marriage after the death of a spouse*
Endogamy........................... *marriage between members of a group or lineage*
Exogamy .... *marriage between members of different groups or lineages*
Heterogamy............................ *marriage between different social backgrounds*
Hierogamy .... *a sacred marriage (e.g. that between Europa and Zeus)*
Homogamy .... *marriage within a shared social background*
Hypergamy............................. *marriage into an equal or higher social group*
Lavender marriage† .... *of convenience or companionship where either party is gay*
Matrilocal .... *married couples living with or near the wife's parents*
Misalliance .... *a marriage between people unsuited to each other*
Misogamy.................................... *antipathy towards or hatred of marriage*
Monogamy.. *having one spouse*
Morganatic............................... *a marriage between high and low social rank, where the lower-ranking (and any offspring) has no claim to title or property*
Opsigamy .... *marriage late in life*
Pantagamy............... *where members of a community are regarded as intermarried*
Patrilocal .... *married couples living with or near the husband's parents*
Polyandry............................. *a woman who has a number of husbands*
Polygamy.. *having a number of spouses*
Totem exogamy ...... *American Indian tradition of marrying outside one's totem clan*
Trigamy .... *having three spouses simultaneously; or a third marriage*

† After the success of Ang Lee's 2006 film *Brokeback Mountain*, the phrase 'Brokeback marriage' entered popular usage to describe a marriage where one of the partners is (secretly) homosexual.

MARRIAGE & DIVORCE

Below are the US Census rates (per 1,000) of US marriage and divorce (1970–2003):

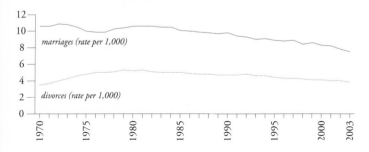

HAPPINESS OF MARRIAGE

The self-reported happiness of marriages in the US in 2004 (General Social Survey):

Very happy	*Pretty happy*	*Not too happy*
62%	35%	3

PREMARITAL SEX

General Social Survey data indicate that attitudes to premarital sex appear to be relaxing. Below are those who consider sex before marriage to be 'not wrong at all':

1972......27·3%	1977......36·5%	1986......40·3%	2000......41·8%
1974......30·7%	1982......42·5%	1990......39·9%	2004..... 44·5%

INTERRACIAL MARRIAGE

Since 1972, the General Social Survey has asked, 'Do you think there should be laws against marriages between (Negroes/Blacks/African Americans) and Whites?'

———————AVERAGE US HOUSEHOLD & FAMILY SIZE———————

Size	1980	1990	1995	2000	2002	2003	2004
Household	2·76	2·63	2·65	2·62	2·58	2·57	2·57
Family	3·29	3·17	3·19	3·17	3·15	3·13	3·13

———HOUSEHOLD TYPE———

Nonfamily households
35,783,000 (32%)

Family households
76,217,000 (68%)

of all family households

61,287,000 (80·4%)
have no members ≥65

14,930,000 (19·6%)
have members ≥65

———SIZE OF HOUSEHOLD———

Persons	%		
1	29·6	4	16·1
2	37·4	5	7·2
3	18·0	6	2·5
		≥7	1·4

—AGE OF HOUSEHOLDER—

Age	%		
15–24	6·6	55–64	16·8
25–29	8·7	65–74	11·5
30–34	10·4	≥75	11·6
35–44	23·2	[2004 figures · US	
45–54	23·1	Stat. Abstract, 2006]	

—————————UNMARRIED-PARTNER HOUSEHOLDS—————————

In 2003, there were 5,571,436 unmarried-partner households in the US – these represented 5·1% of the 108,419,506 US household total. They brokedown thus:

Unmarried-partner household type	*number*	%	*% US total*
Male householder and male partner	363,072	6·5	0·3
Male householder and female partner	2,457,557	44·1	2·3
Female householder and female partner	338,661	6·1	0·3
Female householder and male partner	2,412,146	43·3	2·2

—————————————LIVING ALONE—————————————

The age breakdown of the 29,586,000 people >15 living alone in the US in 2004:

15–19	20–24	25–34	35–44	45–54	55–64	64–74	≥75
8·9%	8·9%	17·2%	19·2%	18·1%	12·5%	8·0%	7·2%

───────── FAMILY SIZE BY RACE & ETHNICITY ─────────

Family type	% childless	1 child	2	≥3
All	53	20	18	10
White	55	19	18	9
Black	44	24	19	13
Asian	46	24	21	8
Hispanic	37	23	23	18
Non-Hispanic White	57	18	17	8

[This table shows families by race and Hispanic origin, with the number of children >18, in 2004. 'All' includes races not shown separately; Hispanics may be of any race. Source: US Census]

───────── IDEAL NUMBER OF CHILDREN ─────────

Since 1972, the General Social Survey has asked, 'What do you think is the ideal number of children for a family to have?' Below is a range of results over time:

Children (%)	1972	1982	1990	2000	2004
None	1·9	1·0	1·2	1·5	1·1
1 child	1·3	3·2	2·0	3·9	1·9
2 children	43·8	55·0	58·6	57·4	55·1
3 children	25·8	20·6	25·4	26·6	28·3
4 children	19·7	15·3	10·5	9·3	11·2
5 children	3·4	2·2	1·4	0·8	0·8
6 children	3·0	1·4	0·8	0·4	1·3
≥7 children	1·2	1·3	0·1	0·1	0·4

───────── FOOD INSECURE HOUSEHOLDS ─────────

Households that are FOOD SECURE have 'access at all times to enough food for an active healthy life for all household members, with no need for recourse to socially unacceptable food sources or extraordinary coping behaviors to meet their basic food needs'. FOOD INSECURE households have 'limited or uncertain ability to acquire acceptable foods in socially acceptable ways'. HUNGER is where 'one or more household members were hungry at least sometime during the period due to inadequate resources for food'. Below is the 2003 analysis of households and food:

Food secure households
99,631,000 (88·8%)

Food insecure households
12,583,000 (11·2%)

Of the households that suffered from food insecurity:
3,920,00 (3·5%) experienced hunger, and 207,000 (0·5%) had children who experienced hunger

The omission of homeless persons may be a cause of underreporting. Data refer to the previous 12 months. Excludes dieting or busy schedules. [Source: US Statistical Abstract, 2006 · See p.319]

——— US SEX(UALITY) ———

Below are the latest measures of sexual behavior among US males and females (aged 15–44) collected during the 2002 National Survey of Family Growth.

Sexual orientation stated†	♂	♀
Heterosexual	90·2	90·3
Homosexual	2·3	1·3
Bisexual	1·8	2·8
Other	3·9	3·8
No response	1·8	1·8
Sexual attraction stated†		
Only opposite sex	92·2	85·7
Mostly opposite sex	3·9	10·2
Both	1·0	1·9
Mostly same sex	0·7	0·8
Only same sex	1·5	0·7
Not sure	0·7	0·8
No. of opposite sex partners		
in previous 12 months		
0 partners	16·4	15·3
1 partner	62·7	68·2
2 partners	8·0	7·6
≥3 partners	10·4	6·8
Did not report	2·5	2·1
No. of opposite sex partners		
within lifetime		
0 partners	9·6	8·6
1 partner	12·5	22·5
2 partners	8·0	10·8
3–6 partners	27·2	32·6
7–14 partners	19·5	16·3
≥15 partners	23·2	9·2
Median no. of partners	5·6	3·3
Sexual contact in lifetime‡		
Any w. opposite sex	97·3	98·4
vaginal sex	97·1	98·2
oral sex	90·1	88·3
anal sex	40·0	34·7
Any with same sex	6·5	10·7
15- to 24-year-olds who have		
had no sexual contacts	21·9	21·9

†18–44 · ‡25–44 · [Source: CDC Vital & Health Statistics No. 362, 2005. See this report for detailed definitions and methodology.]

——— HIV/AIDS ———

By the end of 2003, *c.*1·1m in the US had HIV, *c.*¼ of whom were unaware of being infected. *c.*42,514 were diagnosed with AIDS in 2004, taking the cumulative total to 944,305. Below is a breakdown of the 2004 AIDS cases:

♂ · 73%	♀ · 27%

White, not Hispanic	28·26
Black, not Hispanic	49·31
Hispanic	20·40
Asian/Pacific Islander	1·15
American Indian/Alaska Native	0·45

Age group	%		
<13	0·11	35–39	18·89
13–14	0·14	40–44	20·57
15–19	0·77	45–49	14·69
20–24	4·21	50–54	9·25
25–29	8·41	55–59	4·89
30–34	13·61	60–64	2·34
		≥65	2·12

Exposure category	%
Male-to-male sexual contact	41·7
Injection drug use	21·6
– *above two in combination*	4·5
Heterosexual contact	30·9
Other	1·4

[Source: CDC, Surveillance Report, 2004]

——— SEXUAL PARTNERS ———

A 2005 survey by Durex of the number of sexual partners in a lifetime:

Turkey	14·5	France	8·1
Australia	13·3	Singapore	7·2
Italy	11·8	Taiwan	6·6
Switzerland	11·1	Germany	5·8
USA	10·7	Indonesia	5·1
UK	9·8	China	3·1
Austria	9·7	India	3·0

[Global average = 9 · ♂ = 10·2 · ♀ = 6·9]

——— ABORTION ———

According to the US Census, 1,293,000 legal abortions were performed in the US in 2002 – 20·8 per 1,000 women (15–44) and 319 per 1,000 live births. 2005 Guttmacher Institute data show: half of all pregnancies to US women are unintended, of which 4 in 10 end in abortion ❦ at current rates, about one in three American women will have had an abortion by the time she reaches age 45 ❦ 88% of abortions occur in the first 12 weeks of pregnancy ❦ of those women who have had abortions:

56% .... are in their 20s
61% .... have one or more children
67% .... have never married
57% .. are economically disadvantaged
88% .... live in a metropolitan area
78% .... report a religious affiliation

US Statistical Abstract data show the decline of abortion, by racial group:

Abortion rates per 1,000 women by race

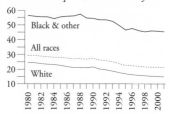

In March 2006, South Dakota passed a law that made terminations illegal unless the mother's life is at risk (no exceptions are made in cases of rape or incest). It is expected that this law will bring about a challenge to *Roe* vs *Wade* (1973) in the light of changes to the Supreme Court [see p.306]. An *LA Times* poll in April showed that 34% of US citizens approved of SD's law, although only 24% of Democrats approved – compared to 52% of Republicans.

——— OUT OF WEDLOCK ———

The chart below shows the percentage of children born to unmarried mothers:

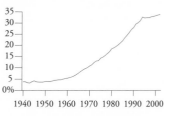

[Source: US Census; US National Center for Health Statistics, 2003]

——— HOMOSEXUALITY ———

Since 1973, the General Social Survey has polled US attitudes on the public acceptance of homosexual sex:

%	always wrong	almost always wrong	sometimes wrong	not wrong at all
1973	72·7	6·6	7·6	11·0
1976	70·1	6·2	7·9	15·9
1980	73·3	6·0	6·1	14·6
1990	76·3	4·8	6·1	12·8
1996	60·4	5·2	6·2	28·2
2000	58·8	4·5	8·0	28·8
2002	55·0	4·9	7·1	33·0
2004	57·5	4·9	6·8	30·8

The GSS also shows that the proportion of the population who would like to see homosexuals prohibited from teaching in colleges or universities has declined from 50·6% in 1973 to 19·7% in 2004. ❦ A 2006 Gallup poll shows that 89% believe that homosexuals should have equal rights in job opportunities (56% in 1977); and 54% believe that homosexuality should be considered an acceptable alternative lifestyle.

———————————UNEMPLOYMENT RATE———————————

The unemployment rate of the civilian noninstitutional population ≥16 (1969–):

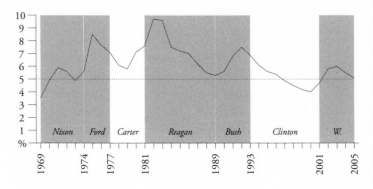

———————OCCUPATIONAL EMPLOYMENT & WAGES———————

Below are the mean hourly wages and percent of workforce, by occupational group:

% of workforce	major occupational group	mean wage/hour
4·7	Management	$41·87
0·8	Legal	$39·03
2·3	Computer and mathematical science	$31·91
1·8	Architecture and engineering	$30·32
5·0	Health care practitioner and technical	$28·03
0·9	Life, physical, and social science	$27·67
4·1	Business and financial operations	$27·46
1·3	Arts, design, entertainment, sports, and media	$21·07
6·2	Education, training, and library	$20·58
4·9	Construction and extraction	$18·21
4·1	Installation, maintenance, and repair	$18·09
1·3	Community and social services	$17·81
2·4	Protective service	$16·94
10·6	Sales and related	$15·52
7·9	Production	$14·18
17·5	Office and administrative support	$14·13
7·4	Transportation and material moving	$13·58
2·6	Health care support	$11·30
2·4	Personal care and service	$10·62
3·3	Building and grounds cleaning and maintenance	$10·42
0·3	Farming, fishing, and forestry	$9·94
8·2	Food preparation and serving related	$8·47

[Source for graph & table: Bureau of Labor Statistics · Table data, as of November 2004]

─────────AMERICANS' USE OF TIME─────────

2005 Bureau of Labor data on how the average American spends an average day:

Activity (hours per day; total = 24 hours)	All	♂	♀
Personal care activities	9·34	9·16	9·51
Sleeping	8·56	8·51	8·61
Eating and drinking	1·24	1·31	1·18
Household activities	1·80	1·32	2·25
Housework	0·59	0·22	0·93
Food preparation and cleanup	0·51	0·25	0·75
Lawn and garden care	0·19	0·25	0·14
Household management	0·14	0·11	0·17
Purchasing goods and services	0·81	0·65	0·96
Consumer goods purchases	0·41	0·30	0·50
Professional and personal care services	0·09	0·07	0·11
Caring for and helping household members	0·56	0·35	0·76
Caring for and helping household children	0·43	0·25	0·59
Caring for and helping nonhousehold members	0·27	0·24	0·30
Caring for and helping nonhousehold adults	0·10	0·11	0·10
Working and work-related activities	3·65	4·37	2·98
Working	3·31	3·96	2·71
Educational activities	0·50	0·49	0·50
Attending class	0·31	0·33	0·29
Homework and research	0·14	0·12	0·16
Organizational, civic, and religious activities	0·32	0·28	0·35
Religious and spiritual activities	0·12	0·12	0·13
Volunteering (organizational and civic activities)	0·15	0·13	0·17
Leisure and sports	5·18	5·56	4·82
Socializing and communicating	0·75	0·71	0·78
Watching television [see p.126]	2·64	2·85	2·44
Participating in sports, exercise, and recreation	0·30	0·40	0·20
Telephone calls, mail, and e-mail	0·18	0·11	0·25
Other activities, not elsewhere classified	0·14	0·13	0·15

─────────UNION MEMBERSHIP─────────

According to the latest data from the Bureau of Labor Statistics, 12·5% of wage and salary workers belonged to a union in 2005 (compared to 20·1% in 1983):

2005 union membership	%
Men	13·5
Women	11·3
Blacks & African Americans	15·1
Whites	12·2
Asians	11·2
Hispanics & Latinos	10·4

Full-time workers	13·7
Part-time workers	6·5
Age 16–24	4·6
Age ≥25	13·9

For complex reasons, in 2005, full-time union workers had median weekly earnings of $801 – compared to a nonunion median of $622.

———— US BIRTH & DEATH RATES · US CENSUS————

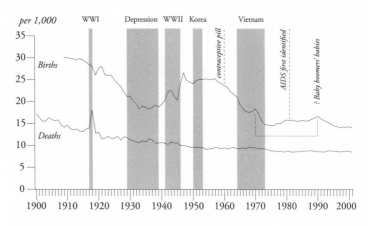

———— US RATES & CHARACTERISTICS OF DISABILITY————

Total population aged >5	All %	♂%	♀%
with no disability	85·7	86·2	85·2
with one type of disability	6·7	6·8	6·5
with two or more types of disabilities	7·6	6·9	8·3
Population 5–15 years			
any disability	6·3	8·0	4·5
a sensory disability	1·1	1·2	1·1
a physical disability	1·1	1·3	1·0
a mental disability	5·1	6·7	3·4
a self-care disability	0·8	0·9	0·7
Population 16–64 years			
any disability	11·6	11·5	11·6
a sensory disability	2·6	3·1	2·2
a physical disability	7·0	6·5	7·4
a mental disability	4·2	4·3	4·2
a self-care disability	1·9	1·7	2·1
a go-outside-home disability	2·8	2·5	3·2
an employment disability	6·6	6·4	6·8
Population ≥65 years			
any disability	39·6	37·1	41·4
a sensory disability	16·0	17·4	15·0
a physical disability	30·2	26·7	32·8
a mental disability	10·9	10·1	11·5
a self-care disability	9·3	7·5	10·6
a go-outside-home disability	16·3	11·9	19·5

[Source: US Census Bureau, American Community Survey, 2004]

———————— HEALTH (CARE) OF THE NATION————————

In 2003, Americans made 1,114,504,000 visits to doctors, outpatient departments, and E.R.s, or 3·9 visits per person. Of course, certain groups are heavier users than others. The average >75-year-old made 8·5 visits, and women (4·4) made more visits than men (3·4). Below are some statistics relating to the health(care) of the nation:

❦ The US spends a greater proportion of its GROSS DOMESTIC PRODUCT on health care than any other developed country. The 2003 total was 15·3% of GDP – $1·7 trillion, or $5,671 per person. Private insurance paid for 35% of this sum; 'out of pocket' payments 16%; state & local government 11%. Below is the trend in % GDP on health:

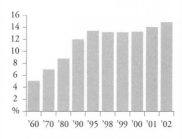

❦ In 2003, 736,211 medical DOCTORS were active in the US – 26·6 doctors per 10,000 population. 139,252,000 CIVILIANS worked in health service sites – 9·9% of all US workers.

During 1999–2002, 40% (♂) and 50% (♀) took at least one PRESCRIPTION DRUG. In 2003, the total spent on prescription drugs was $179·2bn; the most prescribed-for conditions were pain relief; depression (&c.); allergies; asthma (&c.); high cholesterol; and high blood pressure. ❦ In 2003, there were 5,764 hospitals in the US, offering 965,256 beds, with an average occupancy rate of 68·1%. ❦ Health insurance is a key factor in determining health care. Below are the trends in insurance among <65-year-olds (17% of whom were uninsured in 2003):

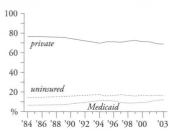

Below are some of the leading causes of death in the US (2002) broken down by sex:

Leading cause of death	♀%	♂%	Leading cause of death
Diseases of heart	28·6	28·4	Diseases of heart
Malignant neoplasms (i.e. cancer)	21·6	24·1	Malignant neoplasms (i.e. cancer)
Cerebrovascular diseases	8·0	5·8	Unintentional injuries
Chronic lower respiratory diseases	5·2	5·2	Cerebrovascular diseases
Alzheimer's disease	3·4	5·1	Chronic lower respiratory diseases
Diabetes mellitus	3·1	2·9	Diabetes mellitus
Unintentional injuries	3·0	2·4	Influenza and pneumonia
Influenza and pneumonia	3·0	2·1	Suicide
Nephritis, nephrosis, &c.	1·7	1·6	Nephritis, nephrosis, &c.
Septicemia	1·5	1·5	Chronic liver disease and cirrhosis

[Source for the page: Health, US, 2005, published 2006]

─────────── SOME HEALTH SCARES OF NOTE ───────────

{JAN} A study by Inserm, France's national institute for medical research, suggested that children who are exposed to household insecticides and head lice shampoos could double their risk of contracting leukemia. ❧ A study in the *New England Journal of Medicine* showed that African American male smokers were more likely to develop lung cancer than white or Latino male smokers. ❧ Findings from a US government-sponsored study suggested that *c.*3 million American women may have a hidden coronary disease that greatly increases their risk of heart attack. {FEB} An advisory panel convened by the Food and Drug Administration [FDA] warned that stimulants like Ritalin should carry warning labels because of possible adverse effects on the heart; the advice came after 25 people using the drug died suddenly. ❧ The *New York Times* reported that the babies of mothers who took anti-depressants late in their pregnancy were more likely to have a rare but serious lung disorder. {MAR} The *New York Times* reported that the popular sleeping pill Ambien was increasingly a factor in dangerous 'sleep-driving' and traffic arrests. Several studies also linked Ambien to night-time binge eating, with some users consuming thousands of calories while 'sleep-eating'. ❧ The US Centers for Disease Control reported that syphilis rates have been on the rise among young men since 2000. ❧ Homeland Security Secretary Michael Chertoff warned of a 'reasonable possibility' that bird flu could hit the US within months [see pp.19 & 181]. ❧ A national telephone survey of students and adults found that >50% of students surveyed had >1 symptom of hearing loss associated with portable music players. ❧ A federal drug panel said that stimulants such as Ritalin caused some children to suffer hallucinations involving snakes, insects, or worms. ❧ High concentrations of fluoride in the drinking water of 200,000 Americans could damage teeth and bones, according to the National Academy of Sciences. ❧ Physicians writing in the *Lancet* linked the Atkins diet to one patient's ketoacidosis, a serious metabolic condition, and warned that 'low-carb' diets may be 'far from healthy'. ❧ 2 women died after taking the abortion pill RU-486, leading the FDA to warn doctors to watch for a deadly blood infection that may be associated with the drug. ❧ A public health group that tested the raw tuna at 6 LA sushi restaurants found average levels of mercury at nearly twice the FDA-approved limit; some portions were deemed 'unsafe for anyone to eat'. The findings led one advocate to declare sushi 'the new Russian roulette'. ❧ Scientists at Leiden University said that low cabin pressure, cramped conditions, and lack of oxygen could all add to the risk of 'deep vein thrombosis' during long-haul flights. ❧ Researchers and federal health officials at the International Conference on Emerging Infectious Diseases suggested there was some evidence that staphylococci bacteria were being transmitted between humans and their pets. {APR} *c.*1,000 people in the Midwest became infected with the mumps, the largest US outbreak in 20 years. ❧ The Centers for Disease Control and Prevention reported 109 suspected or confirmed cases of the eye

─────── SOME HEALTH SCARES OF NOTE cont. ───────

fungus Fusarium, which can scar the cornea and cause blindness. The fungus was later linked to a popular contact lens solution, which was permanently withdrawn from the shelves. ❦ An LA woman was hospitalized with bubonic plague, the first confirmed human case in LA County in >2 decades. ❦ The *New York Times* reported on several studies showing that grapefruit juice can enhance the potency of, or otherwise interfere with, several widely used medicines, such as antihistamines and anti-depressants. {MAY} In a letter to doctors, GlaxoSmithKline warned that the anti depressant drug Paxil may increase the risk of suicide in young adults. ❦ A report showed that 15% of Asians in NYC were chronically infected with Hepatitis B – 35 times the rate in the general population. ❦ Data on the painkiller Vioxx showed an increased risk of heart attack and stroke after a few months of use, rather than after 18 months as had previously been reported. ❦ Children who are exposed to cats soon after birth have a greater risk of developing eczema, according to a team from the University of Arizona. ❦ The *New York Times* reported on evidence that bisphosphonates, a class of drugs used to strengthen bones, can cause an adverse reaction whereby parts of the jawbone die. ❦ A study in the *Journal of the American Medical Association* claimed that poor teenagers aged 15–17 were 50% more likely to be overweight than their richer peers. ❦ A study in *Pediatrics* found that 1 in 5 Cornell and Princeton students had purposefully cut, burned, or otherwise injured themselves at least once. ❦ Mothers who took ACE inhibitors (a class of blood pressure lowering drug) were more than twice as likely to have babies born with serious heart and brain problems, according to a study in the *New England Journal of Medicine*. ❦ A study by the National Institute of Occupational Safety and Health found that a flavor additive used in microwave popcorn produces hazardous fumes that may cause lung disease. ❦ A University of California study found that a type of ionic air purifier can produce toxic levels of ozone worse than high smog days in LA. {JUN} Evidence was presented that suggested exposure to artificial light at night can increase the risk of cancer; night workers such as air stewardesses and nurses are *c.*60% more likely to develop breast cancer. {JUL} The FDA warned that combining anti-depressants with triptans, a type of antimigraine drug, can cause the rare but life-threatening serotonin syndrome. ❦ An article in *Newsday* warned of a rise in 'BlackBerry thumb' [see p.192]. ❦ A report from the National Academy of Sciences claimed that trichloroethylene, a common drinking-water contaminant, can cause a variety of serious medical problems. ❦ The Institute of Medicine reported that medication mistakes harm 1·5m Americans each year, with each hospitalized patient subject to an average >1 medication error per day. ❦ A study in *Occupational & Environmental Medicine* found a probable link between indoor pools and childhood asthma. ❦ A federal government study found that 4 in 10 who undergo weight-loss surgery develop complications within 6 months. {AUG} A study in *Pediatrics* found that teens who listened to explicit music had sex earlier than their peers who did not.

———————————— OBESITY ————————————

Obesity is generally measured by the Body Mass Index (BMI), derived by dividing weight by the square of height (e.g. kg/m^2). A BMI >30 defines an individual as obese.

CLASS	underweight	normal	overweight	obese		(extreme)
BMI	<18·5	18·5–24·9	25–29·9	class I 30–34·9	class II 35–39·9	class III >40
RISK	varies	average	increased	moderate	severe	very severe

[See *Schott's Food & Drink Miscellany* for a complete schematic of BMI calculations]

The consensus of medical opinion concludes that excess body weight is associated with higher rates of morbidity and mortality, and, specifically, elevated risks of diabetes, heart disease, some cancers, hypertension, arthritis, and other musculo-skeletal problems. The National Institutes of Health estimate that *c.*300,000 US deaths a year are linked to obesity. Below are recent trends in US rates of obesity:

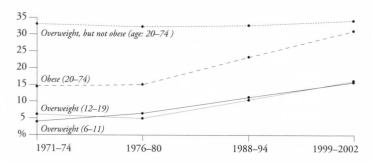

The 2003–4 *National Health & Nutrition Examination Survey* of 20–74-year-olds:

BMI <25 · 33·8%	Overweight · 33·3%	Obese · 32·9%

A range of factors influence America's obesity growth (not least poor diet), and the 2003 rates of leisure time (in)activity[†] in the population illustrate this correlation:

Regular activity · 32·8%	Some activity · 29·5%	Inactive · 37·6%

The most recent statistical analysis (1999–2002[†]) of obesity among 20–74-year-olds:

♂ & ♀, all races (rate of obesity).. 31·1%	Black/African American ♂ ..... 27·9%
♂, all races .... 28·1%	Black/African American ♀...... 49·6%
♀, all races...................... 34·0%	Mexican ♂ .... 29·0%
White ♂.......................... 28·7%	Mexican ♀...................... 38·9%
White ♀ .... 31·3%	[† Source: Health, US, 2005, Dept Health]

A 2006 study by Dr Majid Ezzati (Harvard School of Public Health) notes that obesity phone surveys may be flawed, since women tend to underestimate their weight, and men overestimate their height.

———————SMOKING: SOME FIGURES———————

The latest CDC figures (2005) indicate that 44·5m adults (20·9% of the adult population) currently smoke cigarettes. Smoking remains the leading US cause of preventable death, accounting for *c.*438,000 deaths a year – or 1:5 of all deaths. (2004 American Lung Association data indicate that 19·6% of US adults smoke cigars, and in 2003 *c.*15% of high school students smoked cigars.) Below is a breakdown of the current characteristics of cigarette smoking amongst US adults:

Men	(%) 23·4	GED diploma	39·6
Women	18·5	9–11 years of school	34
Am. Indians†	33·4	Undergrad. degree	11·7
Whites	22·2	Graduate degree	8
African Americans	20·2	Living in poverty	29·1
Hispanics	15·0	Not living in poverty	20·6
Asians‡	11·3	[† Incl. Alaskan Natives · ‡ Excl. Pacific Is]	

The chart below illustrates the prevalence of smoking in the US (1965–2003):

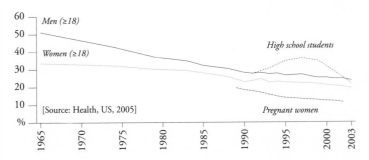

Men (≥18) · *Women (≥18)* · *High school students* · *Pregnant women* · [Source: Health, US, 2005]

The Federal Trade Commission's 2005 report gives the latest cigarette industry data:

		1965	1970	1980	1990	2000	2003
Cigarettes sold	bn	521·1	534·2	628·2	523·7	413·9	360·5
– given away	bn	–	–	–	–	–	7·1
Domestic ad spend	$	–	361m	1·2b	3·9b	9·6b	15·2b
Filtered cigarettes	%	64	80	92	95	98	99
Menthol cigarettes	%	18	23	28	26	26	27
Tar yield ≤15mg	%	–	3·6	44·8	60·6	87·1	84·9
Tar yield ≤12mg	%	–	–	–	51·5	50·4	59·5
Tar yield ≤9mg	%	–	–	–	25·5	23·7	22·5
Tar yield ≤6mg	%	–	–	–	12·2	13·6	12·6
Tar yield ≤3mg	%	–	–	–	2·8	1·3	1·0
Regular (68–72mm)	%	–	9	3	2	1	1
Kingsize (79–88)	%	–	73	63	57	60	61
Long (94–101)	%	–	18	32	39	37	36
Ultra-Long (110–121)	%	–	–	2	2	2	2

———————————————— DRUG ABUSE ————————————————

The most recent findings on drug use from the US Substance Abuse and Mental Health Services Administration (SAMHSA) show that, in 2004, 14·5% of those aged ≥12 had used illicit drugs (marijuana/hashish, cocaine, crack, heroin, hallucinogens, inhalants, psychotherapeutics) during the past *year*. The age breakdown of use was:

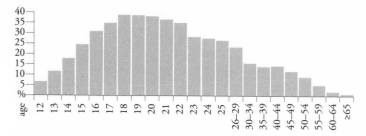

SAMHSA estimates that, in 2004, 19·1m Americans (≥12) were current illicit drug users – i.e. they had used an illicit drug in the preceding *month*. This represented 7·9% of the ≥12 population (8·2% in 2003, and 8·3% in 2002). The drugs were:

Drug	No. of users	%
Any illicit drug	19,071,000	7·9
Marijuana/hashish	14,576,000	6·1
Cocaine	2,021,000	0·8
Crack	467,000	0·2
Heroin	166,000	0·1
Hallucinogens	929,000	0·4
LSD	141,000	0·1
PCP	49,000	–
Ecstasy	450,000	0·2
Inhalants	638,000	0·3
Psychotherapeutics	6,007,000	2·5
Pain relievers	4,404,000	1·8
OxyContin	325,000	0·1
Tranquilizers	1,616,000	0·7
Stimulants	1,189,000	0·5
Methamphetamine	583,000	0·2
Sedatives	265,000	0·1

Of the 19·1m US drug users in 2004, 57% used marijuana alone and 20% used it with some other drug. 13% of marijuana users used the drug on ≥300 days per year. However, only 40% of users purchased their own supply of marijuana. Of 12–17-year-olds who bought marijuana, 15% purchased it on school property. Below is the average age of new users in 2004 of a selection of substances (for those ≥12). So, for example, the average age that Americans started using crack was 21·9.

Substance	age		age		age
Inhalants	16·0	PCP	18·9	Pain relievers	23·3
Cigarettes	16·7	Ecstasy	19·5	Stimulants	24·1
Alcohol	17·5	Smokeless tobacco	19·7	Heroin	24·4
Marijuana/hashish	18·0	Cocaine	20·0	OxyContin	24·5
LSD	18·4	Illicit drugs	20·1	Tranquilizers	25·2
Hallucinogens	18·7	Cigars	21·3	Sedatives	29·3
Daily cigarette use[†]	18·8	Crack	21·9	[† defined as smoking
		Methamphetamine	22·1	every day for >30 days]

SAMHSA cautions against inferring a *sequence* of drug use (e.g. 'soft' to 'hard') from these data.

——————————ALCOHOL——————————

The 2005 *Dietary Guidelines for Americans* issued by the Departments of Health & Human Services and Agriculture warns that 'the hazards of heavy alcohol consumption are well known and include increased risk of liver cirrhosis, hypertension, cancers of the upper gastrointestinal tract, injury, violence, and death'. Yet, it also notes that 'alcohol may have beneficial effects when consumed in moderation. The lowest all-cause mortality occurs at an intake of one to two drinks per day. The lowest coronary heart disease mortality also occurs at an intake of one to two drinks per day'. The government's advice is to drink in 'moderation' – defined as 1 drink/day for women and 2 drinks/day for men, where a 'drink' is:

12 fl.oz *regular beer* · 5 fl.oz *wine* · 1·5 fl.oz *80°-proof distilled spirits*

Most drinking guides employ the following definitions of alcohol consumption:

REGULAR DRINKING .... ≥12 drinks in a year
INFREQUENT DRINKING .... <12 drinks in a year
LIGHT DRINKING .... ≤3 drinks per week
MODERATE DRINKING .... 3–14 (♂) or 3–7 (♀) drinks per week
HEAVY DRINKING .... >14 (♂) or >7 (♀) drinks per week
BINGE DRINKING... ≥5 (♂) or ≥4 (♀) 'drinks' in a row >once in a 2-week period

Below are the latest (2003) figures of alcohol consumption among ≥18-year-olds:

Characteristic	*All* %	♂ %	♀ %
DRINKERS	60·8	67·1	55·2
regular	47·4	56·7	39·0
infrequent	12·9	9·8	15·9
light	68·4	58·9	78·9
moderate	23·7	32·8	13·7
heavy	7·9	8·3	7·4
binge	30·8	40·3	20·3
NONDRINKERS	39·2	33·0	44·9
lifetime abstainers	24·9	17·8	31·3
former drinkers	14·3	15·2	13·6

[Source: Health, US, 2005, Department of Health]

Because alcohol diminishes attention, coordination, skills, inhibition, &c., its (ab)use touches upon many aspects of society. According to data collated in the CDC's *General Alcohol Information*: binge drinkers were 14x more likely to report alcohol-impaired driving ❦ *c.*23% of suicide deaths are attributable to alcohol ❦ *c.*40% of all crimes are committed under the influence of alcohol ❦ excessive drinkers are at greater risk of cancers: liver cancer x3, esophageal cancer x4, oral cancer x6 ❦ *c.*50% of child abuse cases are associated with parental alcohol or drug abuse ❦ increasing the drinking age to 21 saved *c.*917 lives in traffic accidents in 2002 ❦ alcohol use by young adults is linked to earlier initiation of sexual activity, multiple partners, unprotected and nonconsensual sex, increased STDs, &c.

———————————— US GUN OWNERSHIP ————————————

Since 1973, the General Social Survey has asked Americans whether they have a gun in their home. In 1973, 47·3% did, compared to 36·5% in 2004. The only survey year in which the majority had a gun in their home was 1977, when 50·7% did.

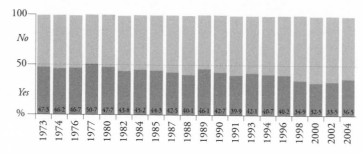

———————————— GUNS & VIOLENT CRIME ————————————

Below are the percentages of murders, robberies, and aggravated assaults in which firearms were used. In 2004, 70·3% of murders, 40·6% of robberies, and 19·3% of aggravated assaults reported to the police were committed with a firearm.

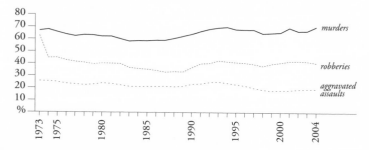

In 2001, *c.*39% of the deaths that resulted from firearms injuries were homicides, *c.*57% were suicides, *c.*3% were unintentional, and *c.*1% were of undetermined intent. [Source: Dept Justice]

———————————— US ARMS MANUFACTURE & EXPORT ————————————

PISTOLS 728,511	REVOLVERS....294,099	RIFLES....... 1,325,138
– to .22.........211,473	– to .22..........88,570	SHOTGUNS 731,769
– to .25..........10,140	– to .32........... 3,446	MISC............19,508
– to .32..........32,435	– to .357 MAG ..62,640	TOTAL....... 3,099,025
– to .380 68,291	– to .38 SPEC....54,842	*Exported* ....4·6%
– to 9mm.......182,493	– to .44 MAG....35,097	[Source: Bureau AT&F, 2004,
– to .50.........223,679	– to .50..........49,504	for 74% of manufacturers]

——————————CRIME IN THE US · 2004——————————

Below are the relative frequencies of crimes in the US, if averaged across the year:

1 VIOLENT CRIME ......*every* 23·1 sec	1 PROPERTY CRIME...... *every* 3·1 sec
1 murder .... 32·6 min	1 burglary ....14·7 sec
1 forcible rape.................5·6 min	1 larceny-theft.................. 4·5 sec
1 robbery......................1·3 min	1 motor vehicle theft..........25·5 sec
1 aggravated assault............36·9 sec	[Source: FBI Crime Clock, 2004]

——————————US CRIME RATES · 1985–2004——————————

The rates of violent and property crime (1985–2004) per 100,000 US population:

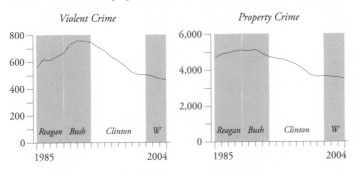

[Source: FBI, US Dept of Justice: Uniform Crime Reports, 2004]

——————US VIOLENT CRIME VICTIMIZATION RATES——————

The 2003–4 average rate of violent crimes per 1,000 people (>12 years old) by group:

Male	27·5	Urban	28·6
Female	18·6	Suburban	19·6
Never married	40·5	Rural	19·2
Married	9·9	12–15 years	50·7
Widowed	3·8	16–19 years	49·4
Divorced/separated	34·0	20–24 years	43·2
Income <$7,500	44·0	25–34 years	25·0
$7,500–14,999	34·8	35–49 years	18·2
$15,000–24,999	25·3	50–64 years	10·6
$25,000–34,999	23·5	≥65 years	2·0
$35,000–49,999	21·5	Northeast	18·5
$50,000–74,999	22·5	Midwest	23·8
≥$75,000	17·2	South	20·4
[Nat. Crime Victimization Survey, 2004]		West	25·7

———————MURDER———————

Murder fell in 2004 for the first time in 4 years: 16,137 offenses were recorded (5·5/100,000 population). This represented a fall of 2·4% from 2003, and 25·3% from 1995. Below are some of the statistics pertaining to perpetrators and their victims in 2004:

% of murders by month

Jan	7·9	May	8·8	Sep	8·6
Feb	6·7	Jun	8·3	Oct	8·3
Mar	8·4	Jul	9·5	Nov	7·9
Apr	8·0	Aug	9·4	Dec	8·1

murder offenders by race, sex, and age %

♂ (known)	90·1	White	33·5
♀ (known)	9·9	Black	35·2
<18-yr-old	20·6	Other	1·7
>18-yr-old	79·4	*unknown*	29·6

murder victims by race and sex

%	all	♂	♀	?
White	49·1	45·8	61·2	6·3
Black	47·0	50·6	34·4	9·4
Other	2·6	2·4	3·1	3·1
?	1·4	1·2	1·3	81·3
Total	—	77·8	21·9	0·2

In single victim–offender murders, 92·2% of blacks were killed by blacks; 84·8% of whites by whites. ❧ Where a murder weapon was specified, 70·3% were killed with a firearm; 14·1% with a knife (&c.); 7% with 'personal weapons' of hands, feet, teeth, &c.; 5% with a blunt object; &c. ❧ Where known, 76·8% of victims knew their killers (29·8% were family members), and 23·2% were killed by strangers. 33% of female victims were killed by husbands or boyfriends; only 2·7% of male victims died at the hands of wives or girlfriends. ❧ Nationally, 62·6% of murders were 'closed' or 'cleared'.

———————LAW ENFORCERS———————

2004 law enforcement personnel data:

Total law enforcement		970,588
– *civilians*	(30%)	294,854
– *sworn officers*	(70%)	675,734
Personnel/1,000 pop.		3·5

Sworn officers are defined as '*individuals who ordinarily carry a firearm and a badge, have full arrest powers, and are paid from governmental funds set aside specifically for sworn law enforcement representatives*'. ❧ Of all sworn officers, 88·4% are male, and 11·6% female. ❧ Since 1995, 566,523 law enforcement officers have been assaulted, and 594 feloniously killed (excluding 72 deaths as a consequence of the 9/11 attacks):

1995	74	2000	51
1996	61	2001	70
1997	70	2002	56
1998	61	2003	52
1999	42	2004	57

These killings can further be categorized by time and day of death of officers:

00:01–06:00	21·7%
06:01–12:00	17·8%
12:01–18:00	25·6%
18:01–24:00	34·3%

Sunday	10·1%
Monday	12·6%
Tuesday	13·5%
Wednesday	15·7%
Thursday	16·2%
Friday	16·7%
Saturday	15·3%

Of the 594 officers killed (1995–2004), 54 were murdered with their own gun. The average age of their killers was 29.

[Sources: Crime in the US, 2004; Law Enforcement Officers Killed & Assaulted, 2004; FBI]

——————————— PRISONS & PRISONERS ———————————

In December 2004, US federal, state, and local jails held the following prisoners:

2,135,901 people incarcerated	724 inmates per 100,000 population	1 in 138 of population in prison	1 in 109 US males in prison†	1 in 1,563 US females in prison†

This represented a 2·6% growth in the US prison population since 2003 – although this rate is slower than the 3·4% average yearly increase recorded since 1995. The total of all those incarcerated in the US (including military and juvenile facilities, territorial prisons, local jails, immigration & customs facilities, &c.) was 2,267,787. Including probation and parole, the US 'correctional population' totals *c.*7 million.

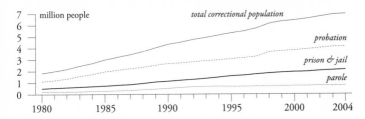

Below are some state incarceration rates per 100,000 population, with worldwide comparisons from the annual survey of the International Centre for Prison Studies:

Rate/100,000 population	Russia....... 581	*Minnesota*....171	France 88
Louisiana 816	Cuba........ 487	*Maine*........148	Switzerland...83
USA 724	S. Africa 344	England 144	Sweden 78
Texas.........694	Israel........ 209	Scotland.... 138	Denmark.....77
Mississippi ...669	Mexico 191	Canada 107	Japan 60
Oklahoma ...649	*Rhode Is.*......175	Germany 97	India..........31

A breakdown by race and ethnicity shows that at year end 2004, 41% of the prison population (serving >1 year) were Black (compared to 12% in the population); 34% of inmates were White (compared to 75%); and 19% were Hispanic (14%). 8·4% of all US Black males aged 25–29 were in prison in 2004, compared to 1·2% White and 2·5% Hispanic males of that age. In 2004, 7% of all prisoners were female. Below is the breakdown of sentenced state inmates by category of serious offense:

Serious offense	1995	2002	No. 1995	No. 2002
Violent	47%	51%	459,600	624,900
Property	23%	20%	226,600	253,000
Drug	22%	21%	212,800	265,100
Public order	9%	7%	86,500	87,500

[† Refers to prisoners in state or federal prisons only. Sources: Bureau of Justice Statistics, 2005; The International Centre for Prison Studies, 2006]

CAPITAL PUNISHMENT

60 prisoners in 16 States were executed during 2005 (59 in 2004) – of which 68% were white and 32% black. All but one of those executed were male, and all died by lethal injection. ❧ At 2am on December 2, 2005, Kenneth Boyd became the 1,000th person to be executed since capital punishment was reintroduced in 1976. Boyd was put to death in North Carolina for the murder of his estranged wife and her father in 1988. ❧ Below are the number of those executed in the US from 1930–2005:

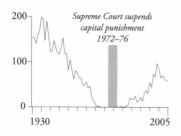

Supreme Court suspends
capital punishment
1972–76

A May 2006 *USA Today* poll indicated the following support for the death penalty for those convicted of murder:

favor 65% · *oppose* 28% · *unsure* 7%

However, 48% said that they would favor a life imprisonment sentence if 'life' meant life without parole.

The table opposite gives a snapshot of the death penalty in the 50 states, DC, the federal system, and the US. It shows: the methods allowed by state statute; state minimum age; if mentally ill patients may be executed; the numbers executed between 1977–2005, and in 2005; and the state's 2004 murder rate per 100,000.

Key to table – Lethal [I]njection · [G]assing
[E]lectrocution · [H]anging · [F]iring squad
ns=not stated · *na*=not applicable · ?=not known
[Sources: US Department of Justice; FBI]

	legal methods	minimum age	mentally ill	executed post '77	executed in '05	murder rate '04
AL	I·E	16	Y	34	4	5·6
AK	·	·	·	·	·	5·6
AZ	I·G	*ns*	N	22	0	7·2
AR	I·E	14	N	27	1	6·4
CA	I·G	18	N	12	2	6·7
CO	I	18	N	1	0	4·4
CT	I	18	N	0	1	2·6
DC	·	·	·	·	·	35·8
DE	I·H	16	N	14	1	2·0
FL	I·E	17	N	60	1	5·4
GA	I	17	N	39	3	6·9
HI	·	·	·	·	·	2·6
ID	I·F	*ns*	N	1	0	2·2
IL	I	18	N	12	0	6·1
IN	I	18	N	16	5	5·1
IA	·	·	·	·	·	1·6
KS	I	18	N	0	0	4·5
KY	I·E	16	N	2	0	5·7
LA	I	*ns*	N	27	0	12·7
ME	·	·	·	·	·	1·4
MD	I	18	N	5	1	9·4
MA	·	·	·	·	·	2·6
MI	·	·	·	·	·	6·4
MN	·	·	·	·	·	2·2
MS	I	16	Y	7	1	7·8
MO	I·G	18	N	66	5	6·2
MT	I	*ns*	Y	2	0	3·2
NE	E	18	N	3	0	2·3
NV	I	16	N	11	0	7·4
NH	I·H	17	Y	0	0	1·4
NJ	I	18	N	0	0	4·5
NM	I	18	N	1	0	8·9
NY	I	18	N	0	0	4·6
NC	I	17	N	39	5	6·2
ND	·	·	·	·	·	1·4
OH	I	18	Y	19	4	4·5
OK	I·E·F	16	Y	79	4	5·3
OR	I	18	Y	2	0	2·5
PA	I	*ns*	Y	3	0	5·2
RI	·	·	·	·	·	2·4
SC	I·E	*ns*	?	35	3	6·9
SD	I	18	N	0	0	2·3
TN	I·E	18	N	1	0	5·9
TX	I	17	Y	355	19	6·1
UT	I·F	14	N	6	0	1·9
VT	·	·	·	·	·	2·6
VA	I·E	14	N	94	0	5·2
WA	I·H	18	N	4	0	3·1
WV	·	·	·	·	·	3·7
WI	·	·	·	·	·	2·8
WY	I·G	18	Y	1	0	2·2
Fed.	I	18	?	3	0	*na*
USA	*na*	*na*	*na*	1004	60	5·5

Media & Celebrity

A celebrity is a person who works hard all his life to become known,
then wears dark glasses to avoid being recognized. — FRED ALLEN

—————'PEOPLE' vs 'US WEEKLY' COVER STARS—————

Date	People	Us Weekly
1·09·06	People who lost half their size	Nick Lachey & Jessica Simpson
1·16·06	Sharon Rocha	Angelina Jolie
1·23·06	Angelina Jolie & Maddox	Lindsay Lohan
1·30·06	Brad Pitt & Angelina Jolie	Jennifer Aniston
2·06·06	Jennifer Aniston	Angelina Jolie
2·13·06	Neil, Rachel, & Lillian Entwistle	Jessica Simpson
2·20·06	Heather Locklear	Denise Richards
2·27·06	Britney Spears	Jessica Simpson
3·06·06	Nick Lachey & Jessica Simpson	Nick Lachey & Jessica Simpson
3·13·06	Sheryl Crow	Angelina Jolie & Brad Pitt
3·20·06	'Oscar secrets'	Jessica Simpson & Kristin Cavallari
3·27·06	Christopher & Dana Reeve	Kristin Cavallari
4·03·06	Princess Diana	Keven Federline & Britney Spears
4·10·06	The Winkler family	Jessica Simpson
4·17·06	Julia Roberts	Tom Cruise & Katie Holmes
4·24·06	Katie Holmes	Jessica Simpson & Lindsay Lohan
5·01·06	Tom Cruise & Katie Holmes	Nick Lachey
5·08·06	Angelina Jolie	Denise Richards & Heather Locklear
5·15·06	Heather Locklear	Denise Richards
5·22·06	Brooke Shields & her children	Britney Spears
5·29·06	People who lost half their size	Britney Spears & Kevin Federline
6·05·06	Sir Paul McCartney & Heather Mills McCartney	Janet Jackson
6·12·06	Angelina Jolie	Angelina Jolie
6·19·06	Angelina Jolie, Brad Pitt, & Shiloh	Britney Spears & Sean Preston
6·26·06	Taylor Hicks	Angelina Jolie & Brad Pitt
7·03·06	Kirstie Alley	Britney Spears, Kevin Federline, Sean Preston
7·10·06	Nicole Kidman & Keith Urban	Tori Spelling
7·17·06	Faith Hill & Tim McGraw	Tom Cruise & Katie Holmes
7·24·06	Jennifer Aniston	Keira Knightley & Kate Bosworth
7·31·06	Sandra Bullock	Pamela Anderson
8·07·06	Lance Bass	Tori Spelling
8·14·06	Mel Gibson	Nick Lachey
8·21·06	Brad Pitt	Vince Vaughn & Jennifer Aniston
8·28·06	Britney Spears	Kate Hudson & Owen Wilson

Angelina Jolie appeared 5 times each on *People* and *Us Weekly* covers during the months surveyed.

——————SOME HATCHED, MATCHED, & DISPATCHED——————

HATCHED

Ava [♀]...*born to* Kevin Dillon & Jane Stuart
Barron William [♂]......................Donald Trump & Melania Knauss Trump
Bluebell Madonna [♀] .... Geri Halliwell
Grier Hammond [♀]............................. Brooke Shields & Chris Henchy
Isabella [♀]..Matt Damon & Luciana Bozan
Johnny [♂] ....Mira Sorvino & Chris Backus
Kingston James McGregor [♂] .... Gwen Stefani & Gavin Rossdale
Moses [♂].. Gwyneth Paltrow & Chris Martin
Samuel Jason [♂]...Jack Black & Tanya Haden
Shiloh Nouvel† [♀] ....Angelina Jolie & Brad Pitt
Suri† [♀] ....Katie Holmes & Tom Cruise
Tennyson Spencer [♂] ....Russell Crowe & Danielle Spencer
Violet Maye [♀] ....Dave Grohl & Jordyn Blum

MATCHED

Avril Lavigne & Deryck Whibley............................Montecito, California
Eminem & Kimberly Mathers ....Rochester Hills, Michigan
Glenn Close & David Shaw......................................Prouts Neck, Maine
Jack Black & Tanya Haden.................................... Big Sur, California
Kevin Dillon & Jane Stuart ....Las Vegas, Nevada
Marcia Cross & Tom Mahoney............................ San Gabriel, California
Nicole Kidman & Keith Urban....................................Manly, Australia
Patricia Arquette & Thomas Jane.......................................Venice, Italy
Pink & Carey Hart...Costa Rica
Tori Spelling & Dean McDermott... Fiji
Pamela Anderson & Kid Rock...............................San Tropez, France

DISPATCHED

Hilary Swank & Chad Lowe (*after* 8 years) ....separated
Jessica Simpson & Nick Lachey (2 years)................................. divorced
Heather Locklear & Richie Sambora (11 years).................... filed for divorce
Phil Collins & Orianne Cevey (6 years)..................................separated
Eminem & Kimberly Mathers (81 days) .... divorced
Eddie & Nicole Murphy (12 years)....................................... divorced
Paul McCartney & Heather Mills (4 years) ....separated
Selma Blair & Ahmet Zappa (2 years)............................ filed for divorce
David Lynch & Mary Sweeney (1 month) .... filed for divorce
Dave Navarro & Carmen Electra (2½ years).................... filed for divorce
Christie Brinkley & Peter Cook (10 years)...............................separated
Kate Hudson & Chris Robinson (6 years) ....separated

---

† Shiloh and Suri join the children of other celebs who may face playground taunts: Phinnaeus
to Julia Roberts; Scout LaRue to Demi Moore; Sage Moonblood to Sylvester Stallone; Banjo to
Rachel Griffiths; Sailor to Christie Brinkley; Blue Angel to The Edge; Moxie CrimeFighter to Penn
Jillette; and, of course, Moon Unit, Dweezil, Ahmet Emuukha Rodan, & Diva to Frank Zappa.

VANITY FAIR'S HOLLYWOOD · 2006

The stars featured on the cover of the 2006 *Vanity Fair* 'Hollywood issue' were:

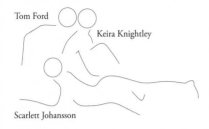

Tom Ford

Keira Knightley

Scarlett Johansson

The cover of the 2006 Hollywood edition caused a degree of controversy, since it featured a very clothed Tom Ford alongside the very naked Knightley and Johansson. The girls' arms and legs were strategically placed to avoid embarrassment – though Johansson's bare buttocks were exposed on page 2 of the gatefold pullout cover. Ford claims he stepped in to the frame after Rachel McAdams decided she was not comfortable appearing unclad.

The 2005 *Vanity Fair* cover stars: Kate Winslet, Cate Blanchett, Uma Thurman, Rosario Dawson, Ziyi Zhang, Scarlett Johansson, Claire Danes, Kate Bosworth, Sienna Miller, and Kerry Washington.

THE FACE OF...

Celebrity	face of ...
Kirstie Alley	*Jenny Craig*
Christina Applegate	*Hanes*
Halle Berry	*Revlon*
Mischa Barton	*Keds*
Penélope Cruz	*L'Oréal Natural Match*
Carmen Electra	*Max Factor*
George Hamilton	*Nabisco Toasted Chips*
Teri Hatcher	*Clairol Nice 'n Easy*
Angelina Jolie	*St. John*
Scarlett Johansson	*L'Oréal Sublime Glow*
Nicole Kidman	*Chanel No.5*
Keira Knightley [from '07]	*Chanel No.7*
Evangeline Lilly	*Michelle K*
Kate Moss	*Nikon Coolpix S6*
Gwyneth Paltrow	*Estée Lauder Pleasures*
Danica Patrick	*Secret*
Anna Nicole Smith	*TrimSpa*
Molly Sims	*CoverGirl*
Hilary Swank	*Guerlain Insolence*
Lindsay Lohan	*Louis Vuitton*
Carrie Underwood	*Skechers*
Tiger Woods	*TAG Heuer*
Catherine Zeta-Jones	*T-Mobile*

CELEBRITY SKIN

The startling clarity of High Definition TV (HDTV) magnifies the flaws of even the most pampered of faces. In a poll commissioned to coincide with Britain's first HDTV broadcast, the National Association of Screen Makeup Artists and Hairdressers listed which celebrities it thought had the most naturally flawless skin, and which required a touch of concealer. Below are the best and worst celebrity complexions:

flawless, absolutely flawless
Scarlett Johansson · Orlando Bloom
Kate Winslet · Jake Gyllenhaal
Catherine Zeta-Jones · Johnny Depp

not so flawless
Cameron Diaz · Michael Douglas
Keira Knightley · Bryan Adams
Joan Collins · Brad Pitt

[Source: NASMAH/Telewest · March 2006]

CELEBRITY RANKINGS

· FHM's SEXIEST ♀ ·

1 .....Scarlett Johansson
2 .... Angelina Jolie
3 .... Jessica Alba
4 .... Jessica Simpson
5 .... Keira Knightley
6 .... Halle Berry
7 ...... Jenny McCarthy
8 ...... Maria Sharapova
9 ....Carmen Electra
10.........Teri Hatcher
[Source: *FHM*, 2006]

· PEOPLE's SEXIEST ♂ ·

1 .....M. McConaughey
2 ...... Patrick Dempsey
3 .....Terrence Howard
4 ..... Viggo Mortensen
5 .... Vince Vaughn
6 ....Nick Lachey
7 ....Heath Ledger
8 ....Daniel Dae Kim
9 ....Keith Urban
10......... Ian McShane
[Source: *People*, 2005]

Taylor Hicks was named
People's sexiest bachelor of
2006. Jake Gyllenhaal,
Nick Lachey, and 12 other
soulful-looking leading
men also appeared on the list.

· UNSEXIEST ♂ ·

In 2006 the *Boston
Phoenix* named the
world's 100 Unsexiest
Men: owlish comedian
Gilbert Gottfried 'won',
followed by Yankees
pitcher Randy Johnson,
and Roger Ebert.
Osama bin Laden was
No. 8. Curiously, Brad
Pitt was No. 100, due
to alleged poor hygiene.

· HOT HOLLYWOOD ·

Some winners of
Us Weekly's 2006
Hot Hollywood awards:

Athlete Style
Maria Sharapova
Body Style
Jennifer Love Hewitt
Breakout Style
Jamie-Lynn Sigler
Cast Style
Entourage (HBO)
Couple Style
Tori Spelling &
Dean McDermott
Hip-hop Style
Ludacris
Movie Star Style
Brittany Murphy
Reality Style
Stacy Keibler
Red Carpet Style
Paris Hilton
Rock Star Style
Avril Lavigne
Sexy Style
Carmen Electra
Style Icon of the Year
Jessica Alba

· FORBES CELEBRITY POWER RANKING ·

The most powerful stars
in the media firmament:
1 ....Tom Cruise
2 .... The Rolling Stones
3 ....Oprah Winfrey
4 .... U2
5 ....Tiger Woods
6 ....Steven Spielberg
7 .... Howard Stern
8 ....50 Cent
9 ....*Sopranos* cast
10...........Dan Brown
[Source: *Forbes*, 2006]

· MAXIM's HOT 100 ·

Desperate Housewives
star Eva Longoria
topped *Maxim*'s Hot
100 list for the second
year in a row (the
list ranks the 'most
successful' women in
film, TV, music, sports,
and fashion). Others
listed included:

2 .... Jessica Alba
3 ....Lindsay Lohan
4 ....Angelina Jolie
5 .... Stacy Keibler
6 .....Scarlett Johansson
7 ....Cameron Diaz
8 ....Kate Bosworth
9 ...... Keira Knightley
10......Christina Milian

· PEOPLE's 100 MOST BEAUTIFUL ·

People expanded
its famed *50 Most
Beautiful* list to *100
Most Beautiful* for 2006.
Angelina Jolie was
named number one,
and joined Brad Pitt
and children Zahara &
Maddox in the *World's
Most Beautiful Family*.
Jessica Simpson
won *Best Smile*,
Halle Berry won *Best
Brows*, and Scarlett
Johansson won *Best
Cleavage*. The lavish
issue also featured
celebrities with their
favorite pets, *Beauties
Around the Globe*, and
the pronouncements of
a Chinese face analyst.

CELEBRITY AUTOGRAPHS

Autograph Collector magazine published in May 2006 a list of celebrities judged the best and worst to approach with a request for an autograph. The results were:

the best signers	*the worst signers*
Johnny Depp · George Clooney	Cameron Diaz · Bruce Willis
Matt Damon · Al Pacino	Demi Moore · Tobey Maguire
Tom Cruise · Angelina Jolie	Alan Alda · Halle Berry
Elijah Wood · Brittany Murphy	Winona Ryder · Teri Hatcher

DAVID BLAINE'S 'DROWNED ALIVE'

On May 1, 2006, 'showman' David Blaine submerged himself in a saltwater-filled acrylic sphere (8' diameter) at Lincoln Center in NY. Among other devices, he was equipped with an oxygen mask, 2-way communication, and a catheter. Blaine's aim was to stay underwater for 7 days before attempting the world underwater-breath-holding record of 8 min 58 sec. Though he accomplished 177 hours submerged in the sphere, he could hold his breath for only 7 min 8 sec before he was rescued on the verge of unconsciousness. Blaine's previous exploits include being buried in a glass coffin for 7 days, being encased in ice for *c.*61 hours, standing atop a 90' pillar for *c.*34 hours, and spending 44 days in a transparent box suspended from a crane.

CELEBRITY VOICE-OVERS

In a rejection of the baritone 'voice of God' voice-over, advertising agencies are increasingly turning to the warmer, congenial, familiar tones of Hollywood stars:

Celebrity	voice-overs for		
Jeff Bridges	*Duracell*	Queen Latifah	*Pizza Hut*
George Clooney	*Anheuser-Busch*	Charlie Murphy	*Boost Mobile*
Sean Connery	*Level 3 Comm.*	Julia Roberts	*America Online*
Richard Dreyfuss	*Honda*	Christian Slater	*Panasonic*
Kelsey Grammer	*Disney*	Kevin Spacey	*Honda*
Gene Hackman	*Oppenheimer Funds*	Donald Sutherland	*Volvo*
		Kiefer Sutherland	*Apple*

2005 research in the *Journal of Consumer Research* suggests that celebrity voice-overs are more likely to create positive brand associations when listeners *cannot* identify the particular celebrity's voice.

MEDIA PERSON OF THE YEAR · 2005

Media news website *I Want Media* named CNN's Anderson Cooper its 2005 Media Person of the Year. Other 2005 nominees included founder of the *Gawker* blog empire, Nick Denton; '*Google* guys' Sergey Brin and Larry Page; *Apple* CEO Steve Jobs; tycoon Rupert Murdoch; and founder of *Craigslist*, Craig Newmark.

─────CELEBRITY BLOGS AND QUOTES OF NOTE─────

Wisdom from celebrity interviews and blogs:

SCARLETT JOHANSSON
(to *People*, on Woody Allen)
I sometimes find him to be overwhelming, maybe not sexually, but before he eats his muffins in the morning.

PINK (blog)
There is absolutely nothing wrong with being sexy, feeling sexy, or dressing sexy. My point is only this: 'SMART' and 'SEXY' are not oil and water. They can actually work together. You don't need to dumb yourself down in order to be cute.

SASHA COHEN (blog)
The question I am asked most lately is what does it feel like to win the national championship? It feels great! I am real excited that my name will be on the US Trophy as the 2006 US National Champion. ... On tour and shows I will now be announced as 'US National Champion', not four-time silver medalist! It has a better ring to it!

MADONNA
(to *Harper's Bazaar*)
What's the difference between a pop star and a terrorist? You can negotiate with a terrorist.

DAVID BLAINE (blog)
The most courageous act a man can do is cry.

KATE BECKINSALE
(in *Us Weekly*, on false internet rumors)
I eat cotton wool to stay in shape. I have slept with everyone on the planet. There's a photograph of me doing unfortunate things with vegetables.

KEVIN FEDERLINE
(to *Newsweek*) · If I was that bad, you think anyone, let alone Britney, would put up with it?

TOM CRUISE
(to *GQ*, on Katie Holmes)
I went, 'You're gonna tell me if you're pregnant, aren't you?' ... And I knew at that moment she was pregnant. 'Cuz I notice things in people.

GENE SIMMONS (blog)
Some of you get sick and tired of seeing GENE SIMMONS in front of every project. Not my problem. I like it. I like me. And, I am unabashed and unapologetic of being in the Gene Simmons Business. If there can be Geffen Records and Bloomberg TV and Walt Disney Pictures ... there can be GENE SIMMONS EVERYTHING. Those guys did it right. And, I certainly intend to do the same.

MOBY (blog)
they should prescribe waffles to people suffering from depression. waffles and puppies. how could anyone [be] depressed while eating waffles and playing with puppies? just imagine: a plate of waffles and maple syrup and a little box with jack russell puppies leaping around?

JENNY McCARTHY
(to *People*)
A psychic [once] told me I was going to be a writer. I was like, 'What?! I've read one book in my entire life'.

SUSAN SARANDON
(in *Us Weekly*, after Tom Cruise and Brooke Shields had children on the same day)
That's so cool: they have something to talk about other than antidepressants.

BRITNEY SPEARS
(blog) · In some ways, people are a lot like animals. We all hunger for the same things. Love, lust, danger, warmth and adventure. Like people, animals all have their own rhythm to life. I'm mesmerized by tigers.

LINDSAY LOHAN
(to British *GQ*)
I find myself pretty darn intelligent.

——— CELEBRITY BLOGS AND QUOTES OF NOTE cont. ———

OPRAH WINFREY
(to *Oprah Magazine*, on
her best friend, Gayle King)
I understand why people
think we're gay. There
isn't a definition in our
culture for this kind of
bond between women.
… How can you be this
close without it being
sexual?

NICK LACHEY
(in *Us Weekly*, denying being
gay) · While I respect the
other team and recog-
nize the other team and
recognize that they too
play ball, I am not interested in playing for the
other team.

MARY J. BLIGE
(in *Us Weekly*)
My god is a god who
wants me to have things.
He wants me to bling!

PARIS HILTON (in *Us
Weekly*) · There's nobody
in the world like me. I
think every decade has
an iconic blonde – like
Marilyn Monroe or
Princess Diana – and
right now, I'm that icon.

PAMELA ANDERSON
(blog) · I'm finally getting
remarried … it's been a
whirlwind. … Feels like
I've been stuck in a time
warp. Not able to let go
of MY family picture …
it's been sad and lonely
and frustrating. … I've
raised my kids alone in
hope of a miracle. Well
my miracle came and
went. And came back
and came back because
he knew that I'd wake up
one day and realize that I
was waiting for nothing.
I'm moving on.

DAVID BLAINE (blog)
Soft is stronger than
hard; love is stronger
than hate; water is
stronger than stone;
silence is stronger than
screams.

PAUL McCARTNEY
(web site statement on the
day he announced his separation from Heather Mills)
In reading the media
reports that are coming
out, I would urge peo-
ple not to believe them.
Almost everything I'm
reading is 100% untrue.
I urge people not to read
this stuff and support
Heather and myself at
this difficult time.

BRAD PITT
(to NBC *Today*)
I am so tired of thinking
about myself.

——— GAWKER STALKER ———

In March 2006, influential media and
celebrity blog *gawker.com* launched
Gawker Stalker, a mash-up [see p.192]
overlaying NYC celebrity sightings
(sent in by readers) with Google Maps.
Thus Gawker seeks to 'visually pinpoint the location of every stalkworthy
celebrity as soon as they're spotted'.
Unsurprisingly perhaps, a number of
celebrities and their PRs were less than
amused. The Associated Press reported
that George Clooney had urged people
to send in dozens of false reports, 'a
couple hundred conflicting sightings
and this web site is worthless'.

——— FASHION OFFENDERS ———

Each year a fashion guru and former
designer known only as Mr Blackwell
produces a list of Tinseltown's worst
style offenders. His top ten of 2005:

1	Britney Spears
2	Mary-Kate Olsen
3	Jessica Simpson
4	Eva Longoria
5	Mariah Carey
6	Paris Hilton
7	Anna Nicole Smith
8	Shakira
9	Lindsay Lohan
10	Renée Zellweger

MISS AMERICA · 2006

The winner of the 2006 *Miss America* pageant was 22-year-old brunette Jennifer Berry – an aspiring teacher from Tulsa and 2005's *Miss Oklahoma*. In the 'talent section' of the show, Berry performed a *ballet en pointe* to William Joseph's 'Within', and she confessed to host James Denton that she enjoys nothing more than dipping French fries into ranch dressing. Berry received a $30,000 college scholarship to continue her education, and embarked on a yearlong (20,000 miles per month) speaking tour to promote her pageant 'platform issue': *Building Intolerance to Drunk Driving and Underage Drinking* (at 15, Jennifer lost a friend in an alcohol-related accident). ❦ The Miss Congeniality Prize, awarded by the contestants to the entrant they most like and respect, was given for the first time since 1974 – to Miss Hawaii, Malika Dudley, for her kindness, generosity, and 'addictive smile'.

18% of a PBS online poll said that *Miss America* was 'an event that's really about looking at women's bodies'; 27% said the pageant was 'a fun American tradition'; and 36% 'a good scholarship opportunity for women'. However, 23% said they would not walk down a runaway in a swimsuit 'at any price'. ❦ The preliminary rounds of the 2007 *Miss America* pageant will be incorporated into a reality TV show. The 7-episode series will follow 52 *Miss America* hopefuls, living together (in groups of 7) and competing in preliminary evening gown, swimwear, and talent competitions. Viewers will be able to select 5 contestants to go through to the final; a panel of judges will select another 8. The final 15 will be revealed during the pageant's live broadcast, which will follow the traditional format.

SOME CELEBRITY 'GOT MILK' MUSTACHES · 2006

Ben Roethlisberger · *The View* · Matt Hasselbeck · Sheryl Crow
Brandon Routh · Elizabeth Hurley · Mischa Barton · Lindsay Davenport

SCENTS OF THE FAMOUS

Jennifer Lopez......................*Glow*	Paris Hilton.................*Paris Hilton*
Britney Spears......*Curious; In Control*	Celine Dion..............*Always Belong*
Sarah Jessica Parker...............*Lovely*	Bo Derek...*Bless the Beasts* [a dog perfume]
Donald Trump...........*The Fragrance*	Sean 'Diddy' Combs......*Unforgivable*
Beyoncé Knowles.............*True Star*	Alan Cumming..............*Cumming*
Jessica Simpson ....*Taste*	Antonio Banderas.................*Spirit*

The Fragrance Foundation's annual 'FiFi Awards' honor the creative achievements of the perfume industry. In 2006, *euphoria* by Calvin Klein (a mix of pomegranate, persimmon, and black orchid) won the 'Women's Luxe' award, while *Armani Code* by Giorgio Armani (made of lemon and bergamot, with hints of orange tree blossom) won 'Men's Luxe'. *Fracas de Robert Piguet* (tuberose, jasmine, and jonquil) was entered into the prestigious 'Fragrance Hall of Fame'. At a New York ceremony, each of the winners was presented with a crystal sculpture of two abstract columns embracing a droplet.

AMERICAN IDOL 5

Gray-haired Alabaman TAYLOR HICKS was crowned the fifth *American Idol* on May 24, 2006, during a 2-hour finale watched by 36 million. Upon winning, Hicks shouted, '*Soul Patrol*', the 'official' nickname for his fans. Told at his first audition that he wasn't 'Idol material', Hicks went on to amass such a passionate fan base that his eventual win over crooner Katharine McPhee was almost a foregone conclusion. However, 'rocker dad' Chris Daughtry's elimination on May 10 was less expected, especially after his cover of Fuel's *Hemorrhage* led the band to offer him a job as lead singer. (Mostly) minor scandals and feuds kept viewers entertained throughout the season, as did British judge Simon Cowell's famously biting pronouncements. *American Idol 5*'s top twelve contestants were sent packing in the following order:

March 15	Melissa McGhee	April 26	Kellie Pickler
March 22	Kevin Covais	May 3	Paris Bennett
March 29	Lisa Tucker	May 10	Chris Daughtry
April 5	Mandisa	May 17	Elliott Yamin
April 12	Bucky Covington	May 24	Katharine McPhee
April 19	Ace Young	WINNER	Taylor Hicks

According to a Pursuant Inc. poll, 10% of all US adults voted during *American Idol*'s fifth season. The final vote tally was 63·4m, which host Ryan Seacrest claimed was more than any US President had ever received. *American Idol* was the top-rated TV show in the US in the 2005–6 season, with an average weekly audience of 30 million; the finale was the third most-watched 'TV event' of the year.

QUOTES OF NOTE

SIMON COWELL · [to Ryan Seacreast] Lose the beard. ❦ MANDISA · [dedicating the song *Praise You*] To everybody that wants to be free! Your addiction, your lifestyle, or situation may be big, but God is bigger. ❦ PAULA ABDUL · [inexplicably, after being asked why two contestants got low votes] Simon said because one of them ate pizza and the other ate salad. ❦ RANDY JACKSON · [after Paula Abdul asked contestant Ace Young how he got the scar on his chest] Oh, listen! Paula! Oh, no no no! Control yourself! ❦ KATHARINE MCPHEE · [after a wardrobe mishap] I hope I didn't offend anybody. ❦ TAYLOR HICKS · [at the end of the finale] Thank you, America! I'm living the American dream!

OTHER REALITY SHOW WINNERS

Network	show	winner (prize)
ABC	*American Inventor*	Janusz Liberkowski ($1m)
ABC	*Dancing with the Stars*	Drew Lachey (disco ball 'inspired' trophy)
VH1	*Flavor of Love*	Hoopz (set of gold teeth)
UPN	*Next Top Model 6*	Danielle Evans (Ford Model & CoverGirl contracts; *Elle* shoot)
Fox	*Skating with Celebrities*	Kristy Swanson & Lloyd Eisler (Lucite trophies)
CBS	*Survivor Panama: Exile Island*	Aras Baskauskas ($1m)
BRAVO	*Top Chef*	Harold Dieterle ($100,000)
NBC	*The Apprentice 4*	Randal Pinkett (job with Donald Trump)
BRAVO	*Project Runway*	Chloe Dao ($100,000 for a clothes line; *Elle* spread; &c.)

—HOUSEHOLDS WITH...—

Telephone service .... 95·5%
Radio .... 99·0%
    average number of radios 8
Televisions .... 98·2%
    average number of TV sets .... 2·4
Cable TV .... 69·8%
VCRs .... 91·5%
Computers .... 61·8%

[Source: US Statistical Abstract, 2006]

—— TV HOUSEHOLDS ——

Of the 110,213,910 homes with TV:

Have color TV	99%
Have ≥2 sets	81%
Have ≥3 sets	50%
Have a VCR	89%
Have wired cable	66%
Have wired pay cable	31%

[Source: Nielsen Media Research, 2006 ©]

—— DAILY TV VIEWING DURATION ——

Average daily viewing	Total US	African Americans	Hispanic Americans
All people	4h 44m	6h 36m	3h 53m
Women 18+	5h 27m	7h 51m	4h 32m
Men 18+	4h 45m	6h 44m	3h 52m
Teens 12–17	3h 26m	4h 59m	3h 10m
Children 2–11	3h 23m	4h 34m	3h 13m

Below are the Nielsen Media Research historical daily viewing figures for US *households* (Sept–Sept), along with some notable milestones in TV broadcasting:

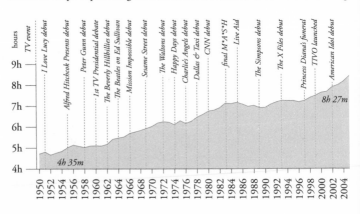

—— US TV 'INDECENCY' TIMELINE ——

1st broadcast of...	1976 .... ♀ *nipple*	1994 ...... 'screw'	1997 .... 'tits'
1971 ... 'goddam'	1986 ... 'condom'	1994 .... 'piss'	1997 ... 'bullshit'
1973 ... ♀ *nudity*	1991. *lesbian kiss*	1995 .... 'dick'	[Sources: Parents TV
1975 .... 'shit'	1993 .... 'asshole'	1997 .... 'fuck'	Council; & others]

———— TOP TELECASTS ————

The top network telecasts, ranked by household ratings, with viewer millions:

Program	audience (m)	year
M*A*S*H Special	50·15	1983
Dallas (who shot JR?)	41·47	1980
Roots Pt. VIII	36·38	1977
Super Bowl XVI Game	40·02	1982
Super Bowl XVII Game	40·48	1983
XVII Winter Olympics	45·69	1994
Super Bowl XX Game	41·49	1986
Gone with the Wind (I)	33·96	1976
Gone with the Wind (II)	33·75	1976
Super Bowl XII Game	34·41	1978
Super Bowl XIII Game	35·09	1979
Bob Hope Christmas Show	27·26	1970
Super Bowl XVIII Game	38·88	1984
Super Bowl XIX Game	39·39	1985
Super Bowl XIV Game	35·33	1980
Super Bowl XXX Game	44·15	1996
The Day After	38·55	1983
Roots Pt. VI	32·68	1977
The Fugitive	25·70	1967
Super Bowl XXI Game	40·03	1987
Roots Pt. V	32·54	1977
Super Bowl XXVIII Game	42·86	1994
Cheers (finale)	42·36	1993
Ed Sullivan (*The Beatles*)	23·24	1964
Super Bowl XXVII	41·99	1993
Bob Hope Christmas Show	27·05	1971
Roots Pt. III	31·90	1977
Super Bowl XXXII Game	43·63	1998
Super Bowl XI Game	31·61	1977
Super Bowl XV Game	34·54	1981
Super Bowl VI Game	27·45	1972
XVII Winter Olympics	41·54	1994
Roots Pt. II	31·40	1977
Beverly Hillbillies	22·57	1964
Roots Pt. IV	31·19	1977
Ed Sullivan (*The Beatles*)	22·44	1964
Super Bowl XXIII Game	39·32	1989
Academy Awards	25·39	1970

[Excludes programs <30 minutes and unsponsored or joint network telecasts.
Source: Nielsen Media Research ©]

———— TV PRIMETIME ————

Persons watching TV in primetime[†]:

Monday	114,430,000
Tuesday	113,873,000
Wednesday	109,459,000
Thursday	110,308,000
Friday	100,307,000
Saturday	100,658,000
Sunday	121,695,000

[† defined: Mon–Sat 8–11pm; Sunday 7–11pm
Source: Nielsen Media Research ©, 2006]

———— TOP SHOWS ————

The primetime top 20 programs
(September 2005–May 2006)

Network	show	share %
Fox	*American Idol* [Tue]	27
Fox	*American Idol* [Wed]	26
CBS	*CSI*	24
ABC	*Desperate Housewives*	20
ABC	*Grey's Anatomy*	20
CBS	*Without a Trace*	20
ABC	*Dancing with the Stars*	18
CBS	*CSI: Miami*	19
CBS	*Survivor: Guatemala*	17
Fox	*House*	16
ABC	*NFL Monday Night Football*	17
CBS	*NCIS*	15
CBS	*Survivor:Panama-Exile Is.*	15
CBS	*Two and a Half Men*	14
CBS	*The Unit*	14
ABC	*Dancing w/Stars Results*	16
NBC	*Deal or No Deal* [Mon]	15
CBS	*Cold Case*	14
CBS	*CSI: NY*	15
NBC	*Law and Order: SVU*	15

The top show in 1996 was *E.R.*;
in 1986, *The Bill Cosby Show*;
in 1976, *All In The Family.*

[Source: Nielsen Media Research ©]

——————— PRIMETIME EMMYS · 2006 ———————

Award	winner
Drama series	*24* · Fox
Drama, actor	Kiefer Sutherland · *24*
Drama, actress	Mariska Hargitay · *Law & Order: Special Victims Unit*
Drama, directing	Jon Cassar · *24*, '7:00–8:00'
Drama, writing	Terence Winter · *The Sopranos*, 'Members Only'
Comedy series	*The Office* · NBC
Comedy, actor	Tony Shalhoub · *Monk*
Comedy, actress	Julia Louis-Dreyfus · *The New Adventures of Old Christine*
Comedy, directing	Marc Buckland · *My Name Is Earl*, 'Pilot'
Comedy, writing	Greg Garcia · *My Name Is Earl*, 'Pilot'
Miniseries	*Elizabeth I* · HBO
Made-for-TV movie	*The Girl in the Café* · HBO
Miniseries or movie, actor	Andre Braugher · *Thief*
Miniseries or movie, actress	Helen Mirren · *Elizabeth I*
Variety, music, or comedy series	*The Daily Show w. Jon Stewart* · Comedy Central
Reality-competition program	*The Amazing Race* · CBS

Primetime Emmy nomination rules changed in 2006. Nominations had previously gone to those receiving the most votes from the Academy of Television Arts & Sciences membership. In 2006, a screening panel assisted with the process; it was hoped the change would 'invigorate' the awards.

——————— DAYTIME EMMYS · 2006 ———————

Award	winner
Drama series	*General Hospital* · ABC
Drama, lead actress	Kim Zimmer · *Guiding Light*
Drama, lead actor	Anthony Geary · *General Hospital*
Drama, supporting actress	Gina Tognoni · *Guiding Light*
Drama, supporting actor	Jordan Clarke · *Guiding Light*
Children's series	*Zoom* · PBS
Children's series, performer	Kevin Clash · Elmo, *Sesame Street*
Preschool children's series	*Sesame Street* · PBS
Talk show	*The Ellen Degeneres Show* · Syndicated
Talk show host	Ellen Degeneres · *The Ellen Degeneres Show*
Game show	*Jeopardy!* · Syndicated
Game show host	Alex Trebek · *Jeopardy!*
Service show	*30 Minute Meals with Rachel Ray* · Food Network
Children's animated program	*Jakers! The Adventures of Piggley Winks* · PBS
Original song	*Sunshine* · *The Young and the Restless*

In 2006, an Emmy for 'Outstanding Achievement in Video Content for Non-Traditional Delivery Platforms' was added to the Daytime roster. The award was designed to recognize programming created specifically to be viewed online, via cellphone, iPod, or video on demand, and is not limited to content traditionally shown during the day (such as soaps). The 2006 winner was *Live8 on AOL*.

―――――――――― RADIO LISTENING ――――――――――

Commercial radio continues to enjoy a wide listenership in the US: 93% of all American adults listened to the radio at least once a week in 2005. News, talk, and information was the most popular genre, accounting for an average 17·1% of listeners. Below, the share of listeners who chose each radio genre in winter 2005:

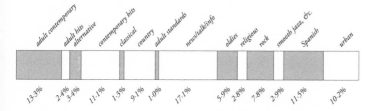

[% of listeners tuned to each format in an average 15 min. 2005–2006 winter · Source: Arbitron Inc.]

Location of radio listening	%
Home	38·8
Car	34·6
Work	24·0
Other	2·6

[Spring 2005; 6–12am. Source: Arbitron Inc.]

Most popular radio hour	7–8 am
Least popular radio hour	3–4 am
Group listening the most[†]	25–34♀
Group listening the least[†]	≥65♀

[† Based on the % of radio listeners in total demographic. Source: Arbitron Inc, Spring 2005]

―――――――――― 65th PEABODY AWARDS ――――――――――

Some of the programming chosen by the Peabody Awards, which honor the previous year's best in electronic media. (The awards do not recognize specific categories.)

Hurricane Katrina · WLOX-TV
Preparation and coverage of Hurricane Katrina · WWL-TV
NBC Nightly News with Brian Williams: After the Storm: The Long Road Back · NBC
CNN Coverage of Hurricane Katrina and Aftermath · CNN
China: A Million Steps Ahead · TVE
American Experience: Two Days in October · PBS
This World BBC: Bad Medicine · BBC2
Boston Legal · ABC
House · FOX
Edge of America · Showtime
South Park · Comedy Central

Classical Baby · HBO
A Room Nearby · PBS
Burning Questions · KNBC-TV
How Far Will the Army Go? KCNC-TV
Radio Rookies Project · WNYC Radio
American Masters: No Direction Home – Bob Dylan · PBS
Save Our History: Voices of Civil Rights The History Channel
Viva Blackpool · BBC America
The Staircase · Sundance Channel
Yesterday · HBO
The Queen of Trees · BBC2
Bleak House · BBC
The Shield · FX

———————————————— MAGAZINES ————————————————

According to the National Directory of Magazines, a total of 18,267 magazine titles were available in the US at the end of 2005 (350 were new that year). Those winning General Excellence prizes at the 2006 National Magazine Awards were:

Circulation >2m.................... *Time*	250k–500k........ *New York Magazine*
1m–2m............ *ESPN the Magazine*	100k–250k.........*Harper's Magazine*
500k–1m.......................*Esquire*	<100k........ *Virginia Quarterly Review*

TOP MAGAZINE CIRCULATION

Average 2005 sales of top magazines:

AARP the Magazine†	22,675,655
AARP Bulletin†	22,075,011
Reader's Digest	10,111,773
TV Guide	 8,211,581
Better Homes & Gardens	 7,620,932
National Geographic	 5,403,934
Good Housekeeping	 4,634,763
Family Circle	 4,296,370
Ladies' Home Journal	 4,122,460
Woman's Day	 4,048,799

† Membership publications of the AARP, an association for those >50. [Per issue average; members of the Audit Bureau of Circulations]

MAGAZINE CATEGORY GROWTH

Number of new magazines launched (1995–2005), by subject matter:

College & alumni...................	268
Interior design & decoration.......	98
Travel................................	93
Golf.................................	61
Automotive..........................	54
Dogs.................................	51
Crossword puzzles	35
Architecture.........................	34
Guns & firearms.....................	30
Collectibles..........................	24

MAGAZINE PAGES BY CONTENT

The percentage of editorial pages devoted to various subjects in 2005‡:

Entertainment/celebrity	%16·7
Apparel/accessories.................	13·4
Home furnishing/management.....	7·8
Travel/transportation	6·9
Food & nutrition	6·7
Business & industry	6·5
Culture...............................	6·1
Health/medical science	5·1
Beauty & grooming.................	4·9
Sports/recreation/hobby............	4·2

‡ Of the 141 magazines measured by Hall's Magazine Reports Co.

MAGAZINE DEATHS

Some of the magazines that met an untimely demise during 2006, with the number of years published:

Absolute (1) · *Budget Living* (4)
Cargo (2) · *Bundle* (1)
Business Traveler (30) · *CMO Mag.* (3)
Fuego (1) · *Inspired House* (3)
IT Architect (20) · *Secure Enterprise* (2)
Elle Girl (5) · *Travel Savvy* (3)
Celebrity Living (<1) · *MPH* (2)
Red (1) · *Shape en Español* (3) · *Sync* (2)
Teen People (8) · *The New Leader* (79)

[Source: Mag. Publishers of America] 'Pass-along rates' are also used to measure popularity. Enthusiast titles often dominate – as of fall 2005, *Handguns* magazine had the most readers per copy, at 41·46.

——————————— TRUSTED NEWS SOURCES ———————————

The percentage of those who believe 'all or most' of what a news organization reports, based on those able to rate the organization, and shown by partisan split:

Republicans (%)	Independents (%)	Democrats (%)
Fox News (29)	*60 Minutes* (29)	*CNN* (45)
CNN (26)	*CNN* (28)	*60 Minutes* (42)
60 Minutes (25)	*C-SPAN* (26)	*C-SPAN* (36)
Wall Street Journal (23)	*US News* (26)	*ABC News* (34)
C-SPAN (22)	*NBC News* (24)	*CBS News* (34)
Local TV news (21)	*NewsHour* (24)	*NPR* (33)

[Source: Pew Research Center · Trends 2005]

——————————— CONFIDENCE IN THE PRESS ———————————

The chart below indicates the percentage of the US public that has 'a great deal of confidence' in the press (and, by way of comparison, the scientific community):

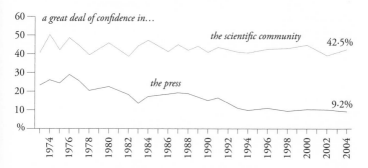

[Source: General Social Survey, 1972–2004]

——————————— TOP US NEWSPAPERS BY CIRCULATION ———————————

Title	reported circulation		
USA Today	2,528,437	*Chicago Tribune*	957,212
Wall Street Journal	2,058,342	*New York Daily News*	795,153
New York Times	1,683,855	*Philadelphia Inquirer*	705,965
Los Angeles Times	1,231,318	*Denver Post/Rocky Mt. News*	704,806
Washington Post	960,684	*Houston Chronicle*	692,557

[Source: Audit Bureau of Circulations, March 2006]

According to the World Association of Newspapers, the five largest global markets for newspapers in 2005 were – China (96·6m copies sold daily); India (78·7m copies); Japan (69·7m copies); the US (53·3m copies); and Germany (21·5m copies).

─────────── THE MILITARY & THE MEDIA ───────────

Below are some selected excerpts from *Meeting the Media* – a manual for military personnel, produced in 2003 by the Air Force Public Affairs Center of Excellence:

❦ Because the very existence of the Air Force depends on the 'consent of the governed', we have a duty to keep the citizenry informed. ❦ The news media are neither our friend nor our enemy. They are a conduit, albeit filtered, to the American public. ❦ Bad news does not improve with age. ❦ In this technologically advanced era, reality is not what actually exists, but what is perceived to exist. ❦ Prepare for [the media] by identifying and organizing predetermined, positive messages. No matter what the interviewer asks, you should feel free to steer your response to the related message. ❦ Let the media know your plans in as much detail as practical. ❦ Treat the media as you would want others to treat you. ❦ Make short, simple, and direct statements. ❦ Don't pretend to be perfect. ❦ Discuss only matters of which you have direct knowledge. ❦ When given a multiple-part question, answer the one segment that allows you to make a positive point. ❦ Prior planning is critical; don't 'wing it'. ❦ Speak conversationally, as you would to a non-military high school friend. ❦ Avoid repeating or using 'color words' that may have a negative connotation. Words such as 'massacre', 'scandal', 'deaths', 'corruption', etc., induce overly strong, emotional reactions and may be counterproductive to your objectives. ❦ People will remember their impression of you, not necessarily what you said. ❦ By assuming an assertive and positive attitude, you will not be victimized by events no matter how disastrous.

────── THE PULITZER PRIZE · JOURNALISM · 2006 ──────

PUBLIC SERVICE AWARD
The *Sun Herald* for its '*valorous and comprehensive coverage of Hurricane Katrina, providing a lifeline for devastated readers, in print and online, during their time of greatest need*'. And the *Times-Picayune* for its '*heroic, multi-faceted coverage of Hurricane Katrina and its aftermath, making exceptional use of the newspaper's resources to serve an inundated city even after evacuation of the newspaper plant*'.

BREAKING NEWS REPORTING
The *Times-Picayune* for its '*courageous and aggressive coverage of Hurricane Katrina, overcoming desperate conditions facing the city and the newspaper*'.

INVESTIGATIVE REPORTING
Susan Schmidt, James V. Grimaldi, and R. Jeffrey Smith of the *Washington Post* for their '*indefatigable probe of Washington lobbyist Jack Abramoff that exposed congressional corruption and produced reform efforts*'.

INTERNATIONAL REPORTING
Joseph Kahn and Jim Yardley of the *New York Times* for their '*ambitious stories on ragged justice in China as the booming nation's legal system evolves*'.

BREAKING NEWS PHOTOGRAPHY
Dallas Morning News staff for their '*vivid photographs depicting the chaos and pain after Hurricane Katrina engulfed New Orleans*'.

——————————— WORLD PRESS FREEDOM INDEX ———————————

Reporters Without Borders, a group working to protect freedom of the press, annually compiles an index of press freedom. The ranking is created by assessing the degree of freedom that journalists and news organizations experience in each country. The index for 2005 shows that Europe enjoys the greatest freedom (the top 10 countries are exclusively European) – the United Kingdom ranked 24th. The United States dropped over 20 places from 2004, to 44th – because of the imprisonment of *New York Times* reporter Judith Miller. The countries with the least press freedom are those where privately owned media is not permitted and freedom of expression does not exist. The ten most and least free countries are shown below:

Most free press	*Least free press*
Denmark[†] · Finland · Iceland · Ireland	North Korea · Eritrea · Turkmenistan
Netherlands · Norway · Switzerland	Iran · Burma · Libya
Slovakia · Czech Republic · Slovenia	Cuba · Nepal · China · Vietnam

[†Denmark's ranking is of special interest given the Muhammad cartoon crisis; see p.17]

——————————— JOURNALISTS AT RISK ———————————

The Committee to Protect Journalists (CPJ) is a group of US foreign correspondents working to promote freedom of the press worldwide. The CPJ highlights abuses of the press, publicizes the plight of imprisoned journalists, and records how many reporters are killed in the course of duty. In January 2006, the CPJ stated that during the previous year, 47 journalists had been killed worldwide – the majority of whom were victims of murder. Iraq was by far the most dangerous location: 22 journalists were killed there in 2005. In the Philippines, 4 reporters died (a fall from 8 in 2004); Lebanon, Russia, Bangladesh, Pakistan, Sri Lanka, and Somalia all recorded 2 deaths. 'Gulf War II' and its aftermath have made Iraq the deadliest conflict for journalists since the CPJ was established 24 years ago.

Conflict	*date*	*total killed*			
Iraq	2003–	60	Colombia	1986–	52
Algeria	1993–96	58	Balkans	1991–95	36
			Philippines	1983–87	36

The CPJ also reports how many journalists are imprisoned worldwide: as of December 2005, the total was 125. The countries with most jailed journalists were:

China	32	Ethiopia	13	USA	5
Cuba	24	Uzbekistan	6	Algeria	3
Eritrea	15	Burma	5	The Maldives	3

In November 2005 the International Federation of Journalists (IFJ) and the International News Safety Institute (INSI) presented a draft UN resolution to Kofi Annan. The resolution proposed the pursuit of governments that fail to prosecute those responsible for killing reporters. The IFJ and INSI hope to garner enough support to put the resolution before the United Nations Security Council.

─────────── INTERNET USAGE · US & ELSEWHERE ───────────

According to research by comScore Networks, 694m people (aged ≥15) worldwide used the internet (in March 2006) – 14% of the population in that age group. And, though the US accounts for about ⅓ of global users, this represents a decline from a decade ago, when it had ⅔ of users. Below are some online populations:

Online population	*visitors* (m)	%			
Worldwide	694·3	100·0	Germany	31·8	4·6
United States	152·1	21·9	United Kingdom	30·2	4·3
China	74·7	10·8	South Korea	24·7	3·5
Japan	52·1	7·5	France	23·9	3·4
			Canada	18·9	2·7

comScore further analyzed average monthly hours spent online in various countries:

hours/month online			
World average	31·3	Taiwan	43·2	Germany	37·2
Israel	57·5	Sweden	41·4	Denmark	36·8
Finland	49·3	Brazil	41·2	France	36·8
South Korea	47·2	Hong Kong	41·2	(US	29·3)
Netherlands	43·5	Portugal	39·8	(UK	29·2)
		Canada	38·4	[March 2006 data]	

Research by the widely respected Pew Internet and American Life Project gives the following insight into the demographic breakdown of internet users in the States:

US group	*% who use the internet*		
All adults	73	White, non-Hispanic	73
♂	74	Black, non-Hispanic	61
♀	71	English-speaking Hispanic	76
18–29 years	88	Income >$30,000/year	53
30–49 years	84	– $30,000–$49,999/year	80
50–64	71	– $50,000–$74,999/year	86
≥65	32	– ≥$75,000/year	91
		[February–April 2006 data]	

A detailed Pew report in April 2006 by John Horrigan and Lee Rainie illustrates the increasingly important role the internet plays in the day-to-day life of Americans:

The internet played a major role in	%
... *helping them cope with a major illness*	40
... *assisting another to cope with a major illness*	54
... *pursuing further training for their careers*	50
... *making major investment or financial decisions*	45
... *looking for a new place to live*	43
... *purchasing a car*	23
... *switching jobs*	14

Additional Pew data show that the rate of broadband adoption in the US is fast accelerating. In March 2006, 42% of adults had home broadband (30% in 2005).

──────── BLOGGING ────────

According to a 2005–2006 study by the Pew Internet and American Life Project, 12 million American adults currently have a blog, and 57 million read blogs (8% and 39% of all internet users, respectively). The Pew research also showed that bloggers tend to be young (54% are under 30) and suburban (51%), but are about as likely to be male as female [see below]. Most bloggers described their primary urge as the desire to express themselves creatively (52%). Other Pew data follow:

Bloggers who …	%
Post new material each day	13
Spend 1 or 2 hours a week maintaining their blog	59
Use a pseudonym	55
Mostly blog for themselves, rather than for an audience	52
Consider their blog a form of journalism	34
Have never been published anywhere else	54
'Sometimes' or 'often' spend time verifying facts they include in a post	56
Say their blog is very important to them	13

Bloggers who are …	%		%
♂	54	White (non-Hispanic)	60
♀	46	Black (non-Hispanic)	11
18–29 years old	54	Hispanic (English-speaking)	19
30–49	30	Other ethnicity	10
50–64	14	Suburban	51
≥65	2	Urban	36
		Rural	13

Many bloggers (37%) described the primary topic of their blog as 'my life and experiences'. Other subjects drew considerably less interest, as is illustrated below:

Politics and government	11	Religion, spirituality, or faith	2
Entertainment	7	Specific hobby	1
Sports	6	Specific health problem	1
General news & current events	5	Specific illness	1
Business	5	Other blog topics mentioned included opinion,	
Technology	4	volunteering, photography, and education.	

──── THE BROADCAST DECENCY ENFORCEMENT ACT ────

On June 15, 2006, President Bush signed the *Broadcast Decency Enforcement Act of 2005*, which raised the maximum penalty for 'obscene, indecent, or profane language' on TV or radio broadcasts from $32,500 to $325,000 per station, per violation. The Federal Communications Commission defines indecency as '*language or material that, in context, depicts or describes, in terms patently offensive as measured by contemporary community standards for the broadcast medium, sexual or excretory organs or activities*'. In March 2006 CBS was fined $3·3m for an episode of *Without a Trace* depicting group sex, reportedly the highest such fine imposed [see p.126].

———————— ON ADVERTISING ————————

US advertising spending totaled $143 billion in 2005, with internet display and cable TV enjoying the fastest rates of growth. Further advertising figures are below:

TOP 2005 ADVERTISERS
Top advertisers by total US spending

Procter & Gamble Co.........$3,237m
General Motors Corp. 2,986
Time Warner Inc.................2,043
Verizon Comm. Inc..............1,652
Ford Motor Co...................1,636
AT&T Inc.......................1,584
DaimlerChrysler AG.............1,584
Walt Disney Co. 1,365

TOP 2005 CATEGORIES
Top ad categories and spending

Auto, nondomestic...........$8,686m
Auto, domestic..................8,452
Financial services...............8,279
Telecom 8,078
Retail other......................7,991
Miscellaneous services 7,759
Direct response..................6,099
Personal care products 5,624

2005 SPENDING BY MEDIA
Total ad spending by type of media

Newspapers (local)..........$25,090m
Network TV.....................22,455
Consumer magazines 21,688
Cable TV........................15,874
Sport TV 15,529
Internet...........................8,322
Local radio 7,364
Business-to-business magazines . 4,471
Syndication, national 4,222
Spanish-language media 4,219
Outdoor..........................3,528
National newspapers.............3,466

[Source: TNS Media Intelligence]

TOP 2005 GLOBAL BRANDS
BusinessWeek/Interbrand's *ranking of 2005's most valuable global brands*

Brand	estimated 2005 value $m
Coca-Cola	67,525
Microsoft	59,941
IBM	53,376
GE	46,996
Intel	35,588
Nokia	26,452
Disney	26,441
McDonald's	26,014

BEST LOGOS
The best logos, according to a 2006 *Graphic Design USA* magazine reader survey:

Nike · Apple · Target
Starbucks · FedEx · Coca-Cola
UPS · CBS · BP · I♡NY

TARGET was voted 'most influential corporate design of the era', followed by Apple, Herman Miller, Adobe, Nike, IBM, Disney, and Fossil.

CELEBRITY SELLING POWER

In 2006, media research company NPD surveyed 11,000 people (≥13) about the influence of celebrity endorsements in 86 advertisements. It was found that a celebrity appearance did not always translate into an intent to purchase the advertised product. Of the celebrities tested, Ty Pennington of *Trading Spaces* had the highest positive 'purchase impact'. James Earl Jones, Emeril Lagasse, and Olympic swimming medalist Summer Sanders also scored highly. Donald Trump, Britney Spears, and Paris Hilton had a negative influence on intent to purchase – only 4% said that they trusted Paris Hilton.

Music & Movies

Keep it simple, keep it sexy, keep it sad.
— MITCH MILLER *on pop music,* 1950

———————————— PIMP CHIC ————————————

The 2006 Best Song Oscar went to *It's Hard out Here for a Pimp* from *Hustle & Flow*. Although for the live performance many of the song's more offensive lyrics were censored, this Academy Award recognized the popularity of 'pimp chic' and secured (for a time) its place in the cultural mainstream. ❦ From as early as the C17th, a pimp was a panderer (a man who controlled or procured prostitutes and lived off their earnings) and the word is found in Pepys, Dryden, and Pope. Because pimping is both illegal and immoral, 'pimp' has long been considered an insult – so much so that, even in the 1960s, some US papers refused to print the word. Yet, in the 1970s, a modern, cool, and essentially African American pimp aesthetic was born, derived from blaxploitation films like *Shaft, Superfly, Hit Man, The Mack,* and *Black Caesar,* their soundtracks, and the ostentatious street fashions they depicted. ❦ In recent years, the notion of the pimp has evolved – 'to pimp' now also means any elaborate modification for show or effect where excess trumps taste. In the MTV series *Pimp My Ride* (first shown in 2004), unfashionable cars are 'tricked out' with 'flames, wings, superchargers, chrome tailpipes, and more'. And, just as the phrase '__ *is the new black*' has entered the vernacular, so '*pimp my* __' has become a ubiquitous media cliché.

A brief search of recent news reveals a plethora of imprecations to pimp: 'my husband', 'my librarian', 'my WMD', 'my Vespa', 'my life', and so on. In certain bars, 'pimp my drink' means either to use only the most expensive brands of liquor, or to add a dash of champagne. By extension, a number of hip-hop artists have popularized 'pimp cups' – capacious, gaudy, bejeweled goblets with 'pimp', 'playa', or the drinker's name spelled out in (semi-) precious stones. ❦ Yet, some have noted that, even in its dilute pop form, pimp culture is rooted in misogyny, the (violent) exploitation of women, and the stereotyping of black men as criminal. Director Spike Lee lamented that 'no one gets upset anymore that pimpdom gets elevated on a pedestal'; and *Body Shop* founder Dame Anita Roddick criticized 'pimp and ho chic' for masking the 'dark' and 'evil' reality of the sex trade. ❦ Inevitably, high street fashion and mainstream advertising have seized on pimp culture. Burger King ran a 'pimp my burger' promotion, and Virgin Atlantic promoted their refurbished *Upper Class* clubhouse with the slogan 'pimp my lounge'. It seems likely that such campaigns will prove to be the high-water mark of 'pimp chic' – the corporate embrace finally suffocating a controversial and inherently ambiguous street culture.

———————————— MUSIC DOWNLOADING ————————————

According to a January 2006 Ipsos poll, 25% of all US music fans have downloaded music to their computer – legally or otherwise. And, as CD sales slipped in 2005, so downloading rates rose dramatically [see below]. Although concerns over the ease and proliferation of illegal downloading persist, many feel that downloading music allows fans the chance to explore new genres and niche bands: in April 2006 the track *Crazy* by Gnarls Barkley[†] made musical history by soaring to the top of the UK charts based solely on downloading, even before the record was released. Below is a snapshot of American CD sales, downloading behavior, and the like:

Sales of CDs · 2004–05 percentage change . . . .–7%
Single track downloads · 2004–05 percentage change . . . .+147%
Total CDs sold in 2005 . . . . 618·9m
Total number of single track downloads, 2005 . . . . 353m
Total number of album downloads, 2005 . . . . .16m
 – as a share of 2005 total album market . . . . .2·6%
Number of music downloading sites worldwide (estimated) 230
 – iTunes share of legal US downloads 80%
Number of iPods sold in 2005 (net) 4,540m
 – percentage change from 2004 . . . . 248%
Americans ≥12 who own a portable MP3 player 20%
US music fans who think downloading without permission is stealing 80%
US music fans who say 99 cents is a fair price or better for a song 71%
Downloaders ≥12 who have paid a fee to download music or MP3s 52%

† Charles Wade Barkley (*b.*1963) is an American basketball player who won Olympic gold playing in the 1992 US 'dream team'. However, the band 'Gnarls Barkley' (producer Danger Mouse and rapper/singer Cee-Lo) dismisses this obvious connection, claiming, 'it's a name and that's it'. ❧ In February 2006, iTunes announced that Alex Ostrovsky from West Bloomfield, MI, had downloaded the store's billionth song. Sadly, it was Coldplay's *Speed of Sound*. Rewarding this numerical coincidence, Apple gave Ostrovsky 10 iPods and an iMac, and it established a Juilliard School of Music scholarship in his name. [Sources: Int. Federation of the Phonographic Industry; BBC; Ipsos Insight; Apple; &c.]

———————————— iPODS OF THE FIRST COUPLES ————————————

Presidential media adviser Mark McKinnon revealed in 2005 that George W. Bush enjoys listening to his iPod (dubbed 'iPod One') while mountain biking around his Texas ranch. His favorite songs were *(You're So Square) Baby, I Don't Care* by Joni Mitchell; *Brown Eyed Girl* by Van Morrison; *Say It Ain't So* by The Thrills; *Centerfield* by John Fogerty; *Circle Back* by John Hiatt; and *My Sharona* by The Knack. McKinnon stressed that 'no one should psychoanalyze the song selection – it's music to get over the next hill'. Laura Bush confessed that she preferred Tina Turner and Dolly Parton on her iPod, and said she particularly enjoyed listening to Parton's epic rendition of *Stairway to Heaven*. ❧ In May 2006, Hillary Clinton said her iPod featured a 'smorgasbord' of '60s and '70s tunes, including Aretha Franklin's *Respect*, the Beatles' *Hey Jude*, and *Take It to the Limit* by the Eagles.

CELEBRITY PLAYLISTS

Apple's iTunes music store has canvassed personalized celebrity playlists from a wide range of musicians and Hollywood stars. Selections encompass everything from the dreary to the opportunistic (Beyoncé's list includes 8 tracks performed by relatives, former bandmates, or the singer herself). The compilations are accompanied by comments explaining (or justifying) each choice of track. Below are some examples:

ALICE COOPER
Nirvana · *Smells Like Teen Spirit*
'One of those songs I kick myself
for not writing'

ANDERSON COOPER
R.E.M · *What's the Frequency, Kenneth?*
'Might be tempting fate to pick a
song inspired by the mugging
of a news anchor'

GARRISON KEILLOR
Chopin · *Etude No. 3 in E Major,
Op. 10, 'Tristesse'* · V. Ashkenazy
'It transports [me] to Minneapolis in
the summer of 1960, but that's just me'

MANDY MOORE
Colin Hay · *Waiting for My
Real Life to Begin*
'I think everyone feels this way
sometimes … ya' know?'

ASHLEE SIMPSON
Björk · *All Is Full of Love*
'This has such a cool vibe to it. It's a
song that connects everyone'

STEPHEN KING
Donna the Buffalo · *Love and Gasoline*
'The kind of song you're supposed to
hear at the bottom of the FM dial
late at night on the interstate'

'BLINGTONES'

The Recording Industry Association of America updated its awards program in 2006 to include gold, platinum, and multiplatinum designations for ringtones. The Master Ringtone Sales Award is given only to ringtones based on original recordings, rather than synthesized versions. Ringtones must sell the same number of units as traditional formats [see below] to earn the awards, which come in the form of a plaque decorated with a golden cellphone. On June 14, 2006, 84 ringtones were given gold awards, 40 platinum, and 4 multiplatinum. The 4 multiplatinum tones:

T-Pain ...... *I'm N Luv (Wit a Stripper)*
D4L .... *Laffy Taffy*

Black Eyed Peas .... *My Humps*
Chamillionaire .... *Ridin'*

MUSIC SALES AWARDS

Album, single, or ringtone	Recording Industry Association of America Award	Internet downloads
500,000	Gold	100,000
1,000,000	Platinum	200,000
2,000,000	Multiplatinum	400,000
10,000,000	Diamond [albums & singles only]	—

GLOBAL BEST-SELLING ALBUMS · 2005

Album	artist	publisher	global sales
X&Y	Coldplay	EMI	8·3m
The Emancipation of Mimi	Mariah Carey	Universal	7·7m
The Massacre	50 Cent	Universal	7·5m
Monkey Business	Black Eyed Peas	Universal	6·8m
American Idiot	Green Day	Warner	6·4m
Confessions on a Dance Floor	Madonna	Warner	6·3m
Breakaway	Kelly Clarkson	Sony BMG	6·1m
Curtain Call	Eminem	Universal	5·5m
Back to Bedlam	James Blunt	Warner	5·5m
Intensive Care	Robbie Williams	EMI	5·4m

WORLDWIDE MUSIC SALE REVENUE BY FORMAT

Format	2004 ($m)	2005 ($m)	% change
CD	18,109	17,019	−6%
DVD	1,610	1,540	−4%
Digital sales	397	1,143	+188%
Singles	821	721	−12%
Tapes, LPs, VHS, &c.	531	372	−30%

[Sources for albums & formats: International Federation of the Phonographic Industry; BBC]

POP'S TOP EARNERS

U2 topped *Rolling Stone* magazine's 2006 top moneymakers' poll, having earned over $139 million touring across North America. The top ten bands were as follows:

U2............$154·2m	Elton John........48·9m	Dave Matthews Band...
Rolling Stones....92·5m	Neil Diamond....44·7m	39·6m
Eagles.............63·2m	Jimmy Buffett......44m	Celine Dion......38·5m
Paul McCartney....56m	Rod Stewart......40·3m	[All figures are estimates]

MUSICIANS HALL OF FAME

The Musicians Hall of Fame and Museum opened in Nashville on June 9, 2006, to honor backing musicians and session artists who have made key contributions to musical history. The 30,000ft^2 complex features instruments, photos, recordings, and other artifacts, with displays honoring famous second-fiddles, like Floyd 'Lightnin' Chance (responsible for the bass line in Hank Williams' *Your Cheatin' Heart*) and Chad Smith (the drummer behind the Red Hot Chili Peppers' *Give It Away*). Besides the renowned Rock & Roll Hall of Fame, music halls of fame also exist for gospel, classical, dance, country, and Hawaiian music, and for songwriters.

ROCK & ROLL HALL OF FAME

The following were inducted into the American *Rock & Roll Hall of Fame* in 2006:

Black Sabbath (Geezer Butler, Tony Iommi, Ozzy Osbourne, Bill Ward)
Miles Davis · *Blondie* (Clem Burke, Jimmy Destri, Nigel Harrison,
Debbie Harry, Frank Infante, Chris Stein, Gary Valentine)
Sex Pistols (Paul Cook, Steve Jones, Glen Matlock, Johnny Rotten, Sid Vicious)
Lynyrd Skynyrd (Bob Burns, Allen Collins, Steve Gaines, Ed King, Billy Powell,
Artimus Pyle, Gary Rossington, Ronnie Van Zant, Leon Wilkeson)

Artists are eligible for induction 25 years after their first record release. In February 2006, the Sex Pistols released a statement saying: 'That hall of fame is a piss stain. Your museum. Urine in wine. Were [sic] not coming. Were [sic] not your monkey and so what? Fame at $25,000 if we paid for a table, or $15,000 [sic] to squeak up in the gallery, goes to a non-profit organization selling us a load of old famous'.

NOMS DE RAP

The stage names of some illustrious rappers: [For other *noms de* ..., see p.161].

50 Cent	*Curtis James Jackson III*	Ice-T	*Tracy Morrow*
Andre 3000	*Andre Benjamin*	Ja Rule	*Jeffrey Atkins*
Busta Rhymes	*Trevor Smith*	Jay-Z	*Shawn Carter*
Cee-Lo	*Thomas Calloway*	KRS-One	*Kris Parker*
Common	*Lonnie Rashid Lynn*	Lil' Kim	*Kimberly Jones*
DMX	*Earl Simmons*	LL Cool J	*James Todd Smith*
Eminem	*Marshall Mathers III*	Ludacris	*Christopher Bridges*
Foxy Brown	*Inga Marchand*	Mos Def	*Dante Smith*
The Game	*Jayceon Taylor*	Notorious BIG	*Christopher Wallace*
Ghostface Killah	*Dennis Coles*	Snoop Dogg	*Calvin Broadus*
Grandmaster Flash	*Joseph Saddler*	T.I.	*Clifford Harris Jr*
Ice Cube	*O'Shea Jackson*	[Some spellings are debated]	

The musician and mogul born Sean Combs began recording as Puff Daddy in the 1990s. He changed his name to 'P. Diddy' in 2001, and took the 'P' from himself in 2005 to become simply 'Diddy'.

HIP-HOP AT THE SMITHSONIAN

In February 2006, the Smithsonian National Museum of American History in Washington, DC, announced a project to archive objects from hip-hop culture. Early donations included: custom-made jackets from the rap collective Zulu Nation; a Zulu warrior beaded necklace and red fez (with the 'proud Nuwaubian' logo) donated by Afrika Bambaataa; Fab 5 Freddy's vintage boombox; MC Lyte's handwritten journal; Ice-T's tour T-shirts; and Grandmaster Flash's turntable. The museum planned to create both a permanent exhibition and a traveling display.

————————GRAMMY AWARDS · 2006————————

While media speculation leading up to the 48th Grammys was preoccupied with Mariah 'comeback kid' Carey and rapper Kanye West, Irish rockers U2 stole the LA spotlight by taking 5 awards, bringing their all-time tally to 21. Kelly Clarkson's 2 awards were (significantly ?) the first Grammys for an American Idol. Dr John led a musical tribute to New Orleans, and a host of stars (from Paul McCartney to Jay-Z) performed, including a rare and brief outing from über-funkster Sly Stone.

> *He was the atomic bomb in question and when he died, set off kind of a chain*
> *reaction in me, and I've been shoutin' about him ... for the last few years.*
> *And maybe, maybe, tonight is the time to stop.* — BONO, on his father

Record of the year	Green Day · *Boulevard of Broken Dreams*
Album of the year	U2 · *How to Dismantle an Atomic Bomb*
Song of the year	U2 · *Sometimes You Can't Make It on Your Own*
New artist	John Legend
Female pop vocal performance	Kelly Clarkson · *Since U Been Gone*
Male pop vocal performance	Stevie Wonder · *From the Bottom of My Heart*
Pop vocal album	Kelly Clarkson · *Breakaway*
Dance recording	The Chemical Brothers featuring Q-Tip · *Galvanize*
Electronic/dance album	The Chemical Brothers · *Push the Button*
Solo rock vocal performance	Bruce Springsteen · *Devils & Dust*
Rock song	U2 · *City of Blinding Lights*
Rock album	U2 · *How to Dismantle an Atomic Bomb*
Alternative music album	The White Stripes · *Get Behind Me Satan*
Female R&B vocal performance	Mariah Carey · *We Belong Together*
Male R&B vocal performance	John Legend · *Ordinary People*
R&B song	J. Austin *et al.* · *We Belong Together*
R&B album	John Legend · *Get Lifted*
Contemporary R&B album	Mariah Carey · *The Emancipation of Mimi*
Rap song	D. Harris and Kanye West · *Diamonds from Sierra Leone*
Rap album	Kanye West · *Late Registration*
Country song	Bobby Boyd *et al.* · *Bless the Broken Road*
Country album	Alison Krauss and Union Station · *Lonely Runs Both Ways*
Bluegrass album	The Del McCoury Band · *The Company We Keep*
Contemporary jazz album	Pat Metheny Group · *The Way Up*
Gospel performance	CeCe Winan · *Pray*
Reggae album	Damian Marley· *Welcome to Jamrock*
Polka album	Jimmy Sturr and His Orchestra · *Shake, Rattle, and Polka!*
Spoken word album	Sen. Barack Obama · *Dreams from My Father*
Compilation soundtrack album (motion picture, TV, &c.)	*Ray* score
Soundtrack album (motion picture, TV, &c.)	*Ray*
Album notes	John Szwed, album notes writer
	The Complete Library of Congress Recordings by Alan Lomax
Classical album	Leonard Slatkin, Jerry Blackstone *et al.*
	Bolcom: Songs of Innocence and of Experience
Opera recording	Verdi: *Falstaff ·* Sir Colin Davis

OTHER NOTABLE MUSIC AWARDS

Awards	prize	winner
	Pop album	Mariah Carey · *The Emancipation of Mimi*
	Country album	Tim McGraw · *Live Like You Were Dying*
	Soul/R&B album	Destiny's Child · *Destiny Fulfilled*
American Music ['05]	*Rap/hip-hop album*	50 Cent · *The Massacre*
	Artist, adult contemporary	Kelly Clarkson
	Artist, Latin	Shakira
	Artist, alternative	Green Day
	Century award	Tom Petty
	Artist achievement	Kanye West
	Artist of the year	50 Cent
	Artist, R&B/hip-hop, female	Mariah Carey
	Artist, R&B/hip-hop, male	50 Cent
Billboard Music ['05]	*Artist, country*	Toby Keith
	Artist, rock	Green Day
	Artist, R&B/hip-hop	Destiny's Child
	Artist, comedy	Larry the Cable Guy
	Artist, rhythmic top 40	50 Cent
	Artist, dance club-play	Destiny's Child
	Entertainer of the year	Keith Urban
	Vocalist of the year, female	Gretchen Wilson
	Vocalist of the year, male	Keith Urban
	Horizon award	Dierks Bentley
Country Music ['05]	*Single*	Lee Ann Womack
		I May Hate Myself in the Morning
	Musician	Jerry Douglas
	Album	Lee Ann Womack
		There's More Where That Came From
	Artist, mainstream hit radio	Kelly Clarkson
	Artist, urban and rhythmic radio	Mariah Carey
	Artist, alternative and active rock radio	Green Day
Radio Music ['05]	*Artist, country radio*	Keith Urban
	Artist, rock radio	Green Day
	Artist, adult hit radio	Goo Goo Dolls
	Single, female	Mariah Carey · *We Belong Together*
	Single, male	John Legend · *Ordinary People*
Soul Train ['06]	*Album, female*	Mariah Carey · *The Emancipation of Mimi*
	Album, male	John Legend · *Get Lifted*
	Song	Alicia Keyes · *Unbreakable*
NAACP Image ['06]	*Album*	Mariah Carey · *The Emancipation of Mimi*
	Artist, male	Jamie Foxx
	Artist, female	Alicia Keys
	Video of the year	Green Day · *Boulevard of Broken Dreams*
MTV VMAs ['05]	*Video, male*	Kanye West · *Jesus Walks*
	Video, female	Kelly Clarkson · *Since U Been Gone*
	Viewer's choice award	Green Day · *Blvd of Broken Dreams*

———————————— WORLD'S SLOWEST RECITAL ————————————

In January 2006, a rare chord was sounded in the slowest recital in history, scheduled to last 639 years. The recital is the premiere of *Organ²/ASLSP* ('as slow as possible'), adapted from a piano composition by the American composer John Cage† (1912–92) by a group of philosophers and physicists; its length is intended to match the estimated lifespan of the organ itself. Every year, more than 10,000 devotees of experimental music flock to the small Saxony town of Halberstadt, Germany, to witness the phenomenon firsthand. The concert began on September 5, 2001, when the composer would have turned 89, and there followed 1½ years of silence. Cage's piece cannot, for obvious reasons, be performed by a single organist; a combination of sandbags and lead weights is used in the rare event that a new note requires articulation. The work has been divided into 9 sections, each lasting 71 years. The opening notes, and the dates on which they are played:

Date	pitch		
February 5, 2003	G♯, B, G♯	August 5, 2011	C, D♭
July 5, 2004	E, E	October 5, 2013	D♯, A♯, E
January 5, 2006	A, C, F♯	September 5, 2020	G♯, E
July 5, 2008	C, A♭	February 5, 2024	D
February 5, 2009	D, E	August 5, 2026	A
		April 5, 2028	G

† Cage is perhaps best known to the public for his 1952 composition *4'33"*, which consists of 4 minutes and 33 seconds of silence. In 2002, the Cage Trust took Mike Batt, creator of *The Wombles*, to court for plagiarism, following the inclusion of the track *A Minute's Silence* on his album *Classical Graffiti*, recorded with rock band the Planets. The ensuing trial featured a simultaneous 'performance' of the two silences; Cage's publishers even hired a clarinetist for the purpose. Batt, though, was vehement: 'I certainly wasn't quoting his silence. I claim my silence is original silence'.

———————————— MOZART'S BIRTHDAY ————————————

On January 27, 2006, the world celebrated Wolfgang Amadeus Mozart's 250th birthday (1756–91). Born in Salzburg, Austria, the composer was christened Johannes Chrysostomus Wolfgangus Theophilus Mozart, but he preferred to go by the more snappy Wolfgango Amadeo and, later in his life, just plain Wolfgang Amadé†.

Mozart chocolates ('*Mozartkugeln*'‡) produced annually 90m
Google search results for 'Mozart' [April '06]..............................81,700,000
Annual visitors to Mozart's birthplace in Salzburg...........................500,000
Number of days Mozart spent traveling through Europe 3,720
Germans who think Mozart more important than modern pop stars 84%
Number of 'Mozart cities' and towns worldwide.................................70

† In letters to his sister, however, he liked to write his name backward, thus signing with the silly 'Gnagflow Trazom'. ‡ The tasty rotund chocolates named after the composer are said to be an 1890 invention of Paul Fürst, an expert pastry cook from Salzburg. The core is pistachio-flavored almond paste, wrapped in a layer of nougat, and enveloped in a sumptuous jacket of fine dark chocolate.

ELAINE LEBENBOM AWARD

In 2006, the Detroit Symphony Orchestra announced the formation of the Elaine Lebenbom Memorial Award, named after the late Detroit-born composer, teacher, artist, and poet. The contest was praised in classical music for being the first major prize specifically for female composers. The winner will receive $10,000, and premiere an original piece of work at the DSO's Classical Subscription Series. The prize (to be judged by a panel of composers, musicians, DSO staff, and the DSO conductor) is open to an international field, and will be first awarded in fall 2006.

SOME CLASSICAL ANNIVERSARIES · 2007

2007 marks two major classical music anniversaries – the 150th anniversary of the birth of self-taught British composer EDWARD ELGAR (6·2·1857); and the 75th anniversary of the death of the composer and conductor JOHN PHILIP SOUSA[†] (3·6·1932). Other classical musical births and deaths of note during 2007 include:

b. 1567	Claudio Monteverdi	*d.* 1897	Johannes Brahms
d. 1757	Domenico Scarlatti	*b.* 1897	Alexandre Tansman
d. 1827	Ludwig Van Beethoven	*d.* 1937	George Gershwin
b. 1877	Ernst von Dohnányi	*d.* 1957	Jean Sibelius
b. 1887	Ernst Toch	*d.* 1987	Dmitry Kabalevsky

† The esteemed musical instrument maker J.W. Pepper named his somewhat elaborate bass tuba the Sousaphone in gratitude for John Philip Sousa's helpful suggestions during its design and construction in *c.*1893. In the same year, Sousa composed his jaunty *Liberty Bell March*, which went on to be used as the theme tune to *Monty Python's Flying Circus*, first aired in Britain during 1969.

HERBERT VON KARAJAN PRIZE

Valery Gergiev won the 2006 Herbert von Karajan Prize, an annual €50,000 award for contemporary musicians given by the Festspielhaus Baden-Baden in Germany. Gergiev is credited with helping the historic Mariinsky Theater in St Petersburg, Russia, survive the collapse of the Soviet Union; in 1996 he was named its Artistic & General Director. He is also principal guest conductor of the Metropolitan Opera and music director of the Rotterdam Philharmonic. In 2007 he will be the principal guest conductor of the London Symphony Orchestra. Gergiev is known for his 'emotional interpretations' of Italian, German, and Russian works.

GILMORE ARTIST AWARD · 2006

The $300,000 Gilmore Artist Award is given by the Irving S. Gilmore Foundation every four years to a 'superb pianist and profound musician' of any age or nationality. The 2006 winner was Ingrid Fliter, an Argentine pianist living in Milan who had not (then) recorded commercially. Fliter was the first female to win the award.

———— TRADITIONAL ORCHESTRA SCHEMATIC ————

PERCUSSION · TIMPANI

FRENCH HORNS · TRUMPETS · TROMBONES · TUBAS

CLARINETS · BASSOONS · CONTRA-BASSOONS

PICCOLOS · FLUTES · OBOES · CORS ANGLAIS

FIRST VIOLINS · SECOND VIOLINS · VIOLAS · CELLOS · DOUBLE BASSES

PIANO · HARP

CONDUCTOR

———————— THEMATIC CATALOGS ————————

The work of some composers, especially those prolific in the C18–19th, has been organized and cataloged – often by a dedicated scholar – to aid the identification of each piece. To take a famous example, the work of Mozart was chronologically ordered by the Austrian naturalist Ludwig von Köchel (1800–77), who gave each piece a number prefixed with his initial 'K'. So, Mozart's *Eine Kleine Nachtmusik* (1787) is commonly referred to as K525. Some other thematic catalogs include:

Code	composer	cataloger
BWV	Johann Sebastian Bach	Wolfgang Schmieder
BuxWV	Dietrich Buxtehude	Georg Karstadt
HWV	George Frederick Handel	Bernd Bäselt
H(ob)	Franz Joseph Haydn	Anthony Van Hoboken
S	Franz Liszt	Humphrey Searle
TFV	Richard Strauss	Franz Trenner
RV	Antonio Vivaldi	Peter Ryom
WWV	Richard Wagner	Deathridge, Geck, & Voss

———————— VAN CLIBURN COMPETITION · 2005 ————————

Alexander Kobrin won the gold medal at the 2005 Van Cliburn International Piano Competition. Kobrin played Mozart's *Piano Concerto No. 20 in D Minor, K466* and Rachmaninoff's *Rhapsody on a Theme of Paganini, Op. 43* in the final round to win $20,000, major concert tours, and other prizes. The competition was founded by American pianist Van Cliburn in 1962, 4 years after he became the first American to win the International Tchaikovsky Piano Competition in Moscow.

GRAMOPHONE AWARDS · 2005

The Gramophone Awards, presented annually by *Gramophone* magazine, are chosen by a panel of critics, members of the industry, broadcasters, and 'celebrity' jurors.

Record of the year.................................*cond.* Sir John Eliot Gardiner; Monteverdi Choir & Orchestra, Bach *Cantatas Vol. 1*
Artist of the year ....Michael Tilson Thomas
Label of the year ....Naxos
Best of category (chamber) ....Takács Quartet · Beethoven *Late String Quartets*
Best of category (choral) ...*cond.* René Jacobs; Marlis Petersen, Werner Güra, *et al.* RIAS-Kammerchor & Freiburger Barockorchester · Haydn *The Seasons*
Best of category (DVD) ....*dir.* Peter Maniura; *cond.* Sir John Eliot Gardiner; Susan Graham *et al.*, Monteverdi Choir *et al.* · Berlioz *Les Troyens*
Best of category (orchestral) ....*cond.* Nikolaus Harnoncourt; Concentus Musicus Wien · Haydn *Paris Symphonies*
Best of category (recital) .... Rolando Villazón · Gounod & Massenet *Arias*

OPERA'S 'GRAND SLAM'

For an opera singer to score a 'Grand Slam' they must perform at these four venues:

LA SCALA · Milan
opened 1778 · capacity: 2,400
Musical director: Stéphane Lissner
Notable premieres:
Verdi – *Otello* (1887)
Puccini – *Madama Butterfly* (1904)

STATE OPERA HOUSE · Vienna
opened 1869 · capacity: 2,282
Musical director: Seiji Ozawa
Notable premieres: R Strauss –
Die Frau ohne Schatten (1919)
Meyerbeer – *Le Prophète* (1998)

ROYAL OPERA HOUSE · London
opened 1732 · capacity: 2,267
Music director: Antonio Pappano
Notable premieres:
Birtwistle – *Gawain* (1991)
Maw – *Sophie's Choice* (2002)

METROPOLITAN OPERA · New York
opened 1883 · capacity: 2,065
Musical director: James Levine
Notable premieres: R Strauss –
Salome (1907) · Puccini – *The Girl of the Golden West* (1910)

MOST-PERFORMED OPERAS

The operas most frequently staged by members of OPERA America and Opera.ca during the 2004–2005 season, with the number of productions during the season:

Puccini · *Madama Butterfly*..........21
Mozart · *Don Giovanni*.............14
Puccini · *La Bohème*.................13
Bizet · *Carmen* 13
Mozart · *The Marriage of Figaro*.....12

Puccini · *Tosca*.........................12
Verdi · *Rigoletto* 10
Verdi · *Aida*........................... 9
Gilbert & Sullivan · *The Mikado* 9
Verdi · *La Traviata* 9

———————————— JUILLIARD'S TREASURES ————————————

In one of the largest ever gifts of its kind, hedge fund billionaire and amateur pianist Bruce Kovner donated 139 classical music manuscripts to Juilliard in March 2006. Highlights of the collection include the printer's manuscript of Beethoven's *Symphony No. 9*, Mozart's autograph of one section of *The Marriage of Figaro*, Schumann's working draft of his *Symphony No. 2*, a manuscript of Brahm's *Symphony No. 2*, and other astonishing first editions, scores, and sketches. The destination surprised some, since Juilliard is primarily known as a performing arts conservatory rather than a repository of musical heritage. However, the school is not taking its new responsibility lightly – a special room is being built and a curator hired to oversee the collection, which will be made available to scholars by September 2009.

———————————— CLASSICAL MUSIC'S 'BIG FIVE' ————————————

Although the designation is now controversial, the following venerable symphony orchestras are traditionally called the Big 5, and considered the most prestigious:

BOSTON SYMPHONY ORCHESTRA
founded 1881
Symphony Hall
301 Massachusetts Avenue
Boston, MA 02115
Music Director: James Levine

NEW YORK PHILHARMONIC
founded 1842
Avery Fisher Hall
10 Lincoln Center Plaza
New York, NY 10023
Music Director: Lorin Maazel

CHICAGO SYMPHONY ORCHESTRA
founded 1891
Symphony Center
220 South Michigan Avenue
Chicago, IL 60604
Principal Conductor: Bernard Haitink

PHILADELPHIA ORCHESTRA
founded 1900
Kimmel Center for the Performing Arts
Broad and Spruce Streets
Philadelphia, PA 19102
Music Director: Christoph Eschenbach

CLEVELAND ORCHESTRA
founded 1918
Severance Hall
11001 Euclid Avenue
Cleveland, OH 44106
Music Director: Franz Welser-Möst

Although the precise origin of the term is unclear, the 'Big Five' designation seems to have been in common usage by the 1960s. ❧ During WWII, the Big 5 were: Franklin D. Roosevelt, Winston Churchill, Joseph Stalin, Chiang Kai-shek, and Charles de Gaulle.

———————————— UNESCO INTERNATIONAL MUSIC PRIZE ————————————

UNESCO's International Music Prize is given to musicians and institutions who have 'served peace, understanding between peoples, (and) international cooperation', in addition to enriching the world of music. The 2005 winner was Greek composer and activist Mikis Theodorakis (formerly both a member of the Greek parliament and a Greek prisoner), who composed the theme for the 1964 film *Zorba the Greek*.

US TOP-GROSSING MOVIES · 2005

Film	US box office gross ($m)	director
Star Wars: Ep. III – Revenge of the Sith[†]	380·3	George Lucas
Harry Potter and the Goblet of Fire[†]	289·2	Mike Newell
The Chronicles of Narnia	288·8	Andrew Adamson
War of the Worlds	234·3	Steven Spielberg
King Kong	216·9	Peter Jackson
Wedding Crashers	209·2	David Dobkin
Charlie and the Chocolate Factory	206·5	Tim Burton
Batman Begins[†]	205·3	Christopher Nolan
Madagascar	193·2	Eric Darnell & Tom McGrath
Mr and Mrs Smith	186·3	Doug Liman
Hitch	177·8	Andy Tennant
The Longest Yard	158·1	Peter Segal
Fantastic Four	154·7	Tim Story
Chicken Little	134·8	Mark Dindal
Robots	128·2	Chris Wedge & Carlos Saldanha
Walk the Line	118·2	James Mangold
The Pacifier	113·1	Adam Shankman
Fun with Dick and Jane	110·3	Dean Parisot
The 40-Year-Old Virgin	109·4	Judd Apatow
Flightplan	89·7	Robert Schwentke

[Source: MPAA · † indicates a prequel or sequel]

US MOVIE ATTENDANCE & PRICE

Annual US ticket cost and admissions, according to the Motion Picture Association of America (MPAA) and the National Association of Theater Owners (NATO):

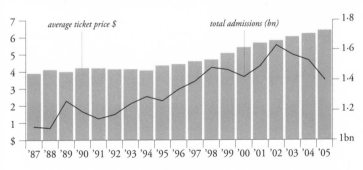

In 2006, Nielsen asked people to list reasons why they did not go to the movies:

High ticket prices	47·4%	Expensive concessions	36·5%
Bad movies	44·4%	Too many ads	26·7%
Lifestyle changes/less time	39·6%	Prefer movies on DVD	22·6%

——————THE 63rd GOLDEN GLOBES · 2006——————

The 2006 Golden Globes were awarded primarily to politically charged, low(er) budget films. A gay love story set in the mountains of Wyoming won Best Picture, and Best Actress went to a portrayal of a transgendered man. Yet the mood of the awards was light, and most winners resisted calling their films 'message movies'.

I want to give my ... thanks to my fellow filmmakers for strengthening my faith in movies, and in the power of movies to change the way we're thinking. — ANG LEE

Award	winner
Dramatic picture	*Brokeback Mountain*
Dramatic actress	Felicity Huffman · *Transamerica*
Dramatic actor	Philip Seymour Hoffman · *Capote*
Picture, musical or comedy	*Walk the Line*
Actress, musical or comedy	Reese Witherspoon · *Walk the Line*
Actor, musical or comedy	Joaquin Phoenix · *Walk the Line*
Supporting actress	Rachel Weisz · *The Constant Gardener*
Supporting actor	George Clooney · *Syriana*
Director	Ang Lee · *Brokeback Mountain*
Screenplay	Larry McMurtry and Diana Ossana · *Brokeback Mountain*
Original score	John Williams · *Memoirs of a Geisha*
Original song	*A Love That Will Never Grow Old* · *Brokeback Mountain*
Foreign language film	*Paradise Now* · Palestine
Dramatic TV series	*Lost*
Actress, dramatic TV series	Geena Davis · *Commander in Chief*
Actor, dramatic TV series	Hugh Laurie · *House*
TV series, musical or comedy	*Desperate Housewives*
TV actress, musical or comedy	Mary-Louise Parker · *Weeds*
TV actor, musical or comedy	Steve Carell · *The Office*
TV miniseries or movie	*Empire Falls*
TV actress, miniseries or movie	S. Epatha Merkerson · *Lackawanna Blues*
TV actor, miniseries or movie	Jonathan Rhys Meyers · *Elvis*
TV supporting actress, miniseries or movie	Sandra Oh · *Grey's Anatomy*
TV supporting actor, miniseries or movie	Paul Newman · *Empire Falls*
Cecil B. DeMille award	Anthony Hopkins

NOTABLE QUOTES ❦ GEORGE CLOONEY, on *Syriana* · *This was not an attack on the Bush administration, it was an attack on 60 years of failed Mideast policy.* ❦ LARRY McMURTRY · *I thank my typewriter. [It's] a Hermes 3000 – surely one of the noblest instruments of European genius.* ❦ FELICITY HUFFMAN · *I think as people our job is to become who we really are, and so I would like to salute the men and women who brave ostracism, alienation, and a life lived on the margins to become who they really are.*

Globes & Oscars · The Golden Globes are often considered a good predictor of Oscar results. In the last 13 years, 10 films have won Best Picture awards at both ceremonies: *Schindler's List* (1994), *Forrest Gump* (1995), *The English Patient* (1997), *Titanic* (1998), *Shakespeare in Love* (1999), *American Beauty* (2000), *Gladiator* (2001), *A Beautiful Mind* (2002), *Chicago* (2003), *Lord of the Rings* (2004).

──────── SOME 2006 MOVIE TAGLINES OF NOTE ────────

Captain Jack is back . . . . *Pirates of the Caribbean: Dead Man's Chest*
A story like mine has never been told . . . . *Memoirs of a Geisha*
The eighth wonder of the world . . . . *King Kong*
Love is a burning thing . . . . *Walk the Line*
With no power comes no responsibility . . . . *Clerks II*
Love is a force of nature . . . . *Brokeback Mountain*
Look up in the sky . . . . *Superman Returns*
Welcome to the suck . . . . *Jarhead*
Nick Naylor doesn't hide the truth … he filters it . . . . *Thank You for Smoking*
At the end of the day, what will you hang on to? . . . . *Get Rich or Die Tryin'*
Passion, temptation, obsession . . . . *Match Point*
… pick a side . . . . *The Break-Up*
Unlock the code . . . . *The Da Vinci Code*
Oh yes, there will be blood . . . . *Saw II*
Afraid of the dark? You will be . . . . *The Descent*
The lucky ones die first . . . . *The Hills Have Eyes*
Radio like you've never seen it before . . . . *A Prairie Home Companion*

──────────── COMAS IN MOVIES ────────────

Research by Dr Eelco Wijdicks on the depiction of comas in movies was published
in *Neurology* in May 2006. Dr Wijdicks studied 30 films (made between 1970–
2004) that portrayed actors in prolonged comas, and he concluded that only two
films accurately depicted the state of a coma victim and the agony of waiting for a
patient to awaken: *Reversal of Fortune* (1990) and *The Dreamlife of Angels* (1998).
The remaining 28 were criticized for portraying miraculous awakenings with no
lasting side effects; unrealistic depictions of treatments and equipment required; and
comatose patients remaining tanned, muscular, and suspiciously well turned out.

──────────── FILM CREDIT GLOSSARY ────────────

Gaffer . . . . *senior electrician who sets up lighting*
Best Boy . . . . *head electrician responsible for set power; reports to Gaffer*
Electrician . . . . *member of the electrical crew; reports to the Best Boy*
Grip . . . . *stagehand responsible for moving and setting up equipment*
Key Grip . . . . *the head of the Grips*
Best Boy Grip . . . . *assistant to the Key Grip*
Dolly[†] Grip . . . . *prepares and operates the camera dolly*
Craft Services[‡] . . . . *provides refreshment for cast and crew*
Foley Artist . . . . *sound-effects artist who matches sounds to visuals*
Wrangler . . . . *handles any animals used in the film*

† The 'dolly' is a moving platform on which the camera is mounted for tracking shots. ‡ Some craft
services vie for the most inventive name – one of the best goes by the name of 'Cecil B. deMeals'.

——————————78th ACADEMY AWARDS——————————

Hosted by Jon Stewart, the 78th Academy Awards celebrated the glamour of old-school Hollywood in an effort to entice the public back into theaters. With no one film dominating, the surprise of the night came when *Crash* snatched the Best Picture Oscar from the favorite *Brokeback Mountain*. And the winners were:

Leading actor.................................... Philip Seymour Hoffman · *Capote*
Leading actress................................. Reese Witherspoon · *Walk the Line*
Supporting actor...George Clooney · *Syriana*
Supporting actress ....Rachel Weisz · *The Constant Gardener*
Best picture ....*Crash*
Director .... Ang Lee · *Brokeback Mountain*
Animated feature......Nick Park · *Wallace & Gromit: The Curse of the Were-Rabbit*
Art direction .... John Myhre & Gretchen Rau · *Memoirs of a Geisha*
Cinematography...................................Dion Beebe · *Memoirs of a Geisha*
Costume design...........................Colleen Atwood · *Memoirs of a Geisha*
Doc. feature............... Luc Jacquet & Yves Darondeau · *March of the Penguins*
Doc. short subject ...... Corinne Marrinan & Eric Simonson · *A Note of Triumph*
Film editing... Hughes Winborne · *Crash*
Foreign language film.. Gavin Hood · *Tsotsi*
Screenplay (adapted).....Larry McMurtry & Diana Ossana · *Brokeback Mountain*
Screenplay (original)........................ Paul Haggis & Bobby Moresco · *Crash*
Makeup .... Howard Berger & Tami Lane · *Chronicles of Narnia*
Music (score)............................Gustavo Santaolalla · *Brokeback Mountain*
Music (song) .... *It's Hard out Here for a Pimp · Hustle & Flow* [see p.137]
Short film (animated).... John Canemaker & Peggy Stern · *The Moon and the Son*
Short film (live)......................................Martin McDonagh · *Six Shooter*
Sound ....C. Boyes, M. Semanick, M. Hedges & H. Peek · *King Kong*
Sound editing................... Mike Hopkins & Ethan Van der Ryn · *King Kong*
Visual effects ....J. Letteri, B. Van't Hul, C. Rivers & R. Taylor · *King Kong*
Honorary award .... Robert Altman

SOME OSCAR-NIGHT QUOTES

❦ GEORGE CLOONEY · I guess this means I'm not going to win best director. ❦ PAUL HAGGIS · I just want to thank people who take big risks in their daily lives when there aren't cameras rolling. ❦ CHRISTOPHE LIOUD (producer of *March of the Penguins*) · Looking at all the tuxedos tonight, it's like seeing the movie all over again. ❦ JON STEWART · Björk could not be here ... she was trying on her Oscar dress and Dick Cheney shot her. ❦ REESE WITHERSPOON · People used to ask June how she was doing, and she would say, 'I'm just trying to matter'. I know what she means. ❦ RACHEL WEISZ · He [John le Carré] really paid tribute to the people who are willing to risk their own lives to fight injustice. And they're greater men and women than I. ❦ PHILIP SEYMOUR HOFFMAN · My mom's name is Marilyn O'Connor, and she's here tonight. And I'd like if you see her tonight to congratulate her. Because she brought up four kids alone, and she deserves a congratulations for that ... be proud, Mom, because I'm proud of you. ❦

———————————OSCAR-NIGHT FASHION · 2006———————————

Actor	dress	designer
Keira Knightley	*burgundy, single strap, fishtail*	Vera Wang
Uma Thurman	*cap-sleeved, slinky, draped cream silk*	Versace
Jennifer Lopez	*olive-green, toga-style, vintage, cinched waist*	Jean Dessès
Charlize Theron	*green/black silk, huge bow on shoulder*	Christian Dior
Michelle Williams	*saffron chiffon, deep V-neck*	Vera Wang
Dolly Parton	*candyfloss-pink chiffon, crisscross bodice*	Robert Behar
Reese Witherspoon	*long, pale, vintage, tiered net*	Christian Dior
Nicole Kidman	*strapless, white, structured column dress*	Balenciaga
Naomi Watts	*nude and bunched tulle, single strap, net skirt*	Givenchy
Salma Hayek	*long, aqua, draped frock*	Versace
Rachel Weisz	*simple, black, embroidered, empire line*	Narciso Rodriguez

———————————CELEBRITY GIFT BASKETS———————————

Burdening celebrities with gift baskets of 'swag' has become an integral part of Hollywood awards shows. The total value of these baskets in 2006 was estimated to be: Grammys $54,000, Golden Globes $62,000, and Oscars $100,000. However, in April, the IRS reminded stars that 'merchants who participate in giving the gifts do not do so solely out of affection, respect or similar impulses. ... In general, the person has received taxable income equal to the fair market value of the bag and its contents'. Consequently, celebrities can expect to receive a tax demand for the swag they were given at 2006's Oscars, and the Academy has agreed to pay the tax on gift baskets from previous years. ❦ In 2006, the official Oscar haul of swag included: a 4-night stay in Honolulu, worth $25,000; $600 Krups kitchen set; 3-night stay for 2 (with 'personal surf-butler') at St Regis Monarch Beach Resort & Spa in CA; case of Shu Uemura cosmetics, including mink eyelashes; year's supply of Vonage phone service; dinner party at Morton's; &c. [Sources: *USA Today*, *NYT*, CBC]

———————————OSCAR MISCELLANY———————————

First held	May 16, 1929 (tickets cost $10; 250 attended)
First televised	1953 (25th Academy Awards, hosted by Bob Hope)
Most nominations: film	(14) *All About Eve* (1950) won 6; *Titanic* (1997) won 11
Most wins: film	(11) *Ben-Hur* (1959); *Titanic* (1997); *The Lord of the Rings – The Return of the King* (2003)
Most nominations: actor	(12, won 3) Jack Nicholson
Most nominations: actress	(13, won 2) Meryl Streep
Most nominations: director	(12, won 3) William Wyler
Most awards	(4) Katharine Hepburn
Oldest winner: actor	(76y 317d) Henry Fonda · *On Golden Pond* (1981)
Youngest winner: actor	(29y 343d) Adrien Brody · *The Pianist* (2002)
Oldest winner: actress	(80y 293d) Jessica Tandy · *Driving Miss Daisy* (1989)
Youngest winner: actress	(21y 218d) Marlee Matlin · *Children of a Lesser God* (1986)

OTHER MOVIE AWARDS OF NOTE

ANNIE AWARDS 2005· *annieawards.com*

Best animated feature.............. *Wallace & Gromit: The Curse of the Were-Rabbit*
Best animated television production...... *Star Wars: Clone Wars II Chapters 21–25*

DIRECTORS GUILD AWARDS 2006 · *dga.org*

Feature .... Ang Lee · *Brokeback Mountain*
Documentary .... Werner Herzog · *Grizzly Man*
Comedy series............................Marc Buckland · *My Name Is Earl* (pilot)
Reality.. Tony Croll · *Three Wishes* (pilot)
Commercials.........Craig Gillespie · *'Surprise Dinner', 'Mini-Mart'* (Ameriquest)
'People of Pain,' 'Fable of the Fruit Bat' (Altoids)

GOLDEN RASPBERRIES 2006 · *razzies.com*

Worst picture .... *Dirty Love*
Worst actor........................Rob Schneider · *Deuce Bigalow: European Gigolo*
Worst actress..Jenny McCarthy · *Dirty Love*
Most tiresome tabloid targets[†] ....Tom Cruise, Katie Holmes, the Eiffel Tower,
Oprah Winfrey's Couch & 'Tom's Baby'

INDEPENDENT SPIRIT AWARDS 2006 · *filmindependent.org*

Best feature...*Brokeback Mountain*
Best director... Ang Lee · *Brokeback Mountain*
Best male lead.................................. Philip Seymour Hoffman · *Capote*
Best female lead.................................Felicity Huffman · *Transamerica*

MTV MOVIE AWARDS 2006 · *mtv.com*

Best movie.. *Wedding Crashers*
Best performance .... Jake Gyllenhaal · *Brokeback Mountain*
Best villain ...... Hayden Christensen · *Star Wars: Episode III – Revenge of the Sith*
Best fight.............................Angelina Jolie *vs* Brad Pitt · *Mr & Mrs Smith*
Best frightened performance ...... Jennifer Carpenter · *The Exorcism of Emily Rose*
Best kiss .... Jake Gyllenhaal & Heath Ledger · *Brokeback Mountain*

NATIONAL BOARD OF REVIEW 2005 · *nbrmp.org/awards*

Best film... *Good Night, And Good Luck*
Best actor... Philip Seymour Hoffman · *Capote*
Best actress ....Felicity Huffman · *Transamerica*
Career achievement award... Jane Fonda

SCREEN ACTORS GUILD AWARDS 2006 · *sagawards.org*

Cast performance..*Crash*
Best actor... Philip Seymour Hoffman · *Capote*
Best actress .... Reese Witherspoon · *Walk the Line*
Life achievement award...Shirley Temple Black

† New for 2006, this offscreen Razzie category saluted 'the Celebs We're ALL Sick & Tired Of!'

———————————— GRAUMAN'S CHINESE THEATRE ————————————

A curious fusion of oriental and Art Deco architecture, Grauman's Chinese Theatre [sic] is famed for its collection of stars' concrete foot- and handprints, and for hosting Hollywood film premieres. Since its construction in 1927, when it opened Cecil B. DeMille's *King of Kings*, the theater has hosted a wealth of glittering premieres, including: *King Kong* (1933); *The Wizard of Oz* (1939); *Mary Poppins* (1964); and *Star Wars* (1977). Some of the films that premiered at the Chinese Theatre in 2006:

> *Ant Bully · ATL · Big Momma's House 2 · Bloodrayne · Ice Age 2*
> *Final Destination 3 · Firewall · Mission Impossible 3 · Poseidon*

The décor at Grauman's Chinese Theatre features huge stone Heaven Dogs imported from China, gigantic wrought iron masks, temple bells, pagodas, a 30' dragon, and 10' lotus-shaped fountains.

———————————— HOLLYWOOD WALK OF FAME ————————————

In 1960, the Hollywood Chamber of Commerce created its world-famous *Walk of Fame* by placing some 2,500 blank stars along (and around) Hollywood Boulevard. To date, approximately 2,130 of these stars have been occupied. Each year, the Hollywood Walk of Fame Committee considers the nominations for this honor. The stars are divided into five categories (each with its own symbol): singers & songwriters (a record); film stars & directors (a film camera); television stars (a TV set); radio stars (a microphone); and stage performers (theatrical masks). In 2006, the following celebrities were presented with a star – at a cost of $15,000:

FILM · Annette Bening	Robert Osborne	LIVE THEATER &c.
Matthew Broderick	Ray Romano	Shecky Greene
Holly Hunter	Vanna White	Jack Cassidy†
William Hurt	Leonard Goldenson†	Milt & Bill Larsen
Nathan Lane		
Steve Martin	RECORDING	RADIO · Dan Avey
Charlize Theron	Lou Adler	Mark Wallengren
	Alejandro Fernandez	Kim Amidon
TV · Jim Hill · Judge Judy	Mötley Crüe	Wink Martindale
David Milch	Isaac Hayes	† awarded posthumously

———————————— ADULT VIDEO NETWORK AWARDS · 2006 ————————————

The Adult Video Network (AVN) Awards are the highest accolades in pornography. The 2006 Best Feature went to *Pirates*, a high-budget (for porn) romp featuring a group of sailors searching for evil pirates and booty (of every kind). Evan Stone, winner of Best Actor for his performance as the ship's captain, told the *New York Times* that the movie's authenticity was a crucial part of its success: 'Take the sex out of this movie and it's Walt Disney'. Held on January 8 at the Venetian Hotel in Las Vegas, AVN recognized 104 categories – some more 'specialist' than others.

——————————— THE MOVIE RATING SYSTEM ———————————

The movie rating system operates under the jurisdiction of the Motion Picture Association of America (MPAA) and National Association of Theater Owners (NATO). Ratings are given by the Classification and Rating Administration, a board of parents who view each film and assess its suitability for children based on 'theme, language, violence, nudity, sex, and drug use', among other considerations. The rating system is voluntary, but the vast majority of producers submit their films.

G · *General Audiences* · all ages admitted. Contains nothing most parents will consider offensive for even their youngest children to see or hear. Nudity, sex scenes, and scenes of drug use are absent; violence is minimal; snippets of dialogue may go beyond polite conversations but do not go beyond common everyday expressions.

PG · *Parental Guidance* · some material may not be suitable for children. May contain some material parents may not like to expose to their young children – material that will clearly need to be examined or inquired about before children are allowed to attend the film. Explicit sex scenes and scenes of drug use are absent; nudity, if present, is seen only briefly; horror and violence do not exceed moderate levels.

PG-13 · *Parents strongly cautioned* · some material may be inappropriate for children under 13. Parents should be especially careful about letting their younger children attend. Rough or persistent violence is absent; sexually-oriented nudity is generally absent; some scenes of drug use may be seen; some use of one of the harsher sexually derived words may be heard.

R · *Restricted* · those under 17 require accompanying parent or adult guardian (age varies in some jurisdictions). May contain some adult material. Parents are urged to learn more about the film before taking their children to see it. An R may be assigned due to, among other things, a film's use of language, violence, sex or its portrayal of drug use.

NC-17 · *No one 17 or under admitted* · most American parents would feel the film is patently adult and that children age 17 and under should not be admitted to it. The film may contain explicit sex scenes, an accumulation of sexually oriented language, and/or scenes of excessive violence. The NC-17 designation does not, however, signify that the film is obscene or pornographic in terms of sex, language, or violence.

MPAA analysis of top-20 grossing films shows the following breakdown of ratings:

Rating	G	PG	PG-13	R
2005	5%	25%	60%	10%
2004	5%	25%	55%	15%
2003	5%	15%	60%	20%
2002	5%	30%	65%	
2001	10%	20%	55%	15%

─────── MOST CONTROVERSIAL MOVIES ───────

The five most controversial movies, as judged in 2006 by *Entertainment Weekly*:

2004	*The Passion of the Christ*	*(directed by)* Mel Gibson
1971	*A Clockwork Orange*	Stanley Kubrick
2004	*Fahrenheit 9/11*	Michael Moore
1972	*Deep Throat*	Gerard Damiano
1991	*JFK*	Oliver Stone

─────── SUNDANCE · 2006 ───────

The Sundance Film Festival is a key marketplace for American and international independent film – and an excellent opportunity to spot celebrities in furry boots. Though smaller, 'arty' movies once dominated the festival, in recent years Sundance films (such as 2004's *Sideways*) have enjoyed major commercial success. Productions that secured major deals in 2006 included: *Little Miss Sunshine*, a family road-trip comedy, to Fox Searchlight for $10·5m (a Sundance record); and *Science of Sleep*, about one man's dream life, to Warner Independent Pictures for $6m. For the first time in the festival's 22 years, audience and festival jurors concurred on the Grand Prize for both Documentary and Drama. *Quinceañera* [Hispanic girl in LA], won the Grand Jury Prize and the Audience Award in the Dramatic category. *God Grew Tired of Us* [Sudanese 'lost boys' move to America] won in the Documentary category (in both cases the Audience Awards were for American films; other Audience Awards were given for world cinema). These films addressed cultural assimilation and alienation, which emerged as major themes of Sundance and of many acclaimed 2006 films.

Sundance in Quotes

PARIS HILTON [to *People*] · It's like LA in the snow! ✸ ROSIE O'DONNELL [on her film, to the BBC] · I just hope it opens people's hearts. ✸ ROB LOWE [on his swag, to *People*] · I'm making Paris Hilton look like an Amish person! ✸ LUCY LIU [to *People*] · We're all here to encourage each other. ✸ ROBERT DOWNEY JR [on his alcoholic past] · Thank you, I'll be drunk by 10! ✸ ROBERT REDFORD [to the BBC] · Sundance is about storytelling.

The Sundance Institute celebrated its 25th anniversary in 2006. It was founded by Robert 'Sundance Kid' Redford in Sundance, Utah, to promote 'the development of artists of independent vision'.

─────── FILM FESTIVAL PRIZES · 2006 ───────

Berlin · Golden Bear [FEB]	*Grbavica*	· Jasmila Zbanic
Tribeca · Best Narrative Feature [APR]	*Iluminados por el Fuego*	· Tristán Bauer
Cannes · Palme d'Or [MAY]	*The Wind That Shakes the Barley*	· Ken Loach
Moscow · Golden St George [JUN]	*About Sara*	· Karim Othman
Venice · Golden Lion [SEP '05]	*Brokeback Mountain*	· Ang Lee
Toronto · People's Choice Award [SEP '05]	*Tsotsi*	· Gavin Hood
London · Sutherland Trophy [OCT '05]	*For the Living and the Dead*	· K. Paljakka

—————————————— GREATEST SCREENPLAYS ——————————————

Premiere magazine and the Writers Guild of America West and East named the '101 Greatest Screenplays of All Time' in the magazine's May 2006 issue. Their top 10:

Casablanca (1942) ....*(screenplay by)* Julius J. & Philip G. Epstein & Howard Koch
The Godfather (1972) .... Mario Puzo & Francis Ford Coppola
Chinatown (1974) .... Robert Towne
Citizen Kane (1941)..............................Herman Mankiewicz & Orson Welles
All About Eve (1950) .... Joseph L. Mankiewicz
Annie Hall (1977) .... Woody Allen & Marshall Brickman
Sunset Boulevard (1950) ....Charles Brackett, Billy Wilder, & D.M. Marshman Jr
Network (1976)..Paddy Chayefsky
Some Like It Hot (1959)...................................Billy Wilder & I.A.L. Diamond
The Godfather Part II (1974) .... Francis Ford Coppola & Mario Puzo

————————————————— ALAN SMITHEE —————————————————

Alan Smithee was responsible for some of the worst Hollywood films, and yet the man did not exist. The name Alan Smithee was the sole pseudonym sanctioned by the Directors Guild of America (DGA) for use when directors felt the need to distance themselves from a movie. However, the DGA would not grant the use of a Smithee to hide a director's shame about a terrible production. Smithees were granted only when creative differences destroyed a director's 'vision'. Those allowed to hide behind a Smithee were required to keep their reasons secret. *Death of a Gunfighter* (1969) was the first movie to credit Alan Smithee, after director Robert Totten fell out with the star, Richard Widmark, and was replaced by Don Siegel. At the end of filming, neither director wanted to be credited. Since the DGA demands that all films list a director, Alan Smithee was created to take their place. In 1997, a comedy titled *An Alan Smithee Film: Burn*

Some Alan Smithee
movies:
Hellraiser: Bloodline
The Barking Dog
Putz
I Love N.Y.
Appointment with Fear
The Shrimp on the Barbie
Ghost Fever
Solar Crisis

Hollywood Burn was released, which told the story of a director actually called Alan Smithee who wanted his name removed from a movie. Bizarrely (or for reasons of publicity) the director of the film, Arthur Hiller, was himself granted an Alan Smithee for the piece. After that, the DGA retired Alan and now grants each director a new pseudonym. ❦ George & Georgina Spelvin were pseudonyms traditionally used by actors in American theaters when they were playing more than one part. Georgina Spelvin lost favor when it was adopted as a screen name by porn star Dorothy May. Walter Plinge was similarly used by actors in London theaters. In the 1970s, the BBC used the pseudonym David Agnew when a writer's name could not be used for contractual reasons. ❦ The DGA only allows one director to be listed on the credits of a film, even if more were actually involved. The only exception to this is if there is a death mid-production.

Books & Arts

It's all very well to be able to write books, but can you waggle your ears?
— J.M. BARRIE

NOBEL PRIZE IN LITERATURE

The 2005 Nobel Prize in Literature was awarded to HAROLD PINTER (1930–),

Who in his plays uncovers the precipice under everyday prattle and forces entry into oppression's closed rooms.

Illness prevented Pinter from receiving the award in person on December 10, and it was accepted on his behalf by his publisher at Faber & Faber, Stephen Page. However, Pinter prerecorded a pugnacious Nobel Lecture, broadcast by video to the Swedish Academy in Stockolm on December 7. Speaking from his wheelchair (in a manner that provoked comparisons to Hamm in Beckett's *Endgame*) Pinter poured ironic scorn on postwar American foreign policy, and George W. Bush's presidency in particular: 'I put it to you that the United States is without doubt the greatest show on the road. Brutal, indifferent, scornful, and ruthless it may be, but it is also very clever'. ❦ Pinter's work has long been concerned with the oppression of authoritarian intervention. In *The Dumb Waiter* (1959), *The Birthday Party* (1958), and *The Hothouse* (1958), this oppression is manifest respectively in the power of state, family, and religion; in *One for the Road* (1984), *Mountain Language* (1988), and *Ashes to Ashes* (1996),

it is stated more explicitly. It was perhaps *The Homecoming* (1964) and *The Caretaker* (1959) that made the strongest impression on critics; they prominently featured the relentless rhythms that became the hallmark of Pinter's style. The 'Pinteresque' (a term that entered the *Oxford English Dictionary* in 1989) constitutes a cocktail of 'menace, erotic fantasy, and mental disequilibrium'. ❦ Pinter was diagnosed with cancer of the oesophagus in January 2002, but in August of that year stated his intention to be 'even more of a pain in the arse' to the British government than before. Upon accepting the Nobel Laureateship, Pinter declared that he would be writing no further drama, and planned instead to devote all his time to poetry. ❦ Pinter's Nobel lecture was above all concerned with the themes central to his work: 'What is true? What is false?', personal responsibility, 'the dignity of man', and the 'crucial obligation which devolves upon us all' to 'define the truth of our lives and our societies'.

The 2004 winner was the Austrian writer Elfriede Jelinek (1946-), whose novels and plays *'with extraordinary linguistic zeal reveal the absurdity of society's clichés'*.

—————————— BEST-SELLING POTENTIAL ——————————

Literary website lulu.com undertook research into what makes a successful book title. By analyzing 700 titles from the *New York Times* best-seller lists over 50 years, Dr Atai Winkler, the statistician who led the project, was able to pinpoint the common attributes of top-selling titles. According to Winkler's model, metaphorical titles are more popular than literal ones, and the length of title seems not to affect sales. The survey concluded that the following books had the most successful titles:

Sleeping Murder · Agatha Christie	*Presumed Innocent* · Scott Turow
Something of Value · Robert Ruark	*Everything's Eventual* · Stephen King
Looking for Mr Goodbar · J. Rossner	*Rising Sun* · Michael Crichton

—————————— TOP 10 BEST-SELLING US BOOKS · 2005–06 ——————————

Title	author	sales
A Million Little Pieces	James Frey [see p.27]	2,448,584
Marley & Me	John Grogan	1,336,836
The Da Vinci Code [mass market paperback ed.]	Dan Brown [see p.164]	1,230,733
Eldest	Christopher Paolini	1,034,331
The Kite Runner	Khaled Hosseini	1,023,050
The Broker	John Grisham	965,640
Night	Elie Wiesel	859,630
The World Is Flat	Thomas L. Friedman	843,385
Harry Potter and the Half-Blood Prince	J.K. Rowling	754,695
The Da Vinci Code [original hardcover ed.]	Dan Brown [see p.164]	741,339

[Source: Nielsen BookScan © · August 2005–August 2006]

—————————— BOOKSELLER OF THE YEAR · 2006 ——————————

Northshire Books in Manchester, Vermont, won *Publishers Weekly*'s 2006 Bookseller of the Year Award. The venerable 30-year-old store, housed in an old inn, features books of all types, in addition to music, author events, and a splendid 70-seat café.

—————————— STRIKEOUT NUMBER ——————————

It is common for books to have *strikeout numbers* printed on their copyright page:

1 2 3 4 5 6 7 8 9 10   (or, sometimes)   1 3 5 7 9 10 8 6 4 2

The purpose of these numbers is to indicate the impression, or printing, from which the book came. The lowest number visible indicates the book's impression. (The term 'strikeout' comes from the practice of literally scratching the numbers from the printing plate as the impression changed.) So, if on the strikeout line there is a '1', the book is a first printing; if there is a '5', it is a fifth; and so on.

──────THE PULITZER PRIZE · LETTERS & DRAMA──────

The 2006 Pulitzer Prizes in Letters & Drama awarded Special Citations to Edmund S. Morgan for a 'creative and deeply influential body of work as an American historian'; and Thelonious Monk for his 'enduring impact on the evolution of jazz' (Monk's award was posthumous; he died in 1982). The other 2006 Pulitzers went to:

Fiction...Geraldine Brooks · *March*
Drama... no award (Awards administrator Sig Gissler said, 'sometimes you don't get a winner')[†]
History...............................David M. Oshinsky · *Polio: an American Story*
Biography ....Kai Bird & Martin J. Sherwin
          American Prometheus: The Triumph and Tragedy of J. Robert Oppenheimer
Poetry...Claudia Emerson · *Late Wife*
General Nonfiction ....Caroline Elkins
          Imperial Reckoning: the Untold Story of Britain's Gulag in Kenya
Music...........................Yehudi Wyner · *Piano Concerto: 'Chiavi in Mano'*

† 2006 was the first year since 1997 that no Pulitzer Drama Prize was awarded, and the 15th such occurrence since the Prize was founded in 1917. The three nominees were: Adam Rapp · *Red Light Winter*; Rolin Jones · *The Intelligent Design of Jenny Chow*; and Christopher Durang · *Miss Witherspoon*.

──────────── NOMS DE ... ────────────

Nom de plume........... a pseudonymous name assumed by authors, for example:

Nom de plume	real name		
John le Carré	*David Cornwell*	George Orwell	*Eric Arthur Blair*
Lewis Carroll	*Charles Lutwidge Dodgson*	Dr Seuss	*Theodor Seuss Geisel*
George Eliot	*Mary Ann Evans*	Iceberg Slim	*Robert Beck*
O. Henry	*William Sydney Porter*	Lemony Snicket	*Daniel Handler*
Hergé	*Georges Rémi*	Stendhal	*Marie Henri Beyle*
James Herriot	*James Alfred Wight*	Mark Twain	*Samuel Langhorne Clemens*
P.D. James	*Phyllis Dorothy James White*	Barbara Vine	*Ruth Rendell*
Ann Landers	*Esther P.F. Lederer*	Voltaire	*François-Marie Arouet*
		Mary Westmacott	*Agatha Christie*

Nom de Dieu ....a French oath of exasperation (literally, 'name of God')
Nom de guerre[†] .... a fictitious name assumed during war or espionage
Nom de théâtre[‡] .... a stage name assumed by actors
Nom de vente ....an assumed name under which one bids at an auction

† At one time it was customary for all those who entered the French army to assume a *nom de guerre*; indeed, during the time of chivalry, knights were often known only by the devices on their shields. Perhaps the most famous contemporary *nom de guerre* is 'P. O'Neill', the name which is usually signed on statements issued by the Irish Republican Army (IRA). There are some suggestions that Osama bin Laden fought (and perhaps still does) under the *nom de guerre* 'Abu Abdullah'. ‡ See also Alan Smithee on p.158, Noms de Rap on p.141, and Truthiness in Fiction on p.27.

ODDEST BOOK TITLE OF THE YEAR

The Diagram Group's *Oddest Book Title of the Year* has been contested annually since 1978. Previous winners have included: *Living with Crazy Buttocks*; *Proceedings of the Second International Workshop on Nude Mice*; *How to Avoid Huge Ships*; and *The Big Book of Lesbian Horse Stories*. 2005's winning title and runners-up were:

People Who Don't Know They Are Dead: How They Attach Themselves to Unsuspecting Bystanders and What to Do About It
Gary Leon Hill [WINNER]

Rhino Horn Stockpile Management: Minimum Standards and Best Practices from East and Southern Africa
Simon Milledge

Ancient Starch Research
Robin Torrence & Huw J. Barton

Soil Nailing: Best Practice Guidance
A. Phear, C. Dew, B. Ozsoy

Bullying and Sexual Harassment: A Practical Handbook
T. Stephens & J. Hallas

Nessus, Snort & Ethereal Powertools
B. Caswell, G. Ramirez, J. Beale, N. Rathaus

[The contest is run by UK magazine *The Bookseller* and voted on by the book trade.]

INTERNET ABECEDARIAN

The alphabet of words most commonly looked up on dictionary.com in 2005:

Affect · Benevolent · Cynical · Definitely · Effect · Fallacious · Gregarious · Hyperbole Irony · Jaded · Karma · Love · Metaphor · Naive · Oxymoron · Paradox · Quixotic Rhetoric · Sex · Theme · Ubiquitous · Virtue · Whether · Xenophobia · Yield · Zeal

---

'PEN' PRISON WRITING CONTEST · 2006

Winners of the prison writing contest held by literary/human rights group PEN:

Fiction............................ Brian Chase · *Willie en Las Cruces* (Beaver, WV)
Nonfiction/essay .... Patricia Prewitt · *Contraband* (Vandalia, MO)
Memoir............ Richard Parker · *Land of Opportunity – Or Else* (Rosharon, TX)
Poetry....................................... Erin George · *Origami Heart* (Troy, VA)
Drama............................... Laos Schman · *Sisters* (San Luis Obispo, CA)

ISBN-13

Due to growth in publishing, the International Standard Book Number (ISBN) is changing. The existing 10-digit system, introduced in the 1960s, is running out of numbers. So, the International Organization for Standardization (ISO) has ruled that ISBNs will grow from 10 digits to 13 digits, as of January 1, 2007.

─────────────── BAD SEX IN FICTION PRIZE ───────────────

Each year the UK *Literary Review* awards its 'Bad Sex in Fiction' prize to a novel featuring the most 'inept, embarrassing, and unnecessary' sex scene. The 2005 winner was the columnist and food critic GILES COREN, for his debut, *Winkler.*

And he came hard in her mouth and his dick jumped around and rattled on her teeth and he blacked out and she took his dick out of her mouth and lifted herself from his face and whipped the pillow away and he gasped and glugged at the air, and he came again so hard that his dick wrenched out of her hand and a shot of it hit him straight in the eye and stung like nothing he'd ever had in there, and he yelled with the pain, but the yell could have been anything, and as she grabbed at his dick, which was leaping around like a shower dropped in an empty bath, she scratched his back deeply with the nails of both hands and he shot three more times, in thick stripes on her chest. Like Zorro.

─────────── OTHER BOOK PRIZES OF NOTE · 2006 ───────────

Bollingen Prize in Poetry	Jay Wright
Caldecott Medal Chris Raschka & Norton Juster · *The Hello, Goodbye Window*	
Costa Book Award [formerly Whitbread prize] Hilary Spurling · *Matisse the Master*	
Guardian First Novel	Alexander Masters · *Stuart: A Life Backwards*
Kingsley Tufts Poetry Prize	Lucia Perillo · *Luck Is Luck*
Man Booker Prize [2005]	John Banville · *The Sea*
National Book Awards: Fiction	William T. Vollmann · *Europe Central*
Nonfiction	Joan Didion · *The Year of Magical Thinking*
Poetry	W.S. Merwin · *Migration: New and Selected Poems*
Young People's Literature	Jeanne Birdsall · *The Penderwicks*
National Book Critics Circle Awards: Fiction	E.L. Doctorow · *The March*
Nonfiction	Svetlana Alexievich · *Voices from Chernobyl*
Autobiography	Francine du Plessix Gray · *Them: A Memoir of Parents*
Newbery Medal	Lynne Rae Perkins · *Criss Cross*
Orange Prize	Zadie Smith · *On Beauty*
PEN/Faulkner Award	E.L. Doctorow · *The March*
PEN/Nabokov Award	Philip Roth
Truman Capote Award for Literary Criticism	*The Geoffrey Hartman Reader* ·
	Co-eds. Geoffrey Hartman & Daniel T. O'Hara

─────────────── MOST LITERATE CITIES ───────────────

Central Connecticut State University conducts an annual assessment of the literary vitality of the nation's largest cities [pop. >250,000]. Data are collected in 6 categories: newspaper circulation, number of bookstores, number of periodical publishers, library resources, educational attainment, and internet resources. 2005's top 10:

Seattle · Minneapolis · Washington, DC · Atlanta · San Francisco
Denver · Boston · Pittsburgh · Cincinnati · St Paul

──────── 'THE DA VINCI CODE' RULING ────────

In February 2006, Richard Leigh and Michael Baigent sued Random House, in the British High Court, claiming that Dan Brown's (>40m) best-selling novel, *The Da Vinci Code* (DVC), had copied the central ideas of their 1982 nonfiction book, *Holy Blood & Holy Grail* (HBHG), also published by Random House. Baigent and Leigh argued that DVC appropriated 'the whole architecture' of their theory that Jesus and Mary Magdalene were married and that their bloodline lasts to this day. Because copyright infringement is notoriously difficult to prove, many legal pundits

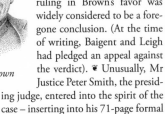

Dan Brown

were skeptical as to the plaintiffs' case. Intense media interest faded as the trial progressed and the evidence against Brown appeared to be weak. During testimony, Baigent was forced to retract a number of his claims, and the eventual ruling in Brown's favor was widely considered to be a foregone conclusion. (At the time of writing, Baigent and Leigh had pledged an appeal against the verdict). ❦ Unusually, Mr Justice Peter Smith, the presiding judge, entered into the spirit of the case – inserting into his 71-page formal judgment a set of seemingly random letters, singled out in bold italic type:

s, m, i, t, h, y, c, o, d, e, J, a, e, i, e, x, t, o, s, t, g, p, s, a, c, g, r, e, a, m, q, w, f, k, a, d, p, m, q, z, v, z

A London lawyer, Dan Tench, spotted these anomalies and soon, after hints from the judge to refer to his *Who's Who* entry and employ the Fibonacci sequence, journalists uncovered the disappointingly naval message '*Smithy Code Jackie Fisher who are you Dreadnought*'. It seems that this statement refers only to Justice Smith's passion for obscure Royal Navy history and not, as hoped, the meaning of life.

──────── AMAZON'S TEXT STATS ────────

By analyzing the entire text of individual works, Amazon.com created its *Text Stats* service which enables purchasers to compare the readability and complexity of books featured on the site. Below are the *Text Stats* for selected recent works:

Author *Benchmark · Book*	M. Gladwell *Blink*	Dan Brown *Da Vinci Code*	Levitt & Dubner *Freakonomics*	Zadie Smith *On Beauty*
Fog Index[†]	11·6	9·1	11·1	8·7
Complex words[‡]	12%	12%	14%	9%
Syllables per word	1·5	1·6	1·6	1·5
Words per sentence	17·0	11·1	14·1	13·0
Total characters	408,390	821,310	399,657	880,751
Total words	70,731	137,100	63,809	154,512
Total sentences	4,172	12,354	4,511	11,913

† The Fog Index measures readability by suggesting how many years of formal education would be required to comprehend the text. ‡ A word is classed as complex if it has 3 or more syllables.

BULWER-LYTTON FICTION CONTEST

In 1982, the English Department of San José State University created a literary contest in honor of E.G.E. Bulwer-Lytton (1803–73), who famously opened his book *Paul Clifford* with, 'It was a dark and stormy night'. The contest rewards the best 'bad' opening line to an imaginary novel. The 2006 prize went to Jim Guigli, for:

Detective Bart Lasiter was in his office studying the light from his one small window falling on his super burrito when the door swung open to reveal a woman whose body said you've had your last burrito for a while, whose face said angels did exist, and whose eyes said she could make you dig your own grave and lick the shovel clean.

US LIBRARY USAGE

Ohio has the highest number of public library visits per capita, according to the latest US Department of Education figures (2003). Ohio had 7·1 visits per person that year, followed by Connecticut and Colorado (6·6 and 6·4 visits per capita, respectively). Mississippi had 2·6, the fewest of any state. Below is charted patron use of key library services, according to the American Library Association (2005):

Activity	%		± from 2002
Borrow books	81		+14%
Consult the librarian	54		+7%
Borrow CDs, videos, or software	38		+13%
Attend a special program	22		+8%

MOST FREQUENTLY CHALLENGED BOOKS · 2005

The American Library Association annually compiles a list of the books most often challenged by the public. A 'challenge' is a formal, written complaint requesting the removal of a book from a library or school due to 'content or appropriateness'. Below are the top ten most frequently challenged books (or series) during 2005:

Book & author	reason challenged
It's Perfectly Normal · Robie H. Harris	homosexuality, nudity, sex education, abortion, religious viewpoint, unsuited to age group
Forever · Judy Blume	sexual content and offensive language
The Catcher in the Rye · J.D. Salinger	sexual content, offensive language, unsuited to age group
The Chocolate War · Robert Cormier	sexual content and offensive language
Whale Talk · Chris Crutcher	racism and offensive language
Detour for Emmy · Marilyn Reynolds	sexual content
What My Mother Doesn't Know · Sonya Sones	sexual content and unsuited to age group
Captain Underpants · D. Pilkey	anti-family content, unsuited to age group, violence
Crazy Lady! · Jane Leslie Conly	offensive language
It's So Amazing! · Robie H. Harris	sex education and sexual content

—————— BOOK RECOMMENDATIONS ——————

Celebrities are often asked to list books they would recommend. Below are J.K. Rowling's list from a Royal Society of Literature report, and First Lady Laura Bush's tips from her *Ready to Read, Ready to Learn* literacy initiative.

J.K. ROWLING

Wuthering Heights · Emily Brontë
Charlie & the Chocolate Factory
Roald Dahl
Robinson Crusoe · Daniel Defoe
David Copperfield · Charles Dickens
Catch-22 · Joseph Heller
To Kill a Mockingbird · Harper Lee
Animal Farm · George Orwell
The Tale of Two Bad Mice
Beatrix Potter
The Catcher in the Rye · J.D. Salinger
Hamlet · William Shakespeare

LAURA BUSH

Ship of Fools; The Collected Stories of Katherine Anne Porter
Katherine Anne Porter
The Brothers Karamazov
Fyodor Dostoyevsky
Beloved · Toni Morrison
Music for Chameleons · Truman Capote
Goodbye to a River · John Graves
Mornings on Horseback
David McCullough
Bless Me, Ultima · Rudolfo A. Anaya
My Antonia; Death Comes to the Archbishop · Willa Cather
All the Pretty Horses
Cormac McCarthy

In an audiotape Aljazeera aired January 19, 2006, Osama bin Laden declared, 'If Bush declines but to continue lying and practicing injustice [against us], it is useful for you to read the book of *The Rogue State*'. Within 24 hours William Blum's *Rogue State: a Guide to the World's Only Superpower* had surged from 205,000th to 30th on Amazon.com's chart.

The power of Oprah Winfrey to create best-sellers is both admired and feared by the publishing industry. Books featured on *Oprah's Book Club* can expect a massive boost in sales that in turn feeds into further media interest – the so-called 'Oprah effect'. Winfrey has been credited with changing the fortunes of dozens of authors [for better or worse, see p.27] as well as the reading habits of America – in 2005, after her advocacy, William Faulkner hit number three in the book charts, 43 years after his death. Below are some of Winfrey's personal book favorites:

The Bible
The Color Purple · Alice Walker
The Education of Little Tree
Forrest Carter & Rennard Strickland
The Grapes of Wrath
[and anything else by ...]
John Steinbeck
Jubilee · Margaret Walker
The Power of Now: a Guide to Spiritual Enlightenment
Eckhart Tolle
Strawberry Girl · Lois Lenski
Sula · Beloved · and
The Bluest Eye · Toni Morrison
A Tree Grows in Brooklyn
Betty Smith
White Oleander · Janet Fitch
Reflections on the Art of Living: A Joseph Campbell Companion
Diane K. Osborne (Ed.)
The Seat of the Soul · Gary Zukav
I Know Why the Caged Bird Sings
Maya Angelou
Discover the Power Within You
Eric Butterworth
Their Eyes Were Watching God
Zora Neale Hurston
A Return to Love
Marianne Williamson
To Kill a Mockingbird · Harper Lee

BEST US FICTION

In 2006, the *New York Times Book Review* asked critics, writers, and editors to name the best work of US fiction in the last 25 years. Winners were determined by the number of multiple votes:

WINNER
Beloved · Toni Morrison

RUNNERS-UP
Underworld · Don DeLillo
Blood Meridian · Cormac McCarthy
Rabbit Angstrom: the Four Novels
John Updike
American Pastoral · Philip Roth

MULTIPLE VOTES
A Confederacy of Dunces · John K. Toole
Housekeeping · Marilynne Robinson
Winter's Tale · Mark Helprin
White Noise · Don DeLillo
The Counterlife · Philip Roth
Libra · Don DeLillo
Where I'm Calling From · R. Carver
The Things They Carried · Tim O'Brien
Mating · Norman Rush
Jesus' Son · Denis Johnson
Operation Shylock · Philip Roth
Independence Day · Richard Ford
Sabbath's Theater · Philip Roth
Border Trilogy · Cormac McCarthy
The Human Stain · Philip Roth
The Known World · Edward P. Jones
The Plot Against America · Philip Roth

* * *

The *New York Times* 10 Best Books of 2005:

Kafka on the Shore by Haruki Murakami; *On Beauty* by Zadie Smith; *Prep* by Curtis Sittenfeld; *Saturday* by Ian McEwan; *Veronica* by Mary Gaitskill; *The Assassin's Gate: America in Iraq* by George Packer; *De Kooning: An American Master* by Mark Stevens & Annalyn Swan; *The Lost Painting* by Jonathan Harr; *Postwar: A History of Europe Since 1945* by Tony Judt; and *The Year of Magical Thinking* by Joan Didion.

PUBLIC & THE ARTS

Selected statistics on arts participation and preferences amongst US adults:

% who attended/visited the following at least once in the past year:
Any arts activity....................65·1
Visual arts ....41·9
Plays................................22·3
Music performances ....18·8
Dance performances................8·7

% performing or creating the following at least once in the past year:
Photography (incl. filming)........11·5
Painting/drawing....................8·6
Creative writing....................7·0
Musical plays.......................2·4
Classical music.....................1·8
Jazz ....1·3
Ballet ....0·3

% who participated in the following at least once in the past year:
Buying artwork ....29·5
Singing in groups ....4·8
Writing or composing music ....2·3

% who participated in literary activities at least once in the past year:
Read any book ....56·6
Read literature ....46·7
Read novels or short stories.......45·1
Read or listened to poetry ....14·3
Read a play.........................3·6

% who liked these types of music:
Classic rock/oldies ....48·3
Country and Western..............40·4
Blues/R&B.........................29·9
Mood/easy ....29·1
Jazz ....27·5
Classical/chamber..................27·4

[Source: NEA 2002 Survey of Public Participation in the Arts · The survey is undertaken every ten years.]

—————————— THE TURNER PRIZE · 2005 ——————————

Founded in 1984, the Turner Prize is awarded each year to a British artist, under 50, for an outstanding exhibition or other presentation in the 12 months prior to each May. The winner receives £25,000, and three runners-up receive £5,000.

Simon Starling, 38, won the 2005 Turner prize amidst the usual media uproar. The Glaswegian, whose past works include an attempt to create an 'island of weeds' in the middle of Loch Lomond, describes his works as 'the physical manifestation of my thought process'. The centrepiece of his Turner entry, *Shedboatshed* (Mobile Architecture No. 2) is a dilapidated former guard-hut. Having discovered it in the Swiss town of Schweizerhalle, Starling turned it into a boat and paddled it for 7 miles down the Rhine to Basel, where he rebuilt it in its original incarnation. He said of the piece, 'You can start to sort of read the shed and rebuild the boat in your mind.' Another exhibit, *Tabernas Desert Run 2004*, saw him cross the Spanish desert on an improvised hydrogen bicycle, then use the waste water it produced to paint a watercolor cactus. Painting and vehicle are exhibited side by side

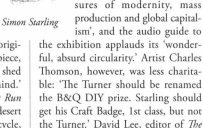

Simon Starling

in a glass cabinet. Starling will spend a portion of his Turner winnings placing a replica Henry Moore sculpture in Lake Ontario and growing zebra mussels on its surface. He also has plans to construct a replica of the car built by erotic photographer Carlo Mollino for the Le Mans 24 Hour Race, and drive it around the Turin ring road for an entire day. *Shedboatshed* was hailed by Tate Britain Curators as 'poetic … a buttress against the pressures of modernity, mass production and global capitalism', and the audio guide to the exhibition applauds its 'wonderful, absurd circularity.' Artist Charles Thomson, however, was less charitable: 'The Turner should be renamed the B&Q DIY prize. Starling should get his Craft Badge, 1st class, but not the Turner.' David Lee, editor of *The Jackdaw* magazine, concluded: 'He's got some quaint charm, provided you don't take him too seriously.'

Year	previous winner				
'84	Malcolm Morley	'91	Anish Kapoor	'98	Chris Ofili
'85	Howard Hodgkin	'92	Grenville Davey	'99	Steve McQueen
'86	Gilbert & George	'93	Rachel Whiteread	'00	Wolfgang Tillmans
'87	Richard Deacon	'94	Antony Gormley	'01	Martin Creed
'88	Tony Cragg	'95	Damien Hirst	'02	Keith Tyson
'89	Richard Long	'96	Douglas Gordon	'03	Grayson Perry
		'97	Gillian Wearing	'04	Jeremy Deller

2006 NOMINATIONS

It was announced in May 2006 that the following four artists are shortlisted for the 2006 Turner Prize, the winner of which will be announced on December 4:

Sculptor Rebecca Warren; German-born abstract painter Tomma Abts; video artist and photographer Phil Collins; and installation artist Mark Titchener.

———————————ARTIST RANKINGS · 2005———————————

The Artist Ranking system, developed by Artfacts.net, employs an algorithm to rank artists according to their international prestige. Each time an artist exhibits, they are awarded points based on the international importance of the gallery that hosts the exhibition. The database includes 60,000 artists, and tracks exhibitions within the last 5 years. The top-ranked artist, living or dead, in 2005 was Pablo Picasso, followed by Andy Warhol. The top 5 *living* artists in 2005 were as follows:

Artist	*points*	
Bruce Nauman	55,486·21	Sol LeWitt................40,335·57
Gerhard Richter	53,037·16	Robert Rauschenberg.......39,510·74
		Sigmar Polke................37,688·71

———————————WHITNEY BIENNIAL · 2006———————————

The Whitney Museum of American Art, NYC, hosts the lavish survey of American contemporary art known as the Whitney Biennial. In 2006, *c.*100 artists were featured, with artwork apportioned more or less equally across painting, sculpture, photography, film, video, and performance. Works of note included: *Peace Tower*, the work of 180 artists erected in the Whitney's Sculpture Court; the film *Trailer for a Remake of Gore Vidal's 'Caligula'* (starring Courtney Love, Benicio Del Toro, Milla Jovovich, and Helen Mirren, and narrated by Gore Vidal); the puppet show *Don't Trust Anyone Over Thirty*; and Marilyn Minter's paintings of decadent glamour. The exhibition, curated by Chrissie Iles and Philippe Vergne, ran March 2 to May 28.
❦ Los Angeles artist Mark Bradford won the 2006 Bucksbaum Award, given to an artist exhibiting in the Whitney Biennial whose work combines 'talent and imagination'. Bradford's work tends to be inspired by LA's environment, combining materials and urban, pop, and street culture references, to create pieces that comment on the 'aesthetics and the economics' of urban interactions. He has said, 'Like those tagged up, repainted, tagged up, sanded, and repainted walls you pass every day on the street, my process is both reductive and additive'. Bradford received $100,000 and was invited to mount a solo exhibition at the museum. He is the second consecutive LA artist to win the Bucksbaum; Raymond Pettibon won in 2004.

2006 was the first year the Biennial had a formal title, *Day for Night* – the English title of François Truffaut's *La Nuit Américaine* (1973), noted for using filters allowing night scenes to be shot in the day.

———————————ORDWAY PRIZE · 2005———————————

In 2005, the Penny McCall Foundation announced the inauguration of the Ordway Prize to honor the achievements of mid-career artists, curators, and arts writers from around the world. The award is given every other year in two categories: to a working artist, and to an arts writer or curator. In 2005, Colombian artist Doris Salcedo, whose work addresses political violence, won in the first category; Ralph Rugoff, director of the California College of the Arts Wattis Institute for Contemporary Arts won in the second. Both received an award of $100,000.

──────────── TOP EXHIBITIONS · 2005 ────────────

The *Art Newspaper*'s figures for the most popular art exhibitions around the world:

2005 exhibition	museum	daily attendance
Hokusai	Tokyo National	9,436
Treasures of the Toshodaiji Temple	Tokyo National	8,678
C19th Masterpieces from the Louvre	Yokohama Museum of Art	7,066
Vincent Van Gogh: The Drawings	Metropolitan, NY	6,571
Cézanne and Pissarro 1865–85	Museum of Modern Art, NY	6,387
Turner, Whistler, Monet	Grand Palais, Paris	6,043
C19th Masterpieces from the Louvre	Kyoto City Museum	5,992
Thomas Demand	Museum of Modern Art, NY	5,991
Tutankhamun and the Pharaohs	LACMA, Los Angeles	5,934
Van Gogh in Context	Nat. Museum of Modern Art, Tokyo	5,890

──────────── A SMASHING TIME, DADA, & GUM ────────────

In January 2006, an unfortunate visitor to the Fitzwilliam Museum in Cambridge, England, stumbled on his loose shoelace and tumbled into a trio of priceless vases, smashing them to pieces. The 300-year-old Qing vases had been displayed, perhaps recklessly, on a windowsill. Margaret Greeves, the museum's assistant director, said 'they are in very, very small pieces, but we are determined to put them back together'. The plot thickened in April 2006, when, after studying CCTV footage of the incident, the police arrested the culprit, Nick Flynn, on suspicion of causing criminal damage (charges were dropped in June 2006). ❦ Also in January, French performance artist Pierre Pinoncelli attacked Marcel Duchamp's *Fountain* with a small hammer while it was on display in Paris. The urinal was slightly chipped, but spared the treatment it received in 1993, when Pinoncelli urinated on the same work. ❦ In March 2006, Helen Frankenthaler's *The Bay* was damaged when a boy of 12 stuck chewing gum on the canvas during a school trip to the Detroit Institute of Arts.

──────────── MOST EXPENSIVE PAINTINGS ────────────

In June 2006, Gustav Klimt's 1907 portrait of Adele Bloch-Bauer was auctioned for a record $135m. The painting sold to billionaire Ronald Lauder, after a court ordered the Austrian government to return the Nazi-looted painting to Bloch-Bauer's descendants. Lauder will hang the work in his New York Neue Galerie. The following are the world's most expensive paintings, according to the London *Times*:

Painting	artist	year of sale	cost
Adele Bloch-Bauer I	Gustav Klimt	2006	$135m
Garçon à la Pipe	Pablo Picasso	2004	$104m
Dora Maar au Chat	Pablo Picasso	2006	$95m
Portrait du Dr Gachet	Vincent Van Gogh	1990	$82m
Au Moulin de la Galette	Pierre Auguste Renoir	1990	$78m

──────── TOP TEN ARTISTS BY REVENUE · 2005 ────────

Artprice annually publishes a ranking of artists based on sales generated by their works at auction. In 2005, revenue from the top ten artists reached $576 million:

Rank artist ('04 rank)	2005 sales ($)
1 .... Pablo Picasso (1) .... 153·2m	6 .... Marc Chagall (11)......... 36·6m
2 .... Andy Warhol (3) .... 86·7m	7 .... Willem de Kooning (36).. 36·6m
3 .... Claude Monet (2)......... 61·5m	8 .... Fernand Léger (23)........ 35·7m
4 .... Canaletto (239)............ 55·5m	9 .... Jean-Michel Basquiat (16) 35·6m
5 .... Mark Rothko (13)......... 41·6m	10... Lucian Freud (81)......... 33·7m
	[Source: artprice.com]

──────────── FBI's TOP TEN ART CRIMES ────────────

In November 2005, the FBI's Art Theft program released a list of the worlds' most significant art heists in a bid to raise public awareness of the works still unrecovered. The works of art, the country of their theft, and their estimated value are below:

Item(s)	stolen from	in	$ value
7,000–10,000 Iraqi artifacts	Iraq	2003	'priceless'
12 Isabella Stewart Gardner Museum paintings	USA	1990	300m
Munch · *The Scream* and *The Madonna*	Norway	2004	102m
Da Vinci · *Madonna with the Yarnwinder*	Scotland	2003	65m
Cellini · *The Salt Cellar*†	Austria	2003	55m
2 Renoirs and 1 Rembrandt‡	Sweden	2000	36m
2 Van Goghs	Netherlands	2002	30m
Caravaggio · *Nativity with San Lorenzo and San Francesco*	Italy	1969	20m
Cézanne · *View of Auvers-sur-Oise*	England	1999	3m
Davidoff-Morini Stradivarius violin	USA	1995	3m

† Cellini's sculpture *The Salt Cellar* was found by Austrian police in January 2006. ‡ These works were recovered in 2001 & 2005. The list is regularly updated and can be seen at fbi.com.

──────────── GLOBAL TRADE IN CULTURAL GOODS ────────────

UNESCO analyzed cross-border trade data for 120 countries (1994–2002), to determine the leading importers and exporters of books, CDs, video games, statuary (statues, sculpture, &c.), and other cultural goods. The top three exporting countries in 2002 are shown below, with their share of exports in each cultural category:

Export category	1st	2nd	3rd
Printed media	US (18%)	UK (17%)	Germany (12%)
Recorded media	US (17%)	Germany (12%)	Ireland (12%)
Visual arts	UK (22%)	China (19%)	US (8%)
Audiovisual media	China (32%)	Japan (17%)	Mexico (11%)
Overall exports	UK ($8·5bn)	US ($7·6bn)	China ($5·2bn)

——————WHERE TO SEE MAJOR WORKS OF ART——————

Garden of Earthly Delights	Bosch	Prado, Madrid
The Birth of Venus	Botticelli	Galleria degli Uffizi, Florence
Massacre of the Innocents	Bruegel (Elder)	Hampton Court, Middlesex
Venice: Regatta on Grand Canal	Canaletto	National Gallery, London
I and the Village	Chagall	Museum of Modern Art, NY
Persistence of Memory	Dalí	Museum of Modern Art, NY
The Last Supper	da Vinci	Santa Maria delle Grazie, Milan
Mona Lisa	da Vinci	Louvre, Paris
The Dancing Lesson	Degas	Musée National d'Orsay, Paris
Fountain	Duchamp	Centre Pompidou, Paris
The Swing	Fragonard	Wallace Collection, London
Girl with a White Dog	Freud	Tate Britain, London
The Blue Boy	Gainsborough	Huntington Library, CA
Merry-Go-Round	Gertler	Tate Britain, London
Turin Shroud	God	Cathedral of St John the Baptist, Turin
Saturn Devouring His Children	Goya	Prado, Madrid
Single Form	Hepworth	United Nations HQ, NY
Nighthawks	Hopper	The Art Institute of Chicago
Composition VIII	Kandinsky	Guggenheim, NY
Magic Garden	Klee	Guggenheim, NY
The Kiss	Klimt	Belvedere, Vienna
Washington Crossing the Delaware	Leutze	Metropolitan Museum of Art, NY
Coming from the Mill	Lowry	Salford Museum and Art Gallery
Le Double Secret	Magritte	Centre Pompidou, Paris
Creation of Adam	Michelangelo	Sistine Chapel, Rome
David	Michelangelo	Accademia, Florence
Broadway Boogie Woogie	Mondrian	Museum of Modern Art, NY
Nympheas	Monet	Orangerie, Paris
Reclining Figure	Moore	UNESCO HQ, Paris
Guernica	Picasso	Reina Sofía Museum, Madrid
Lavender Mist: Number 1	Pollock	National Gallery of Art, D.C.
Almanac	Rauschenberg	Tate Modern, London
Self-Portrait (1661)	Rembrandt	Kenwood House, London
Luncheon of the Boating Party	Renoir	Phillips Collection, Washington
The Thinker	Rodin	Musée Rodin, Paris
Bacchus	Rubens	Hermitage, St Petersburg
At the Moulin Rouge	Toulouse-Lautrec	Art Institute of Chicago
Ulysses Deriding Polyphemus	Turner	National Gallery, London
Rosetta Stone	unknown	British Museum, London
Tutankhamun's gold mask	unknown	Egyptian Museum, Cairo
The Arnolfini Portrait	Van Eyck	National Gallery, London
Starry Night	Van Gogh	Museum of Modern Art, NY
Girl with a Pearl Earring	Vermeer	Mauritshuis, The Hague
100 Soup Cans	Warhol	Albright-Knox Gallery, Buffalo
Marilyn Monroe print	Warhol	The Warhol Museum, Pittsburgh

Because of sales, restoration, loans, multiple copies, and other factors, the location of some works may vary.

---------- TOP-GROSSING BROADWAY SHOWS ----------

The top-grossing 2005 Broadway shows, including total sales and attendance:

$ total gross	[Source: League of American Theaters & Producers Inc.]	total attendance
66,421,803	*Wicked*	752,226
59,917,875	*The Lion King*	729,055
49,161,427	*Mamma Mia!*	614,503
43,594,101	*Spamalot*	518,049
42,701,058	*The Producers*	591,946
37,556,566	*The Phantom of the Opera*	622,583
36,242,571	*Hairspray*	529,339
35,497,898	*Dirty Rotten Scoundrels*	477,181
32,261,756	*Beauty and the Beast*	518,377
27,196,334	*Fiddler on the Roof*	464,354

---------- STAGE DIRECTIONS & LAYOUT ----------

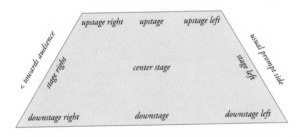

---------- LONGEST-RUNNING BROADWAY SHOW ----------

Andrew Lloyd Webber's *The Phantom of the Opera* broke the record for the longest-running Broadway show with its 7,486th performance on January 9, 2006. The previous record-holder was *Cats* (also from Lloyd Webber), which played 7,485 times during its 1982–2000 run. The record-breaking *Phantom* performance was marked with a ceremony featuring a woman dressed as a cat passing a baton to the Phantom, followed by a rain of silver confetti and balloons, and a masked ball at the Waldorf-Astoria. ✸ Since its opening in 1988, *c.*11m have seen *Phantom*, generating $600m in box office sales. Other statistics for the first 7,486 shows include: 6,850 people employed; 3,038,400 pounds of dry ice used; 1,832 Kryolan TV paint sticks (No. 3W) daubed; 7,486 loaves of Italian bread eaten; and 1 mechanical elephant.

The Mousetrap, the Agatha Christie whodunit at London's St Martin's Theatre, purports to be the longest-running show of any kind in the world. Since opening in 1952, 336 actors and actresses have appeared in more than 21,000 performances of the play; 101 miles of shirts have been ironed; and at least 395 tons of ice cream have been slurped during intermissions.

TONY AWARDS · 2006

Best play.. *The History Boys*
Best musical.. *Jersey Boys*
Best original score.................................... *The Drowsy Chaperone*
Best revival of a play .... *Awake and Sing!*
Best revival of a musical .... *The Pajama Game*
Best leading actor in a play .... Richard Griffiths · *The History Boys*
Best leading actress in a play............................ Cynthia Nixon · *Rabbit Hole*
Best leading actor in a musical .... John Lloyd Young · *Jersey Boys*
Best leading actress in a musical....................... LaChanze · *The Color Purple*
Best featured actor in a play .... Ian McDiarmid · *Faith Healer*
Best featured actress in a play.............. Frances de la Tour · *The History Boys*
Best featured actor in a musical .... Christian Hoff · *Jersey Boys*
Best featured actress in a musical.............. Beth Leaval · *The Drowsy Chaperone*
Best direction of a play .... Nicholas Hytner · *The History Boys*
Best direction of a musical............................... John Doyle · *Sweeney Todd*
Best choreography .... Kathleen Marshall · *The Pajama Game*
Best orchestrations.. Sarah Travis · *Sweeney Todd*
Regional theater Tony Award........................... Intiman Theater, Seattle, WA
Special Tony Award.................................... Sarah Jones · *Bridge and Tunnel*
Special Tony Award for lifetime achievement in the theater .... Harold Prince

Due to a lack of competition, there was no 'special theatrical event' category in 2006 – however, the Tony committee gave Sarah Jones a special award for her one-woman show *Bridge & Tunnel*.

SOME CAUSES OF THEATRICAL BAD LUCK

❦ Actors and stagehands alike believe WHISTLING or CLAPPING backstage to be bad luck. This may derive from the time when sailors operated the scenery, since they were handy with knots. The sailors communicated with one another by a system of whistles and claps that, if inadvertently used by an actor, might result in scenery falling on their head. ❦ Wishing an actor GOOD LUCK is unlucky, since folklore tells that to fool evil spirits, actors should request the very opposite of what they want – hence the phrase BREAK A LEG. ❦ Never say MACBETH in a theater, since the play is associated with many tragedies and mishaps; instead call it THE SCOTTISH PLAY. If you do happen to utter *Macbeth* in a theater, there are several ways to counteract the curse: turn around three times; spit over your left shoulder; say the rudest word you can imagine (yes, that one); or speak a line from *A Midsummer Night's Dream*. ❦ WEARING GREEN is considered unwise in any theater, since green is the fairies' favorite color, and to wear it will provoke their jealousy and ire. ❦ Using a MIRROR on stage is considered taboo – possibly due to the technical difficulty of lighting mirrors, but also because of the age-old belief that mirrors can open one's soul to the devil. ❦ Some theater-hands believe in leaving a GHOST LIGHT lit when the stage is not in use. It is said that such lights keep alive the spirit of theaters. ❦

—— HASTY PUDDING MAN & WOMAN OF THE YEAR ——

Harvard University's Hasty Pudding Theatricals, America's oldest student drama troupe, presents each year a Pudding award to actors who have made a 'lasting and impressive contribution to the world of entertainment'. In 2006 the Puddings were presented to Halle Berry and Richard Gere. To celebrate, Halle Berry led a parade through the streets of Cambridge, MA. Previous recipients of the award include:

Woman of the year		*Man of the year*
Catherine Zeta-Jones	2005	Tim Robbins
Sandra Bullock	2004	Robert Downey Jr
Anjelica Huston	2003	Martin Scorsese
Sarah Jessica Parker	2002	Bruce Willis
Drew Barrymore	2001	Anthony Hopkins

Hasty pudding is a not very pleasant version of porridge, usually made with corn (recipes differ). The Harvard troupe took its curious name from the pledge made when the society was created in 1795 – 'the members in alphabetical order shall provide a pot of hasty pudding for every meeting'. Harvard has strong ties to the history of American theater: the first play written by an American was *Gustavus Vasa*, penned by Harvard grad Benjamin Colman and acted by Harvard students in 1690.

———— OBIE AWARDS · 2006 ————

A selection of the 2006 Village Voice OBIE awards, given since 1955 to 'publicly acknowledge and encourage' off-Broadway and off-off-Broadway productions:

PERFORMANCE
Reed Birney · 'sustained excellence'†
Michael Cumpsty · *Hamlet*
Christine Ebersole · *Grey Gardens*
Ari Fliakos
Poor Theater: A Series of Simulacra
Edwin Lee Gibson · *The Seven*
Peter Francis James · *Stuff Happens*
Byron Jennings · *Stuff Happens*
Marin Ireland · *Cyclone*
Dana Ivey
Mrs. Warren's Profession
Meg MacCary · *What Then*
S. Epatha Merkerson · *Birdie Blue*
Euan Morton · *Measure for Pleasure*
Sherie R. Scott · *Landscape of the Body*
Scott Shepherd
Poor Theater: A Series of Simulacra
Lois Smith · *The Trip to Bountiful*
Julie White · *The Little Dog Laughed*
Gary Wilmes · *Red Light Winter*

DIRECTION
John Clancy · 'sustained excellence'†
Daniel Sullivan · *Stuff Happens*

PLAYWRITING
Rolin Jones
The Intelligent Design of Jenny Chow
Martin McDonagh
The Lieutenant of Inishmore

SPECIAL CITATION
Hunter Bell, Michael Berresse, Jeff
Bowen · *[title of show]* [sic]
Ricky Ian Gordon, Jane Moss, Jon
Nakagawa, Doug Varone
Orpheus and Euridyce
Danai Gurira, Robert O'Hara,
Nikkole Salter · *In the Continuum*
Adam Rapp · *Red Light Winter*

† Awards are given for overall achievement

KENNEDY CENTER AWARDS · 2005

The annual Kennedy Center Honors award achievement in the performing arts:

Tony Bennett (*singer*) · Suzanne Farrell (*dancer and teacher*) · Julie Harris (*actress*)
Robert Redford (*actor, director, producer*) · Tina Turner (*singer*)

ARTS & HUMANITIES NATIONAL MEDALS · 2005

NATIONAL MEDAL OF ARTS
Paquito D'Rivera
(*jazz musician, writer*)
James DePreist (*conductor*)
Tina Ramirez (*choreographer, dancer*)
Louis Auchincloss (*author*)
Robert Duvall (*actor*)
Leonard Garment
(*arts patron & advocate*)
Ollie Johnston (*film animator, artist*)
Wynton Marsalis (*musician*)
Dolly Parton (*musician*)
Pennsylvania Academy
of the Fine Arts

NATIONAL HUMANITIES MEDAL
Walter Berns (*historian*)
Matthew Bogdanos (*US Marine Corps
Reserves Colonel, Asst District Attorney*)
Eva Brann (*philosophy professor*)
John L. Gaddis (*historian*)
Leigh & Leslie Keno
(*art historians & appraisers*)
Alan Kors (*historian*)
Judith Martin (*writer*) · Richard Gilder
& Lewis Lehrman (*history patrons*)
Mary Ann Glendon (*legal scholar*)
The Papers of George Washington
(*Univ. of VA publication project*)

NATIONAL ARTS AWARDS · 2005

The National Arts Awards, presented by Americans for the Arts, honor artistic achievement as well as 'exemplary national leadership'. On October 11, 2005, the National Endowment for the Arts was honored, in addition to the following:

Lifetime achievement award..John Baldessari
Kitty Carlisle Hart award...Mikhail Baryshnikov
Frederick R. Weisman award for philanthropy in the arts..................... Eli Broad
Arts education award............................ Pierre Dulaine and Yvonne Marceau
Young artist award for artistic excellence.............................Kerry Washington
Corporate citizenship in the arts award...Target

THURBER PRIZE FOR AMERICAN HUMOR · 2005

The annual Thurber Prize for American Humor awards the US's 'most outstanding' book of humor writing. The 2005 runners-up were Firoozeh Dumas's *Funny in Farsi: A Memoir of Growing Up Iranian in America* and Andy Borowitz's *The Borowitz Report: The Big Book of Shockers*. The winners of $5,000 (and a commemorative crystal plaque) were Jon Stewart and *The Daily Show* writers David Javerbaum and Ben Karlin for *America (The Book): A Citizen's Guide to Democracy Inaction*.

WARTIME ATTACKS ON ARCHITECTURE

In his 2006 book, *The Destruction of Memory: Architecture at War*, Robert Bevan notes that Slobodan Milosevic's trial at The Hague marked the first time an individual had been formally charged with wartime attacks on architecture. Milosevic had been accused of 'the intentional and wanton destruction of religious and cultural buildings of the Bosnian Muslim and Bosnian Croat communities'. Among the important structures damaged during the conflict were the Stari Most Bridge; the Old Town of Dubrovnik; Orthodox churches and monasteries; and Belgrade's only mosque. ❦ Milosevic's indictment at The Hague included allegations that he contravened the *Convention for the Protection of Cultural Property in the Event of Armed Conflict*. Adopted in 1954, this convention is the primary international agreement protecting art and other cultural properties in wartime. Countries that have ratified the treaty place special emblems on buildings deemed worthy of protection, which are to be preserved except in the case of 'military necessity'. Milosevic's Hague indictment noted that he ignored such symbols on buildings in Dubrovnik. Although 105 states have ratified the treaty, including France, Germany, Italy, Greece, Israel, Zimbabwe, and Iraq, America has not, placing the US in the company of North Korea and Turkmenistan.

AMERICAN INSTITUTE OF ARCHITECTS AWARDS

Gold Medal · 2006
Antoine Predock of Albuquerque won for his 'personal and place-inspired vision', which reflects the landscapes of the American Southwest. Predock's work includes the San Diego Padres stadium, buildings at Stanford and Rice universities, and the Turtle Creek House – built for bird-watchers along a prehistoric trail in Texas.

Architecture Firm Award · 2006
Moore Ruble Yudell Architects and Planners of Santa Monica, California, are noted for their 'deep commitment to humanistic architecture'. The firm concentrates on housing, mixed-use urban projects, and community planning. Key works include Berlin's Tegel Harbor, and St Matthew's Church in California.

PRITZKER ARCHITECTURE PRIZE

The international *Pritzker Architecture Prize*, founded by the Hyatt Foundation in 1979, aims to honor living architects who have created buildings that have significantly contributed to the beauty and functionality of the built environment. In 2006 the prize was awarded to the Brazilian Paulo Mendes da Rocha, whose work includes the Brazilian Sculpture Museum and renovation of the Pinacoteca do Estado. The winner receives a $100,000 prize and a tasteful bronze medallion.

Some previous Pritzker winners	
1990 . . . . Aldo Rossi [ITA]	1998 . . . . Renzo Piano [ITA]
1991 . . . . Robert Venturi [USA]	1999 . . . . Sir Norman Foster [UK]
	2004 . . . . Zaha Hadid [UK]

———————————— A DANCING GENE (?) ————————————

Research published in the September 2005 issue of *Public Library of Science Genetics* suggested that genetics may in part explain why some are more interested in dance than others. Researchers examined three groups: current performing dancers and advanced dancing students, competitive athletes, and those who were neither dancers nor athletes. Researchers found that dancers were much more likely to carry variants of the genes AVPR1a and SLC6A4. Animal studies have shown that AVPR1a may influence social communication and bonding, and SLC6A4 regulates the level of the neurotransmitter serotonin, which has been linked to the experience of spirituality. A further personality questionnaire indicated that dancers tended to be more spiritual, with a greater need for social contact. The researchers concluded that as a 'type', dancers tend to have a 'heightened sense of communication, often of a symbolic and ceremonial nature, and a strong spiritual personality trait'. A fondness for tulle is not thought to be genetically determined.

——————— USA INTERNATIONAL BALLET COMPETITION ———————

The USA International Ballet Competition has been held every 4 years in Jackson, Mississippi, since 1979. The 2-week 'Olympic style' competition confers medals, awards, scholarships, and (often) contracts on contestants. Some 2006 winners:

Daniil Simkin (Germany) .... Men's Gold Medal (senior division)
Misa Kuranaga (Japan)........................... Women's Gold Medal (senior division)
Isaac Hernandez (Mexico)........................... Men's Gold Medal (junior division)
Denys Cherevychko (Ukraine) .... Men's Silver Medal (junior division)

——————— 'DANCE MAGAZINE' AWARDS · 2005 ———————

Dance Magazine's 2005 awards honored individuals from across the dance world:

Clive Barnes..*respected dance and theater critic*
Alessandra Ferri .... *ballerina with the American Ballet Theater, noted for her expressivity*
Donald McKayle............... *modern dance choreographer known for African American themes*
Jimmy Slyde..................................... *tap-dancing legend, called the 'King of Slides'*
Christopher Wheeldon .... *New York City Ballet choreographer with more than 30 works*

——————— CAPEZIO DANCE AWARD · 2006 ———————

Donald Saddler was the recipient of the 55th Capezio Dance Award, presented since 1952 by the Capezio Ballet Makers Dance Foundation. The award is given in celebration of those who bring 'respect, stature, and distinction to dance'. Saddler's work as dancer and choreographer spans ballet, theater, and opera, and has included 2 Tony Awards (for *Wonderful Town* in 1953, and *No, No Nanette* in 1971). He received his $10,000 honorarium at the Pierre Hotel in New York in June 2006.

———————————HOUSE DESIGNERS———————————

Aquascutum..............Michael Hertz	*Gucci* .... Frida Giannini
Burberry ....Christopher Bailey	*Lanvin*......................Alber Elbaz
Balenciaga .... Nicolas Ghesquière	*Louis Vuitton* .... Marc Jacobs
Chanel..................Karl Lagerfeld	*Marni*........... Consuelo Castiglioni
Christian Dior..........John Galliano	*Missoni* .... Angela Missoni
Fendi.....................Karl Lagerfeld	*Prada* ....Miuccia Prada
Givenchy.................Riccardo Tisci	*Yves Saint Laurent*.......Stefano Pilati

———————————CFDA AWARDS · 2006———————————

The Council of Fashion Designers of America Awards were presented on June 5, 2006. Winners received a specially designed arch studded with Swarovski crystals.

Womenswear designer of the year....................Francisco Costa for Calvin Klein
Menswear designer of the year...Thom Browne
Accessory designer of the year...Tom Binns
Swarovski's Perry Ellis award, emerging talent womenswear...........Doo-Ri Chung
Swarovski's Perry Ellis award, emerging talent menswear.................Jeff Halmos,
               Josia Lamberto-Egan, Sam Shipley, and John Whitledge for Trovata
Swarovski's Perry Ellis award, emerging talent accessory design ....Devi Kroell
Lifetime achievement award..Stan Herman
International award ....Olivier Theyskens for Rochas
Eugenia Sheppard award for fashion journalism..........................Bruce Weber
Eleanor Lambert award ....Joan Kaner
Board of Directors' special tribute ....Stephen Burrows

According to the Bureau of Labor Statistics, in 2004 the average 'consumer unit' (resource-sharing household or independent individual) spent $1,816 on apparel and related services (dry cleaning, &c.).

—ACCESSORIES COUNCIL EXCELLENCE AWARDS · 2005—

The US Accessories Council awards those who have raised 'awareness of the accessories industry' and stimulated the purchase of accessories in the past year.

Hall of fame.. Kenneth Cole
Lifetime achievement.. Betsey Johnson
Marylou Luther Award for fashion journalism ......Teri Agins · *Wall Street Journal*
Retailer of the year... NeimanMarcus.com
Accessory brand launch...Juicy Couture
Magazine of the year...*InStyle*
Designer of the year... Oscar de la Renta
Fashion icon...Jessica Simpson
Fashion influencer .... Sean 'Diddy' Combs [see p.141]
Accessories Council excellence award ....Mary-Kate & Ashley Olsen

COLOR FORECAST · 2006–07

Color forecasts for 2006–07 indicate that reds and blues will continue to dominate. According to the Color Marketing Group, red shades are both 'cooling down' and 'warming up', while blues 'inspired by spa influences and ocean hues' will likely color everything from paint to cushions. The raspberry-hued 'Rubino' was said to be an important newcomer, while the rich 'Marrakesh Red' was the best-selling consumer red of 2005–06. Below, some of the colors forecasted to be hot in 2006–07:

Benjamin Moore & Co. · *'soft heathery hues' such as Pale Sea Mist · 'organic and radiant' shades like Pumpkin Patch · 'sensuous and sultry' Stone Brown and Currant Red*

Color Marketing Group · *Trench Coat ('reminiscent of tumbled stones') · Creamy Hollandaise · Franciscan Fog ('mysterious') · Beep-Beep ('vivid yellow') · Blue Bling*

Pantone Color Inst. Fashion Forecast
'the constancy of nightfall', in shades like Purple Magic · Apple Cinnamon ('the essence of freshly brewed tea') Frost Gray ('a quiet winter morning')

Lee Eiseman, Pantone Consultant
'bright, juicy' oranges and apricots … 'shades of earth, wood, grass, and patina blue' … 'pink lemonade, cool aqua, and buttery yellow'

Color Association of the US
'new-trals' and 'metallic-inspired hues like Pewter and Bronze' · the 'wistful nostalgia' of 'purpled browns' and 'sepia tones' such as Ashes, Foundation, and Victoriana · floral pinks & reds

Pantone Color Inst. Home Forecast
High Risk Red · Purple Passion · Mineral Yellow Champagne Beige · Frosted Almond · Antelope

[Sources: MSN Lifestyle; Benjamin Moore & Co.; Graphic Design USA]

READY-TO-WEAR FASHION WEEKS

NEW YORK
February & September
olympusfashionweek.com
Who shows: *Ralph Lauren, Zac Posen, Marc Jacobs, Diane von Furstenberg, Calvin Klein, Oscar de la Renta, Michael Kors, Donna Karan*

MILAN
February & September/October
cameramoda.it
Who shows: *Gucci, Armani, Prada, Dolce & Gabbana, Moschino, Versace, Roberto Cavalli, Max Mara Burberry Prorsum, Fendi*

LONDON
February & September
londonfashionweek.co.uk
Who shows: *Aquascutum, Ben de Lisi, Paul Smith Women, Nicole Farhi, Clements Ribeiro, Betty Jackson, Margaret Howell, Ghost*

PARIS
February/March & October
modeaparis.com
Who shows: *Stella McCartney, Chanel, Vivienne Westwood, Jean Paul Gaultier, John Galliano, Issey Miyake, Christian Dior, Chloé, Lanvin*

According to *Style.com* the key trends for Fall 2006 include the following: The Bubble – voluminous skirts; fur (especially on coats); metallics, lamés, and brocades; oversize slouchy trousers and coats; layering (with dresses and skirts worn over pants or leggings); Napoleonic and militaristic details.

Sci, Tech, Net

Technology, sufficiently advanced, is indistinguishable from magic.
— ARTHUR C. CLARKE

TAMIFLU · OSELTAMIVIR PHOSPHATE

Tamiflu is the proprietary name for *oseltamivir phosphate* – an oral antiviral treatment for influenza, designed to prevent flu viruses from replicating within the body (it is neither a vaccine nor a substitute for one). A neuraminidase inhibitor (NAI), Tamiflu targets neuraminidase – the enzyme found on the surface of flu viruses – and hinders the virus from traveling cell to cell to spread the infection. The drug can be used both for prevention and treatment of flu, though for full efficacy, the manufacturers recommend taking Tamiflu within 48 hours of the onset of flu symptoms. The adult dose is one oral 75mg capsule taken twice a day for 5 days. ❦ Tamiflu is one of two main drugs thought to be effective against avian flu H5N1 [see p.19] – the other drug, *zanamivir*, less conveniently, has to be inhaled. ❦ The drug company Roche acquired the rights to manufacture and distribute Tamiflu from Gilead Sciences in 1996, and the drug's patent expires in 2016[†]. ❦ As the threat of an H5N1 pandemic grew [see p.19], demand for Tamiflu threatened to outstrip supply. Real and counterfeit supplies of the drug flooded the web (Tamiflu-related spam became rife), and in December 2005 eBay halted a British auction where a 10-capsule course reached >£100.

Under political pressure from governments worldwide[†] (and market pressure to maximize profits), Roche took steps to increase production. One of the issues affecting Tamiflu's supply is the complexity of its manufacture: the 10-step process takes 6–8 months, and currently starts with the extraction of shikimic acid from star anise pods grown in the Guanxi, Sichuan, Yunnan, and Guizhou mountain provinces of SW China. In March 2006, Roche pledged to manufacture *c.*400m treatments annually by the end of the year, using 15 external contractors in 9 countries. Roche claim to have fulfilled Tamiflu 'pandemic orders' from >65 countries, with some governments stockpiling treatments for 20–40% of their population. Roche has also donated 5·125m courses of Tamiflu to the WHO for rapid response in flu-hit areas. ❦ While some reports have questioned the effectiveness of *oseltamivir* for bird flu, Tamiflu remains the drug of choice. Roche announced a 22% growth in sales during the first 3 months of 2006, to 7·7bn Swiss Francs ($6bn; £3·4bn).

† Patents for new drugs allow the creators a 20-year monopoly of supply. However, international law permits governments to break patents, and 'compulsory license' generic versions in the event of severe national health emergencies.

—————— NOBEL PRIZES IN SCIENCE · 2005 ——————

THE NOBEL PRIZE IN PHYSICS

One half to Roy J. Glauber, *Harvard*

'for his contribution to the quantum
theory of optical coherence'

one half jointly to John L. Hall
JILA, University of Colorado & NIST
Theodor W. Hänsch
*Max-Planck-Institut & Ludwig-
Maximilians-Universität, Munich*

'for their contributions to the
development of laser-based precision
spectroscopy, including the optical
frequency comb technique'

Glauber's work into how quantum
theory relates to the field of optics
led him to establish the principles of
Quantum Optics. This allowed him
to explore the fundamental differences in frequency and phase between
sources of light – for example lasers
and lightbulbs. Hall and Hänsch built
on Glauber's work to develop laser-
based precision spectroscopy, encom-
passing the optical frequency comb
technique. This allows the quantum
structure of matter to be determined
with greater accuracy, facilitating the
creation of technologies such as ultra-
accurate clocks and improved Global
Positioning Systems.

THE NOBEL PRIZE IN CHEMISTRY

Yves Chauvin
Institut Français du Pétrole, France
Robert H. Grubbs
Caltech, USA
Richard R. Schrock
Massachusetts Institute of Technology

'for the development of the metathesis
method in organic synthesis'

Chauvin, Grubbs, and Schrock each
contributed to the development of
'metathesis reactions'. These reactions
occur in organic substances and cause
the double bonds between carbon
atoms to break, thereby allowing atom
groups to change places. Metathesis
is now widely used by the chemical
industry to make synthesis methods
easier, more environmentally friendly,
and efficient.

THE NOBEL PRIZE IN PHYSIOLOGY OR MEDICINE

Barry J. Marshall
Australia
J. Robin Warren
Australia

'for the discovery of the bacterium
Helicobacter pylori and its role in
gastritis and peptic ulcer disease'

Marshall and Warren's research challenged the established scientific view
that peptic ulcers and gastritis were
caused by lifestyle or stress. Through
careful observation of ulcer patients,
they discovered the bacterium
Helicobacter pylori was the cause of most
types of ulcers. Marshall even went so
far as to infect himself with bacteria in
order to prove the theory and monitor
the curative effects of antibiotics.

It is an oft-repeated myth that no Nobel Prize in mathematics exists because Alfred Nobel's wife had
an affair with a mathematician. However, Nobel was unmarried and there seems to be no evidence
of any similar scandal. Nobel may have been discouraged by the existence of a math prize created by
Oscar II, King of Sweden and Norway, or simply by the fact that he wasn't overfond of the subject.

— MATHEMATICS · THE ABEL PRIZE & FIELDS MEDAL —

The Abel Prize was created in memory of Norwegian mathematician Niels Henrik Abel (1802–29) who is famous for proving that the general quintic equation is unsolvable algebraically. In 2006 the Abel was awarded to Lennart Carleson for his 'profound and seminal contributions to harmonic analysis and the theory of smooth dynamical systems'. The Fields Medal is awarded every 4 years at the International Congress of Mathematicians to recognise past achievements in mathematics and future promise. In 2006, Medals were presented to Andrei Okounkov, Terence Tao, and Wendelin Werner. Notably, the reclusive Russian 'genius' Grigori Perelman was offered a Fields Medal for his proof of the Poincaré Conjecture, but turned down the award, lamenting that he had become disillusioned with mathematics. It was unclear whether Perelman would accept a separate $1m prize for his proof.

——————————— IG NOBEL PRIZE ———————————

Ig Nobel prizes are awarded for scientific 'achievements that cannot or should not be reproduced.' In 2005 the esteemed honours were presented to the following:

PHYSICS · John Mainstone and Thomas Parnell (University of Queensland, Australia) *for conducting a very long-term experiment that began in 1927, in which a blob of black tar drips through a funnel, at the rate of approximately one drop every nine years.*

MEDICINE · Gregg A. Miller (Oak Grove, Missouri) *for the invention of 'neuticles' – artificial testicles for dogs who have lost their own.*

CHEMISTRY · Edward Cussler and Brian Gettelfinger (University of Minnesota) *for their tireless investigation into whether people swim faster in syrup or in water.*

BIOLOGY · Benjamin Smith, Michael Tyler, Brian Williams (University of Adelaide &c), Craig Williams (James Cook University), Yoji Hayasaka (Australian Wine Research Institute) *for their work smelling and compiling the different odors produced by 131 species of frogs while stressed.*

FLUID DYNAMICS · Victor Benno Meyer-Rochow (International University, Bremen) and Jozsef Gal (Loránd Eötvös University, Hungary) *for their seminal paper 'Pressures Produced when Penguins Pooh* [sic] *– Calculations on Avian Defaecation'.*

[Source: www.improb.com/ig/ig-top.html]

——————————— DARWIN AWARDS ———————————

The annual Darwin Awards '*salute the improvement of the human genome by honoring those who accidentally kill themselves in really stupid ways*'. In 2005, the dubious honour went to 'Marko', a 55-year-old Croatian man who wanted to clean his chimney but lacked a broom long enough for the job. He improvised a makeshift device by attaching a brush to a chain and, requiring a heavy object to weigh it down, chose a hand grenade, which exploded when he tried to weld it in place.

—NATIONAL MEDALS FOR SCIENCE & TECHNOLOGY—

President Bush presented the National Medal of Science and the National Medal of Technology (both for 2004) at the White House on February 13, 2006. The Medal of Science, given for pioneering scientific research, is administered by the National Science Foundation, while the Commerce Department administers the Medal of Technology to honor 'individuals who embody the spirit of American innovation'.

Medal of Science	*Medal of Technology*
KENNETH J. ARROW (Stanford University) *For contribution to economics*	RALPH H. BAER (engineering consultant, Manchester, NH) *For work developing and commercializing interactive video games*
NORMAN E. BORLAUG (Texas A&M University) · *For work on wheat breeding and cultivation education*	ROGER L. EASTON (founder of RoBarCo in Canaan, NH) *For achievements leading to the development of the NAVSTAR Global Positioning System*
ROBERT N. CLAYTON (University of Chicago) · *For work on the evolution of the solar system*	
EDWIN N. LIGHTFOOT (University of Wisconsin) · *For research in how the body controls insulin levels and oxygenates blood*	GEN-PROBE INC. (San Diego, CA) · *For work on new blood-testing technologies and systems for the direct detection of viral infections*
STEPHEN J. LIPPARD (Massachusetts Institute of Technology) *For research in bioinorganic chemistry*	IBM MICROELECTRONICS DIVISION (Armonk, NY) · *For innovation in semiconductor technology*
PHILLIP A. SHARP (MIT) · *For genetic research, including work on split genes*	INDUSTRIAL LIGHT AND MAGIC (San Francisco, CA) · *For innovation in visual effects technology for the motion picture industry*
THOMAS E. STARZL (University of Pittsburgh School of Medicine) *For work in liver transplantation*	MOTOROLA INC. (Schaumburg, IL) *For work in mobile communications*
DENNIS P. SULLIVAN (City University of New York Graduate Center and State University of NY) · *For his work in mathematics, including the creation of new fields*	PACCAR INC. (Bellevue, WA) *For pioneering work in the development and commercialization of aerodynamic, lightweight trucks*

—CONGRESSIONAL SPACE MEDAL OF HONOR—

Former astronaut Robert L. Crippen was awarded the Congressional Space Medal of Honor on April 26, 2006, for his work as the pilot of the first-ever space shuttle mission, STS-1 (*Columbia*) in 1981. Crippen spent 2 days in flight (36 orbits) testing the shuttle's systems before landing safely in California. Congress created the medal in 1969 to recognize '*any astronaut who in the performance of his duties has distinguished himself or herself by exceptionally meritorious efforts and contributions to the welfare of the nation and mankind.*' It was first presented in 1978 to 6 astronauts, including Neil Armstrong; 28 astronauts have since received the medal.

WOO SUK HWANG

In January 2006, an investigation by Seoul National University revealed that the celebrated South Korean scientist Dr Woo Suk Hwang had faked data on human cloning. The announcement was deeply embarrassing to the scientific community – tarnishing the integrity of published research and setting back fellow researchers working on cloning technology. Things started to go wrong for Hwang in November 2005, when he was forced to admit that female researchers from his team had supplied their own eggs for use in his research. Further questions from collaborators about his methods led to a full investigation. ❦ Hwang's groundbreaking work rested on two papers published in the prestigious journal *Science*. The first, published in February 2004, claimed that Hwang's team had created the world's first cloned human embryos. The second, in May 2005, went one step further, reporting that he had created 11 stem cell lines tailored to individual patients. Such therapeutic cloning has the potential to provide new treatments for diseases like Parkinson's and diabetes. Since others had based their research on the techniques described by Hwang, the news that his results were falsified left many scientists with no working blueprint. ❦ Hwang's fall from grace was spectacular: he had been treated like a superstar in South Korea; granted the title of 'Supreme Scientist' by the government; given large sums of money to fund his research; and gifted as many free first-class flights on Korean Air as he desired. Despite his public disgrace, Hwang claimed that the fabrications were carried out without his knowledge. He nevertheless stated that he could not lift his head for shame and added, 'The use of fake data … is what I have to take full responsibility for as first author. I acknowledge all of that and apologize once again'. (Hwang's only comfort was the confirmation that his Afghan hound Snuppy was indeed the world's first cloned dog.) ❦ In March 2006, Hwang was sacked from his professorship at Seoul National University. At the time of writing, Hwang was on trial in South Korea for fraud and embezzlement.

BREAKTHROUGHS OF THE YEAR · 2005

Science magazine's prestigious list of the major scientific breakthroughs of 2005:

Evolution in Action......... *genome sequencing advanced understanding of evolution*
Planetary Blitz............*a plethora of space explorations shed new light on the galaxy*
Blooming Marvelous.... *new discoveries into genes that control the flowering of plants*
Neutron Stars ....*advances in technology gave more information on neutron stars*
Miswiring the Brain .... *research into genes produced links to brain disorders*
Geochemical Turmoil.... *isotopes revealed the formation of Earth was not as supposed*
Protein Portrait...... *model of nerve & muscle protein revealed its molecular structure*
Change in Climate......... *further evidence for human influence on global warming*
Systems Biology Signals Its Arrival ....*new methods for understanding cell signals*
ITER .... *International Thermonuclear Experimental Reactor to be built in France*

—— SOME NOTABLE SCIENTIFIC RESEARCH · 2005–06 ——

{OCT 2005} · Scientists at the University of Tasmania found that eating chilies can help people to sleep better and feel more alert the next day. ❦ A study in the *Lancet* reported that those in their late 40s and early 50s can cut their risk of Alzheimer's by *c.*50% by exercising twice a week. {NOV} · Research in the *Lancet* suggested that the 'hip-to-waist ratio' gave a better indication of the risks of heart attack than weight or Body Mass Index. (Those with a 'beer belly' are most at risk.) ❦ The Common Cold Centre in Wales tested the belief that exposure to cold temperatures increases the risk of developing a cold. 90 volunteers immersed their feet in cold water; 90 did not. Over the next few days, >⅓ of those whose feet were chilled developed cold symptoms. ❦ A study in *Neurology* suggested that those with high levels of education or intellectually challenging jobs had an increased risk of developing Parkinson's. {DEC} · Research in the *Proceedings of the National Academy of Science* showed that patients were able to exercise some control over their chronic pain by watching images of their brain's 'pain centers'. {JAN 2006} After years of trial and error, the world's first hydroponically grown rice crop was harvested from a Tokyo bank vault. Hydroponics (growing crops in nutrient solution) could allow for four rice crops a year (rather than one), unaffected by adverse weather. ❦ Scientists at the Max Planck Institute for Nuclear Physics shocked climate-change researchers by suggesting that plants contribute to global warming, since they emit *c.*⅓ of the methane entering the atmosphere. ❦ A study in *Science* suggested that humans have an innate sense of geom-

etry. The researchers discovered that the Munduruku Indians (members of a remote Amazonian tribe) had a natural understanding of basic geometrical images they were shown, even though geometry is absent from their culture. {FEB} · Roger Pitman, a psychiatrist at Harvard University, suggested that giving trauma victims the beta-blocker Propranolol for 10 days after the incident reduced the symptoms of post-traumatic stress disorder. ❦ A British study proposed that forensic scientists might predict a criminal's surname through a DNA sample. Since the Y chromosome is passed down the male line as surnames are, a large enough database of names and DNA could provide police with a possible surname of their suspect. ❦ A study of Romanian orphans found that children who grow up in deprived conditions suffer from impaired growth and lower IQs. {MAR} · A trial began in the Black Mountains of Wales to harvest daffodils grown at high altitude; it was suggested that these plants may contain high levels of galantamine, which has been used in the treatment of Alzheimer's disease. ❦ Paleontologist Dr Neil Clark proposed that sightings of Scotland's mythical Loch Ness Monster were in fact circus elephants bathing in the Loch, leaving only their trunks, the humps of their heads, and their backs on show. ❦ Scientists at MIT and Hong Kong University used nanotechnology to restore the sight of hamsters. The teams cut the optic nerves of the animals, before injecting nanopeptides that formed a bridge of nanofibers to re-connect the severed nerve. ❦ Research presented to the American College of Cardiology

– SOME NOTABLE SCIENTIFIC RESEARCH · 2005–06 cont. –

indicated that a new statin drug, rosu-vastatin, might break down the fatty deposits in arteries that cause heart disease. ❦ A study by researchers at the University of Zurich suggested that phobias may be managed by taking the stress hormone cortisol. ❦ Trials at the University of Edinburgh indicated the success of a new contraceptive pill based on a low dose of RU486 (a drug used in abortions); it was suggested the pill may also protect against breast cancer. {APR} · The *Lancet* published the results of a successful American trial in which seven patients had new bladders, grown from their own cells, transplanted back into their bodies. ❦ A team of researchers at Massachussets General Hospital developed a free-electron laser (FEL) that can target and melt fat under the skin. The FEL could provide treatment for arterial heart disease, cellulite, acne, &c. {MAY} · Researchers from Tufts University in Boston studied the 'gender bending' effects of bisphenol A – an estrogen-mimicking chemical used to make polycarbonate plastics such as bottles and food containers. A mice study by the US Centers for Disease Control and Prevention suggested that bisphenol A 'masculinizes' the brains of female mice. ❦ A study showed that Nigerian putty-nosed monkeys were able to put together a number of sounds to construct a primitive sentence, an ability previously thought to be uniquely human. ❦ Research at the University of Toronto suggested that caffeine may cut the time premature babies spend on ventilators, and protect them from lung diseases. ❦ A study at St Andrew's University, Scotland, suggested that girls from broken homes grow up to be less physically attractive. The research-ers assessed the bodies and faces of 229 women, and found that those from unhappy homes looked more mascu-line. {JUN} · Scientists at Guy's and St Thomas' Hospital, London, devel-oped a new technique – pre-implanta-tion genetic haplotyping (PGH) – that allows more accurate screening of embryos for genetic diseases. ❦ A team from Ohio State University Medical Center presented results of a study into alleviating migraines to the American Headache Society. The research showed that patients using an elec-tronic device that emits a magnetic pulse to the brain reported significant improvements to their condition. ❦ Research by Anthony Bogaert at Brock University, Canada, indicated that men with a biological older brother were 30% more likely to be homosexual. {JUL} · *The Journal of Investigative Dermatology* published the results of an Australian trial of a drug that creates an instant tan. The study indicated the drug may protect against skin cancer, however 30 injections were required to achieve a noticeable tan, and some recipients complained of nausea. {AUG} · Researchers in Singapore suggested that the elderly can boost their brain power by eating turmeric-rich curries. ❦ A study from the University of Buffalo warned that the drug methamphetamine ('crystal meth') appeared to increase the spread of HIV in those already infected. ❦ Scientists in Japan and Hawaii reported in the *Proceedings of the National Academy of Sciences* that they had used IVF to produce healthy pups from the sperm of mice that had died and been frozen 15 years previously.

———————————— DANGEROUS IDEAS ————————————

Each year since 1998, the online magazine edge.org has invited notable scientists and intellectuals to answer one probing question, usually with fascinating results. The 2006 question was, '*What is your dangerous idea? An idea you think about (not necessarily one you originated) that is dangerous not because it is assumed to be false, but because it might be true?*' Below is a small selection from the 119 answers provided:

Everything is pointless · Susan Blackmore (psychologist & skeptic)
Retribution as a moral principle is incompatible with a scientific view of human behavior · Richard Dawkins (evolutionary biologist)
The fight against global warming is lost · Paul Davies (physicist)
The human brain and its products are incapable of understanding the truths about the universe · Karl Sabbagh (writer & TV producer)
Groups of people may differ genetically in their average talents and temperaments · Steven Pinker (psychologist)

———————— NASA'S CENTENNIAL CHALLENGES ————————

NASA has established a series of cash prizes called 'Centennial Challenges', to encourage innovation in areas of technical development that would benefit both space exploration and NASA. The first four Centennial Challenges to be issued are:

Challenge	prize
Design a powerful tether for a space elevator	$50,000
Create a robot that can climb a cable in space while carrying a load	$50,000
Extract breathable oxygen from lunar soil	$250,000
Develop space gloves to maximize movement but maintain protection	$25,000

———————————— ANIMAL 'EXTREMISTS' ————————————

In response to an escalation in criminal incidents, the FBI has classified the 'animal rights' movement as the greatest domestic terrorist threat in the USA. Figures released in February 2006 by the Foundation for Biomedical Research, an organization working to promote understanding for humane and responsible animal research, showed that over the last 25 years criminal activities against medical research have greatly increased. Vandalism saw the greatest increase, with 189 cases in the last five years, compared to just 49 incidents in the preceding twenty years. The following table illustrates the illegal 'animal rights' incidents that have occurred in the US:

	1985	1990	1995	2000	2005	*total* (1981–2005)
Arson	0	0	0	7	2	53
Theft	2	4	0	5	11	123
Bombing	0	0	0	6	7	36
Vandalism	3	0	3	8	48	238
Harassment	2	1	0	2	14	79

─────── SOME INVENTIONS OF NOTE · 2005–06 ───────

{OCT} · Nicholas Negroponte of MIT designed a cheap laptop (*c.*$100) that he hopes will appeal to the 3rd World. The laptop can be powered by a hand crank, includes wireless connectivity, and is encased in indestructible rubber. ❦ Stephen Salter, an engineer at Edinburgh University, proposed a system to reduce global warming: a fleet of yachts that spray water droplets into the sky, increasing the whiteness of low-lying clouds that reflect more heat back into space. ❦ Japanese company Denso is developing an in-car system to stop drivers falling asleep at the wheel. The device monitors the blink rate of drivers and makes a bleeping noise to wake them up should they doze off. {NOV} · Canon of Japan developed a high-resolution ink-jet printer that can print hard copies of images directly from a flat-screen TV. {DEC} · Nissan invented a self-repairing paint for cars. The paint is blended with an elastic resin that, when warmed by the sun, expands to cover small scratches. {JAN 2006} · Elmo-Tech developed an automated home-curfew system using voice-recognition. Offenders are phoned at home and prove their identity and whereabouts by repeating a series of set phrases. ❦ Plastic Logic has developed a 10" flexible screen that, when plugged into a hand-held device, re-creates the resolution of a computer monitor. The screen (which can be rolled up) has a number of applications – not least in the future of e-books. {FEB} · Kurita Water Industries of Japan developed a fuel cell that can power a cellphone for days on a small drop of methanol. {MAR} · Researchers at Boston's MIT Media Lab created a WiFi wine glass that glows when an absent partner takes a sip, allowing long-distance lovers to share a drink. ❦ A prototype eco-friendly cellphone has been unveiled. The phone has a biodegradable cover that contains a sunflower seed; when discarded, the phone will break down organically and produce a plant. {APR} · Menssana Research has developed a breath analyzer that

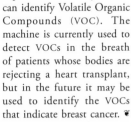

can identify Volatile Organic Compounds (VOC). The machine is currently used to detect VOCs in the breath of patients whose bodies are rejecting a heart transplant, but in the future it may be used to identify the VOCs that indicate breast cancer. ❦ Scientists at the University of Southern California are developing a new wafer-thin material that creates a bright white light when plugged in to an electricity supply. The organic light-emitting diode (OLED) is more energy efficient than standard lightbulbs and gives off a pleasing natural light. {MAY} · US defense researchers have patented a device inspired by circus 'human cannonballs'. The machine uses compressed air to propel firefighters or special forces to the top of a 5-story building in just a few seconds. {JUN} · Japanese company Lofty has developed a pillow (the 'Sleep Doctor') that uses sensors to measure body movements and judge the quality of sleep. To aid sleep, the pillow offers helpful suggestions and encouragement, such as: '*You've been sleeping great! Keep it up!*'. {AUG} · Zenph Studios, NC, have developed software that allows old audio recordings to be programmed into a computerized grand piano, thereby allowing modern audiences to hear 'live' performances from deceased virtuosos like Rachmaninov.

HABSTARS

At the 2006 meeting of the American Association for the Advancement of Science, astronomer Margaret Turnbull of the Carnegie Institution in Washington, DC, proposed a list of 'habstars' (stars most likely to have habitable zones). Turnbull analyzed a number of criteria, such as the age of the star (it should be over 3bn years old to allow complex life to develop), and the amount of iron in its atmosphere (stars need at least 50% of the iron content of our Sun for planets to form). From over 17,000 habitable stellar systems, Turnbull advised that those seeking radio signals from intelligent life should focus their efforts on the following 5 habstars:

Beta CVn....................*part of constellation Canes Venatici, 26 light-years away*
HD 10307 ....*similar mass, temperature, and iron content to the Sun*
HD 211415........................ *cooler than the sun with 50% of its metal content*
18 Sco .... *part of constellation Scorpio; very similar in form to the Sun*
51 Pegasus......*planet similar to Jupiter orbits the star; terrestrial planets a possibility*

PLANETARY EVENTS · 2007

January 3......................Perihelion: Earth is at orbital position closest to Sun
February 10 ....Saturn at opposition (closest approach to Earth)
March 3 .... total lunar eclipse
March 19..partial solar eclipse
March 21............. Equinox: Sun passes northward over equator at 0007 GMT
June 6 ....Jupiter at opposition
June 21 ....Solstice: Sun directly above Tropic of Cancer at 1806 GMT
July 7 ....Aphelion: Earth is at orbital position farthest from Sun
August 13 ....Neptune at opposition
August 28 .... total lunar eclipse
September 9...Uranus at opposition
September 11 ....partial solar eclipse
September 23 .... Equinox: Sun passes southward over equator at 0951 GMT
December 22......Solstice: Sun directly above Tropic of Capricorn at 0608 GMT
December 24..Mars at opposition

NASA'S SPACE SHUTTLES

Shuttle	operational	years operational	crew carried	no. flights
Atlantis	Y	1985–	167	27
Challenger	N	1983–86	60	10
Columbia	N	1981–2003	160	28
Discovery	Y	1984–	191	31
Endeavour [sic]	Y	1992–	130	19

The first commercial space flight in 2004 by SpaceShipOne hinted at the future of space tourism. *Virgin Galactic* is now taking bookings for a planned 2008 space flight; tickets cost $200,000.

——————————KEY SPACE MISSIONS OF 2006——————————

MARS RECONNAISSANCE ORBITER (MRO) · NASA's MRO arrived at Mars on March 10, 2006, and spent the first phase of its mission 'aerobraking' to gain the correct orbit to enable it to collect data. The mission's objective is to investigate the history of water on the planet, and discover if it was present long enough to have sustained life.

STARDUST · On January 15, 2006, after a 7-year mission, the NASA probe Stardust delivered dust samples from the comet Wild-2 to Earth. Scientists hope that the interstellar dust collected from the tail of the comet might provide insights into the formation of the universe which, like Wild-2, is 4·6bn years old. The samples of dust are currently being investigated by *c.*150 scientists across the globe.

VENUS EXPRESS · A European Space Agency (ESA) probe, launched in November 2005, reached Venus in April 2006. Since then, the probe has sent back to Earth groundbreaking images that show a huge 'double-eye' atmospheric vortex over Venus's south pole. It is hoped that further infrared images of the vortex will reveal more about its structure.

CASSINI-HUYGENS · A joint ESA and NASA effort to study Saturn and its moons. In 2006, Cassini sent back radar images that revealed that the areas once thought to be oceans on Saturn's moon Titan were, in fact, large sand dunes. Data from the mission also suggested that Enceladus (another of Saturn's moons) may have a liquid ocean under a layer of ice. Geysers of water were observed erupting from the Moon's polar region, implying the Moon may be geologically active.

NEW HORIZONS · A NASA mission launched on January 19, 2006, with the aim of being the first to reach Pluto and its moon Charon. The probe (which is roughly the size of a piano) is expected to reach its final destination by 2015.

DISCOVERY · In July 2006, *Discovery* undertook a 13-day mission during which the crew tested new shuttle safety features and repaired a rail car on the International Space Station. Throughout the flight a number of high-resolution photos of the shuttle were taken, which provided the ground crew with proof that no major damage had occurred during its voyage.

——————————THE PUZZLE OF RED RAIN——————————

In January 2006, Godfrey Louis of Mahatma Gandhi University published a paper in *Astrophysics and Space Science*, which suggested that the mysterious red rain which fell over Kerala, India, for a number of weeks in 2001 may have had an extraterrestrial origin. Louis saw no natural explanation for the 'striking' red rain – samples of which were found to contain cell-like structures with no traces of DNA. Further analysis of the cells was undertaken at Cardiff University by Chandra Wickramasinghe, an expert in 'panspermia' – the theory that life on Earth came from primitive cells carried by comets. Wickramasinghe's research indicated that the red rain cells did in fact contain very simple DNA and might, therefore, be of terrestrial origin. Investigation continues into the origin of the Kerala downpour.

————— SCI, TECH, NET WORDS OF NOTE —————

RINGXIETY *or* FAUXCELLARM ·
[1] the false sensation of hearing a
cellphone ring or feeling one vibrate.
The phenomenon, akin to 'phantom
limbs' felt by amputees, is exacerbated
by adverts that use ringtones to jog
listeners' attention; [2] when a group of
people scramble for their cellphones on
hearing a ringtone. *Also* RAINXIETY ·
the stress of driving in driving rain.

SPIM · instant messaging spam.

BLACKBERRY THUMB · the repetitive
strain injury caused by excessive use of
a PDA. *Also* GAMEBOY PALM.

VIRAL VIDEO · a video clip that is
passed around by email. They feature on
websites like *youtube.com* and are said
to form part of the CLIP CULTURE.

15 MEGS OF FAME · internet equivalent
of Andy Warhol's 15 minutes of fame.

PIGGYBACKING · 'stealing' WiFi access
from unsecured wireless networks.

CYBERCHONDRIACS · people who use
the internet to self-diagnose illnesses.

MASHUP · websites or web applications
that mix content from two or more
sources to create new services, e.g.
Gawker Stalker [see p.123].

HTM · internet material that is deemed
Harmful to Minors.

PROOF-OF-CONCEPT BUGS · viruses
created to demonstrate flaws in an
operating system that have not (yet)
been released 'INTO THE WILD'.

VAMPIRE LOAD · 'always on' features
(like TV 'standby') that suck energy.

SLIVERCAST *or* NARROWCAST ·
directing media messages to a specific
audience. *Also* SILVERCAST · directing
media messages to retired people.

NERD BIRDS · airplanes on routes
that connect high-tech capitals, such
as Silicon Valley (San José, CA) and
Silicon Forest (Seattle). Such planes
have become networking magnets for
executives in high-tech companies.

RING-BACK TONES · where telephone
callers hear as the ringing tone sounds
(music, special effects, &c.) selected by
the party they are calling.

REBAY · to sell unloved gifts on eBay.

VIRTUAL VISITATION · long-distance
access to a child by a divorced parent
using webcams, VOIP, IM, &c.

DUMB TERMINALS · basic computers
that draw down applications and other
software from the internet.

MP-SHEs · term to describe women
who download music from the net.

CYBER FOOTPRINT · what can be
discerned about an individual or entity
by its presence online.

GOOGLEJUICE · the ability of a website
to appear near the top of Google (or
other) search results.

BOOT CAMP · software that allows Mac
computers to run Windows software.

VINGLE · video singles that can be
mixed by DJs like traditional records.

SPOETRY · Poems created (or emerging
serendipitously) from spam email.

———————SCI, TECH, NET WORDS OF NOTE cont.———————

BOOK · another word for 'cool', derived from cellphone predictive text: on many phones, the first word that pops up if you enter the letters c-o-o-l is 'book'. In the same way, 'pint' becomes SHOT, 'Smirnoff' becomes POISONED, 'lips' becomes KISS, 'shag' becomes RICH, 'home' becomes GOOD, &c.

ARTCASTING · when museums, galleries, &c. place their audio tours online to attract more visitors. *Also* GODCASTING · religious podcasting.

THE LONG TAIL · the notion (first popularized by Chris Anderson) that the net allows the sale of a vast array of low-demand items as well as the mainstream hits. Crucially, the Long Tail theory posits that the sum of the former may be as valuable as the latter (e.g. the combined sales of all the niche songs on iTunes generating income at least as valuable as the Top 10 'hits').

GENERATION M · *myspace.com* users.

FOLKSONOMICS · the organization of digital content in a transparent and community-minded manner.

NET NEUTRALITY · the increasingly controversial idea that all internet content and applications should be treated equally, and that service providers should not discriminate in favor of their internet content or against the content of another's. (In the same way that phone companies do not ensure faster connections to numbers within their own networks.)

ECOLONOMICS · sustainable living via environmentally friendly (e)business.

GREENWASH · to fraudulently portray something as environmentally sound.

NOPE · Not On Planet Earth: a global expansion of Not In My Back Yard.

GEOCACHING · a treasure hunt where players use GPS coordinates (from sites like *navicache.com*) to hide and seek caches of 'treasure'. The waterproof box 'caches' contain logbooks (to record discoveries) and low-value trinkets that players can take if they leave something of similar or higher value in their place.

DEAD TREE EDITION · a book.

———————COMPUTER STORAGE CAPACITY———————

Memory				approximate storage capacity
Bit				single binary digit (1 or 0)
Byte		8 bits		a single character
Kilobyte	kB	1,024 bytes		half a page of typed text
Megabyte	MB	1,024 kB	10^6 bytes	novella of text
Gigabyte	GB	1,024 MB	10^9 bytes	500,000 pages of text
Terabyte	TB	1,024 GB	10^{12} bytes	1 million books
Petabyte	PB	1,024 TB	10^{15} bytes	200 NY Public Libraries
Exabyte	EB	1,024 PB	10^{18} bytes	200,000 NY Public Libraries
Zettabyte	ZB	1,024 EB	10^{21} bytes	incomprehensibly large

A CD-ROM can hold 650–700 MB, which roughly equates to *c.*75 minutes of recorded music.

– CONTINUOUS PARTIAL – ATTENTION

Continuous Partial Attention [CPA] is the trend of stretching our 'attention bandwidth' to cope with the myriad demands on our concentration posed by technology. The term was coined by the writer Linda Stone, formerly of Apple and Microsoft, who describes CPA as 'the behavior of continuously monitoring as many inputs as possible, paying partial attention to each'. According to Stone, CPA is 'post-multitasking behavior'. If multi-tasking is 'motivated by a desire to be more productive and more efficient', CPA is 'motivated by a desire to be a live node on the network'. Anxious to connect and desperate not to miss an opportunity, CPA 'contributes to a feeling of overwhelm, over-stimulation, and a sense of being unfulfilled'. Indeed, the 'always on' character of technology (emails, PDAs, IM, VOIP) compromises 'normal' social interactions (checking your BlackBerry or cell during lunch) and, in Stone's analysis, 'has created an artificial sense of constant crisis'. Like wild animals in a continuous state of alert, an 'adrenalized fight or flight mechanism kicks in'. Of the hundreds of emails received each day, Stone asks, how many are 'tigers', requiring immediate action, and how many are merely 'mice'? (Most, in fact, are likely to be spam.) Faced with this profusion of inputs we increasingly turn to *filters* (TiVo) and *blocks* (iPods) to find a signal amidst the noise. ❦ Stone suggests that 'the world may continue to be noisy, but our yearning and fulfilment are more likely to come from getting to the bottom of things, from stillness, and from opportunities for meaningful connection'. And, perhaps presciently, she describes committed and undivided attention as 'the real aphrodisiac'.

WEBLOG AWARDS

The 6th annual Weblog Awards are independent, unsponsored awards, nominated and voted for by the public. Some of the 2005 awards included:

Best new blog... *bobgeiger.blogspot.com*
Oz or NZ .... *timblair.net*
Asian blog.......... *xiaxue.blogspot.com*
Afr./M.East.. *iraqthemodel.blogspot.com*
British/Irish ..... *normblog.typepad.com*
Europe...*medienkritik.typepad.com/blog*
Canadian........ *smalldeadanimals.com*
Latin Amer... *blogs.salon.com/0001330*
Journalism....... *michaelyon-online.com*
Group ....*reason.com/hitandrun*
Blog design...................*ljcfyi.com*
Photo...................*zombietime.com*
Video................*crooksandliars.com*
Humorous...... *patriotboy.blogspot.com*
Weblog of the year........ *dailykos.com*

BLOOKER PRIZES

In April 2006, the first 'Blooker Prizes' were awarded to books that started life as blogs. The top prize of £1,140 went to:

Julie Powell
Julie and Julia: 365 Days, 524 Recipes, One Tiny Apartment Kitchen

INTERNET LEAGUE

The following ranks countries making the greatest and most constructive use of computers and the internet in 2006:

1	US	6	Canada
2	Singapore	7	Taiwan
3	Denmark	8	Sweden
4	Iceland	9	Switzerland
5	Finland	10	UK

[Source: WEF Networked Readiness Index]

—WEBBY AWARDS · 2006—

Awarded by the International Academy of Digital Arts and Sciences, the Webby Awards reward excellence in web design, innovation, and functionality. The following represents a selection of the winners at the 10th annual awards:

Breakout of the year ...... *myspace.com*
Webby artist of the year ... *gorillaz.com*
Activism .... *youthink.worldbank.org*
Best writing .... *newyorker.com*
Best homepage *remembersegregation.org*
Blog – political ...... *huffingtonpost.com*
Celebrity/fan .... *npgmusicclub.com*
Humor .... *theonion.com*
Lifestyle .... *epicurious.com*
Magazine .... *ngm.com*
Movies *festival.sundance.org/2006/*
Music .... *fabchannel.com*
News .... *bbc.co.uk/news*
Newspaper .... *guardian.co.uk*
Politics .... *opensecrets.org*
Sports .... *espn.com*

At the Webby awards ceremony all winners are limited to a five-word acceptance speech. In 2005 Al Gore, recipient of a lifetime achievement award, asked the audience, 'Please don't recount this vote'.

—WIRELESS CITIES—

According to Intel's 2005 survey, the top 5 areas for wireless accessibility are:

1 .. *Seattle/Bellevue/Everett/Tacoma* WA†
2 .. *San Francisco/San José/Oakland* CA
3 .... *Austin/San Marcos* TX
4 .... *Portland* OR/*Vancouver* WA
5 .... *Toledo* OH

† The Seattle area is home to many high-tech companies, including the HQs of Microsoft, Amazon.com, Nintendo, and Starbucks – whose WiFi-equipped cafés blanket the area. [Source: Intel's Most Unwired Cities Survey, 2005, by Burt Sterling. Based on the number of wireless hotspots, broadband availability, wireless networks, and wireless email devices.]

WARDRIVING is the practice of scanning for available wireless networks in a car equipped with WiFi-spotting technology. 'Wardrivers' often pinpoint the GPS coordinates of any wireless networks they find, adding them to websites (such as wigle.net) in order to build collective maps of the wireless landscape. Wardriving seems to derive from 'wardialing' (randomly dialing phone lines to see which are connected to a modem), a technique popularized by the 1983 thriller *War Games*.

—WEB MOMENTS THAT CHANGED THE WORLD—

To celebrate 10 years of the Webby Awards [see above], the International Academy of Digital Arts and Sciences listed the 10 web moments that changed the world:

1 ....the dotcom boom and bust, 1995–2001
2 .... Drudge Report, a one-man news site, broke Monica Lewinsky scandal, 1998
3 .... Amazon's Jeff Bezos named *Time*'s Man of the Year, 1999
4 .... worldwide elections – widespread use of internet to garner support, 2004
5 .... 9/11 – people turned to email and internet for immediate news, 2001
6 .... Asian tsunami, citizen reporters first on scene to document disaster, 2004
7 .... court ruling shut down innovative file-sharing site Napster, 2001
8 .... internet coverage of Live8 concert on AOL, 2005
9 ...... Match.com booms – internet became the place to make connections, 2002
10 .... web played central role in discovery of SARS virus, 2003

——————————— SOME WEBSITES OF THE YEAR ———————————

archibot.com/ratings/index.html...........................*rate your favorite buildings*
craignotbond.com ....*Bond fans urge a boycott of* Casino Royale
deadbodyguy.com.............. *man stages photos of himself dead to get part in film*
deathlist.net ....*predictions of which celebs will die in the coming 12 months*
dontdatehimgirl.com ....*women expose their ex-boyfriends online*
gethuman.com ....*cheat sheets to get through automated answering systems*
housingmaps.com......................*Google's maps with Craigslist's property listings*
kittenwars.com...*pussycats battle it out to be the cutest*
littlegreenfootballs.com................. *site that broke the 'fake' Lebanon photo story*
milliondollarhomepage.com...........................*selling pixels to pay for college*
myspacesucks.8m.com..*myspace backlash*
narniarapbattle.com...................... *West Coast response to SNL's 'Lazy Sunday'*
nbc.com/Video/videos/snl_1432_narnia.shtml ....*SNL's 'Lazy Sunday' rap*
ocweekly.com/columns/ask-a-mexican...........*ask questions of a real-life Mexican*
popvssoda.com...........................*is that fizzy stuff called pop, soda, or Coke?*
president.ir/eng ....*official website of the President of Iran* [see pp. 11 & 34]
productinvasion.com .... *Writers Guild of America mocks product placement*
ready.gov/kids/home.html......................*US homeland security advice for kids*
riverbendblog.blogspot.com......... *Iraqi blog nominated for Samuel Johnson Prize*
savethe76ball.com ....*campaign to save iconic balls atop Union 76 gas stations*
sfcompact.blogspot.com...............................*surviving without shopping*
siteinstitute.org..*tracks terrorist sources on the net*
stuffonmycat.com.................. *cats with various objects loving placed upon them*
the-bc.com ....The OC, *but now with Jesuits*
thefatmanwalking.com ....*journal of Steve Vaught walking across USA*
underneaththeirrobes.blogs.com .... *Supreme Court gossip blog*
usinfo.state.gov/media/misinformation.html .. *official response to conspiracy theories*
youtube.com ....*watch and share homemade video*

——————————— GOOGLE ZEITGEIST ———————————

Ubiquitous search engine Google [see p.198] regularly publishes its *Zeitgeist* list of popular search queries. Below are the 'top gaining' search queries during 2006:

Week ending	search						
Jan 2	2006 new year	Feb 20	Richard Bright	Apr 24	420†	Jun 26	World Cup 2006
Jan 9	Vince Young	Feb 27	Sasha Cohen	May 1	NFL draft	Jul 3	Star Jones
Jan 16	Joe Pichler	Mar 6	Oscars	May 8	Chernobyl	Jul 10	Zidane
Jan 23	Anna Benson	Mar 13	Dana Reeve	May 15	Maggie Q	July 17	Zidane headbutt
Jan 30	Chris Penn	Mar 20	St Patrick's Day	May 22	Barbaro		video
Feb 6	Super Bowl	Mar 27	Debra Lafave	May 29	Clay Aiken	July 24	storm large
	commercials	Apr 3	Whitney Houston	Jun 5	The Omen	Jul 31	Reichen Lehmkuhl
Feb 13	Torino games	Apr 10	Masters	Jun 12	2006 World Cup	Aug 7	Scrabble
		Apr 17	happy easter	Jun 19	World Cup 2006	Aug 14	Segolene Royal

[*Zeitgeist* is German for 'spirit of the age' (*Zeit* time + *Geist* spirit). † '420' is a slang term for smoking marijuana]

———— SPAM & UCE ————

SPAM is the proprietary name of a brand of tinned meat, mainly pork, that was first marketed by George A. Hormel & Co. in 1937. The word, a blend of 'spiced' and 'ham', was apparently the brainchild of actor Kenneth Daigneau. It seems that the use of the word in association with junk email derives from the 1971 *Monty Python* sketch where – at The Green Midget Café, Bromley – Mr and Mrs Bun (Eric Idle and Graham Chapman) attempt to order a meal without SPAM from the waitress (Terry Jones). Their attempts are drowned out by a horde of SPAM-loving Vikings, whose chanting of the word SPAM crescendoes into the now-famous 'SPAM song'. Some 20 years later, the relentless Viking chanting became forever linked with the equally relentless bombardment of junk email. Hormel & Co. are, understandably, keen to protect their trademark from association with junk email and prefer the term UCE (unsolicited commercial email). However, like Hoover, Biro, and others, the pressure on proprietary

names is intense once they become used generically. This seems especially so with the word *spam*. Despite a prediction by Bill Gates that spam would be eradicated by 2006, and a plethora of spam-canning laws around the world, *c.*45% of all emails are unsolicited and unwanted. According to *spamhaus.org*, the 'worst spam origin countries' are: USA, China, Japan, Russia, Taiwan, Canada, South Korea, UK, Netherlands, and Hong Kong. *commtouch.com* analyzed *c.*256 million emails in January 2006, and confirmed (what most email users will know) that the major spam types are:

Pharmaceutical	52·5%
Gifts	14·1%
'Enhancers' & diets	13·4%
Finance/loans	7·6%
Software	6·4%
Pornography & 'dating'	5·3%
'Fraud' notification	1%

Despite a slight recent decline in spam volume, eradication has proved elusive.

———— LOVE ONLINE ————

Increasingly people are using the internet to find love. A study by the PEW Internet & American Life Project found that 74% of unattached web users in America have taken part in at least one online dating activity. The following shows the percentage of people who have used the internet to establish romantic connections:

Flirted with someone online	40%
Visited an online dating site	37%
Asked someone on a date online	28%
Searched online for location for date	27%
Searched online for information on someone you dated in the past	18%
Maintained a long-distance relationship online	18%
Searched for information about someone you are currently dating online	17%
Broken up with someone online	9%

——————————— GOOGLE CHINA ———————————

Google announced in January 2006 that it would allow the Chinese government to censor its services in return for being granted access to China's fast-growing and potentially vast online market. Google has been available in China for a number of years via a US server, but government blocks and lengthy delays frustrated users. The new service will use a server based in China that automatically restricts access to sites the Chinese State deems unacceptable. Yahoo and Microsoft already run censored services in China and, in a bid to appear more transparent, Google promises to inform surfers when pages are removed from search results by order of the government. China is one of the most heavily censored societies in the world, and it is thought that >30,000 online police monitor websites, chatrooms, and blogs for subversion. Groups fighting for press freedom have criticized Google for facilitating China's suppression of information – highlighting the fact that of the 64 known internet dissidents in prison worldwide, 54 are Chinese. Furthermore, some have questioned whether Google's decision to engage with China in this way is in keeping with the company's goal 'to make all possible information available to everyone who has a computer', or their mission statement: 'Don't be evil'. Below are examples of the searches that *www.google.cn* censors from Chinese users:

'TIANANMEN SQUARE' · Whereas google.com returns sites about the massacre of student protesters in 1989, Chinese users are directed to positive, tourist sites about the square.

'FALUN GONG' · Information on the spiritual group that has been labeled an 'evil cult' by the Chinese government is heavily censored – returning results that are universally negative.

'TAIWANESE INDEPENDENCE' · A very sensitive subject for the Chinese government; Chinese users are taken to sites that quote Foreign Minister Li Zhaoxing, warning that China could not tolerate such an outcome.

'DONGZHOU' · Any reference to the recent killing by paramilitary police of protesters in Dongzhou village has been removed.

Western users can compare results for a search of 'Tiananmen Square' on *google.com/images* with those on *google.cn/images*. ❦ In June 2006, Sergey Brin (Google's cofounder) signaled a possible reverse of the plan to censor Chinese content, saying, 'Perhaps now the principled approach makes more sense'.

——————————— GOOGLE PORN SEARCHES ———————————

Google Trends, which analyzes internet search patterns across the world, found that in 2005 searching for 'porn' had reached an all-time high. The most prolific enthusiasts were British, followed by the Australians. The top ten are shown below:

1	Birmingham, UK	6	St Louis, US
2	Manchester, UK	7	Sydney, Australia
3	Brisbane, Australia	8	Brentford, UK
4	Melbourne, Australia	9	San Diego, US
5	Delhi, India	10	Seattle, US

———————————— MMORPGs & REAL LIFE ————————————

Massive Multiplayer Online Role-Playing Games (MMORPGs, or simply MMOs) are simulated, online gaming environments to which players anywhere in the world can log on, usually for a monthly subscription. In most games, players control and customize characters ('avatars'), guiding them through virtual landscapes. The most successful MMOs are set in worlds inspired by Dungeons & Dragons role-playing, Tolkien-esque fantasy, and science fiction. Thus, orcs, goblins, ogres, elves, dragons, druids, shamans, and warlocks abound, as do spells, potions, swords, and armor. (Inevitably, spaceships and extraterrestrials also feature). In June 2006, mmogchart.com estimated there were *c.*12·5m MMO subscriptions, of which *World of Warcraft* (WoW) had a 53% share. Below is mmogchart.com's estimate of MMO and WoW subscriptions since 1998 – with some comparative populations:

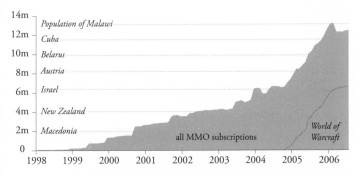

The online gaming economy is impressive. NDP Research estimated that in 2005 MMO subscriptions (in the US alone) generated >$290m. Yet, a novel feature of MMOs is Real Money Trading (RMT) in virtual goods, where in-game objects (weapons, spells, gold, &c.) are sold for hard cash (often via eBay). Some players ('gold farmers') 'grind' out repetitive tasks to create objects to sell; others play a character to a high level before selling it. In 2005, an *Entropia* player bought a virtual space station for $100,000; he now makes $12,000 a month rent. And, in a disturbing parallel to real-life capitalism, workers in Mexico, China, Vietnam, Eastern Europe, &c., play MMOs for sweatshop wages to create online goods for affluent players. Despite most games prohibiting RMT, estimates of this gray market range from $300m–$800m. Keen to cash in, some games now have their own RMT markets, and in *Entropia*, the Project Entropia Dollar (PED) can be exchanged for real money via ATMs (10 PED=1 US$). While the tax implications of RMT remain baffling, they may prove simple compared to the ethical and legal dilemmas posed by MMOs, in which real-life (im)morality is mirrored online. Many players now join together to protect themselves from online 'griefers' (bullies), 'PKers' (player killers), cheats, and mercenaries. As 'criminal' acts increase online, real-life risks also grow. Already, courts are ruling on virtual theft and fraud (and, presumably, soon assault), and on the legality of online punishments (like account suspension, banishment, or crucifixion). As MMOs become more complex, popular, and lucrative, it seems inevitable that the boundary between the virtual and the real will increasingly blur.

─────── HACKER, CRACKER, & GEEK SPEAK ───────

HACKER. . . . . *an expert computer programmer*
CRACKER . . . . *a* HACKER *who uses his/her skill for malicious/illegal purposes*
WHITE HAT. . . . . *one who breaks into computer systems to identify security flaws*
BLACK HAT . . . .*a* CRACKER
SNEAKER. . . . .*a* WHITE HAT
PHREAKER . . . . *one who tampers with telephone systems (e.g. to avoid paying)*
GEEK . . . .*one fascinated by technology; not necessarily a pejorative term*
NERD. . . . . . . *above-average IQ; below-average social skills and, often, personal hygiene*
DWEEB. . . . . *a clueless though inoffensive* NERD
DORK . . . . *an offensive* DWEEB
SPOD . . . . *a* NERD/GEEK *without the interest or skill in computing*
PROPELLER HEAD. . . . . *an expert in any field of technology*
NEWBIE . . . .*a newcomer to a technology or environment (e.g. chatrooms)*
LUSER . . . . *an annoying, incompetent computer user*
LAMER . . . . *one who downloads but seldom uploads; also a* LUSER
TREKKIE . . . .*obsessive fan of* Star Trek† *in its myriad incarnations*
ANORAK . . . .*one obsessed with an unfashionable interest or technology (e.g. trains)*

† Other sci-fi fan nicknames are: x-philes, *The X Files*; scapers, *Farscape*; dwarfers, *Red Dwarf*.

─────────────────── FLOPS ───────────────────

Flops, short for ᶠᴸoating point ᴼperations ᴾer ˢecond, are the units used to measure how many calculations per second a computer can make. Standard SI prefixes are employed to show the relative performance level of a given computer:

Megaflops . . . . . 10^6 flops	Teraflops. . . . . . 10^{12} flops	Exaflops . . . . . . 10^{18} flops
Gigaflops . . . . . . 10^9 flops	Petaflops. . . . . . 10^{15} flops	Zettaflops. . . . . 10^{21} flops

Home computers generally perform at gigaflops, compared to supercomputers which are capable of teraflops. Supercomputers are used to process calculations with a vast array of variables, such as climate-change models, DNA mapping, and military simulations. To date, only one computer has exceeded 100 teraflops, but new models are improving all the time. The TOP500 project tracks the performance of supercomputers and biannually releases a ranking. Its latest top five were:

Computer	manufacturer	country	teraflops
BlueGene/L eServer Blue Gene	IBM	USA	280·60
BGW eServer Blue Gene	IBM	USA	91·29
ASC Purple eServer pSeries p575	IBM	USA	63·39
Columbia, Altix, Infiniband	SGI	USA	51·87
Thunderbird	Dell	USA	38·27

[Incidentally, the 'Fosbury Flop' high-jump approach (a backward jump arching over the bar) became popular after its pioneer, Richard 'Dick' Douglas Fosbury, won Olympic gold in 1968.]

——————— ON CELLPHONES, TEXTING, &c. ———————

Very orthodox Jews are forbidden from using new-generation cellphones because they offer access to the worldly temptations of film, internet, photos, and text messaging. However, in 2006, Mirs Communication, a subsidiary of Motorola, developed a 'kosher cell' approved by the Rabbinical Committee for Communications. It is a call-only service stripped of potential distractions (>10,000 numbers for phone sex and dating services are blocked), and it has a biased tariff structure that encourages members of the network to stick to 'kosher-to-kosher' calls. The service was launched in Israel and is expected to spread to America and beyond. (It has, ironically, already been embraced by conservative Islamic groups who are equally concerned with moral rectitude.) The invention of kosher cells is the latest development in 'faith phones' that offer services like: religious ringtones; prayers and sermons by text; digital *muezzin* calls to prayer; and internal compasses to identify the direction of Mecca. ❦ The think tank *Future Laboratory* recently reported that the old Australian custom of burying the dead with their favorite status symbol has been revived, with more people requesting to be buried with their cellphones. The cellphone market has also benefited from the rise in taphephobia – the primal (and perhaps reasonable) fear of being buried alive. In South Africa, taphephobia is compounded by the widespread belief that witches can cause a deathlike trance. To counteract this menace, morticians have begun advertising special 'burial' cellphones, with extralong battery life. ❦ In the Muslim world even marriage customs have been affected by the rise of the cellphone. Islamic Sharia law allows instant divorce by repeating *talaq* (I divorce you) three times. Nowadays, an alarming number of (callous or busy) men use three *talaq* text messages to effect a divorce. However, in April 2006, Malaysia's Minister for Women and Family, Shahrizat Abdul Jalil, condemned the practice, calling it 'disrespectful and impolite'. ❦ At a charity event in Doha, Qatar, in May 2006, an anonymous bidder paid a record $2·75m for the cell number 666 6666 (the number 6 is considered lucky). ❦ Publisher Harlequin Books introduced a daily text message service to send snippets of its romantic novels for fans to read on the go. ❦ Specialized internet- and GPS-enabled cells in Japan allow tourists to point their handset at historical monuments, restaurants, &c. and receive relevant data about them on their screens. ❦ In August, Sweden became the first country in Europe to introduce a law preventing the use of cellphones in designated areas of public transport. ❦ Korean cellphone manufacturer LG Electronics has produced a new phone to prevent drunk dialing. The LP4100 includes a built-in Breathalyzer which can be linked to certain numbers in the phone book, to prevent embarrassing late-night drunken rants to an ex. ❦ The 'Mosquito' is a device that emits a particularly unpleasant noise at a frequency so high that only those <20-years-old can usually hear it; it has been used to clear youths from congregating and causing trouble in urban areas. Recently, the Mosquito's buzz has been converted into a cellphone ringtone that can be heard only by youthful ears – causing some trouble in classrooms.

—————————— SI PREFIXES ——————————

Below are the SI prefixes and symbols for the decimal multiples and submultiples of SI Units from 10^{24} to 10^{-24}.

10^{24}	yotta	Y	1 000 000 000 000 000 000 000 000
10^{21}	zetta	Z	1 000 000 000 000 000 000 000
10^{18}	exa	E	1 000 000 000 000 000 000
10^{15}	peta	P	1 000 000 000 000 000
10^{12}	tera	T	1 000 000 000 000
10^9	giga	G	1 000 000 000
10^6	mega	M	1 000 000
10^3	kilo	k	1 000
10^2	hecto	h	100
10	deca	da	10
1			1
10^{-1}	deci	d	0.1
10^{-2}	centi	c	0.01
10^{-3}	milli	m	0.001
10^{-6}	micro		0.000 001
10^{-9}	nano	n	0.000 000 001
10^{-12}	pico	p	0.000 000 000 001
10^{-15}	femto	f	0.000 000 000 000 001
10^{-18}	atto	a	0.000 000 000 000 000 001
10^{-21}	zepto	z	0.000 000 000 000 000 000 001
10^{-24}	yocto	y	0.000 000 000 000 000 000 000 001

—————— SOME USEFUL CONVERSIONS ——————

A	A *to* B *multiply by*	B *to* A *multiply by*	B
inches	25·4	0·0397	millimeters
inches	2·54	0·3937	centimeters
feet	0·3048	3·2808	meters
yards	0·9144	1·0936	meters
miles	1·6093	0·6214	kilometers
acres	0·4047	2·471	hectares
square feet	0·0929	10·76	square meters
square miles	2·5899	0·3861	square kilometers
UK pints	0·5682	1·7598	liters
UK gallons	4·546	0·2199	liters
cubic inches	16·39	0·0610	cubic centimeters
ounces	28·35	0·0353	grams
pounds	0·4536	2·2046	kilograms
stones	6·35	0·157	kilograms
miles/gallon	0·3539	2·825	kilometers/liter
miles/US gallon	0·4250	2·353	kilometers/liter
miles/hour	1·609	0·6117	kilometers/hour

—— °C – °F ——

°C	°F			
100	212		49	120·2
99	210·2		48	118·4
98	208·4		47	116·6
97	206·6		46	114·8
96	204·8		45	113
95	203		44	111·2
94	201·2		43	109·4
93	199·4		42	107·6
92	197·6		41	105·8
91	195·8		40	104
90	194		39	102·2
89	192·2		38	100·4
88	190·4		37	98·6
87	188·6		36	96·8
86	186·8		35	95
85	185		34	93·2
84	183·2		33	91·4
83	181·4		32	89·6
82	179·6		31	87·8
81	177·8		30	86
80	176		29	84·2
79	174·2		28	82·4
78	172·4		27	80·6
77	170·6		26	78·8
76	168·8		25	77
75	167		24	75·2
74	165·2		23	73·4
73	163·4		22	71·6
72	161·6		21	69·8
71	159·8		20	68
70	158		19	66·2
69	156·2		18	64·4
68	154·4		17	62·6
67	152·6		16	60·8
66	150·8		15	59
65	149		14	57·2
64	147·2		13	55·4
63	145·4		12	53·6
62	143·6		11	51·8
61	141·8		10	50
60	140		9	48·2
59	138·2		8	46·4
58	136·4		7	44·6
57	134·6		6	42·8
56	132·8		5	41
55	131		4	39·2
54	129·2		3	37·4
53	127·4		2	35·6
52	125·6		1	33·8
51	123·8		0	32
50	122		–1	30·2
			–2	28·4

Normal body temp.
= 98·6°F (37°C)
range 97·7–98·9°F
(36·1–37·2°C)

Travel & Leisure

I have recently been all round the world and have formed a very poor opinion of it.
— SIR THOMAS BEECHAM

DOMESTIC TRAVEL

Below is a snapshot of how Americans traveled within the country during 2004:

The top 5 states visited by US residents
California · Florida · Texas
New York · Pennsylvania

Method of transportation used	%
Auto, truck, or RV	73
Airplane	16
Train/ship/other	4
Rental car (as primary mode)	3
Bus/motorcoach	2

Lodging type	%
Hotel/motel/bed & breakfast	54
Private home	40
RV or tent	5
Condo or time-share	4

Trip duration	%
0 nights	23
1–2 nights	35
3–6 nights	29
≥7 nights	13

Purpose of trip	%
Pleasure activities	81
Business	12
Business and pleasure combined	7

The percentage of domestic trips undertaken for leisure in 2004, by activity type

Activity	%
Shopping	30%
Social events	27%
Outdoor activities	11%
Urban or rural sightseeing	10%
Beach activities	9%
Historic sites or museums	8%
Gambling	7%
Theme or amusement park	7%
National or state park	6%
Nightlife/dancing	6%

[Source: Travel Industry Assoc. of America]

DREAM VACATION LOCATIONS

A Gallup Poll in May 2006 asked American adults, 'If money were no object, where would you go on your dream vacation?' The top 12 locations selected were these:

	%		%
Hawaii	17%	Florida	2
Europe	11	Greece	2
Australia	6	London/England	2
Italy	5	Ireland	2
Alaska/Alaskan cruise	4	Fiji	2
California	2	Bahamas	2

———————————————ON COMMUTING———————————————

On average, Americans spend >100 hours commuting each year, 20 hours more than spent vacationing. Below, some additional data on the commuting experience:

Daily commute	%
<10 minutes	14·9
10–14	14·6
15–19	15·5
20–24	14·6
25–29	6·1
30–34	13·0
35–44	6·2
45–59	7·5
≥60	7·6

[Mean travel time to work is 24·7 minutes]

Time commuters leave for work	%
00:00–04:59	3·8
05:00–05:29	3·4
05:30–05:59	4·9
06:00–06:29	8·9
06:30–06:59	10·8
07:00–07:29	14·8
07:30–07:59	14·0
08:00–08:29	10·9
08:30–08:59	5·5
09:00–23:59	23·1

Method of commuting	%
Driving alone	77·7
Carpooling†	10·1
2-person carpool	7·9
3-person carpool	1·3
≥4 person carpool	0·9
Public transportation	4·6
Walking	2·4
Bicycling	0·4

Experience of delays	%
Do not experience delays	22
Delays 1–3 days per week	40
Delays ≥4 days per week	38

Satisfaction with commute	%
Very satisfied	43
Somewhat satisfied	37
Dissatisfied	20

† High Occupancy Vehicle (HOV) lanes (aka 'carpool lanes' or, because of their markings, 'diamond lanes') were first used near Washington, DC, during the 1960s, and *c*.100 localities nationwide now have them. Initially, HOV lanes were designed to encourage multiple occupancy, but recently there have been moves to allow low-emission hybrid cars into the diamonds. Inevitably, HOV lanes have been abused by ingenious fraud – as the California Department of Transportation notes, 'each child counts as an occupant, but pets, infants still in the womb, inflatable dolls, or ghosts do not'. [Sources: US Census Bureau, 2004; Federal Highway Admin., 2005] ❦ The term 'commuting' seems to derive from American 'commutation tickets' – train season tickets for workers.

———————————IN-CAR RADIO & CELLPHONES———————————

Research by Bridge Ratings (February 2006) indicates that 56% of US commuters used cellphones while driving – talking for an average of 13½ minutes per daily commute. Such gabbiness (which has increased annually since 1990) may represent a challenge to in-car radio, which is usually turned down (79%) or switched off (19%) during calls. Below are comparative minutes of in-car radio and cell usage:

Activity while driving	1990	1995	2000	2005
Radio listening (mins)	29	27	30	26
Cell calls (mins)	2·55	3·08	6·63	13·49

─────────────── CARS & DRIVING ───────────────

Americans drove roughly 10,077 miles per capita in 2004, and spent an average of $3,397 per person buying vehicles – roughly equivalent to what they spent on groceries. More on cars:

Some of the sexiest cars of 2006 as named by Road & Travel
Chevrolet Corvette
Ford Mustang
BMW Z4
Hyundai Tiburon
Honda S2000
Mazda MX-5 Miata
Mercedes Benz SLK

Most-stolen cars, as named by the Insurance Institute for Highway Safety
Cadillac Escalade
Mitsubishi Lancer Evolution
Dodge Ram 1500 quad cab
Ford F-250/350 supercrew
Chrysler Sebring
[Based on loss rates for cars 1–3 years old]

States that drive the greatest number of miles per capita[†]
Wyoming........................18,485
Mississippi......................13,588
Oklahoma......................13,450
Indiana 13,113
Alabama.........................12,926

States that drive the fewest miles per capita[†]
New York........................7,198
Alaska 7,630
Hawaii............................7,774
New Jersey 8,374
Massachusetts 8,535

† The number of miles traveled by trucks and cars within each state in 2004.
[Source: US Department of Transportation Federal Highway Administration highway statistics; Indiana data are from 2003.]

Max speed limit (mph)		% using safety belts
70	Alabama	81·8
65	Alaska	78·4
75	Arizona	94·2
70	Arkansas	68·3
70	California	92·5
75	Colorado	79·2
65	Connecticut	81·6
65	Delaware	83·8
55	DC	88·8
70	Florida	73·9
70	Georgia	81·6
60	Hawaii	95·3
75	Idaho	76·0
65	Illinois	86·0
70	Indiana	81·2
70	Iowa	85·9
70	Kansas	69·0
65	Kentucky	66·7
70	Louisiana	77·7
65	Maine	75·8
65	Maryland	91·1
65	Massachusetts	64·8
70	Michigan	92·9
70	Minnesota	82·6
70	Mississippi	60·8
70	Missouri	77·4
75	Montana	80·0
75	Nebraska	79·2
75	Nevada	94·8
65	New Hampshire	NA
65	New Jersey	86·0
75	New Mexico	89·5
65	New York	85·0
70	North Carolina	86·7
75	North Dakota	76·3
65	Ohio	78·7
75	Oklahoma	83·1
65	Oregon	93·3
65	Pennsylvania	83·3
65	Rhode Island	74·7
70	South Carolina	69·7
75	South Dakota	68·8
70	Tennessee	74·4
80	Texas	89·9
75	Utah	86·9
65	Vermont	84·7
70	Virginia	80·4
70	Washington	95·2
70	West Virginia	84·9
65	Wisconsin	73·3
75	Wyoming	NA

[Source: NHTSA · As of July 2006]

———————————— DRUNK DRIVING ————————————

According to the Department of Transportation, 39% of all traffic-related deaths in 2004 occurred in crashes in which alcohol was involved[†]. The risk of being in such an accident is higher for young people (peak age for death is 25–34), and male drivers are almost twice as likely as female drivers to have a BAC [see below] above the legal limit. The following is a look at the deaths from alcohol-related crashes in 2004:

Car occupants killed.............14,196
– in 1-car crashes................ 8,808
– in 2-car crashes................ 4,492
– in >2-car crashes 896
Pedestrians killed 2,2110
– in 1-car crashes................ 1,976

– in multiple-car crashes.......... 234
Bicyclists killed..................... 248
– in 1-car crashes.................. 237
– in multiple-car crashes............11
Others/unknown 39
Total deaths 16,694

Illegal blood alcohol concentration (BAC) in most states   ≥0·08 grams per deciliter
Arrests for driving under the influence of alcohol or drugs, 2004   1·4m
Estimated cost of alcohol-related crashes annually $51b
– 1 death from alcohol-related crash   *every* 31 minutes
– 1 injury from alcohol-related crash   *every* 2 minutes
Peak hours for deaths from alcohol-related crashes   24:00–02:59

† Crashes are considered to be alcohol-related if at least one driver or nonoccupant (such as a pedestrian or cyclist) is determined to have had a blood alcohol concentration ≥0·01 grams per deciliter.
[Sources: National Center for Injury Prevention and Control; Department of Transportation]

———————————— WORLDWIDE ROAD RISKS ————————————

Country	population	No. of cars	pedestrian deaths	car deaths
Germany	83m	44·7m	812	3,774
Japan	128m	54·5m	2,739	2,230
Netherlands	16m	6·9m	97	483
UK	60m	27m	802	1,861
USA	291m	131m	4,749	19,460

[Source: International Road Traffic and Accident Database · Latest figures, 2003]

———— US TRANSPORTATION-RELATED DEATHS · 2004 ————

Method of transportation   2004 deaths
Large air-carrier 14
On-demand air taxi.................65
General aviation.................... 556
Highway.........................42,636
Railroad 528
Transit (train accidents, &c.) 248

Commercial ship......................36
Commercial ship, non-vessel[†] 57
Recreational boating.............. 676

US deaths; aviation includes deaths on the ground. † Fatalities unrelated to the vessel itself, such as falling overboard. [Source: DOT, 2006]

——————— CAR COLOR AND SAFETY ———————

Research published in the *British Medical Journal* in 2003 proposed a correlation between car color and likelihood of being in a car accident. A research team analyzed car accidents in New Zealand during a 15-month period in 1998–99. The research indicated that SILVER cars were the safest, being involved in 50% fewer accidents than WHITE cars. BROWN, BLACK, and GREEN cars showed an increased risk of accident, whereas the risk of serious injury arising from driving a YELLOW, RED, or BLUE car was not significantly higher than that of driving a WHITE car.

——————— UNUSUAL STREET NAMES ———————

The 7 'wackiest' street names, according to a 2006 poll by Car Connection website:

1 .. Psycho Path .... Traverse City, MI
2 .. Divorce Court .... Heather Highlands, PA
3 .. Farfrompoopen Road [the only road leading to Constipation Ridge] .... Story, AK
4 .. The intersection of Lonesome & Hardup .... Albany, GA
5 .. The intersection of Clinton & Fidelity .... Houston, TX
6 .. Bucket of Blood Street .... Holbrook, AZ
7 .. Unexpected Road .... Buena, NJ

——————— THOMAS THE TANK ENGINE ———————

Thomas the Tank Engine was created by the Reverend W. Awdry in 1945. He wrote twenty-six volumes about the charismatic engine before his son Christopher took over and added forty more books to the series. Below are tabulated the names of some of the engines and carriages – along with their characteristic colors:

Thomas	blue	Percy	green	Diesel	black
Henry	green	James	red	Edward	blue
Donald & Douglas	black	Gordon	blue	Bill & Ben	orange
		Toby	brown	Daisy	green
Duck (Montague)	green	Mavis	black	Duncan	yellow

——————— VANITY PLATES ———————

Vanity plates are issued by the Department of Motor Vehicles in each state. Rules for choosing character combinations vary, but choices are generally screened to weed out those that might cause offense. This screening can be controversial, however, and plate choices occasionally make their way into court. In 2005, a Utah court heard a case over the plate 'GAYSROK'; in 2006, an Anchorage woman was ordered by the DMV to surrender her plate reading 'XONSUX' (she appealed). ❦ Vanity plates with a special design or background are sometimes issued for a specific cause; a 'California Arts' plate has so far generated more than $6m for local arts programs.

———————————— AMTRAK ————————————

Amtrak was created by the Rail Passenger Service Act of 1970, which seized control of passenger rail services from private railroads. Currently, the quasi-public agency (technically called the National Railroad Passenger Corporation) has 500 destinations in 46 states[†], and in 2005 carried over 25·4 million passengers – 69,000 passengers per day. Below, a list of Amtrak's routes and the number of 2005 riders:

Route	2005 riders[‡]
Acela/Metroliner	1,283,475
Pacific Surfliner	1,209,196
Capitols	614,814
Empire	440,568
Keystone	400,262
San Joaquins	374,404
Cascades	281,139
Hiawatha	276,752
Empire Builder	226,301
Wolverine	200,209
Washington–Newport News	186,532
California Zephyr	157,818
Downeaster	157,422
New Haven–Springfield	157,010
Coast Starlight	153,918
Lake Shore Ltd	151,016
Silver Star	149,564
Albany–Niagara Falls–TO	137,781
Southwest Chief	132,427
Silver Meteor	128,692
Chicago–St Louis	122,204
Carolinian	118,286
Crescent	111,451
Texas Eagle	105,536
Auto Train	96,544
Pennsylvanian	87,494
Capitol Ltd	86,938
City of New Orleans	79,398
Illini	66,676
Kansas City–St Louis	64,080
Palmetto	61,650
Blue Water	56,972
Illinois Zephyr	56,104
Pere Marquette	44,882
Cardinal	43,157
Adirondack	37,470
Heartland Flyer	29,109
Piedmont	27,315
Vermonter	25,376
Sunset Ltd	22,102
Ethan Allen	20,076
Hoosier State	9,409
Total	11,559,330

‡ Excluding contract commuter trains and special trains. [Source: Amtrak, Oct '05–Mar '06]

† Hawaii, Alaska, South Dakota, and Wyoming lack Amtrak service. ⚓ 70% of Amtrak train trips were on time in 2005. 10 minutes late was considered 'delayed' for journeys <250 miles; other delays varied by trip length. Host railroads were the major cause of delay, accounting for 64,097 hours of delay in 2005, followed by Amtrak itself (25,549 hours), and other issues such as weather and customs searches.

———————— BUSIEST AMTRAK STATIONS ————————

Amtrak's busiest stations, based on number of boardings and alightings combined:

New York, NY	8,497,212	Baltimore, MD	980,122
Philadelphia, PA	3,742,630	Boston, MA	971,196
Washington, DC	3,734,287	Sacramento, CA	932,853
Chicago, IL	2,451,293	Trenton, NJ	901,429
Los Angeles, CA	1,373,740		
Newark, NJ	1,214,800		

[Source: Amtrak.com; fiscal year 2005 data]

—————————— US PASSPORT WORDING ——————————

The Secretary of State of the United States of America hereby requests all whom it may concern to permit the citizen/national of the United States named herein to pass without delay or hindrance and in case of need to give all lawful aid and assistance.

The allegedly low rate of US citizens holding passports has long been a source of scorn for those Europeans who see it as evidence of American insularity. However, the comparatively miserly US rates of vacation and (until recently) the opportunities for passport-free travel within America and its near neighbors, meant that the requirement for passports in America was not as pressing as in Europe. Considerable debate surrounds the percentage of US citizens holding passports (and, for various technical reasons, most countries are able to give only broad estimates). Many claim the US rate is as low as 20–30%, but the State Department press office (in February 2006) asserted that *c.*60% of the US population hold a passport. (The British rate in 2003 was 72–84% of adults, according to the Home Office.) It is likely that, whatever the current rate, US passport ownership will grow, as various new security initiatives demand passports for travel to and from the Americas, the Caribbean, and Bermuda. Below are recent US passport issue rates:

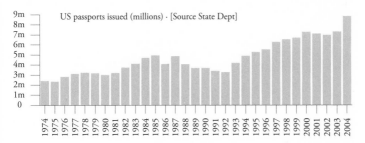

—————————— TO-FROM TOURISM FIGURES ——————————

Americans visiting	to or from	visiting America
12·4m	Europe	10·3m
5·6m	Mexico	12·9m
5·3m	Caribbean	1·1m
4·8m	Asia	6·2m
3·9m	Canada	14·9m
2·3m	Central America	0·7m
2·2m	South America	1·8m
0·8m	Oceania	1·3m
0·5m	Middle East	0·5m
0·2m	Africa	0·3m

[Source: US Dept of Commerce, Int. Trade Admin; preliminary 2005 data. Data for Americans visiting Mexico and Canada are air only; inbound data are air & ground; Oceania includes Australia.]

BUSIEST US AIRPORTS

Airport	million passengers
Atlanta International	41·6
Chicago International	34·5
Dallas–Fort Worth International	27·7
Los Angeles International	22·9
Las Vegas International	20·7
Denver International	20·5
Phoenix International	20·1
Houston Intercontinental	18·4
Minnesota-St Paul Intl	17·9
Detroit Metro	17·4

[Passengers boarding domestic & international flights, 2005. Source: Dept of Transportation]

DELAYED AIRLINES

Airlines with the most delayed departures, as a percentage of total flights[†]

Southwest Airlines	16·3%
American Airlines	9·4
Delta Air Lines	8·6
American Eagle Airlines	7·6
United Air Lines	6·6
Northwest Airlines	6·2
US Airways	6·1
Atlantic Southeast Airlines	6·0
Skywest Airlines	5·9
Expressjet Airlines	5·0

LOST LUGGAGE

Airlines with the most reports of lost luggage, as reports per 1,000 passengers[‡]

Atlantic Southeast	17·4
Comair	10·8
American Eagle	10·3
Skywest	10·1
US Airways	9·6
Delta	7·1
Expressjet	6·6
American Airlines	5·9
Alaska Airlines	5·0
Northwest Airlines	4·9

† Departures ≥15 min. late, & canceled. ‡ Domestic system only. [Source: Dept of Transport, 2005]

DANGEROUS ITEMS

In 2005, US airport security personnel confiscated the following prohibited items[†]:

lighters: 8,124,525 · *sharp objects (scissors, meat cleavers, ice picks, &c.)*: 3,041,218
knives and blades (except for plastic & butter knives): 1,650,894
tools (screwdrivers, axes, hatchets, &c.): 819,450
flammables/irritants (aerosols, paint thinner, &c.): 362,613
box cutters: 19,499 · *clubs, bats, and bludgeons*: 19,183

[† Jan–Nov 2005 · Source: *USA Today*] In response to an alleged British plot to bomb transatlantic airplanes using liquid explosives, on 8·10·2006 the Transportation Security Administration banned all liquids and gels in carry-on baggage [see p.31]. Beverages, lotions, perfumes, and non-solid cosmetics were included in the restrictions, but medicine and baby formula were exempt after passing inspection. It was unclear how long the restrictions would remain in effect. *Also prohibited in carry-on baggage*: lighters, spillable batteries, bows & arrows, sabers, swords, ice picks, meat cleavers, tear gas, and dynamite. *Acceptable items*: scissors with cutting edges ≤4", screwdrivers, wrenches, and pliers <7", eyelash curlers, tweezers, canes, and toy transformer robots. See tsa.gov for a definitive list.

———————————— DUTY-FREE ALLOWANCES ————————————

Travelers who are US residents may bring home $200, $800, or $1,600 of goods without paying duty, depending on the country visited and the time spent away. Generally, these exemptions apply if the goods are: for the use of the traveler or their household, or are to be given as 'bona fide' gifts; are in the traveler's possession (rather than being shipped); are declared to Customs and Border Protection; and are not on the list of prohibited or restricted items. Rough guidelines for the exemption follow:

$200	$800	$1,600
Applies: if away less than 48 hours; or out of the country more than once in 30 days	*Applies*: if arrival is from any country but a US insular possession; from Caribbean Basin or Andean countries; if away more than 48 hours	*Applies*: if returning directly or indirectly from a US insular possession; away for more than 48 hours
Allowed: 50 cigarettes, 10 cigars, and 150 milliliters of alcohol or perfume containing alcohol	*Allowed*: 1 liter of alcohol, or 2 if 1 liter was produced in a listed country [see cbp.gov]. Antiques ≥100 years old and fine art are duty free	*Allowed*: 1,000 cigarettes, but ≥800 of them must have been acquired in an insular possession, 4 liters of alcohol – 5 if one is a product of an insular possession
[For detailed guidelines on all exemptions, see cbp.gov]		

[Travelers may import more than these amounts, but must pay duty and other taxes if they do so.]

———————————— THE 'NO FLY' LIST ————————————

The Transportation Security Administration maintains a 'No Fly' list of passengers prohibited from boarding aircraft. Developed after 9/11, this list includes the name, nationality, date of birth, and passport number of individuals who may pose a 'threat to civil aviation', based on intelligence from the FBI and CIA. The TSA also maintains a 'Selectee' list of those who must pass through extensive screening before boarding. The exact number on the 'No Fly' list is classified, but, according to the American Civil Liberties Union, it numbers in the tens of thousands. The FBI states that as of 2004 the List had caused some 350 Americans to be delayed or denied boarding. ❦ The 'No Fly' list has prompted numerous complaints from those given 'false positives', according to TSA logs. In March 2004, Sen. Ted Kennedy was stopped 5 times at airports because his name was on the list, even though he was known to the airline; it was later revealed that 'T. Kennedy' is the alias of a terrorist suspect. Others delayed by the list have included State Department officials, a man with Energy Dept security clearance, airline employees, a reservist returning from Iraq, and an 82-year-old veteran who claimed he had never had a traffic ticket.

The 'No Fly' list is currently administered by airlines. Since 2003, the TSA has been developing a program that would allow the government to screen passenger lists themselves. The TSA hopes the program will reduce the number of false positives by standardizing and centralizing the process. ❦ In 2004, the ACLU filed a lawsuit against the TSA challenging the list; in response, Congress directed the TSA to maintain the list in a manner that 'will not produce a large number of false positives'.

————————GENERALLY APPROVED PRODUCTS————————

The following are some plants and other products generally allowed into the US:

aloe vera (aboveground parts) · bat nut or devil pod (*Trapa bicornis*)
baked goods · candies · canned fruit · canned & processed sauces
canned & processed vegetables · cannonball fruit · Chinese water chestnut
coffee (roasted beans only) · fish · garlic cloves (peeled) · maguey leaf
matsutake · mushrooms · nuts (roasted only) · palm hearts (peeled)
seaweed · shamrock leaves (without roots or soil) · St John's Bread†
singhara nut (*Trapa bispinosa*) · tamarind bean pod · truffles

[Source: Customs and Border Patrol] Most (but not all) produce from Canada and Mexico is allowed into the US. † St John's Bread, also called carob, derives its name from the belief that it was the 'locust' eaten by John the Baptist while in the wilderness. Today it is often used as a chocolate substitute.

————————THE COST OF TRAVEL————————

A snapshot of the average costs of international travel for Americans in 2004:

Average total trip cost, per visitor $2,916
Average international airfare...$1,405
Average package price...$2,266
Average amount spent outside the US
– total per visitor...$1,317
– per visitor/per day $81
Percent who used the following methods to pay for their trip
– credit cards..55%
– cash...33%
– debit cards...7%
– travelers checks..4%

[Source: US Department of Commerce, International Trade Administration; air travelers only]

————————THE MONTREAL CONVENTION————————

The Montreal Convention established the liability of airlines for passengers and their luggage. Ratified by the US in July 2003, the Convention replaced the much-maligned Warsaw Convention (1929), which was criticized for 'unconscionably low limits of liability' on passenger death, and for lost-luggage payments calculated according to the weight of luggage rather than the value of its contents. Under the Montreal Convention, air carriers are required to make payments of up to roughly $141,000 in proven damages on behalf of accident victims, regardless of whether the airline is ruled negligent. A limit of roughly $6,000 per passenger also exists for travelers who incur costs as result of airline delays. In addition, the Convention ensures that Americans have access to US courts in most cases of death or injury.

COSTLIEST PRIVATE ISLANDS

Isla de sa Ferradura, Spain *(14 acres)* .... $39·7m
Pakatoa Isl., NZ *(59 acres)*, & Cerralvo Island, Mexico *(35,000 acres)* [TIE] $35m
Temptation Island, Thailand *(20 acres)* $30m
Caritas Island, Fairfield County, CT *(4 acres)* .... >$25m
Allan Island, WA *(292 acres)*, Grand Bogue Caye, Belize *(314 acres)*,
& Blue Lagoon, Fiji *(225 acres)* [TIE] $25m
Thatch Cay, US Virgin Islands *(230 acres)* $24m
Isola Santo Stefano, Italy *(62 acres)* $24m
Little Ragged Island, Bahamas *(700 acres)* .... $23·5m
Leaf Cay 2, Bahamas *(25 acres)* $19m
Coakley Cay, Bahamas *(340 acres)* .... $18·2m
Magic Island, French Polynesia *(2 islands; 2·4 acres & 1·09 acres)* $18m

[Source: Forbes.com · 2006]

MARINE DISTRESS SIGNALS

Some of the internationally recognized marine distress signals:

Continuous sounding of any fog-signaling apparatus
Gun or other explosive device fired at intervals of a minute
Rockets or shells with red stars fired singly at short intervals
The spoken word 'MAYDAY' repeated where possible
Signaling SOS (· · · – – – · · ·) in Morse code by any method
Displaying 'N C' (November, Charlie) in flags
Square flag with ball (or anything similar) above or below it
Flames on a vessel, including a burning tar or oil barrel
Rocket parachute or hand flare showing a red light
Smoke signal giving off orange smoke
Raising and lowering arms outstretched to each side
Radiotelegraphy alarm · Dye marker
Orange-colored canvas with black square and circle

BEST BEACHES · 2006

Stephen Leatherman (aka 'Dr Beach'), director of the coastal research lab at Florida International University, produces a list every year rating America's best beaches:

Fleming Beach Park .... Maui, HI	*Coast Guard Beach* ..... Cape Cod, MA
Caladesi Isl. State Park ... Dunedin, FL	*Coronado Beach* .... San Diego, CA
Ocracoke Island ...... Outer Banks, NC	*Hamoa Beach* .... Maui, HI
Coopers Beach .... Southampton, NY	*Barefoot Beach Prk.* . Bonita Springs, FL
Hanalei Beach .... Kauai, HI	
Main Beach .... East Hampton, NY	[Previous winners are excluded from the survey]

──────── UNESCO WORLD HERITAGE SITES · 2006 ────────

The United Nations Educational, Scientific, and Cultural Organization (UNESCO) seeks to encourage the worldwide identification, protection, and preservation of cultural and natural heritage considered to be of outstanding value to humanity. To this end, UNESCO has granted World Heritage Status to 830 sites across the globe. Listed below are the heritage sites that were 'newly inscribed' on the list in 2006:

Cultural Properties: Aflaj Irrigation System of Oman · Aapravasi Ghat, Mauritius
Agave Landscape and Ancient Industrial Facilities of Tequila, Mexico
Bisotun, Iran · Centennial Hall in Wroclaw, Poland
Chongoni Rock Art Area, Malawi
Cornwall and West Devon Mining Landscape, UK
Crac des Chevaliers and Qal'at Salah El-Din, Syria
Le Strade Nuove and the system of the Palazzi dei Rolli, Genoa, Italy
Harar Jugol, the Fortified Historic Town, Ethiopia
Kondoa Rock Art Sites, Tanzania
Old town of Regensburg with Stadtamhof, Germany
Sewell Mining Town, Chile · Stone Circles of Senegambia, Gambia/Senegal
Vizcaya Bridge, Spain · Yin Xu, China
Natural Properties: Malpelo Fauna and Flora Sanctuary, Colombia
Sichuan Giant Panda Sanctuaries, China
Extensions approved for: Medieval Monuments in Kosovo, Serbia
Kvarken Archipelago & High Coast, Finland/Sweden

After the 2003 Iraq invasion, American soldiers damaged the ancient site of Babylon. Col. John Coleman offered an apology, but claimed that looters would have caused more serious damage.

──────── WORLD HERITAGE SITES IN DANGER ────────

War, natural disaster, pollution, unchecked urban sprawl, and unregulated tourism all pose significant threats to some World Heritage Sites. Consequently, UNESCO classifies a number of World Heritage Sites in Danger to highlight their plight and encourage dialogue with host nations to find ways of protecting the sites. At present, 32 of 812 World Heritage Sites are considered to be 'in danger', including:

Minaret and Archaeological Remains of Jam............................Afghanistan
Comoé National Park .... Côte d'Ivoire
Garamba National Park .... Democratic Republic of Congo
Abu Mena... Egypt
Río Plátano Biosphere Reserve...Honduras
Manas Wildlife Sanctuary.. India
Air and Ténéré Natural Reserves..Niger
Kathmandu Valley.. Nepal
Fort and Shalamar gardens in Trahore......................................Pakistan
Everglades National Park...USA
Historic town of Zabid.. Yemen

——————— MOST ENDANGERED HISTORIC PLACES ———————

Below are some of the most endangered historic places in America, according to the annual report produced by the US National Trust for Historic Preservation:

The Smithsonian Arts & Industries Building (Washington, DC) – *first museum of the Smithsonian Institution*

Blair Mountain Battlefield (Logan County, WV) – *site of a 1921 armed insurrection of unionized coal miners*

Doo Wop Motels (Wildwood, NJ) – *considered the largest collection of mid-C20th commercial resort architecture*

Fort Snelling Upper Post (Hennepin County, MN) – *fort complex overlooking the Mississippi and Minnesota rivers*

Historic Communities and Landmarks of the Mississippi Coast – *historic homes and landmarks damaged by Hurricane Katrina*

The Historic Neighborhoods of New Orleans – *shotgun houses, craftsman bungalows, Creole cottages, &c., damaged by Hurricane Katrina*

Kenilworth, IL – *Built as an 'ideal suburban village' with a diverse collection of stately homes; now being replaced by 'hulking McMansions'*

Kootenai Lodge, Bigfork, MT – *40-acre property built as a summer retreat, now threatened by development*

Mission San Miguel Arcangel, San Miguel, CA – *Superb example of Franciscan Mission architecture known for its original murals*

Over-the-Rhine Neighborhood, Cincinnati, OH – *known for its large collection of C19th Italianate, Federal, Greek Revival, and Queen Anne buildings; now plagued by crime*

World Trade Center Vesey Street Staircase[†], New York, NY – *Lone aboveground remnant of the Twin Towers, known as the 'Survivors' Staircase', threatened by construction*

† The two major American disasters of the 21st century to date (September 11 and Hurricane Katrina) are jointly commemorated in the building of the *USS New York*. At the time of writing, the $1bn ship was being constructed by workers in New Orleans, with a hull made of 24 tons of steel taken from the ruins of the World Trade Center. The ship is expected to join the Navy's fleet in 2007.

——————— HAWAIIAN NATIONAL MONUMENT ———————

On June 15, 2006, President Bush signed a proclamation creating the Northwestern Hawaiian Islands Marine National Monument. Located northwest of Hawaii's main islands, the 140,000-square-mile stretch is the single largest area dedicated to conservation in US history and the world's largest protected marine area. It is also:

>7x larger than all US National Marine Sanctuaries combined · home to 7,000 species (¼ of which are found nowhere else) · the largest coral reef system in the United States · larger than 46 of the 50 States larger than all US National Parks combined · roughly the distance from Chicago to Miami

The Antiquities Act of 1906 authorizes US Presidents to proclaim as National Monuments 'historic landmarks, historic and prehistoric structures, and other objects of historic or scientific interest' without necessarily having the consent of Congress. Wyoming's Devils Tower, a rock formation considered sacred by the area's Native Americans, was the first monument so designated, by T. Roosevelt in 1906.

—— WHEN IN ROME ... ——

Some elementary etiquette for the world traveler:

SOUTHEAST ASIA · outside of tourist resorts it is polite to dress modestly, especially when visiting holy sites or important buildings ❦ remove shoes before entering temples, mosques, pagodas, and private homes ❦ Buddhist monks are not allowed to have close contact with women, so do not stand or sit too near ❦ in most Southeast Asian cultures the head is considered sacred, therefore it is very rude to touch another person's head ❦ feet are considered unclean, so avoid pointing them at any person or religious image ❦ as the left hand is used for personal hygiene, it is impolite to shake hands or eat with it ❦ THAILAND · visitors are advised not to criticize the much-revered Thai royal family. The National Anthem is played daily in public spaces, like stations, and visitors should stand for its duration ❦ LAOS · it is considered taboo for women to sit on a roof (e.g. of a bus or boat) – Laotians believe that boats possess magical spirits who take offense at women sitting on their roofs; it is thought to portend bad luck for all aboard ❦ JAPAN · it is polite to remove your shoes on entering a home or restaurant ❦ bowing is the traditional Japanese greeting, though in a business context handshakes are common ❦ if giving a present in Japan, do not use black, white, or blue wrapping paper as these colors are associated with funerals; present any gift with both hands [see p.328] ❦ INDIA · apart from shaking hands, strangers should avoid touching one another, especially with their feet ❦

offensive in Brazil

a side-to-side sway of the head means 'yes' ❦ THE MIDDLE EAST · respect the area's religious practices; keep dress modest and remove your shoes when entering a home or mosque ❦ it is rude to show the soles of your shoes, and never place your feet on a chair or table ❦ a raised thumb is an insulting gesture ❦ SAUDI ARABIA · do not expect to be introduced to any veiled woman ❦ men often hold hands in friendship ❦ when inviting Saudis to dine, ask a number of times, since it is considered polite to decline at least once before accepting ❦ OCEANIA · FIJI · be cautious about admiring an object in someone's home, since they may feel obliged to give it to you ❦ LATIN AMERICA · personal body space is not as well defined as in Europe, and people like to stand close ❦ it is considered aggressive to stand with your hands on your hips ❦ COLOMBIA · it is rude to yawn in public ❦ BRAZIL · forming an 'O' with finger and thumb is considered offensive ❦ squeezing one's earlobe between the thumb and index finger demonstrates approval. ❦ ARGENTINA · it is rude to point with a finger; indicate instead with your whole hand ❦ CHILE · hitting the open palm of the left hand with the clenched right fist is an obscene gesture ❦ AFRICA · remove your shoes before entering any mosque ❦ it is rude to point the sole of your shoe at anyone ❦ items should not be passed, nor food consumed, with the left hand, as it is the hand used for personal hygiene ❦ people may try to attract your attention by snapping their fingers or hissing ❦ RUSSIA · it is considered (more) offensive (than usual) to drop anything in the street.

———— LEISURE PARTICIPATION ————

America's favorite leisure activities are dining out (48·1% did so in 2004) and entertaining at home (38·2%), according to data from Mediamark Research. Below, the percent of US adults who participated in other leisure activities in 2004:

Activity	%		Activity	%
BBQ-ing	32·1		Country music performances	5·3
Surfing the net	26·8		Woodworking	5·2
Playing cards	23·6		Bird-watching	4·7
Beachgoing	22·1		Bingo	4·3
Bars/nightclubs	19·0		Album 'scrapbooking'	4·2
Baking	17·7		Dance performances	3·7
Board games	16·7		Furniture refinishing	3·6
Cooking for fun	16·3		Chess playing	3·6
Crossword puzzles	15·7		Kite flying	3·3
Other music performances†	14·1		Book clubs	3·2
Theatergoing	13·5		Horse races	2·5
Video games	12·9		Model making	1·6
Zoo attendance	11·8			
Picnicing	11·5		† Other than rock or country performances.	
Dance/go dancing	9·2		[Source: Mediamark Research Inc. © · Participa-	
Rock music performances	9·2		tion is once in the 12 months ending fall 2004.]	

———— TOP US AMUSEMENT PARKS ————

The best-attended US amusement parks in 2005, along with that year's attendance:

1	Magic Kingdom	Walt Disney World, FL	16·1m
2	Disneyland	Anaheim, CA	14·5m
3	Epcot	Walt Disney World, FL	9·9m
4	Disney-MGM Studios	Walt Disney World, FL	8·6m
5	Disney's Animal Kingdom	Walt Disney World, FL	8·2m

[Source: *Amusement Business* magazine] According to a survey by the International Association of Amusement Parks and Attractions, 46% of American adults say roller coasters are their favorite type of amusement park ride; 13% chose bumper cars; 10% log flumes; 9% Ferris wheels; 7% carousels.

———— TOP US WATERPARKS ————

US waterparks with the highest 2005 attendance, according to *Amusement Business*:

1	Typhoon Lagoon	Walt Disney World, FL	1·9m
2	Blizzard Beach	Walt Disney World, FL	1·8m
3	Wet 'n' Wild	Orlando, FL	1·3m
4	Schlitterbahn	New Braunfels, TX	0·9m
5	Water Country USA	Williamsburg, VA	0·7m

—————————————— NATIONAL PARKS ——————————————

America's National Parks are part of the National Park Service (NPS), created when President Woodrow Wilson signed the National Park Service Organic Act in 1916. According to the Act, the primary purpose of the NPS is to: 'conserve the scenery and the natural and historic objects and the wild life [of the parks] and to provide for the enjoyment for the same in such manner and by such means as will leave them unimpaired for the enjoyment of future generations'. Currently, there are 388 NPS areas, which cover over 83 million acres (slightly more land than the US devoted to growing corn in 2005), and include every state but Delaware†. Some of the many notable features within the 58 designated National Park areas:

CARLSBAD CAVERNS, NM
Deepest limestone cave in the US
(Lechuguilla Cave)

CONGAREE, SC
Largest tract of US old-growth
hardwood forest

DEATH VALLEY, CA/NV
Lowest point in the western hemisphere
(nr Badwater; 282 ft below sea level)

DENALI, AK
North America's highest mountain
(Mt McKinley, 20,320 ft)

MESA VERDE, CO
Best-preserved prehistoric
cliff dwellings in the US

REDWOOD, CA
World's tallest known tree
(a redwood 369·2ft tall)
[Incidentally, a 350-year-old, 260ft
eucalyptus was the world's tallest
hardwood until it burnt down in 2003.]

WRANGELL–ST ELIAS, AK
Second highest peak in the US
(Mt St Elias; 18,008 ft)

YELLOWSTONE, WY/MT/ID
World's tallest active geyser
(Steamboat; Norris Geyser Basin)

2005 National Park visit statistics:

Recreation visits	63,546,297
Overnight stays	9,151,802
Lodging	3,019,226
Tent camping	2,209,149
RV camping	1,449,512
Backcountry camping	1,000,456
Campgrounds	842,256
Misc. camping	598,985

Per capita visits to National Parks have been declining since 1988. One study suggests that between 1988–2003 this decrease in visits was linked to the rise in the average annual number of hours spent watching TV, going to the movies, watching movies at home, using the internet, and playing video games.

† The House is currently considering a bill to start the process of creating Delaware's first National Park: the *Delaware National Coastal Heritage Park*. The bill passed the Senate in 2005. The Park would celebrate the landing of the Swedes and Finns in America, among other events. ❧ In 2005, *National Geographic Traveler* rated the condition of 55 parks in the US and Canada. The *Gwaii Haanas National Park Reserve & Haida Heritage Site* in BC, Canada, won top marks, followed by the *Apostle Islands National Lakeshore* in WI and the *Cape Breton Highlands National Park* in NS, Canada. In fact, 8 of the 10 Canadian parks in the survey scored above average, which the magazine attributed in part to a willingness of Canadian authorities to spend money on their natural treasures.

—— HOW TO SURVIVE ... ——

BEAR ATTACK · If you see a bear and can escape without being spotted, do so! Do not shout. If you cannot escape, show the bear you are human by waving your arms slowly and speaking to the bear, then back away. If attacked, 'shoot to kill' (at the heart), and continue firing until the bear is dead. *Never* try to outswim a bear [CBC News]

SNAKEBITE · Keep bite below heart level, remove restrictive clothing, and go to a hospital. Do not eat or drink, cut into the bite with a blade, 'use a stun gun', 'freeze or apply extreme cold to the area' [Savannah River Ecology Lab]

CIVIL UNREST · If you are caught in the middle of the unrest, 'do not take sides'. If you are abroad when unrest begins, stay in your hotel and contact the embassy. If phones are down, 'hire someone to take a note'. 'Do not watch activity from your window', and choose a room that 'provides greater protection from gunfire, rocks, grenades, etc'. [US State Dept]

SHARK ATTACK · 'Punch and kick at the animal's nose and eyes'; shout for help. Raise one arm, but 'do not wave', as others on the beach may simply wave back [Bugbog.com]

HOTEL FIRE · Crawl to the door; if it is cool, 'open the door slowly'. If your exit is clear, crawl to the hallway and walk carefully down the stairs. If you meet heavy smoke, do not run through it – go to the roof, find the windward side, and wait for help. If exits are blocked and the hallway is constricted by smoke, stay in your room, 'open a window and turn on the bathroom vent'. 'Hang a sheet out the window' to alert firefighters', 'tie a wet towel over your mouth and nose to help filter out smoke', and 'stuff wet towels into cracks under and around doors' [Dept of State]

SCORPION STING · Try to remain calm as the effects will be exacerbated by anxiety. Clean affected area with soap and water and apply a cold compress, then 'lift the limb to heart level': chances of death are low [Bugbog.com]

HIJACKING · 'Stay alert, but do not challenge [captors] physically or verbally'; follow their instructions. 'If interrogated, keep answers short and limited to non-political topics'. 'Carry a family photo ... you may be able to appeal to captors' family feeling'. 'Give innocuous reasons for traveling' [Dept of State]

KIDNAPPING · 'If drugs are administered, do not resist'; 'if conscious, follow your captors' instructions'. Establish rapport; 'family is a universal subject'. 'Plan on a lengthy stay', and find a way to track the passage of time. 'Devise ways to communicate' with other hostages. 'Take note of the characteristics of your captors and surroundings'. 'Establish exercise and relaxation programs'. (The US government does not pay ransoms.) [Dept of State]

ALLIGATOR ATTACK · If you can, run away in a straight line; otherwise strike the animal repeatedly on its nose; 'poke it in the eyes and scream'. If all else fails, 'play dead' [Bugbog.com]

KILLER BEE ATTACK · 'Run for shelter' in a straight line, covering your face. Remove stingers promptly; victims of swarming may require hospitalization. 'Do not try to hide underwater' [insecta-inspecta.com; *Webster's New World Medical Dictionary*]

MOOSE ATTACK · Generally when a moose charges, it is merely a warning. 'Get behind something solid'; 'it is okay to run'. If a moose knocks you down, do not try to fight back, but 'curl up in a ball and protect your head' [Kenai Fjords National Park]

———————HUNTING & FISHING———————

The latest US Fish & Wildlife Service figures (2001†) on hunting and fishing show that 82 million US residents (≥16) participate in wildlife-related recreation: 34·1m fished, 13m hunted, and 66·1m participated in at least one type of wildlife-watching activity (observing, feeding, photographing). As might be expected, there was some overlap in participation: 71% of hunters fished; 27% of anglers hunted; 62% of hunters and 58% of anglers participated in wildlife-watching activities; and 33% of all wildlife watchers hunted and/or fished. In total, it was estimated that in 2001 wildlife recreation-related spending totaled $108bn – or 1·1% of US GDP. Below is charted the percentage of the US population (≥16) who hunt or fish:

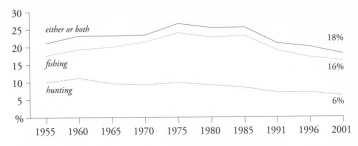

Hunting

National participation	6%
– participation in 1991	7%
% of US ♂ who hunt	12%
% of US ♀ who hunt	1%
Number of hunters	13m
– ♂	91%
– ♀	9%
– White	96%
– Black & other	4%
– big game	84%
– small game	42%
– migratory birds	23%
– other animals	8%
– modal age group	35–44
Days spent hunting	228·4m
– big game	67%
– small game	26%
– migratory birds	13%
– other animals	8%
Total 2001 expenditure	$20·6b
– 1996 expenditure	$23·3b
– 1991 expenditure	$16·0b

Fishing

National participation	16%
– participation in 1991	19%
% of US ♂ who fish	25%
% of US ♀ who fish	8%
Number of anglers	34·1m
– freshwater	28·4m
– saltwater	9·1m
– ♂	74%
– ♀	26%
– White	93%
– Black	5%
– Asian	1%
– other	1%
Days spent angling	557m
– freshwater	467m
– saltwater	91m
Total 2001 expenditure	$35·6b
– 1991 expenditure	$31·2b

Wildlife watching

National participation	30%
Total 2001 expenditure	$38·4b

[Source: US Fish & Wildlife Service, 2001 Survey of Fishing, Hunting, &c. † New data due in 2007]

———— THE WORLD'S TOP TABLES ————

Restaurant Magazine's 2006 survey of the world's finest tables listed the following:

El Bulli†	Girona, Spain	*Bras*	Laguiole, France
The Fat Duck	Bray, UK	*Le Louis XV*	Monte Carlo, Monaco
Pierre Gagnaire	Paris, France	*Per Se*	New York City, US
French Laundry	Yountville, CA, US	*Arzak*	San Sebastián, Spain
Tetsuya's	Sydney, Australia	*Mugaritz*	San Sebastián, Spain

† El Bulli chef Ferrán Adrià is perhaps the best-known proponent of *molecular gastronomy*, a cooking style that uses techniques generally reserved for science experiments. His menus have featured dishes such as Rice Krispies paella, rose petal tempura, injected goose barnacles, and caramelized cough drops.

———— CHICAGO & FOIE GRAS ————

In April 2006, Chicago became the first US city to outlaw the sale of foie gras when the City Council prohibited all 'food dispensing establishments' from selling the delicacy, and sanctioned a $500 fine. The law stems from welfare concerns relating to the production of foie gras: force-feeding fowl with a tube until their livers balloon to many times their normal size. The ban caused some in Chicago to complain about state interference in private consumption – and at least one chef was inspired to new culinary heights: Graham Elliot Bowles of Avenues at the Peninsula Hotel created a 10-course foie gras tasting menu, featuring delights such as kangaroo carpaccio with lime, eucalyptus, and melon, dusted with foie gras snow. At the time of writing, a number of chefs planned to challenge the ban.

Legislation again collided with culinary matters when in March 2006 the NYC health department prohibited chefs from cooking food '*sous vide*'. French for 'under vacuum', *sous vide* refers to the technique of vacuum-packing food into plastic bags, whereupon it is poached, simmered, or stored. Chefs claim the technique renders food more tender and flavorful than conventional methods, but the trend worries some health officials, who are concerned that food *sous vide* could harbor botulism. At the time of writing, NYC was in the process of establishing strict guidelines for *sous vide* cooking.

—— 'FOOD & WINE' MAGAZINE'S BEST NEW CHEFS · 2006 ——

Cathal Armstrong	*Restaurant Eve*	Alexandria, Virginia
Jonathan Benno	*Per Se*	New York City
Michael Carlson	*Schwa*	Chicago, Illinois
David Chang	*Momofuku*	New York City
Mary Dumont	*Dunaway Restaurant at Strawbery Banke*	Portsmouth, NH
Douglas Keane	*Cyrus*	Healdsburg, California
Christopher Lee	*Striped Bass*	Philadelphia, Pennsylvania
Pino Maffeo	*Restaurant L*	Boston, Massachusetts
Jason Wilson	*Crush*	Seattle, Washington
Stewart Woodman	*Five*	Minneapolis, Minnesota

——————— 2006 JAMES BEARD AWARDS ———————

The James Beard Foundation, named after the American culinary legend (1903–85), celebrates the 'heritage and diversity' of US cuisine. Some of the 2006 awards:

Outstanding restaurateur .... Daniel Boulud · Dinex Group, NYC
Outstanding restaurant .... *The French Laundry* · Yountville, CA
Best new restaurant .... *The Modern* · NYC
Rising star chef .... Corey Lee, *The French Laundry* · Yountville, CA
Outstanding pastry chef. .... Chef Johnny Iuzzini, *Jean Georges* · NYC
Outstanding wine service .... *Aureole* · Las Vegas
Outstanding wine and spirits professional ..... Daniel Johnnes · Dinex Group, NYC
Outstanding service award .... Gary Danko, *Gary Danko* · San Francisco
Best California chef. .... Suzanne Goin, *Lucques* · West Hollywood
Best Mid-Atlantic chef .... Fabio Trabocchi, *Maestro* · McLean, VA
Best Midwest chef. .... Shawn McClain, *Spring* · Chicago
Best NYC chef .... Dan Barber, *Blue Hill* · NYC
Best Northeast chef .... Jean-Louis Gerin, *Jean-Louis* · Greenwich, CT
Best Northwest/HI chef .... Scott Carsberg, *Lampreia* · Seattle
Best Southeast chef. .... John Besh, *Restaurant August* · New Orleans
Best Southwest chef .... Bradford Thompson, *Mary Elaine's* · Scottsdale, AZ

The James Beard Foundation also awards cookbooks, journalism, and broadcast media. In 2006, Cookbook of the Year went to *Hungry Planet: What the World Eats* by Peter Menzel and Faith D'Aluisio. *An Invitation to Indian Cooking* by the splendid Madhur Jaffrey entered the Cookbook Hall of Fame. *How to Cook Everything* with Mark Bittman won for Best National TV Show, and a new category, Website for Food, was added, won by David Leite and Linda Avery's leitesculinaria.com.

——————— RED OR WHITE? ———————

Data on wine sales by volume since 1991 reveal a US trend toward red wines:

Color	1991	1995	2004	2005
Red	17%	25%	41%	42%
White	49%	41%	40%	41%
Blush	34%	34%	19%	18%

[Sources: Wine Institute; ACNielsen supermarket data] A 2005 Gallup poll found that 39% of US drinkers prefer wine, while only 36% prefer beer (21% chose spirits). Notably, this was the first time that wine supplanted beer as the American drink of choice since Gallup began the poll in 1992.

——————— WINE IMPORTS INTO THE US · 2005 ———————

Country	$				
France	1·11b	Australia	765m	Germany	99m
Italy	1·06b	Spain	209m	[Imports to the US. Source:	
		Chile	166m	US Dept of Commerce]	

2005 TOP COFFEE EXPORTERS

Brazil .... *bags* 26m

Vietnam 13m

Colombia 11m

Indonesia 6m

Guatemala 3m

[Source: International Coffee Organization]

World coffee production for the 2005–06 crop year was 107m bags, of which 64·31% were Arabica beans (grown from *C. arabica* and considered superior), and 35·69% Robusta (*C. canephora*).

FAVORITE ICE CREAM FLAVORS

The top 5 ice cream flavors in the United States, based on their share of total sales:

Vanilla .... 26·0%

Chocolate .... 12·9%

Neapolitan .... 4·8%

Strawberry .... 4·3%

Cookies 'n' cream .... 4·0%

[Source: Intl Dairy Foods Association]

For the year ending July 2005, the best-selling frozen novelty brand (after in-house labels) was Nestlé Drumstick, followed by Klondike, Dreyer's/Edy's Whole Fruit, and Popsicle. According to the International Dairy Foods Association, over 90% of American households purchase ice cream.

TOY OF THE YEAR AWARDS

The Toy Industry Association's Toy of the Year Awards (the 'TOTYs') honor the best toys developed for the North American consumer. The big winner at the 2006 awards, presented February 11 at the 103rd American International Toy Fair in NYC, was a pen-based computer that performs math and basic translations.

Toy of the year .... FLY Pentop Computer
Infant/preschool toy of the year .... Weebles Weebly Wobbly Tree House
Girl toy of the year .... Dora's Talking Kitchen
Boy toy of the year [sic] .... Tyco R/C Shell Shocker
Game of the year .... Apples to Apples & Hullabaloo [TIE]
Outdoor toy of the year .... Air Hogs R/C Dominator
Educational toy of the year .... FLY Pentop Computer
Activity toy of the year .... LEGO Star Wars
Electronic entertainment toy of the year 20Q
Most innovative toy of the year .... FLY Pentop Computer
Specialty toy of the year .... 3-D Pool Table & UGLYDOLL [TIE]
Property of the year .... Dora the Explorer
Retailer of the year .... Target

According to a retailer survey conducted by trade magazine *TDmonthly*, the best-selling toys of Christmas 2005 included the V.Smile TV Learning System, featuring educational games played on a set that connects to the television; the 20Q Challenge, a handheld brainteaser featuring 'artificial intelligence'; the remote-controlled Roboraptor, a robotic dinosaur; and the FLY Pentop Computer.

—————————————— SUDOKU ——————————————

'Sudoku' is the Japanese term for an American adaptation of a puzzle devised by a Swiss mathematician. In 1783, Leonhard Euler (the man who gave us 'i' for the square root of –1) created a new kind of magic square that he called 'Latin Squares'. These were grids of equal dimension in which every symbol or number appeared once in each row or column. In the 1970s, a variant of Latin Squares was introduced into the US magazine *Math Puzzles & Logic Problems*, under the title 'Number Place'. Grids are solved by placing a number (1–9) in each blank cell so that each row and column of 9 cells, and every internal 3x3 block, contains a digit from 1–9. In 1984, Japanese publisher Nikoli ran the puzzle under the name *Suuji wa dokushin ni kagiru* ('the numbers must be unmarried'). This was swiftly abbreviated to *Su*[number] *doku*[single].

The man responsible for importing Sudoku to the West was retired judge Wayne Gould. He saw the puzzles when in Tokyo and approached the London *Times*, which began publishing them in November 2004. The popularity of Sudoku quickly blossomed, and soon other newspapers realized the potential of a number puzzle that requires no mathematical ability, costs little to produce, and boosts circulation without the need for prizes. In April 2005, the *New York Post* (re)introduced Sudoku into the US and over half the major US newspapers soon followed. In March 2006, the first World Sudoku Championships were held in Italy (the winner was Czech Jana Tylova). However, it remains to be seen whether Sudoku ('broadsheet bingo' and the 'C21st Rubik's Cube') will have the staying power of the crossword [started in 1913].

In 2006, UK paper the *Independent* reported a 700% increase in pencil sales thanks to Sudoku.

—————————— MOST POPULAR GYM MACHINES ——————————

Treadmills	28%	Stationary bikes	17%
Free weights	28%	Elliptical motion trainers	10%
Weight machines	17%	[Source: Sporting Goods Mnf. Assoc./*NYT*]	

—————————— TOP LEISURE SPORTS ——————————

The most popular recreational sports and fitness activities in the US for 2005 were:

Bowling	53·5m	Day hiking	36·6m
Treadmill exercise	48·0m	Fitness walking	36·3m
Stretching	42·3m	Billiards/pool	35·2m
Freshwater fishing	42·1m	Basketball	32·0m
Tent camping	38·6m	[Source: Sporting Goods Mnf. Association	
Running/jogging	37·8m	· Participated ≥1 time in the past year]	

PET OWNERSHIP

Pet	% own				
Dog	43·5	Freshwater fish	13·9	Equine	4·2
Cat	37·7	Bird	6·4	Reptile	4·4
		Other small animal	5·7	Saltwater fish	0·8

[Source: American Pet Products Manufacturers Association 2005–06 survey]

DOGS

Top purebreed dogs
Labrador retrievers
Golden retrievers
Yorkshire terriers
German shepherds
Beagles

Most popular dog names
♂ ...... *Buddy, Max, Jake, Jack, Charlie*
♀ .... *Daisy, Molly, Sadie, Lucy, Lady*

CATS

Top purebreed cats
Persian
Maine Coon
Exotic
Siamese
Abyssinian

Most popular cat names
♂ ... *Smokey, Max, Charlie, Simon, Jack*
♀ ..... *Molly, Angel, Lucy, Princess, Chloe*

[Sources: American Kennel Club, 2005; Cat Fanciers' Association, 2005; Petfinder.com, 2005]

DESIGNER DOG MIXED BREEDS

Designer dog mixed breeds are increasingly popular. A few breeds of note follow:

Basselier	Cavalier King Charles Spaniel & Basset Hound
Boxador	Boxer & Labrador
Bug	Boston Terrier & Pug
Chiweenie	Chihuahua & Dachshund
Cockeranian	Cocker Spaniel & Pomeranian
Doodleman Pinscher	Doberman & Standard Poodle
Dorgi	Dachshund & Corgi
Goldendoodle	Golden Retriever & Poodle
Labradoodle	Labrador & Poodle†
Peek-a-pom	Pekingese & Pomeranian
Saint Berdoodle	Saint Bernard & Poodle
Schnoodle	Schnauzer & Poodle
Saint Weiler	Rottweiler & Saint Bernard
Taco Terrier	Chihuahua & Toy Fox Terrier

† Labradoodles have the distinct advantage of a nonmolting coat, and were first bred in Australia as assistance dogs for people with asthma or severe allergies. Because breeding programs are still in development, labradoodle appearance is unpredictable, but the dogs generally have woolly or curly coats and come in a range of colors and sizes. Costs range from $900 to $2,100, depending on color.

───────────── WESTMINSTER DOG SHOW · 2006 ─────────────

The 130th Westminster Kennel Club Dog Show (first staged in 1877) saw 2,500 dogs in 165 breeds compete in 7 groups. The best in each group advanced to the Best in Show, which was won by Champion† Rocky Top's Sundance Kid, aka 'Rufus'.

Group	winner (nickname)	breed
Working	*Ch. Carter's Noble Shaka Zulu (Shaka)*	Rottweiler
Terrier	*Ch. Rocky Top's Sundance Kid (Rufus)*	Bull Terrier (Colored)
Toy	*Ch. Kendoric's Riversong Mulroney (Dermot)*	Pug
Nonsporting	*Ch. Merry Go Round Mach Ten (Boomer)*	Dalmatian
Sporting	*Ch. Chuckanut Party Favor O Novel (Andy)*	Retriever (Golden)
Hound	*Ch. Thistleglen Margot (Margot)*	Scottish Deerhound
Herding	*Ch. Bugaboos Big Resolution (Smokin')*	Old English Sheepdog

† 'Champion' denotes a dog who has earned 15 points at other AKC shows, a requirement to enter Westminster. ❦ The 2006 Westminster Dog Show had an unfortunate postscript when prize whippet *Ch. Bohem C'est La Vie*, who won an award of merit at the show, escaped from her cage at JFK airport and vanished. As of the time of writing, an extensive ground search (including psychics) had failed.

───────────── TOP BIRDS · 2006 ─────────────

The 5 most frequently reported birds of the 2006 'Great Backyard Bird Count' were: Northern Cardinals, Mourning Doves, Dark-eyed Juncos, American Goldfinches, and Downy Woodpeckers. The count, which takes place across North America, is conducted by the Cornell Lab of Ornithology and National Audubon Society.

───────────── SPENDING ON LEISURE ─────────────

Americans spent $702 billion on leisure in 2004. A look at where the money went:

Commercial participant amusements (bowling alleys, pool halls, &c.) ..... $99·4b†
Video and audio goods, including musical instruments .... 79·8
Wheel goods, sports, and photographic equipment .... 70·4
Nondurable toys and sport supplies .... 64·0
Computers, peripherals, and software .... 51·0
Books and maps .... 41·4
Magazines, newspapers, and sheet music .... 38·7
Admissions to spectator amusements (sports events, movies, &c.) .... 37·4
Clubs and fraternal organizations, except insurance .... 23·2
Flowers, seeds, and potted plants .... 18·2
Pari-mutuel net receipts (betting) .... 5·3
Radio and television repair .... 4·5
Other (film processing, lotteries, pet purchases, cable TV, &c.) .... 169·0

† Total spending by individuals and nonprofits. [Source: US Department of Commerce, latest figs.]

Sports

I was 9½ years old in 1974 when Hank Aaron hit his 714th home run to tie Babe Ruth. Never at that time could I have ever imagined achieving the same numbers. — BARRY BONDS [see p.234]

──────── 'SPORTS ILLUSTRATED' COVERS OF NOTE ────────

Date	Cover star(s)
01·09·06	Vince Young, Texas Longhorns
01·16·06	Jerome Bettis, Pittsburgh Steelers
01·23·06	Ben Roethlisberger, Pittsburgh Steelers
01·30·06	Jerome Bettis, Pittsburgh Steelers
02·06·06	US Olympic Ski Team
02·13·06	Hines Ward, Pittsburgh Steelers
02·20·06	Shaun White, US Olympic Snowboarding Team
02·27·06	US Olympic Snowboarding Medalists
03·06·06	J.J. Redick, Duke Blue Devils, & Adam Morrison, Gonzaga Bullfrogs
03·13·06	Barry Bonds, San Francisco Giants
03·20·06	*March Madness*†
03·27·06	*March Madness* specials
04·03·06	Albert Pujols, St Louis Cardinals
04·10·06	Joakim Noah, Florida Gators
04·17·06	Phil Mickelson
04·24·06	Lebron James, Cleveland Cavaliers, & Gary Payton, Miami Heat
05·01·06	Vince Young, Texas Longhorns
05·08·06	Lance Armstrong
05·15·06	Barry Bonds, San Francisco Giants
05·22·06	Albert Pujols, St Louis Cardinals
05·29·06	Carson Palmer, Cincinnati Bengals
06·05·06	US Men's National Soccer Team
06·12·06	Dwyane Wade, Miami Heat
06·19·06	David Ortiz, Boston Red Sox
06·26·06	Phil Mickelson
07·03·06	Lawrence Taylor, ex New York Giants
07·17·06	Paul Lo Duca & New York Mets
07·24·06	Larry Johnson, Kansas City Cheifs
07·31·06	Tiger Woods
08·07·06	Joe Mauer, Minnesota Twins
08·14·06	Hank Frayley & Jamal Jackson, Philadelphia Eagles
08·21·06	College Football specials
08·28·06	Justin Verlander, Detriot Tigers

[† For a discussion of things March, and an indication as to why it is linked with madness, see p.346]

───── WINTER OLYMPICS · TORINO 2006 ─────

Preparations for the Torino 2006 Olympics were beset by financial difficulty and organizational strife. The Italian government was obliged to rescue the Games from bankruptcy, and international concern over transport venues, and security was compounded by disappointing attendance figures. ❦ The US medal tally (25) was impressive (second only to the 2002 Salt Lake City Games total of 34) and several American performances stood out. In SPEED SKATING, Chad Hedrick became only the 3rd American to win 3 medals; Shani Davis's 1,000m victory was the first Winter Gold won by an African American; Joey Cheek collected Gold and Silver, donating his winnings to a Sudanese charity; and Apolo Anton Ohno, after a disastrous fall in his first event, went on to claim a surprise win in his weakest discipline, the 500m. FIGURE SKATER Sasha Cohen fell at the start of her program, but fought doggedly to take Silver. Ted Ligety and Julia Mancuso[†] both took Gold in ALPINE SKIING, and in the SNOWBOARD disciplines, 19-year-old Shaun 'Flying Tomato' White (half-pipe), Hannah Teter (half-pipe), and Seth Wescott (snowboard X) all claimed Gold. ❦ However, the achievements of the US team were overshadowed time and again by the showboating, partying, and ultimate underperformance of hotly tipped and heavily trailed 'sports celebs'. Lindsey Jacobellis, on course for Gold in the first-ever Snowboard Cross, fell while attempting a showy 'backside method' grab on her final jump, and gifted victory to Tanja Frieden of Switzerland. Skiier Bode Miller entered the Games in a vortex of public expectation stoked by sponsorship commerce and media hype (he featured simultaneously on the covers of *Time* and *Newsweek*). Yet, an *après-ski* attitude to preparation and a disregard for traditional technique saw Miller fail to win a single medal in any of his five events. Commentators lambasted his arrogance and indiscipline – but Miller was unrepentant: 'I got to party and socialize at an Olympic level ... the expectations were other people's'. ❦ The media's tendency to inflate hope and then dwell on high-profile failure left many Americans largely indifferent to the Games. This was exacerbated by sneaky TV counterprogramming (Fox's *American Idol* regularly beat NBC's Olympic coverage), and Italy's timezone (+6 EST), which meant that most results were old news by the time the events were broadcast. ❦ Despite this, it seems likely that by the Games of Vancouver 2010, the public debate will focus less on the froth of celebrity than how Team USA can live up to their 2006 haul of medals.

Country	G	S	B	All
GER	11	12	6	29
USA	9	9	7	25
AUT	9	7	7	23
RUS	8	6	8	22
CAN	7	10	7	24
SWE	7	2	5	14
KOR	6	3	2	11
SUI	5	4	5	14
ITA	5	0	6	11
FRA	3	2	4	9
NED	3	2	4	9
EST	3	0	0	3
NOR	2	8	9	19
CHN	2	4	5	11
CZE	1	2	1	4
CRO	1	2	0	3
AUS	1	0	1	2
JPN	1	0	0	1
FIN	0	6	3	9
POL	0	1	1	2
BLR	0	1	0	1
BUL	0	1	0	1
GBR	0	1	0	1
SVK	0	1	0	1
UKR	0	0	2	2
LAT	0	0	1	1

61 countries won no medals

─────────── NEVE & GLIZ ───────────

The twin mascots of Torino 2006 were 'best friends' NEVE (a snowball) and GLIZ (an ice cube). The bizarre male and female duo issued from the pencil of Portuguese designer Pedro Albuquerque, who described the genesis of these characters thus:

> *'Like all Lusitanians, I feel a natural attraction for the sea. That is why I am intrigued by the incredible shapes that this element takes on when it is transformed into snow and ice. And it was just this aesthetic passion ... that inspired the creative process that gave birth to Neve and Gliz.'*

─────────── US TORINO MEDALS ───────────

	Event	*winner*	*medal*
♀	Alpine skiing · giant slalom	Julia Mancuso	G
♂	Alpine skiing · combined	Ted Ligety	G
♀	Bobsled	S. Rohbock/V. Fleming	S
♂	Curling	♂ team	B
♀	Figure skating	Sasha Cohen	S
♂♀	Figure skating · ice dancing	T. Belbin/B. Agosto	S
♂	Freestyle skiing · moguls	Toby Dawson	B
♀	Ice Hockey	♀ team	B
♂	Snowboard · half-pipe	Shaun White	G
♀	Snowboard · half-pipe	Hannah Teter	G
♂	Snowboard · snowboard X	Seth Wescott	G
♂	Snowboard · half-pipe	Daniel Kass	S
♀	Snowboard · half-pipe	Gretchen Bleiler	S
♀	Snowboard · snowboard X	Lindsey Jacobellis	S
♀	Snowboard · parallel giant slalom	Rosey Fletcher	B
♂	Speed skating · 5,000m	Chad Hedrick	G
♂	Speed skating · 500m	Joey Cheek	G
♂	Speed skating · 1,000m	Shani Davis	G
♂	Speed skating · 1,000m	Joey Cheek	S
♂	Speed skating · 1,500m	Shani Davis	S
♂	Speed skating · 10,000m	Chad Hedrick	S
♂	Speed skating · 1,500m	Chad Hedrick	B
♂	Short track speed skating · 500m	Apolo Anton Ohno	G
♂	Short track speed skating · 1,000m	Apolo Anton Ohno	B
♂	Short track speed skating · 5,000m relay	♂ team	B

† Mancuso designed a 'Super Jules' underwear line that she wears for races. It is rumored that her grandfather acted as a rum-runner for Al Capone. ❦ Boosting morale in the figure skating camp was the flamboyant Johnny Weir, whose fashion sense and refreshing frankness with journalists won him numerous followers. For example: 'My glove's name is Camille, two 'l's ... when I skate badly, I blame it on him!' and '[skating] takes you from feeling like the lowest scum, like two hours ago. And now I feel like a flower growing out of the pond'. ❦ The US Olympic Committee presented US winners with substantial cash rewards: Gold earned an athlete $25,000, Silver $15,000, and Bronze $10,000.

─────────────── THE 'S.I.' SWIMSUIT ISSUE ───────────────

Sports Illustrated's 2006 Swimsuit Issue featured 8 women disporting themselves in a 'cover model beach party', *Project Runway* hostess Heidi Klum wearing only body-paint, and photo shoots from the Bahamas and other exotic locales. The cover stars:

Carolyn Murphy · Daniela Pestova · Elle Macpherson · Elsa Benitez
Rachel Hunter · Rebecca Romijn · Veronica Varekova · Yamila Diaz-Rahi

─────────────── CHEERLEADING & INJURY ───────────────

Though cheerleaders are known for their flashy outfits, athletic routines, and toned, nubile bodies, less attention has been paid to their injuries. A January 2006 study in *Pediatrics* showed that between 1990–2002, 208,800 children aged 5–18 were seen in emergency rooms for cheerleading-related injuries. 52·4% of the accidents were strains and sprains, 18·4% involved soft tissues, 16·4% were fractures and dislocations, 3·8% were lacerations or avulsions (tearings or detachments), and 3·5% were concussions and closed head injuries (5·5% were 'other', such as dental injuries, hemorrhage, or crushing). The number of injuries increased 110% in the years studied. In response, a national database to track cheerleading injuries is being developed, in part to determine the most dangerous stunts. Thus far, it seems probable that the human pyramid and basket toss are most likely to imperil participants.

─────────────── THE SOCCER WORLD CUP 2006 & USA ───────────────

Despite the desire to prove their 2002 World Cup quarterfinal appearance was no fluke (and live up to an inflated top-10 world ranking), Team USA failed to make it out of a difficult Group E in Germany 2006. They lost their first round-robin game 3–0 to the Czech Republic – a drubbing that the *Chicago Tribune* could not resist calling a 'reality Czech'. In their second match they fared better, scraping a 1–1 draw against Italy, despite the dismissal of 3 players (Mastroeni for a foul, Pope for 2 yellow cards, and Italian De Rossi for a nasty elbow to McBride). After the Czechs unexpectedly lost to the Ghanaians, Group E opened up for the US – who could have made the knock-outs with a win against Ghana in their final Group match. In a very physical game, Dramani scored first for Ghana, only for Dempsey to level the score in the 43rd minute. A controversial penalty to Ghana in the final minutes of the first half (after Pimpong theatrically collapsed in the box) put the game beyond America's reach. Ultimately, the USA salvaged just 1 point to finish at the bottom of their Group, a position that did little to inspire a passion for soccer at home. The USA's performance was blamed on everything from 'unhelpful' refereeing to the tactics of manager Bruce Arena, whose contract was not renewed.

During the Italy–France final (which Italy won 5–3 on penalties), French captain Zinedine Zidane was sent off for head-butting Marco Materazzi. Zidane claimed that Materazzi had insulted his mother and sister, but Materazzi countered that the comments he made were not 'racist, religious, or political … I also said nothing about his mother'. Both players received fines and match bans from FIFA.

FIFA · SOCCER WORLD CUP · GERMANY 2006

Group A

Germany [1]	4–2	Costa Rica
Poland	0–2	Ecuador
Germany	1–0	Poland
Ecuador [2]	3–0	Costa Rica
Ecuador	0–3	Germany
Costa Rica	1–2	Poland

Group B

England [1]	1–0	Paraguay
Trin & Tob	0–0	Sweden
England	2–0	Trin & Tob
Sweden	1–0	Paraguay
Sweden [2]	2–2	England
Paraguay	2–0	Trin & Tob

Group C

Argentina [1]	2–1	Ivory Coast
Serbia & Mon	0–1	Holland
Argentina	6–0	Serbia & Mon
Holland [2]	2–1	Ivory Coast
Holland	0–0	Argentina
Ivory Coast	3–2	Serbia & Mon

Group D

Mexico [2]	3–1	Iran
Angola	0–1	Portugal
Mexico	0–0	Angola
Portugal [1]	2–0	Iran
Portugal	2–1	Mexico
Iran	1–1	Angola

Group E

Italy [1]	2–0	Ghana
USA	0–3	Czech Rep
Italy	1–1	USA
Czech Rep	0–2	Ghana
Czech Rep	0–2	Italy
Ghana [2]	2–1	USA

Group F

Brazil [1]	1–0	Croatia
Australia [2]	3–1	Japan
Brazil	2–0	Australia
Japan	0–0	Croatia
Japan	1–4	Brazil
Croatia	2–2	Australia

Group G

France [2]	0–0	Switzerland
Korea	2–1	Togo
France	1–1	S Korea
Togo	0–2	Switzerland
Togo	0–2	France
Switzerland [1]	2–0	S Korea

Group H

Spain [1]	4–0	Ukraine
Tunisia	2–2	Saudi Arabia
Spain	3–1	Tunisia
Saudi Arabia	0–4	Ukraine
Saudi Arabia	0–1	Spain
Ukraine [2]	1–0	Tunisia

2nd Round

Germany	2	
Sweden	0	
Argentina	2	
Mexico	1	
Italy	1	
Australia	0	
Switzerland	0 (0)	
Ukraine	0 (3)	

England	1	
Ecuador	0	
Portugal	1	
Holland	0	
Brazil	3	
Ghana	0	
Spain	1	
France	3	

QUARTERFINAL

June 30 · Berlin

Germany	1 (4)	
Argentina	1 (2)	

June 30 · Hamburg

Italy	3	
Ukraine	0	

QUARTER FINAL

July 1 · Gelsenkirchen

England	(1) 0	
Portugal	(3) 0	

July 1 · Frankfurt

Brazil	1	
France	0	

SEMIFINAL

July 4 · Dortmund

Germany	0	
Italy	2	

SEMIFINAL

July 5 · Munich

Portugal	0	
France	1	

· FINAL ·

July 9 2006
Berlin 20:00

Italy
bt
France
5–3
on penalties
[1–1 AET]

July 8 · *Stuttgart* · Germany *bt* Portugal 3–1 for 3rd place

─────────── SPORTS BROADCASTING RIGHTS ───────────

Rights	*broadcaster*	*until*
BCS title game	Fox	2009
Daytona 500	Fox	2014
Final Four	CBS	2013
Indy 500	ABC Sports/ESPN	2009
The Masters	USA/CBS	*negotiated year-to-year*
NBA Finals	ABC	2008
Olympics	NBC	2012 Summer Games
Stanley Cup	OLN† (games 1–2)	2008
	NBC (games 3–7)	2007
Super Bowl	CBS/Fox/NBC	'07 (CBS); '08 (FOX); '09 (NBC); '10 (CBS)
US Open (tennis)	USA/CBS	2008
World Series	Fox	2013

† OLN was renamed Versus as of September 2006. [Sources: MLB; NCAA; *USA Today*; &c.]

─────────── ATHLETES AND THEIR AGENTS ───────────

A selection of notable sports agents, their companies, and some famous clients:

Tom Condon, Creative Artists Agency.....Peyton and Eli Manning, Matt Leinart, Marvin Harrison, LaDainian Tomlinson
Mark Steinberg, IMG .... Tiger Woods, Annika Sörenstam
Bill Duffy, BDA .... Carmelo Anthony, Steve Nash, Yao Ming
Scott Boras, Scott Boras Corporation............ Alex Rodriguez, Johnny Damon, Barry Zito, Greg Maddux, Jason Giambi
Arn Tellem ................................J.J. Redick, Hideki Matsui, Ben Wallace
Lowell Taub, GFHF Marketing & Management........Bode Miller, Julia Mancuso

[Current at the time of writing.] ❦ Tom Cruise's Jerry Maguire character was based on agent Leigh Steinberg. According to an interview in *SportsHollywood*, the phrase 'Show me the money!' emerged when director Cameron Crowe was researching the film with Steinberg and (then-unrepresented) Tim McDonald. When Crowe asked McDonald what he was looking for in the bidding process, McDonald replied, 'the money' – though, according to Steinberg, McDonald actually meant respect.

─────────── TOP-SELLING JERSEYS ───────────

The National Basketball Association's list of the best-selling player jerseys in 2005:

1	Dwyane Wade, Heat	6	Shaquille O'Neal, Heat
2	Allen Iverson, 76ers	7	Tracy McGrady, Rockets
3	LeBron James, Cavaliers	8	Carmelo Anthony, Nuggets
4	Stephon Marbury, Knicks	9	Tim Duncan, Spurs
5	Kobe Bryant, Lakers	10	Vince Carter, Nets

──────── 2005 SPORTSMAN OF THE YEAR ────────

Each year, *Sports Illustrated* anoints its 'Sportsman of the Year', a team or athlete who 'embodies the spirit of sportsmanship and achievement.' New England Patriots quarterback Tom Brady, winner of 3 Super Bowls by age 27, was the 2005 recipient.

Sports Illustrated Sportsmen of the Year, since the magazine (and the prize) began:

2005......................Tom Brady	1979...Terry Bradshaw/Willie Stargell
2004..................Boston Red Sox	1978......................Jack Nicklaus
2003...Tim Duncan/David Robinson	1977......................Steve Cauthen
2002................Lance Armstrong	1976........................Chris Evert
2001...Curt Schilling/Randy Johnson	1975..........................Pete Rose
2000......................Tiger Woods	1974..................Muhammad Ali
1999..............US Women's Soccer	1973..................Jackie Stewart
1998.....Mark McGwire/Sammy Sosa	1972...Billie Jean King/John Wooden
1997......................Dean Smith	1971........................Lee Trevino
1996......................Tiger Woods	1970........................Bobby Orr
1995......................Cal Ripken Jr	1969........................Tom Seaver
1994..Bonnie Blair/Johann Olav Koss	1968........................Bill Russell
1993......................Don Shula	1967..................Carl Yastrzemski
1992......................Arthur Ashe	1966..........................Jim Ryun
1991..................Michael Jordan	1965......................Sandy Koufax
1990....................Joe Montana	1964......................Ken Venturi
1989..................Greg LeMond	1963......................Pete Rozelle
1988.................. Orel Hershiser	1962........................Terry Baker
1987..............Athletes Who Care	1961........................Jerry Lucas
1986......................Joe Paterno	1960....................Arnold Palmer
1985............Kareem Abdul-Jabbar	1959..........Ingemar Johansson
1984....Edwin Moses/Mary L. Retton	1958....................Rafer Johnson
1983..................Mary Decker	1957........................Stan Musial
1982..................Wayne Gretzky	1956..................Bobby Morrow
1981..............Sugar Ray Leonard	1955..................Johnny Podres
1980......................US Hockey	1954..................Roger Bannister

──────── MOST COMPETITIVE (EXCITING?) SPORT ────────

Researchers at Los Alamos National Laboratory assessed the competitiveness of five professional sports: American hockey, football, baseball, basketball, and English Premiership soccer. Competitiveness was assessed by measuring the unpredictability of each sport, determined by 'upset frequency', or how often a superior team is beaten by lesser opponents. After reviewing 300,000 C20th matches, the researchers concluded that soccer had the greatest 'upset frequency', and consequently was the most competitive. To the delight of soccer fans, press reviews of this study noted that the most competitive sports tended to be the most exciting and, therefore, the 'best'. (Baseball fans were reassured to discover that, when reviewing games from only the previous 10 years, baseball triumphed over soccer as the most competitive.)

————————— STEROIDS &c. IN SPORTS —————————

2006 saw further scandal intensify the debate about drugs in sports, and, again, baseball was the main focus. In 2005, players and owners agreed to Commissioner Bud Selig's new punishments for steroid abuse: a 50-game suspension for the 1st offense, a 100-game suspension for the 2nd, and a lifetime ban thereafter. (Testing for amphetamines was instituted, with less severe punishments.) Yet, this attempt at a fresh start was undermined by the March publication of Williams and Fainaru-Wada's *Game of Shadows*, which accused Barry Bonds and others of using steroids. In response, Selig asked former Senator George Mitchell to launch an investigation into past steroid use in baseball. In June, pitcher Jason Grimsley was released by the Arizona Diamondbacks and suspended for 50 games after allegedly admitting human growth hormone abuse and naming other drug-abusing players. ❦ An AP/AOL Sports poll in April 2006 showed that 63% of baseball fans cared 'a lot' if pro players used performance-enhancing drugs like steroids. A *USA Today* poll in June 2006 asked baseball fans to explain the most likely cause of the rise in home runs:

performance-enhancing drugs, 47% · *better hitting*, 27% · *worse pitching*, 9%
changes to the way baseballs are designed, 8% · *other/unsure*, 8%

However, baseball was not the only sport to be embroiled in doping. The 2006 Tour de France descended into farce after 13 riders withdrew because of a doping probe, and the US winner Floyd Landis risked being stripped of his title after failing two drug tests [see p.245]. In April, Olympic and world 100m champion sprinter Justin Gatlin tested positive for testosterone and faced a minimum 4-year ban. And, at the time of writing, former triple Olympic champion Marion Jones faced a possible 2-year ban after she tested positive for a banned substance. [All named have denied wrongdoing.] ❦ Steroids were first developed in the 1930s, when a method of creating synthetic male sex hormones was discovered while searching for ways to treat hypogonadism (where the testes produce insufficient testosterone). The drugs caught on among bodybuilders, who valued their ability to increase muscle development and strength, and then spread across the world of sports. ❦ The term 'steroids' (aka *Arnolds*, *gym candy*, *pumpers*, *roids*, *stackers*, *weight trainers*, *gear*, *juice*) most often refers to anabolic androgenic steroids – the effects of which include gains in skeletal muscle and increased strength, libido, and appetite. However, steroids also increase the risk of heart attacks and strokes, and can cause liver damage, impotence, and outbursts of 'roid rage'. While steroids are prescribed to those suffering from various diseases, illegal use far outstrips legal prescriptions.

The Drug Enforcement Agency notes that steroids are often obtained through the internet, with supplies illegally diverted from pharmacies, produced in secret laboratories, or smuggled into the US (usually from Mexico and Europe). ❦ Data on the extent of steroid abuse by adults are limited. According to the National Institute on Drug Abuse estimates, hundreds of thousands of adults use illegal steroids each year. And, a brief web search yields a plethora of sites where users trade tips and review drugs. Use by teenagers is far better documented. According to the 2005 Monitoring the Future study, 2·6% of 12th graders have used steroids at least once; 2% of 10th graders said the same; along with 1·7% of 8th graders. 39·7% of 12th graders said that steroids would be 'fairly' or 'very' easy to obtain.

BASEBALL · THE 2005 WORLD SERIES

CHICAGO WHITE SOX *bt* HOUSTON ASTROS 4–0

2005 saw the Chicago White Sox win their first World Series in 88 years, in only the 19th-ever four-game sweep. The last two games were hard fought, and the third was the longest in World Series history (5 hours, 41 minutes). Sox outfielder Jermaine Dye earned Most Valuable Player, declaring: 'It means a lot, not only to us in the clubhouse, but to the organization, to the fans, to the city, and it's just a great feeling'.

> *With the birth of my kids, this is the most wonderful day of my life.*
> — OZZIE GUILLEN, White Sox manager

No.	date	result	city	*sang* God Bless America
1	10·22·05	White Sox 5, Astros 3	Chicago	Liz Phair
2	10·23·05	White Sox 7, Astros 6	Chicago	Chris Botti
3	10·25·05	White Sox 7, Astros 5	Houston	Aaron Neville
4	10·26·05	White Sox 1, Astros 0	Houston	Lyle Lovett

In honor of the White Sox's World Series win, *Wheaties* produced a special-edition package featuring pitcher Mark Buehrle. This marked the first time the White Sox had been featured on a *Wheaties* box.

2005 MLB PLAYOFFS

American League Division Series

White Sox *bt* Red Sox† 3–0
10·04·05	White Sox	14–2
10·05·05	White Sox	5–4
10·07·05	White Sox	5–3

Angels *bt* Yankees 3–2
10·04·05	Yankees	4–2
10·05·05	Angels	5–3
10·07·05	Angels	11–7
10·09·05	Yankees	3–2
10·10·05	Angels	5–3

American League Championship Series

White Sox *bt* Angels 4–1
10·11·05	Angels	3–2
10·12·05	White Sox	2–1
10·14·05	White Sox	5–2
10·15·05	White Sox	8–2
10·16·05	White Sox	6–3

† Wild card team

National League Division Series

Cardinals *bt* Padres 3–0
10·04·05	Cardinals	8–5
10·06·05	Cardinals	6–2
10·08·05	Cardinals	7–4

Astros† *bt* Braves 3–1
10·05·05	Astros	10–5
10·06·05	Braves	7–1
10·08·05	Astros	7–3
10·09·05	Astros	7–6

National League Championship Series

Astros *bt* Cardinals 4–2
10·12·05	Cardinals	5–3
10·13·05	Astros	4–1
10·15·05	Astros	4–3
10·16·05	Astros	2–1
10·17·05	Cardinals	5–4
10·19·05	Astros	5–1

—————2005 BATTING STATS & THE TRIPLE CROWN—————

American League		National League
Michael Young, Rangers [0·331]	*batting average*	Derrek Lee, Cubs [0·335]
Alex Rodriguez, Yankees [48]	*home runs*	Andruw Jones, Braves [51]
David Ortiz, Red Sox [148]	*runs batted in*	Andruw Jones, Braves [128]

Players who lead either league in batting average, home runs, and runs batted in are said to have won the batting Triple Crown. For obvious reasons, this is rare – only 9 have been so crowned in the American League, and 7 in the National League.

American League		National League	
Nap Lajoie, Philadelphia	1901	Paul Hines, Providence	1878
Ty Cobb, Detroit	1909	Hugh Duffy, Boston	1894
Jimmie Foxx, Philadelphia	1933	Heinie Zimmerman, Chicago	1912
Lou Gehrig†, New York	1934	Rogers Hornsby, St Louis	1922
Ted Williams, Boston	1942	Rogers Hornsby, St Louis	1925
Ted Williams, Boston	1947	Chuck Klein, Philadelphia	1933
Mickey Mantle, New York	1956	Joe Medwick, St Louis	1937
Frank Robinson, Baltimore	1966	† After whom amyotrophic lateral sclerosis (a	
Carl Yastrzemski, Boston	1967	form of motor neuron disease) is often called.	

—————SOME ANNUAL BASEBALL AWARDS OF NOTE—————

National League MVP 2005 ....Albert Pujols, St Louis Cardinals
American League MVP 2005 ....Alex Rodriguez, New York Yankees
Cy Young† National League 2005 ....Chris Carpenter, St Louis Cardinals
Cy Young American League 2005..........Bartolo Colon, LA Angels of Anaheim

† Honors the best pitcher in each league. Denton True 'Cy' Young was one of the finest pitchers of all time, winning 511 games in his career – almost 100 more than any other pitcher in history.

—————1st WORLD BASEBALL CLASSIC · 2006—————

The inaugural World Baseball Classic ran March 3–20 at 8 fields in the US and Japan. 16 territories competed in a 4-round tournament that comprised 39 games. On March 16, Mexico defeated the US 2–1, denying the US a place in the semi-finals and undermining their claim to be the world's top baseball nation. Japan was crowned champion after beating Cuba 10–6 in an electrifying game March 20.

On a somewhat tangential note – a persistent myth attributes the title of baseball's World Series to the tournament's sponsorship by the *New York World* newspaper. However, there is no evidence that the paper ever sponsored the series, and it seems likely that, because the winners of the National and American leagues were both already referred to as the baseball champions of the United States, any game they played against each other would require a much grander title.

—————————— SUPER BOWL XL · 2006 ——————————

PITTSBURGH STEELERS *bt* SEATTLE SEAHAWKS 21–10

Field: Ford Field, Detroit, MI · Viewers: 90·7m
National Anthem performed by: Aaron Neville, Aretha Franklin, and Dr John

The Pittsburgh Steelers won their first Super Bowl since 1980 to take their tally of
Super Bowl victory rings to five – IX, X, XIII, XIV, XL – 'one for the thumb' according
to the fans. Although the Seahawks had the better 1st quarter after a 42-yard field
goal from Brown, the Steelers recovered with a dramatic 37-yard pass by 'Big Ben'
Roethlisberger, who went on to score a much-disputed touchdown to give Pittsburgh
a 7–3 half-time lead. After 2004's 'wardrobe malfunction', the Rolling Stones' half-
time show was eagerly anticipated. The sexagenarians performed with their usual
vigor (Jagger even showing a little midriff), and two of their three songs (*Start Me
Up, Satisfaction, Rough Justice*) were censored for sexual references ('you make a
dead man come'). The 3rd quarter exploded with a record-breaking 75-yard run by
Parker (the longest touchdown run in Super Bowl history) that gave Pittsburgh an
11-point lead. Although a touchdown by Stevens from a Hasselbeck pass brought
Seattle back into the running, the Seahawks, already jittery, became increasingly
accident-prone. In the 4th quarter, Pittsburgh's victory was sealed by the 'play of
the game' – Randle El's (record-breaking) 43-yard touchdown pass to (MVP) Hines
Ward: the kind of trick play for which Steelers coach Bill Cowher is renowned.

Super Bowl XL TV ads (≤$2·5m for a 30-second spot) included: *Bud Light*'s 'secret fridge' – one
man's device for keeping his beer safe; *Sprint*'s 'crime deterrent' – a cellphone enthusiast throws his
phone at a friend to demonstrate its safety feature; *FedEx*'s 'caveman' – a prehistoric man is fired
for not using FedEx; and *Burger King*'s 'Whopperettes', with women dressed as burger toppings.

—————————— 2006 NFL PLAYOFFS ——————————

Though 26 years had passed since the Steelers' last Super Bowl, and the Seahawks had
spent their whole history without a championship win, both teams won their playoffs
with room to spare. Quarterback Ben Roethlisberger was the Steelers' hero, making
21 of the final game's 29 passes, while the Seahawks could thank quarterback Matt
Hasselbeck and running back Shaun Alexander (who played despite a concussion).

AFC Wild Card Playoffs	*NFC Wild Card Playoffs*
01·07·06........ Patriots 28 – Jaguars 3	01·07·06.Redskins 17 – Buccaneers 10
01·08·06...... Steelers 31 – Bengals 17	01·08·06....... Panthers 23 – Giants 0
AFC Divisional Playoffs	*NFC Divisional Playoffs*
01·14·06..... Broncos 27 – Patriots 13	01·14·06... Seahawks 20 – Redkins 10
01·15·06........Steelers 21 – Colts 18	01·15·06....... Panthers 29 – Bears 21
AFC Championships	*NFC Championships*
01·22·06.....Broncos 17 – Steelers 34	01·22·06...Seahawks 34 – Panthers 14

2006 BOWL CHAMPIONSHIP SERIES

THE ROSE BOWL: TEXAS LONGHORNS *bt* USC TROJANS 41–38

The USC Trojans entered the 2006 Rose Bowl on a 34-game winning streak and with a claim to being one of college football's great dynasties. However, in a spectacular upset, the Texas Longhorns triumphed, winning their first national championship since 1970. The Texas victory prevented USC from becoming the first team to win 3 consecutive Associated Press national titles, and dented their dynastic pedigree. Texas's win was in large part thanks to quarterback Vince Young, who rushed 19 times for 200 yards and was named Rose Bowl MVP in recognition.

FIESTA BOWL	SUGAR BOWL	ORANGE BOWL
1·2·06 · Tempe	1·2·06 · Atlanta	1·3·06 · Miami
Ohio State Buckeyes (4)	W. Virginia Mt. (5)	Penn State Nt. Lions
bt Notre Dame Fighting	*bt* Georgia Bulldogs	(3) *bt* Florida State
Irish (9) 34–20	(10) 38–35	Seminoles (23) 26–23

2005 HEISMAN TROPHY

Reggie Bush of the USC Trojans won the 2005 Heisman Trophy (given to the most outstanding college player, as voted annually since 1935 by fans, media, and former winners). Bush, who is valued for his incredible speed and agility, won with 784 first-place votes – second only to fellow USC player O.J. Simpson, who won in 1968.

NFL ANNUAL AWARDS OF NOTE · 2006

Some of the major awards given by the Associated Press for the 2005–6 season:

Most Valuable Player	Shaun Alexander, Seattle Seahawks
Offensive Player of the Year	Shaun Alexander, Seattle Seahawks
Defensive Player of the Year	Brian Urlacher, Chicago Bears
Coach of the Year	Lovie Smith, Chicago Bears

2006 NCAA WOMEN'S CHAMPIONSHIP

MARYLAND TERRAPINS *bt* DUKE BLUE DEVILS 78–75

Maryland won their first NCAA women's title in a stunning game featuring a comeback from a 13-point deficit – a triumph thanks largely to freshman Kristi Toliver, whose 3-point shot at the end of regulation sent the game into overtime.

	1	*2*	*OT*
Maryland Terrapins	28	42	8
Duke Blue Devils	38	32	5

NCAA 'MARCH MADNESS' · 2006

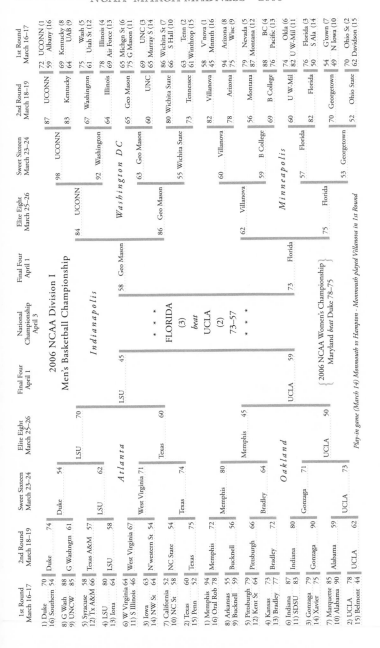

2006 NBA FINALS

MIAMI HEAT *bt* DALLAS MAVERICKS 4–2

The Miami Heat won the first national title of their 18-year history in 2006, beating the Dallas Mavericks 95–92 in Game 6 of the Finals. The win marked the third time ever that a team has triumphed from a 0–2 deficit to take the Finals. Guard Dwyane Wade impressed with a series of dramatic moves and took home MVP.

No.	date	result	city
1	06·08·06	Mavericks–90, Heat–80	Dallas
2	06·11·06	Mavericks–99, Heat–85	Dallas
3	06·13·06	Heat–98, Mavericks–96	Miami
4	06·15·06	Heat–98, Mavericks–74	Miami
5	06·18·06	Heat–101, Mavericks–100	Miami
6	06·20·06	Heat–95, Mavericks–92	Dallas

2006 NBA PLAYOFFS

Eastern Conference Quarterfinals
Pistons *bt* Bucks, 4–1 [games]
Heat *bt* Bulls, 4–2
Nets *bt* Pacers, 4–2
Cavaliers *bt* Wizards, 4–2

Eastern Conference Semifinals
Pistons *bt* Cavaliers, 4–3
Heat *bt* Nets, 4–1

Eastern Conference Finals
Heat *bt* Pistons, 4–2

05·23·06	Heat	91–86
05·25·06	Pistons	92–88
05·27·06	Heat	98–83
05·29·06	Heat	89–78
05·31·06	Pistons	91–78
06·02·06	Heat	95–78

Western Conference Quarterfinals
Spurs *bt* Kings, 4–2 [games]
Suns *bt* Lakers, 4–3
Clippers *bt* Nuggets, 4–1
Mavericks *bt* Grizzlies, 4–0

Western Conference Semifinals
Mavericks *bt* Spurs, 4–3
Suns *bt* Clippers, 4–3

Western Conference Finals
Mavericks *bt* Suns, 4–2

05·24·06	Suns	121–118
05·26·06	Mavericks	105–98
05·28·06	Mavericks	95–88
05·30·06	Suns	106–86
06·01·06	Mavericks	117–101
06·03·06	Mavericks	102–93

2006 NBA ANNUAL AWARDS

Most Valuable Player .... Steve Nash[†], Phoenix Suns
Rookie of the Year .... Chris Paul, New Orleans/Oklahoma City Hornets
Coach of the Year .... Avery Johnson, Dallas Mavericks

[†] Nash's win was his second in a row, the second time in league history that a point guard has won multiple MVP trophies. Only nine NBA players have won the MVP trophy in consecutive seasons.

STANLEY CUP CHAMPIONSHIP · 2006

CAROLINA HURRICANES *bt* EDMONTON OILERS, 4–3

The Edmonton Oilers suffered a bitter loss in 2006 to the Carolina Hurricanes, who won Game 7 of the finals 3–1 with 1 minute, 1 second left. Their victory was thanks in large measure to rookie goalie Cam Ward who finished with 22 saves, winning the Conn Smythe Trophy (for Most Valuable Player in the playoffs) in the process.

No.	date	result	city
1	06·05·06	Hurricanes–5, Oilers–4	Raleigh
2	06·07·06	Hurricanes–5, Oilers–0	Raleigh
3	06·10·06	Oilers–2, Hurricanes–1	Edmonton
4	06·12·06	Hurricanes–2, Oilers–1	Edmonton
5	06·14·06	Oilers–4, Hurricanes–3	Raleigh
6	06·17·06	Oilers–4, Hurricanes–0	Edmonton
7	06·19·06	Hurricanes–3, Oilers–1	Raleigh

STANLEY CUP PLAYOFFS · 2006

Western Conference Quarterfinals
Oilers *bt* Red Wings, 4–2 [games]
Avalanche *bt* Stars, 4–1
Mighty Ducks *bt* Flames, 4–3
Sharks *bt* Predators, 4–1

Western Conference Semifinals
Oilers *bt* Sharks, 4–2
Mighty Ducks *bt* Avalanche, 4–0

Western Conference Finals
Oilers *bt* Mighty Ducks, 4–1

05·19·06	Oilers	3–1
05·21·06	Oilers	3–1
05·23·06	Oilers	5–4
05·25·06	Mighty Ducks	6–3
05·27·06	Oilers	2–1

Eastern Conference Quarterfinals
Senators *bt* Lightning, 4–1 [games]
Hurricanes *bt* Canadiens, 4–2
Devils *bt* Rangers, 4–0
Sabres *bt* Flyers, 4–2

Eastern Conference Semifinals
Sabres *bt* Senators, 4–1
Hurricanes *bt* Devils, 4–1

Eastern Conference Finals
Hurricanes *bt* Sabres, 4–3

05·20·06	Sabres	3–2
05·22·06	Hurricanes	4–3
05·24·06	Sabres	4–3
05·26·06	Hurricanes	4–0
05·28·06	Hurricanes	4–3
05·30·06	Sabres	2–1
06·01·06	Hurricanes	4–2

2006 ANNUAL NHL AWARDS

Lester B. Pearson Award, Players' MVP	Jaromir Jagr, NY Rangers
Hart Trophy, NHL MVP	Joe Thornton, San Jose Sharks
Vezina Trophy, Top Goaltender	Miikka Kiprusoff, Calgary Flames
Norris Trophy, Top Defenseman	Nicklas Lidstrom, Detroit Red Wings

—MARATHONS OF NOTE—

2005/6 results of the 'Big Five' major marathons run in the US and Europe:

BERLIN	*first run* 1974
2005 · Sep 24–25	sunny, warm
♂ .... Philip Manyim · 2:07:41	
♀ ....Mizuki Noguchi · 2:19:22	
Purse........................*c.*$50,848	

CHICAGO	*first run* 1977
2005 · Oct 9	overcast, then sunny
♂ .... Felix Limo · 2:07:02	
♀ ....Deena Kastor · 2:21:25	
Purse........................ $650,000	

NEW YORK CITY	*first run* 1970
2005 · Nov 6	warm, humid
♂ ....Paul Tergat · 2:09:30	
♀ ....Jelena Prokopcuka · 2:24:41	
Purse........................$>600,000	

BOSTON	*first run* 1897
2006 · Apr 17	cloudy, cool
♂ ....Robert Cheruiyot · 2:07:14	
♀ ....Rita Jeptoo · 2:23:38	
Purse........................ $575,000	

LONDON	*first run* 1981
2006 · April 23	cool, drizzly
♂ .... Felix Limo · 2:06:39	
♀ ....Deena Kastor · 2:19:36	
Purse........................ $295,000	

In 2006, these five marathons joined to create the World Marathon Majors. The World Marathon Majors *Series* was also announced; the Series includes the WMM Majors as well as the International Association of Athletics Federation World Marathon Championships, and Olympic marathons. Males and females are judged separately, and runners earn points toward winning the Series when they place within the top 5. The winning man and woman share a $1m prize purse. The inaugural series started with Boston in 2006, and will end with the New York City run in the fall of 2007.

—2006 TRIPLE CROWN—

· KENTUCKY DERBY ·
Purse: $2m
Churchill Downs, Louisville, KY
May 6, 6:10pm · Distance: 1¼ miles

BARBARO†
Edgar Prado *(j)* · Michael Matz *(tr)*

BLUEGRASS CAT
Ramon Dominguez *(j)* · Todd Pletcher *(tr)*

STEPPENWOLFER
Robby Albarado *(j)* · Danny Peitz *(tr)*

· PREAKNESS ·
Purse: $1m
Pimlico Race Course, Baltimore, MD
May 20, 6:15pm · Distance: 1³⁄₁₆ miles

BERNARDINI
Javier Castellano *(j)* · Tom Albertrani *(tr)*

SWEETNORTHERNSAINT
Kent Desormeaux *(j)* · Michael Trombetta *(tr)*

HEMINGWAY'S KEY
Jeremy Rose *(j)* · Nick Zito *(tr)*

· BELMONT ·
Purse: $1m
Belmont Park, Elmont, NY
June 10, 6:38pm · Distance: 1½ miles

JAZIL
Fernando Jara *(j)* · Kiaran McLaughlin *(tr)*

BLUEGRASS CAT
John Velazquez *(j)* · Todd Pletcher *(tr)*

SUNRIVER
Rafael Bejarano *(j)* · Todd Pletcher *(tr)*

Key: *(j)*ockey · *(tr)*ainer
[† For the fate of Barbaro, see p.250]

THE MASTERS · 2006

The 2006 Masters (April 6–9) was won by Phil Mickelson, who finished 7 under par 281; it was his 2nd Masters title in 3 years. Below are the prizes and final scores:

Phil Mickelson	$1,260,000...–7	Angel Cabrera	$210,000...–3
Tim Clark	$756,000...–5	Vijay Singh	$210,000...–3
Jose Maria Olazabal	$315,700...–4	Stewart Cink	$189,000...–2
Retief Goosen	$315,700...–4	Mike Weir	$161,000...–1
Tiger Woods	$315,700...–4	Miguel Angel Jimenez	$161,000...–1
Fred Couples	$315,700...–4	Stephen Ames	$161,000...–1
Chad Campbell	$315,700...–4	[Total prize purse for the event was $7m.]	

AUGUSTA · CHANGES TO THE 'BIG GREEN'

The Augusta National golf course, among the most famous in the sport, was designed by golfer and engineer Bobby Jones (1902–71) in 1934. Since then, the 'big green' has been subject to numerous remodelings. Some of the most controversial changes† were made before the 2006 tournament. The changes were as follows:

Hole	par	alteration
1st	4	was 398m, now 416m · trees added · bunker expanded
4th	3	was 187m, now 219m
7th	4	was 376m, now 411m · trees added both sides of fairway
11th	4	was 447m, now 461m · trees added · extra wooded area
15th	5	was 457m, now 484m · tee moved 20m to left
17th	4	was 389m, now 402m

† Former champions Jack Nicklaus and Arnold Palmer criticized the alterations, arguing that they favored bigger hitters like Tiger Woods. However, Augusta chairman Hootie Johnson stuck to his guns and offered the rejoinder, 'I didn't know that a tough golf course was supposed to be a lot of fun'.

GOLF MAJORS · 2006

♂	course		winner
US OPEN	Winged Foot, NY	Geoff Ogilvy [AUS]	+5
BRITISH OPEN	Hoylake, England	Tiger Woods [USA]	–18
USPGA	Medinah, IL	Tiger Woods† [USA]	–18
♀			
KRAFT NABISCO	Rancho Mirage, CA	Karrie Webb [AUS]	–9
LPGA	Bulle Rock, MD	Se Ri Pak [KOR]	–8
US OPEN	Newport, RI	Annika Sörenstam [SWE]	par
BRITISH OPEN	Royal Lytham, England	Sherri Steinhauer [USA]	–7

† Woods won his 12th major at Medinah, edging closer to Jack Nicklaus' record 18 wins. In 2006, Woods became the youngest golfer to win 50 PGA Tour titles, beating Nicklaus' 1973 record.

———————————TRACK & FIELD RECORDS———————————

Event		set by	when	record
♂	100m	Asafa Powell [JAM]	2005	9·77s
♀	100m	Florence Griffith-Joyner [USA]	1988	10·49s
♂	110m hurdles	Xiang Liu [CHN]	2006	12·88s
♀	100m hurdles	Yordanka Donkova [BUL]	1988	12·21s
♂	200m	Michael Johnson [USA]	1996	19·32s
♀	200m	Florence Griffith-Joyner [USA]	1988	21·34s
♂	400m	Michael Johnson [USA]	1999	43·18s
♀	400m	Marita Koch [GER]	1985	47·60s
♂	400m hurdles	Kevin Young [USA]	1992	46·78s
♀	400m hurdles	Yuliya Pechonkina [RUS]	2003	52·34s
♂	800m	Wilson Kipketer [DEN]	1997	1:41·11
♀	800m	Jarmila Kratochvilova [TCH]	1983	1:53·28
♂	1,500m	Hitcham El Guerrouj [MAR]	1998	3:26·00
♀	1,500m	Yunxia Qu [CHN]	1993	3:50·46
♂	Mile	Hitcham El Guerrouj [MAR]	1999	3:43·13
♀	Mile	Svetlana Masterkova [RUS]	1996	4:12·56
♂	5,000m	Kenenisa Bekele [ETH]	2004	12:37·35
♀	5,000m	Meseret Defar [ETH]	2006	14:24·53
♂	10,000m	Kenenisa Bekele [ETH]	2005	26:17·53
♀	10,000m	Junxia Wang [CHN]	1993	29:31·78
♂	Marathon	Paul Tergat [KEN]	2003	2:04·55
♀	Marathon	Paula Radcliffe [GBR]	2003	2:15·25
♂	High jump	Javier Sotomayor [CUB]	1993	2·45m
♀	High jump	Stefka Kostadinova [BUL]	1987	2·09m
♂	Long jump	Mike Powell [USA]	1991	8·95m
♀	Long jump	Galina Christiakova [URS]	1988	7·52m
♂	Triple jump	Jonathan Edwards [GBR]	1995	18·29m
♀	Triple jump	Inessa Kravets [UKR]	1995	15·50m
♂	Pole vault	Sergey Bubka [UKR]	1994	6·14m
♀	Pole vault	Yelena Isinbayeva [RUS]	2005	5·01m
♂	Shot put	Randy Barnes [USA]	1990	23·12m
♀	Shot put	Natalya Lisovskaya [URS]	1987	22·63m
♂	Discus	Jürgen Schult [GER]	1986	74·08m
♀	Discus	Gabriele Reinsch [GER]	1988	76·80m
♂	Hammer	Yuriy Sedykh [URS]	1986	86·74m
♀	Hammer	Tatyana Lysenko [RUS]	2006	77·80m†
♂	Javelin	Jan Zelezny [CZE]	1996	98·48m
♀	Javelin	Osleidys Menéndez [CUB]	2005	71·70m
♂	Decathlon	Roman Sebrle [CZE]	2001	9,026pts
♀	Heptathlon	Jackie Joyner-Kersee [USA]	1988	7,291pts
♂	4x100m relay	USA	1992	37·40s
♀	4x100m relay	Germany	1985	41·37s
♂	4x400m relay	USA	1998	2:54·20
♀	4x400m relay	USSR	1988	3:15·17

[Records correct as of 8·22·06 · † awaiting ratification]

———————————— THE TOUR DE FRANCE · 2006 ————————————

The 2006 (93rd) Tour de France thoroughly earned its 'Tour de Farce' nickname, living down to the standards of the 1998 'Tour of Shame'. Before the race had even started, 13 riders (including favorites Jan Ullrich and Ivan Basso) were withdrawn amidst controversy surrounding a Spanish doping probe. American Floyd Landis won the 3-week, 2,267-mile race in 89h 39' 30" – despite riding while in need of a hip replacement. However, his jubilation was cut short when both his 'A' and 'B' drug-test samples indicated excessive levels of testosterone. Landis denied any wrongdoing, and insisted that these high levels were a 'natural occurrence'. At the time of writing, Landis pledged a legal challenge against any attempt to strip him of his title. Should his challenge fail, Landis will face a two-year ban, and his title and yellow jersey will be transferred to the Spanish runner-up, Óscar Pereiro Sio.

———————————— MLS CUP · 2005 ————————————

LOS ANGELES GALAXY *bt* NEW ENGLAND REVOLUTION 1–0
November 13, 2005 · Field: Pizza Hut Park, Frisco, TX · Attendance: 21,193
Honda MLS Cup MVP · Guillermo Ramirez

	total shots	shots on goal	fouls	offsides	corner kicks	saves
Los Angeles Galaxy	25	8	27	1	7	2
New England Revolution	11	2	24	5	7	7

———————————— FINA WORLD CHAMPIONSHIPS · 2005 ————————————

FINA's biannual World Championships were held in Montreal July 17–31, 2005.

Event		winner [country]	(World or Championship record)	time
♂	50m butterfly	Roland Schoeman [RSA]	WR	22·96
♀	50m butterfly	Danni Miatke [AUS]		26·11
♀	50m breaststroke	Jade Edmistone [AUS]	WR	30·45
♂	100m freestyle	Filippo Magnini [ITA]	CR	48·12
♀	100m freestyle	Jodie Henry [AUS]		54·18
♂	100m breaststroke	Brendan Hansen [USA]	CR	59·37
♀	100m breaststroke	Leisel Jones [AUS]		1:06·25
♂	100m butterfly	Ian Crocker [USA]	WR	50·40
♀	100m butterfly	Jessica Schipper [AUS]	CR	57·23
♂	200m backstroke	Aaron Peirsol [USA]	WR	1:54·66
♀	200m breaststroke	Leisel Jones [AUS]	WR	2:21·72
♂	200m freestyle	Michael Phelps [USA]		1:45·20
♀	200m freestyle	Solenne Figues [FRA]		1:58·60
♀	200m butterfly	Otylia Jedrzejczak [POL]	WR	2:05·61
♂	400m freestyle	Grant Hackett [AUS]		3:42·91
♀	400m freestyle	Laure Manaudou [FRA]		4:06·44
♂	800m freestyle	Grant Hackett [AUS]	WR	7:38·65

——2006 · WIMBLEDON——

All England Lawn Tennis and Croquet
Club, London, UK
June 26–July 9, 2006
Purse: £10,378,710
Attendance: 447,126

MEN'S SINGLES
Roger Federer [SUI]
bt Rafael Nadal [ESP]
6–0, 7–6 (7–5), 6–7 (2–7), 6–3

LADIES' SINGLES
Amélie Mauresmo [FRA]
bt Justine Henin-Hardenne [BEL]
2–6, 6–3, 6–4

MEN'S DOUBLES
Bob Bryan [USA]
& Mike Bryan [USA]
bt Fabrice Santoro [FRA] &
Nenad Zimonjic [SCG]
6–3, 4–6, 6–4, 6–2

LADIES' DOUBLES
Zi Yan [CHN]
& Jie Zheng [CHN]
bt Virginia Ruano Pascual [ESP]
& Paola Suarez [ARG]
6–3, 3–6, 6–2

MIXED DOUBLES
Andy Ram [ISR]
& Vera Zvonareva [RUS]
bt Bob Bryan [USA]
& Venus Williams [USA]
6–3, 6–2

Fastest serve ♂.....A. Roddick 143mph
Fastest serve ♀.... V. Williams 121mph
Most aces ♂ R. Stepanek 90 in 5 matches
Most aces ♀ ......A. Mauresmo 35 in 7

Andre Agassi chose the 2006 Wimbledon to
announce he would retire following the 2006
US Open. Agassi has won 8 Grand Slam singles
titles; the first was at Wimbledon in 1992.

——2005 · US OPEN——

Flushing Meadows Corona Park,
Queens, NY
August 29–September 11, 2005
Purse: >$17·7m
Attendance: 659,538[†]

MEN'S SINGLES
Roger Federer [SUI]
bt Andre Agassi [USA]
6–3, 2–6, 7–6 (7–1), 6–1

WOMEN'S SINGLES
Kim Clijsters [BEL]
bt Mary Pierce [FRA]
6–3, 6–1

MEN'S DOUBLES
Bob Bryan [USA] &
Mike Bryan [USA]
bt Jonas Bjorkman [SWE] &
Max Mirnyi [BLR]
6–1, 6–4

WOMEN'S DOUBLES
Lisa Raymond [USA] &
Samantha Stosur [AUS]
bt Elena Dementieva [RUS] &
Flavia Pennetta [ITA]
6–2, 5–7, 6–3

MIXED DOUBLES
Daniela Hantuchova [SVK] &
Mahesh Bhupathi [IND]
bt Katarina Srebotnik [SLO] &
Nenad Zimonjic [SCG]
6–4, 6–2

The US Open celebrated its 125th anniversary
in 2005. The amazing Bill Tilden [1893–1953]
holds the men's record for the most US
Open titles, having won 7 singles, 5 doubles,
and 4 mixed between 1913–29. Tilden also
won 3 Wimbledons, 2 professional singles
championships, and 7 Davis Cups in the course
of his spectacular career. † The 2005 attendance
totals set an all-time attendance record.

──────── TENNIS GRAND SLAM TOURNAMENTS ────────

Event	month	surface	♂	winner	♀
Australian Open	Jan	Rebound Ace	Roger Federer	Amélie Mauresmo	
French Open	May/Jun	clay	Rafael Nadal	J. Henin-Hardenne	
Wimbledon	Jun/Jul	grass	Roger Federer	Amelie Mauresmo	
US Open [2005]	Aug/Sep	cement	Roger Federer	Kim Clijsters	

Winning all four Grand Slam games in one year is exceedingly rare; the only people to have achieved the feat are: Don Budge [USA] (1938), Maureen Connoly [USA] (1953), Rod Laver [AUS] (1962 & '69), Margaret Smith Court [AUS] (1970), Steffi Graf [GER] (1988) – Steffi Graf also won the Olympic Gold in that year, earning a 'Golden Slam'.

──────────── THE DAVIS CUP ────────────

The Davis Cup was begun in 1900 by Harvard student Dwight F. Davis and now involves 134 countries, of which only 16 qualify to play in the World Group. The rest fight it out in continental leagues, in an effort to gain promotion into the elite World Group. The US has belonged to the World Group since 1989, the longest uninterrupted run in the Cup's history, and has won 31 times – though not since 1995. Current 2006 results appear below, along with some previous winners:

February 10–12 · 2006 WORLD GROUP 1ST ROUND
Croatia *bt* Austria 3–2
Argentina *bt* Sweden 5–0
Belarus *bt* Spain 4–1
Australia *bt* Switzerland 3–2
France *bt* Germany 3–2
Russia *bt* Netherlands 5–0
USA *bt* Romania 4–1
Chile *bt* Slovak Republic 4–1

April 7–9 · 2006 WORLD GROUP QUARTERFINALS
Argentina *bt* Croatia 3–2
Australia *bt* Belarus 5–0
Russia *bt* France 4–1
USA *bt* Chile 3–2

[The World Group semifinals are Sep 22–24, 2006, and finals Dec 1–3, 2006. See daviscup.com]

────────────

Previous winners			
2005.....Croatia	2000.......Spain	1994.... Sweden	1988.. Germany
2004.......Spain	1999...Australia	1993.. Germany	1987.... Sweden
2003...Australia	1998.... Sweden	1992....... USA	1986...Australia
2002......Russia	1997.... Sweden	1991..... France	1985.... Sweden
2001..... France	1996..... France	1990....... USA	1984.... Sweden
	1995....... USA	1989.. Germany	1983...Australia

———WORLD BOXING CHAMPIONS · AS OF 8·25·2006———

Weight	WBC	WBA	IBF	WBO
Heavy	Maskaev [KAZ]	Valuev [RUS]	Klitschko [UKR]	Lyakhovich [BEL]
Cruiser	Bell [JAM]	Bell [JAM]	*vacant*	Nelson [GBR]
Light heavy	Adamek [POL]	Tiozzo [FRA]	Woods [GBR]	Erdei [HUN]
Super middle	Beyer [GER]	Kessler [DEN]	Calzaghe [GBR]	Calzaghe [GBR]
Middle	Taylor [USA]	Castillejo [ESP]	Abraham [AUS]	Taylor [USA]
Junior middle	De la Hoya [USA]	Rivera [USA]	Spinks [USA]	Dzindziruk [UKR]
Welter	Baldomir [ARG]	Hatton [GBR]	*vacant*	Margarito [MEX]
Junior welter	*vacant*	*vacant*	Urango [COL]	Cotto [PUR]
Light	Corrales [USA]	Diaz J [USA]	Chavez [USA]	Freitas [BRA]
Junior light	Barrera [MEX]	Valero [PAN]	St Clair [AUS]	Barrios [ARG]
Feather	Lopez [KOR]	John [INA]	Aiken [USA]	Harrison [GBR]
Junior feather	Vazquez [MEX]	Sithchatchawal [THA]	*vacant*	De Leon [MEX]
Bantam	Hasegawa [JAP]	Sidorenko [UKR]	Marquez [MEX]	Gonzalez [MEX]
Junior bantam	Tokuyama [JAP]	Castillo [MEX]	Perez [NCA]	Montiel [MEX]
Fly	Wonjongkam [THA]	Parra [VEN]	Darchinyan [AUS]	Narvaez [ARG]
Junior fly	Romero [MEX]	Kameda [JAP]	Solis [MEX]	Cazares [MEX]
Straw	Kyowa [JAP]	Niida [JAP]	Rachman [INA]	Calderon [PUR]

Category	lb						
Straw	105	Jr bantam	115	Jr light	130	Jr middle	154	Cruiser	200
Jr fly	108	Bantam	118	Light	135	Middle	160	Heavy	>200
Fly	112	Jr feather	122	Jr welter	140	Spr middle	168	*[different names*
		Feather	126	Welter	147	Light heavy	175	*are used in UK]*

———————————NIKOLAY VALUEV———————————

In December 2005 Russian pugilist Nikolay Valuev became the tallest and heaviest champion in boxing history when he took the World Boxing Association (WBA) heavyweight title from John Ruiz. The giant, perhaps unsurprisingly, drew a record number of uppercuts from his opponent (a mere 6'3") before claiming the points victory, which also made him the first Russian ever to take the title. ❦ Valuev is something of a national hero: Putin personally commended him for a heroic display, and he has starred as a bungling decorator in a popular TV show. Despite his astonishing dimensions, Valuev is known as a sensitive and cultured man; he is an avid reader of Tolstoy and Jack London, and regularly composes poetry for his wife. Below are some specifications and particulars of the mighty 'Beast from the East':

Date of birth	08·21·73	Stance	orthodox
Height	7'2"	Trainer	Manuel Gabrielian
Weight	*c.*320lbs	Manager	Wilfried Sauerland
Reach	85"	Fights	44; won 43; 31 K.O.s

One adversary, Larry Donald, referred to Valuev as a 'Neanderthal man, like something from the Dark Ages'. Another, Clifford Etienne, was so intimidated at the weigh-in by Valuev's mammoth stature that he reportedly returned to his hotel, began drinking, and later attempted to flee the city.

48th DAYTONA 500

February 19, 2006 · Estimated crowd: 175,000
Distance: 500 miles · Average speed: 142·667mph · Cautions: 11

Driver (start)	team	points	earnings
Jimmie Johnson (9)	Lowe's Chevrolet	185	$1,505,124
Casey Mears (14)	Texaco/Havoline Dodge	170	$1,095,770
Ryan Newman (18)	Alltel Dodge	170	$796,116
Elliott Sadler (3)	M&Ms Ford	165	$684,076
Tony Stewart (15)	Home Depot Chevrolet	160	$537,944

NEXTEL CUP LEADERS AS OF 8·25·2006

Rank	driver	points	poles	wins	winnings
1	Jimmie Johnson	3365	1	4	$6,645,770
2	Matt Kenseth	3307	0	3	$4,611,890
3	Kevin Harvick	3048	0	2	$4,064,510
4	Mark Martin	2970	0	0	$2,925,450
5	Tony Stewart	2959	0	2	$4,655,390
6	Jeff Gordon	2931	0	2	$4,072,280
7	Kyle Busch	2922	1	1	$3,268,290
8	Denny Hamlin	2920	2	2	$2,991,550
9	Jeff Burton	2916	4	0	$3,301,240
10	Dale Earnhardt Jr.	2881	0	1	$3,592,200

The 2005 Nextel Cup Champion was Tony Stewart, who ended the season with 5 wins and 6,533 pts.

90th INDIANAPOLIS 500

May 28, 2006 · Estimated crowd: 300,000
Distance: 500 miles · Average speed: 157·085mph · Cautions: 5

Driver (start)	team	total points	total earnings
Sam Hornish Jr (1)	Marlboro Team Penske	144	$1,744,855
Marco Andretti (9)	NYSE Group	88	$688,505
Michael Andretti (13)	Jim Beam/Vonage	35	$455,105
Dan Wheldon (3)	Target Chip Ganassi Racing	139	$571,405
Tony Kanaan (5)	Team 7-Eleven	119	$340,405
Scott Dixon (4)	Target	120	$361,005
Dario Franchitti (17)	Klein Tools/Canadian Club	89	$307,905
Danica Patrick (10)	Rahal Letterman Racing Team Argent	83	$285,805
Scott Sharp (8)	Delphi	82	$283,805
Vitor Meira (6)	Harrah's Panther	84	$267,705

The 2005 IndyCar Series Champion was Dan Wheldon, who had 6 wins – an IRL season record.

──────OTHER SPORTS STORIES & RESULTS──────

· IDITAROD ·

The Iditarod Trail was once a mail and supply route serving small Alaskan villages and mining communities. Since 1973, it has been the location of the Iditarod annual dogsled race across 1,150 miles of frozen river, forest, and tundra from Anchorage to Nome. In 2006, 83 mushers competed in the race, each leading a team of 12–16 dogs. The winner (determined by the wet nose of the first dog to cross the finish line) was 3-time champion Jeff King, who completed the race in 9 days, 11 hours, 11 minutes, and 36 seconds. King won a brand-new car and a sizable share of the $835,000 prize purse. Though the winners of the Iditarod are guaranteed certain glory, finishing the grueling race at all is considered an accomplishment, and in 2006, 22 mushers withdrew. Thus, the last team to reach Nome is honored with the gift of a red lantern, and celebrated at a special 'red lantern banquet'; in 2006, Glenn Lockwood won this award. [*Iditarod* is a native Alaskan word meaning 'clear water' or 'distant place'.]

· FAVORITE SPORTSCASTERS ·

The Davie-Brown Index tracks celebrity marketing power using variables from influence to trust. The top 5 sportscasters, as of May 2006, were:

Terry Bradshaw · John Madden
Mike Ditka · Bryant Gumbel
Troy Aikman

· BARBARO ·

Moments after the Preakness Stakes began on May 20, 2006, Barbaro, the Kentucky Derby winner and Triple Crown hopeful, shattered three bones in his right hind leg. A dismayed Preakness crowd of 118,402 watched in horror as jockey Edgar Prado struggled to control the injured horse. Because of their delicate physiology, thoroughbreds often do not survive such injuries, and Barbaro later endured over six hours of surgery. His plight provoked a national outpouring of sympathy as well as gifts of cards, flowers, and carrots. At the time of writing, Barbaro showed excellent progress despite developing a severe case of laminitis in his left hind hoof. Sadly, he will never race again.

· LAUREUS AWARDS ·

The Laureus World Sporting Academy encourages the 'positive and worthwhile in sport', presenting awards to athletes in all disciplines. Some 2006 winners were:

World sportsman of the year
Roger Federer (tennis)
World sportswoman of the year
Janica Kostelic (skiing)
Comeback of the year
Martina Hingis (tennis)
Sportsperson with a disability
Ernst van Dyk (wheelchair racing)
Alternative sportsperson of the year
Angelo d'Arrigo (aviation)

· NBA ALL-STAR DUNKFEST ·

Nate Robinson won the 2006 Sprite Rising Stars Slam Dunk Contest, part of the NBA's All-Star Saturday extravaganza in February. Robinson took the title with a stunt that celebrated Spud Webb's win 20 years earlier. While Webb (5'7") stood in the lane, Robinson (5'9") backed up to half-court, sprinted, and caught the ball from Webb, jumping over him in the process. Despite the move's nod to history, some fans felt that the graceful behind-the-backboard dunk by (6'6") Andre Iguodala should have won, and argued that Iguodala had been 'Nate-Robbed'.

—————— OTHER SPORTS STORIES & RESULTS cont. ——————

· HOT DOG EATING ·

The 2006 winner of Nathan's Famous Fourth of July International Hot Dog Eating Contest was Takeru 'Tsunami' Kobayashi, who consumed a record-breaking 53¾ hot dogs (with buns) in 12 minutes. The 160lb 27-year-old from Japan edged out 220lb American Joey Chestnut, who managed only 52 hot dogs. Despite his loss, Chestnut's performance set an American record and thrilled patriotic fans. The win was Kobayashi's 6th consecutive such title, earning him the prized 'Yellow Mustard Belt'. Sometimes called the 'World Cup' of competitive eating, Nathan's is one of the highlights of the International Federation of Competitive Eating's year. Other contests feature such delicacies as bratwurst, wings, pizza, and Shoo-Fly Pie.

· 2005–2006 PBA BOWLING ·

The first major championship of the Professional Bowlers Association Tour, the 2005 USBC Masters, was won by Mike Scroggins, who defeated 22-time PBA Tour winner Norm Duke 245–238 to earn a two-season tour exemption. Tommy Jones defeated Ryan Shafer 237–223 at the 63rd US Open, winning $100,000 and a spot on the PBA Tour through the 2008–9 season. Walter Ray Williams Jr defeated Pete Weber 236–213 at the 2006 Denny's World Championship, winning $100,000 and a four-season exemption. Chris Barnes defeated defending champion Steve Jaros 234–227 at the Dexter Tournament of Champions in April, earning his 7th career title. Barnes also triumphed for the second time in a row at the Motel 6 Roll to Riches, winning $200,000 – the biggest grand prize in PBA history. Notably, at the 2006–7 tour

trials, Kelly Kulick (a 29-year-old from Union, NJ) made history by becoming the first woman to earn a full-season exemption on the (traditionally male) PBA Tour – garnering comparisons to Billie Jean King's tennis victory over Bobby Riggs in 1973.

· 2006 ESPYS ·

Lance Armstrong was the host of the 2006 ESPY awards, created by ESPN to 'celebrate the best sports stories of the year'. Armstrong was the first athlete to host the awards, and his performance included several 'memorable' comments about the French soccer team and Jake Gyllenhaal. Some 2006 winners:

Male athlete · Lance Armstrong
Best female athlete · Annika Sörenstam
Team · Pittsburgh Steelers
Game · Southern California *vs* Texas, 2006 Rose Bowl
Play · Tyrone Prothro
Sports movie · Glory Road
US Olympian · Shaun White
Arthur Ashe Courage Award
Afghanistan female soccer players

· WORLD SERIES OF POKER ·

The appropriately named Jamie Gold from California won the $12m grand prize at the close of the 37th World Series of Poker. A record 8,773 players entered the 12-day contest at the Rio Hotel and Casino in Las Vegas; the game was $10,000, no-limit Hold'em. Nine players reached the final, just four of whom were poker professionals. After thirteen hours of play, two players remained: 25-year-old bartender Paul Wasicka and 36-year-old TV producer Jamie Gold. Eventually, Wasicka fell for a bluff by Gold and went all in with a pair of tens, only to come up against Gold's paired queens.

———————READY RECKONER OF OTHER RESULTS———————

AMATEUR ATHLETICS · AAU James E. Sullivan Award	J.J. Redick
AUTO RACING · F1 US Grand Prix	Michael Schumacher
F1 World Constructors Championship [2005]	Renault [FR]
F1 World Drivers Championship [2005]	Fernando Alonso [ESP]
Champ. Car Atlantic Championship [2005]	Charles Zwolsman [NL]
Champ. Car World Series Season Champion [2005]	Sebastien Bourdais [FR]
NHRA Funny Car Champion [2005]	Gary Scelzi
NHRA Top Fuel Champion [2005]	Tony Schumacher
NHRA Pro Stock Bike Champion [2005]	Andrew Hines
NHRA Pro Stock Champion [2005]	Greg Anderson
BADMINTON · World Ch. [2005] ♂ Taufik Hidayat [INA] *bt* Dan Lin [CHI]	15–3, 15–7
♀ Xingfang Xie [CHI] *bt* Ning Zhang [CHI]	11–8, 9–11, 11–3
BASEBALL · MLB All-Star Game	American League *bt* National League 3–2
BASKETBALL · NBA All-Star Game	Eastern Conf. *bt* Western Conf. 125–115
BOG SNORKELING · World Championships [2005]	Iain Hawkes [GBR]
BOWLING · USBC Queens Tournament	Shannon Pluhowsky [203]
BOXING · *Ring Mag.* Fight of the Year [2005]	Diego Corrales *bt* Jose Luis Castillo
Ring Magazine Fighter of the Year [2005]	Ricky Hatton
BRIDGE · World Bridge Championships	
Rosenblum Cup	Rose Meltzer team
McConnell Cup	Carlyn Steiner team
CHEESE ROLLING · Cooper's Hill ♂ Jason Crowther [WAL]	♀ Dione Carter [NZL]
CHESS · FIDE World Chess Championship [2005]	Veselin Topalov
US Chess Championships ♂ Alexander Onischuk	♀ Anna Zatonskih
CROQUET · World Croquet Championship [2005]	Reg Bamford [RSA]
ELEPHANT POLO · World Champ. [2005] Scotland *bt* National Parks of Nepal 6–5	
FISHING · Bassmaster Classic Championship	Luke Clausen
Rolex/IGFA Inshore Championship	Joe Lopez
Rolex/IGFA Offshore Championship	Schramm, Segal, & Rosher [USA]
GOLF · Solheim Cup [2005]	USA *bt* Europe 15·5–12·5
GYMNASTICS · World Acrobatic Gymnastics Championships	
Mixed Pairs	Revaz Gurgenidze/Anna Katchalova [RUS] 29·252
Women's Group	Elena Moiseeva/Elena Kirilova/Tatiana Alexeeva [RUS] 28·800
Men's Group	Adam Smith/Adam Dobbs/Adam Denny/Andrew Price [GBR] 28·450
ICE CREAM EATING · World Championships	Patrick Bertoletti (1¾ gallons)
LACROSSE · Division I NCAA Men's Champ.	Virginia *bt* Massachusetts 15–7
Division I NCAA Women's Champ.	Northwestern *bt* Dartmouth 7–4
LITTLE LEAGUE BASEBALL · World Series [2005]	West Oahu Little League [USA]
LITTLE LEAGUE SOFTBALL · World Championships	Central [USA]
MOTORCYCLE RACING · US Grand Prix	Nicky Hayden [USA]
NACDA DIRECTORS' CUP · NCAA Division I	Stanford
Division II	Grand Valley State
Division III	Williams
NAIA	Azusa Pacific
PARACHUTING · World Championships 8-way	France
POWER BOAT RACING · APBA Gold Cup	Jean Theoret

——— READY RECKONER OF OTHER RESULTS cont. ———

RODEO · World Championships [2005]   All-Around Champion · Ryan Jarrett
   Bareback Riding Champion   Will Lowe
   Steer Wrestling Champion   Lee Graves
   Saddle Bronc Riding Champion   Jeffery Willert
   Steer Roping Champion   Guy Allen
   Bull Riding Champion   Matt Austin
RUGBY · Zurich Premiership Championship   Sale Sharks 45–20 Leicester Tigers
   Guinness Premiership   Sale Sharks
   Heineken Cup   Munster 23–19 Biarritz
   European Challenge Cup   Gloucester 36–34 London Irish
SOAP BOX RACING · All-American Soap Box Derby
   Masters   Garrett Kysar [40]
   Super Stock   Sally Sue Thornton [234]
   Stock   Michael Neely [302]
SOFTBALL · Men's major fast pitch   Circle Tap
   Men's major slow pitch [2005]   AM/Las Vegas/Benfield/Reece & co.
   Women's major fast pitch   Stratford Brakettes
SQUASH · Super Series Finals   Anthony Ricketts [AUS] *bt*
                Lee Beachill [GBR] 11–7, 6–11, 11–4, 12–10
   World Men's tournament [2005]   England *bt* Egypt 2–0
SUMMER X GAMES · Skateboarding Big Air   Danny Way 95
   Skateboard street   ♂ Chris Cole ♀ Elissa Steamer
   Moto X freestyle   Travis Pastrana 94·20
   BMX freestyle dirt   Corey Bohan 91·66
   BMX Big Air   Kevin Robinson 95
SWIMMING · ConocoPhillips National Championships
   200m backstroke   ♂ Aaron Peirsol 1:56·36
   200m breaststroke   ♂ Brendan Hansen 2:08·74† ♀ Tara Kirk 2:28·46
   1,500m freestyle   ♂ Erik Vendt 15:05·41
   400m medley relay   ♂ Club Wolverine A 3:41·96 ♀ California Aquatics A 4:03·32
   100m freestyle   ♀ Amanda Weir 53·58
   800m freestyle   ♀ Hayley Peirsol 8:26·45
   FINA Short Course World Championships medal leader   AUS [25]
TENNIS · Fed Cup [2005]   Russia *bt* France 3–2
   WTA Champ [2005]   Amelie Mauresmo *bt* Mary Pierce 5–7, 7–6 (7–3), 6–4
TRIATHLONS · ITU Age Group World Champ. [2005]   Diogo Sclebin [BRA] 1:55·38
   Aquathalon World Championship [2005]   Jonny Collett [NZL] 32:08
   Ironman World Championship [2005]   Faris Al-Sultan [GER] 8:14:17
WOMEN'S HOCKEY · NWHL Ch. Cup   Montreal Axion *bt* Brampton Thunder 1–0
YACHTING · Valencia 32nd America's Cup
   Act 10   BMW Oracle Racing [USA]
   Act 11   Alinghi [SUI]
   Act 12 & ACC Championship   Emirates Team New Zealand

All events are 2006 unless otherwise stated. † Hansen broke his own world record in the 200m and
100m breaststroke at the 2006 National Championships; both had been set in 2004 Olympic trials.

The Nation

*Columbus did not find out America by chance, but God directed him
at that time to discover it; it was contingent to him, but necessary to God.*
— ROBERT BURTON, *The Anatomy of Melancholy,* 1621

US GEOGRAPHIC SPECIFICATIONS & EXTREMES

Highest point .... Mount McKinley, Alaska (20,320ft above sea level)
Lowest point .... Death Valley, California (282ft below sea level)
Mean elevation.. ≈2,500ft
Northernmost point .... Point Barrow, Alaska
Southernmost point .... Ka Lae (South Cape), Hawaii
Easternmost point .... West Quoddy Head, Maine
Westernmost point.. Cape Wrangell, Alaska

GEOGRAPHIC AREA
Total....................9,631,418 km²
Land....................9,161,923 km²
Water.................... 469,495 km²
[includes only the 50 States and DC]
LAND BOUNDARIES
Total....................... 12,034 km
Canada ....8,893 km
[including 2,477 km with Alaska]
Mexico ....3,141 km
Guantánamo Bay† .... 29 km
Coastline .... 19,924 km
MARITIME CLAIMS
Territorial sea.........12 nautical miles
Contiguous zone............... 24 nm
Exclusive economic zone ......200 nm
Continental shelf.........not specified
LAND USE (2005)
Arable land.....................18·01%
Permanent crops .... 0·21%
Other...........................81·78%
different calculations exist
[Sources: USGS; CIA; Dept of Interior]

US Commonwealth & Territories
American Samoa · Guam
Northern Mariana Islands
Puerto Rico · Virgin Islands

Freely Associated States
Republic of the Marshall Islands
Federated States of Micronesia
Republic of Palau (status review in 2009)

Other areas under US jurisdiction
Midway Atoll · Palmyra Atoll
Wake Atoll · Baker Island
Howland Island · Jarvis Island
Johnston Atoll · North Island
Sand Island · Kingman Reef
Navassa Island (claimed by Haiti)

† The oldest base outside the US, Guantánamo
Bay has been leased from Cuba (*c.*$4,000/year)
since 1903. The naval base is now home to the
highly controversial 'terrorist' detention camp.

There are 633 WILDERNESS AREAS in the US covering 105,764,330 acres (an area
greater than California). The 1864 Wilderness Act gave Congress the authority to
designate and protect these unique areas 'where the earth and its community of life
are untrammeled by man, where man himself is a visitor who does not remain…'.

─────────────LARGEST US CITIES─────────────

City, State		2002 pop.	± since 2000 (%)	nickname(s)
New York	NY	8,084,316	76,038 (0·9)	*The Big Apple; Gotham City*
Los Angeles	CA	3,798,981	104,239 (2·8)	*City of Angels; La La Land*
Chicago	IL	2,886,251	–9,796 (–0·3)	*The Windy City; Big Town*
Houston	TX	2,009,834	56,201 (2·9)	*Magnolia City; Clutch City*
Philadelphia	PA	1,492,231	–25,319 (–1·7)	*City of Brotherly Love*
Phoenix	AZ	1,371,960	50,770 (3·8)	*Valley of the Sun*
San Diego	CA	1,259,532	36,116 (3·0)	*Plymouth of the West*
Dallas	TX	1,211,467	22,878 (1·9)	*The Big D*
San Antonio	TX	1,194,222	42,954 (3·7)	*Alamo City; Mission City*
Detroit	MI	925,051	–26,219 (–2·8)	*Motor City*

[As of July 1, 2002 · Source: US Census · Some cities have additional or alternative nicknames]

───────────AMERICAN SUPERLATIVES OF NOTE───────────

Highest active volcano ...... Wrangell, Alaska 4,316m
Highest dam .... Oroville Dam, California 770ft
Highest waterfall .... Yosemite Falls, California 2,425ft
Biggest waterfall (volume) .. Niagara Falls, New York 168,000m³/s
Deepest depression .... Death Valley, California .... 282ft below sea level
Largest lake .... Michigan-Huron, USA/Canada 45,300m²
Longest suspension bridge ... Verrazano Narrows, New York 1,298m
Largest geyser .... Steamboat, Yellowstone National Park .... >300ft
Tallest inhabited building ... Sears Tower, Chicago .... 110 stories, 443m
Tallest structure .... KVLY TV mast, North Dakota 629m
Longest rail tunnel .... New Cascade, Washington 12,537m
Longest road tunnel .... Ted Williams/I-90 Extension, MA 4,200m

Unsurprisingly, a degree of uncertainty and debate surrounds some of these entries and their specifications.

───────────THE CENTER OF AMERICA───────────

The US Geological Survey, admitting that there is no universally accepted or utterly satisfactory definition of the 'geographic center' of an area, offers one definition as 'the center of gravity of the surface, or that point on which the surface of an area would balance if it were a plane of uniform thickness'. Clearly a number of factors will influence any measurement of the center of America (large bodies of water, the curvature of the Earth, &c.), not to mention the exact definition of the landmass:

Geographic area   *location*
Conterminous US (48 States) ....*nr Lebanon, Smith County, KS* · 39°50'N 98°35'W
Continental US (49 States).......*nr Castle Rock, Butte County, SD* · 44°59'N 103°38'W
The US (50 States) ....*W. of Castle Rock, Butte County, SD* · 44°58'N 103°46'W
N. American Continent .... *6 mi W. of Balta, Pierce County, ND* · 48°10'N 100°10'W

—ALLEGIANCE PLEDGE—

According to the US Code, the PLEDGE OF ALLEGIANCE should be made facing the flag, standing to attention, with the right hand over the heart. Men not in uniform should remove their headdress with their right hand and hold it at the left shoulder. Those in uniform should remain silent, face the flag, and salute. The Pledge of Allegiance is:

I pledge allegiance to the flag of
the United States of America and
to the Republic for which it stands,
one Nation, under God, indivisible,
with Liberty and Justice for all.

The Youth's Companion, a magazine in Boston, first published the Pledge of Allegiance in 1892 to celebrate the 400th anniversary of America's discovery. However, the publication of the Pledge was not without controversy, since two writers at the *Companion*, James B. Upham and Francis Bellamy, both claimed authorship. A number of tribunals ruled in favor of Bellamy, and in 1957 the Library of Congress confirmed his claim. The original text pledged allegiance to 'my flag', and in 1923 the National Flag Conference added a specification of the US flag (presumably a bid to avoid confusion and prevent any possible ambiguity amongst those who were born in other countries). In 1942, the Pledge was given official recognition by Congress; and, on June 14, 1954, the phrase 'under God' was added by Congressional decree. President Eisenhower stated, 'In this way we are reaffirming the transcendence of religious faith in America's heritage and future; in this way we shall constantly strengthen those spiritual weapons which forever will be our country's most powerful resource in peace and war'.

—AMERICAN'S CREED—

The AMERICAN'S CREED is as follows:

I believe in the United States of America as a government of the people, by the people, for the people; whose just powers are derived from the consent of the governed; a democracy in a republic; a sovereign Nation of many sovereign States; a perfect union, one and inseparable; established upon those principles of Freedom, Equality, Justice, and Humanity for which American patriots sacrificed their lives and fortunes. I therefore believe it is my duty to my country to love it, to support its Constitution, to obey its laws, to respect its flag, and to defend it against all enemies.

It was written by William Tyler Page (a descendent of President Tyler) in 1917, as an entry for a national competition for a composition that embodied the principles of America. The competition, conceived by Henry Sterling Chapin, the Commissioner of Education in NY, prompted over 3,000 entries. Page's text was formally adopted by the House of Representatives in April 1918.

—NATIONAL MOTTO—

The NATIONAL MOTTO, 'In God We Trust', was established by the 84th Congress, and approved by Eisenhower in 1956. It seems the motto dates from a popular movement during the Civil War to recognize God on US coinage. Secretary of the Treasury Salmon P. Chase declared in 1861, 'No nation can be strong except in the strength of God, or safe except in His defense. The trust of our people in God should be declared on our national coins'. 'In God We Trust', which first appeared on US notes in 1957, may be based on 'In God is our trust' from the fourth verse of *The Star-Spangled Banner* [see p.260].

UNCLE SAM

The exact origins of UNCLE SAM – the tall, gaunt, be-goateed, top-hat-wearing, red-white-and-blue sporting personification of the United States – are uncertain. Some claim he is based on Samuel Wilson, a New York meatpacker who *c.*1812 supplied beef to the army in barrels labeled 'US'. Popular use transmogrified these initials into 'Uncle Sam', and the link between Wilson and the Union stuck. This theory was given official recognition by the 87th Congress, which in 1961 recognized 'Uncle Sam Wilson of Troy, NY, as the progenitor of America's national symbol of Uncle Sam'. Oddly, Wilson looked little like his graphic depiction (he was, for example, clean-shaven), and it seems that German-born artist Thomas Nast first drew Uncle Sam (*c.*1840) as we know him today [see p.300]. Nast may have borrowed the stylings of Dan Rice, a jockey, strong-man, blackface minstrel, and clown, who performed in the mid-C19th with an educated pig ('Lord Byron') and a trick horse ('Excelsior'). Rice's costume matched Nast's Uncle Sam to a tee: red and white star-spangled striped suit, a top hat, and chin whiskers. [Some have suggested that Nast's Uncle Sam may have preceded Rice.] Yet the image that cemented Uncle Sam in the nation's consciousness was James Montogomery Flagg's iconic WWI recruiting poster, where an imposing Uncle Sam declares: 'I Want YOU For US Army'. ❦ According to official figures from the Social Security Administration, the popularity of the name Sam has declined over the centuries. In 1880, Sam was the 36th most popular boy's name; by 2005, Sam had dropped to 463th [see also p.92]. ❦ Google users may search within US government web sites at google.com/unclesam. ❦ To *Stand Sam* is to be obliged to pay for something – or to be left to pick up the check (as Uncle Sam did for his troops). ❦ For WWII-era federal workers and soldiers, *Uncle Sam's Party* was payday.

LIBERTY BELL

THE LIBERTY BELL is inscribed with the Biblical text '*Proclaim liberty throughout the land unto all the inhabitants thereof*' [Leviticus 25:10]. The bell (*c.*1 ton in weight and 3·7m around the lip) was first rung on July 8, 1776, to celebrate the first public reading of the Declaration of Independence; it was rung for the final time in 1846 on the anniversary of Washington's birthday, when it cracked irreparably. Today, the bell hangs in Philadelphia's Liberty Bell Pavilion and is, apparently, still gently tapped each July 4.

THE BALD EAGLE

The national bird of the US since 1782, the BALD EAGLE is represented on a number of American icons, including the Great Seal, the President's flag, and the $1 bill. It was chosen, after 6 years of Congressional wrangling, because it symbolized strength, courage, freedom, and immortality – and because it was unique to America. Not folliculary challenged but 'piebald' (i.e. marked with white), the bald eagle (*Haliaeetus leucocephalus*) is currently designated 'threatened' by the US Fish & Wildlife Service.

——FLORAL EMBLEM——

'... *we hold the rose dear as the symbol of life and love and devotion, of beauty and eternity. For the love of man and woman, for the love of mankind and God, for the love of country...*' – with these words President Ronald Reagan, on November 20, 1986, proclaimed the ROSE America's National Floral Emblem. Reagan said that 'Americans who would speak the language of the heart do so with a rose' – yet he did not specify a type of rose. In the traditional Courtly 'language of flowers', different roses would be sent between suitors to signify a panoply of emotions:

Burgundy rose.... *simplicity and beauty*
China rose.....*grace or beauty ever fresh*
Daily rose .... *a smile*
Dog rose...... *pleasure mixed with pain*
A faded rose .... *fleeting beauty*
Japan rose ... *beauty your sole attraction*
Moss rose................*voluptuous love*
Musk rose ....*capricious beauty*
Provence rose........ *my heart is aflame*
White rosebud .... *too young to love*
White rose in full bloom ....*secrecy*
Wreath of roses......... *virtue rewarded*
Yellow rose .... *infidelity*

——NATIONAL MARCH——

John Philip Sousa's 1896 composition *The Stars and Stripes Forever* (noted for its elaborate piccolo part) is the US National March. Sousa declared that 'march music is for the feet, not for the head' and that 'a march speaks to a fundamental rhythm in the human organization and is answered. A march stimulates every center of vitality, wakens the imagination'. (It was falsely suggested that the composer fabricated his surname so that it would include the letters USA.)

——FEDERAL HOLIDAYS——

Federal law [5 U.S.C. 6103] establishes the following public holidays for all federal employees:

New Year's Day
Birthday of Martin Luther King Jr
Washington's Birthday · Memorial Day
Independence Day · Labor Day
Columbus Day · Veterans Day
Thanksgiving · Christmas Day

[See also the Ephemerides chapter, p.342]

——THE GREAT SEAL——

The Great Seal of the US, adopted in 1782, validates a range of government documents (Presidential proclamations, foreign treaties, commissions of office, ambassadorial accreditation, &c.). The Seal itself is suffused with imagery, as befits a design that took 6 years to finalize, and was intended to reflect the hopes, values, and beliefs of America's Founding Fathers. The front (obverse) shows an American eagle in whose beak is a scroll inscribed with the 13-letter motto *E pluribus unum* [out of many, one]. In one talon, the eagle grips an olive branch [peace] with 13 leaves and 13 olives; in the other, a bundle of 13 arrows [war]. A shield with 13 red and white stripes [the States] covers the eagle's breast, and overhead is a blue crest with 13 stars [America in the world]. The 'spiritual' reverse depicts a 13-step pyramid [strength and durability], with 1776 [Declaration of Independence] in Roman numerals at its base and the motto *Novus Ordo Seclorum* [a new order of the ages]. At the pyramid's summit is the glowing Eye of Providence with the words *Annuit Coeptis* [He (God) favors our undertakings]. The number 13 symbolizes the number of original states in 1776.

THE STARS & STRIPES

The correct proportions of the United States flag (the Stars & Stripes) were laid down on August 21, 1959, by Executive Order of President Dwight D. Eisenhower:

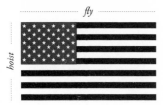

If hoist = 1, the flag's proportions are:

Fly . . . . 1·9
Union hoist . . . . 0·5385
Union fly . . . . 0·76
Width of stripe . . . . 0·0769
Diameter of star . . . . 0·0616

The history of the US flag is steeped in myth and dispute. However, no one disputes the resolution passed by the Marine Committee of the 2nd Continental Congress at Philadelphia (June 14, 1777) that reads: '*That the flag of the United States be thirteen stripes, alternate red and white; that the union be thirteen stars, white in a blue field, representing a new constellation*'. The 1777 flag was used until 1795, when 2 more stars and stripes were added for the admission of Vermont and Kentucky. To avoid excess clutter, Congress decreed in 1818 the flag should have 13 stripes, and that new admissions should be recognized with a star. The 50-star flag was first raised at 12:01am on July 4, 1960, at Fort McHenry National Monument, when Hawaii joined the Union. Below are some of the US Code's numerous flag rules:

It is the universal custom to display the flag only from sunrise to sunset on buildings and on stationary flagstaffs in the open. However, when a patriotic effect is desired, the flag may be displayed 24 hours a day if properly illuminated during the hours of darkness ✇ the flag should be hoisted briskly and lowered ceremoniously ✇ the flag should not be displayed on days when the weather is inclement, except when an all-weather flag is displayed ✇ the flag should be displayed in or near every polling place on Election Day ✇ the flag should never touch anything beneath it, such as the ground, the floor, water, or merchandise ✇ the flag should never be used as a covering for a ceiling ✇ the flag should never be used as a receptacle for receiving, holding, carrying, or delivering anything ✇ the flag should never be used for advertising purposes in any manner whatsoever ✇ no part of the flag should ever be used as a costume or athletic uniform ✇ the flag, when it is in such condition that it is no longer a fitting emblem for display, should be destroyed in a dignified way, preferably by burning [see below]

Curiously, while the US Code recommends that worn-out flags be destroyed by fire, the burning of the Stars & Stripes remains controversial and legally ambiguous. Although *c.*43 States have laws that protect the flag (and Congress passed the 1989 Flag Protection Act), since 1969 the Supreme Court has twice narrowly ruled that flag desecration is a form of free speech protected by the 1st Amendment: '*We do not consecrate the flag by punishing its desecration, for in doing so we dilute the freedom that this cherished emblem represents*'. A number of attempts have been made to amend the Constitution to protect the flag. In June 2006 the Senate failed by 1 vote to achieve the two-thirds majority needed to send an amendment to the individual states for ratification; a CNN poll in the same month showed that 56% favored some Constitutional protection of the Stars & Stripes.

——THE NATIONAL ANTHEM & NUESTRO HIMNO——

Francis Scott Key (1779–1843) was a wealthy Georgetown, MD, lawyer with a penchant for poetry. He penned the four verses of *The Star-Spangled Banner* in 1814, after being inspired by seeing the US flag flying over Fort McHenry, MD, despite heavy night-time bombardment by the British.

Key had the poem (then called *Defence of Fort McHenry*) printed up as a broadside, with instructions for the words to be set to the English tune *To Anacreon in Heaven*, by John Stafford Smith. After publication in many newspapers, the song became a patriotic favorite – finding inclusion in most songbooks of the day. In 1889 the Secretary of the Navy ordered *The Star-Spangled Banner* to be played each morning as the flag was raised, and by the time of WWI, both the navy and the army used the song as an unofficial anthem. The song was given official status in 1916 by Executive Order of President Wilson, and was confirmed as the US national anthem by Congress on March 3, 1931. ❧ 75 years later, in 2006, a new Spanish adaptation of the anthem was recorded by a group of Latin musicians, to coincide with mass protests against proposed US immigration reforms [see p.28]. *Nuestro Himno* ('Our Anthem') received wide airplay on Spanish-language radio, and was immediately denounced – not least by Key's great-great grandson, Charles, who said, 'I think it's a despicable thing that someone is going into our society from another country and … changing our national anthem'. To critics of 'The Illegal Alien Anthem', any translation

O say, can you see, by the dawn's early light, | What so proudly we hailed at the twilight's last gleaming? | Whose broad stripes and bright stars, through the perilous fight, | O'er the ramparts we watched, were so gallantly streaming? | And the rockets' red glare, the bombs bursting in air, | Gave proof through the night that our flag was still there. | O say does that star-spangled banner yet wave | O'er the land of the free, and the home of the brave?

of Key's work challenges America's tradition of assimilation. George W. Bush said, 'I think people who want to be a citizen of this country ought to learn English. And they ought to learn to sing the national anthem in English'. However, Sec. of State Condoleezza Rice told CBS, 'I've heard the national anthem done in rap versions, country versions, classical versions. The individualization of the American national anthem is quite underway'. A Fox News poll in May 2006 indicated that 78% of Americans thought the anthem should be sung only in English – even though a Harris poll 2 years earlier showed that 61% did not know all of the words. ❧ It appears that the 2006 *Nuestro Himno* debate concerned immigration and national identity more than the merits of the anthem – as did associated political attempts to constitutionally establish English as the official language of the US. *The Star Spangled Banner* has weathered interpretations by Duke Ellington, Marvin Gaye, Dolly Parton, Jimi Hendrix, and Aerosmith, and a disturbingly crude rendition by Roseanne Barr, and it looks likely to survive. Indeed, even the issue of translation is not new. In 1919 the Bureau of Education commissioned a Spanish version of *The Star Spangled Banner* that is now held by the Library of Congress. Since then, Key's words have been translated into dozens of languages, including Dr Abraham Asen's rather splendid Yiddish version, the opening line of which is: *O'zog, kenstu sehh, wen bagin licht dervacht.*

─────────────── US TIME ZONES ───────────────

Pacific   *Mountain*   *Central*   *Eastern*

*Hawaii
-Aleutian   Alaska*

Hatched areas do not observe Daylight Saving
[Adapted from *The National Atlas*]

± hours from UTC	DST	Standard
Atlantic	–3	–4
Eastern	–4	–5
Central	–5	–6
Mountain	–6	–7
Pacific	–7	–8
Alaska	–8	–9
Hawaii-Aleutian	–9	–10
Samoa†	NA	–11
Chamorro‡	NA	+10

Coordinated Universal Time (UTC or just UT) is an international time standard essentially identical to good old-fashioned Greenwich Mean Time (GMT). † Samoa Standard Time Zone includes that part of the US that is between 169°30'W–172°30'W, but does not include any part of Hawaii or Alaska. ‡ The 9th US Time Zone was established by Congress in December 2000, for Guam and the Northern Marianas west of the International Date Line. The Chamorro Time Zone, named after the region's indigenous people, is 14 hours ahead of Eastern Standard Time.

Daylight Saving Time (DST) is not observed in Hawaii, American Samoa, Guam, Puerto Rico, the Virgin Islands, or the state of Arizona, with the exception of the Navajo Indian Reservation, which does observe DST. (Indiana adopted DST in 2006; 18 counties use Central Daylight Time, and 74 Eastern Daylight Time.) The Energy Policy Act, 2005, extended DST for one month so that, where it is observed in the United States, it will start and end on the following days:

DST *begins* at 2am	year	DST *ends* at 2am
[Spring forward, Fall back]		
Mar 11	2007	Nov 4
Mar 9	2008	Nov 2
Mar 8	2009	Nov 1
Mar 14	2010	Nov 7
Mar 13	2011	Nov 6
Mar 11	2012	Nov 4
Mar 10	2013	Nov 3
Mar 9	2014	Nov 2

———— LONGEST US RIVERS ————

River	mouth	source	miles
Missouri	Missouri	Red Rock Creek, MT	2,540
Mississippi	Louisiana	Mississippi River, MN	2,340
Yukon	Alaska	McNeil River, Canada	1,980
St Lawrence	Canada	North River, MN	1,900
Rio Grande	Mexico-Texas	Rio Grande, CO	1,900
Arkansas	Arkansas	East Fork Arkansas River, CO	1,460
Colorado	Mexico	Colorado River, CO	1,450
Atchafalaya	Louisiana	Tierra Blanca Creek, NM	1,420
Ohio	Illinois-Kentucky	Allegheny River, PA	1,310
Red	Louisiana	Tierra Blanca Creek, NM	1,290

[Source: US Geological Survey]

— MASON-DIXON LINE —

The Mason-Dixon Line (or, originally 'Mason & Dixon's line') is the southernmost boundary that divided Pennsylvania from Maryland. The Line was set at *c.*39° 43' 26" north by the two British surveyors (and astronomers) Charles Mason and Jeremiah Dixon, who marked out the land between 1763–67 at the behest of William Penn and Lord Baltimore. Before the Civil War, the line represented the division between the Southern pro-slavery and the Northern free states. In common usage nowadays it represents the informal division between the North and the South. The Line is one of the possible etymological sources for the terms 'Dixie' and 'Dixieland'.

——— URBAN vs RURAL———

The latest (2000) Census classified as URBAN 'all territory, population, and housing units located within an Urbanized Area or an Urban Cluster', where 'core census block groups or blocks have a population density of at least 1,000 people per square mile' and 'surrounding census blocks have an overall density of at least 500 people per square mile'. RURAL is defined as everything not counted as URBAN. The 2000 Census calculation was as follows:

79% Urban
(222,361,000)

21% Rural
(59,061,000)

————— LONGEST COMMUNITY NAMES —————

With hyphens	*characters*
Winchester-on-the-Severn, MD	24
Linstead-on-the-Severn, MD	22
Lauderdale-by-the-Sea, FL	21
Vermillion-on-the-Lake, OH	21
Wymberly-on-the-March, GA	21
Kentwood-in-the-Pines, CA	21

Without hyphens	*characters*
Mooselookmeguntic, ME	17
Kleinfeltersville, PA.	17
Chickasawhatchee, GA	16
Chancellorsville, VA.	16
Eichelbergertown, PA	16

[Sources: Dept of Interior; USGS]

—— USA TERRITORIAL —— EXPANSION

Accession	year	sq. miles
Total	——	3,540,558
United States	——	3,536,288
Territory in 1790[1]	——	895,415
Louisiana Purchase	1803	909,380
Purchase of Florida[2]	1819	58,666
Texas	1845	388,687
Oregon Territory	1846	286,541
Mexican Cession	1848	529,189
Gadsden Purchase	1853	29,670
Alaska	1867	570,374
Hawaii	1898	6,423

Other areas

Puerto Rico[3]	1898	3,427
Guam[4]	1898	210
American Samoa[5]	1899	77
US Virgin Islands	1917	134
Palau[6]	1947	179
N. Mariana Is.[7]	1947	177
All other	——	16

[1] Includes part of drainage basin of Red River of the North, south of 49th parallel, often considered part of the Louisiana Purchase. [2] Also acquired 22,834 sq. mi. west of the Mississippi River but relinquished to Spain 97,150 sq. mi. [3] Ceded by Spain in 1898; ratified in 1899; became Commonwealth of Puerto Rico July 25, 1952. [4] Acquired 1898; ratified 1899. [5] Acquired 1899; ratified 1900. [6] Remaining portion of the Trust Territory of the Pacific Islands under UN trusteeship since 1947. The Federated States of Micronesia and the Marshall Islands, also formerly part of the TTPI, became freely associated States in 1986 and are not included in this table. [7] Attained Commonwealth status in 1986, separate from the TTPI, of which it had been a part since 1947. Land areas are approximate and may not add to totals. 1 sq. mi. = 2·59 sq. km. [Sources: US Census; US Geological Survey, which see for more detailed notes].

—— 13 COLONIES ——

The colonies that signed the Declaration of Independence in 1776:

the New England colonies
Massachusetts, Rhode Island,
Connecticut, New Hampshire

the middle colonies
New York, New Jersey,
Pennsylvania, Delaware

the southern colonies
Maryland, Virginia, North Carolina,
South Carolina, Georgia.

By 1770, the population of these 13 colonies had reached almost 2 million.

—— COUNTIES, &c. ——

3,141 counties and their equivalents presently exist in the 50 States and Washington, DC. They are categorized:

3,007 entities named 'County'
16 Boroughs in Alaska
11 Census Areas in Alaska (for areas not organized into Boroughs by the State)
64 Parishes in Louisiana
42 Independent Cities
(1 in Maryland, 1 in Missouri,
1 in Nevada, 39 in Virginia)
1 District – the Federal District, or
District of Columbia

This excludes Commonwealths and territories with county equivalents:

Puerto Rico – 78 Municipios
US Virgin Islands – 2 Districts
Guam – 19 Election Districts
Northern Mariana Is. – 17 Districts
American Samoa – 5 Districts

[Sources: Dept of Interior; USGS]

BILLION $ WEATHER DISASTERS

The National Climatic Data Center, part of the US Dept of Commerce, compiles data on severe weather events – analyzing their social, economic, and environmental effects. Below are 'billion dollar weather disasters' that have hit the US since 2000:

Date	event	category	damage/costs	deaths
October 2005	Hurricane Wilma	5	>$10bn	c.35
September 2005	Hurricane Rita	3	>$8bn	119
August 2005	Hurricane Katrina	3	>$100bn	>1,300
July 2005	Hurricane Dennis	3	>$2bn	≥12
Summer 2005	Midwest drought	–	>$1bn	none
September 2004	Hurricane Jeanne	3	>$7bn	≥28
September 2004	Hurricane Ivan	3	>$14bn	≥57
September 2004	Hurricane Francis	2	>$9bn	≥48
August 2004	Hurricane Charley	4	>$15bn	≥34
Oct–Nov 2003	Southern CA wildfires	–	>$2·5bn	22
September 2003	Hurricane Isabel	2	>$5bn	≥55
May 2003	Storms & tornadoes	–	>$3·4bn	51
April 2003	Storms & hail	–	$1·6bn	3
Fall 2002	Widespread drought	–	>$10bn	none
Fall 2002	Western fires	–	$2·0bn	21
June 2001	Tropical Storm Allison	–	>$5bn	≥43
April 2001	Midwest hail & tornadoes	–	>$1·9bn	≥3
Summer 2000	Southern heat & drought	–	>$4bn	c.140
Summer 2000	Western fires	–	>$2bn	none

LIGHTNING

Often underestimated as a threat, lightning kills more people in the US each year than tornadoes and, after flooding, is the second most frequent fatal weather event. Below are NOAA's figures for fatalities from lightning strikes in the US from 1940:

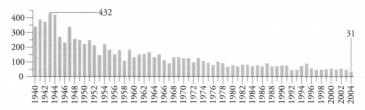

It seems the dramatic decline from prewar rates is mainly due to better education and technological innovation. However, the advent of the car and the decline in rural population have also had effects. NOAA and the National Weather Service estimate that across the States >30 million points on the ground are hit by lightning each year; that based on actual reports the chances of being struck in a given year are 1 in 700,000; and that c.10% of those struck by lightning die as a consequence.

———— RECENT SEVERE WEATHER FATALITIES ————

Year	lightning	tornado	flooding	hurricane	heat	cold	winter	total cost $m
2004	31	34	82	34	6	27	28	26,761·0
2003	43	54	86	14	36	20	37	11,409·5
2002	51	55	49	53	167	11	17	5,674·8
2001	44	40	48	24	166	4	18	11,839·2
2000	51	41	38	0	158	26	41	8,950·1

[Sources: National Weather Service; NOAA · See p.264 for further data on lightning fatalities]

———————— RAIN GODS OF NOTE ————————

Imdugud was the lion-headed eagle of Mesopotamian myth, whose wings were storm clouds that, when beaten, made thunder and rain. ❦ The Iroquois worshipped *Oshadagea* ('great dew-eagle'), who carried water from the oceans in his wings. ❦ *Haddad*, one of sea goddess Asherat's seventy children, was the thunder god and bringer of rain in Sumerian myth. ❦ In Nordic myth, *Frigg* (sister of Thor) was the goddess of clouds and rain whose robes were spun from mist. ❦ The rain goddess of Chaco myth was *Kasogonaga,* an anteater who took human form and created rain by urination. ❦ *Parjanya*, in Vedic myth, was the god of clouds who navigated a cart across the sky, dispensing rain from sacks. ❦ Aztec priests would sacrifice children in the hope that their tears would appeal to their rain god, *Tláloc.* ❦ *Alrinach* was an Eastern demon of floods, earthquakes, rain, and hail, responsible for shipwrecks.

———————— WEATHER RECORDS OF NOTE ————————

			date
Highest recorded temperature			
US · Death Valley, CA	134ºF	57ºC	07·10·1913
World · El Azizia, Libya	136ºF	58ºC	09·13·1922
Lowest recorded temperature			
US · Prospect Creek, AK	–80ºF	–62·2ºC	01·23·1971
World · Vostok, Antarctica	–129ºF	–89ºC	07·21·1983
Greatest recorded rainfall (24h)			
US · Alvin, TX	43"	109mm	07·25–26·1979
World · Foc-Foc, La Réunion	72"	182·5mm	01·07–08·1966
Minimum average yearly rainfall			
US · Death Valley, CA	1·63"	41·4mm	42-year average
World · Arica, Chile	0·03"	8mm	59-year average
Snowfall records · US			
daily snowfall	Georgetown, CO	63"	12·04·1913
monthly snowfall	Thompson Pass, AK	346·1"	February 1964
daily snow depth	Timberline Lodge, OR	448"	11·19·1951

[Sources: National Weather Services; National Climatic Data Center; NOAA; US Army; &c.]

———PRESIDENTIAL & CONGRESSIONAL AWARDS———

The President and Congress are entitled to bestow a host of awards and medals to those they deem deserving of recognition. Below are some of the major awards:

Originally presented to military leaders (the first recipient was Washington in 1776), the *Congressional Gold Medal* is now the highest civilian award and the greatest honor Congress can bestow. No law regulates when or to whom the Gold Medal is given. From time to time Congress selects individuals who have made a significant contribution in their field (e.g. medicine, public service, the arts, entertainment, &c.) and passes legislation authorizing the award that must be signed by the President. The US Mint strikes a bespoke design for each award. Notable recent recipients include Frank Sinatra (1997); Rosa Parks (1999); Charles M. Schulz (2000); and UK PM Tony Blair (2003) [see p.267].

The *Medal of Honor*, presented by the President in the name of Congress, is the US's highest military award, given for acts of bravery above and beyond the call of duty. Nominations from military commanders are reviewed and adjudicated by the Dept of Defense. Recipients are entitled to a monthly pension of $1,000 and a number of military courtesies. To date, since the first award in 1863, 3,461 Medals of Honor have been bestowed for 3,456 acts of heroism by 3,442 individuals (9 of whom remain 'unknown').

The highest civilian award bestowed by the executive is the *Presidential Medal of Freedom*. It was instigated by Truman to honor those who served with merit during WWII, and reestablished by JFK in 1963 as a peacetime award for meritorious service. It is given each year, around July 4, to several people and, because it is in the sole gift of the President, the recipients tend to reflect the interests of the Oval Office's occupant. Recent awards have been made to Paul Bremer, Tommy Franks, and George Tenet. (The Presidential Medal of Freedom may also be awarded with Distinction.)

In 1969, Richard Nixon established the *Presidential Citizens Medal* – the second highest civilian honor for those who have performed exemplary acts for their country or fellow citizens. *c.*100 individuals have received the medal, including Strom Thurmond (1989); and Muhammad Ali (2001).

In 2003, George W. Bush instituted two military medals to honor those who, after 9/11, have served in the Global War on Terrorism (GWOT): the GWOT Expeditionary Medal, for those who served in Operation Enduring Freedom; and the GWOT Service Medal, for those who served in Operation Noble Eagle or assisted in Enduring Freedom. Both awards may be presented posthumously.

In addition, the President is able to award a myriad of other honors and prizes, including: *Enrico Fermi Award* [for nuclear energy, see p.183]; *President's Award for Distinguished Federal Civilian Service*; *Presidential Award for Excellence in Mathematics and Science Teaching*; *Preserve America Presidential Awards* [heritage protection]; *Presidential Awards for Design Excellence; The President's Environmental Youth Award*; &c.

[Sources: Congressional Research Service, &c.]

——TONY BLAIR'S CONGRESSIONAL GOLD MEDAL——

British Prime Minister Tony Blair was awarded the Congressional Gold Medal in 2003, in recognition of his staunch 'shoulder-to-shoulder' support of the United States in the aftermath of 9/11. The rules of Congress require that the recipient of the award 'shall have performed an achievement that has an impact on American history and culture that is likely to be recognized as a major achievement in the recipient's field long after the achievement'. It was unanimously agreed that Blair had met this test. However, a number of his political opponents, and elements of the British press, cast doubt on Blair's good faith when it transpired in 2006 that he had still not collected the award. The London *Times* dismissed reports that the medal was still being designed 3 years after it was announced (Nelson Mandela collected his medal in under 2 months) and suggested that Blair was deliberately delaying his approval. The *Guardian* mooted that a 'likely explanation [of the delay] is that with Blair's plummeting poll ratings and backbench hostility to the Iraq war, the last thing he needs is a ceremony celebrating his steadfastness as an American ally'.

——————HONORARY CITIZENSHIP——————

To date, only six foreigners have been awarded Honorary Citizenship of the US:

Winston Churchill · *British Prime Minister and wartime leader* 1963
Raoul Wallenberg · *Swedish diplomat who aided Jews escaping the Nazis* 1981
William & Hannah Callowhill Penn · *founders of the colony of Pennsylvania* .. 1984
Anges Gonxha Bojaxhiu · *also known as Mother Theresa of Calcutta* 1996
Marquis de Lafayette · *French nobleman who fought alongside G. Washington* .. 2002

A number of others have, from time to time, been proposed for Honorary Citizenship based upon exceptional merit including, in May 2005, Anne Frank.

——————————THE SPINGARN MEDAL——————————

Since 1914, the National Association for the Advancement of Colored People (NAACP) has annually awarded the Spingarn Medal for achievements in any field or endeavor by an African American during the preceding year. The medal is intended 'to bring attention to notable merit among Americans of African descent, to reward such accomplishment, and stimulate ambition for today's youth'. The roster of recipients includes: Martin Luther King Jr, Rosa Parks, Duke Ellington, Bill Cosby, Colin Powell, Maya Angelou, and Oprah Winfrey. The medal is named in honor of the late J.E. Spingarn, former NAACP Chairman. The 2006 Medal was awarded to Dr Benjamin S. Carson Sr who, in 1987, made medical history when he led a 70-strong surgical team in a 22-hour operation to separate conjoined twins who were born joined at the back of the head. Carson has since participated in the surgical separation of four further twins conjoined at the head. On receiving his Medal, Carson said, 'I am deeply honored by this award and will continue to strive to present a model of excellence that will encourage and inspire the next generation'.

———— US HOMELAND SECURITY, BIKINI, & JTAC ————

In response to the terrorist outrages of September 11, 2001, President George W. Bush created the Department of Homeland Security to 'anticipate, pre-empt and deter' terrorist and other threats. The Department employs a five-point, color-coded Security Advisory System to indicate the perceived level of risk – the higher the 'threat condition', the greater the risk of an attack in probability and severity:

Threat	*color*	GUARDED.........Blue	HIGH...........Orange
LOW.............. Green		ELEVATED.......Yellow	SEVERE............ Red

The threat condition was established at YELLOW; since then its changes have been:

Period	*shift*	*cause*
09·10·02–09·24·02	yellow–orange	*1st anniversary of the September 11 attacks*
02·07·03–02·27·03	yellow–orange	*the time of the Muslim Hajj*
03·17·03–04·16·03	yellow–orange	*start of allied military attacks on Iraq*
05·20·03–05·30·03	yellow–orange	*intelligence reports of potential attacks*
12·21·03–01·09·04	yellow–orange	*intelligence reports of holiday season attacks*
08·01·04–11·10·04	yellow–orange	*specific warning for East Coast financial areas*
07·07·05–08·12·05	yellow–orange	*specific mass-transit warning after London bombs*
08·10·06–	yellow–orange (& briefly red)	*specific shift for the airline industry*

Although many states have similar national security alert systems (especially in the military), few make them as public as the United States. France uses the *Plan Vigipirate* – four color-coded steps (*Jaune, Orange, Rouge, Écarlate*) – each signaling a greater degree of threat. British forces across the world and some British government departments use the 'Bikini'[†] alert status to indicate the perceived level of terrorist threat at specific locations. The Bikini alert states range from *White* (no specific threat), through *Black, Black Special, Amber,* to *Red*. In July 2006, the British government made public their previously covert 7-point risk status: *Negligible, Low, Moderate, Substantial, Severe General, Severe Defined, Critical.* Assessed by the Joint Terrorism Analysis Centre (JTAC) and MI5, the British system has no color coding. The status was set at Severe General, but rose to Critical on August 10, 2006, when an alleged plot to blow up a number of transatlantic planes was foiled. [† The etymology of 'Bikini' is unknown.]

———— US VETERAN POPULATION ————

Total US pop. ≥18 212,052,116		Median income for veterans.. $32,657	
Veteran pop. ≥18...........23,756,268		– non-veterans $23,291	
– aged 18–64 ....61·9%		Persian Gulf War veterans ...... 16·4%	
– aged 65–74....................19·3%		Vietnam era veterans............32·9%	
– aged ≥75 ....18·9%		Korean War era veterans........ 14·0%	
% veterans in the US pop.......11·2%		World War II era veterans ...... 15·9%	
Total US pop. ♀ (18–64) ....50·9%		[service periods not mutually exclusive; veterans	
Total veteran pop. ♀ (18–64)...... 8·7%		may have served in more than one conflict.]	

[Source: US Census Bureau, American Community Survey, 2004]

───────── US DEFENSE PERSONNEL ─────────

Below is shown the US's average military strength, from the Korean War onward:

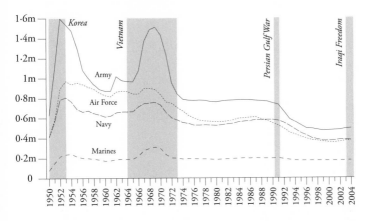

[Average military strength, man years; fiscal years · Source: DoD Washington HQ Services]

── US DEATHS FROM SELECTED WARS, CONFLICTS, &c. ──

War/conflict/incident/operation	date	No. serving	total deaths	%
Revolutionary War	1775–83	—	4,435	—
War of 1812	1812–15	286,730	2,260	0·79
Mexican War	1846–48	78,718	13,283	16·87
Civil War (Union forces only)	1861–65	2,213,363	364,511	16·47
Spanish-American War	1898	306,760	2,446	0·80
World War I	1917–18	4,734,991	116,516	2·46
World War II	1941–46	16,112,566	405,399	2·52
Korean War	1950–53	5,720,000	36,574	0·64
Vietnam Conflict	1964–73	8,744,000	58,209	0·67
Iranian hostage rescue	1980	—	8	—
Lebanon peacekeeping	1982–84	—	265	—
Urgent Fury, Grenada	1983	—	19	—
Just Cause, Panama	1989	—	23	—
Persian Gulf War	1990–91	2,225,000	383	0·02
Restore Hope, Somalia	1992–94	—	43	—
Uphold Democracy, Haiti	1994–96	—	4	—
Enduring Freedom, Afghanistan	2001–	*ongoing*	*ongoing*	—
Iraqi Freedom, Iraq	2003–	*ongoing*	*ongoing*	—

[Source: Dept of Defense. Estimates for Union Forces in the Civil War range from 180,000 –250,000. These above data represent headline figures, see the Dept of Defense detailed official report for further information. Operations *Enduring Freedom* & *Iraqi Freedom* are still to be counted: see also p.22]

—————————SPENDING ON NATIONAL DEFENSE—————————

Federal spending on national defense as % of the total federal budget, and of GDP:

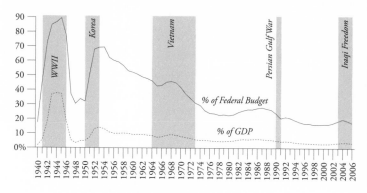

[Source: National Defense Budget Estimates, Dept of Defense, 2006]

——————————DoD PRIME CONTRACT AWARDS——————————

Ranking		parent company	awards ($bn)	
'05	'04	[Source: Dept of Defense]	'04	'05
1	1	Lockheed Martin Corporation	20·7	19·4
2	2	The Boeing Company	17·1	18·3
3	3	Northrop Grumman Corporation	11·9	13·5
4	4	General Dynamics Corporation	9·6	10·6
5	5	Raytheon Company	8·5	9·1
6	6	Halliburton Company	8·0	5·8
7	12	BAE Systems	2·2	5·6
8	7	United Technologies Corporation	5·1	5·0
9	10	L-3 Communications Holdings	2·3	4·7
10	9	Computer Sciences Corporation	2·4	2·8

——————————MUSTACHES & THE ARMY——————————

'Mustaches are permitted; if worn, males will keep mustaches neatly trimmed, tapered, and tidy. Mustaches will not present a chopped off or bushy appearance, and no portion of the mustache will cover the upper lip line or extend sideways beyond a vertical line drawn upward from the corners of the mouth. Handlebar mustaches, goatees, and beards are not authorized. If appropriate medical authority prescribes beard growth, the length required for medical treatment must be specified. ... Soldiers will keep the growth trimmed to the level specified by appropriate medical authority, but they are not authorized to shape the growth into goatees, or "Fu Manchu" or handlebar mustaches.' [Army Regulation 670–1, Pt.1 Ch.1–8a(c)]

US MILITARY RANKS

PAY	ARMY	NAVY & COAST GUARD†	MARINES	AIR FORCE	Number
O-11‡	General of the Army	Fleet Admiral	—	General of the Air Force	—
O-10	General	Admiral	General	General	38
O-9	Lieutenant General	Vice Admiral	Lieutenant General	Lieutenant General	131
O-8	Major General	Rear Admiral (Upper Half)	Major General	Major General	266
O-7	Brigadier General	Rear Admiral (Lower Half)	Brigadier General	Brigadier General	439
O-6	Colonel	Captain	Colonel	Colonel	11,391
O-5	Lieutenant Colonel	Commander	Lieutenant Colonel	Lieutenant Colonel	28,037
O-4	Major	Lieutenant Commander	Major	Major	43,600
O-3	Captain	Lieutenant	Captain	Captain	72,037
O-2	First Lieutenant	Lieutenant Junior Grade	First Lieutenant	First Lieutenant	28,729
O-1	Second Lieutenant	Ensign	Second Lieutenant	Second Lieutenant	23,378
W-5	Chief Warrant Officer	Chief Warrant Officer	Chief Warrant Officer	—	580
W-4	Chief Warrant Officer	Chief Warrant Officer	Chief Warrant Officer	—	2,179
W-3	Chief Warrant Officer	Chief Warrant Officer	Chief Warrant Officer	—	4,548
W-2	Chief Warrant Officer	Chief Warrant Officer	Chief Warrant Officer	—	6,185
W-1	Warrant Officer	Warrant Officer	Warrant Officer	—	2,470
E-9	Sgt Major of the Army	MCPO of the Navy	Sgt Major of the Marine Corps	Ch. Master Sgt of the Air Force	10,508
E-9	Command Sgt Major/Sgt Major	Fleet/Command MCPO	Sgt Major/Master Gunnery Sgt	Command Chief Master Sgt	↑
E-9		Master Chief Petty Officer		Chief Master Sgt/First Sgt	↑
E-8	First Sgt/Master Sgt	Senior Chief Petty Officer	First Sgt/Master Sgt	Senior Master Sgt/First Sgt	27,579
E-7	Sgt First Class/Platoon Sgt	Chief Petty Officer	Gunnery Sergeant	Master Sgt/First Sgt	96,648
E-6	Staff Sergeant	Petty Officer First Class	Staff Sergeant	Technical Sergeant	173,162
E-5	Sergeant	Petty Officer Second Class	Sergeant	Staff Sergeant	249,845
E-4	Corporal/Specialist	Petty Officer Third Class	Corporal	Senior Airman	260,895
E-3	Private First Class	Seaman	Lance Corporal	Airman First Class	194,676
E-2	Private	Seaman Apprentice	Private First Class	Airman	69,593
E-1	Private	Seaman Recruit	Private	Airman Basic	58,374

† The US Coast Guard is a part of the Dept of Transportation in peacetime and the Navy in times of war. Coast Guard ranks are essentially the same as Navy ranks. ‡ Reserved for wartime only. Within the O-10 rank, each service has a Chief of Staff or Commandant. · Numbers are Active Duty Military Personnel as of 12-31-2005. Source: Department of Defense

The States

No political dreamer was ever wild enough to think of breaking down the lines which separate the States, and of compounding the American people into one common mass. — Chief Justice JOHN MARSHALL, 1819

MANIFEST DESTINY

Manifest Destiny was a popular mid-C19th slogan expressing the conviction that no less than Divine Providence destined the United States to stretch (geographically and ideologically) from the Atlantic to the Pacific. Manifest Destiny justified the imperialist land acquisition westward, by force if necessary – as Native Americans learned. The philosophy was expounded by followers of President Jackson, but the term was coined by journalist John L. O'Sullivan in 1845, as settlers moved west to California and Oregon. He wrote of '*our manifest destiny to overspread the continent allotted by Providence for the free development of our yearly multiplying millions*'.

C19th STATE NICKNAMES

Alabama	Lizards	New Jersey	Clam Catchers
Connecticut	Wooden Nutmegs	New York	Knickerbockers
Delaware	Muskrats	North Carolina	Tar Boilers
Florida	Fly Up the Creeks	Ohio	Buckeyes
Georgia	Buzzards	Oregon	Hard Cases
Illinois	Suckers	Pennsylvania	Logher Heads
Indiana	Hoosiers	Rhode Island	Gun Flints
Iowa	Hawkeyes	South Carolina	Weasels
Kentucky	Corn Crackers	Vermont	Green Mountain Boys
Louisiana	Creoles	Virginia	Beagles
Maine	Foxes	Wisconsin	Badgers
Maryland	Claw Thumpers		
Massachusetts	Bay Staters		
Michigan	Wolverines		
Mississippi	Tad Poles		
Missouri	Pukes		
New Hampshire	Granite Boys		

These nicknames are commonly said to have been collected by Walt Whitman in 'Slang in America' (*North American Review*, 1885). Yet it seems likely that they originated from an article in the *Broadway Journal* of May 1845.

CONFEDERATE STATES

Organized in February 1861, the Confederacy consisted of eleven states that seceded from the Union: Alabama, Arkansas, Florida, Georgia, Louisiana, Mississippi, North Carolina, South Carolina, Tennessee, Texas, and Virginia.

THE UNITED STATES

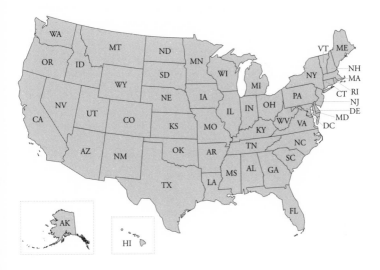

KEY TO TABLES OVERLEAF

Overleaf are a range of tables designed to allow comparisons to be made between the various states and, where relevant, Washington, DC, and the USA as a whole. A degree of debate and dispute surrounds a number of entries, and data sources have been the most recent at the time of writing. Below is a key to some entries:

Land area	US Census Bureau
Resident population	July 2005 · US Census Bureau
Unemployment rate	% of civilian labor force · 2004 · US Bureau of Labor Statistics
Home ownership rate	% of owner households · 2004 · US Census Bureau
Persons below poverty line	2003 · US Census Bureau
Average annual pay	2004 · Bureau of Labor Statistics
Violent crime	per 100,000 population · 2004 · FBI
Racial & ethnic breakdown	2000 · US Census Bureau
Infant mortality rate	deaths of infants <1/1,000 live births · 2002 · US NCHS
Doctors	per 100,000 resident population · 2003 · American Medical Association
Traffic fatalities	per 100 million vehicle miles · 2003 · US NHSTA
Energy consumption	million Btus per person · 2001 · US Energy Information Admin
Mobile homes	% of total housing units · 2003 · US Census Bureau
Degree	persons ≥25 with a Bachelor's degree or higher · 2004 · US Census
Highway miles	miles of functional roads (interstate–local) · 2003 · US Fed. Highway Admin
Temperatures	April 2002 · National Oceanic and Atmospheric Administration (NOAA)
Highest & lowest points & geographic center	US Geographic Survey
Morgan Quitno state rankings	morganquitno.com
State Quarter Program	date of release · US Mint

STATES · MAPS, CAPITALS, ADMISSION, &c.

California · CA
155,959 sq mi
Sacramento
31st State on
9.9.1850

Georgia · GA
57,906 sq mi
Atlanta
4th State on
1.2.1788

Iowa · IA
55,869 sq mi
Des Moines
29th State on
12.28.1846

Maryland · MD
9,774 sq mi
Annapolis
7th State
on 4.28.1788

Missouri · MO
68,886 sq mi
Jefferson City
24th State on
8.10.1821

Arkansas · AR
52,068 sq mi
Little Rock
25th State on
6.15.1836

Florida · FL
53,927 sq mi
Tallahassee
27th State on
3.3.1845

Indiana · IN
35,867 sq mi
Indianapolis
19th State on
12.11.1816

Maine · ME
30,862 sq mi
Augusta
23rd State on
3.15.1820

Mississippi · MS
46,907 sq mi
Jackson
20th State on
12.10.1817

Arizona · AZ
113,635 sq mi
Phoenix
48th State on
2.14.1912

Delaware · DE
1,954 sq mi
Dover
1st State on
12.7.1787

Illinois · IL
55,584 sq mi
Springfield
21st State on
12.3.1818

Louisiana · LA
43,562 sq mi
Baton Rouge
18th State on
4.30.1812

Minnesota · MN
79,610 sq mi
St Paul
32nd State on
5.11.1858

Alaska · AK
571,951 sq mi
Juneau
49th State on
1.3.1959

Connecticut · CT
4,844 sq mi
Hartford
5th State on
1.9.1788

Idaho · ID
82,747 sq mi
Boise
43rd State on
7.3.1890

Kentucky · KY
39,728 sq mi
Frankfort
15th State
on 6.1.1792

Michigan · MI
56,804 sq mi
Lansing
26th State on
1.26.1837

Alabama · AL
50,744 sq mi
Montgomery
22nd State on
12.14.1819

Colorado · CO
103,717 sq mi
Denver
38th State on
8.1.1876

Hawaii · HI
6,423 sq mi
Honolulu
50th State on
8.21.1959

Kansas · KS
81,815 sq mi
Topeka
34th State on
1.29.1861

Massachusetts · MA
7,840 sq mi
Boston
6th State
on 2.6.1788

STATES · MAPS, CAPITALS, ADMISSION, &c.

New Jersey · NJ 7,417 sq mi *Trenton* 3rd State on 12-18-1787	Ohio · OH 40,948 sq mi *Columbus* 17th State on 3-1-1803	South Carolina · SC 30,109 sq mi *Columbia* 8th State on 5-23-1788	Vermont · VT 9,250 sq mi *Montpelier* 14th State on 3-4-1791	Wyoming · WY 97,100 sq mi *Cheyenne* 44th State on 7-10-1890
New Hampshire NH · 8,968 sq mi *Concord* 9th State on 6-21-1788	North Dakota · ND 68,976 sq mi *Bismarck* 39th State on 11-2-1889	Rhode Island · RI 1,045 sq mi *Providence* 13th State on 5-29-1790	Utah · UT 82,144 sq mi *Salt Lake City* 45th State on 1-4-1896	Wisconsin · WI 54,310 sq mi *Madison* 30th State on 5-29-1848
Nevada · NV 109,826 sq mi *Carson City* 36th State on 10-31-1864	North Carolina · NC 48,711 sq mi *Raleigh* 12th State on 11-21-1789	Pennsylvania · PA 44,817 sq mi *Harrisburg* 2nd State on 12-12-1787	Texas · TX 261,797 sq mi *Austin* 28th State on 12-29-1845	West Virginia · WV 24,077 sq mi *Charleston* 35th State on 6-20-1863
Nebraska · NE 76,872 sq mi *Lincoln* 37th State on 3-1-1867	New York · NY 47,214 sq mi *Albany* 11th State on 7-26-1788	Oregon · OR 95,997 sq mi *Salem* 33rd State on 2-14-1859	Tennessee · TN 41,217 sq mi *Nashville* 16th State on 6-1-1796	Washington · WA 66,544 sq mi *Olympia* 42nd State on 11-11-1889
Montana · MT 145,552 sq mi *Helena* 41st State on 11-8-1889	New Mexico · NM 121,356 sq mi *Santa Fe* 47th State on 1-6-1912	Oklahoma · OK 68,667 sq mi *Oklahoma City* 46th State on 11-16-1907	South Dakota · SD 75,885 sq mi *Pierre* 40th State on 11-2-1889	Virginia · VA 39,594 sq mi *Richmond* 10th State on 6-25-1788

—————————— STATES · RESIDENTS, SYMBOLS, &c. ——————————

State	Residents called	State tree	State flower	State bird	Abbreviation
Alabama	Alabamian, Alabaman	Southern Longleaf Pine	Camellia	Yellowhammer	Ala.
Alaska	Alaskan	Sitka Spruce	Forget-me-not	Willow Ptarmigan	Alaska
Arizona	Arizonan, Arizonian	Palo Verde	Blossom of the Saguaro Cactus	Cactus Wren	Ariz.
Arkansas	Arkansan	Loblolly Pine	Apple Blossom	Mockingbird	Ark.
California	Californian	California Redwood	Golden Poppy	California Valley Quail	Calif.
Colorado	Coloradan, Coloradoan	Colorado Blue Spruce	Rocky Mountain Columbine	Lark Bunting	Colo.
Connecticut	Connecticuter, Nutmegger	White Oak	Mountain Laurel	American Robin	Conn.
Delaware	Delawarean	American Holly	Peach Blossom	Blue Hen Chicken	Del.
DC	Washingtonian	Scarlet Oak	American Beauty Rose	Wood Thrush	D.C.
Florida	Floridian, Floridan	Sabal Palm	Orange Blossom	Mockingbird	Fla.
Georgia	Georgian	Live Oak	Cherokee Rose	Brown Thrasher	Ga.
Hawaii	Hawaiian	Kukui or Candlenut	Native Yellow Hibiscus	Nene or Hawaiian Goose	Hawaii
Idaho	Idahoan	Western White Pine	Syringa	Mountain Bluebird	Idaho
Illinois	Illinoisan	White Oak	Purple Violet	Cardinal	Ill.
Indiana	Indianan, Indianian, Hoosier	Tulip Tree	Peony	Cardinal	Ind.
Iowa	Iowan	Oak	Wild Rose	Eastern Goldfinch	Iowa
Kansas	Kansan	Cottonwood	Native Sunflower	Western Meadowlark	Kans.
Kentucky	Kentuckian	Tulip Poplar	Goldenrod	Cardinal	Ky.
Louisiana	Louisianan, Louisianian	Bald Cypress	Magnolia	Eastern Brown Pelican	La.
Maine	Mainer	Eastern White Pine	White Pinecone and Tassel	Chickadee	Maine
Maryland	Marylander	White Oak	Black-eyed Susan	Baltimore Oriole	Md.
Massachusetts	Bay Stater	American Elm	Mayflower	Chickadee	Mass.
Michigan	Michigander(-ian), Michiganite	Eastern White Pine	Apple Blossom	Robin	Mich.
Minnesota	Minnesotan	Red or Norway Pine	Pink & White Lady's Slipper	Common Loon	Minn.
Mississippi	Mississippian	Magnolia	Magnolia	Mockingbird	Miss.
Missouri	Missourian	Flowering Dogwood	Hawthorn	Eastern Bluebird	Mo.

STATES · RESIDENTS, SYMBOLS, &c.

State	Residents called	State tree	State flower	State bird	Abbreviation
Montana	Montanan	Ponderosa Pine	Bitterroot	Western Meadowlark	Mont.
Nebraska	Nebraskan	Cottonwood	Goldenrod	Western Meadowlark	Nebr.
Nevada	Nevadan, Nevadian	Singleleaf Pinyon & Pine	Sagebrush	Mountain Bluebird	Nev.
New Hampshire	New Hampshirite	White Birch	Purple Lilac	Purple Finch	N.H.
New Jersey	New Jerseyite, New Jerseyan	Northern Red Oak	Purple Violet	Eastern Goldfinch	N.J.
New Mexico	New Mexican	Pinyon Pine / Pinon	Yucca	Roadrunner	N.Mex.
New York	New Yorker	Sugar Maple	Rose	Eastern Bluebird	N.Y.
North Carolina	North Carolinian	Longleaf Pine	Dogwood	Cardinal	N.C.
North Dakota	North Dakotan	American Elm	Wild Prarie Rose	Western Meadowlark	N.Dak.
Ohio	Ohioan	Buckeye	Scarlet Carnation	Cardinal	Ohio
Oklahoma	Oklahoman	Redbud	Mistletoe	Scissor-tailed Flycatcher	Okla.
Oregon	Oregonian	Douglas Fir	Oregon Grape	Western Meadowlark	Oreg.
Pennsylvania	Pennsylvanian	Eastern Hemlock	Mountain Laurel	Ruffed Grouse	Pa.
Rhode Island	Rhode Islander	Red Maple	Blue Violet	Rhode Island Red Hen	R.I.
South Carolina	South Carolinian	Sabel Palm / Palmetto Tree	Yellow Jessamine	Great Carolina Wren	S.C.
South Dakota	South Dakotan	Black Hills Spruce	Pasqueflower	Ring-necked Pheasant	S.Dak.
Tennessee	Tennessean, Tennesseean	Tulip Poplar	Iris	Mockingbird	Tenn.
Texas	Texan	Pecan	Bluebonnet	Mockingbird	Tex.
Utah	Utahn, Utahn	Blue Spruce	Sego Lily	California Seagull	Utah
Vermont	Vermonter	Sugar Maple	Red Clover	Hermit Thrush	Vt.
Virginia	Virginian	Flowering Dogwood	American Dogwood	Northern Cardinal	Va.
Washington	Washingtonian	Western Hemlock	Western Rhododendron	Willow Goldfinch	Wash.
West Virginia	West Virginian	Sugar Maple	Big Rhododendron	Cardinal	W. Va.
Wisconsin	Wisconsinite	Sugar Maple	Wood Violet	Robin	Wis.
Wyoming	Wyomingite	Plains Cottonwood	Indian Paintbrush	Western Meadowlark	Wyo.

State · Nickname – motto [translation]

Alabama · Yellowhammer State; Heart of Dixie – Audemus jura nostra defendere [we dare defend our rights] ❦ Alaska · The Last Frontier; Land of the Midnight Sun – North to the Future ❦ Arizona · Grand Canyon State – Ditat Deus [God enriches] ❦ Arkansas · Natural State – Regnat populus [the people rule] ❦ California · Golden State – Eureka [I have found it] ❦ Colorado · Centennial State · Nil sine Numine [nothing without Providence] ❦ Connecticut · Constitution State; Nutmeg State – Qui transtulit sustinet [he who transplanted still sustains] ❦ Delaware · Diamond State; First State; Small Wonder; Blue Hen State – Liberty and independence ❦ DC · DC; the District – Justia omnibus [justice for all] ❦ Florida · Sunshine State – In God we trust ❦ Georgia · Peach State; Empire State of the South – Wisdom, justice, and moderation ❦ Hawaii · Aloha State – Ua Mau Ke Ea O Ka Aina I Ka Pono [the life of the land is perpetuated in righteousness] ❦ Idaho · Gem State – Esto perpetua [it is forever] ❦ Illinois · Prairie State – State sovereignty, national union ❦ Indiana · Hoosier State – The Crossroads of America ❦ Iowa · Hawkeye State – Our liberties we prize and our rights we will maintain ❦ Kansas · Sunflower State; Jayhawk State – Ad astra per aspera [to the stars through difficulties] ❦ Kentucky · Bluegrass State – United we stand, divided we fall ❦ Louisiana · Pelican State – Union, justice, and confidence ❦ Maine · Pine Tree State – Dirigo [I lead] ❦ Maryland · Free State; Old Line State – Fatti maschii, parole femine [manly deeds, womanly words] ❦ Massachusetts · Bay State; Old Colony State – Ense petit placidam sub libertate quietem [by the sword we seek peace, but peace only under liberty] ❦ Michigan · Wolverine State; Great Lakes State – Si quaeris peninsulam amoenam circumspice [if you seek a pleasant peninsula, look around you] ❦ Minnesota · North Star State; Land of 10,000 Lakes; Gopher State – L'Etoile du Nord [the North Star] ❦ Mississippi · Magnolia State – Virtute et armis [by valor and arms] ❦ Missouri · Show-me State – Salus populi suprema lex esto [the welfare of the people shall be the supreme law] ❦ Montana · Treasure State – Oro y plata [gold and silver] ❦ Nebraska · Cornhusker State; Beef State – Equality before the law ❦ Nevada · Sagebrush State; Silver State; Battle Born State – All for Our Country ❦ New Hampshire · Granite State – Live free or die ❦ New Jersey · Garden State – Liberty and prosperity ❦ New Mexico · Land of Enchantment – Crescit eundo [it grows as it goes] ❦ New York · Empire State – Excelsior [ever upward] ❦ North Carolina · Tar Heel State; Old North State – Esse quam videri [to be rather than to seem] ❦ North Dakota · Sioux State; Flickertail State; Peace Garden State; Rough Rider State – Liberty and union, now and forever; one and inseparable ❦ Ohio · Buckeye State – With God all things are possible ❦ Oklahoma · Sooner State – Labor omnia vincit [labor conquers all] ❦ Oregon · Beaver State – Alis volat Propriis [she flies with her own wings] ❦ Pennsylvania · Keystone State – Virtue, liberty, and independence ❦ Rhode Island · Ocean State · Hope ❦ South Carolina · Palmetto State · Animis opibusque parati [prepared in mind and resources] & Dum spiro spero [while I breathe, I hope] ❦ South Dakota · Mount Rushmore State; Coyote State – Under God the people rule ❦ Tennessee · Volunteer State – Agriculture and Commerce ❦ Texas – Lone Star State – Friendship ❦ Utah · Beehive State – Industry ❦ Vermont · Green Mountain State – Freedom and Unity ❦ Virginia – Old Dominion State; Mother of Presidents – Sic semper tyrannis [thus always to tyrants] ❦ Washington · Evergreen State – Al-Ki [Indian for 'by and by'] ❦ West Virginia · Mountain State – Montani semper liberi [mountaineers are always free] ❦ Wisconsin · Badger State – Forward ❦ Wyoming · Equality State – Equal rights · [Alternative names & mottos exist]

—————— STATES · MISCELLANY ——————

State	State Quarter	Presidents	Highway mi	Fed. Court	Census region
AL	03-17-03	0	94,434	Eleventh	ES Central
AK	tba	0	14,230	Ninth	Pacific
AZ	tba	0	57,529	Ninth	Mountain
AR	10-20-03	1	98,541	Eighth	WS Central
CA	01-31-05	1	169,549	Ninth	Pacific
CO	tba	0	86,821	Tenth	Mountain
CT	10-12-99	1	21,089	Second	New England
DE	01-04-99	0	5,894	Third	S Atlantic
DC	–	0	1,536	DC	S Atlantic
FL	03-29-04	0	120,375	Eleventh	S Atlantic
GA	07-19-99	1	116,534	Eleventh	S Atlantic
HI	tba	0	4,309	Ninth	Pacific
ID	tba	0	46,927	Ninth	Mountain
IL	01-02-03	1	138,526	Seventh	EN Central
IN	08-02-02	0	94,597	Seventh	EN Central
IA	08-30-04	1	113,516	Eighth	WN Central
KS	08-29-05	0	135,012	Tenth	WN Central
KY	10-15-01	1	77,011	Sixth	ES Central
LA	05-20-02	0	60,937	Fifth	WS Central
ME	06-02-03	0	22,693	First	New England
MD	03-13-00	0	30,688	Fourth	S Atlantic
MA	01-03-00	4	35,590	First	New England
MI	01-26-04	0	122,222	Sixth	EN Central
MN	04-04-05	0	131,893	Eighth	WN Central
MS	10-15-02	0	74,105	Fifth	ES Central
MO	08-04-03	1	124,685	Eighth	WN Central
MT	tba	0	69,450	Ninth	Mountain
NE	03-03-06	1	93,198	Eighth	WN Central
NV	01-31-06	0	33,977	Ninth	Mountain
NH	08-07-00	1	15,630	First	New England
NJ	05-17-99	1	38,952	Third	Middle Atlantic
NM	tba	0	63,953	Tenth	Mountain
NY	01-02-01	4	113,124	Second	Middle Atlantic
NC	03-12-01	2	102,160	Fourth	South Atlantic
ND	tba	0	86,782	Eighth	WN Central
OH	03-11-02	7	123,522	Sixth	EN Central
OK	tba	0	112,578	Tenth	WS Central
OR	06-06-05	0	65,951	Ninth	Pacific
PA	03-08-99	1	120,423	Third	Middle Atlantic
RI	05-21-01	0	6,415	First	New England
SC	05-22-00	1	66,230	Fourth	S Atlantic
SD	tba	0	83,688	Eighth	WN Central
TN	01-02-02	0	88,518	Sixth	ES Central
TX	06-01-04	2	301,987	Fifth	WS Central
UT	tba	0	42,716	Tenth	Mountain
VT	08-06-01	2	14,359	Second	New England
VA	10-16-00	8	71,242	Fourth	South Atlantic
WA	tba	0	82,264	Ninth	Pacific
WV	10-14-05	0	36,993	Fourth	South Atlantic
WI	10-25-04	0	113,270	Seventh	EN Central
WY	tba	0	27,482	Tenth	Mountain

STATES · RACE & ETHNICITY

Race and Ethnicity 2000	White %	Black & African American %	American Indian & Alaskan Native %	Asian %	Hawaiian & Pacific Islands %	Other %	2 or more races %	Hispanic or Latino (Any Race) %	White alone, not Hispanic or Latino %	State Population 2000
Alabama	71.1	26.0	0.5	0.7	0.0	0.7	1.0	1.7	70.3	4,447,100
Alaska	69.3	3.5	15.6	4.0	0.5	1.6	5.4	4.1	67.6	626,932
Arizona	75.5	3.1	5.0	1.8	0.1	11.6	2.9	25.3	63.8	5,130,632
Arkansas	80.0	15.7	0.7	0.8	0.1	1.5	2.9	3.2	78.6	2,673,400
California	59.5	6.7	1.0	10.9	0.3	16.8	4.7	32.4	46.7	33,871,648
Colorado	82.8	3.8	1.0	2.2	0.1	7.2	2.8	17.1	74.5	4,301,261
Connecticut	81.6	9.1	0.3	2.4	0.0	4.3	2.2	9.4	77.5	3,405,565
Delaware	74.6	19.2	0.3	2.1	0.0	2.0	1.7	4.8	72.5	783,600
DC	30.8	60.0	0.3	2.7	0.1	3.8	2.4	7.9	27.8	572,059
Florida	78.0	14.6	0.3	1.7	0.1	3.0	2.4	16.8	65.4	15,982,378
Georgia	65.1	28.7	0.3	2.1	0.1	2.4	1.4	5.3	62.6	8,186,453
Hawaii	24.3	1.8	0.3	41.6	9.4	1.3	21.4	7.2	22.9	1,211,537
Idaho	91.0	0.4	1.4	0.9	0.1	4.2	2.0	7.9	88.0	1,293,953
Illinois	73.5	15.1	0.2	3.4	0.0	5.8	1.9	12.3	67.8	12,419,293
Indiana	87.5	8.4	0.3	1.0	0.0	1.6	1.2	3.5	85.8	6,080,485
Iowa	93.9	2.1	0.3	1.3	0.0	1.3	1.1	2.8	92.6	2,926,324
Kansas	86.1	5.7	0.9	1.7	0.0	3.4	2.1	7.0	83.1	2,688,418
Kentucky	90.1	7.3	0.2	0.7	0.0	0.6	1.1	1.5	89.3	4,041,769
Louisiana	63.9	32.5	0.6	1.2	0.0	0.7	1.1	2.4	62.5	4,468,976
Maine	96.9	0.5	0.6	0.7	0.0	0.2	1.0	0.7	96.5	1,274,923
Maryland	64.0	27.9	0.3	4.0	0.0	1.8	2.0	4.3	62.1	5,296,486
Massachusetts	84.5	5.4	0.2	3.8	0.0	3.7	2.3	6.8	81.9	6,349,097
Michigan	80.2	14.2	0.6	1.8	0.0	1.3	1.9	3.3	78.6	9,938,444
Minnesota	89.4	3.5	1.1	2.9	0.0	1.3	1.7	2.9	88.2	4,919,479
Mississippi	61.4	36.3	0.4	0.7	0.0	0.5	0.7	1.4	60.7	2,844,658
Missouri	84.9	11.2	0.4	1.1	0.1	0.8	1.5	2.1	83.8	5,595,211

————— STATES · RACE & ETHNICITY —————

Race and Ethnicity 2000	White %	Black & African American %	American Indian & Alaskan Native %	Asian %	Hawaiian & Pacific Islands %	Other %	2 or more races %	(Any Race) Hispanic or Latino %	White alone, not Hispanic or Latino %	State Population 2000
Montana	90.6	0.3	6.2	0.5	0.1	0.6	1.7	2.0	89.5	902,195
Nebraska	89.6	4.0	0.9	1.3	0.0	2.8	1.4	5.5	87.3	1,711,263
Nevada	75.2	6.8	1.3	4.5	0.4	8.0	3.8	19.7	65.2	1,998,257
New Hampshire	96.0	0.7	0.2	1.3	0.0	0.6	1.1	1.7	95.1	1,235,786
New Jersey	72.6	13.6	0.2	5.7	0.0	5.4	2.5	13.3	66.0	8,414,350
New Mexico	66.8	1.9	9.5	1.1	0.1	17.0	3.6	42.1	44.7	1,819,046
New York	67.9	15.9	0.4	5.5	0.0	7.1	3.1	15.1	62.0	18,976,457
North Carolina	72.1	21.6	1.2	1.4	0.0	2.3	1.3	4.7	70.2	8,049,313
North Dakota	92.4	0.6	4.9	0.6	0.0	0.4	1.2	1.2	91.7	642,200
Ohio	85.0	11.5	0.2	1.2	0.0	0.8	1.4	1.9	84.0	11,353,140
Oklahoma	76.2	7.6	7.9	1.4	0.1	2.4	4.5	5.2	74.1	3,450,654
Oregon	86.6	1.6	1.3	3.0	0.2	4.2	3.1	8.0	83.5	3,421,399
Pennsylvania	85.4	10.0	0.1	1.8	0.0	1.5	1.2	3.2	84.1	12,281,054
Rhode Island	85.0	4.5	0.5	2.3	0.1	5.0	2.7	8.7	81.9	1,048,319
South Carolina	67.2	29.5	0.3	0.9	0.0	1.0	1.0	2.4	66.1	4,012,012
South Dakota	88.7	0.6	8.3	0.6	0.0	0.5	1.3	1.4	88.0	754,844
Tennessee	80.2	16.4	0.3	1.0	0.0	1.0	1.1	2.2	79.2	5,689,283
Texas	71.0	11.5	0.6	2.7	0.1	11.7	2.5	32.0	52.4	20,851,820
Utah	89.2	0.8	1.3	1.7	0.7	4.2	2.1	9.0	85.3	2,233,169
Vermont	96.8	0.5	0.4	0.9	0.0	0.2	1.2	0.9	96.2	608,827
Virginia	72.3	19.6	0.3	3.7	0.1	2.0	2.0	4.7	70.2	7,078,515
Washington	81.8	3.2	1.6	5.5	0.4	3.9	3.6	7.5	78.9	5,894,121
West Virginia	95.0	3.2	0.2	0.5	0.0	0.2	0.9	0.7	94.6	1,808,344
Wisconsin	88.9	5.7	0.9	1.7	0.0	1.6	1.2	3.6	87.3	5,363,675
Wyoming	92.1	0.8	2.3	0.6	0.1	2.5	1.8	6.4	88.9	493,782
USA	75.1	12.3	0.9	3.6	0.1	5.5	2.4	12.5	69.1	281,421,906

STATES · SOCIAL INDICATORS

State (& rank)	Resident population		Unemployment %		Home ownership %		% of people below the poverty line		Av. annual pay $		Violent crime rate per 100,000 pop.	
Alabama	4,557,808	23rd	5·8	13th	78.0	2nd	17.1	6th	33,414	31st	427	22nd
Alaska	663,661	47th	7·5	2nd	67.2	42nd	9.7	40th	39,062	15th	635	7th
Arizona	5,939,292	17th	5·1	27th	68.7	40th	15.4	10th	36,646	21st	504	13th
Arkansas	2,779,154	32nd	5·9	12th	69.1	37th	16.0	9th	30,245	45th	499	15th
California	36,132,147	1st	6·2	6th	59.7	49th	13.4	18th	44,641	5th	552	10th
Colorado	4,665,177	22nd	5·4	19th	71.1	30th	9.8	39th	40,276	12th	374	25th
Connecticut	3,510,297	29th	4·9	31st	71.7	26th	8.1	48th	51,007	1st	286	34th
Delaware	843,524	45th	3·9	42nd	77.3	3rd	8.7	45th	42,487	7th	568	9th
DC	550,521	–	8·2	–	45.6	–	19.9	–	63,887	–	1,371	–
Florida	17,789,864	4th	4·6	38th	72.2	23rd	13.1	20th	35,186	25th	711	2nd
Georgia	9,072,576	9th	4·7	36th	70.9	32nd	13.4	18th	37,866	18th	456	19th
Hawaii	1,275,194	42nd	3·4	49th	60.9	48th	10.9	30th	35,198	24th	254	39th
Idaho	1,429,096	39th	5·3	22nd	73.7	13th	13.8	15th	29,871	46th	245	41st
Illinois	12,763,371	5th	6·1	9th	72.7	20th	11.3	26th	42,277	8th	543	11th
Indiana	6,271,973	15th	5·3	22nd	75.8	7th	10.6	34th	34,694	30th	325	29th
Iowa	2,966,334	30th	4·6	38th	73.2	17th	10.1	38th	32,097	36th	271	37th
Kansas	2,744,687	33rd	5·5	18th	69.9	35th	10.8	32nd	32,738	34th	375	24th
Kentucky	4,173,405	26th	5·2	26th	74.3	11th	17.4	5th	33,165	33rd	245	41st
Louisiana	4,523,628	24th	6·0	10th	70.6	33rd	20.3	1st	31,880	38th	639	6th
Maine	1,321,505	40th	4·7	36th	74.7	10th	10.5	36th	31,906	37th	104	49th
Maryland	5,600,388	19th	4·2	40th	72.1	24th	8.2	47th	42,579	6th	701	3rd
Massachusetts	6,398,743	13th	5·1	27th	63.8	46th	9.4	43rd	48,916	3rd	459	18th
Michigan	10,120,860	8th	7·0	3rd	77.1	4th	11.4	25th	40,373	11th	490	17th
Minnesota	5,132,799	21st	4·8	34th	76.4	5th	7.8	49th	40,398	10th	270	38th
Mississippi	2,921,088	31st	6·2	6th	74.0	12th	19.9	2nd	28,535	48th	295	32nd
Missouri	5,800,310	18th	5·7	15th	72.4	21st	11.7	22nd	34,845	27th	491	16th

—————————— STATES · SOCIAL INDICATORS ——————————

State (& rank)	Resident population		Unemployment %		Home ownership %		% of people below the poverty line		Av. annual pay $		Violent crime rate per 100,000 pop.	
Montana	935,670	44th	4.9	31st	72.4	21st	14.2	11th	27,830	50th	294	33rd
Nebraska	1,758,787	38th	3.8	44th	71.2	29th	10.8	32nd	31,507	40th	309	30th
Nevada	2,414,807	35th	4.2	40th	65.7	44th	11.5	24th	37,106	20th	616	8th
New Hampshire	1,309,940	41st	3.7	46th	73.3	15th	7.7	50th	39,176	14th	167	47th
New Jersey	8,717,925	10th	4.8	34th	68.8	39th	8.4	46th	48,065	4th	356	26th
New Mexico	1,928,384	36th	5.6	16th	71.5	28th	18.6	3rd	31,411	41st	687	5th
New York	19,254,630	3rd	5.8	13th	54.8	50th	13.5	17th	49,941	2nd	442	21st
North Carolina	8,683,242	11th	5.4	19th	69.8	36th	14.0	13th	34,791	28th	448	20th
North Dakota	636,677	48th	3.4	49th	70.0	34th	11.7	22nd	28,987	47th	79	50th
Ohio	11,464,042	7th	6.3	5th	73.1	18th	12.1	21st	36,441	22nd	342	28th
Oklahoma	3,547,884	28th	4.9	31st	71.1	30th	16.1	8th	30,743	43rd	501	14th
Oregon	3,641,056	27th	7.6	1st	69.0	38th	13.9	14th	35,630	23rd	298	31st
Pennsylvania	12,429,616	6th	5.6	16th	74.9	8th	10.9	30th	38,555	16th	411	23rd
Rhode Island	1,076,189	43rd	5.4	19th	61.5	47th	11.3	26th	37,651	19th	247	40th
South Carolina	4,255,083	25th	6.9	4th	76.2	6th	14.1	12th	31,839	39th	784	1st
South Dakota	775,933	46th	3.7	46th	68.5	41st	11.1	28th	28,281	49th	172	46th
Tennessee	5,962,959	16th	5.1	27th	71.6	27th	13.8	15th	34,925	26th	695	4th
Texas	22,859,968	2nd	6.0	10th	65.6	45th	16.3	7th	38,511	17th	541	12th
Utah	2,469,585	34th	5.3	22nd	74.9	8th	10.6	34th	32,171	35th	236	43rd
Vermont	623,050	49th	3.7	46th	72.0	25th	9.7	40th	33,274	32nd	112	48th
Virginia	7,567,465	12th	3.9	42nd	73.4	14th	9.0	44th	40,534	9th	276	35th
Washington	6,287,759	14th	6.2	6th	66.0	43rd	11.0	29th	39,361	13th	344	27th
West Virginia	1,816,856	37th	5.3	22nd	80.3	1st	18.5	4th	30,382	44th	271	36th
Wisconsin	5,536,201	20th	5.0	30th	73.3	15th	10.5	36th	34,743	29th	210	45th
Wyoming	509,294	50th	3.8	44th	72.8	19th	9.7	40th	31,210	42nd	230	44th
USA	296,410,404	–	5.5	–	69.0	–	12.7	–	39,354	–	466	–

—————————— STATES · SOCIAL INDICATORS ——————————

State (& rank)	Infant mortality rate		Doctors per 100,000 resident population		Traffic fatalities per 100m vehicle miles		Energy consumption million Btu/person		Mobile homes as % of all housing units		% of >25s with a BA or higher	
Alabama	9·1	5th	212	40th	1·71	17th	435	9th	14·3	8th	22·3	45th
Alaska	5·5	43rd	222	35th	1·92	11th	1,164	1st	7·6	25th	25·5	25th
Arizona	6·4	31st	209	43rd	2·08	4th	255	43rd	13·1	10th	28·0	16th
Arkansas	8·3	10th	202	44th	2·05	5th	411	11th	12·6	11th	18·8	49th
California	5·5	43rd	261	18th	1·30	35th	227	48th	4·4	40th	31·7	10th
Colorado	6·1	35th	255	21st	1·46	26th	287	39th	5·4	34th	35·5	2nd
Connecticut	6·5	29th	362	5th	0·94	48th	249	45th	1·0	47th	34·5	6th
Delaware	8·7	8th	253	23rd	1·57	22nd	368	21st	11·1	16th	26·9	20th
DC	11·3	–	768	–	1·61	–	294	–	0·1	–	45·7	–
Florida	7·5	17th	248	25th	1·71	17th	253	44th	10·8	17th	26·0	22nd
Georgia	8·9	7th	221	36th	1·47	25th	343	26th	11·7	13th	27·6	17th
Hawaii	7·3	22nd	310	8th	1·45	29th	230	47th	0·2	50th	26·6	21st
Idaho	6·1	35th	170	50th	2·05	5th	379	19th	11·6	14th	23·8	40th
Illinois	7·4	20th	272	12th	1·36	34th	309	35th	2·9	43rd	27·4	18th
Indiana	7·7	15th	215	38th	1·15	43rd	457	7th	6·6	29th	21·1	46th
Iowa	5·3	46th	188	46th	1·42	30th	392	14th	4·8	37th	24·3	37th
Kansas	7·1	24th	218	37th	1·64	19th	387	15th	5·0	35th	30·0	13th
Kentucky	7·2	23rd	227	33rd	1·99	9th	462	6th	14·7	6th	21·0	47th
Louisiana	10·3	1st	265	15th	2·02	7th	784	3rd	12·6	11th	22·4	44th
Maine	4·4	49th	267	13th	1·39	33rd	382	17th	10·2	18th	24·2	39th
Maryland	7·5	17th	414	2nd	1·19	40th	264	41st	1·9	45th	35·2	4th
Massachusetts	4·9	48th	443	1st	0·86	49th	242	46th	1·0	47th	36·7	1st
Michigan	8·1	12th	238	30th	1·27	37th	312	34th	6·2	32nd	24·4	36th
Minnesota	5·4	45th	278	10th	1·19	40th	350	23rd	3·5	42nd	32·5	9th
Mississippi	10·3	1st	182	48th	2·32	3rd	410	12th	14·5	7th	20·1	48th
Missouri	8·5	9th	241	28th	1·81	14th	322	29th	7·1	27th	28·1	15th

STATES · SOCIAL INDICATORS

State (& rank)	Infant mortality rate		Doctors per 100,000 resident population		Traffic fatalities per 100m vehicle miles		Energy consumption million Btu/person		Mobile homes as % of all housing units		% of >25s with a BA or higher	
Montana	7.5	17th	227	34th	2.41	1st	404	13th	13.5	9th	25.5	25th
Nebraska	7.0	25th	242	26th	1.54	23rd	365	22nd	4.9	36th	24.8	32nd
Nevada	6.0	37th	185	47th	1.91	13th	301	37th	7.9	23rd	24.5	34th
New Hampshire	5.0	47th	263	16th	0.96	47th	256	42nd	6.3	31st	35.4	3rd
New Jersey	5.7	41st	310	7th	1.07	46th	294	38th	0.9	49th	34.6	5th
New Mexico	6.3	33rd	239	29th	1.92	11th	371	20th	18.7	1st	25.1	30th
New York	6.0	37th	391	3rd	1.10	44th	217	49th	2.6	44th	30.6	12th
North Carolina	8.2	11th	253	22nd	1.63	21st	316	33rd	17.6	3rd	23.4	41st
North Dakota	6.3	33rd	241	27th	1.41	32nd	640	4th	7.3	26th	25.2	29th
Ohio	7.9	14th	255	20th	1.17	42nd	350	24th	4.1	41st	24.6	33rd
Oklahoma	8.1	12th	172	49th	1.46	26th	444	8th	9.4	19th	22.9	42nd
Oregon	5.8	39th	262	17th	1.46	26th	307	36th	9.1	20th	25.9	23rd
Pennsylvania	7.6	16th	295	9th	1.48	24th	319	31st	4.7	38th	25.3	28th
Rhode Island	7.0	25th	350	6th	1.24	38th	215	50th	1.4	46th	27.2	19th
South Carolina	9.3	4th	230	32nd	2.01	8th	382	18th	17.9	2nd	24.9	31st
South Dakota	6.5	29th	215	39th	2.38	2nd	327	28th	11.2	15th	25.5	25th
Tennessee	9.4	3rd	260	19th	1.73	16th	382	16th	9.1	20th	24.3	37th
Texas	6.4	31st	212	42nd	1.64	19th	564	5th	8.0	22nd	24.5	34th
Utah	5.6	42nd	212	41st	1.29	36th	318	32nd	4.5	39th	30.8	11th
Vermont	4.4	49th	363	4th	0.83	50th	267	40th	7.0	28th	34.2	7th
Virginia	7.4	20th	274	11th	1.23	39th	322	30th	6.4	30th	33.1	8th
Washington	5.8	39th	267	14th	1.09	45th	339	27th	7.7	24th	29.9	14th
West Virginia	9.1	5th	230	31st	1.96	10th	423	10th	17.5	4th	15.3	50th
Wisconsin	6.9	27th	252	24th	1.42	30th	345	25th	6.1	33rd	25.6	24th
Wyoming	6.7	28th	192	45th	1.79	15th	890	2nd	15.2	5th	22.5	43rd
USA	7.0	–	266	–	1.48	–	338	–	7.2	–	27.2	–

STATES · CENTER & ELEVATIONS

State	Geographic center	Highest elevation	feet (′)	Lowest elevation	feet (′)	difference (′)
Alabama	12 mi SW of Clanton	Cheaha Mountain	2,405	Gulf of Mexico	0	2,405
Alaska	60 mi NW of Mount McKinley	Mount McKinley (Denali)	20,320	Pacific Ocean	0	20,320
Arizona	55 mi ESE of Prescott	Humphreys Peak	12,633	Colorado River	70	12,563
Arkansas	12 mi NW of Little Rock	Magazine Mountain	2,753	Ouachita River	55	2,698
California	38 mi E of Madera	Mount Whitney	14,494	Death Valley	-282	14,776
Colorado	30 mi NW of Pikes Peak	Mount Elbert	14,433	Arikaree River	3,350	11,083
Connecticut	Hartford at East Berlin	Mount Frissell	2,380	Long Island Sound	0	2,380
Delaware	11 mi S of Dover	Ebright Road	448	Atlantic Ocean	0	448
Florida	12 mi NNW of Brooksville	Walton County	345	Atlantic Ocean	0	345
Georgia	18 mi SE of Macon	Brasstown Bald	4,784	Atlantic Ocean	0	4,784
Hawaii	20°15' N 156°20' W, off Maui Island	Pu'u Wekiu	13,796	Pacific Ocean	0	13,796
Idaho	At Custer, SW of Challis	Borah Peak	12,662	Snake River	710	11,952
Illinois	28 mi NE of Springfield	Charles Mound	1,235	Mississippi River	279	956
Indiana	14 mi NNW of Indianapolis	Franklin Township	1,257	Ohio River	320	937
Iowa	5 mi NE of Ames	Oscola County	1,670	Mississippi River	480	1,190
Kansas	15 mi NE of Great Bend	Mount Sunflower	4,039	Verdigris River	679	3,360
Kentucky	3 mi NNW of Lebanon	Black Mountain	4,139	Mississippi River	257	3,882
Louisiana	3 mi SE of Marksville	Driskill Mountain	535	New Orleans	-8	543
Maine	18 mi N of Dover	Mount Katahdin	5,267	Atlantic Ocean	0	5,267
Maryland	4 ½ mi NW of Davidsonville	Backbone Mountain	3,360	Atlantic Ocean	0	3,360
Massachusetts	12 mi NW of Worcester	Mount Greylock	3,487	Atlantic Ocean	0	3,487
Michigan	5 mi NNW of Cadillac	Mount Arvon	1,979	Lake Erie	571	1,408
Minnesota	10 mi SW of Brainerd	Eagle Mountain	2,301	Lake Superior	601	1,700
Mississippi	9 mi WNW of Carthage	Woodall Mountain	806	Gulf of Mexico	0	806
Missouri	20 mi SW of Jefferson City	Taum Sauk Mountain	1,772	Saint Francis River	230	1,542

—————— STATES · CENTER & ELEVATIONS ——————

State	Geographic center	Highest elevation	feet (')	Lowest elevation	feet (')	difference (')
Montana	11 mi W of Lewistown	Granite Peak	12,799	Kootenai River	1,800	10,999
Nebraska	10 mi NW of Broken Bow	Johnson Twp., Kimball Co.	5,424	Missouri River	840	4,584
Nevada	26 mi SE of Austin	Boundary Peak	13,140	Colorado River	479	12,661
New Hampshire	3 mi E of Ashland	Mount Washington	6,288	Atlantic Ocean	0	6,288
New Jersey	5 mi E of Trenton	High Point	1,803	Atlantic Ocean	0	1,803
New Mexico	12 mi SSW of Willard	Wheeler Peak	13,161	Red Bluff Reservoir	2,842	10,319
New York	12 mi S of Oneida; 26 mi SW of Utica	Mount Marcy	5,344	Atlantic Ocean	0	5,344
North Carolina	10 mi NW of Sanford	Mount Mitchell	6,684	Atlantic Ocean	0	6,684
North Dakota	5 mi SW of McClusky	White Butte	3,506	Red River	750	2,756
Ohio	25 mi NNE of Columbus	Campbell Hill	1,549	Ohio River	455	1,094
Oklahoma	8 mi N of Oklahoma City	Black Mesa	4,973	Little River	289	4,684
Oregon	25 mi SSE of Prineville	Mount Hood	11,239	Pacific Ocean	0	11,239
Pennsylvania	2½ mi SW of Bellefonte	Mount Davis	3,213	Delaware River	0	3,213
Rhode Island	1 mile SSW of Crompton	Jerimoth Hill	812	Atlantic Ocean	0	812
South Carolina	13 mi SE of Columbia	Sassafras Mountain	3,560	Atlantic Ocean	0	3,560
South Dakota	8 mi NE of Pierre	Harney Peak	7,242	Big Stone Lake	966	6,276
Tennessee	5 mi NE of Murfreesboro	Clingmans Dome	6,643	Mississippi River	178	6,465
Texas	15 mi NE of Brady	Guadalupe Peak	8,749	Gulf of Mexico	0	8,749
Utah	3 mi N of Manti	Kings Peak	13,528	Beaver Dam Wash	2,000	11,528
Vermont	3 mi E of Roxbury	Mount Mansfield	4,393	Lake Champlain	95	4,298
Virginia	5 mi SW of Buckingham	Mount Rogers	5,729	Atlantic Ocean	0	5,729
Washington	10 mi WSW of Wenatchee	Mount Rainier	14,410	Pacific Ocean	0	14,410
West Virginia	4 mi W of Sutton	Spruce Knob	4,861	Potomac River	240	4,621
Wisconsin	9 mi SE of Marshfield	Timms Hill	1,951	Lake Michigan	579	1,372
Wyoming	58 mi ENE of Lander	Gannett Peak	13,804	Belle Fourche River	3,099	10,705

STATES · RANKINGS & TEMPERATURES

State	2006 Morgan Quinto State Rankings (morganquinto.com)				Record State Temperatures				
	Smartest	Healthiest	Dangerous	Livable	Highest	recorded at	Lowest	recorded at	difference
Alabama	43rd	42nd	18th	39th	112°F	Centerville	-27°F	New Market	139°F
Alaska	44th	39th	9th	23rd	100°F	Fort Yukon	-80°F	Prospect Creek Camp	180°F
Arizona	50th	40th	4th	29th	128°F	Lake Havasu City	-40°F	Hawley Lake	168°F
Arkansas	37th	36th	15th	48th	120°F	Ozark	-29°F	Pond	149°F
California	46th	19th	10th	34th	134°F	Greenland Ranch	-45°F	Boca	179°F
Colorado	23rd	32nd	22nd	20th	118°F	Bennett	-61°F	Maybell	179°F
Connecticut	2nd	9th	39th	10th	106°F	Danbury	-32°F	Falls Village	138°F
Delaware	25th	37th	24th	18th	110°F	Millsboro	-17°F	Millsboro	127°F
Florida	36th	41st	7th	31st	109°F	Monticello	-2°F	Tallahassee	111°F
Georgia	40th	44th	13th	38th	112°F	Greenville	-17°F	CCC Camp F-16	129°F
Hawaii	42nd	10th	26th	22nd	100°F	Pahala	12°F	Mauna Kea Obs 111.2	88°F
Idaho	28th	18th	40th	18th	118°F	Orofino	-60°F	Island Park Dam	178°F
Illinois	32nd	33rd	19th	28th	117°F	East St. Louis	-36°F	Congerville	153°F
Indiana	26th	28th	28th	36th	116°F	Collegeville	-36°F	New Whiteland	152°F
Iowa	14th	5th	43rd	3rd	118°F	Keokuk	-47°F	Elkader	165°F
Kansas	13th	12th	25th	15th	121°F	Alton (near)	-40°F	Lebanon	161°F
Kentucky	35th	26th	33rd	47th	114°F	Greensburg	-37°F	Shelbyville	151°F
Louisiana	45th	48th	2nd	50th	114°F	Plain Dealing	-16°F	Minden	130°F
Maine	5th	4th	49th	17th	105°F	North Bridgton	-48°F	Van Buren	153°F
Maryland	19th	35th	5th	16th	109°F	Cumberland & Frederick	-40°F	Oakland	149°F
Massachusetts	3rd	6th	30th	7th	107°F	New Bedford & Chester	-35°F	Chester	142°F
Michigan	27th	23rd	12th	35th	112°F	Mio	-51°F	Vanderbilt	163°F
Minnesota	6th	3rd	35th	2nd	114°F	Moorhead	-60°F	Tower	174°F
Mississippi	49th	50th	21st	49th	115°F	Holly Springs	-19°F	Corinth	134°F
Missouri	21st	34th	20th	27th	118°F	Warsaw & Union	-40°F	Warsaw	158°F

—STATES · RANKINGS & TEMPERATURES—

State	2006 Morgan Quitno State Rankings (morganquitno.com)				Record State Temperatures				
	Smartest	Healthiest	Dangerous	Livable	Highest	recorded at	Lowest	recorded at	difference
Montana	9th	27th	42nd	21st	117°F	Medicine Lake	-70°F	Rogers Pass	187°F
Nebraska	12th	7th	34th	9th	118°F	Minden	-47°F	Oshkosh	165°F
Nevada	47th	47th	1st	24th	125°F	Laughlin	-50°F	San Jacinto	175°F
New Hampshire	15th	2nd	47th	1st	106°F	Nashua	-47°F	Mt. Washington	153°F
New Jersey	4th	16th	32nd	5th	110°F	Runyon	-34°F	River Vale	144°F
New Mexico	48th	49th	3rd	41st	122°F	Waste Isolation Pilot Plant	-50°F	Gavilan	172°F
New York	10th	31st	31st	32nd	108°F	Troy	-52°F	Old Forge	160°F
North Carolina	22nd	30th	17th	40th	110°F	Fayetteville	-34°F	Mt. Mitchell	144°F
North Dakota	20th	11th	50th	12th	121°F	Steele	-60°F	Parshall	181°F
Ohio	31st	24th	23rd	37th	113°F	Gallipolis (near)	-39°F	Milligan	152°F
Oklahoma	39th	45th	14th	43rd	120°F	Tipton	-27°F	Watts	147°F
Oregon	38th	15th	27th	33rd	119°F	Pendleton	-54°F	Seneca	173°F
Pennsylvania	11th	29th	29th	30th	111°F	Phoenixville	-42°F	Smethport	153°F
Rhode Island	16th	13th	38th	26th	104°F	Providence	-23°F	Kingston	127°F
South Carolina	29th	42nd	6th	46th	111°F	Camden	-19°F	Caesars Head	130°F
South Dakota	18th	17th	45th	13th	120°F	Gannvalley	-58°F	McIntosh	178°F
Tennessee	41st	38th	8th	45th	113°F	Perryville	-32°F	Mountain City	145°F
Texas	24th	46th	11th	41st	120°F	Seymour	-23°F	Seminole	143°F
Utah	33rd	8th	36th	11th	117°F	Saint George	-69°F	Peter's Sink	186°F
Vermont	1st	1st	48th	4th	105°F	Vernon	-50°F	Bloomfield	155°F
Virginia	7th	21st	37th	8th	110°F	Balcony Falls	-30°F	Mtn. Lake Bio. Stn.	140°F
Washington	30th	20th	16th	25th	118°F	Ice Harbor Dam	-48°F	Mazama & Winthrop	166°F
West Virginia	34th	22nd	41st	44th	112°F	Martinsburg	-37°F	Lewisburg	149°F
Wisconsin	8th	14th	44th	14th	114°F	Wisconsin Dells	-55°F	Couderay	169°F
Wyoming	17th	25th	46th	6th	115°F	Basin	-66°F	Riverside R.S.	181°F

Government

*Politics are such a torment that I would advise
every one I love not to mix with them.*
— THOMAS JEFFERSON

GEORGE WALKER BUSH · 43rd PRESIDENT

Sworn into office: January 20, 2001 & January 20, 2005 · *Affiliation*: Republican
Born: July 6, 1946, New Haven, Connecticut · *Professed religion*: Methodist
Yale University (graduated 1968) & Harvard University Business School (graduated 1975)
Served as 46th Governor of Texas 1994–2000
Marriage: November 5, 1977, to Laura Welch (born November 4, 1946, in Midland, Texas)
Children: twins Barbara (1981–), Jenna (1981–)
Pets: Barney & Miss Beazley (dogs); India 'Willie' Bush (cat)

Height.....71·50 inches	Body fat .... 16·8%	Blood pressure ..108/68
Weight..........196·0 lb	Pulse (resting) .. 46 bpm	Temperature..... 97·5°F
Cholesterol.. 174 mg/dl	Pulse (active) ..179 bpm	[2006 annual medical checkup]

THE CABINET & CABINET RANKING MEMBERS

Vice President	Richard B. Cheney
Secretary of State	Condoleezza Rice
Secretary of the Treasury	Henry M. Paulson Jr
Secretary of Defense	Donald H. Rumsfeld
Attorney General	Alberto R. Gonzales
Secretary of the Interior	Dirk Kempthorne
Secretary of Agriculture	Michael O. Johanns
Secretary of Commerce	Carlos M. Gutierrez
Secretary of Labor	Elaine Chao
Secretary of Health & Human Services	Michael O. Leavitt
Secretary of Housing & Urban Development	Alphonso Jackson
Secretary of Transportation	Mario Cino (acting Sec.)
Secretary of Energy	Samuel W. Bodman
Secretary of Education	Margaret L. Spellings
Secretary of Veterans Affairs	Robert J. 'Jim' Nicholson
Secretary of Homeland Security	Michael Chertoff
Administrator, Environmental Protection Agency	Stephen Johnson
Director, Office of Management and Budget	Rob Portman
Director, Office of National Drug Control Policy	John Walters
US Trade Representative	Ambassador Susan Schwab
White House Chief of Staff	Joshua B. Bolten

—— PRESIDENTIAL SUCCESSION & QUALIFICATION ——

Under the 1947 Presidential Succession Act, if the President is incapacitated, dies, resigns, is for any reason unable to hold the office, or is removed from office (impeached and convicted), he/she is to be replaced by those holding the following offices, in order, provided that they are legally qualified to be President [see below].

Vice President
Speaker of the House [see p.298]
President Pro Tempore of the Senate
Secretary of State
Secretary of the Treasury
Secretary of Defense
Attorney General
(proposed: Secretary of Homeland Security)
Secretary of the Interior

Secretary of Agriculture
Secretary of Commerce
Secretary of Labor
Sec. of Health & Human Services
Secretary of Housing & Urban Dev.
Secretary of Transportation
Secretary of Energy
Secretary of Education
Secretary of Veterans Affairs

To qualify as President, candidates must be at least 35 years old and natural-born US citizens who have lived in the US for at least 14 years. Each term is 4 years and, since the 22nd Amendment was ratified in 1951, Presidents are limited to 2 terms.

—— NICKNAMES, THE 'POTUS', & THE 'W' KEYS ——

Most Presidents of the United States (POTUS) have earned nicknames, such as:

G. Washington.....*Father of His Country*
Martin Van Buren........*Old Kinderhook*
A. Lincoln .... *The Great Emancipator*
Zachary Taylor.....*Old Rough and Ready*

Thomas Jefferson.. *The Sage of Monticello*
Richard Nixon .... *Tricky Dick*
Ronald Reagan............... *The Gipper*
Bill Clinton .... *Slick Willie; Bubba*

George Bush (himself nicknamed *W*[†], *Dubya, Shrub, 43*, amongst others) has taken the tradition one step further, instigating a set of his own nicknames, including:

Dick Cheney............*Big Time; Veep*
Condoleezza Rice.................*Guru*
Karl Rove .... *The Boy Genius*

Tony Blair.................... *Landslide*
Kenneth Lay [see p.18] .... *Kenny Boy*
Vladimir Putin..............*Pootie-Poot*

As 'Big Time' said in an interview, 'In our White House, the President is the one who passes out nicknames. He does it very effectively and he has a great ability to sort of identify people's unique characteristics that stand out. He does it on a regular basis. It's always done in good humor, with no feelings hurt. When I talk to him, I always refer to him as Mr President … He calls me "Veep"'.
† After George W. Bush's election, rumors abounded that outgoing White House Democrats played pranks on Republican replacements – like removing the 'W' keys from keyboards. In 2002, the GAO published an obsessively detailed 220-page report of the various allegations of acts by Clinton's supporters. The investigation concluded that 'damage, theft, vandalism, and pranks occurred in the White House complex during the 2001 presidential transition. Incidents such as the removal of keys from computer keyboards; the theft of various items; the leaving of certain voice mail messages, signs, and written messages; and the placing of glue on desk drawers clearly were intentional acts'.

US PRESIDENTS

president	born	star sign	birth state	age at inaug.	dates of term	political party	religion	handedness	owned slaves	facial hair	red-headed	Mt Rushmore	assassinated	served as VP	went to Harvard	Nobel Prize	children	salary	died in office	dates of death	age
George Washington	02-22-1732	♓	VA‡	57	1789–1797	F	E	r	■			■						$25k		12-14-1799	67
John Adams	10-30-1735	♏	MA‡	61	1797–1801	F	U	r						■	■		5	$25k		07-04-1826	90
Thomas Jefferson	04-13-1743	♈	VA‡	57	1801–1809	DR	D	r	■		□	■		■			6	$25k		07-04-1826	83
James Madison	03-16-1751	♓	VA‡	57	1809–1817	DR	E	r	■									$25k		06-28-1836	85
James Monroe	04-28-1758	♉	VA‡	58	1817–1825	DR	E	r	■								2	$25k		07-04-1831	73
John Q. Adams	07-11-1767	♋	MA‡	57	1825–1829	DR	U	r							■		4	$25k		02-23-1848	80
Andrew Jackson	03-15-1767	♓	SC‡	61	1829–1837	D	P	r	■									$25k		06-08-1845	78
Martin Van Buren	12-05-1782	♐	NY	54	1837–1841	D	Re	r	■	■	□			■			4	$25k		07-24-1862	79
William Harrison	02-09-1773	♒	VA‡	68	1841	W	E	r	■								10	$25k	■	04-04-1841	68
John Tyler	03-29-1790	♈	VA	51	1841–1845	W	E	r	■					■			14	$25k		01-18-1862	71
James Knox Polk	11-02-1795	♏	NC	49	1845–1849	D	M	r	■									$25k		06-15-1849	53
Zachary Taylor	11-24-1784	♐	VA	64	1849–1850	W	E	r	■								6	$25k	■	07-09-1850	65
Millard Fillmore	01-07-1800	♑	NY	50	1850–1853	W	U	r						■			2	$25k		03-08-1874	74
Franklin Pierce	11-23-1804	♐	NH	48	1853–1857	D	E	r									3	$25k		10-08-1869	64
James Buchanan	04-23-1791	♉	PA	65	1857–1861	D	P	r										$25k		06-01-1868	77
Abraham Lincoln	02-12-1809	♒	KY	52	1861–1865	R	L	r		■		■	■				4	$25k	■	04-15-1865	56
Andrew Johnson	12-29-1808	♑	NC	56	1865–1869	D/U/R	?	r	■					■			5	$25k		07-31-1875	66
Ulysses S. Grant	04-27-1822	♉	OH	46	1869–1877	R	M	r	■	■							4	$25k		07-23-1885	63
Rutherford Hayes	10-04-1822	♎	OH	54	1877–1881	R	M	r		■					■		8	*$50k		01-17-1893	70
James Garfield	11-19-1831	♏	OH	49	1881	R	Di	l		■			■				7	$50k	■	09-19-1881	49
Chester Arthur	10-05-1829	♎	VT	50	1881–1885	R	E	r		■				■			3	$50k		11-18-1886	56
Grover Cleveland	03-18-1837	♓	NJ	47	1885–1889	D	P	r									5	$50k		06-24-1908	71
Benjamin Harrison	08-20-1833	♌	OH	55	1889–1893	R	P	r		■							3	$50k		03-13-1901	67
Grover Cleveland	03-18-1837	♓	NJ	55	1893–1897	D	P	r									5	$50k		06-24-1908	71

——————— US PRESIDENTS cont. ———————

president	born	star sign	birth state	age at inaug.	dates of term	political party	religion	handedness	owned slaves	facial hair	red headed	Mt Rushmore	assassinated	served as VP	at Harvard	on a banknote	Nobel Prize	children	Gft or tallest	salary	died in office	date of death	age
William McKinley	01-29-1843	♒	OH	54	1897–1901	R	M	r	·	·	·	·	■	·	·	□	·	2	·	$50k	■	09.14.1901	58
Theodore Roosevelt	10-27-1858	♏	NY	42	1901–1909	R	Re	r	·	■	·	■	□	■	·	·	■	6	·	$50k	·	01-06-1919	60
William Taft	09-15-1857	♍	OH	51	1909–1913	R	U	r	·	■	·	·	·	·	·	·	·	3	■	$75k	·	03-08-1930	72
Woodrow Wilson	12-28-1856	♑	VA	56	1913–1921	D	P	r	·	·	·	·	·	·	·	□	■	3	·	$75k	·	02-03-1924	67
Warren Harding	11-02-1865	♏	OH	55	1921–1923	R	B	r	·	·	·	·	·	·	·	·	·	2	·	$75k	■	08-02-1923	57
Calvin Coolidge	07-04-1872	♋	VT	51	1923–1929	R	C	?	·	·	·	·	·	■	·	·	·	2	·	$75k	·	01-05-1933	60
Herbert Hoover	08-10-1874	♌	IO	54	1929–1933	R	Q	?	·	·	·	·	·	·	·	·	·	2	·	$75k	·	10-20-1964	90
Franklin D. Roosevelt	01-30-1882	♒	NY	51	1933–1945	D	E	l	·	·	·	·	□	□	■	·	·	6	·	$75k	■	04-12-1945	63
Harry S. Truman	05-08-1884	♉	MO	60	1945–1953	D	B	l	·	·	·	·	□	■	·	·	·	1	·	*$100k	·	12-26-1972	88
Dwight Eisenhower	10-14-1890	♎	TX	62	1953–1961	R	P	r	·	·	·	·	·	·	·	·	·	2	·	$100k	·	03-28-1969	78
John F. Kennedy	05-29-1917	♊	MA	43	1961–1963	D	Ro	r	·	·	·	·	■	·	■	·	·	3	■	$100k	■	11-22-1963	46
Lyndon B. Johnson	08-27-1908	♍	TX	55	1963–1969	D	Di	r	·	·	·	·	·	■	·	·	·	2	■	$100k	·	01-22-1973	64
Richard Nixon	01-09-1913	♑	CA	56	1969–1974	R	Q	r	·	·	·	·	·	■	·	·	·	2	■	$200k	·	04-22-1994	81
Gerald Ford	07-14-1913	♋	NE	61	1974–1977	R	E	l	·	·	·	·	□	■	·	·	·	4	·	$200k	·		
James 'Jimmy' Carter	10-01-1924	♎	GA	52	1977–1981	D	So	r	·	·	·	·	·	·	·	·	·	4	·	$200k	·		
Ronald Reagan	02-06-1911	♒	IL	69	1981–1989	R	Di	?	·	·	·	·	□	·	·	·	·	4	·	$200k	·	06-05-2004	93
George Bush	06-12-1924	♊	MA	64	1989–1993	R	E	l	·	·	·	·	·	■	·	·	·	6	■	$200k	·		
William 'Bill' Clinton	08-19-1946	♌	AR	46	1993–2001	D	B	r	·	·	·	·	·	·	·	·	·	1	·	$200k	·		
George W. Bush	07-06-1946	♋	CT	54	2001–	R	M	r	·	·	·	·	·	·	■	·	·	2	·	p.290 $400k	·		

NOTES: Considerable debate and dispute surround a number of these entries. ‡ = Born British; *Party*: [F]ederalist; [D]emocratic; [R]epublican; [W]hig; [U]nion. *Religion at election*: [E]piscopalian; [C]ongregationalist; [U]nitarian; [D]eist; [P]resbyterian; [Re]formed Dutch; [M]ethodist; [L]iberal; [Di]sciples of Christ; [B]aptist; [Q]uaker; [Ro]man Catholic; [So]uthern Baptist. A number of Presidents changed their religion. *Left-handedness* data are equivocal. *Slave ownership* is disputed and not necessarily while in office. *Heights* are problematic, often subjective (e.g. JFK). *Children* includes those who died as infants; Jefferson's activity with the slave Sally Hemings is disputed; one of Reagan's sons was adopted. *Salary*: * indicates the President also received the preceding salary. Hollow boxes indicate an assassination attempt, an obsolete banknote design, or uncertain hair color.

—————— 2006 STATE OF THE UNION ADDRESS ——————

Delivered by President George W. Bush · January 31, 2006
Start: 9·12pm EST · *Finish*: 10·03pm EST · *Duration*: 51 mins
Words: 5,309 · *Interruptions*: applause, 66; laughter, 2 [White House analysis]

Some thematic extracts

AMERICA · The only way to protect our people, the only way to secure the peace, the only way to control our destiny is by our leadership – so the United States of America will continue to lead.

IRAN · a nation now held hostage by a small clerical elite that is isolating and repressing its people … and the nations of the world must not permit the Iranian regime to gain nuclear weapons. … Let me speak directly to the citizens of Iran: America respects you, and we respect your country. We respect your right to choose your own future and win your own freedom.

IRAQ · We are on the offensive in Iraq. … I am confident in our plan for victory – I am confident in the will of the Iraqi people – I am confident in the skill and spirit of our military. Fellow citizens, we are in this fight to win, and we are winning.

PALESTINE · The Palestinian people have voted in elections – now the leaders of Hamas must recognize Israel, disarm, reject terrorism, and work for lasting peace.

ECONOMY · We will build the prosperity of our country by strengthening our economic leadership in the world. … In the last two-and-a-half years, America has created 4·6 million new jobs – more than Japan and the European Union combined. … The American economy is preeminent, but we cannot afford to be complacent.

ENERGY · America is addicted to oil, which is often imported from unstable parts of the world. … We will invest more in zero-emission coal-fired plants; revolutionary solar and wind technologies; and clean, safe nuclear energy. Breakthroughs on … new technologies will help us reach another great goal: to replace more than 75% of our oil imports from the Middle East by 2025.

CLONING · I ask you to pass legislation to prohibit the most egregious abuses of medical research – human cloning in all its forms: creating or implanting embryos for experiments; creating human-animal hybrids; and buying, selling, or patenting human embryos. Human life is a gift from our Creator – and that gift should never be discarded, devalued, or put up for sale.

SURVEILLANCE · Based on authority given to me by the Constitution and by statute, I have authorized a terrorist surveillance program to aggressively pursue the international communications of suspected Al Qaeda operatives and affiliates to and from America. … if there are people inside our country who are talking with Al Qaeda, we want to know about it, because we will not sit back and wait to be hit again.

AMERICANS · Our greatness is not measured in power or luxuries, but by who we are and how we treat one another. So we strive to be a compassionate, decent, hopeful society.

——————2006 SOTU · REACTION & ANALYSIS——————

New York Times · While the goal was grand, the means were minuscule. The President has never been serious about energy independence.

Wall Street Journal · Absent was the sort of bold thrust that marked last year's push for Social Security overhaul, which failed in a hail of partisan recriminations.

LA Times · It was bracing to hear [Bush] state bluntly that 'America is addicted to oil' … but the President often musters laudable principles to avoid specifics or deflect unpleasant realities.

Chicago Tribune · Bush reminded us of our most crucial common purpose. For a President, for a Congress, for each of us in a citizenry of 300 million, the security of this nation is Job One.

Washington Post · The President's future horizons are constrained by his past choices, budgetary and political. The speech reflected Mr. Bush's changed political circumstances, and it displayed little ambition to tackle some of America's greatest challenges.

Le Monde (France) · The modesty of his proposals is a spectacular contrast to the ambition and confidence of the 2003 and 2004 versions.

The Times (UK) · The path Mr Bush can now follow is dramatically narrowed by the press of events and the mistakes of his last year.

The Late Show with David Letterman The State of the Union address was stopped 72 times last night for applause and another 30 for subpoenas.

WORD FREQUENCY & MICROSOFT'S AUTO SUMMARY

Afghanistan....... 2	Democracy(ies) ... 7	Israel............. 1	Pollution 1
AIDS/HIV 8	Economy(ic)..... 23	Job(s) 7	Poor/Poverty...... 2
Alito 1	Education 2	Medicaid(are)..... 4	Prison............. 1
America(n)(ns) ... 72	Enemy(ies) 8	Military 8	Al Qaeda 3
Battlefield 1	Energy 8	New Orleans...... 2	Reform(s) 9
Bipartisan 2	Europe(an) 3	Nuclear 3	School(s) 4
Burma 1	Family(ies)........ 4	Oil............... 3	Science(s)......... 7
Business(es)....... 2	Fight(ing) 13	Osama bin Laden . 2	Social security..... 3
Churches......... 1	Freedom......... 18	Others 3	September 11 2
Cloning 1	God 2	Our(selves) 109	Surveillance....... 2
Competitive(ness) 10	Iran(ian)......... 6	Palestinian........ 2	Tax(es)(payer).... 10
Crime............ 4	Iraq(i)(is) 16	Peace(ful)......... 8	Terrorist(s)(ism).. 20
Deficit(s) 2	Islam............. 2	Petroleum 1	WMD 1

When the text of George W. Bush's speech is entered into Microsoft Word's Auto Summarize feature, and distilled down to *c.*1% of its original length, the result is:

Keeping America competitive begins with keeping our economy growing.
Keeping America competitive requires affordable health care.
Keeping America competitive requires affordable energy. If we ensure that America's children succeed in life, they will ensure that America succeeds in the world. America is a great force for freedom and prosperity. May God bless America.

————————— PRESIDENTIAL MISCELLANY —————————

HAIL TO THE CHIEF · Written *c.*1812 by English composer James Sanderson, 'Hail to the Chief' was performed for a number of Presidents before being used at James Polk's inauguration in 1845. In 1954 the Dept of Defense made it the President's official musical tribute:

Hail to the Chief we have chosen for the nation, | *Hail to the Chief!*
We salute him, one and all. | *Hail to the Chief, as we pledge cooperation* | *In proud fulfillment of a great, noble call.* | *Yours is the aim to make this grand country grander,* | *This you will do, That's our strong, firm belief.* | *Hail to the one we selected as commander,* | *Hail to the President! Hail to the Chief!*

AIR FORCE ONE · The President usually travels on one of two customized Boeing 747-200B airplanes (tail Nos. 28000 & 29000). An abundance of communications equipment allows the business of government to be transacted at heights of 45,100ft, and although the planes have a range of 7,800 miles, they are capable of midair refueling. Every aircraft is allocated a call sign which allows it to be identified by air-traffic control – however these call signs change if the President is aboard, depending on who operates the flight:

Operator	*Call sign*
US Air Force	Air Force One
US Army	Army One
US Navy	Navy One
US Marines	Marine One
Civilian	Executive One

When members of the President's family travel on a plane its call sign is 'Executive One Foxtrot'. Similar call signs are used for the Vice President: in each case the suffix One becomes Two.

SKULL & BONES · Established in 1832, the Skull & Bones is a secret senior society at Yale that each year 'taps' 15 juniors to join its ranks. It is likely that the Skull & Bones would have piqued little curiosity outside of Yale had not many of the 'establishment' been members, including 3 Presidents: Taft, Bush Sr, and George W. Bush. The 2000 Presidential race was given added spice, for conspiracy theorists at least, by the fact that Senator John Kerry is also a 'Bonesman'. The exact nature, purpose, membership, and intent of Skull & Bones are little known and much debated. As Lyman Bagg, himself a Bonesman, wrote in 1871: 'The mystery now attending [the club's] existence forms the one great enigma which college gossips never tire of discussing'. Over the years, a plethora of rumors have dogged the society, alleging bizarre initiation rituals and dark, fraternal codes of loyalty.

CAMP DAVID · The Presidential retreat in Catoctin Mountain Park was created in 1943 for Franklin D. Roosevelt – who sought somewhere near to (but cooler than) Washington, DC, to relax and ease his sinus troubles. FDR named the camp 'Shangri-La', from James Hilton's novel *Lost Horizon*. Truman made Shangri-La the official Presidential retreat in 1945; and in 1953 Eisenhower renamed it Camp David, after his grandson. A majority of Presidents have used Camp David to host foreign leaders (the first such guest was Winston Churchill in May 1943), and the camp has been the location of many significant historical events, including: the planning of the Normandy invasion, the Bay of Pigs, Vietnam, and the Camp David Accords between Israel and Egypt.

---------- PRESIDENTIAL MISCELLANY cont. ----------

THE WHITE HOUSE · Designed by Irish-born architect James Hoban, the White House was started in 1792 and completed in 1800, when President John Adams moved in. Until Theodore Roosevelt officially named the building in 1901, the White House was known variously as the 'President's Palace', the 'President's House', and the 'Executive Mansion'. According to White House records, the building has 132 rooms, 35 bathrooms, and 6 levels in the Residence; 412 doors, 147 windows, 28 fireplaces, 8 staircases, and 3 elevators. And President Nixon would no doubt have been interested to learn that it takes about 570 gallons of paint to whitewash the White House.

OVAL OFFICE · Supposedly symbolizing democracy, the White House Oval Office dates back to Washington, whose Philadelphia home had a similar room. Here he held levees in a circle so that all were at an equal distance to the President. The White House Oval Office is the work of President Taft, who first occupied it in 1909. Over the years, in photographs and on film, the Oval Office has become one of the world's most famous political stages. President Clinton's infamous dalliance with Monica Lewinsky led wags to re-name the room the 'Oral Office'.

MOUNT RUSHMORE · A mountain 5,600ft high in the Black Hills of South Dakota, Mount Rushmore is carved with the faces of four great Presidents: Washington, Jefferson, Lincoln, and Theodore Roosevelt. The heads, each *c.*60ft high, are the work of American sculptor Gutzon Borglum, who began in 1927 and continued until his death in 1941; they were completed by his son Lincoln Borglum.

'THE BUCK STOPS HERE' · Famously, Truman had a sign on his Oval Office desk that declared 'The Buck Stops Here'. The phrase originates in poker, where the buck is a marker that indicates the dealer. To pass the buck is to transfer the job of dealing and, by extension, to shift responsibility or blame. Of course, since 'buck' has been slang for the dollar since the 1850s, it is likely that Truman was also alluding to the economic element of his political responsibility.

21-GUN SALUTE · Why 21 guns salute the President is unknown. It might date from a 1688 British army regulation that mandated 19 guns for Admirals and 21 for Royalty. Superstition dictates that gun salutes are fired in odd numbers – the VP's salute is 19 guns.

SALARY · In 2001, the President's salary doubled to $400,000 (the first raise since 1969). In addition, the President receives an additional (untaxed) $50,000 expense allowance. (Under the Constitution, the President's salary may not be altered during his/her period in office.) [Previous salary changes can be seen in the table on pp.292–3.] The Vice President receives a salary of $208,100, plus a taxable allowance for expenses of $10,000.

FIRST LADY · Describing the wife of the President as the First Lady dates back to Zachary Taylor's 1849 description of 'Dolley' Madison as 'our First Lady for half a century'. Even now the title is colloquial, and the position of Presidential wife (or husband) has no constitutional basis and carries no formal power. Apropos of nothing, Theodore Roosevelt's second wife's middle name was Kermit; in her honor, one assumes, his son, grandson, and great-grandson were also named Kermit. (The name, apparently, is Gaelic for 'without envy'.)

─────────── 109th CONGRESS ───────────

HOUSE		SENATE	
Republican	231 (53·1%)	Republican	55 (%)
Democrat	202 (46·4%)	Democrat	44 (%)
Independent	1 (0·2%)	Independent	1 (%)
Vacancy	1 (0·2%)	Vacancy	0 (%)
Members	435	Members	100
Delegates	4	(Vice President votes in event of a tie)	
Resident Commissioner	1	Vice President	Richard B. Cheney
Women members	68 (15·6%)	Women members	14 (%)
Black members	42	Black members	1
Hispanic members	26	Hispanic members	2
Asian Pacific members	6	Asian Pacific members	2
American Indian members	1	American Indian members	0
Foreign-born members	9	Foreign born-members	0
Average age	54·99 years	Average age	60·4 years
Prior military service	110 (25·3%)	Prior military service	31(%)

CONSTITUTIONAL QUALIFICATION
Article I, Section 2

No person shall be a Representative who shall not have attained to the Age of twenty five Years, and been seven Years a Citizen of the United States, and who shall not, when elected, be an Inhabitant of that State in which he shall be chosen.

CONSTITUTIONAL QUALIFICATION
Article I, Section 3

No Person shall be a Senator who shall not have attained to the Age of thirty Years, and been nine Years a Citizen of the United States, and who shall not, when elected, be an Inhabitant of that State for which he shall be chosen.

Speaker
J. Dennis Hastert [R-IL]
Majority Leader
John A. Boehner [R-OH]
Minority Leader
Nancy Pelosi [D-CA]

President Pro Tempore
Theodore (Ted) Stevens [R-AK]
Majority Leader
William (Bill) H. Frist [R-TN]
Minority Leader
Harry M. Reid [D-NV]

Speaker's salary	$212,100	President Pro Tempore slry	$183,500
Maj. & Min. Leaders' slry	$183,500	Maj. & Min. Leaders' slry	$183,500
Members' salary	$165,200	Senators' salary	$165,200

Chaplain
Rev. Daniel P. Coughlin
Clerk of the House
Karen L. Haas
Sergeant at Arms
Wilson (Bill) Livingood

Chaplain
Barry C. Black
Secretary
Emily J. Reynolds
Sergeant at Arms
William H. Pickle

[Congressional membership data as at election · Sources: Congressional Research Service; & others]

79th–109th CONGRESSES

Congress	Year	Senate Rep	Dem	Other	Total	President	House Rep	Dem	Other	Total
109	'05–'07	55	44	1	100	W. Bush	232	202	1	435
108	'03–'05	51	48	1	100	W. Bush	229	204	2	435
107	'01–'03	50	50	0	100	W. Bush	221	212	2	435
106	'99–'01	55	45	0	100	Clinton	223	211	1	435
105	'97–'99	55	45	0	100	Clinton	228	206	1	435
104	'95–'97	52	48	0	100	Clinton	230	204	1	435
103	'93–'95	43	57	0	100	Clinton	176	258	1	435
102	'91–'93	44	56	0	100	Bush	167	267	1	435
101	'89–'91	45	55	0	100	Bush	175	260	0	435
100	'87–'89	45	55	0	100	Reagan	177	258	0	435
99	'85–'87	53	47	0	100	Reagan	182	253	0	435
98	'83–'85	54	46	0	100	Reagan	166	269	0	435
97	'81–'83	53	46	1	100	Reagan	192	242	1	435
96	'79–'81	41	58	1	100	Carter	158	277	0	435
95	'77–'79	38	61	1	100	Carter	143	292	0	435
94	'75–'77	38	60	2	100	Ford	144	291	0	435
93	'73–'75	42	56	2	100	Nixon	192	242	1	435
92	'71–'73	44	54	2	100	Nixon	180	255	0	435
91	'69–'71	43	57	0	100	Nixon	192	243	0	435
90	'67–'69	36	64	0	100	LBJ	187	247	1	435
89	'65–'67	32	68	0	100	LBJ	140	295	0	435
88	'63–'65	34	66	0	100	JFK	176	259	0	435
87	'61–'63	36	64	0	100	JFK	174	263	0	437
86	'59–'61	35	65	0	100	Eisenhower	153	283	1	437
85	'57–'59	47	49	0	96	Eisenhower	201	234	0	435
84	'55–'57	47	48	1	96	Eisenhower	203	232	0	435
83	'53–'55	48	47	1	96	Eisenhower	221	213	1	435
82	'51–'53	47	49	0	96	Truman	199	235	1	435
81	'49–'51	42	54	0	96	Truman	171	263	1	435
80	'47–'49	51	45	0	96	Truman	246	188	1	435
79	'45–'47	38	57	1	96	Truman	191	242	2	435

SENATE SEATS   HOUSE SEATS

——————————— POLITICAL BESTIARY ———————————

Animal symbolism is a central element of art, literature, myth, and belief in every culture. Different animals have been ascribed a range of characteristics and associations, which translate into symbolic shorthand: the cunning fox, the wise owl, &c. In the West, the linking of animals with politics was formalized by heraldry's complex menagerie of real and fabled beasts. Below are some notes on recent political animal symbolism. ❦ The Democrat DONKEY and the Republican ELEPHANT probably date to the Congressional elections of 1874, and the work of German-born artist Thomas Nast – the 'father' of US caricature and cartoon. (Although some say that in the 1820s, Andrew Jackson was portrayed by cartoonists as a 'jackass'.) It seems that in 1874 the *New York Herald* ran a hoax about animals escaping the Central Park Zoo and scavenging for food. In a cartoon for *Harper's Weekly*, Nast combined the *Herald*'s joke with Ulysses S. Grant's bid for reelection, depicting the *Herald* as a donkey disguised as a lion, trying to scare away a Republican elephant. (In 1877 Nast also depicted a Democratic TIGER licking his chops while waiting for a Republican LAMB.) Depending on your partisan persuasion, the donkey (an C18th euphemism for 'ass') represents either stubbornness and braying stupidity or cleverness, courage, and likeableness. (In Biblical times, donkeys were thought suitable mounts for royalty in peacetime.) The elephant symbolizes either sturdiness, toughness, and a preternatural memory, or blundering clumsiness and pachydermal insensitivity. Unlike the Republicans, the Democrats have never formally adopted their animal as a symbol. ❦

Two recent additions to the political menagerie are the RINO (*Republican in Name Only*) and the DINO (*Democrat in Name Only*) to represent politicians whose beliefs do not always match their party's line. ❦ British politicians are familiar with STALKING HORSES. In the C17th these were horses trained to conceal hunters as close as possible to their quarry. In modern politics a stalking horse is a 'no-hoper' who challenges an incumbent to gauge their popularity while providing cover for stronger candidates. ❦ Amongst a number of symbols adopted by Gandhi was the COW – a beast sacrificed by Muslims but held sacred by Hindus. The cow was a paradoxical (and unsuccessful) attempt to bridge this divide and create a symbol of national Indian unity, religious tolerance, and respect for all life. ❦ The DOVE has long been associated with goodness, but of three different types: the dove of Noah symbolizes *rest*; the dove of David, *peace*; and the dove of Christ, *salvation*. In contrast, from the earliest days of falconry, the HAWK has symbolized war. (A CHICKENHAWK is one who advocates war despite never having had personal military experience.) ❦ The SCAPEGOAT, so often discussed in politics, dates to Jewish ritual [Lev. XVI] and the Day of Atonement, when one of two goats was chosen to be sent into the wilderness (the sins of the people having been symbolically laid upon it), while the other was sacrificed. ❦ LAME DUCK was originally a London stock market term [see also Bulls, Bears, & Stags p.311] for one who defaulted on a debt. It is now used to describe a discredited politician or a President in (roughly) the second half of their second term.

—————————— BEST & WORST PRESIDENTS ——————————

A Quinnipiac University poll in May 2006 asked registered American voters which US Presidents since World War II they considered to be the best and the worst:

Best Postwar President	%	*Worst Postwar President*	%
Ronald Reagan	28	George W. Bush	34
Bill Clinton	25	Richard Nixon	17
John Kennedy	18	Bill Clinton	16
Harry Truman	7	Jimmy Carter	13
Jimmy Carter	5	Lyndon Johnson	4
Dwight Eisenhower	5	George Bush Senior	3
George W. Bush	3	Ronald Reagan	3
George Bush Senior	2	Gerald Ford	2
Gerald Ford	1	John Kennedy	1
Lyndon Johnson	1	Harry Truman	1
Richard Nixon	1	Dwight Eisenhower	−
No opinion	4	No opinion	5

[A May 2006 *Newsweek* poll showed 50% thought George W. Bush would be viewed as a 'below average President' (32% said 'average', 16% 'above average'.) A December 2005 Diageo/Hotline poll found that 34% thought history would judge W. Bush as having done a 'good' or 'excellent' job.]

—————————— RED & BLUE ——————————

Since the Presidential election of 2000, Republican and Democrat states have been represented on TV and in the press by red and blue respectively. (The FEC's 2004 election report uses the same coding.) Yet, prior to this, most used the opposite colors: Reagan's 'lake' in 1980, for example, turned blue. The reason for the switch in colors is unclear. The *Washington Post* apportioned blame to the NBC graphics department and to a joke by David Letterman who, during the lengthy 2000 recount, suggested a compromise to 'make George W. Bush President of the red states and Al Gore head of the blue ones'. The resulting (and seamless) shift into 'red' and 'blue' state thinking was elegantly captured (and perhaps catalyzed) by David Brooks's 2001 *Atlantic Monthly* essay, 'One Nation, Slightly Divisible'. ❦ One curiosity of associating red with the political right and blue with the left is that it bucks historical precedent. Red has long been the color of revolution, Socialism and Communism (red-Russia, red-China, reds under the bed), yet red is also regal and was the uniform of British soldiers in the Revolutionary War (the Continental army sported blue). In heraldry, red signifies magnanimity and fortitude; in folklore red is linked to magic. Blue is associated with the aristocracy (blue blood), the sea, the sky, and constancy (true blue). Yet it is also the color of depression, and was worn by the lower classes: servants, paupers, charity-school boys, and licensed beggars. ❦ In military planning, allied troops are blue and enemy troops are red – thus 'friendly fire' is known as 'blue on blue'. It seems that the divide exposed by Bush *vs* Gore was only exacerbated by Bush *vs* Kerry, the war on terror, and the Iraq conflict. Consequently, red state/blue state 'unfriendly fire' looks set to continue.

———————— PARTISAN POLITICS & THE BRAIN ————————

Research published in January 2006 by psychologists at Emory University, Atlanta, suggested that both liberals and conservatives may be equally irrational when discussing politics. The study utilized functional MRI brain scanning to examine which parts of the brain appeared to activate during political discourse. In 2004, 30 adult men were recruited: half committed supporters of George W. Bush; the other half, supporters of John Kerry. Each man was asked to consider a series of doctored statements that portrayed both Bush and Kerry as dishonest. The study's authors concluded that partisan supporters denied obvious contradictions made by their own candidate, but spotted contradictions when they were made by the 'opposition'. Interestingly, the MRI scans seemed to indicate that participants activated *emotional* rather than *analytical* centers of their brains. Drew Westen, Director of Clinical Psychology, stated, 'We did not see any increased activation of the parts of the brain normally engaged during reasoning ... what we saw instead was a network of emotion circuits lighting up'. Westen suggested that once partisans had formed utterly biased conclusions (ignoring information that did not fit their preconceptions), circuits that mediate negative emotions (sadness and disgust) 'turned off' and subjects 'activated' circuits involved in reward and pleasure. The research team hypothesized that this kind of emotional reasoning reinforces itself (since it produces feelings of pleasure) which in turns leads to the hardening of defensive, partisan beliefs.

> *It appears as if partisans twirl the cognitive kaleidoscope until they get the conclusions they want ... then they get massively reinforced for it, with the elimination of negative emotional states and activation of positive ones.*
> — Drew Westen

———————— POTUS & SOTU ————————

The State of the Union [SOTU] is presented before a joint session of Congress and held in the House of Representatives Chamber at the US Capitol. It is in fulfillment of Article II, Sec. 3, Cl. 1, of the US Constitution, which requires that '*the President shall from time to time give to Congress information on the State of the Union and recommend to their Consideration such measures as he* [sic] *shall judge necessary and expedient*'. From 1790–1934, the address was informally called the Annual Message.

Longest address . . . . Truman, 1946, >25,000 words
Shortest address . . . . Washington, 1790, 833 words
Average length . . . . C19th: *c*.10,000 words; late C20th: *c*.5,000 words
First broadcasts... *radio*: Coolidge, 1923; *TV*: Truman, 1947; *web*: W. Bush, 2002

By tradition, one member of the Cabinet does not attend the address, in case a disaster in the Capitol kills or incapacitates the line of succession [see p.291]. In response to 9/11, two Senators and two Representatives also absent themselves.

[Sources: Office of the Clerk of the House; The Congressional Research Service]

PRESIDENTIAL VOTES 1952–2004

Year	Democrat candidate	% popular vote	electoral vote	Republican candidate	% popular vote	electoral vote
1952	Stevenson	44·4	89	EISENHOWER	54·9	442
1956	Stevenson	43·1	73	EISENHOWER	57·4	457
1960	[†]KENNEDY	49·7	303	Nixon	49·5	219
1964	JOHNSON	61·1	486	Goldwater	38·7	52
1968	Humphrey	42·4	191	[†]NIXON	43·4	301
1972	McGovern	37·2	17	NIXON	60·2	520
1976	CARTER	50·0	297	Ford	48·0	240
1980	Carter	41·0	49	REAGAN	50·5	489
1984	Mondale	40·4	13	REAGAN	58·5	525
1988	Dukakis	45·5	111	BUSH SR	53·1	426
1992	[†]CLINTON	42·9	370	Bush Sr	37·1	168
1996	[†]CLINTON	49·2	379	Dole	40·7	159
2000	Gore	48·3	266	[†]BUSH JR	47·8	271
2004	Kerry	48·1	251	BUSH JR	50·6	286

[† minority vote · pre-1960, excludes AK & HI, pre-1964, excludes DC. Source: Office of the Clerk]

ELECTORAL PARTICIPATION

Voter participation in Presidential elections between 1932–2004 is charted below:

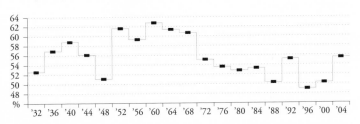

Below, voter turnout in the 2004 Presidential election, charted by individual state:

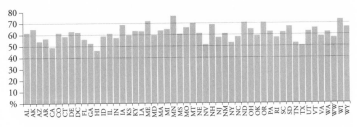

[Source: US Statistical Abstract, 2006 · See this report for detailed notes on data]

——————— EXECUTIVE CLEMENCY ———————

The power of the President to exercise Executive Clemency is enshrined in Article II, Section 2, of the Constitution. Clemency can apply only to federal criminal offenses and can take a number of forms including: pardon, commutation of sentence, remission of fine or restitution, and reprieve. The exercise of Executive Clemency has a long and controversial history, since it has been used both for political gain as well as to right a judicial wrong. Perhaps the most famous pardon in American history was that granted by President Gerald Ford to ex-President Richard Nixon. In Proclamation 4311, September 8, 1974, Ford issued his pardon on the grounds that judicial action against Nixon would 'cause prolonged and divisive debate over the propriety of exposing to further punishment and degradation a man who has already paid the unprecedented penalty of relinquishing the highest elective office of the United States'. Below are some recent statistics:

Pardon petitions granted		
Wilson............2,480	Truman...........2,044	Carter..............566
Harding 800	Eisenhower.......1,157	Reagan..............406
Coolidge..........1,545	Kennedy............575	Bush Sr..............77
Hoover 1,385	Johnson...........1,187	Clinton.............459
F.D. Roosevelt....3,687	Nixon..............926	Bush Jr [to date].......82
	Ford 409	[Source: US Pardon Attorney]

Although the first official Thanksgiving Presidential Turkey Pardon was issued in 1947 by President Harry S. Truman, the now-annual event dates back to the Civil War, when Abraham Lincoln's son Tad beseeched his father to spare a turkey named Jack. Now, the turkeys are donated by the National Turkey Federation which hand-rears birds to acclimatize them for the Rose Garden ceremony.

——————— PROTECTING THE PRESIDENT ———————

After the assassination of President William McKinley on September 6, 1901, by Leon Czolgosz, Congress charged the Secret Service with protecting the President of the United States. Nowadays, the Secret Service is mandated by law to protect:

the President, the Vice President (or other individuals next in order of succession to the Office of the President) ❦ the President-elect and Vice President-elect ❦ the immediate families of the above individuals ❦ former Presidents, their spouses for their lifetimes, except when the spouse remarries (in 1997, Congressional legislation became effective limiting Secret Service protection to former Presidents for a period of not more than 10 years from the date the former President leaves office†) ❦ children of former Presidents until age 16 ❦ visiting heads of foreign states or governments and their spouses traveling with them, other distinguished foreign visitors to the United States, and official representatives of the United States performing special missions abroad ❦ major Presidential and Vice Presidential candidates and their spouses, within 120 days of a Presidential election.

[Source: US Secret Service · † Bill Clinton will be the last President to enjoy lifelong protection]

2004 PRESIDENTIAL VOTES BY STATE

State	Presidential candidates		electoral college vote
AL	Bush 62.5%	Kerry 36.8%	R-9
AK	Bush 61.1%	Kerry 35.5%	R-3
AZ	Bush 54.9%	Kerry 44.4%	R-10
AR	Bush 54.3%	Kerry 44.5%	R-6
CA	Bush 44.4%	Kerry 54.3%	D-55
CO	Bush 51.7%	Kerry 47.0%	R-9
CT	Bush 43.9%	Kerry 54.3%	D-7
DE	Bush 45.8%	Kerry 53.3%	D-3
DC	Bush 9.3%	Kerry 89.2%	D-3
FL	Bush 52.1%	Kerry 47.1%	R-27
GA	Bush 58.0%	Kerry 41.4%	R-15
HI	Bush 45.3%	Kerry 54.0%	D-4
ID	Bush 68.4%	Kerry 30.3%	R-4
IL	Bush 44.5%	Kerry 54.8%	D-21
IN	Bush 59.9%	Kerry 39.3%	R-11
IA	Bush 49.9%	Kerry 49.2%	R-7
KS	Bush 62.0%	Kerry 36.6%	R-6
KY	Bush 59.5%	Kerry 39.7%	R-8
LA	Bush 56.7%	Kerry 42.2%	R-9
ME	Bush 44.6%	Kerry 53.6%	D-4
MD	Bush 43.0%	Kerry 56.0%	D-10
MA	Bush 36.6%	Kerry 61.6%	D-12
MI	Bush 47.8%	Kerry 51.2%	D-17
MN	Bush 47.6%	Kerry 51.1%	D-9
MS	Bush 59.0%	Kerry 40.2%	R-6
MO	Bush 53.3%	Kerry 46.1%	R-11
MT	Bush 59.1%	Kerry 38.6%	R-3
NE	Bush 65.9%	Kerry 32.7%	R-5
NV	Bush 50.5%	Kerry 47.9%	R-5
NH	Bush 48.9%	Kerry 50.2%	D-4
NJ	Bush 46.2%	Kerry 52.9%	D-15
NM	Bush 49.8%	Kerry 49.0%	R-5
NY	Bush 37.7%	Kerry 56.1%	D-31
NC	Bush 56.0%	Kerry 43.6%	R-15
ND	Bush 62.9%	Kerry 35.5%	R-3
OH	Bush 50.8%	Kerry 48.7%	R-20
OK	Bush 65.6%	Kerry 34.4%	R-7
OR	Bush 47.2%	Kerry 51.3%	D-7
PA	Bush 48.4%	Kerry 50.9%	D-21
RI	Bush 38.7%	Kerry 59.4%	D-4
SC	Bush 58.0%	Kerry 40.9%	R-8
SD	Bush 59.9%	Kerry 38.4%	R-3
TN	Bush 56.8%	Kerry 42.5%	R-11
TX	Bush 61.1%	Kerry 38.2%	R-34
UT	Bush 71.5%	Kerry 26.0%	R-5
VT	Bush 38.8%	Kerry 58.9%	D-3
VI	Bush 53.7%	Kerry 45.5%	R-13
WA	Bush 45.6%	Kerry 52.8%	D-11
WV	Bush 56.1%	Kerry 43.2%	R-5
WI	Bush 49.3%	Kerry 49.7%	D-10
WY	Bush 68.7%	Kerry 29.0%	R-3

———————————— SUPREME COURT JUSTICES ————————————

Justice	*date of birth*	*state*	*law school*	*appointed by*		*term began*
John G. Roberts Jr†	01·27·1955	NY	Harvard	Bush Jr	[R]	09·29·2005
John Paul Stevens	04·20·1920	IL	Northwestern	Ford	[R]	12·19·1975
Antonin Scalia	03·11·1936	NJ	Harvard	Reagan	[R]	09·26·1986
Anthony M. Kennedy	07·23·1936	CA	Harvard	Reagan	[R]	02·18·1988
David H. Souter	09·17·1939	MA	Harvard	Bush Sr	[R]	10·09·1990
Clarence Thomas	06·23·1948	GA	Yale	Bush Sr	[R]	10·23·1991
Ruth Bader Ginsburg	03·15·1933	NY	Columbia	Clinton	[D]	08·10·1993
Stephen G. Breyer	08·15·1938	CA	Harvard	Clinton	[D]	08·03·1994
Samuel A. Alito Jr	04·01·1950	NJ	Yale	Bush Jr	[R]	01·31·2006

[† The 17th Chief Justice · Sources: Supreme Court; Cornell Law School] · The appointment of Alito was not without dispute since some Democrats feared he would swing the Court to the right over issues like abortion. Yet, the real controversy surrounded Bush's first candidate. Harriet Miers, White House counsel and Bush's former personal attorney, was roundly attacked by both parties for lacking judicial experience, and she was forced to resign her nomination.

———————————— SUPREME COURT LAWGIVERS ————————————

On the north and south walls of the Supreme Court (opened in 1935), above the Chief Justice's bench, is a marble frieze that depicts the following famous lawgivers:

Menes (*c.*3200 BC) . . . . *ancient Egyptian king, unifier of Upper and Lower Egypt*
Hammurabi (*c.*1700s BC) . . . . . . *Babylonian ruler, creator of one of the earliest legal codes*
Moses (*c.*1300s BC) . . . . *ancient Israelite leader, lawgiver, and prophet*
Solomon (*c.*900s BC) . . . . *ancient Israelite king, renowned for his wisdom and justice*
Lycurgus (*c.*800 BC) . . . . *semi-mythical ancient Spartan lawgiver*
Solon (*c.*638 BC) . . . . *famous Athenian statesman and legal reformer*
Draco (*c.*600s BC) . . . . *responsible for the first written code of law in Athens*
Confucius (*b.*551 BC) . . . . *ancient Chinese philosopher, founder of Confucianism*
Augustus (*b.*63 BC) . . . . *first Roman Emperor, significant reformer*
Justinian (*c.*483) . . . . *Byzantine Emperor who codified Roman law*
Muhammad† (*c.*570) . . . . *prophet, founder of Islam*
Charlemagne (*c.*742) . . . . *King of France, first Holy Roman Emperor*
King John (*b.*1166) . . . . *King of England, signed the Magna Carta*
Louis IX (*b.*1214) . . . . *King of France, led crusades, reformed French administration*
Hugo Grotius (*b.*1583) . . . . *Dutch lawyer, legal philosopher, and theologian*
Sir William Blackstone (*b.*1723) . . . . *influential English law professor*
John Marshall (*b.*1755) . . . . *4th Chief Justice, established Supreme Court's authority*
Napoleon (*b.*1769) . . . . *French Emperor, established the Napoleonic Code*

The carvings are listed in order of appearance: Menes to Augustus appear on the Court's south wall, left to right; Justinian to Napoleon appear on the north wall, right to left. † Interestingly, Muhammad appears on the frieze even though Islam traditionally decries any depictions of the Prophet, a fact that became controversial in 2006 during the international furor over the Danish cartoons [see p.17].

—————————— CONSTITUTIONAL AMENDMENTS ——————————

1st ....guarantees freedom of religion, speech, press, assembly, and petition
2nd .... guarantees the right to keep and bear arms
3rd..prevents compulsory billeting during peacetime
4th........ guarantees security of person and possessions against search and seizure
5th..........prevents double-jeopardy; guarantees right against self-incrimination
6th............... guarantees fair, speedy, and public trial by jury; right to counsel
7th............................ guarantees right to trial by jury in common law suits
8th.................... prevents cruel or unusual punishments, and excessive fines
9th............................ protects rights not enumerated in the Constitution
10th .... reserves the rights of individual states
11th ....delineates judicial powers of the US in certain cases
12th .... sets procedures for electing President & Vice President
13th .... outlaws slavery
14th ....guarantees the rights of citizenship
15th .... guarantees right to vote regardless of race, color, or previous servitude
16th .... sets the powers of Congress to levy income taxes
17th ....enumerates procedure for electing Senators
18th .... introduced prohibition
19th .... guarantees the right of women to vote
20th ....sets Presidential term and succession, and terms of other offices
21st...repeals prohibition (18th Amendment)
22nd.. limits Presidents to two terms
23rd .... grants Washington, DC, residents a vote in Presidential elections
24th ....bars poll (voting) tax in federal elections
25th .... sets the order of Presidential succession
26th .... guarantees right to vote at age eighteen
27th ....postpones Representatives' pay raises until after new elections

—————————————— FEDERAL JURY SERVICE ——————————————

Eligibility for federal jury service depends upon being drawn at random from voter (or driver) lists, and being legally qualified to serve: QUALIFICATIONS · *United States citizen · at least 18 years of age · reside in the judicial district for 1 year · adequate proficiency in reading, writing, speaking, and understanding English · no disqualifying mental or physical condition · not currently subject to felony charges · never convicted of a felony (unless civil rights have been legally restored)* · EXEMPTIONS · *active-duty members of the armed forces · members of police and fire departments · certain public officials · others based on individual court rules (e.g. members of voluntary emergency service organizations, and people who recently have served on a jury)* · EXCUSALS · *may be granted for undue hardship or extreme inconvenience* · TIME · *trial jury service varies by court · some courts require service for one day or for the duration of one trial; others require service for a fixed term · Grand Jury service may be up to 18 months* · PAYMENT · *$40 per day (+ allowances)* · EMPLOYMENT · *By law, employers must allow employees time off (paid or unpaid) for jury service. The law prohibits employers from dismissing, intimidating, or coercing any permanent employee because of their federal jury service.*

—CLASSIFIED MATERIAL—

Executive Orders 12958 & 12829 set rules for the classification of information relating to national security. Only specifically authorized individuals may classify data, and documents may be classified only in the interests of national security. In order to access classified material, individuals must have the appropriate level of security clearance, have signed a nondisclosure agreement, and have a 'need to know'. Classified documents must indicate the individual who classified them, the expected date of declassification, and one of the following 3 classifications:

TOP SECRET

[T] · shall be applied to information, the unauthorized disclosure of which reasonably could be expected to cause exceptionally grave damage to the national security that the original classification authority is able to identify or describe.

SECRET

[S] · shall be applied to information, the unauthorized disclosure of which reasonably could be expected to cause serious damage to the national security that the original classification authority is able to identify or describe.

CONFIDENTIAL

[C] · shall be applied to information, the unauthorized disclosure of which reasonably could be expected to cause damage to the national security that the original classification authority is able to identify or describe.

The US Information Security Oversight Office reported that in 2005 classification decisions fell by 9%, from 15,645,237 classifications in 2004 to 14,206,773. In 2005, 29,540,603 pages of classified material were declassified, adding to the 'permanently valuable historical record'.

—POLITICAL ETHICS—

Code of Ethics for Government Service

Any person in Government
service should:

[1] Put loyalty to the highest moral principals and to country above loyalty to Government persons, party, or department. ❦ [2] Uphold the Constitution, laws, and legal regulations of the United States and of all governments therein and never be a party to their evasion. ❦ [3] Give a full day's labor for a full day's pay; giving to the performance of his duties his earnest effort and best thought. ❦ [4] Seek to find and employ more efficient and economical ways of getting tasks accomplished. ❦ [5] Never discriminate unfairly by the dispensing of special favors or privileges to anyone, whether for remuneration or not; and never accept for himself or his family, favors or benefits under circumstances which might be construed by reasonable persons as influencing the performance of his governmental duties. ❦ [6] Make no private promises of any kind binding upon the duties of office, since a Government employee has no private word which can be binding on public duty. ❦ [7] Engage in no business with the Government, either directly or indirectly, which is inconsistent with the conscientious performance of his governmental duties. ❦ [8] Never use any information coming to him confidentially in the performance of governmental duties as a means for making private profit. ❦ [9] Expose corruption wherever discovered. ❦ [10] Uphold these principles, ever conscious that public office is a public trust.

— Passed July 11, 1958.

Money

For the love of money is the root of all evil: which while some coveted after,
they have erred from the faith, and pierced themselves through with many sorrows.
— I TIMOTHY 6:10

MONEY · MANUFACTURE & LIFESPAN

Currency	No. produced in 2005	average lifespan	animal equivalent
$1 bill	3,475,200,000	18 months	deer mouse
$2 bill	(none in 2005; 2004 = 121,600,000)	9 years	fox
$5 bill	576,000,000	15 months	worker bee
$10 bill	512,000,000	18 months	deer mouse
$20 bill	3,059,200,000	2 years	field mouse
$50 bill	345,600,000	5 years	rabbit
$100 bill	668,800,000	8½ years	fox
Coins	15,302,690,500	25–30 years	hippopotamus

[Sources: US Mint; Dept Treasury · Note production for fiscal year; coin production, calendar year]

PRESIDENTS &c. ON BANK NOTES

Portrait	bill
George Washington	$1
Thomas Jefferson	$2
Abraham Lincoln	$5
Alexander Hamilton	$10
Andrew Jackson	$20
Ulysses S. Grant	$50
Benjamin Franklin	$100
†William McKinley	$500
†Grover Cleveland	$1,000
†James Madison	$5,000
†Salmon P. Chase	$10,000
†‡Woodrow Wilson	$100,000

† These notes are no longer in production. ‡ Wilson $100,000 bills were produced 1934–35, and were issued by the Treasury to Federal Banks based upon held gold bullion stocks; they were used only for official transactions.

CASH IN CIRCULATION

Year	cash ($) in circulation	cash ($) per capita
1910	3,148,700,000	34·07
1920	5,698,214,612	53·18
1930	4,521,987,962	36·74
1940	7,847,501,324	59·40
1950	27,156,290,042	179·03
1960	32,064,619,064	177·47
1970	54,350,971,661	265·39
1980	127,097,192,148	570·51
1990	266,902,367,798	1,062·86
2000	571,121,194,344	2,075·63

[Source: Federal Reserve Bank of Atlanta · Cash per capita applies to the United States]

—MISSION STATEMENTS—

A few mission statements of interest:

ENRON · [extracts] *Enron's Vision and Values comprise the platform upon which our human rights principles are built. ... Ruthlessness, callousness and arrogance don't belong here. ... When we say we will do something, we will do it; when we say we cannot or will not do something, then we won't do it. ... We have an obligation to communicate. ... We believe that information is meant to move and that information moves people. ... We are satisfied with nothing less than the very best in everything we do. ... The great fun here will be for all of us to discover just how good we can really be.*

PHILIP MORRIS USA · *Our goal is to be the most responsible, effective and respected developer, manufacturer and marketer of consumer products, especially products intended for adults. Our core business is manufacturing and marketing the best quality tobacco products to adults who use them.*

US STATE DEPT · *Create a more secure, democratic, and prosperous world for the benefit of the American people and the international community.*

GOOGLE · *Don't be evil.*

COCA-COLA · *The Coca-Cola Company exists to benefit and refresh everyone who is touched by our business.*

STARBUCKS · *To establish Starbucks as the premier purveyor of the finest coffee in the world while maintaining our uncompromising principles as we grow.*

Splendidly, the *dilbert.com* website has a mission statement generator which shuffles the standard buzzwords of corporate gibberish.

——— COLLAR COLOR———

BLUE-COLLAR workers are manual laborers who, traditionally, wore blue uniforms. In prewar slang, blue shirts were called '1,000-mile shirts' because of their ability to hide dirt for so long. WHITE-COLLAR workers are non-manual (usually clerical) workers after whom, as early as 1932, a segment of 'victimless', non-violent, and usually financial crime was named. Other collar colors include: GRAY-COLLAR for mechanics, maintenance men, and janitors, or those in semiskilled technical work. ❦ PINK-COLLAR for women working in 'traditional' female jobs like teaching and secretarial work. ❦ GREEN-COLLAR for environmental workers and BROWN-COLLAR for those working in recycling. ❦ GOLD-COLLAR for CEOs and those considered vital to a company. ❦ SCARLET-COLLAR for women working in prostitution or porn. ❦ BLACK-COLLAR for those working in 'creative' industries and the media, or those in industrial jobs like mining[†]. ❦ SILVER-COLLAR for robots, or workers of retirement age. ❦ OPEN-COLLAR for those working from home. ❦ and, inevitably, DOG-COLLAR for priests.

[†] 'Black-collar crime' has been used to describe both sexual abuse within the Church and judicial corruption.

——— MONEY & SEX———

A 2006 UK survey by French insurance agency AXA indicated that 20% of those with financial problems said the worry had adversely affected their sex lives. Of those who had experienced money-related relationship problems, 37% said they spent less 'quality time' with their partners, and 50% said they had more arguments as a result.

—BULLS, BEARS, & STAGS—

A BEAR MARKET is one where the price of stocks, shares, commodities, &c. is falling or is expected to fall. Conversely, a BULL MARKET is one where the price of stocks, shares, commodities, &c. is rising or is expected to rise. A BULL is one who, expecting the market to rise, buys in the hope of realizing a profit on a later sale. A BEAR is one who expects the market to fall, and trades accordingly. Some Bears sell stocks they do not hold for delivery at a future date ('shorting'), hoping on delivery to buy the stock more cheaply than they sold it. Both terms originated on the London exchanges (bear *c.*1709; bull *c.*1714). A 'bear-skin jobber' hoped 'to sell the bearskin before he'd caught the bear'. Astute investors know that money can be made in all markets; as the saying goes: 'Bulls make money, Bears make money, Pigs get slaughtered'. A STAG (traditionally one who dealt outside the Stock Exchange) describes traders who buy new issue shares in order to sell them quickly at a profit. ❦ In C16th England, bull- and bear-baiting were popular pastimes, where unfortunate animals would be tied to stakes and set upon by dogs. Shakespeare's *The Winter's Tale* is famous for one of theater's most outlandish stage directions ('*Exit, pursued by a bear*'), that was probably inspired by the proximity of Southwark's bear gardens. (Britain banned bull- and bear-baiting in 1835.)

—GIVING TO UNCLE SAM—

Citizens concerned about the size of the Public Debt can write checks to the Bureau of the Public Debt (the memo section should read 'a gift to reduce Debt Held by the Public'). In 2005, the American public donated $1,455,541·65 to reduce the debt.

—CxOs—

CAO...........	Chief Analytics Officer
CCO	Chief Compliance Officer
CEO...........	Chief Executive Officer
CFO...........	Chief Financial Officer
CIO	Chief Information Officer
CKO	Chief Knowledge Officer
CMO.........	Chief Marketing Officer
CNO	Chief Networking Officer
COO	Chief Operating Officer
CPO.......	Chief Procurement Officer
CRO................	Chief Risk Officer
CSO	Chief Strategy Officer
CTO...........	Chief Technical Officer
CWO	Chief Wisdom Officer
CxO	generic code for such terms

Many of these 'C-suite' initialisms have alternative translations – some sillier than others.

—THE DEVIL'S $—

Ambrose Bierce's 1906 definition of MONEY in *The Devil's Dictionary*:

MONEY · n. *A blessing that is of no advantage to us excepting when we part with it. An evidence of culture and a passport to polite society. Supportable property.*

— FORTUNE'S TOP 10(0) —

The best 10 companies to work for, from *Fortune*'s 2006 Top 100 survey:

1	Genentech
2	Wegmans Food Markets
3	Valero Energy
4	Griffin Hospital
5	W.L. Gore & Associates
6	Container Store
7	Vision Service Plan
8	J.M. Smucker
9	Recreational Equipment (REI)
10	S.C. Johnson

THE TIPPING POINT

In March 2006, Amanda Newkirk, a 7-month pregnant, 19-year-old waitress in Roanoke, VA, was left $1,000 to cover a $26·35 bill, with a note that said, 'Keep the change! Have a great day'. The $973·65 tip (a cool 3,695%) was left by a self-confessed shopaholic, Erin Dogan, who said of leaving the tip (rather than spending the money herself), 'it made me feel phenomenal ... it has changed my life'. ❦ How, when, who, and what to tip are subjects of considerable confusion – exacerbated by local custom, personal mores, and poor mental arithmetic. In certain countries (e.g. Japan) tipping is eschewed altogether. Where tipping is common, seemingly arbitrary conventions govern the jobs deemed worthy of gratuities. (It is no accident that most travel guides have a section on tipping.) ❦ Perhaps the most commonly tipped group of workers are waiters, for whom tips can range from a welcome bonus to their entire salary. The expected tip for US waiters is 15–20%; much of Europe and the rest of the world expects 10–15%. When *New York Times* restaurant critic Frank Bruni worked as a waiter, in 2006, he highlighted the vital importance of tips and exposed the 'verbal tippers', who 'offer extravagant praise in lieu of 20%'. ❦ A 2003 review of research on restaurant tipping by Michael Lynn of Cornell's Center for Hospitality Research offers some hard facts: credit card payers leave better tips than cash payers; large dining parties leave lower percentage tips than small parties; and, inevitably, alcohol, sunny weather, good food, and attractive servers increase tips. Lynn also notes that waiters can increase their tips by writing messages or drawing 'smiley' faces on the back of checks, and by squatting down next to the table when interacting with customers. ❦ The verb 'to tip', in its economic sense, derives from thieves' slang of the C17th–18th, when it described the act of passing, giving, or touching. Elisha Cole's 1676 *Dictionary* contains the entry, '*Tip the cole to Adam Tiler*: give the (stolen) money to your (running) Comrade'. Slightly later, 'tipping' described the passing of a private signal ('tip him the wink'), and the bestowing of a gratuity, either to servants and tradesmen, or to schoolchildren. [There is no evidence to suggest 'tip' derives from 'To Insure Promptness'] ❦ Now certain social scenes (golf clubs, weddings, hunting parties, and country houses) have their own tipping norms. Indeed, tipping aboard cruise ships is so complex that some lines publish lists of expected gratuities. ❦ Emily Post noted in 1922 that 'tipping is undoubtedly a bad system, but it happens to be in force ... one piece of advice: You will not get good service unless you tip generously'. English dandy Wilfred Gowers-Round declared – 'If it moves, tip it!'. And, Groucho Marx famously had the following exchange with a steward in *A Night at the Opera* (1935): 'Do they allow tipping on the boat?' 'Yes, sir.' 'Have you got two fives?' 'Oh, yes, sir.' 'Then you won't need the ten cents I was going to give you.'

Royal Caribbean International suggested tip/guest/day 2006	
Suite Attendant	$5·75
Stateroom Attendant	$3·50
Dining Room Waiter	$3·50
Assistant Waiter	$2·00
Headwaiter	$0·75

FEDERAL & STATE INCOME TAX RATES

Below are the basic rates of federal income tax and an indication of each State's income tax rates. For further information, seek expert advice.

2006 Federal Rate	Single Filers	Married Filing Jointly or Qualifying Widow(er)	Married Filing Separately	Head of Household	
10%	$0–$7,550	$0–$15,100	$0–$7,550	$0–$10,750	10%
15%	$7,550–$30,650	$15,100–$61,300	$7,550–$30,650	$10,750–$41,050	15%
25%	$30,650–$74,200	$61,300–$123,700	$30,650–$61,850	$41,050–$106,000	25%
28%	$74,200–$154,800	$123,700–$188,450	$61,850–$94,225	$106,000–$171,650	28%
33%	$154,800–$336,550	$188,450–$336,550	$94,225–$168,275	$171,650–$336,550	33%
35%	>$336,550	>$336,550	>$168,275	>$336,550	35%
	[Schedule X]	[Schedule Y-1]	[Schedule Y-2]	[Schedule Z]	

State	income tax rate (%)
Alabama	2.0–5.0
Alaska	none
Arizona	2.87–5.04
Arkansas	1.0–7.0
California	1.0–10.3
Colorado	4.63
Connecticut	3.0–5.0
Delaware	2.2–5.95
Florida	none
Georgia	1.0–6.0
Hawaii	1.4–8.25
Idaho	1.6–7.8
Illinois	3
Indiana	3.4
Iowa	0.36–8.98
Kansas	3.5–6.45
Kentucky	2.0–6.0
Louisiana	2.0–6.0
Maine	2.0–8.5
Maryland	2.0–4.75
Massachusetts	5.3 & 12
Michigan	3.9
Minnesota	5.35–7.85
Mississippi	3.0–5.0
Missouri	1.5–6.0
Montana	1.0–6.9
Nebraska	2.56–6.84
Nevada	none
New Hampshire	5 (intrst & dvend)
New Jersey	1.4–8.97
New Mexico	1.7–5.7
New York	4.0–7.7
North Carolina	6.0–8.25
North Dakota	2.1–5.54
Ohio	0.712–7.185
Oklahoma	0.5–6.65
Oregon	5.0–9.0
Pennsylvania	3.07
Rhode Island	3.75–9.9
South Carolina	2.5–7.0
South Dakota	none
Tennessee	6 (intrst & dvend)
Texas	none
Utah	2.3–7.0
Vermont	3.6–9.5
Virginia	2.0–5.75
Washington	none
West Virginia	3.0–6.5
Wisconsin	4.6–6.75
Wyoming	none
Washington, DC	5.0–9.0

———————————————— 'GOING POSTAL' ————————————————

At *c*.9.15pm on January 30, 2006, a female ex-postal worker shot dead 6 workers at a mail processing plant in Santa Barbara, CA, before turning the gun on herself.

This tragedy was the latest in a series of attacks by United States Postal Service workers on their colleagues – the most notorious of which occurred in 1986, when letter carrier Patrick Henry Sherrill shot dead 14 and wounded 6 postal employees in Edmond, OK, before killing himself. Over time, the phrase 'going postal' entered the language to describe both random shooting sprees (especially of coworkers) and, more generally, excessive and irrational anger. The 1995 film *Clueless* has been credited with popularizing the phrase, and the American Dialect

God, I totally choked. My father's going to go postal on me!
— CLUELESS (1995)

Society nominated 'going postal' as one of its words of 1995. Quite reasonably, the USPS objects to the term as unrepresentative of the dedication of its *c*.700,000 staff.

In August 2000, at the request of the Postmaster General, the National Center on Addiction and Substance Abuse at Columbia Univ. published a 250-page report on the safety of USPS workers. It concluded that postal employees are only a third as likely as those in the national workforce to be victims of homicide at work, and that '"Going postal" is a myth, a bad rap'. However, now that 'going postal' has entered the vernacular (and, in 2002, the *Oxford English Dictionary*), this statistically unjust stereotyping of postal workers looks set to continue.

———————————————— USPS SLANG GLOSSARY ————————————————

Like many organizations, the USPS has its own vocabulary of formal and slang terms. For example, envelopes that enter the automatic canceler back to front are called *Smiles* if the flap makes a 'V', or *Frowns* if the flap is inverted. Others include:

Balloon	an unusually large sack or pouch of mail
Elbow and eyeball	to check empty mail sacks for trapped items
Bulkie; Heavy	a regular envelope containing an irregular object (e.g. a pen)
Bum	bundle of empty mail sacks or pouches
Bump	additional help because of unusually heavy mail volume
Chunk	a small parcel
Drop day	scheduled day off for a USPS employee
Dump up	to empty sacks for sorting
Flagpole	overseas military post office
Hit	to postmark mail by hand
Hot mail	preferential mail
Log; Truck	a heavy parcel
Red	registered mail
Skin sack	a sack or pouch containing few items
Skip	an item of mail that accidentally escapes machine cancelation
Tap	to collect mail from a box

---------------- USPS BASIC RATES & FEES ----------------

First-Class Mail		Priority Mail		Media Mail (Book Rate)	
Ounces	$	*Pounds*	$	*Pounds*	$
≤1	0·39	≤1	4·05	≤1	1·59
≤2	0·63	≤2	4·20	≤2	2·07
≤3	0·87	≤3	5·00	≤3	2·55
≤4	1·11	≤4	5·60	≤4	3·03
≤5	1·35	≤5	6·15	≤5	3·51
≤6	1·59	(for Zones local–3)		≤6	3·99
≤7	1·83			≤7	4·47
≤8	2·07	Express Mail		≤8	4·81
≤9	2·31	*Pounds*	$	≤9	5·15
≤10	2·55	≤8 ounces	14·40	≤10	5·49
≤11	2·79	≤2	18·80		
≤12	3·03	≤3	22·20	Certificate of Mailing	
≤13	3·27	≤4	25·50	postage + $0·95	
>13	goes Priority	≤5	28·75		
Postcard	0·24	≤6	32·05	Certified Mail	
USPS card	0·26	≤7	35·25	postage + $2·40	

[Rates effective from January 8, 2006. These are necessarily simplified tables;
for more detail on pricing, services, and restrictions on size and weight, see usps.com]

---------------- ZIP CODES & MR ZIP ----------------

The Zone Improvement Plan (ZIP) Code was introduced on July 1, 1963, to cope with a business demand that had grown to 80% of all mail. A number of coding systems had been mooted in the past, and the ZIP Code grew out of a 'zoning address' system developed in 1943, and the later 'Metro System' of 552 sectional centers, each serving 40–150 post offices. The 5-digit ZIP Code was structured thus:

First digit....................broad geographical area in the USA (e.g. 0=Northeast)
2nd & 3rd digits...............sectional center accessible to the transport network
4th & 5th digits ....small post offices or postal zones in large cities

Initially, ZIP Codes were optional. In 1967 bulk senders of 2nd- and 3rd-class mail were obliged to use the Codes and over time the use of ZIP Codes became commonplace. In 1983, primarily to cater for business mass-mailing, the ZIP Code was expanded by an optional extra 4 digits. This 'ZIP+4' Code helps identify a specific geographical segment within the delivery zone, such as a city block, an office building, or an organization that receives an unusually large volume of mail.

In 1962, the cartoon character 'Mr ZIP' was unveiled to announce the new Codes and promote their use. Mr ZIP was originally created by adman Harold Wilcox (himself the son of a postman) for a New York bank. The Post Office Department acquired and modified the design (adding a mailbag), and Mr ZIP's promotion was abetted by Ethel '*I Got Rhythm*' Merman, who sang his television jingle.

———————————————— THE FISCAL YEAR ————————————————

The 'fiscal year' is a period used for the purposes of financial accounting. For the federal government, the fiscal year begins on October 1 and ends September 30. The four quarters of this federal year are subdivided in the following manner:

1st Quarter..............Oct 1–Dec 31		3rd Quarter .... Apr 1–Jun 30	
2nd Quarter............. Jan 1–Mar 31		4th Quarter .... Jul 1–Sep 30	

All but four of the States start their fiscal year on July 1. The exceptions are: New York (April 1); Texas (September 1); and Alabama & Michigan (October 1).

———————————————— TAX FREEDOM DAY ————————————————

America's annual 'Tax Freedom Day' is announced by The Tax Foundation, a 'non-partisan tax research organization based in Washington, DC'. It is the theoretical day when the average taxpayer has paid off their debt to the state and starts to earn for themselves. It is calculated by dividing the total tax collected by total income, and extrapolating the results into the calendar year. The Tax Foundation declared that Tax Freedom Day in 2006 fell on April 26: 3 days later than in 2005, and 10 days later than in 2003 and 2004. Below the date is charted since 1980.

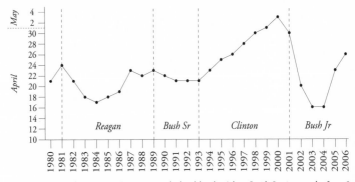

In 2006, Tax Freedom Day in Britain was calculated by the Adam Smith Institute to be June 3.

———————————————— BUY NOTHING DAY ————————————————

Buy Nothing Day (BND) is a global movement encouraging people not to purchase anything for (at least) a day a year. It began in 1992 as No Shop Day, the brainchild of former ad-exec Ted Dave, and was taken up by *Adbusters* magazine and advocates in 35 countries. In the US and Canada, BND falls on the 'Black' Friday after Thanksgiving (the start of Christmas shopping); elsewhere BND is the following Saturday. The movement is self-organizing, and motives for participation vary: for some it is a day of reflection, for others a chance to campaign against consumerism.

—INTEREST RATES · FEDERAL RESERVE PRIME RATE—

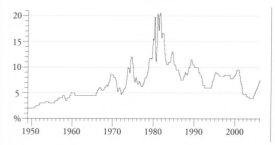

Recent rates	
Month	%
Dec '05	7·15
Jan '06	7·26
Feb '06	7·50
Mar '06	7·53
Apr '06	7·75
May '06	7·93
Jun '06	8·02
Jul '06	8·25

—NATIONAL HOUSING CHARACTERISTICS & PRICE—

Number of rooms	%	*Value ($)* [occupied]	%	*Year structure built*	%
1	0·4	<10,000	2·6	2000–2004	5·2
2	1·2	10–20k	1·9	1995–1999	7·3
3	9·1	20–30k	2·0	1990–1994	5·9
4	19·3	30–40k	2·3	1985–1989	7·3
5	23·2	40–50k	2·7	1980–1984	6·3
6	20·4	50–60k	3·4	1975–1979	10·2
7	12·1	60–70k	3·9	1970–1974	9·3
8	6·9	70–80k	5·0	1960–1969	12·8
9	3·2	80–100k	10·3	1950–1959	11·1
≥10	4·2	100–120k	8·0	1940–1949	6·7
Number of bedrooms	%	120–150k	11·8	1930–1939	5·3
0	1·0	150–200k	13·8	1920–1929	4·5
1	11·9	200–250k	8·8	1919 or earlier	8·0
2	28·8	250–300k	6·3	*Median year*	1971
3	40·4	>300,000	17·2		
≥4	17·8	*Median value* . $140,201		[American Housing Survey · '03]	

Below are the percentage changes in house prices, ranked by Census division, for the year ending March 31, 2006. [Source: Office of Federal Housing Enterprise Oversight]

	Census division (% change)	*1 year*	*quarter*	*5 year*	*since 1980*
1	Pacific	18·02	2·98	95·57	474·89
2	Mountain	17·80	2·29	54·77	262·23
3	South Atlantic	17·23	2·86	69·32	308·03
4	Middle Atlantic	13·33	2·19	71·42	419·27
5	New England	8·67	1·16	66·28	527·92
6	East South Central	7·74	1·36	26·04	172·44
7	West South Central	7·69	1·77	26·17	113·25
8	West North Central	6·21	0·65	36·34	197·4
9	East North Central	5·56	0·74	28·58	216·36
–	United States	12·54	2·03	57·28	293·78

―――――――――FORBES MAGAZINE RICH LIST · 2006―――――――――

No.	billionaire	age	$ billion	activity	2005 rank
1	William Gates III†	50	50·0	Microsoft	1
2	Warren Buffett	75	42·0	investing	2
3	Carlos Slim Helu	66	30·0	telecoms	4
4	Ingvar Kamprad	79	28·0	Ikea	6
5	Lakshmi Mittal	55	23·5	Mittal Steel	3
6	Paul Allen	53	22·0	Microsoft	7
7	Bernard Arnault	57	21·5	LVMH	16
8	Prince Alwaleed	49	20·0	investing	5
9	Kenneth Thomson & family	82	19·6	publishing	14
10	Li Ka-Shing	77	18·8	investing	21

† Gates's fortune is roughly 5 times the GDP of Iceland; in January 2006, he said at a Microsoft conference, 'My tax return in the US has to be kept on a special computer because their normal computers can't deal with the numbers. ... So I am constantly getting these notices telling me I haven't paid something when really it is just on the wrong computer. ... Then they will send me another notice telling me how bad they feel that they sent me a notice that was a mistake'.

―――――――――――――― MINIMUM WAGE ――――――――――――――

The federal minimum wage was introduced in 1938 at the rate of $0·25 per hour. The current hourly rate (set 9·1·1997) is $5·15 for all covered, nonexempt workers. In addition, overtime pay at a rate of not less than one and one half times the regular rate of pay is required after 40 hours of work in a workweek. The minimum wage generally applies to employees of enterprises with annual turnovers >$500,000, as well as smaller firms engaged in interstate business. All federal, state, and local government employees are covered, as are domestic workers. That said, a complex range of exceptions apply, for example, to workers with disabilities, full-time students, those under 20 early in their employment, tipped employees [see p.312], &c. In addition, a number of states have their own minimum wages and regulations. Where state and federal wages differ, employees are entitled to the provisions of each law that provide them the greater benefits [data at 4·6·2006]:

AL.......no law	HI....... $7·25	MA...... $6·75	NM...... $5·15	SD....... $5·15
AK...... $7·15	ID....... $5·15	MI....... $5·15	NY ...... $7·15	TN ......no law
AZ.......no law	IL .... $6·50	MN...... $5·25	NC..federal rate	TX ..federal rate
AR...... $5·15	IN .... $5·15	MS ......no law	ND...... $5·15	UT ..federal rate
CA ...... $6·75	IA ...federal rate	MO..federal rate	OH...... $5·15	VT ...... $7·25
CO ..... $5·15	KS....... $6·25	MT..federal rate	OK..federal rate	VA...federal rate
CT ...... $7·65	KY...federal rate	NE ...... $5·15	OR ...... $7·50	WA...... $7·63
DE ...... $6·15	LA.......no law	NV..federal rate	PA...federal rate	WV...... $5·15
FL....... $6·40	ME...... $6·50	NH...... $5·15	RI .... $7·10	WI....... $5·70
GA ...... $5·15	MD...... $6·15	NJ...federal rate	SC.......no law	WY...... $5·15

This is an elementary guide. Further data are available from the Dept of Labor and individual states.

———————————— FOOD STAMP PROGRAM ————————————

The war against hunger is truly mankind's war of liberation.
— John F. Kennedy, World Food Congress, 1963

The Food Stamp Program (FSP) traces its origins to 1939, when those on relief could purchase $1 orange food stamps, each of which entitled them to a 50-cent blue stamp. Orange stamps could be spent on any foodstuff; blue stamps could only be redeemed for food deemed to be 'surplus'. Over 20 million participated in the scheme before it ended in 1943 due to decline in mass unemployment and in food surpluses. In 1961, President John F. Kennedy used his first Executive Order to call for a pilot FSP; and in 1964, President Johnson called for Congress to make the FSP permanent. In 1974, Congress required all states to offer food stamps to low-income households; since then, administrations in succession have sought to amend the FSP to streamline administration, cut costs, target recipients, and eliminate fraud. Currently, the FSP provides low-income households with coupons and (increasingly) electronic benefits that can be exchanged in grocery stores like cash. The FSP is governed federally via the Dept of Agriculture and is administered locally by state agencies. The uptake and cost of the FSP have been:

Year	recipients	cost $			
2005	25·7m	31·1bn	1985	19·9m	11·7bn
2000	17·2m	17·1bn	1980	21·1m	9·2bn
1995	26·2m	24·6bn	1975	17·1m	4·6bn
1990	20·1m	15·5bn	1970	4·3m	577m

[Source: Food & Nutrition Service, FNS]

To be eligible, households must meet (and prove) certain criteria, for example: having <$2,000 in countable resources, such as bank accounts (excluding home and lot), and having a gross monthly income ≤130% of the federal poverty guidelines (*c.* $1,700 for a family of 3). Stamps can be used to buy breads and cereals, fruits and vegetables, meats, fish, poultry, and dairy products. Additionally, seeds and plants which produce food can also be purchased. Beer, wine, liquor, tobacco, nonfood items (like pet food, toiletries, or household supplies), vitamins, medicines, and hot food cannot be purchased. The current maximum stamp allotment levels are:

Household size	max monthly benefit				
1	$152	3	$399	7	$798
2	$278	4	$506	8	$912
		5	$601	Thereafter +1	+$114
		6	$722		

[Source: FNS]

The latest (2004) FNS figures indicate the character of Food Stamp households:

Of all food stamp recipients, 50% were children; 8% were ≥60; 28% were working-age women; and 13% working-age men. 29% of households receiving food stamps have earned income, 71% had no earnings at all. The typical food stamp household had a gross income of $643 per month and possessed only $143 in countable resources. In 2003, 41% of recipients were white; 36% African American; 18% Hispanic; 3% Asian; and 2% Native American; and 1% unknown.

——— MEAN EARNINGS BY HIGHEST QUALIFICATION———

Below are the average annual earnings of workers >18 with different levels of education – broken down by sex, race, ethnicity, and age. As one might expect, as educational attainment rises, so too does income. For example, the average income of Americans with professional qualifications is almost 6 times that of those who never graduated from high school. And, even within educational bands, significant inequalities persist between all groups. Interestingly, the greatest disparity between male and female earnings occurs between those with a professional qualification.

2003	Not high school graduate	High school graduate only	Some college, no degree	Associate's degree	Bachelor's degree	Master's degree	Doctorate	Professional qualification
All	$18,734	$27,915	$29,533	$35,958	$51,206	$62,514	$88,471	$115,212
proportion								
Male	21,447	33,266	36,419	43,462	63,084	76,896	95,894	136,128
Female	14,214	21,659	22,615	29,537	38,447	48,205	73,516	72,445
difference	+33.7%	+34.9%	+37.9%	+32.0%	+39.1%	+37.3%	+23.3%	+46.8%
White	19,110	28,708	30,316	36,881	52,259	62,981	89,640	119,712
Black	16,201	23,777	25,616	31,415	42,968	57,449	81,457	87,713
difference	+15.2%	+17.2%	+15.5%	+14.8%	+17.8%	+8.8%	+9.1%	+26.7%
Hispanic	18,349	23,472	27,586	31,032	43,676	56,486	N/A	78,190
25–34	18,920	26,073	28,954	32,276	43,794	51,040	62,109	74,120
35–44	22,123	31,479	36,038	38,442	57,438	66,264	101,382	126,165
45–54	23,185	32,978	40,291	41,511	59,208	68,344	92,229	132,180
55–64	23,602	31,742	38,131	39,147	57,423	66,760	98,433	138,845
≥65	17,123	20,618	28,017	23,080	41,323	42,194	56,724	77,312

[Source: US Statistical Abstract · 2006]

——————— PRESIDENTIAL TAX RETURNS———————

On April 14, 2006, the White House released details of the First and Second Couple's 2005 tax returns. President and Mrs George W. Bush reported taxable income of $618,694 for the tax year 2005, which resulted in a total federal income tax bill of $187,768. The Bushes contributed $75,560 (*c.*17½% of their posttax income) to churches and charities. The Cheneys owed federal taxes for 2005 of $529,636 on taxable income of $1,961,157. The Cheneys adjusted gross income in 2005 was $8,819,006 – largely as a result of the exercise by an independent gift administrator of stock options that had been irrevocably set aside in 2001 for charity. Jointly, the Cheneys donated $6,869,655 to charitable causes in 2005.

US COINAGE

	Cent	Nickel	Dime	Quarter	Half Dollar	Dollar*	Golden Dollar*
2005 Production	7,700,050,500	1,741,200,000	2,835,500,000	3,013,600,000	7,300,000		5,040,000
Composition	copper-plated Zn	cupro-nickel	cupro-nickel	cupro-nickel	cupro-nickel	cupro-nickel	manganese-brass
Weight	2.500g	5.000g	2.268g	5.670g	11.340g	8.1g	8.1g
Diameter	19.05mm	21.21mm	17.91mm	24-26mm	30-61mm	26.50mm	26-50mm
Thickness	1.55mm	1.95mm	1.35mm	1.75mm	2.15mm	2.00mm	2.00mm
Edge	plain	plain	reeded	reeded	reeded	reeded	plain
No. of Reeds†	none	none	118	119	150	133	none
Obverse	Lincoln	Jefferson	Roosevelt	Washington	Kennedy	Susan B. Anthony	Sacagawea & son
Designed by	V.D. Brenner	Felix Schlag	John R. Sinnock	John Flannagan	Gilroy Roberts	Frank Gasparro	Glenna Goodacre
Issue	1909	1938	1946	1932	1964	1979,1980,1999	2000
Reverse	Lincoln Memorial	Monticello	Torch, oak, &c.	Eagle	Presidential Arms	Apollo 11 Insignia	Eagle in Flight
Designed by	Frank Gasparro	Felix Schlag	John R. Sinnock	John Flannagan	Frank Gasparro	Frank Gasparro	Thomas D. Rogers
Date of Issue	1959	1938	1946	1932‡	1964‡	1979,1980,1999	2000

[Source: US Mint] The above specifications are for US Mint legal tender coins currently in circulation.

* In fulfillment of the 1997 $1 Coin Act (Public Law 104–124 §4), the Golden Dollar replaced the Susan B. Anthony Dollar, first issued in 1979. Golden Dollars were released into circulation on January 27, 2000. Sacagawea (also spelled Sacajawea) was a young Shoshone interpreter who translated, guided, and navigated for the Lewis and Clark expedition to the Pacific Ocean from 1804–06. The 'Golden Dollar' is actually 88.5% Cu; 6.0% Zn; 3.5% Mn; 2.0% Ni.

† Traditionally, when coins were minted from precious metals (silver, gold, &c.), they were milled with 'reeding', or grooves, in order to foil counterfeiters and protect their edges (reeded edges show when coins have been clipped or filed for their precious metals). Although no gold coins have circulated in the US since 1934, and by the 1980s silver had also been abandoned, reeded edges remain to help the visually impaired distinguish similar size coins by touch.

‡ 1975–6 Bicentennial reverses were minted. These coins are dated 1776–1976; none was individually dated 1975 or 1976. ❧ The Mint classifies coins unfit for circulation as *uncurrent* (worn yet recognizable as to genuineness and denomination, and machine countable); and *mutilated* (chipped, fused, and not machine countable). Uncurrent coins may be redeemed at Federal Reserve Banks; mutilated coins are redeemable only through the Philadelphia Mint facility. All redeemed coins unfit for circulation are melted down and recycled in the manufacture of new coins. ❧ The US Mint has no plans to discontinue the one-cent coin (penny) from circulation at present.

—————————————————————————— THE EURO ——————————————————————————

The euro has been in circulation since January 1, 2002, when 7·8bn notes and 40·4bn coins were issued by the central banks of the twelve participating countries. (On February 28, 2002, the old national currencies were effectively withdrawn.)

€ *is the official currency*	€ *used by special arrangement*
Belgium, Germany, Greece,	Monaco, Vatican City,
Spain, France, Ireland, Italy,	San Marino
Luxembourg, the Netherlands,	
Austria, Portugal, Finland	*overseas territories of* € *states*
	Guadeloupe, French Guiana,
€ *is the de facto currency*	Martinique, Mayotte, Réunion,
without formal agreement	Saint Pierre and Miquelon, French
Andorra, Kosovo, Montenegro	Southern & Antarctic Territories

Officially, *euro* and *cent* are written lowercase and, in English, the spelling does not change when plural (e.g. 100 euro; 100 cent). Oddly, the plurals *euros* and *cents* are permitted with languages like French and Spanish. [See p.323 for the euro symbol.] Euro coins share common faces – three designs that supposedly 'symbolize the unity of the EU' – the reverse faces are country-specific and designed by each country. Euro notes have common designs that depict one of seven architectural periods.

Coin	common face design
€2, €1	EU map before enlargement of 2004
50¢, 20¢, 10¢	individual EU countries before enlargement of 2004
5¢, 2¢, 1¢	Europe in relation to Africa and Asia

Note	color	size (mm)	architecture				
€5	gray	120x62	Classical	€50	orange	140x77	Renaissance
€10	red	127x67	Romanesque	€100	green	147x82	Baroque/Rococo
€20	blue	133x72	Gothic	€200	yellow	153x82	C19th iron/glass
				€500	purple	160x82	C20th modern

Britain's relationship with the euro is ambivalent. The Labour government's policy has been to join the euro if the *economic* conditions are right, based on 5 'economic tests'. The Conservative Party, traditionally 'Euro-skeptic' on *constitutional* grounds, is divided, and opinion polls indicate that British voters are skeptical both of Europe and the euro. All major parties have pledged to hold a referendum before any entry into the 'euro-zone'. Below, the Dollar is charted against the euro and the Pound.

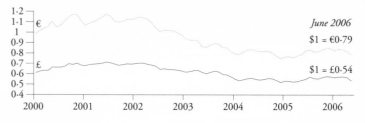

—————————— CURRENCY SYMBOLS ——————————

**$** The origin of the dollar sign is controversial and a host of explanations have been given – some more likely than others. For example: that it derives from the superimposition of the 'U' and 'S' of 'United States'. One curious and highly unlikely theory is that the sign is linked to the slave trade, and the Spanish words for a slave (*esclavo*) and the nail (*clavo*) that locked the shackles. It is suggested that an 'S' with a nail ('S' and *clavo*) was written '$'. Perhaps the most plausible suggestion is that the sign was created when the letters 'P' and 'S' from the Spanish *Pesos* were conflated if written at speed. Oddly, neither US notes nor coins feature the $ sign.

£ The Pound sign derives from the capital 'L' written in cursive script, with one or two horizontal bars bisecting it to indicate it is an abbreviation. ('L' stood for *libre*, the Latin for a pound in weight; a pound of silver was the standard on which the monetary unit was based.) The £ sign is also used for pounds in Syria, Egypt, Lebanon, Turkey, &c.

€ The design of the euro sign was required to be 'a highly recognizable symbol of Europe; easy to write by hand; and to have an aesthetically pleasing design'. [Two out of three is not bad.] The EC claims that the symbol was 'inspired by the Greek letter epsilon, harking back to Classical times and the cradle of European civilization'. The two parallel lines apparently 'indicate the stability of the euro'. At best, this is fanciful twaddle. The EC claims that the euro symbol was the product of 'teamwork', but most agree that it is really the unsung work of Arthur Eisenmenger – graphic designer for the EEC. Eisenmenger designed the European Union flag and the 'CE' logo, and recalls that sometime in 1974 he simply fused the letters 'C' and 'E' using Indian ink on an 8"-wide cardboard sheet 'without giving it much thought'. For type designers, the euro has proved problematic. Not only is it hard to 'retro-fit' a new symbol into many existing fonts, but the strict design set by the EC has effectively to be ignored to make the logo work as a character.

¥ The design of the Yen (the Japanese unit of currency since 1871) is much less problematic, being, like the Pound, a letter slashed with lines to show it is an abbreviation. In the 1990s, London city traders knew it by the rhyming slang 'Bill & Ben'.

¤ This is a generic currency symbol, used with a three-letter currency code, or to indicate that a symbol is missing from a font.

———————————

SPECIAL DRAWING
RIGHTS (SDR)

In 1969, the IMF created the SDR as an 'international reserve asset' in response to fears about an overreliance on gold and the Dollar. The SDR is not actually a currency but a means of accounting by IMF members who agree to accept SDRs in settlement of accounts. SDRs are allocated to countries in proportion to their IMF quotas, and members can trade between themselves. The SDR value was 0·888671g of fine gold, or US$1. But it is now based upon a basket of major currencies. At present 1 SDR=*c*.$1·473.

—US DOLLARS ABROAD—

The US dollar is adopted as a currency of first resort in times of war, crisis, or uncertainty around the world. The dollar has near universal recognition, and is considered a safe and reliable alternative when domestic currencies falter or fail. In 2003, the US Treasury estimated that *c.*60% (*c.*$370bn) of all Federal Reserve notes in circulation were held abroad, in these areas:

Former Soviet Union, &c.........	40%
Latin America....................	25%
Africa & Middle East.............	20%
Asia...............................	15%

Surveys by the Treasury indicate that, in addition to the recently dollarized Ecuador and El Salvador, a number of countries are heavily reliant on the dollar. Russia is thought to hold *c.*10% of its GDP in dollars; Argentina, *c.*17·5%; and Cambodia, *c.*25·2%. The circulation of dollars in Cuba, Africa, Afghanistan, and Iraq is unknown but estimated to be significant. While failed states, war zones, and hyper-inflationary economies are obvious locations for informal dollar use, even stable and developed economies see dollars used in 'gray' and 'black' markets, in cross-border deals, and in the funding of crime and the drug trade. Curiously, the Treasury notes that areas which experience significant dollarization in times of crisis (e.g. Taiwan in 1996) tend to retain their dollars even after the crisis has passed. The introduction of the euro [see p.322] is likely to impact use of the dollar in Eastern Europe, the former Soviet Union, and even the Middle East. However, global confidence and familiarity mean that the 'Greenback' is likely to remain the most trusted currency in times of trouble.

——MONEY SLANG——

American slang has a myriad of terms for money – both specific notes and coins, and also for cash in general:

Note/coin/sum	nickname
1 cent.............................	Red
50 cents	Half
$1.................................	Scrip
$2.............................	2-case note
$5......................	Abe's Cabe; Fin
$10	Sawbuck
$20	Jack(son); Yuppie Single
$50	Pinky; Nifty
$100 . C(entury) Note; Yard; Benjamin	
$500...........................	Madison
$1,000...................	Grand; Large
$1bn..........	Yard [on Foreign Exchanges]

bank (roll) · bean · bone · bones
bread · buck · bullet · cabbage · cake
case note · cheddar · cheese · clam
coconut · cush(ion) · dead presidents
do re mi · dough · duckets · filthy
lucre · fish · folding · frogskin · gee
geetus · geedus · gelt · goo-gobs · jack
kale · lettuce · lizard · lucre · marbles
mazuma · moolah · peso · pisatre
plaster potatoes · presidents · reek
rhino · rock · scratch · scrip · shekel
simoleon · simon · skin · skoon
spinach · spondulix · sugar · tlac
wampum · wonga · yellowback

To aid in translating books and films, below is some British money slang:

£1................	Quid; Nugget; Dollar
£5...........	Jack; Blue; (Lady) Godiva
£10	Tenner; Pavarotti; Cock
£20	Score
£25	Pony
£50	Bull's-eye
£100....................	Ton; Century
£500...........................	Monkey
£1,000..........	Grand; Rio (Grande)
£2,000...........................	Archer

—— HISTORICAL ECONOMIC INDICATORS OF NOTE ——

Indicator · Year		1997	1998	1999	2000	2001	2002	2003	2004	2005
President		Clinton	Clinton	Clinton	Clinton	W. Bush	W. Bush	W. Bush	W. Bush	W. Bush
Gross Domestic Product (GDP)	current $bn	8,304·3	8,747·0	9,268·4	9,817·0	10,128·0	10,469·6	10,971·2	11,734·3	12,485·7
Gross Domestic Product (GDP)	% change	6·2	5·3	6·0	5·9	3·2	3·4	4·8	7·0	6·4
Change in consumer prices (all urban consumers)	%	1·7	1·6	2·7	3·4	1·6	2·4	1·9	3·3	3·4
Unemployment rate (civilian labor force)	%	4·9	4·5	4·2	4·0	4·7	5·8	6·0	5·5	5·1
Average weekly hours worked (non-agricultural)	hours	34·5	34·5	34·3	34·3	34·0	33·9	33·7	33·7	33·8
Average gross weekly earnings (non-agricultural)	current $	431·25	448·04	462·49	480·41	493·20	506·07	517·30	528·36	543·65
Industrial output as a percentage of total capacity	%	83·9	82·7	81·9	81·8	76·3	75·1	75·7	78·6	80·0
Disposable income, per capita	current $	21,940	23,161	23,968	25,472	26,235	27,164	28,062	29,477	30,469
Personal expenditure, per capita	current $	20,323	21,291	22,491	23,862	24,722	25,501	26,484	27,964	29,479
Change in real, per capita, personal disp. income	%	2·3	4·6	1·8	3·7	0·9	2·1	1·4	2·4	0·4
Savings as % of disposable income	%	3·6	4·3	2·4	2·3	1·8	2·4	2·1	1·8	-0·5
Consumer credit – total outstanding	$bn	1,323·1	1,420·2	1,533·4	1,710·4	1,842·3	1,925·3	2,006·6	2,091·0	2,147·0
Prime rate charged by banks	%	8·44	8·35	8·00	9·23	6·91	4·67	4·12	4·34	6·19
NYSE Composite index (Dec 2002=5,000)		4,827	5,818	6,546	6,805	6,397	5,578	5,447	6,612	7,349
Dow Jones Industrial Average		7,441	8,625	10,464	10,734	10,189	9,226	8,993	10,317	10,547
NASDAQ Composite (Feb 1971=100)		1,469	1,749	2,782	3,783	2,035	1,539	1,647	1,986	2,099
Net farm income	$bn	51·3	47·1	47·7	48·9	51·5	36·6	59·5	82·5	72·6
Total corporate profits after tax	$bn	552·1	470·0	517·2	508·2	503·8	575·8	705·1	788·2	1,060·2
Federal finance surplus/deficit		-21·9	69·3	125·6	236·2	128·2	-157·8	-377·6	-412·7	-318·3
US Trade - balance on current account	$m	-140,906	-214,064	-300,060	-415,999	-389,456	-475,211	-519,679	-668,074	-804,945
US Dollar/GB Pound ($/£)		1·64	1·66	1·62	1·52	1·44	1·50	1·63	1·83	1·82
US Dollar/euro ($/€) [pre-1999 estimated]		(1·13)	(1·12)	1·06	0·92	0·89	0·94	1·13	1·24	1·24
euro/GB Pound (€/£) [pre-1999 estimated]		(1·45)	(1·49)	1·52	1·64	1·61	1·59	1·45	1·47	1·46
Gold price per Troy ounce	$	331	294	279	279	271	310	364	409	443

[Sources: Economic Indicators, Government Printing Office; US Annual Statistical Abstract; Bank of England]

Form & Faith

I think she must have been very strictly brought up,
she's so desperately anxious to do the wrong thing correctly.
— SAKI (HECTOR HUGH MUNRO), *Reginald on Worries*, 1904

—————————— AMERICANS & CLASS ——————————

Traditionally perceived to be living in a 'classless' society, US citizens are certainly aware of their place in the social pecking order. Since 1972, the General Social Survey has asked respondents to identify their social class, and although 'no class' is one of the five options, only 1 person out of the 44,673 interviewed between 1972–2004 chose it. Charted below are the trends in US self-perception of class:

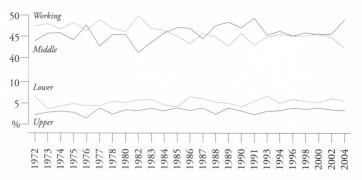

Since the 1970s, the lower- and upper-class bands have remained relatively contained. Interestingly, self-perception as working or middle class appears to be inversely correlated (at least casually), and from the early 1980s, those identifying themselves as middle class began to overtake those in the working class. The 2004 breakdown was: lower 5·5%; working 42·2%; middle 49%; upper 3·3%.

—————————— THE SOCIAL REGISTER ——————————

Founded in 1886, the Social Register claims to be 'among America's oldest and most distinguished private associations', and 'the only reliable and the most trusted, arbiter of Society in America'. Twice a year (summer and winter) the Register publishes a list of the Association's membership (*c.*25,000), with contact information, club and college affiliations, births, debuts, engagements, marriages, and deaths. (The summer edition handily lists yachts and their owners.) Those desirous of inclusion in the Register 'are required to furnish letters of recommendation from several families already listed'. The 2006 edition includes Brooke Astor, the Clintons, and Bush *père et fils* – but not Donald Trump, Martha Stewart, or Rudy Giuliani.

FORMS OF ADDRESS

Personage	envelope	letter opening	verbal address
President	The President, The White House	Dear Mr President	Mr President
Vice President	The Vice President, Old Executive Office Building	Dear Mr Vice President	Mr Vice President
Former US President	The Honorable {A} {B}	Dear Mr {B}	Mr {B}; President {A} {B}
Attorney General	The Honorable {A} {B}	Dear Mr Attorney General	Mr Attorney General
Cabinet Members	The Honorable {A} {B}, Secretary of {department}	Dear Mr Secretary	Mr Secretary
Postmaster General	The Honorable {A} {B}, Postmaster General	Dear Mr Postmaster General	Mr Postmaster G.
President of the Senate	The Honorable {A} {B}, President of the Senate	Dear Mr President	Mr President
Speaker of the House of Rep.	The Honorable {A} {B}, Speaker of the House of Rep.	Dear Mr Speaker	Mr Speaker; Speaker
US Senator	The Honorable {A} {B}, US Senate	Dear Senator {B}	Senator {B}
Congressman/woman	The Honorable {A} {B}, House of Representatives	Dear Mr/Madam {B}	Congressman/woman ({A} {B})
Secretary General of the UN	His Excellency {A} {B}, Secretary General of the UN	Dear Mr Secretary General	Mr Sec. Gen./Excellency
Ambassador of the US	The Honorable {A} {B}, American Ambassador	Dear Mr Ambassador	Mr Ambassador
Foreign Ambassador	His Excellency {A} {B}, Ambassador of {X}	Dear Mr Ambassador	Mr Ambassador
Chief Justice of the Supreme Ct	The Chief Justice, The Supreme Court of the US	Dear (Mr) Chief Justice	Mr Chief Justice ({B})
Assoc. Justice of the Supreme Ct	Mr Justice {B}, The Supreme Court of the US	Dear (Mr) Justice	Mr Justice ({B})
State Governor	The Honorable {A} {B}, The Governor of {X}	Dear Governor {B}	Governor {B}
Lieutenant Governor	The Honorable {A} {B}, Lieutenant Gov. of {X}	Dear Mr {B}	Mr {B}
Mayor	The Honorable {A} {B}, Mayor of {X}	Dear Mayor {B}	Mr Mayor
King/Queen	His/Her Majesty {name}, King/Queen of {X}	Your Majesty	Your Majesty
President of a Republic	His Excellency {A} {B}, President of the Rep. of {X}	Dear Mr President	Mr President
Prime Minister	His Excellency {A} {B}, The Prime Minister of {X}	Dear (Mr) Prime Minister	(Mr) Prime Minister
US Armed Forces	{Rank} {A} {B} {USA, USN, USAF, USMC, USCG}	Dear {Rank} {B}	{Rank} {B}

{A} = first name {B} = last name ❧ Throughout, where appropriate, 'Madam' should be substituted for 'Mr'. ❧ For reasons of space, some titles have been abbreviated; they should not be so truncated in practice. ❧ Considerable debate and dispute surround 'correct' forms of address. The above tabulation has been compiled from a number of, often contradictory, sources. Readers in need of detailed advice, for example on styling of US military ranks, are advised to consult the relevant organization. (The British Peerage is so complex that its customs are the subject of a series of specialist texts that detail, for example, the correct way to address the wives of younger sons of Earls.)

ON VISITING CARDS

The celebrated royal and society printer *Smythson of Bond Street* (London & NY) offers visiting cards in the following traditional sizes, each for a different clientele:

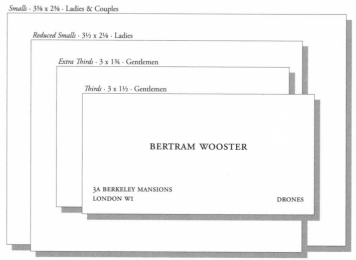

Smalls · 3⅜ x 2⅜ · Ladies & Couples

Reduced Smalls · 3½ x 2⅛ · Ladies

Extra Thirds · 3 x 1¾ · Gentlemen

Thirds · 3 x 1½ · Gentlemen

BERTRAM WOOSTER

3A BERKELEY MANSIONS
LONDON WI

DRONES

[For reasons of space, the above cards are shown at 85% of their actual size · Dimensions in inches]

Since the cards carried by ladies were significantly larger than those carried by gentlemen, in C19th Britain, ladies of dubious repute would have their visiting cards made up in male *Thirds* or *Extra Thirds*. This meant that if one of their married 'friends' chanced to take out his wallet in front of his wife, all of his cards would resemble those of gentlemen – thus averting wifely suspicion and unwanted interrogation. ❧ Much flummery surrounded the text on traditional visiting cards: initials were avoided, as were qualifications; the text was usually elegantly plain black on white unglazed card; and though women and couples would have their address in the lower right-hand corner, many gentlemen (especially bachelors) would just give their club(s). ❧ Some of the complex traditions of folding visiting cards are shown overleaf.

Nowadays, visiting cards have been superseded by business cards cluttered with logos and details of every conceivable form of communication. Different cultures have different attitudes towards cards. Of note are the Japanese, for whom cards are part of a complex etiquette. In Japan, they are exchanged by all participants at the start of a business meeting. You should stand, face your counterpart and bow slightly, while offering your card with the right hand, or both. (If you have your details printed in Japanese on the reverse of your card, offer this side facing upward.) The same procedure should be applied when receiving business cards. It is considered polite to study carefully any cards you receive and to keep them in front of you during meetings. Never fold cards, write on them, or slip them into your back pocket.

————— ON THE FOLDING OF VISITING CARDS —————

In the C19th, an elaborate taxonomy developed regarding how visiting (or calling) cards should be left, folded, and inscribed, when those of 'quality' paid social calls:

Nature of call	style of fold
Visit	*right-hand upper corner folded down*
Felicitation	*left-hand upper corner folded down*
Condolence	*left-hand lower corner folded down*
PPC, PDA†	*right-hand lower corner folded down*
Made on all members of a family	*the lady's card folded in the middle*
Delivered in person	*right-hand side folded down*

† When persons were going abroad or were to be absent for a long period, if they had not the time or inclination to take leave of their friends by making formal calls, they would send cards folded in this manner, or inscribed 'PPC' which stood for *pour prendre congé* (although many assumed the initials to stand for 'presents parting compliments') or 'PDA' which stood for *pour dire adieu*. Other card inscriptions included: 'PC' – *pour condoler*; 'PF' – *pour féliciter*; 'PR' – *pour remercier*; and 'PP' – *pour présenter*. In each case, these inscriptions would be made in ink, in uppercase letters, in the lower left-hand corner. If a card was enclosed within an envelope, it usually indicated that communication between the two parties was at an end. The three exceptions to this rule were: [a] when they were sent to a newly married couple; [b] when they were in reply to a wedding invitation and sent by someone absent from their usual home; [c] when they were PPC or PDA cards. In 1857, the Duke of Parma started the custom of leaving Cartes de Visite with his portrait for the albums of friends. Visiting cards were sometimes nicknamed Paste Boards. So, to 'shoot a PB' was to leave one's card.

————————————————— THE CUT —————————————————

To 'cut' is to affect not to know someone when passing or meeting them. An Edwardian dandy (or 'knut') would have recognized four different forms of cut:

THE CUT DIRECT
To look an acquaintance straight in the face and pretend not to know him.

THE CUT SUBLIME
To admire some object or distant scene until the acquaintance has passed.

THE CUT INDIRECT
To glance another way and pretend not to see an acquaintance.

THE CUT INFERNAL
To stop and attend to your shoes until the acquaintance has walked by.

————— THE PROGRESSION OF FRIENDSHIP —————

2 Glances make 1 Bow ☞ 2 Bows make 1 How d'ye do ☞
6 How d'ye do's make 1 Conversation ☞ 4 Conversations make 1 Acquaintance

DRESS CODES OF NOTE

BLACK TIE (or Tuxedo; Smoking Jacket; Dinner Jacket; DJ; *Cravate Noire*) consists of a single- or double-breasted black (or midnight blue) dinner jacket worn with matching trousers with a single row of braid down the leg, a soft white dress shirt, and a black bow tie. (Wing collars, cummerbunds, white jackets, and showy bow ties are to be avoided.) WHITE TIE consists of a black tailcoat worn with matching trousers with a double row of braid down the leg, a white stiff-fronted wing collar shirt, a white vest, and a white bow tie. MORNING DRESS consists of a morning coat, waistcoat, striped gray trousers, and (often) a top hat. Below are some of the more unusual dress codes to be found on formal invitations:

Bush shirt .... long- or short-sleeved (embroidered) shirt worn outside trousers
Evening dress.. white tie
Informal...................... business suit or jacket with or without tie (not jeans)
Island casual......................Hawaiian shirt and casual (usually khaki) trousers
Lounge suit...business suit and tie
National dress.......... self-explanatory; if one has no national dress, a lounge suit
Planters........................long-sleeved white shirt with a tie and dark trousers
Red Sea Rig; Gulf Rig .... black tie (or lounge suit) without the jacket
Tenue de Ville.............................. business suit (sometimes national dress)
Tenue Decontractée; Tenue de Détente .... smart-casual
Tenue de Gala ....black tie
Tenue de Sport/Voyage .... sporting/traveling attire
Tenue de Cérémonie .... white tie
Windsor Uniform........ dark blue evening tails with scarlet at the collar and cuffs

A degree of debate and dispute exists between different sources, and different rules apply in military, academic, and ecclesiastical settings. The above listing follows the tradition of most formal invitations in giving only the requirements for male attire, on the understanding that women have an intuitive understanding of such matters. ❦ In recent years, a plethora of unusual (and usually unhelpful) dress codes have snuck onto invitations, including: 'Casual Elegance'; 'Downtown Dashing'; 'Fisherman Chic'; 'Sparklingly Flawless'; 'Casual Sheik' (for a Casablanca theme); 'Urban Chic' (never, one assumes, suburban chic); 'Jungle Fresh' (presumably camouflage); and 'Desert Decadence' (pith helmets?). Most of these neologistic dress codes are to be avoided, especially the (oxy)moronic 'Creative Black Tie'. Surely the iconic exception was Truman Capote's 1966 'Black & White Ball'.

ON INTRODUCTIONS

With the exception of reigning Sovereigns (including the Pope), Presidents, and Cardinals, introductions made between strangers should abide by these three rules:

Youth is introduced to age – 'Strom Thurmond, may I present Doogie Howser?'

Men are introduced to women – 'Dame Edna, this is Count Victor Grezhinski.'

Lower ranks are introduced to higher – 'Colonel Sanders, this is Sergeant Bilko.'

MISCELLANEOUS ETIQUETTE

CORRESPONDENCE should always be dated. ❧ If a letter is typed or word-processed, it may be more informal to 'top and tail' the letter by writing the *Dear* —— and *Yours sincerely* by hand. ❧ Personal letters should ideally be handwritten; letters of condolence should always be handwritten. Letters should be written and signed in ink. ❧ EMAIL is a curiously detached form of communication best suited to business transactions. It should be avoided in all formal social situations, and rejected out of hand for the communication of any serious emotion – especially congratulations or condolences. ❧ TEXT MESSAGING and INSTANT MESSAGING are suitable only for the transmission of logistical data – and, of course, for flirtation. ❧ The formality of SIGNING OFF LETTERS has relaxed over the years. The traditional sign-off would have followed the form:

I beg (or *have the honor*) *to remain,*
Sir, Your obedient servant.

Nowadays, the formal sign-off to a letter where the addressee's name is known is *Yours sincerely.* Where the name is not known (letters that start *Dear Sir or Madam*), the sign-off is *Yours faithfully.* The formal sign-off to the Queen of England is:

I have the honor to remain, Madam,
Your Majesty's most humble
and obedient subject.

THANK-YOU LETTERS may be brief, but should be heartfelt and prompt. It is traditional to address thank-you letters for a party to the hostess alone. ❧ FUNERAL CARDS attached to flowers or wreathes should read *In Loving Memory* and never *With Deepest Sympathy.*

Formal INVITATION envelopes to a couple are traditionally addressed just to the lady, whereas the invitation itself is made out to both parties. ❧ Prompt REPLY is essential. The usual forms are:

Mr Wooster thanks Mr & Mrs Glossop
for their kind invitation to dinner on
Friday May 26 and has much
pleasure in accepting.

or

Mr Wooster thanks Mr & Mrs Glossop
for their kind invitation to dinner on
Friday May 26 but regrets
he is unable to accept due to
a previous engagement.

❧ When faced at a meal with complex PLACE SETTING involving a panoply of knives and forks, work from the outside in. ❧ At dessert after a formal meal, port and other wines are PASSED TO THE LEFT and guests usually serve themselves. (It is on occasion acceptable to give a 'BACKHANDER', and fill the glass of the person sitting to your right.) ❧ If SMOKING is allowed at formal dinners in Britain, it should not commence until after the 'Loyal Toast' to the Queen. ❧ When addressing the Queen in person, her moniker MA'AM should be spoken to rhyme with 'ham' not 'harm'. ❧ When formally presented to Royalty, men should BOW from the neck and not from the waist. ❧ When entering a TAXI CAB in America (and in much of the rest of the world), men should enter first, and scoot down the length of the back seat to accommodate the elegant entrance of ladies. In London, where 'black cabs' are the norm, men should hold the door and enter last. If there is inadequate space, men should always take the folding 'cricket' seats.

—ANONYMOUS ALPHABET OF FORM & ADVICE · c.1832—

A*bove* all rules observe this – *honesty is the best policy.*

B*e* just to others, that you may be just to yourself.

C*ut* your coat according to your cloth.

D*esperate* cuts must have desperate cures.

E*nough* is as good as a feast.

F*air* and softly go sure and far.

G*entility* without ability is worse than beggary.

H*alf* a loaf is better than no bread.

I*dle* folks take the most pains.

J*okes* are as bad coin to all but the jocular.

K*eep* your business and conscience well, and they will keep you well.

L*ive* and let live; that is, do as you would be done by.

M*isunderstandings* are best prevented by pen and ink.

N*ever* take credit; as much as possible, avoid giving it.

O*ut* of debt, out of danger.

P*assion* will master you, if you do not master your passion.

Q*uick* at meat, quick at work.

R*evenge* a wrong by forgiving it.

S*hort* reckonings make long friends.

T*he* early bird catcheth the worm.

U*nmannerliness* is not so impolite as overpoliteness.

V*enture* not all you have at once.

W*ade* not into unknown waters.

X*amine* your accounts and your conduct every night.

Y*ou* may find your worst enemy, or best friend, in yourself.

Z*ealously* keep down little expenses, and you will not incur large ones.

ITCHING SIGNIFICANCE

Body part	itching signifies
Ears	longing to hear news or gossip
Palm	the imminent receipt of money
Thumb	the approach of danger or evil[†]
Right eye	imminent laughter or jollity; arrival of a loved one
Left eye	imminent sadness or grief
Lips	imminent prospect of kissing
Nose	imminent arrival of a stranger; the risk of a fire; fighting

† 'By the pricking of my thumbs, Something wicked this way comes.' *Macbeth*, IV, i

──────────────── THE VATICAN SWISS GUARD ────────────────

On January 22, 2006, the Vatican Swiss Guard celebrated 500 years in the service of the Catholic Church. The corps officially assumed Papal defense duties in 1506, when Julius II asked 150 Helvetian mercenaries, renowned for their discipline and hardiness, to march from their native land to the Vatican to act as his personal guard and protect the Apostolic Palace. To commemorate their call to arms, 80 veterans journeyed on foot from Bellinzona, Switzerland, to Rome for the swearing-in of new recruits on May 6, 2006. Competition to join one of the world's smallest armies is fierce, and each guard must still recite and abide by this historic oath:

> *I swear I will faithfully, loyally, and honorably serve the Supreme Pontiff ──*
> *and his legitimate successors and also dedicate myself to them with all my strength,*
> *sacrificing if necessary my life to defend them. I assume this same commitment*
> *with regard to the Sacred College of Cardinals whenever the See is vacant.*
> *Furthermore, I promise to the commanding captain and my other superiors, respect,*
> *fidelity, and obedience. This I swear! May God and our Holy Patrons assist me!*

Recruits must be unmarried, celibate Roman Catholic males, aged 19–30, standing at least 5ft 8in (1·73m) tall, who have completed military training in the Swiss armed forces. Once enlisted, the recruits are taught tactical deployment, security, and counterterrorism, and they learn to handle not only modern firearms but also the unwieldy swords and elaborate halberds of their Renaissance predecessors.

The Vatican Swiss Guard is instantly recognizable by its gaudy apparel – full armor, helmets plumed with ostrich feathers, and striped tunics and breeches in the red, yellow, and blue livery of the Medici family. Popular myth wrongly attributed the design for this garb to Michelangelo (1475–1564); in fact, the design was conceived in 1905 by a Swiss Guard Commander.

──────── RELIGIOUS PERCEPTIONS · INTERNATIONAL ────────

Below is charted how (un)favorably different religions are viewed across the world:

		CHRISTIANS		JEWS		MUSLIMS	
Country	%	*fav.*	*unfav.*	*fav.*	*unfav.*	*fav.*	*unfav.*
China		26	47	28	49	20	50
France		84	15	82	16	64	34
Germany		83	13	67	21	40	47
India		61	19	28	17	46	43
Indonesia		58	38	13	76	99	1
Jordan		58	41	0	100	99	1
Pakistan		22	58	5	74	94	2
Russia		92	3	63	26	55	36
UK		85	6	78	6	72	14
USA [see p.335]		87	6	77	7	57	22

[Source: Pew Global Attitudes Project, 2005]

RELIGIOUS OUTLOOK OF US ADULTS

Religious outlook		all	♂	♀	Black	White	Hispanic	Asian
Religious	} 75% {	37	31	42	49	37	30	28
Somewhat religious		38	41	36	32	40	45	34
Secular	} 16% {	10	12	8	6	10	11	21
Somewhat secular		6	7	5	5	7	5	9
Don't know/refused		9	9	9	7	6	8	8

[Source: 2001 American Religious Identification Survey (ARIS) · Self-described religious outlook of adults]

US RELIGIOUS BELIEF

All Christian .... (%)	76·79
Catholic.....................	24·46
Baptist	16·27
Other Christian............	36·06
Jewish............................	1·36
Muslim/Islamic	0·53
Buddhist...........................	0·52
Hindu	0·37
Unitarian/Universalist	0·30
Pagan	0·07
Spiritualist........................	0·06
Wiccan	0·06
Native American	0·05
Baha'i.............................	0·04
Scientologist.......................	0·03
New Age...........................	0·03
Sikh...............................	0·03
Deity	0·02
Druid.............................	0·02
Taoist.............................	0·02
Eckankar	0·01
Rastafarian	0·01
Santeria...........................	0·01
Ethical Culture...................	<0·01
Other unclassified................	0·19
No religion specified, total.......	14·17
Atheist........................	0·43
Agnostic	0·48
Humanist	0·02
Secular	0·03
No religion	13·22
Refused to reply to question.......	5·41

[Source: 2001 ARIS · Self-described identification]

ON EVOLUTION

Question: Life on Earth has …

Existed in its present form since (%) the beginning of time.............	42
Evolved over time....................	48
guided by a supreme being	18
through natural selection	26
don't know how	4
Don't know...........................	10

[Source: Pew Research Center, 2005]

PRAYER FREQUENCY

Several times a day............ (%)	31·0
Daily................................	27·5
Several times a week	14·1
Weekly	5·7
Less than weekly	10·7
Never...............................	10·2
Don't know/no answer.............	0·6

[Source: General Social Survey, 2004]

GOD IS …

The most common descriptions of God:

1	.... *Love*	6	.. *Supreme being*
2	.... *Creator*	7	.... *Almighty*
3	..........*Power*	8	.... *Awesome*
4	.....*Everything*	9	.... *Being*
5	.... *Father*	10	...... *Forgiving*

[Source: Pew Research Center, 2001]

──────────── BELIEF IN THE BIBLE ────────────

Since 1976, Gallup has asked US adults what they consider the Bible to be, ranging from the literal word of God, to a book of fable and morality written by man.

The Bible is … (%)	Aug 1976	Jul 1980	Feb 2001	Nov 2004	May 2006
Actual word of God to be taken literally, word for word	38	40	27	34	28
Inspired word of God, not all to be taken literally	45	45	49	48	49
An ancient book of fables, legends, &c. written by man	13	10	20	15	19
Unsure	5	6	4	3	3

──────── US PERCEPTIONS OF DIFFERENT RELIGIONS ────────

An April 2006 CBS News poll tested American perceptions of a range of religions:

Perception of	Favorable impression	Unfavorable	Don't know
Protestantism/other Christian …	58	12	30
Catholicism …	48	37	15
Judaism …	47	16	37
Christian Fundamentalism …	31	31	38
Mormonism …	20	39	41
Islam [see below] …	19	45	36
Scientology …	8	52	40

[The 'Don't know' group includes those who 'Haven't heard enough' or are 'Unsure'; the latter category accounted for 3–6%. In contrast to the above Gallup poll, CBS News found that 42% agreed that 'the Bible is the actual word of God and is to be taken literally, word for word'.]

──────── UNDERSTANDING & PERCEPTIONS OF ISLAM ────────

For many reasons, from 9/11 and Iraq to the Muhammad cartoon controversy [see p.17], Islam has featured heavily in recent media coverage. In March 2006, an ABC News/*Washington Post* poll indicated that 59% of US adults did *not* have a 'good basic understanding of the teachings and beliefs of Islam'. Notwithstanding this ignorance, 46% had a 'generally unfavorable opinion of Islam'; 45% thought Islam did not 'teach respect for the beliefs of non-Muslims'; 33% thought mainstream Islam 'encourages violence against non-Muslims'; and 58% thought there were 'more violent extremists within Islam' compared to other religions. (A CNN/*USA Today* poll in February 2006 found that 61% of Americans thought the cartoon controversy was due to 'Muslim intolerance of different points of view', compared to 21% who cited 'Western lack of respect'.) A report in March 2006 by the Pew Forum on Religion and Public Life showed that 55% of Americans had a favorable overall opinion of Muslim Americans, but only 41% had a generally favorable opinion of Islam. Interestingly, those who knew Muslims personally were 24% more likely to think favorably of Muslim Americans than those who knew none.

─────────────── THE FIVE PILLARS OF ISLAM ───────────────

SHAHADA... to affirm there is only one God, and Muhammad was his messenger
SALAT .... to pray five times a day
ZAKAH .... to give alms and charity to the poor
SAUM... to fast during the month of Ramadan
HAJJ [see p.337].................... to pilgrimage to Mecca at least once in a lifetime

─────────────── BUDDHA'S FOUR NOBLE TRUTHS ───────────────

Life involves suffering, and is inevitably sorrowful
Suffering has its roots in desire and craving which arise from ignorance
The end of suffering comes with the cessation of desire
Nirvana can be reached by the Noble Eightfold Path

The Noble Eightfold Path further outlines a method of disciplined behavior:

Right view..................................... understanding the Four Noble Truths
Right aspiration.............having caring thoughts and intent for all living things
Right speech ....speaking kindly, truthfully, without bad language
Right bodily action .... following the Five (or Ten) Moral Precepts
Right livelihood................... undertaking work that will harm nothing living
Right endeavor...........practicing meditation and working to stop bad thoughts
Right mindfulness ....giving full attention and best effort to one's actions
Right concentration .... which leads to enlightenment

─────────────── SIKHISM'S FIVE ARTICLES OF FAITH ───────────────

The 5 *Panj Kakas*, or articles of faith, worn by many Sikhs are: KESH (uncut hair)
KIRPAN (sword) · KARA (steel bangle) · KACHHA (undershorts) · KANGHA (comb)

─────────────── MORMON LIVING PROPHETS ───────────────

The Church of Jesus Christ of Latter-Day Saints (the Mormons) was founded
in 1830 by Joseph Smith, who is believed by Mormons to have been chosen by
God as a Prophet. In 1844, Smith was killed in jail by a mob while facing charges
of conspiracy. Since then, the Church has been led by the following Prophets:

Brigham Young	1844–77	David O. McKay	1951–70
John Taylor	1877–87	Joseph Fielding Smith	1970–72
Wilford Woodruff	1887–98	Harold B. Lee	1972–73
Lorenzo Snow	1898–1901	Spencer W. Kimball	1973–85
Joseph F. Smith	1901–18	Ezra Taft Benson	1985–94
Heber J. Grant	1918–45	Howard W. Hunter	1994–95
George Albert Smith	1945–51	Gordon B. Hinckley	1995–

———————————— THE HAJJ ————————————

The Hajj is the pilgrimage to Mecca, Saudi Arabia, that all Muslims who have the means and ability are obliged to make at least once in their lifetime. It is the fifth and most significant of the five 'Arkan' (or 'Pillars') of Islam. Pilgrims must be sane, healthy, adult Muslims, free from debt, who have provided for their family. ❧ In January 2006, *c.*362 pilgrims were trampled to death at the Jamarat Bridge in Mina. This was not the first time tragedy had struck the Hajj. Prompted by Islam's global growth and facilitated by cheap air travel, participation in the Hajj has risen from *c.*250,000 in 1930 to *c.*2·5 million in 2006. The sheer force of people (measured in 'pilgrims per minute') has caused numerous fatal incidents. In 1990, 1,426 were killed in a tunnel leading to the holy sites; in 1994, 270 died in stampedes; in 1997, 343 pilgrims died in fires; in 1998, >118 were trampled to death; and since 2000, >650 have been crushed, including, in 2004, 251 pilgrims at the Jamarat bridge. ❧ It is hard to overstate the complexity of the various forms of Hajj, which runs from 9th to 13th of *Dhu al-Hijjah* – the 12th Islamic month. Pilgrims arrive in Mecca, where they ablute and exchange their clothes for two simple, white, unstitched pieces of cloth (*Ihram*). Through prayers, pilgrims enter a state of *Ihram* in which they may not have sex, harm another living thing, or cut their hair. During the following five days, pilgrims journey many miles back and forth between Mecca, Mina, Arafat, and Muzdalifah, offering prayers to Allah and performing a series of rituals based upon the lives of Abraham and Muhammad. For example, on arriving in Mecca, pilgrims

Labbayka Allahumma Labbayk
(Here I am at Your service,
O God, Here I am)

perform their first *Tawaf*, 7 counter-clockwise journeys round the *Ka'ba* – a cube-shaped building in the sacred mosque *Masjid al Haram* that was built by Adam, rebuilt by Abraham, and rededicated to Allah by Muhammad. The pilgrims drink water from the Zam Zam well and make 7 journeys between the hills of Safra and Marwa. This commemorates God's benevolence in bringing forth water, after Abraham had been commanded to abandon his wife Hagar and son Ishmael in the desert. On the 2nd day of the Hajj, pilgrims walk to the Plain of Arafat (where Muhammad delivered his last sermon) to perform *Waqoof* – standing in the open, meditating, praising Allah, and praying for forgiveness. The 3rd day celebrates the willingness of Abraham to defy Satan and obey God's demand to sacrifice his son. Pilgrims stone three pillars (*Jamarat*) where Satan appeared, and sacrifice an animal as Abraham did. ❧ While most of the Hajj's many rituals have not changed in 1,400 years, much of the infrastructure has had to adapt. Prompted by tragedies such as those at the Jamarat Bridge (as well as the annual death toll from exhaustion, disease, and dehydration), the Saudi royal family has invested heavily in Mecca. A factory produces some 50m bags of cool water and ice; fire-proof and air-conditioned tents in Mina can house 1·5m; a vast abattoir handles animal sacrifices; and Mecca's morgue can hold >900. It is likely, however, that infrastructural advances will not be enough. In 2006, a number of Saudi newspapers called for Islamic scholars to rethink the ceremonies of the Hajj to protect the lives of 'God's guests'.

——————————— SINS, GIFTS, & VIRTUES ———————————

According to a 2005 survey of BBC Radio 4 listeners, the new 7 Deadly Sins are:

21ST-CENTURY SINS	TRADITIONAL SINS
Cruelty · Adultery · Bigotry · Greed	*Anger · Gluttony · Sloth*
Dishonesty · Hypocrisy · Selfishness	*Envy · Pride · Lust · Greed*

It is said that Mahatma Gandhi (1869–1948) considered the 7 Deadly Sins to be:

[1] Wealth without works · [2] Pleasure without conscience · [3] Knowledge without character · [4] Commerce without morality · [5] Science without humanity · [6] Worship without sacrifice · [7] Politics without principle

Evagrius Ponticus (AD *c*.346–399), Deacon of Constantinople, named his 8 Sins:

[1] Gluttony · [2] Fornication · [3] Avarice · [4] Dejection (lack of pleasure)
[5] Anger · [6] Weariness (acedia) · [7] Vainglory · [8] Pride

——————————— RELIGIOUS VALUES IN THE US ———————————

 67% believe religious freedom is a 'critical' part of their image of America

 62% believe that 'religion is on the decline in America'

 51% would like leaders to keep their religious beliefs mostly to themselves

 55% believe religion provides 'a great deal of guidance' in their daily lives

42% believe the US Constitution strongly reflects Judeo-Christian values

 18% report drawing on faith or religious beliefs when making choices in their lives

[Source: Center for American Progress/Financial Dynamics Poll · June 2006]

——————————— KWANZAA ———————————

Kwanzaa is a secular holiday celebrated from December 26 to January 1 by African Americans. Kwanzaa was proposed in 1966 by Dr Maulana Karenga in response to the race riots of 1965. Dr Karenga felt that Christmas was an overtly 'White' and Eurocentric festival. Consequently, there was a need to create a 'Black' festival that would resonate with the African roots of African Americans. Kwanzaa is based on traditional African harvest festivals, with the additional themes of strong community and family. At the heart of the festival are the *Nguzo Saba*, the seven principles, each of which is celebrated in turn over the course of the festival week:

UMOJA (*unity*) · KUJICHAGULIA (*self-determination*)
UJIMA (*collective works and responsibility*) · UJAMAA (*cooperative economics*)
NIA (*purpose*) · KUUMBA (*creativity*) · IMANI (*faith*)

THE TEN COMMANDMENTS

Exodus 20:1–17 ❧ And God spake all these words, saying, ❧ I am the Lord thy God, which have brought thee out of the land of Egypt, out of the house of bondage. ❧ Thou shalt have no other gods before me. ❧ Thou shalt not make unto thee any graven image, or any likeness of any thing that is in heaven above, or that is in the earth beneath, or that is in the water under the earth: ❧ Thou shalt not bow down thyself to them, nor serve them: for I the Lord thy God am a jealous God, visiting the iniquity of the fathers upon the children unto the third and fourth generations of them that hate me; ❧ And showing mercy unto thousands of them that love me, and keep my commandments. ❧ Thou shalt not take the name of the Lord thy God in vain; for the Lord will not hold him guiltless that taketh his name in vain. ❧ Remember the sabbath day, to keep it holy. ❧ Six days shalt thou labor, and do all thy work: ❧ But the seventh day is the sabbath of the Lord thy God: in it thou shalt not do any work, thou, nor thy son, nor thy daughter, thy manservant, nor thy maidservant, nor thy cattle, nor thy stranger that is within thy gates: ❧ For in six days the Lord made heaven and earth, the sea, and all that in them is, and rested the seventh day: wherefore the Lord blessed the sabbath day, and hallowed it. ❧ Honor thy father and thy mother: that thy days may be long upon the land which the Lord thy God giveth thee. ❧ Thou shalt not kill. ❧ Thou shalt not commit adultery. ❧ Thou shalt not steal. ❧ Thou shalt not bear false witness against thy neighbor. ❧ Thou shalt not covet thy neighbor's house, thou shalt not covet thy neighbor's wife, nor his manservant, nor his maidservant, nor his ox, nor his ass, nor any thing that is thy neighbor's. ❧

In Britain, a Channel 4 *survey (2005) asked the public to create a new set of Ten Commandments that reflected the moral issues of the 21st century. They suggested:*

1 .... Treat others as you would have them treat you
2 .. Take responsibility for your actions
3 .... Don't kill
4 .... Be honest
5 .... Don't steal
6 .... Protect and nurture children
7 .... Protect the environment
8 .... Look after the vulnerable
9 .... Never be violent
10 .... Protect your family

THE THREE JEWELS OF JAINISM

To achieve the goal of the liberation of the soul, Jains attempt to live by the tripartite rules of their ethical code. The 'three jewels' of Jain ethics are as follows:

SAMYAK DARSHANA (right perception) · attempting to perceive the truth clearly without being swayed by superstition or prejudice.

SAMYAK JNANA (right knowledge) · having accurate knowledge of the universe and scripture, and the mental attitude to use this knowledge.

SAMYAK CHARITRA (right conduct) · to live according to Jain ethics, and avoid doing any harm to other living creatures.

THE HINDU TRINITY

All Hindu Gods are part of the Supreme Being Brahman, but beneath him are the Trimurti – three gods who represent the perpetual cycle of creation – Brahma creates the world; while Vishnu sustains it; and Shiva destroys it.

God	consort	vehicle
Brahma *(creator)* . . . . Saraswati *(learning)* . . . . Hamsa – the swan
Vishnu *(preserver)* . . . . Lakshmi *(wealth)* . . . . Garuda – the bird
Shiva *(destroyer)* . . . . Parvati *(mother goddess)* . . . . Nandi – the bull

Vishnu's avatars, below, have appeared in 9 times of crisis; the 10th is yet to come:

Matsya . . . . the fish God . . . . *saved the world from flood*
Kurma . . . . the tortoise God . . . . *created liquid of immortality for Gods*
Varaha . . . . the wild boar . . . . *rescued Earth from a demon*
Nara-Simha . . . . . the man-lion . . . . *killed evil king*
Vamana . . . . the dwarf . . . . *defeated Bali; regained Heaven and Earth*
Parashurama . . . . . Rama with an ax . . . . *defeated oppressor of the people*
Rama . . . . hero of the Ramayana . . . . *killed demon Ravana*
Krishna . . . . the blue God . . . . *lifted mountain; saved village from storm*
Buddha . . . . Siddartha Gautama . . . . *all deities are manifestations of Vishnu*
Kalkin . . . . the horse God . . . . *will come in 428898CE*

RASTAFARIANISM & GANJA

For Rastafarians, the smoking of Ganja (marijuana) is central to their faith. Ganja, the 'wisdom weed', is considered the herb of life which brings believers closer to God. For some, its use is based upon Biblical references, including Genesis I:

11 · *And God said, Let the earth bring forth grass, the herb yielding seed, and the fruit tree yielding fruit after his kind, whose seed is in itself, upon the earth: and it was so.*	12 · *And the earth brought forth grass, and herb yielding seed after his kind, and the tree yielding fruit, whose seed was in itself, after his kind: and God saw that it was good.*

SHINTO & KAMI

Central to Japanese Shinto is the worship of Kami, which might tentatively be translated as 'spirits', except that features such as oceans and forces such as earth-quakes are also Kami. There are many millions of Kami which influence natural and human events and can themselves be influenced by prayer. Kami are not believed to be divine, omnipotent, or supernatural, but are part of the human world and, as such, make mistakes and 'misbehave'. Three types of Kami are worshipped in particular: the ancestors of the clans; the Kami of natural objects, creatures, and forces; and the souls of dead humans who are noted for outstanding achievements.

'SOUTH PARK' & SCIENTOLOGY

The cartoon show *South Park* became the focus of media gossip after a November 2005 episode parodying Scientology allegedly upset Isaac Hayes (who voices the character Chef) and Tom Cruise – both of whom are followers. In the episode, Stan takes a Scientology personality test, scores unprecedented 'Thetan levels', and is declared the reincarnation of Scientology founder L. Ron Hubbard. On hearing the news, a cartoon Tom Cruise hides in Stan's bedroom hoping for a meeting with his new hero. But, after Stan insults his acting, Cruise shuts himself in Stan's closet and refuses to come out. ❦ The episode was due to re-air March 15, 2006, but was abruptly withdrawn after Hayes announced his resignation†, citing the show's 'inappropriate ridicule' of religion. Some media outlets speculated that Tom Cruise may have influenced Comedy Central's decision not to rebroadcast the episode. In response, *South Park* creators Matt Stone and Trey Parker issued this statement:

> *'So, Scientology, you may have won THIS battle, but the million-year*
> *war for Earth has just begun! Temporarily anozinizing our episode will*
> *NOT stop us from keeping Thetans forever trapped in your pitiful man-bodies'*

† After Hayes left, the show spoofed the controversy by depicting Chef as a member of the Super Adventure Club, a group of brainwashing pedophiles. Chef was saved by the children of South Park, but then perished after being set on fire, impaled, shot, and attacked by a mountain lion and a bear.

TEMPLETON PRIZE

The winner of the 2006 *Templeton Prize for Progress Toward Research or Discoveries About Spiritual Realities* was Cambridge University mathematical sciences Professor John D. Barrow. He is best known for his work on the anthropic principle, the notion that Earth is in its present form to allow life capable of observing it to evolve. (In other words, the universe exists as it does because, if it were different, we would not exist to observe it.) Barrow received his prize on May 3 in a ceremony at Buckingham Palace, and was somewhat surprized to have won, saying, 'I thought this particular prize usually went to people who were rather older'. ❦ Sir John Templeton founded his eponymous prize in 1972 'to encourage and honor the advancement of knowledge in spiritual matters'. The prize (currently $1·4m) is said to be the largest annual monetary prize of any kind given to an individual. Templeton stipulated its value always be greater than the Nobel Prize, to 'underscore that research and advances in spiritual discoveries can be quantifiably more significant than disciplines recognized' by the Nobel committees. Previous Templeton winners have included Mother Teresa (1973), Billy Graham (1982), and Alexander Solzhenitsyn (1983). ❦ Born in Winchester, TN, John Templeton once dreamed of a life of religious service. After graduating from Yale University (with a stint at Oxford), he amassed great wealth through success in international investment funds. He was knighted in 1987 for his philanthropy, including his endowment of Templeton College, Oxford, and now lives as a 'full-time philanthropist' in the Bahamas.

Ephemerides

*That Kalendar or Ephemerides which he maketh of the
diversities of times and seasons for all actions and purposes.*
— FRANCIS BACON

———————————————2007———————————————

Roman numerals............. MMVII	Indian (Saka) year...... 1929 (Mar 22)
Dominical letter[1] .... G	Sikh year ... 539 Nanakshahi Era (Mar 14)
Epact[2] XI	Jewish year ....5768 (Sep 13)
Golden number (lunar cycle)[3].....XIII	Roman year [AUC].....2760 (Apr 21)
Chinese New Year.. Pig 4705 (Feb 18)	Masonic year........ 6007 Anno Lucis
Hindu New Year....... 2063 (Mar 19)	Knights Templars' year......889 (AO)
Islamic year............. 1428 (Jan 20)	Queen bee color.......yellow [see p.360]

[1] A way of categorizing years to facilitate the calculation of Easter. If January 1 is a Sunday,
the Dominical letter for the year will be A; if January 2 is a Sunday, it will be B; and so on.
[2] The number of days by which the solar year exceeds the lunar year. [3] The number of
the year (1–19) in the 19-year Metonic cycle; it is used in the calculation of Easter, and
is found by adding 1 to the remainder left after dividing the number of the year by 19.

——————————— THE DIVISION OF MAN'S AGES ———————————

The Ape, the Lion, the Fox, the Ass, Thus sets forth man as in a glass.
APE — Like apes we be toying, till twenty-and-one;
LION — Then hasty as lions, till forty be gone;
FOX — Then wily as foxes, till threescore-and-three;
ASS — Then after for asses accounted we be.

——————————— KEY TO SYMBOLS USED OVERLEAF ———————————

[★ FH]	US Federal Holiday	[§ *patronage*]	Saint's Day
[●]	Clocks change (USA)	[WA *year*]	Wedding Anniversary
[UK]	UK Bank Holiday	[Admis *year*]	Admission Day [US States]
[ND]	National Day	◑	Full Moon
[NH]	National Holiday	[↙]	Annual meteor shower
[ID *year*]	Independence Day	[UN]	United Nations Day
[BD *year*]	Birthday	[◉]	Eclipse
[† *year*]	Anniversary of death	[£]	Union Flag to be flown (UK)

Certain dates are subject to change, or tentative at the time of printing. Zodiac dates are approximate.

———————————— FEDERAL HOLIDAYS ————————————

According to the US Office of Personnel Management, federal law (5 USC 6103) establishes the following public holidays for federal employees. Most federal employees work on a Monday-through-Friday schedule. For these employees, when a holiday falls on a nonworkday, Saturday or Sunday, the holiday is usually observed on Monday (if the holiday falls on a Sunday) or Friday (if on a Saturday).

Holiday	2007	2008	2009	2010
New Year's Day	Jan 1	Jan 1	Jan 1	Jan 1
BD Martin Luther King Jr	Jan 15	Jan 21	Jan 19	Jan 18
Washington's Birthday†	Feb 19	Feb 18	Feb 16	Feb 15
Memorial Day	May 28	May 26	May 25	May 31
Independence Day	Jul 4	Jul 4	Jul 3	Jul 5
Labor Day	Sep 3	Sep 1	Sep 7	Sep 6
Columbus Day	Oct 8	Oct 13	Oct 12	Oct 11
Veterans' Day	Nov 12	Nov 11	Nov 11	Nov 11
Thanksgiving Day	Nov 22	Nov 27	Nov 26	Nov 25
Christmas Day	Dec 25	Dec 25	Dec 25	Dec 24

† This is the official name of the day as specified in Section 6103(a), title 5 of the United States Code.

———————————— FINDING TIME ————————————

The Chancellor of France, Henri François d'Aguesseau (1668–1751), realized that his wife always kept him waiting a quarter of an hour after the dinner bell had rung, and resolved to devote this time to writing a book on jurisprudence. He completed this great task in a work of four quarto volumes.

When asked how he found the time to write books, Archbishop Michael Ramsey (1904–88) is said to have replied: 'Monday, a quarter of an hour; Tuesday, 10 minutes; Wednesday, rather better, half an hour; Thursday, not very good, but 10 minutes; Friday, a lull, an hour; Saturday, half an hour.'

—— TRADITIONAL WEDDING ANNIVERSARY SYMBOLS ——

1st .... Paper	10th .... Tin	35th .... Coral, Jade
2nd .... Cotton	11th .... Steel	40th .... Ruby
3rd .... Leather	12th .... Silk	45th .... Sapphire
4th .... Linen, Silk	13th .... Lace	50th .... Gold
5th .... Wood	14th .... Ivory	55th .... Emerald
6th .... Iron	15th .... Crystal	60th .... Diamond
7th ...... Wool, Copper	20th .... China	70th .... Platinum
8th .... Bronze	25th .... Silver	75th .... Diamond
9th .... Pottery	30th .... Pearl	*British symbols differ*

[Debate rages about the order of paper and cotton, and other symbols exist for certain anniversaries]

———————————— JANUARY ————————————

 Capricorn [♑]   *Birthstone* · GARNET   *Aquarius* [♒]
(Dec 22–Jan 20)   *Flower* · CARNATION   (Jan 21–Feb 19)

1★ ....New Year's Day [★ FH] [UK] · Solemnity of Mary................ M
2 ....Switzerland – Berchtold's Day [NH] · Georgia [Admis 1788]..........Tu
3 ....🌑 · Josiah Wedgewood [† 1795] · Alaska [Admis 1959] ....W
4 ....Albert Camus [† 1960] · Quadrantids [✦] · Utah [Admis 1896] ....Th
5 ....Twelfth Night · Ernest Shackleton [† 1922] ....F
6 ....Epiphany · St Joan of Arc [BD 1412] · New Mexico [Admis 1912]........ Sa
7 ....Catherine of Aragon [† 1536]...........................Su
8 ....David Bowie [BD 1947] · Galileo Galilei [† 1642]................M
9 ....Gracie Fields [BD 1898] · Connecticut [Admis 1788]..............Tu
10 ....Grigori Rasputin [BD 1872] · Rod Stewart [BD 1945].............W
11 ....Nepal – National Unity Day [NH] ....Th
12 ....Hermann Goering [BD 1893] · Agatha Christie [† 1976]............F
13 ....James Joyce [† 1941]..............................Sa
14 ....Edmond Halley [† 1742] · Humphrey Bogart [† 1957]...........Su
15★ ....Martin Luther King Jr [★ FH] · Ivor Novello [BD 1893] ....M
16 ....Kate Moss [BD 1974].............................Tu
17 ....St Anthony of Egypt [§ *basket makers*] ....W
18 ....Cary Grant [BD 1904] · Rudyard Kipling [† 1936] ....Th
19 ....Edgar Allan Poe [BD 1809] · Paul Cézanne [BD 1839]..............F
20 ....Presidential Inauguration Day, USA .... Sa
21 ....Cecil B. DeMille [† 1959]..........................Su
22 ....Francis Bacon [BD 1561] · Lord Byron [BD 1788]...............M
23 ....St John the Almsgiver............................Tu
24 ....Caligula [† AD41 *murdered*] · Winston Churchill [† 1965]............W
25 ....Scotland – Burns' Night · Conversion of St Paul...............Th
26 ....Australia – Australia Day [NH] · Michigan [Admis 1837] ....F
27 ....Lewis Carroll [BD 1832] · Thomas Crapper [† 1910] ....Sa
28 ....King Henry VIII [† 1547]............................Su
29 .....St Julian the Hospitaller [§ *innkeepers and boatmen*] · Kansas [Admis 1861].....M
30 ....Charles I [† 1649 *beheaded*]...........................Tu
31 ....Tallulah Bankhead [BD 1903] · Justin Timberlake [BD 1981].........W

French Rev. calendar..... *Pluviôse* (rain)	Dutch month ...... *Lauwmaand* (chilly)
Angelic governor................*Gabriel*	Saxon month....... *Wulf-monath* (wolf)
Epicurean calendar..... *Marronglaçaire*	Talismanic stone .... *Jasper*

❧ The Latin month *Ianuarius* derives from *ianua* ('door'), since it was the opening of the year. It was also associated with *Janus*, the two-faced Roman god of doors and openings, who guarded the gates of heaven. Janus could simultaneously face the year just past and the year to come. ❧ *If January Calends be summerly gay,'Twill be winterly weather till the calends of May.* ❧ *Janiveer – Freeze the pot upon the fier.* ❧ *He that will live another year, Must eat a hen in Januvere.* ❧ On the stock market, the *January Effect* is the trend of stocks performing especially well that month. ❧

FEBRUARY

 Aquarius [♒]
(Jan 21–Feb 19)

Birthstone · AMETHYST
Flower · PRIMROSE

Pisces [♓]
(Feb 20–Mar 20)

1 .... National Freedom Day, USA · Clark Gable [BD 1901] .... Th
2 .... ☾ · Candlemas · Groundhog Day, USA .... F
3 .... Buddy Holly [† 1959] .... Sa
4 .... Karen Carpenter [† 1983] · Liberace [† 1987] .... Su
5 .... Robert Peel [BD 1788] .... M
6 ....New Zealand – Waitangi Day [NH] · Massachusetts [Admis 1788] .... Tu
7 .... Grenada [ID 1974] · Eddie Izzard [BD 1962] .... W
8 .... St Jerome Emiliani [§ *abandoned children and orphans*] .... Th
9 .... St Apollonia [§ *dentists*] · Mia Farrow [BD 1945] .... F
10 ....Bertolt Brecht [BD 1898] .... Sa
11 .... Burt Reynolds [BD 1936] · Jennifer Aniston [BD 1968] .... Su
12 ....Lady Jane Grey [† 1554 *beheaded*] · Abraham Lincoln [BD 1809] .... M
13 .... St Modomnoc [§ *bee-keepers*] · Oliver Reed [BD 1938] .... Tu
14 ....St Valentine [§ *lovers*] · Oregon [Admis 1859] · Arizona [Admis 1912] .... W
15 ....Susan B. Anthony Day, USA · Nat King Cole [† 1965] .... Th
16 ....Lithuania [ID 1918] .... F
17 .... Ruth Rendell [BD 1930] · Paris Hilton [BD 1981] .... Sa
18 .... 'Bloody' Mary I [BD 1516] · Martin Luther [† 1546] .... Su
19★ ...... Washington's Birthday [★ FH] · Nicolaus Copernicus [BD 1473] .... M
20 ....Sidney Poitier [BD 1927] .... Tu
21 .... Ash Wednesday · International Mother Language Day [UN] .... W
22 ....Feast of Chair of St Peter · St Lucia [ID 1979] .... Th
23 ....John Keats [† 1821] · Stan Laurel [† 1965] .... F
24 .... George Harrison [BD 1943] .... Sa
25 .... Pierre Auguste Renoir [BD 1841] · Tennessee Williams [† 1983] .... Su
26 ....Johnny Cash [BD 1932] .... M
27 .... Dominican Republic [ID 1844] · Chelsea Clinton [BD 1980] .... Tu
28 ....Vincente Minnelli [BD 1903] · Henry James [† 1916] .... W

French Rev. calendar..... *Ventôse* (wind)	Dutch month *Sprokelmaand* (vegetation)
Angelic governor............... *Barchiel*	Saxon month..........*Sol-monath* (Sun)
Epicurean calendar.... *Harrengsauridor*	Talismanic stone .... *Ruby*

❧ Much mythology and folklore consider February to have the bitterest weather: *February is seldom warm.* ❧ *February, if ye be fair, The sheep will mend, and nothing mair; February, if ye be foul, The sheep will die in every pool.* ❧ *As the day lengthens, the cold strengthens.* ❧ That said, a foul February is often said to presage a fine year: *All the moneths in the year curse a fair Februeer.* ❧ The word 'February' derives from *februa* – which means cleansing or purification, and reflects the rituals undertaken before spring. ❧ Having only 28 days in non-leap years [see p.360], February was known in Welsh as '*y mis bach*' – the little month. ❧ February is traditionally personified in pictures either by an old man warming himself by the fireside, or as 'a sturdy maiden, with a tinge of the red hard winter apple on her hardy cheek'. ❧

——————————————MARCH——————————————

Pisces [♓]   *Birthstone* · BLOODSTONE   *Aries* [♈]
(Feb 20–Mar 20)   *Flower* · JONQUIL   (Mar 21–Apr 20)

1 .... St David [§ *Wales*] · Nebraska [Admis 1867] · Ohio [Admis 1803] ....Th
2 ................D.H. Lawrence [† 1930] · John Irving [BD 1942]................F
3 .... ◗ · Doll's Festival, Japan · Bulgaria [ID 1878] · Florida [Admis 1845]...... Sa
4 .... Ronald Reagan & Nancy Davis [WA 1952] · Vermont [Admis 1791]....... Su
5 ....St Piran [§ *tin miners*] · Elaine Paige [BD 1948].................. M
6 .... Gabriel García Márquez [BD 1928] ....Tu
7 ....Aristotle [† 322BC] · Ranulph Fiennes [BD 1944]...............W
8 .... Women's Rights & International Peace Day [UN] ....Th
9 ....Yuri Gagarin [BD 1934] .... F
10.............Prince Edward [BD 1964] · Sharon Stone [BD 1958] .... Sa
11..........[◗ 02:00] · Henry Tate [BD 1819] · Harold Wilson [BD 1916]......... Su
12................. Paul McCartney & Linda Eastman [WA 1969] .... M
13.............. Earl Grey [BD 1764] · William H. Macy [BD 1950]...............Tu
14.......St Matilda [§ *parents with many children*] · Michael Caine [BD 1933] ....W
15...... Elizabeth Taylor & Richard Burton [WA 1964] · Maine [Admis 1820]......Th
16......................St Urho [§ *Finnish immigrants in America*]...................... F
17.............St Patrick's Day [§ *Ireland*] · World Maritime Day [UN] .... Sa
18.........................Fra Angelico [† 1455] ....Su
19...............Wyatt Earp [BD 1848] · Janis Joplin [BD 1943] .... M
20..........John Lennon & Yoko Ono [WA 1969] · Spike Lee [BD 1957]..........Tu
21.... International Day for the Elimination of Racial Discrimination [UN] ....W
22........World Day for Water [UN] · Andrew Lloyd Webber [BD 1948] ....Th
23.......... World Meteorological Day [UN] · Chaka Khan [BD 1953]............ F
24.............. William Morris [BD 1834] · E.H. Shephard [† 1976].............. Sa
25................... Annunciation Day · Elton John [BD 1947]..................Su
26...........Ludwig Van Beethoven [† 1827] · Diana Ross [BD 1944]............ M
27.................Yuri Gagarin [† 1968] · Dudley Moore [† 2002] ....Tu
28.......................Dwight D. Eisenhower [† 1969] ....W
29............... Eric Idle [BD 1943] · Elle Macpherson [BD 1964]...............Th
30.................. Vincent Van Gogh [BD 1853]......................... F
31................ Christopher Walken [BD 1943] .... Sa

French Rev. cal. ..... *Germinal* (budding)	Dutch month ....*Lentmaand* (spring)
Angelic governor............*Machidiel*	Saxon month.....*Hrèth-monath* (rough)
Epicurean calendar.... *Oeufalacoquidor*	Talismanic stone .... *Topaz*

❧ The first month of the Roman year, March is named after Mars – the god of war but also an agricultural deity. ❧ The unpredictability of March weather leads to some confusion (*March has many weathers*), though it is generally agreed that March *comes in like a lion, and goes out like a lamb*. Yet, because March is often too wet for crops to flourish, many considered *a bushel of Marche dust* [a dry March] *is worth a ransom of gold*. ❧ March hares are 'mad' with nothing more than lust, since it is their mating season. ❧ The *Mars* bar is named after its creator, Frank Mars. ❧

—— APRIL ——

Aries [♈]   *Birthstone* · DIAMOND   *Taurus* [♉]
(Mar 21–Apr 20)   *Flower* · SWEET PEA   (Apr 21–May 21)

1 . . . . April Fool's Day [except in Canada] · Marvin Gaye [† 1984 *murdered*] . . . . Su
2 . . . . ◐ · First Seder night · Charlemagne [BD AD742] . . . . M
3 . . . . First day of Passover · Jesse James [† 1882] · Tony Benn [BD 1925] . . . . . . Tu
4 . . . . Charles Siemens [BD 1823] . . . . W
5 . . . . Howard Hughes [† 1976] · Kurt Cobain [† 1994 *suicide*] . . . . Th
6 . . . . Good Friday · Raphael [† 1520] · John Betjeman [BD 1906] . . . . F
7 . . . . World Health Day [UN] · St John Baptist de la Salle [§ *teachers*] . . . . Sa
8 . . . . Easter Sunday · Kofi Annan [BD 1938] · Pablo Picasso [† 1973] . . . . . . Su
9 . . . . Traditionally, slugs and snails start to appear . . . . M
10 . . . . Dante Gabriel Rossetti [† 1882] · Evelyn Waugh [† 1966] . . . . Tu
11 . . . . St Stanislaus of Krakow [§ *Poland*] . . . . W
12 . . . . St Zeno [§ *Verona*] · David Letterman [BD 1947] . . . . Th
13 . . . . Samuel Beckett [BD 1906] · Garry Kasparov [BD 1963] . . . . F
14 . . . . Christiaan Huygens [BD 1629] · John Gielgud [BD 1904] . . . . Sa
15 . . . . Leonardo da Vinci [BD 1452] · Jean-Paul Sartre [† 1980] . . . . Su
16 . . . . Charlie Chaplin [BD 1889] · Peter Ustinov [BD 1921] . . . . M
17 . . . . Benjamin Franklin [† 1790] . . . . Tu
18 . . . . Zimbabwe [ID 1980] · James Woods [BD 1947] . . . . W
19 . . . . Charles Darwin [† 1882] · Dudley Moore [BD 1935] . . . . Th
20 . . . . Canaletto [† 1768] · Bram Stoker [† 1912] . . . . F
21 . . . . Queen Elizabeth II [BD 1926] [£] · St Beuno [§ *sick animals*] · Lyrids [☄] . . . . Sa
22 . . . . Richard Nixon [† 1994] . . . . Su
23 . . . . St George [§ *England*] · World Book & Copyright Day [UN] . . . . M
24 . . . . William I of Orange [BD 1533] . . . . Tu
25 . . . . Australia & New Zealand – Anzac Day · Al Pacino [BD 1940] . . . . W
26 . . . . Marcus Aurelius [BD AD121] · Lucille Ball [† 1989] . . . . Th
27 . . . . St Zita [§ *bakers*] · Ralph Waldo Emerson [† 1882] . . . . F
28 . . . . Francis Bacon [† 1992] · Maryland [Admis 1788] . . . . Sa
29 . . . . Adolf Hitler & Eva Braun [WA 1945] · Andre Agassi [BD 1970] . . . . Su
30 . . . . Édouard Manet [† 1883] · Louisiana [Admis 1812] . . . . M

French Rev. calendar . . . *Floréal* (blossom)	Dutch month . . . . *Grasmaand* (grass)
Angelic governor . . . . *Asmodel*	Saxon month . . . . *Eastre-monath*
Epicurean calendar . . . . *Petitpoisidor*	Talismanic stone . . . . *Garnet*

❦ April, T.S. Eliot's 'cruelest month', heralds the start of spring and is associated with new growth and sudden bursts of rain. ❦ Its etymology might derive from the Latin *aperire* ('to open') – although in Old English it was known simply as the *Eastre-monath*. ❦ *April with his hack and his bill, Plants a flower on every hill.* ❦ The custom of performing pranks and hoaxes on April Fool's Day (or *poisson d'avril* as it is known in France) is long established, although its origins are much disputed. ❦ According to folklore, *If it thunders on All Fools' day, it brings good crops of corn and hay.* ❦ Cuckoos first appear in letters to the London *Times* around April 8. ❦

──────── MAY ────────

Taurus [♉]　　　　*Birthstone* · EMERALD　　　　*Gemini* [♊]
(Apr 21–May 21)　　　*Flower* · LILY OF THE VALLEY　　(May 22–Jun 22)

1 . . . . May Day · Calamity Jane [BD 1852] . . . . Tu
2 . . . . . . ◖ · Engelbert Humperdinck [BD 1936] · David Beckham [BD 1975] . . . . . W
3 . . . . World Press Freedom Day [UN] · St James the Lesser [§ *hatmakers*] . . . . . . Th
4 . . . . Audrey Hepburn [BD 1929] · Diana Dors [† 1984] . . . . F
5 . . . . Japan – Children's Day · Eta Aquarids [☄] . . . . Sa
6 . . . . Orson Welles [BD 1915] . . . . Su
7 . . . . Johannes Brahms [BD 1833] · Eva Perón [BD 1919] . . . . M
8 . . . . VE Day · Paul Gauguin [† 1903] . . . . Tu
9 . . . . Liberation Day – Channel Islands · Billy Joel [BD 1949] . . . . W
10 . . . . Bono [BD 1960] · Joan Crawford [† 1977] . . . . Th
11 . . . . Salvador Dalí [BD 1904] · Bob Marley [† 1981] · Minnesota [Admis 1858] . . . . . F
12 . . . . Katharine Hepburn [BD 1907] . . . . Sa
13 . . . . Mother's Day · Harvey Keitel [BD 1939] . . . . Su
14 . . . . Paraguay [ND] · Frank Sinatra [† 1998] . . . . M
15 . . . . International Day of Families [UN] · St Isidore [§ *rural life*] . . . . Tu
16 . . . . Pierce Brosnan [BD 1953] · Sammy Davis Jr [† 1990] . . . . W
17 . . . . Ascension · Sandro Botticelli [† 1510] . . . . Th
18 . . . . International Museum Day . . . . F
19 . . . . St Yves [§ *lawyers & Brittany*] · Ho Chi Minh [BD 1890] . . . . Sa
20 . . . . St Bernardino of Siena [§ *advertisers*] . . . . Su
21 . . Lauren Bacall & Humphrey Bogart [WA 1945] · Barbara Cartland [† 2000] . . M
22 . . . . International Day for Biological Diversity [UN] . . . . Tu
23 . . . . Feast of Weeks (Shavuot) · South Carolina [Admis 1788] . . . . W
24 . . . . Nicolaus Copernicus [† 1543] . . . . Th
25 . . . . The Venerable Bede [† AD735] · Ian McKellen [BD 1939] . . . . F
26 . . . . Georgia [ID 1991] · John Wayne [BD 1907] . . . . Sa
27 . . . . Pentecost · Isadora Duncan [BD 1878] . . . . Su
28★ . . . . Memorial Day [★ FH] · Ethiopia [ND] · Anne Brontë [† 1849] . . . . M
29 . . . . . Int. Day of UN Peacekeepers [UN] · RI [Admis 1790] · WI [Admis 1848] . . . . . Tu
30 . . . . St Hubert [§ *dogs and hunters*] · Mel Blanc [BD 1908] . . . . W
31 . . . . The Visitation of the Blessed Virgin Mary . . . . Th

French Rev. cal. . . . . *Prairial* (meadow)	Dutch month . . . . . . *Blowmaand* (flower)
Angelic governor . . . . *Ambriel*	Saxon month . . . . *Trimilchi* [see below]
Epicurean calendar . . . . *Aspergial*	Talismanic stone . . . . *Emerald*

❧ Named after *Maia*, the goddess of growth, May is considered a joyous month, as Milton wrote: 'Hail bounteous May that dost inspire Mirth and youth, and warm desire.' ❧ However, May has long been thought a bad month in which to marry: *who weds in May throws it all away.* ❧ Anglo-Saxons called May *thrimilce*, since in May cows could be milked three times a day. ❧ May was thought a time of danger for the sick; so to have *climbed May hill* was to have survived the month. ❧ Kittens born in May were considered to be weak, and were often drowned. ❧

—JUNE—

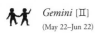 *Gemini* [♊]
(May 22–Jun 22)

Birthstone · PEARL
Flower · ROSE

Cancer [♋]
(Jun 23–Jul 23)

1 .... ● · Morgan Freeman [BD 1937] · KY [Admis 1792] · TN [Admis 1796] .... F
2 ...... Coronation of Elizabeth II [1953] [£] · Marquis de Sade [BD 1740] ..... Sa
3 .... Tony Curtis [BD 1925] · Ayatollah Khomeini [† 1989] .... Su
4 .... Socrates [BD 470BC] · Casanova [† 1798] .... M
5 .... World Environment Day [UN] · Ronald Reagan [† 2004] .... Tu
6 .... D-Day · Robert Kennedy [† 1968 *assassinated*] .... W
7 .... Malta [ND] · Alan Turing [† 1954 *suicide*] .... Th
8 .... The Prophet Muhammad [† AD632] · Bonnie Tyler [BD 1953] .... F
9 .... Cole Porter [BD 1893] .... Sa
10 .... HRH Prince Philip [BD 1921] [£] · Portugal [ND] .... Su
11 .... Gene Wilder [BD 1935] · John Wayne [† 1979] .... M
12 .... Russia [ID 1990] · Anne Frank [BD 1929] .... Tu
13 ... St Anthony of Padua [§ *finder of lost articles*] · Charles the Bald [BD AD823] ... W
14 .... Flag Day, USA · John Logie Baird [† 1946] .... Th
15 .... Edvard Grieg [BD 1846] · Arkansas [Admis 1836] .... F
16 .... Bloomsday (*Ulysses*, James Joyce) · Stan Laurel [BD 1890] .... Sa
17 .... Iceland [ID 1945] · Barry Manilow [BD 1946] .... Su
18 .... Seychelles [ND] · Roald Amundsen [† 1928 *lost in the Arctic*] .... M
19 .... Prince Edward & Sophie Rhys-Jones [WA 1999] .... Tu
20 .... World Refugee Day [UN] · West Virginia [Admis 1863] .... W
21 .... St Aloysius Gonzaga [§ *youth*] · New Hampshire [Admis 1788] .... Th
22 .... Judy Garland [† 1969] · Fred Astaire [† 1987] .... F
23 .... Midsummer's Eve · Vespasian [† AD79] .... Sa
24 .... Midsummer's Day · Juan Manuel Fangio [BD 1911] .... Su
25 .... Slovenia [ID 1991] · Virginia [Admis 1788] .... M
26 .... United Nations Charter Day [UN] · Madagascar [ID 1960] .... Tu
27 .... Jack Lemmon [† 2001] · John 'the Ox' Entwistle [† 2002] .... W
28 .... Peter Paul Rubens [BD 1577] .... Th
29 .... Elizabeth Barrett Browning [† 1861] · Paul Klee [† 1940] .... F
30 .... ● · Stanley Spencer [BD 1891] .... Sa

French Rev. cal. .... *Messidor* (harvest)	Dutch month ... *Zomermaand* (Summer)
Angelic governor .... *Muriel*	Saxon month .... *Sere-monath* (dry)
Epicurean calendar .... *Concombrial*	Talismanic stone .... *Sapphire*

❧ June is probably derived from *iuvenis* ('young'), but it is also linked to the goddess *Juno*, who personifies young women. In Scots Gaelic the month is known as *Ian t-Òg-mbìos*, the 'young month', and in Welsh as *Mehefin*, the 'middle'. ❧ According to weather lore, *Calm weather in June, Sets corn in tune*. ❧ To 'june' a herd of animals is to drive them in a brisk or lively manner. ❧ Wilfred Gowers Round asserts that 'June is the reality of the Poetic's claims for May'. ❧ In parts of South Africa the verb to 'june-july' is slang for shaking or shivering with fear – because these months, while summer in the north, are midwinter in the south. ❧

—— JULY ——

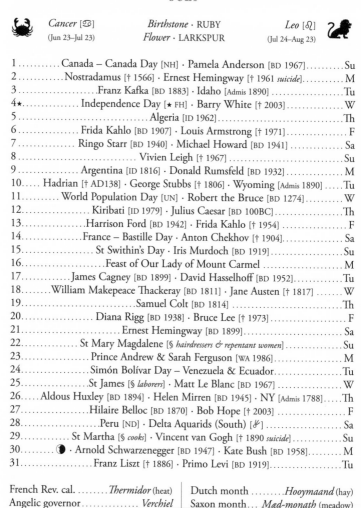

Cancer [♋] (Jun 23–Jul 23)	*Birthstone* · RUBY *Flower* · LARKSPUR	*Leo* [♌] (Jul 24–Aug 23)

1 . . . . Canada – Canada Day [NH] · Pamela Anderson [BD 1967] . . . . Su
2 . . . . Nostradamus [† 1566] · Ernest Hemingway [† 1961 *suicide*] . . . . M
3 . . . . Franz Kafka [BD 1883] · Idaho [Admis 1890] . . . . Tu
4★ . . . . Independence Day [★ FH] · Barry White [† 2003] . . . . W
5 . . . . Algeria [ID 1962] . . . . Th
6 . . . . Frida Kahlo [BD 1907] · Louis Armstrong [† 1971] . . . . F
7 . . . . Ringo Starr [BD 1940] · Michael Howard [BD 1941] . . . . Sa
8 . . . . Vivien Leigh [† 1967] . . . . Su
9 . . . . Argentina [ID 1816] · Donald Rumsfeld [BD 1932] . . . . M
10 . . . . . Hadrian [† AD138] · George Stubbs [† 1806] · Wyoming [Admis 1890] . . . . . Tu
11 . . . . World Population Day [UN] · Robert the Bruce [BD 1274] . . . . W
12 . . . . Kiribati [ID 1979] · Julius Caesar [BD 100BC] . . . . Th
13 . . . . Harrison Ford [BD 1942] · Frida Kahlo [† 1954] . . . . F
14 . . . . France – Bastille Day · Anton Chekhov [† 1904] . . . . Sa
15 . . . . St Swithin's Day · Iris Murdoch [BD 1919] . . . . Su
16 . . . . Feast of Our Lady of Mount Carmel . . . . M
17 . . . . James Cagney [BD 1899] · David Hasselhoff [BD 1952] . . . . Tu
18 . . . . William Makepeace Thackeray [BD 1811] · Jane Austen [† 1817] . . . . . . W
19 . . . . Samuel Colt [BD 1814] . . . . Th
20 . . . . Diana Rigg [BD 1938] · Bruce Lee [† 1973] . . . . F
21 . . . . Ernest Hemingway [BD 1899] . . . . Sa
22 . . . . St Mary Magdalene [§ *hairdressers & repentant women*] . . . . Su
23 . . . . Prince Andrew & Sarah Ferguson [WA 1986] . . . . M
24 . . . . Simón Bolívar Day – Venezuela & Ecuador . . . . Tu
25 . . . . St James [§ *laborers*] · Matt Le Blanc [BD 1967] . . . . W
26 . . . . . Aldous Huxley [BD 1894] · Helen Mirren [BD 1945] · NY [Admis 1788] . . . . . Th
27 . . . . Hilaire Belloc [BD 1870] · Bob Hope [† 2003] . . . . F
28 . . . . Peru [ND] · Delta Aquarids (South) [✦] . . . . Sa
29 . . . . St Martha [§ *cooks*] · Vincent van Gogh [† 1890 *suicide*] . . . . Su
30 . . . . ● · Arnold Schwarzenegger [BD 1947] · Kate Bush [BD 1958] . . . . M
31 . . . . Franz Liszt [† 1886] · Primo Levi [BD 1919] . . . . Tu

French Rev. cal. . . . . *Thermidor* (heat)	Dutch month . . . . *Hooymaand* (hay)	
Angelic governor . . . . *Verchiel*	Saxon month . . . *Mæd-monath* (meadow)	
Epicurean calendar . . . . *Melonial*	Talismanic stone . . . . *Diamond*	

❦ July was originally called *Quintilis* (from *Quintus* – meaning 'fifth'), but it was renamed by Mark Anthony to honor the murdered Julius Caesar, who was born on July 12. ❦ *A swarm of bees in May is worth a load of Hay; A swarm of bees in June is worth a silver spoon; But a swarm of bees in July is not worth a fly.* ❦ *If the first of July be rainy weather, 'Twill rain mair or less for forty days together.* ❦ *Bow-wow, dandy fly – Brew no beer in July.* ❦ July used to be known as the thunder month, and some churches rang their bells in the hope of driving away thunder and lightning. ❦

—AUGUST—

 Leo [♌]
(Jul 24–Aug 23)

Birthstone · AGATE
Flower · GLADIOLUS

Virgo [♍]
(Aug 23–Sep 23)

1 .... Switzerland [ND] · Jerry Garcia [BD 1942] · Colorado [Admis 1876] .... W
2 .... Peter O'Toole [BD 1932] .... Th
3 .... P.D. James [BD 1920] · Joseph Conrad [† 1924] .... F
4 .... St John Vianney [§ *priests*] · Hans Christian Andersen [† 1875] .... Sa
5 .... Oyster Day, UK · Carmen Miranda [† 1955] .... Su
6 .... Delta Aquarids (North) [☄] · Andy Warhol [BD 1928] .... M
7 .... Labor Day – Western Samoa .... Tu
8 .... St Dominic [§ *astronomers*] · Dustin Hoffman [BD 1937] .... W
9 .... International Day of the World's Indigenous People [UN] .... Th
10 .... St Lawrence [§ *cooks, &c.*] · Herbert Hoover [BD 1874] · MO [Admis 1821] .... F
11 .... Hulk Hogan [BD 1953] .... Sa
12 .... Glorious Twelfth – traditional start of the grouse season · Perseids [☄] ... Su
13 .... Fidel Castro [BD 1926] · Madhur Jaffrey [BD 1933] .... M
14 .... Pakistan [ID 1947] · Halle Berry [BD 1968] .... Tu
15 .... VJ Day · Assumption Day · Princess Anne [BD 1950] [£] .... W
16 .... Trevor McDonald [BD 1939] · Idi Amin [† 2003] .... Th
17 .... Davy Crockett [BD 1786] · Mae West [BD 1893] .... F
18 .... Patrick Swayze [BD 1952] .... Sa
19 .... Afghanistan [ID 1919] · Ogden Nash [BD 1902] .... Su
20 .... St Stephen of Hungary [§ *Hungary*] .... M
21 .... Aubrey Beardsley [BD 1872] · Hawaii [Admis 1959] .... Tu
22 .... Claude Debussy [BD 1862] · Michael Collins [† 1922 *assassinated*] .... W
23 .... St Rose of Lima [§ *Latin America and the Philippines*] .... Th
24 .... Ukraine [ID 1991] · George Stubbs [BD 1724] .... F
25 .... St Genesius [§ *actors*] · Sean Connery [BD 1930] .... Sa
26 .... Charles Lindbergh [† 1974] · Haile Selassie [† 1975] .... Su
27 .... Titian [† 1576] .... M
28 .... ◐ · Donald O'Connor [BD 1925] · David Soul [BD 1943] .... Tu
29 .... Michael Jackson [BD 1958] .... W
30 .... St Fiacre [§ *taxi drivers*] · Mary Shelley [BD 1797] .... Th
31 .... Trinidad and Tobago [ND] · Van Morrison [BD 1945] .... F

French Rev. cal. .... *Fructidor* (fruits)	Dutch month ...... *Oostmaand* (harvest)
Angelic governor .... *Hamaliel*	Saxon month ...... *Weod-monath* (weed)
Epicurean calendar .... *Raisinose*	Talismanic stone .... *Zircon*

❧ Previously called *Sextilis* (as the sixth month of the old calendar), August was renamed in 8BC, in honor of the first Roman Emperor, Augustus, who claimed this month to be lucky since it was the month in which he began his consulship, conquered Egypt, and had many other triumphs. ❧ *Greengrocers rise at dawn of sun, August the fifth – come haste away, To Billingsgate the thousands run, Tis Oyster Day! Tis Oyster Day!* ❧ *Dry August and warme, Dothe harvest no harme.* ❧ *Take heed of sudden cold after heat.* ❧ *Gather not garden seeds near the full moon.* ❧ *Sow herbs.* ❧

— SEPTEMBER —

Virgo [♍]   *Birthstone* · SAPPHIRE   *Libra* [♎]
(Aug 23–Sep 23)   *Flower* · ASTER   (Sep 24–Oct 23)

1 .... Uzbekistan [ND] · Barry Gibb [BD 1946] .... Sa
2 ....Jimmy Connors [BD 1952] · Keanu Reeves [BD 1964] .... Su
3★ .... Labor Day [★ FH] · e.e. cummings [† 1962] .... M
4 ....Edvard Grieg [† 1907] · Beyoncé Knowles [BD 1981] .... Tu
5 ....Freddie Mercury [BD 1946] · Mother Teresa [† 1997] .... W
6 ....Greg Rusedski [BD 1973] · Tim Henman [BD 1974] .... Th
7 .... Brazil [ID 1822] · Keith Moon [† 1978] .... F
8 ...... International Literacy Day [UN] · Nativity of Blessed Virgin Mary ...... Sa
9 ...... Japan – Chrysanthemum Day · California [Admis 1850] .... Su
10 .... Karl Lagerfeld [BD 1938] .... M
11 ....New Year – Ethiopia · Nikita Sergeyevich Khrushchev [† 1971] .... Tu
12 ....Elizabeth Barrett & Robert Browning [WA 1846] .... W
13 ......Jewish New Year [AM 5768] · First day of Ramadan · Titus [† AD81] ..... Th
14 .... Exaltation of the Holy Cross · Isadora Duncan [† 1927] .... F
15 .... Battle of Britain Day · Nicaragua [ND] .... Sa
16 .... International Day for the Preservation of the Ozone Layer [UN] .... Su
17 ....Stirling Moss [BD 1929] · Spiro Agnew [† 1996] .... M
18 .... Chile [ND] · Jimi Hendrix [† 1970] .... Tu
19 ....William Golding [BD 1911] · Jeremy Irons [BD 1948] .... W
20 ....Jakob Grimm [† 1863] · Sophia Loren [BD 1934] .... Th
21 .... International Day of Peace [UN] · Belize [ND] .... F
22 ..... Day of Atonement (Yom Kippur) · Mali [ND] · Shaka Zulu [† 1828] ..... Sa
23 .... Wilkie Collins [† 1889] · Mickey Rooney [BD 1920] .... Su
24 .... Howard Hughes [BD 1905] .... M
25 .... Mark Rothko [BD 1903] · Mark Hamill [BD 1951] .... Tu
26 .... ☽ · Olivia Newton-John [BD 1948] .... W
27 .... Feast of Tabernacles (Succoth) · Edgar Degas [† 1917] .... Th
28 .... Louis Pasteur [† 1895] .... F
29 ....Michaelmas Day · Horatio Nelson [BD 1758] .... Sa
30 .... Truman Capote [BD 1924] · James Dean [† 1955] .... Su

French Rev. cal. ... *Vendémiaire* (vintage)	Dutch month .... *Herstmaand* (Autumn)
Angelic governor .... *Uriel*	Saxon month ...... *Gerst-monath* (barley)
Epicurean calendar .... *Hu trose*	Talismanic stone .... *Agate*

❦ September is so named as it was the seventh month in the Roman calendar. ❦ *September blows soft, Till the fruit's in the loft. Forgotten, month past, Doe now at the last.* ❦ *Eat and drink less, And buy a knife at Michaelmas.* ❦ To be 'Septembered' is to be multihued in autumnal colors; as Blackmore wrote: 'His honest face was Septembered with many a vintage'. ❦ *Poor Robin's Almanac* (1666) states, 'now *Libra* weighs the days and nights in an equal balance, so that there is not an hairs breadth difference betwixt them in length; this moneth having an R in it, Oysters come again in season.' ❦ The Irish name *Meán Fómhair* means 'mid-Autumn'. ❦

OCTOBER

 Libra [♎]
(Sep 24–Oct 23)

Birthstone · OPAL
Flower · CALENDULA

Scorpio [♏]
(Oct 24–Nov 22)

1 ....Int. Day of Older Persons [UN] · Julie Andrews [BD 1935]..........M
2 ....Julius 'Groucho' Marx [BD 1890] · Graham Greene [BD 1904]........Tu
3 ....Germany [ND] · William Morris [† 1896]....................W
4 ....Buster Keaton [BD 1895] · Charlton Heston [BD 1924].............Th
5 ......International Teachers' Day [UN] · Louis Jean Lumière [BD 1864] ......F
6 ....Alfred Lord Tennyson [† 1892].........................Sa
7 ....James Whitcomb Riley [BD 1849] · Heinrich Himmler [BD 1900].......Su
8★.. Columbus Day [★ FH] · Chevy Chase [BD 1943] · Clement Attlee [† 1967] ..M
9 ....Uganda [ND] · John Lennon [BD 1940].....................Tu
10..................Edith Piaf [† 1963] · Orson Welles [† 1985]...................W
11...........................Henry John Heinz [BD 1844].........................Th
12..................Spain [ND] · Luciano Pavarotti [BD 1935]....................F
13.............End of Ramadan (Eid al-Fitr) · Paul Simon [BD 1941]............Sa
14.................King Harold [† 1066] · Roger Moore [BD 1927] ....Su
15....................Chris de Burgh [BD 1948]................................M
16.......World Food Day [UN] · Oscar Wilde [BD 1854]................Tu
17.......International Day for the Eradication of Poverty [UN] ....W
18...........Alaska Day, USA · Jean-Claude Van Damme [BD 1960]............Th
19....................John Le Carré [BD 1931].............................F
20..........Christopher Wren [BD 1632] · Viggo Mortensen [BD 1958] ....Sa
21.................St Hilarion [§ *hermits*] · Orionids [☄].....................Su
22.........Derek Jacobi [BD 1938] · Franz Liszt [BD 1811]................M
23.............St John of Capistrano [§ *jurors*] · Al Jolson [† 1950]..............Tu
24..............United Nations Day [UN] · Christian Dior [† 1957]............W
25............Kazakhstan [ND] · Imran Khan [BD 1952] ....Th
26.....................◑ · Joseph Hansom [BD 1803].........................F
27.............Turkmenistan [ND] · Desiderius Erasmus [BD 1466].............Sa
28.......................Bill Gates [BD 1955]...........................Su
29................Turkey [ND] · Joseph Pulitzer [† 1911] ....M
30..............John Chubb [† 1872] · Diego Maradona [BD 1960]..............Tu
31..........Halloween · Harry Houdini [† 1926] · Nevada [Admis 1864] ....W

French Rev. cal. .... *Brumaire* (fog; mist)	Dutch month .... *Wynmaand* (wine)
Angelic governor................*Barbiel*	Saxon month....... *Win-monath* (wine)
Epicurean calendar.......... *Bécassinose*	Talismanic stone ....*Amethyst*

❧ October was originally the eighth month of the calendar. ❧ *Dry your barley land in October, Or you'll always be sober.* ❧ October was a time for brewing, and the month gave its name to a 'heady and ripe' ale: 'five Quarters of Malt to three Hogsheads, and twenty-four Pounds of Hops'. Consequently, *often drunk and seldom sober falls like the leaves in October.* ❧ In American politics, an *October surprise* is an event thought to have been engineered to garner political support just before an election (like the release of US hostages in Tehran in October 1980). ❧

—————————— NOVEMBER ——————————

Scorpio [♏]   *Birthstone* · TOPAZ   *Sagittarius* [♐]
(Oct 24–Nov 22)   *Flower* · CHRSYANTHEMUM   (Nov 23–Dec 21)

1 .... All Saints' Day · L.S. Lowry [BD 1887]..................... Th
2 ..... All Souls' Day · Marie Antoinette [BD 1755] · ND & SD [Admis 1889] ..... F
3 .... Henri Matisse [† 1954] · Dolph Lundgren [BD 1959].............. Sa
4 .... [● 02:00] · St Charles Borromeo [§ *learning and the arts*] .... Su
5 .... Guy Fawkes Night (UK) · Taurids [☄] .... M
6 .... Election Day · Adolphe Sax [BD 1814]..................... Tu
7 .... Marie Curie [BD 1867] · Steve McQueen [† 1980] .... W
8 .... Edmond Halley [BD 1656] · John Milton [† 1674] · Montana [Admis 1889]... Th
9 .... First day of Diwali · Katharine Hepburn [(fake) BD 1909] .... F
10 .... William Hogarth [BD 1697] · Tim Rice [BD 1944] .... Sa
11 .... Veterans' Day · Remembrance Day · Washington [Admis 1889] .... Su
12★ .... Veterans' Day Holiday [★ FH] · Roland Barthes [BD 1915] .... M
13 .... St Homobonus [§ *cloth workers*] · Camille Pissarro [† 1903] .... Tu
14 ...... Prince Charles [BD 1948] [£] · Boutros Boutros-Ghali [BD 1922]...... W
15 .... St Albert the Great [§ *scientists*] · J.G. Ballard [BD 1930]............. Th
16 .... International Day for Tolerance [UN] · Oklahoma [Admis 1907] .... F
17 .... Leonids [☄] · Danny DeVito [BD 1944].................... Sa
18 .... Margaret Attwood [BD 1939] · Kim Wilde [BD 1960].............. Su
19 .... Monaco [ND] .... M
20 .... Queen Elizabeth II & Prince Philip [WA 1947] [£] .... Tu
21 .... North Carolina [Admis 1789]........................... W
22★ ..... Thanksgiving Day [★ FH] · St Cecilia [§ *music*] · Lebanon [ID 1941] ...... Th
23 .... Billy the Kid [BD 1859] · Roald Dahl [† 1990] .... F
24 ...... ◑ · Henri de Toulouse-Lautrec [BD 1864] · Scott Joplin [BD 1868]...... Sa
25 .... Andrew Carnegie [BD 1835] · Joe DiMaggio [BD 1914]............. Su
26 .... William George Armstrong [BD 1810] .... M
27 .... Anders Celsius [BD 1701] · Jimi Hendrix [BD 1942] .... Tu
28 .... East Timor [ND] · Nancy Mitford [BD 1904]................ W
29 .... Jacques Chirac [BD 1932] · Cary Grant [† 1986] .... Th
30 .... St Andrew [§ *Scotland & Russia*] · Jonathan Swift [BD 1667] .... F

French Rev. calendar.... *Frimaire* (frost)	Dutch month ....*Slagtmaand* [see below]
Angelic governor............. *Advachiel*	Saxon month...... *Wind-monath* (wind)
Epicurean calendar....... *Pommedetaire*	Talismanic stone .... *Beryl*

❧ Originally, the ninth (*novem*) month, November has long been associated with slaughter, hence the Dutch *Slaghtmaand* ('slaughter month'). The Anglo-Saxon was *Blotmonath* ('blood' or 'sacrifice month'). ❧ A dismal month, November has been the subject of many writers' ire; as J.B. Burges wrote: 'November leads her wintry train, And stretches o'er the firmament her veil Charg'd with foul vapours, fogs and drizzly rain.' ❧ Famously, Thomas Hood's poem *No!* contains the lines 'No warmth, no cheerfulness, no healthful ease, No shade, no shine, no butterflies, no bees, No fruits, no flowers, no leaves, no birds, —— November!' ❧

DECEMBER

 Sagittarius [♐]   *Birthstone* · TURQUOISE   *Capricorn* [♑]
(Nov 23–Dec 21)   *Flower* · NARCISSUS   (Dec 22–Jan 20)

1 .... World AIDS Day [UN] · Woody Allen [BD 1935] .... Sa
2 .... Kyrgyzstan [ND] · Britney Spears [BD 1981]................... Su
3 .... International Day of Disabled Persons [UN] · Illinois [Admis 1818] ...... M
4 .... Wassily Kandinsky [BD 1866] · Benjamin Britten [† 1976]........... Tu
5 .... First day of Chanukah · Walt Disney [BD 1901] .... W
6 .... St Nicholas [§ *bakers & pawnbrokers*]......................... Th
7 .... Pearl Harbor Day, USA · Delaware [Admis 1787] .... F
8 .... The Immaculate Conception · Mary Queen of Scots [BD 1542]....... Sa
9 .... John Milton [BD 1608] .... Su
10 .... Human Rights Day [UN] · Mississippi [Admis 1817].............. M
11 .... St Damasus [§ *archaeologists*] · Indiana [Admis 1816]............... Tu
12 .... Frank Sinatra [BD 1915] · Pennyslvania [Admis 1787] .... W
13 .... Japan – Soot Sweeping Day .... Th
14 ..... Geminids [♐] · George Washington [† 1799] · Alabama [Admis 1819]..... F
15 .... National Bill of Rights Day, USA · John Paul Getty [BD 1892]....... Sa
16 .... Ludwig Van Beethoven [BD 1770] · Arthur C. Clarke [BD 1917]....... Su
17 .... Bhutan [ND] · Simón Bolívar [† 1830] .... M
18 .... International Migrants Day [UN] · New Jersey [Admis 1787].......... Tu
19 .... William Edward Parry [BD 1790]........................ W
20 .... Yvonne Arnaud [BD 1890] · John Steinbeck [† 1968]............. Th
21 .... Thomas à Becket [BD 1118] · Joseph Stalin [BD 1879] .... F
22 .... First day of Winter · George Eliot [† 1880].................. Sa
23 .... Ursids [♐] · Samuel Smiles [BD 1812] .... Su
24 .... ● · Christmas Eve · Ava Gardner [BD 1922]................. M
25★ .... Christmas Day [★ FH] [UK] · Humphrey Bogart [BD 1899]........... Tu
26 .... Boxing Day [UK] · St Stephen [§ *stonemasons & horses*]............. W
27 .... St John [§ *Asia Minor*] · Marlene Dietrich [BD 1901]............. Th
28 .... Childermass · Denzel Washington [BD 1954] · Iowa [Admis 1846]........ F
29 ... Percy Bysshe Shelley & Mary Wollstonecraft [WA 1816] · TX [Admis 1845]... Sa
30 .... Rudyard Kipling [BD 1865] · L.P. Hartley [BD 1895].............. Su
31 .... New Year's Eve · Scotland – Hogmanay................... M

French Rev. calendar...... *Nivôse* (snow)	Dutch month .... *Wiutermaand* (winter)
Angelic governor............... *Hanael*	Saxon month...... *Mid-Winter-monath*
Epicurean calendar.......... *Boudinaire*	Talismanic stone .... *Onyx*

❧ *If the ice will bear a goose before Christmas, it will not bear a duck afterwards.* ❧ Originally the tenth month, December now closes the year. ❧ *If Christmas Day be bright and clear there'll be two winters in the year.* ❧ The writer Saunders warned in 1679, 'In December, Melancholy and Phlegm much increase, which are heavy, dull, and close, and therefore it behoves all that will consider their healths, to keep their heads and bodies very well from cold'. ❧ Robert Burns splendidly wrote in 1795 – 'As I am in a complete Decemberish humour, gloomy, sullen, stupid'. ❧

—————————— CALENDRICAL MISCELLANY ——————————

DOG DAYS · the hot, muggy days of sultry summer, associated by the Romans (*dies caniculares*) with the influence of the dog star, Sirius, which is high in the sky during summer days. Dog days are said to last for 'more than one month but less than two', from July until early September.

SALAD DAYS · days of inexperience (between youth and maturity) when people are 'green'. As Shakespeare wrote in *Antony & Cleopatra*: 'My salad days, When I was green in judgement, cold in blood, To say as I said then!'

ANNUS HORRIBILIS · a terrible year.
ANNUS MIRABILIS · a miraculous year.

HALCYON DAYS · generally a time of happiness and prosperity; in nautical terms, a period of two weeks of calm seas at the winter solstice.

CAP & FEATHER DAYS · childhood.

HOLOCAUST MEMORIAL DAY · observed across Europe on January 27 each year, the anniversary of the liberation of the Auschwitz-Birkenau concentration camp. (It is also the European Day Against Genocide.)

LUSTRUM · a period of five years.

JOUR MAIGRE · a fast-day *(French)*.

HEXAMERON · 6 days of creation.

CALENDS · in the Roman calendar, the first day of the month. IDES · were the 15th day of March, May, July, and October, and the 13th day of all other months. (Julius Caesar was assassinated on the Ides of March 44BC). NONES · were nine days before the Ides.

MEDICINAL DAYS · according to the Greek 'father of medicine', Hippocrates (*c.*460–*c.*375BC), these are the 6th, 8th, 10th, 12th, 16th, 18th, &c. days of a disease, when no 'crisis' will occur, and medicine may be safely administered. Similarly, MEDICINAL HOURS are those suitable for taking medicine: apparently, an hour before dinner, four hours after dinner, and bedtime.

EQUATION OF TIME · the difference between the time as shown by a clock and the time as shown by a sundial – greatest in November when the sun is 'slow'.

HISTORICAL YEAR · the modern historical convention of measuring the year from January 1, regardless of the system used in the time or culture of the location under discussion.

THE ATOMIC SECOND · is defined as the period of time taken for 9,192,631,770 oscillations of the cesium-133 atom exposed to a suitable excitation.

CLIMACTERIC YEARS · the 7th and 9th years and their multiples by the odd numbers 3, 5, 7, 9 (i.e. 7, 9, 21, 27, 35, 45, 49, 63, and 81) which astrologers predicted would be dismal, since Saturn presided over them. ['Climacteric' is another name for menopause.]

BEGINNING OF THE DAY · varies across history and by culture: modern Western and Chinese cultures follow Roman tradition by starting new days at *midnight*; Egyptians, Armenians, and Persians began their day at *dawn*; Greeks, Jews, and Muslims started their day at *sunset*; some sailors, astronomers, and other cultures began days at *noon*.

—————— FLORA'S CLOCK ——————

Below is one of the fanciful, and essentially theoretical, floral clocks based on the hour certain plants open and close (bracketed names indicate an hour of closing):

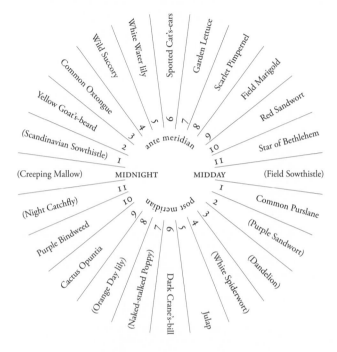

—————— SUPERSTITIONS OF THE YEAR ——————

January . . . . *Of this first month the opening day, and 7th like a sword will slay*
February . . . . . . *The 3rd day bringeth down to death, the 4th will stop a strong man's breath*
March . . . . *The 1st the greedy glutton slays, the 4th cuts short the drunkard's days*
April . . . . *The 10th day and the 11th too, are ready Death's fell work to do*
May . . . . *The 3rd to slay poor men had power, the 7th destroyeth in an hour*
June . . . . *The 10th a pallid visage shows, no faith nor truth the 15th knows*
July . . . . *The 13th is a fatal day, the 10th alike will mortals slay*
August . . . . *The first kills strong men at a blow, the 2nd lays a cohort low*
September . . . . . . *The 3rd day of the month September, and 10th bring evil to each member*
October . . . . *The 3rd and 10th will poisèd breath, to men are foes as foul as death*
November . . . . . *The 5th bears scorpion stings of pain, the 3rd comes with distraction's train*
December . . . . *The 7th is bad for human life, the 10th with serpent's sting is rife*
The lucky have whole days in which to choose; the unlucky have but hours & these they lose.

— ASTRA CIELO, *Signs, Omens, and Superstitions*, 1919

—————————— PHASES OF THE MOON · 2007 ——————————

NEW MOON			FIRST QUARTER			FULL MOON			LAST QUARTER		
d	*h*	*m*	*d*	*h*	*m*	*d*	*h*	*m*	*d*	*h*	*m*
Jan.... 19....	4	...01	Jan.... 25...	23	..01	Jan..... 3	... 13	..57	Jan.... 11...	12	..45
Feb.... 17...	16	..14	Feb.... 24....	7	..56	Feb..... 2	... 5	...45	Feb.... 10....	9	...51
Mar... 19...	2	...43	Mar... 25...	18	..16	Mar....3	... 23	..17	Mar... 12....	3	...54
Apr ... 17...	11	..36	Apr... 24....	6	..36	Apr 2	... 17	..15	Apr ... 10...	18	..04
May... 16...	19	..27	May... 23...	21	..03	May....2	... 10	..09	May... 10....	4	...27
Jun.... 15...	3	...13	Jun.... 22...	13	..15	Jun..... 1	... 1	...04	Jun....8	... 11	..43
Jul..... 14...	12	..04	Jul.... 22....	6	..29	Jun.... 30...	13	..49	Jul.....7	... 16	..54
Aug ... 12...	23	..03	Aug ... 20...	23	..54	Jul..... 30...	0	...48	Aug 5	... 21	..20
Sep.... 11...	12	..44	Sep.... 19...	16	..48	Aug ... 28...	10	..35	Sep....4	2	...32
Oct ... 11....	5	...01	Oct ... 19...	8	..33	Sep.... 26...	19	..45	Oct 3	... 10	..06
Nov....9	... 23	..03	Nov... 17...	22	..33	Oct ... 26....	4	...52	Nov....1	... 21	..18
Dec....9	... 17	..40	Dec... 17...	10	..18	Nov... 24...	14	..30	Dec....1	... 12	..44
[Key: *d*ays, *h*ours, and *m*inutes of Universal Time]						Dec... 24...	1	...16	Dec... 31....	7	...51

new moon · waxing crescent · first quarter · waxing gibbous · full moon · waning gibbous · last quarter · waning crescent · new moon

—————————— FULL MOON NICKNAMES ——————————

Month	*nickname of full moon*
January	Moon after Yule
February	Wolf Moon
March	Lent(en) Moon
April	Egg Moon
May	Milk Moon
June	Flower Moon
July	Hay Moon
August	Grain Moon
September	Fruit Moon
October	Harvest Moon
November	Hunter's Moon
December	Moon before Yule

*A 'Blue Moon' is usually defined as
the second of two full moons that
happens to appear in the same month.*

—————————— EPOCHS & ERAS ——————————

An EPOCH is a fixed point in time (e.g. the birth of Christ), and the succession of
events in the period following is an ERA. Some common epoch abbreviations are:

AD................Anno Domini (*in the year of the Lord*) · after the birth of Christ
AH ....Anno Hegirae (*in the year of the Hegira*) · the Muslim era is dated
from the day of Muhammad's flight from Mecca (July 16, AD622)
AUC........ Ab Urbe Condita (*since the founding of the city* [Rome]) · after 753BC
BC... Before Christ · before the birth of Christ
BCE ....Before the Christian/Common Era · before the birth of Christ
CE................................Christian/Common Era · after the birth of Christ

—————— THE CAD'S AMOROUS WEEK ——————

El lunes me enamro,
martes lo digo,
miércoles me declaro,
jueves consigo;
viernes doy celos,
y sábado y domingo,
busco amor nuevo.

On Monday I fall in love,
On Tuesday I say so,
On Wednesday I make a declaration,
On Thursday I succeed;
On Friday I make her jealous,
On Saturday and Sunday,
I look for new love.

—————— CARDINAL DAYS & THE SEASONS ——————

The adjective *cardinal* derives from the Latin for 'hinge', and tends to be employed for those concepts upon which other things depend. For example, the cardinal points of the compass (N, S, E, W); the cardinal humors of the body (blood, phlegm, yellow bile, and black bile); the cardinal virtues and sins [see p.338]; and so on. In astronomy, the Cardinal Days are the two solstices and the two equinoxes.

SOLSTICES occur when the Sun is at its furthest point from the equator. In the northern hemisphere the Sun's northernmost position occurs at the Summer Solstice (June *c.*21) – the 'longest day'; and its southernmost position occurs at the Winter Solstice (December *c.*22) – the 'shortest day'. EQUINOXES occur when the Sun is directly overhead at the equator, and the hours of daylight and darkness are of equal length at all latitudes. This occurs twice yearly: the Spring or Vernal Equinox (March *c.*21); and the Autumn Equinox (September *c.*23).

—————— THIRTY DAYS... ——————

30 days hath November,
April, June, and September,
February hath 28 alone,
And all the rest have 31

or

30 days hath November,
April, June, and September,
Of 28 there is but one
And the rest 30 and 1

Dirty days hath September,
April, June, and November,
From January up to May
The rain it raineth every day.
February hath twenty-eight alone,
And all the rest have thirty-one.
If any of them had two and thirty
They'd be just as wet and dirty.

THOMAS HOOD (1799–1845)

———————————QUEEN BEE COLOR CODING———————————

Around the world, apiculturists (beekeepers) employ a series of color codes to identify queen bees and indicate their ages. A smudge of harmless quick-drying paint is applied to the thorax of the queen bee so that she stands out within the hive's population. It seems that the origin of this color coding derives from the work of the Nobel Laureate Austrian zoologist Karl Von Frisch, who researched the language, orientation, and direction-finding of bees – as well as their senses of hearing, smell, and taste. The queen bee color coding system operates as follows:

Color	last digit of year	example	mnemonic
White	1 or 6	2006/2011	Will
Yellow	2 or 7	2007/2012	You
Red	3 or 8	2008/2013	Raise
Green	4 or 9	2009/2014	Good
Blue	5 or 0	2010/2015	Bees?

(A number of beekeeping journals change their jacket color annually to match.)

———————————HOURS FOR SLEEP———————————

Nature requires 6 · *Custom* 7 · *Laziness* 9 · and *Wickedness* 11

———————————LEAP YEARS———————————

In the Gregorian calendar, Leap Years have 366 days, with the addition of an extra day: February 29. Any year whose date is a number exactly divisible by four is a leap year, except years ending in '00', which must be divisible by 400. The extra day is added every four years to allow for the difference between a year of 365 days and the actual time it takes the Earth to circle the Sun. The table below shows the recent leap years, as well as the day of the week upon which each February 29 falls:

Monday	1932	1960	1988	2016	2044
Saturday	1936	1964	1992	2020	2048
Thursday	1940	1968	1996	2024	2052
Tuesday	1944	1972	2000	2028	2056
Sunday	1948	1976	2004	2032	2060
Friday	1952	1980	2008	2036	2064
Wednesday	1956	1984	2012	2040	2068

Tradition dictates that the normal conventions of gallantry are suspended on February 29, and a woman may ask for a man's hand in marriage. By custom, if the man declines this request, he is then bound by honor to buy the woman a silk gown by way of recompense. Of course, those born on February 29 (including Pope Paul III and Rossini) celebrate only one birthday in four – which, as Frederic discovered in *The Pirates of Penzance*, can lead to all sorts of elaborate shenanigans.

Index

Should not the Society of Indexers be known as Indexers, Society of, The?
— KEITH WATERHOUSE

2001–6, US OVERVIEW – CAMP DAVID

——CAPITAL OF BURMA – ELEPHANT, REPUBLICAN——

EMMYS – HUMAN RIGHTS, UN

—HUMANITIES, NAT. MEDAL – MOVIE, TOP GROSSING—

MOZART'S BIRTHDAY – RANKINGS, ARTIST

─────── RANKINGS, CELEBRITY – SWIMMING ───────

—— SWISS GUARD, VATICAN – ZIP CODES & MR ZIP ——

ERRATA, CORRIGENDA, &c.

Significant errors and omissions will be corrected here in subsequent editions.

ACKNOWLEDGMENTS

The author would like to thank:

Jonathan, Judith, & Geoffrey Schott · Benjamin Adams, Richard Album,
Joanna Begent, Martin Birchall, Andrew Cock-Starkey, James Coleman,
Gordon Corera, Aster Crawshaw, Jody & Liz Davies, Peter DeGiglio,
Colin Dickerman, Will Douglas, Miles Doyle, Charlotte Druckman,
Stephanie Duncan, Jennifer Epworth, Sabrina Farber, Kathleen Farrar, Josh Fine,
Minna Fry, Alona Fryman, Panio Gianopoulos, Yelena Gitlin, Catherine Gough,
Allison Hatfield, Charlotte Hawes, Mark & Sharon Hubbard, Max Jones,
Amy King, Robert Klaber, Maureen Klier, Alison Lang, Jim Ledbetter,
Suzie Lee, Annik LeFarge, John Lloyd, Ruth Logan, Josh Lovejoy, Chris Lyon,
Sam MacAuslan, Jess Manson, Michael Manson, Sarah Marcus, Blake Martin,
Lauren Mechling, Sara Mercurio, Susannah McFarlane, Colin Midson,
David Miller, Peter Miller, Polly Napper, Nigel Newton, Sarah Norton,
Elizabeth Peters, Cally Poplak, Dave Powell, Alexandra Pringle, Karen Rinaldi,
Pavia Rosati, Jared Van Snellenberg, Bill Swainson, Caroline Turner,
Greg Villepique, David Ward, & Michael Winawer.

Schott's Almanac

2 0 0 8

LIBER PRAETERITORUM ET POSTERITATIS CARMEN

Published Fall 2007
